1990

SOURCES IN SEMIOTICS, V

John Deely and Brooke Williams, Series Editors

CAUSAL REALISM

*An Essay on Philosophical Method
and the Foundations of Knowledge*

by

JOHN C. CAHALAN

UNIVERSITY
PRESS OF
AMERICA

LANHAM • NEW YORK • LONDON

University Press of America,® Inc.

4720 Boston Way
Lanham, MD 20706

3 Henrietta Street
London WC2E 8LU England

This book is published as a volume in the
SOURCES IN SEMIOTICS series
under the General Editorship of
John Deely and Brooke Williams

Library of Congress Cataloging in Publication Data

Cahalan, John C.
  Causal realism.

  (Sources in semiotics ; v. 2)
  Bibliography: p.
  Includes index.
  1. Knowledge, Theory of. 2. Methodology. 3. Causation.
I. Title. II. Series.
BD161.C26 1985   110   85-3309
ISBN 0-8191-4621-8 (alk. paper)
ISBN 0-8191-4622-6 (pbk. : alk. paper)

All University Press of America books are produced on acid-free
paper which exceeds the minimum standards set by the National
Historical Publications and Records Commission.

Editor's Preface

This book is the second volume to be published in the Sources in Semiotics series. Our original announcement of the series described five categories of works suitable for inclusion, the last of which covered "certain works of a 'presemiotic' authorship whose content and problem areas nonetheless touch so centrally on semiotic concerns and tend to transform their subject matter so radically in the direction and line of semiotic consciousness as to constitute in their own right a contribution toward the development of semiotics."

The present book is an extended essay on the subject of philosophical realism. As such, it directly engages a debate that semiotics, in my view, begins by transcending, without by any means being indifferent to the issues at stake in the typically modern oppositions between the varieties of realism and idealism, but by providing a framework within which these oppositions can be construed in the direction of a higher synthesis. For if the doctrine of signs stands, in Sebeok's fine expression, "at the intersection of nature and culture", and—from this standpoint "superior to the division between cognition dependent and cognition independent being" (to borrow Poinsot's forumulary)—contemplates that singular web spun of the collusive workings and interpenetrations of the mind and nature which we call "experience", this would not be were nature not recognizable in something of its own capacity. It is in this way that traditions of so-called "realism" are of interest semiotically.

The confidence and convoluted clarity of the author's argument, sustained over so many topics, is sure to cause consternation among the professors accustomed to presuppose broadly while narrowly analyzing. Cahalan writes directly counter to this contemporary fashion, creating an ambitious and far-ranging work that attempts nothing less than a reconstruction of philosophy from the ground up in what turns out to be a return—but with many new fillips and surprises—to philosophical realism. Insofar, it remains to the end presemiotic in its perspective. But it transforms its subject matter in the direction of seeing how an intersection of mind and nature is possible, and that is precisely what semiotics in its major tradition is all about.

The tone of didacticism in the work will be an irritation for many readers. Underlying tendencies toward dogmatism are a familiar trait of modern realistic philosophy, however, and its greatest weakness in the marketplace. Still, truth in philosophy, although an asymptotic product of inquirers in community, is not, after all, a commodity, and those who dislike tone are always free to deal with substance, and they should. It remains, as a reviewer of the manuscript wrote, that this work, "without question, is a *Lebenswerk*, a monumental work, a complete work" that (within its confines) "touches all the bases."

In particular, I would direct the reader's attention to Cahalan's treatment of Hume and the famous "problem" of causality relative to our experience of the world, and to the corollary exposition—remarkable and unparallelled—of the hoary idea of *propositiones per se notae* (an ancient idea so abused by modern versions of "realism" heretofore as to seem thoroughly discredited: but then Latin thought was no more "realist" in the modern sense than pre-Lutheran Christianity was "Catholic" in the modern sense). It was this feature of the book, this, and the rich discussion of the thing/object distinction which runs throughout, that first interested me in the manuscript, and that seems to me its greatest interest for semiotic.

The book is an exercise in intellectual courage. It may not point to the path of a future era, but it leaves no question that the era of linguistic empiricism, as that of glottocentrism generally, is past. And it most assuredly clarifies the question of method in philosophy, as it digs at foundations of knowledge in what concerns, if not the intersection of nature with culture, at least the way nature is there to be intersected.

John Deely
Stonecliffe Hall
January of 1985

iv

ACKNOWLEDGEMENTS

The publication of this work owes much to the early encouragement of Professor John J. FitzGerald (ret.) of the University of Notre Dame.

The assistance, suggestions, and encouragement of John N. Deely, Editor of Sources in Semiotics, have been invaluable.

The following read portions of the manuscript in various stages of development and made suggestions that helped me substantially: Henry B. Veatch, John Baker, Milton Fisk, Herbert Meyer, James O'Rourke, John Peterson, James Sweeney, Olaf Tollefsen, and Jesse Yoder. John P. Fleming edited the manuscript for style. Vicki Carr proofread the galleys. I owe the title of section 1.1 to James Callero.

At different times, Rita Stevens and Karen Martelucci each typed and proofread almost the entire manuscript. Others who also typed sections of the manuscript are: Beverly Chapman, Maureen Evans, Brenda Ferreira, Donna Frost, Phyllis Krasnowski, Donna McNulty, Laura Nawn, Diane Smelstor. Most of the latter contributed their services.

Assistance of various kinds was generously provided by the following friends: Frederick Blacquier, Earl Brown, Donald Burtt, Richard Cochran, John, Carol, Christa, William, Daniel, and Richard Connors, Phillip Costello, Matthew Deely, Anthony DiPietro, William Garrett, Joseph Lee, Gerald Matross, Kenneth Milik, Stanley Newman, Doris Oden, Frances Palma, Norman Risdal, Martin Saulenas, and Kevin Staid.

Acknowledgement is made to the following publishers and journals for permission to quote copyrighted materials (for which Appendix II has complete bibliographical data):

The American Catholic Philosophical Association for permission to quote from ''The Role of Conceptual and Linguistic Frameworks'' by Edward M. MacKinnon.

The Cambridge University Press for permission to quote from *Patterns of Discovery* by Norwood Russell Hanson.

The Philosophical Quarterly for permission to quote from ''Misleading Analyses'' by Errol E. Harris.

Southern Illinois University Press for permission to quote from *Language and Ontology* by Jack Kaminsky.

The Thomist for permission to quote from ''Maritain's Philosophy of the Sciences'' by Yves R. Simon.

The publication of this book was assisted by a grant from the De Rance Foundation and the American Catholic Philosophical Association. I am grateful for their support.

I wish to thank James H. Miller, Director of Technical Publications, Wang Laboratories, Inc., for giving me a leave of absence in order to complete the manuscript.

This book is dedicated to my mother and to the Community of God's Light, Andover, Massachusetts. I owe whatever value this work may have to their support and that of the other members of my family.

Methuen, Massachusetts
November, 1984

TABLE OF CONTENTS

CAUSAL REALISM

These writers have not, to be sure, done what they hoped to do. They have not provided knock-down, once-and-for-all demonstrations of meaninglessness, conceptual confusion or misuse of language on the part of philosophers they criticized. But that does not matter. . . . Philosophical discussion, by the nature of the subject, is such that the best one can hope for is to put the burden of proof on one's opponent. Linguistic philosophy, over the last thirty years, has succeeded in putting the entire philosophical tradition, from Parmenides through Descartes and Hume to Bradley and Whitehead, on the defensive. (Rorty, 1967, p. 33)

The achievement of linguistic philosophy has been to put all previous philosophy on the defensive. How? By putting the burden of proof on non-linguistic philosophers. But that is where the burden of proof has been all along. When a philosopher makes an assertion, he must be prepared to justify it. Have linguistic philosophers nothing more to show for their efforts than the demand that non-linguistic philosophers be rigorous in providing evidence for their views?

Rorty does say that linguistic philosophers have succeeded in putting others on the defensive "by a careful and thorough scrutiny of the ways in which traditional philosophers have used language in the formulation of their problems" (ibid.). But this is something that linguistic philosophers have done very little of. Only infrequently (and belatedly) have they given detailed textual analyses of the ways traditional philosophers have used language. They often claim to have removed a specific philosophical perplexity by showing some philosopher to have been a victim of linguistic confusion. But the perplexities they claim to remove, at least in the particular formulations for which these claims are made, are usually those of earlier linguistic philosophers, like Russell, the young Wittgenstein and the logical positivists, or empirical philosophers, like Moore and Broad.

In discussing philosophers other than fellow empiricists, instead of scrutinizing the ways they use language, linguistic philosophers are more often than not content to propose hypotheses about these uses of language, hypotheses according to which these ways of using language must be illegitimate and result from linguistic confusions. For something linguistic philosophers have done carefully and thoroughly is to work out theories about the legitimate ways of using language and justifying statements, and about the causes of illegitimate linguistic behavior, theories designed to fit certain preconceived ideas about human knowledge. What Rorty calls "forcing those who wish to propound the traditional problems to admit that they can no longer be put forward in the traditional formulations" (ibid.) is really a matter of accusing traditional philosophers of not measuring up to standards devised for the sake of finding them guilty of abusing language. Linguistic philosophers have little to say about the arguments by which traditional philosophers have defended their assertions and still less about how those philosophers would criticize the presuppositions of the standards brought against them, although Rorty himself has tried to do some of this.

If the current hegemony of the linguistic approach is not due to its having paid close attention to the actual practice of philosophers, what is it due to? Many historical conditions have contributed to it. But the chief reason, and the most important for the purposes of this book, is that the linguistic approach to philosophical questions is the approach that is most consistent with the principles of empiricism. Empirical theories of knowledge leave philosophy with access to no information which is not available to the man on the street or discoverable in the sciences. A philosopher cannot point to a fact that physicists or historians have overlooked without becoming just another physicist or historian. When the physicist and historian have done their work, however, questions arise about the knowledge they have produced. These questions are the business of philosophy: philosophy is a reflection on our empirical, logical and mathematical knowledge. But sound empirical method requires that we approach questions about knowledge as questions about linguistic behavior rather than about postulated abstract entities like propositions. If philosophy is to have something to do over and above what other intellectual pursuits do, there is nothing for it but to comment on the ways language is used in other disciplines and in ordinary life.

A more formal explanation can be given, however, of why empiricism favors the linguistic turn. Truths are either necessary or contingent; that is, their opposites are either contradictory or not contradictory. Necessary truths do not give us information about the world. They concern logical relations between various uses of language, for they are known just by knowing how their terms are being used. If a sentence conveys information about the world, its truth is contingent. And if contingent, it can be verified only by experience. But it is the business of the empirical disciplines to provide us with knowledge of (or good reasons to believe in) truths verified by experience. That is what makes them empirical disciplines. Consequently there is nothing left for philosophy but the logical analysis of language.

Note that the preceding does *not* contain a statement of the verification principle. The verification principle was a theory of meaning. The above contains a statement about two kinds of truth, those that are capable of being false and those that are not, and about two means of verification, by the evidence of experience or by understanding the way words are used. It does not matter whether the verification principle provides a successful test of meaningfulness. What matters is that truths must be either necessary or contingent, and that if they are not known true because the way we used words makes their opposites contradictory, they can only be known true by the evidence of experience. What is left for philosophy, then, but the logical analysis of language?

Many linguistic philosophers have come a long way from the verification principle. And many have even come a long way from the distinction between necessary and contingent truths. The latter make philosophy a part of the empirical enterprise. Still, they place philosophy at that end of the empirical spectrum where language is discussed. For the problems of modern philosophy have largely, though not exclusively, concerned knowledge. And studying knowledge empirically means studying it behavioristically, that is, linguistically.

At the same time, critiques of empiricism are now in fashion among some linguistic philosophers. But most of these critiques are more concerned with empirical accounts of the discovery of truth than with its verification. When empirical accounts of verification are criticized, they are criticized to deny that sentences and theories can be completely verified. The critics do not deny that, no matter how relative and partial verification may be, to whatever degree a belief about the world can be verified, its verification must be empirical. We are going to see that, as radical as some of these so-called critiques of empiricism may appear to be, they are essentially conservative as long as they admit no knowledge of what exists other than empirical knowledge and hence recognize no possibility for philosophy beyond that of being a reflection on other modes of knowing.

1.1 An Essay on Hume and Understanding

This book criticizes linguistic empiricism by defending one of the traditional ways of doing philosophy. Among other things, the methodological principles I am defending will answer the question how metaphysics, in the classical sense of a study of beings as beings, is possible, the question, that is, how verification can take place in metaphysics. But these principles are valid for all areas of philosophy, not just for metaphysics. In particular they will be shown valid for the philosophy of logic (although I would want to classify this as a branch of metaphysics) and the philosophy of science.

Another way of putting it is that I will be challenging the presuppositions on which linguistic philosophers base their judgments about traditional philosophers. Specifically, I will be arguing against the empirical theory of knowledge those presuppositions incorporate. All our knowledge of the world *is* derived from experience; I am not proposing rationalism. But there are more things to know about what is experienced than empirical methods of verification allow us to know. Philosophy is a means of learning truths about what exists, including truths about cognition, which is distinct from the empirical disciplines.

But our philosophy of philosophy and our philosophy of knowledge go hand in hand. In addition to arguing for philosophy as a distinct mode of knowing, my analysis will do something empiricism has always been unable to do: *account for empirical knowledge itself*. For the same principles that make philosophy possible as a distinct mode of knowing solve the problems about empirical knowledge that empiricism itself has been unable to solve: sense data versus physical things, induction, simplicity, contrary-to-fact conditionals, the incompleteness of empirical definitions, the foundations of empirical knowledge. The reason empiricism has been unable to solve these problems is that it is empiricism's theory of knowledge which generates these problems. Whatever else it may be, empiricism is a theory which excludes from knowledge those truths without which these problems are inevitable and insurmountable. It excludes them because it makes all knowledge empirical and thereby rejects modes of knowing like metaphysics.

We have traced the current hegemony of the linguistic turn to empiricism, but how do we explain the hegemony of empiricism? In the present context this question asks why so many philosophers accept empiricism's theory of necessary truth. It cannot be denied that contingent truths can be verified, if at all, only by experience. There are legitimate questions about how much experience, whether external or internal, gives us. But these questions do not cast doubt on the fact that contingent truths are verified only to the extent that experience gives us good reasons to believe in them. If there is any method of verification other than the empirical, it must concern necessary truths. Consequently the question why so many believe that our only knowledge of what exists is empirical is the question why they believe that no truth can both be necessary and convey information about what exists.

It is a mistake to think that the answer to this question is obvious. For most of the history of philosophy it would not have been considered obvious that a necessary truth could not give information about the world. In fact, it would have been considered false. Philosophy has long recognized that necessary truths are known from an understanding of the way their words are used. Yet the conclusion has only lately been drawn that the significance of necessary truth is logical or linguistic in an exclusive sense. For the meanings of the words in question often are not logical or linguistic in character. And from the fact that necessary truths are known by an understanding of their words, it does not follow that a sentence whose truth is necessary *mentions* words instead of *using* them to refer to other things.

If we now do not believe that necessary truths can give information about what exists, it is because an argument to the contrary emerged at a certain point in history and has been found convincing. More than once I have been surprised to find empiricists who were not familiar with the argument to which I am referring: Hume's argument (*Treatise*, 1, 3, 3) that it is impossible for the principle of causality (let us use the formula "Every event has a cause") to be a necessary truth. Before Hume it was believed that "Every event has a cause" was necessarily true. Therefore, and as Hume understood, it was believed that a necessary truth could expand our knowledge of the world beyond what we perceived. For when an event is perceived, we could know that a cause of the event has occurred, even if the cause is unperceived. (An event, of course, will have more than one cause. For the sake of simplicity, I will continue to use the singular when speaking of the necessity of an event's having a cause.)

There is no better example of the unawareness of how important Hume's critique of causal necessity is for empiricism than Beauchamp and Rosenberg's *Hume and the Problem of Causation*. In this attempt at a complete defense of Hume's views on causality, the authors do not even refer to his critique of the necessity of every event's having a cause. Apparently, the issue is not worth mentioning. Causal necessity for them is the forward-looking relation of determination from the cause to the effect. I am using "causal necessity" primarily for the backward-looking relation of an event's dependence on something other than itself. Causal necessity in the sense of an event's need for what is not itself is the crucial relation for human knowledge. It is this necessity that establishes the *existence* of the cause. Our knowledge of the determination by which causes produce effects is a consequence of our knowledge of the existence of things as causes on which other things depend.

Hume's argument has implications far beyond the immediate question of whether we are licensed to posit a cause whenever an event occurs. First, his argument is at the basis of the linguistic turn. If the argument is not conclusive, there is no reason to confine necessity to the domain of the logical (Hume's relations of ideas), and to confine what is true of the existing world (Hume's matters of fact) to the domain of the contingent and empirically verifiable. Second, his rejection of causal necessity prevents us from knowing the truths which solve the main problems about empirical knowledge. And third, it has contributed to problems in all areas of philosophy both by depriving us of tools we need to solve them and by generating fictions that complicate them.

It must be said, however, that the effect on philosophy of Hume's critique of causal necessity has not always been a matter of logical deduction. It has more often been a matter of a sin of omission leading to sins of commission. Accepting Hume has limited the categories in which we allow ourselves to think about philosophical problems. As a result, we do not even set foot on the paths that lead to the correct solutions. The absence of the appropriate conceptual equipment has imposed false dichotomies on us. And we solve problems by constructions whose arbitrariness is hidden from our perception because the constructions fill voids we have no other way to fill. Therefore the method by which I will demonstrate Hume's impact will not be to directly deduce the consequences of rejecting causal necessity. Rather, the method will be to show the consequences, for a variety of foundational philosophical questions, of accepting the fact that events require causes.

For it is my thesis that the problems of philosophy concern causal relations (relations of effects to their causes and causes to their effects) and that philosophy can verify not only by appealing to facts of experience, facts which are to be explained by their causes, but also by appealing to necessary truths concerning causal relations. The existence of this means of verification makes philosophy, including metaphysics, possible as a distinct mode of knowing. Hume's disproof of causal necessity, therefore, is at the heart of the question of philosophical method. If he was right, philosophy must find its means of verification in empirical contingency or logical necessity. But if he was wrong, philosophy should be done quite differently than it has been done.

of causality solely in terms of predictability or universality. In addition to arguing the necessary truth of the principle of causality, therefore, I will argue that causality is not a logical or epistemological relation. It is a relation between things and things, not between things and thought.

The gnoseological understanding of causality has also prevented us from seeing empirical knowledge for what it is. Scientific knowledge does not result from linking events by purely logical relations like class membership or material conditionality. Science discovers causal relations between events, and regularity in nature is relevant to science as evidence for causal relations. Causes are causes of existents. And logical constructs like the negations "non-black" and "non-raven" or the alternation "green and inspected before tomorrow or blue and not inspected before tomorrow" do not exist. The linguistic performances by which we discuss logical constructs exist and hence have causes; logical constructs themselves do not. Therefore the regularities that have given Hempel, Goodman and everyone else so much trouble are no problem if Hume was not correct.

In refuting Hume we are also vindicating the view of empirical knowledge held by the man on the street. Until he is conditioned otherwise by his philosophical education, the man on the street believes that the sciences inform him about causal relations as relations between things and things, not between things and thought. He believes, for instance, that chickens obey the universal law of laying eggs and not puppies because chickens are what they are. Until he is conditioned otherwise by his philosophical education, the man on the street also believes that in understanding causal relations, the sciences are understanding the natures of things. For if causal relations are relations between things, what these relations are must be determined by what these things are. (Rather than being definitive of causality, the universality of laws is an *effect* of things having the causal dispositions their natures determine them to have.)

The idea that we can know the natures of things has come under attack on the basis of evidence from the history of science and cultural linguistics. Allegedly, what we believe about the natures of things is relative to, and cannot be abstracted from, the quite differing and subjective frameworks we must employ in formulating our beliefs. But from the principle of causality follow other necessary truths about causal relations, truths which give us objective reasons for deciding between all genuinely conflicting empirical hypotheses. Because knowledge of what things are is knowledge of causal relations, empirical knowledge has foundations. (I am not saying, by the way, that the empirical scientist should use the concept of causality; it is the philosopher of science who needs that concept in order to understand what science does.)

Clearly a lot depends on the validity of Hume's argument against the necessity of every event having a cause. The nature of both empirical and philosophical knowledge are at stake. And our ability to understand the nature of logical and mathematical knowledge is at stake as well. For if philosophical questions do concern causal relations and if philosophy does verify by causal principles whose opposites are impossible, then we will not succeed in conducting the philosophy of logic or mathematics properly while under the spell of Hume.

1.2 Toward Reconstructing Philosophy

The ways of thinking about causality and necessity that come from Hume are deeply ingrained. My experience discussing these topics indicates they are so deeply ingrained that I cannot begin this reconstruction of our ideas about philosophy and knowledge by demonstrating that every event must have a cause. The demonstration would be prey to objections based on beliefs which are not only false but are so habitual that *they* are considered necessarily true. We must begin, rather, with philosophy as it is today, at the place to which it has come as a result of accepting Hume. From there we must work our way back, cutting away the underbrush of confusions that have sprung up around empiricism's roots. Not that the issues we deal with along the way will be unimportant. They are central to philosophy and, since Hume, have been considered of more significance than causality itself.

To understand the necessity of the principle of causality we must, for example, break loose from the hackneyed and stifling categories in which we have thought about necessary truth. As a step toward this end, Chapter Three begins with a refutation of Quine's attack against the very existence of necessary truth. The refutation of Quine leads to a refutation of the linguistic theory of necessity even for truths like "No unmarried man is married" whose necessity does derive from logical relations. I substantiate my reply to Quine, by the way, by showing how it allows us to escape from Lewis Carroll's Tortoise-Achilles paradox.

Still, we need a general theory of necessary truth. And Chapter Three continues by approaching that subject in a way which is perhaps unprecedented: it bases the theory of necessary truth on a theory of truth; that is, it views the nature of necessary truth as a function of the nature of truth. The theory of truth I defend is a correspondence theory quite different from the kind of theories, like those of the early Wittgenstein or Austin, that have recently gone by that name. To distinguish it from them I call it the "identity theory" of truth, but it could also be justly described as the classical correspondence theory of truth. The identity theory solves the problems other correspondence theories have gotten into. (I present the identity theory as a theory of the truth of sentences. I do not deny the reality or importance of the distinction between sentences and propositions. But that distinction should be justified by means of the method I am defending. The method does not presuppose that distinction.)

The identity theory makes possible a new understanding of necessary truth and a new way to distinguish kinds of necessary truth from each other. There are truths whose necessity derives from logical relations and truths whose necessity derives from causal relations. Chapter Three gives an account of logical relations and an introductory account of necessary causal relations. A necessary causal relation obtains between distinct realities if at least one of them would not exist without the other, where "would not exist without the other" means: if it exists and the other does not, it both is and is not what it is. (I discuss the ontological status of causal relations in Chapter Nine.)

The logical relation/causal relation distinction solves many of the traditional problems with the distinction between necessary and contingent truth. Approaching necessary truth as a kind of truth solves others. For one thing, the question of why a truth is necessary is distinct from, though related to, the question of how the necessity of a truth is known. Thus our account of necessity can bypass the problems of the analytic versus the synthetic and the a priori versus the a posteriori, problems which are usually defined from the point of view of the way truths are known to be necessary.

For a truth to be necessary is for its opposite to be contradictory. We know that the opposite of a truth is contradictory, however, from an understanding of its terms. We cannot recognize the necessity of a truth *solely* by understanding how its terms are used *and* by applying some criterion of necessity. But in knowing the meanings of some terms, we cannot fail to be acquainted with logical relations between them, relations that render certain truths necessary. In knowing the meanings of some other terms, we cannot fail to be acquainted with causal relations between them, relations that likewise render certain truths necessary. One example of a truth whose necessity derives from necessary causal relations is "No two colors can be in the same place at the same time". Another is "The result of adding two objects to a group of two is the same as the result of removing three objects from a group of seven". Chapter Three closes with a section extending the preceding analysis to the truths of mathematics.

Chapter Four focuses on truths whose necessity derives from logical relations. It attempts to explain *how* logical relations make truths necessary—another endeavor that may be unprecedented. And it shows that "truths of logic", truths which do not just use logical relations but concern them, constitute only a subset of logically necessary truths. Truths of logic inform us that sentences employing logical relations in certain ways are necessarily true. But the relations from which logical necessity is derived operate first in sentences about things other than the way some sentences employ logical relations. If not, there would be no logical relations to render truths necessary. Chapter Four continues with an account of negation, a causal analysis explaining how the knowledge of necessary truths comes about and an examination of Quine's alleged doubts about the necessity of the principle of non-contradiction.

The final section applies this account of logical necessity to the formulas of symbolic logic. It is to be noted that in none of this are essences invoked to explain logical necessity. The necessity to which essences are pertinent is causal necessity, not the necessity that derives from logical relations. For as they are usually understood, essences are the antithesis of logical relations.

Chapter Four does not complete the discussion of logical necessity, however. I return to it after cutting away another kind of underbrush that stands in the way of understanding necessary truth, philosophical method and human cognition in general. I have said that causality is neither an empirical nor epistemological concept. What kind of concept is it? As a relation between things, the causal relation is *ontological*, and our definition of a necessary causal relation is an ontological definition. Appreciating what it means to say this requires a re-examination of the function of the verb "exists" and its cognates. For one of those cognates is "ontology", the study of that which exists.

This re-examination is undertaken in Chapter Five. Standard interpretations of the doctrine that "exists" is not a predicate have obscured the true significance of this word. It may be that "exists" should not be considered a predicate; nothing I say will require a commitment one way or the other. But common readings of that doctrine must be rejected out of hand for the simple reason that they imply to exist is to be an object of knowledge (*esse est percipi*). If, for instance, "An F exists" means no more than "The description 'F' has a referent", then things exist only to the extent that they are made the referents of descriptions. Clearly this is not the intention of these interpretations of "exists". But intentions are one thing, implications another.

In a sense, existence is the contrary of being known. Not that what exists cannot be what is known, but the existence of things has a causal priority over their being objects of knowledge, especially over their being referred to in language. To exist is something really distinct from being referred to in language, and without real existents to refer to, we would have no language. This follows from the public character of language. Language can come to be only in a publicly observable, and therefore really existing, world. (This is not the only implication of the public character of language that will be of interest to us.) The causal priority of the fact that things exist over the fact that anything is referred to in language explains the function of "exists". In knowing that an F exists, not only do we know that "F" has a referent, but we also know that a condition obtains for the F which has causal priority over the fact that anything is referred to in language, the condition of existing.

When the meaning of "exists" is seen in the correct light, a possibility for the analysis of experience emerges which empiricists have completely ignored but which has been practiced all along, though with varying degrees of success, by philosophers of the realist tradition: ontological analysis. For once we have freed "exists" from the misinterpretations that usually surround it, we can use it to form concepts by which experience can be articulated otherwise than empirically. (The above definition of causal necessity is such a concept.) And necessary truths employing these concepts can be known. Ontology is not any inquiry into what exists. It is an investigation of what exists from the point of view of necessary truths employing ontological concepts.

The most important of these necessary truths, however, is not the principle of causality; it is the principle of non-contradiction: it is impossible for anything to simultaneously exist and not exist. Thus formulated, the principle of non-contradiction, as also the corresponding principle of excluded middle, is a truth of ontology, not of logic. Its necessity derives from logical relations. But it does not concern logical relations; it concerns existence. The reason it is impossible for a thing to simultaneously exist and not exist cannot be that, if it did, the logical principle that contradictory sentences cannot be true would be violated. On the contrary, the reason it is impossible for contradictory sentences to be true is that, if they were, things could simultaneously exist and not exist.

The goal of making sentences is to know what exists. Logical relations are properties of our apparatus for knowing things sententially. The logical principle of non-contradiction tells us that sentences using the logical relation of negation in a certain manner are necessarily false, that is, cannot achieve the goal for which we make sentences. They cannot achieve the goal of making sentences because the sentential role of negation prevents them from achieving that goal. But it prevents them from achieving that goal because it prevents contradictory sentences from telling us what exists.

The presence of a sign used for negation prevents what ''does not exist'' articulates (that which does not exist) from being the same as what ''exists'' articulates (that which exists). The necessity of the ontological principle of non-contradiction therefore derives from the sentential role of negation. But the necessity that derives from logical relations does not concern other logical relations only. Again, the relations from which logical necessity derives operate first in sentences about things other than such relations. And if the necessity that derives from the role of negation did concern logical relations only, the way things exist would be determined by laws governing the way they are known; things *could* exist and not exist but for the fact that sentences saying as much cannot be true. As it is, things cannot exist and not exist; and as a result, contradictory sentences cannot be true.

But why does the logical principle of non-contradiction govern sentences about the most unworldly of logical constructs? Because of another implication of the fact that language is public. The language we use to discourse about logical constructs is derived from that by which we discourse about real existents. Since the same logical relation is involved in both cases, if contradictions could be true in the domain of logical constructs, they could be true in the domain of real existents. They cannot be true in the latter domain; therefore, they cannot be true in the former. The logical principle of non-contradiction governs our sentences because knowledge of what exists is the teleonomic cause of sentences and because the ontological principle of non-contradiction is true of everything that exists. Necessary truths are not necessary because they extend to all possible worlds; they extend to all possible worlds because their opposites violate a law of all being and, hence, of all discourse. This, by the way, is an ontological analysis of logically necessary truth.

I use the phrase "teleonomic cause" synonymously with "goal". The principle of causality concerns efficient causes, agents. Teleonomic causality refers to the natural determinations of efficient causes to produce certain effects in certain circumstances. That agents act because determined to behave in certain ways does not mean that effects not yet existing produce the exercise of an efficient cause's causality. It simply means that an efficient cause's natural determinations necessitate that it exercise its behavioral dispositions in certain ways in certain circumstances. This necessity is essential to the coming into existence of effects and, therefore, deserves to be described as a mode of causality. (It also deserves this description for another reason explained in Chapter Nine.)

No doubt metaphysicians have abused the notion of teleonomic causality almost to the point where it could not be salvaged. Still, there are problems for which it is needed, especially those dealing with conscious activities like making and using sentences. The job of epistemology is to study the relation of such activities to the goals of truth and knowledge. In doing so, epistemology is examining the teleonomic cause at which an efficient cause (the conscious agent) is directing his activity.

Referring to the terms of *unconscious* causal determinations as goals is not anthropomorphizing. It is a way of calling attention to the fact that the conscious relation to goals by which we direct some of our activity is an instance of a more general relation to terms necessarily found in unconscious as well as conscious causes. The causal analysis of conscious goal-directed activity begins with the recognition that all causal activity requires a mode of acting that is determined to be what it is by the cause's being what it is. Therefore, when the causal analysis of conscious activity includes teleonomic causes, it is not introducing a *causa ex machina* with no legitimate place in our general cast of causal characters. (The teleonomic causes of conscious activity are not necessarily equivalent to the "reasons" of the reasons-versus-causes debate. That debate presupposes a Humean concept of causality.)

To get back to existence, my indifference to the non-predicate theory of "exists" may appear to open the door to Anselmian arguments for the existence of God. Both to meet this objection and to make further clarifications concerning various ways of using "exists" I reformulate a little-known Renaissance refutation of Anselmian arguments that I consider the proper way to refute them. The specifics of the refutation make it appropriate to close Chapter Five with remarks on contrary-to-fact conditionals (which, again, are not central to the issue of causality) and on the use of modal operators in philosophical definitions.

I have said that to get back to empiricism's roots we must begin at the point empiricism has reached today. And today "ontology" means something quite different from what I have in mind. I mean a method of forming non-empirical concepts to articulate, and discover necessary truths about, our experience. Empirical terms are defined by reference to observationally distinguishable features of experience. Ontological terms are defined by reference to existence and functions of existence ("would not exist without", "exists in another or not in another", "capable of being an F", etc.). And existence is not an observationally distinguishable feature of experience. Ontological analysis is the method of philosophy, classical metaphysics included. This is not meant as description of the behavior of most philosophers. Nor does it imply that one cannot find in the writings of philosophers statements that are legitimately empirical, logical or mathematical. But to the extent that philosophy can do something for us that is distinct from what these other modes of knowing can do, philosophy is ontological and should be done ontologically.

Today, however, "ontology" often refers to any kind of belief, philosophical or empirical, about what exists, but to such beliefs viewed from the standpoint of the conceptual framework of the language in which they are expressed. Different languages have different ways of dividing the world and parcelling things into categories. The ways in which a language categorizes things constitutes its ontology. And this ontology is not imposed on any language by experience but is imposed on experience by the language.

This view of ontology is a corollary of what many linguistic empiricists would consider the most important recent development in philosophy. According to them, cultural linguistics and the history of science have shown that our beliefs about what exists result from the imposing of our conceptual frameworks on things and, therefore, that the truth-value of beliefs is relative to the quite adventitious frameworks we must impose on things in knowing them—relative in a sufficiently important way to make it a problem why conflicting ways of describing experience and dividing it into particulars cannot do equally well. Experience itself seems to provide no ultimate ground for deciding between conflicting hypotheses.

I intend to show that necessary truths which are ontological in my sense of the word (the more traditional sense, by the way) defeat this kind of linguistic relativism and provide foundations for empirical knowledge. But because the other use of "ontology" is so closely associated with the latest developments in linguistic philosophy, I have decided to begin my attempt to cut away the underbrush around the roots of empiricism with a critique of the idea that one's ontology is determined by the structural characteristics of one's language. This is done in Chapter Two. Starting this way has the advantage that, in criticizing the linguistic conception of ontology, I have the opportunity to explain some ideas that will be crucial to the arguments of the following chapters. Among other things, Chapter Two will criticize the views of Whorf and Quine, including Quine's definition of existence.

But my own views concerning necessary truth and ontological analysis had to have been explained before I could present my arguments against the relativistic theory of truth that is associated with linguistic ontology. So I do not take up linguistic relativism until Chapter Six. There I argue that truths which will later be derived from the principle of causality give us objective grounds for deciding between conflicting hypotheses. For it is not as easy as the relativists think to find empirically or ontologically significant differences between the framework features of different languages. No matter how diverse languages may be, if the views expressed in them do not require differences in our experience, those views are not conflicting empirical hypotheses about what exists.

But neither must they be conflicting ontological beliefs, since ontological beliefs are not determined by the structural characteristics of our languages. Ontological beliefs are determined by what we rightly or wrongly take to be necessary truths about something non-linguistic, existence and that which exists. If we are mistaken in these beliefs, we may be guilty of reading linguistic categories into reality. But as argued in Chapters Two, Six and Eleven, and as experience shows, the linguistic empiricist is much more apt to be guilty of this fallacy than is the practitioner of ontological analysis. Because they reject modes of knowing other than empirical, empiricists are forced to come up with epistemological accounts of such non-linguistic matters as existence, dispositions and causal relations, not to mention their interpretation of differences between languages as differences in what is believed about reality.

Where neither empirical evidence nor the evidence of necessary ontological truths would be relevant to choosing between two alleged conflicting beliefs, there is no reason to assume these beliefs really are in conflict. Some relativists hold that the meanings of terms must vary from theory to theory or language to language. If so, the sentences of different theories and languages cannot be in contradiction; contradiction is the affirmation and denial of the *same*. Hesse's attempt to avoid this difficulty will be examined and found wanting.

Finally, making truth relative to the structural characteristics of different languages runs into the same difficulty that the later Wittgenstein brought against the picture theory of truth. Random differences in rules of projection (or in the framework features on languages) can make all pictures accurate representations and the same picture both accurate and inaccurate. The identity theory of truth offers the only way to avoid this problem. The accuracy of a description must consist in identity between what the thing we are intending to describe is, at least in part, and the meaning of the word or words by which we describe it. "This is red" is true if and only if that which a certain feature of my visual field in part is, is the same as that which "red" is used for. Anything short of this out-and-out identity and the accuracy of descriptions becomes a matter of whether or not we, either as individuals or as part of a whole linguistic community, *intend* a certain thing to be described by a certain description. And we can intend anything we like. The question is what constitutes the successful accomplishment of the intention to describe something accurately.

But radical identity between the meaning of a description and the nature of the described is compatible with radical diversity between the nature of the described and logical properties of the predicates by which we describe it. The following are logically diverse ways of articulating the same feature of our experience: "is scarlet", "is red", "has redness", "is colored", "has color". Each of these is an accurate description of the same feature of experience; and they are accurate for the same reason. Each of them expresses what something in our experience is, at least in part. Anything that is scarlet is something that is red, has color, etc. The sameness of what is described by each of these predicates is compatible with their logical differences because when a predicate is used to describe things, it is not its logical properties that are attributed to things. These properties are characteristics of the means by which the natures of things are known; they are not that which is known when the natures of things are known. The natures of things become associated with them as a result of being known, that is, of being expressed by predicates; but it does not follow that in being known the natures of things are not known. The identity required for truth is therefore compatible with all degrees of vagueness and abstractness on the part of predicates.

But such distinctions as between "is red" and "has redness" or even "is redding", "is coloring redwise" are taken by many linguistic philosophers as evidence of different ontologies being imposed by different ways of articulating our experience in language. Again, where neither empirical nor philosophical evidence is germane to an apparent conflict between beliefs, there is no reason to believe the conflict is more than apparent. Logical differences in linguistic apparatus do not by themselves amount to differences in what is attributed to reality by means of that apparatus.

This kind of realism can be called "diacritical", a realism that defends itself by making the necessary distinctions. The point is, first, to distinguish between what is true of the means by which something is known and what is true of the end achieved by the use of those means and, second, to recognize that differences between means and end do not prevent the means from achieving the end. What is known about the natures of extramental realities is one thing; what properties can be truthfully attributed to those natures as a result of our ways of making them known are another. Realism of this kind might also be called "teleonomic" since the realism pertains to the end achieved, not to the properties of the means used to achieve it. "Teleonomic" has the advantage of allowing us to emphasize that the same end can be achieved by diverse means.

Whatever this epistemological dimension of causal realism is called, the point being emphasized is that this realism distinguishes the truth that is known from what is true of the means by which it is known, precisely in order to eliminate all distinction between what extramental things are and the goal we achieve in knowing the truth about them. The "correspondence" of the correspondence theory of truth is not a relation between a state of affairs, on the one hand, and some kind of mental entity, on the other. It is identity between a state of affairs and itself. There is truth when what is expressed in language is what exists. The causal analysis of how things come to be expressed in language is a separate question. (For the purposes of this introductory account I have allowed myself to use the terms "extramental" and "meaning" uncritically. The situation is remedied in Chapters Two and Three respectively. In Chapter Three, I introduce the terms "word-function" and "meaning$_T$" to signify that for which words are used, as opposed to any mental entities that may or may not be required as causes of the meaningful use of words.)

When truth is known, what is known about things is what they are. The sentences of any language or theory which do not inform us what the things they intend to describe are, are false—pure and simple. How do we know that a description does express what something is? By the evidence of experience interpreted in the light of necessary ontological truths concerning causal relations.

The most inclusive way to describe this realism, therefore, is causal realism. The phrase "causal realism" has several levels of meaning. It expresses the metaphysical doctrine that there is such a thing as causality in the extramental, not gnoseological, sense. It expresses the epistemological doctrine that we can know the extramental causal dependencies and dispositions of things. And it expresses the epistemological doctrine that knowledge of causal relations provides a means of determining the truth about what things are in their extramental existence.

Now we are ready to discuss causal necessity. The intrinsic significance of the preceding issues aside, this may seem a long prolegomenon to the demonstration that every event must have a cause. But we have been laboring under an illusion, actually several illusions, for two hundred years. Undoing that labor can be expected to take more than a letter to the editor.

1.3 Causality and Causal Knowledge

The principle of causality refers to efficient causality. And another part of our Humean inheritance is the reduction of causality to efficient causality. In philosophy previous to Hume and in everyday language still, the concept of causality extends to other ways in which realities may be so related that one of them would not exist without the other. An event is a change that has not always been occurring. Assume C is a change occurring to something, A, which at some time was not undergoing C. Then the relation between A and C is a necessary causal relation. C is non-identical with, yet would not exist without, A; and it is contradictory for a change occurring to something to exist if that to which it occurs does not exist. For reasons explained in Chapter Seven, I call that to which a change occurs the "component cause" of the change. This is not efficient causality. And to show that events have component causes is not to demonstrate the principle of causality. It is only the first step in the argument.

But it is an important first step. It is a counterexample exposing Hume's argument against causal necessity as a non-sequitur. True, there is no contradiction where there is no denial of something's identity with itself. But to conclude that a thing's relation to another cannot be necessary is to make a false dichotomy between something's identity with itself and its relations to others. Nothing prevents one reality, like a change occurring to something, from being so related to another, like that to which it occurs, that to deny its relation to the other is to deny its identity with itself. Recognizing the dependence of events on their component causes is important for another reason also. As explained in Chapter Ten, it shows that necessary causal relations can be found in sense experience, although it takes ontological analysis to find them there. The arguments of this book do not violate the principle that all knowledge is derived from sense experience.

Why empiricists have overlooked component causality will be explained in Chapter Eleven. Because they have overlooked it, however, it appears to them that it begs the question to argue that events must have efficient causes since otherwise they would either be caused by nothing or be their own causes. It is contradictory to be caused and either to have no cause or to be one's own cause. But these contradictions result only if we presuppose the point at issue, that events would not exist without something other than themselves. Efficient causality is not presupposed, on the other hand, if we ask whether component causes can be the sole causes of the occurrence of events. And it can be shown to be contradictory for events to have component causes *and not* to have efficient causes.

Chapter Seven shows this by means of two arguments. If an event's component causes were its sole causes, it would follow that the event is caused and either has no cause or is cause of itself. The event in question is change C occurring to thing A. At one time A is not undergoing C and is therefore only a potential cause of C. Chapter Six shows potentiality and other dispositional concepts not to be epistemological relations or logical constructs. But that is not pertinent here; if potentiality is a logical construct, all the better. When something is only potentially an F, an F does not exist; and without C, A is only a potential component cause of C. If the only change that occurs is C, therefore, either C occurs with no cause, since nothing else has occurred to make A an actual component cause of C, or C is cause of itself, since it is C that constitutes A the actual component cause without which C would not exist. To avoid contradiction we must posit something other than C without which A's capacity to undergo C would not be fulfilled. This is the efficient cause.

The second argument points out that were A the sole cause of C, the occurrence of C would have necessary but not sufficient causes;

A, the only necessary cause, is not sufficient for C since A can exist without C existing. But C has a necessary cause if and only if that cause provides some condition without which C would not exist. And the necessary cause must be sufficient to provide *that* condition. If not, an infinite regress develops. As insufficient for the existence of that condition, the cause can be necessary for that condition if and only if it provides a (second) condition that is necessary for it (the first condition). And is the cause sufficient to provide this second condition? But A is not sufficient even for there to be a component cause of C since A can be what it is without being a cause for C. There are sufficient causes for A's being a component cause of C if and only if something other than A exists, such that its being what it is and A's being what it is are sufficient for A to become an actual cause of C.

We do not have to know any more than this about the nature of efficient causality in order to know that events must have efficient causes. How do efficient causes bring it about that the potentiality of component causes to undergo changes is fulfilled? Answers differ from efficient cause to efficient cause and component cause to component cause. And we learn those answers from scientists on a daily basis. It is shown in Chapter Seven, finally, that efficient causality is consistent with the existence of time.

The next two chapters explore the implications of causal necessity for empirical and philosophical knowledge respectively. Chapter Eight begins by contrasting our ontological principle of causality with the epistemological principle which has traditionally gone by that name in the philosophy of science. The truth of the ontological principle is indifferent to whether the laws of science are deterministic or statistical.

The remainder of Chapter Eight relies on the previous chapter's explanation of the concepts that entered the demonstration of the principle of causality, but it does not ask us to assume the demonstration has taken place. It considers the necessity of the ontological principle of efficient causality as an hypothesis and asks what consequences for the philosophy of science follow from that hypothesis. This deserves emphasis. We do not have to have proven that every event must have an efficient cause in order to inquire whether the hypothesis that events must have efficient causes is superior to the hypothesis that events can occur without them.

The reason this hypothesis has not been investigated before, in addition to our acceptance of the epistemological concept of causality, is another common belief that was considered false prior to Hume's argument against causal necessity. Until recently, the class of necessary truths has usually been treated as co-extensive with the class of truths *we can know* as necessary because we can derive them from definitions. Before Hume, however, it was believed there were truths whose opposites would require something to both be and not be what it is (in violation of the ontological principle of non-contradiction), even if we cannot arrive at knowledge of such a truth from an understanding of its terms. That there may be such truths is one of the results of Chapter Three's analysis of necessary truth; for the necessity of a truth is defined by reference to the conditions which make it true, not the conditions which make its truth known.

But to know that there can be such truths, we need only have recognized that Hume's argument against causal necessity is a non-sequitur. If things can be so related that one thing could exist without the other only at the price of both being and not being what it is, then there is no reason why sentences like the following cannot be necessary truths: "At standard pressure, when the temperature is 32° on the Fahrenheit scale, water will freeze". And the fact of things undergoing changes establishes that necessary causal relations do obtain. A change is so related to something other than itself, namely, that which undergoes it, that if it existed without that which undergoes it, it would both be and not be what it is.

Nor is there any reason why things should not be so related. Even if true, Hume's principle that "the mind never perceives any real connection between distinct existences" would have an epistemological significance only, and a limited one at that. It would tell us that our knowledge of the truth of a necessary causal relation cannot result solely from an understanding of the way words are used. It could not tell us it is wrong to believe such relations obtain if there are reasons for thinking this hypothesis is superior to its opposite. For it could not tell us that necessary causal relations do not hold ontologically, that is, that things cannot be so related by nature that one thing would not exist without the other.

But if our understanding of some words which are derived from experience allows us to know necessary truths concerning causal relations, and if all the events we experience enter necessary causal relations, why does not our understanding of all words derived from experience give rise to knowledge of causal necessity? Because an application of necessary truths deducible from the principle of causality shows that most empirical concepts must be causally opaque, that is, not revelatory of necessary causal relations. Where effects result from multiple causes, that is, everywhere, acquaintance with an effect sufficient for us to make it the meaning of some word is not sufficient to make us aware of its specific relations to specific causes. Thus the causal opacity of empirical concepts is not an objection to but a conclusion from the hypothesis that "Every event has a cause" is a necessary truth. This is argued at the conclusion of Chapter Eight.

Chapters Nine and Ten, on the other hand, explain why the understanding of some terms derived from experience, especially ontological terms, is an understanding of necessary causal relations. From the fact that an understanding of terms does not reveal the necessity of specific causal relations it does not follow that an understanding of terms cannot reveal the necessity of more general causal relations. Empirical investigation is needed to determine what causes leaves to turn color in autumn. Empirical investigation is not needed to determine that the event of a leaf changing color has causes. Central to this explanation is the logical relation illustrated by this series: "scarlet", "red", "chromatic color", "color". Whatever information is conveyed by the later items in the series is conveyed by the earlier but not vice versa. This relation can be called the logical inclusion of the latter in the former. Although it has been neglected by linguistic empiricists, this relation is crucial to the understanding of several problems. Chapter Four, for instance, shows how it explains the necessary truth of the formulas of the propositional calculus.

What then are the consequences for the philosophy of science of the hypothesis that it is necessary for events to have causes? Using Chapter Seven's explanations of causal concepts, Chapter Eight deduces "the principle of induction" (roughly, that similar causes must have similar effects), "the search warrant" (change C occurs because previous changes have brought sufficient causes for C into existence; therefore we are licensed to look for causes by studying variations in sequences of events), and "the principle of simplicity" (in effect, that there can be no more causes than are necessary for the changes that occur). Like the principle of causality, these necessary truths are ontological, not Kantian. They do not express conditions for the possibility of experience; they express conditions of possibility. For possibility is the possibility of existence. My discussion of induction and simplicity finds these questions related in a way that, to my knowledge, has not been appreciated before. Both are questions of how we are to identify the causes of events. The principles of induction and simplicity allow us to acquire this causal knowledge only because they operate in conjunction with one another.

135; 987

Together, the principles of induction, simplicity and the search warrant constitute foundations of empirical knowledge sufficient to permit us to decide even between hypotheses expressed in languages with apparently conflicting conceptual schemes. For an apparent conflict between two equally simple theories to be empirically significant, the theories must classify events, say, events A, B and C, differently. Where one theory classifies A as similar to B but not to C, the other must classify A as similar to C but not to B. And for this difference in classification to be more than nominal, it must affect our predictions concerning which kind of event will follow which. Induction would therefore tell us which theory we should believe. If the laws of the two theories predict that A, B and C will be preceded by the same kinds of events and succeeded by the same kinds of events, that is evidence that the differences in their way of classifying events are logical or linguistic only, not ontological or empirical. Induction supplies evidence for causal relations. If two theories attribute the same causal relations to things, they are attributing the same natures to things. For knowledge of what things are and knowledge of their causal relations are the same.

Chapter Eight continues by applying its results to the raven and grue paradoxes and by adding some remarks about counterfactuals to those of Chapter Five. Since the truth that a causal relation obtains may be necessary even though we are not able to deduce it from definitions, belief in the truth of a counterfactual may be a belief that a necessary causal relation does obtain. And as indicated above, the role played by logical relations in "non-black" and in the definition of "grue" shows that these are terms for logical constructs. They are therefore outside the domain of causal relations, the domain to which inductive regularities are pertinent.

The upshot of Chapter Eight, then, is that the necessary truth of the principle of causality is superior as an hypothesis to the belief that causal relations must be contingent. If every event must have sufficient component and efficient causes, the outstanding difficulties with empirical knowledge, difficulties that have hitherto been intractable, are done away with in one fell swoop. To object that the hypothesis is an impossible one because necessity is wholly a matter of logical relations would be to assume the very point that is in dispute. Chapter Eight closes with remarks about the use of mathematics in scientific theories, remarks suggesting a different approach from the usual to the question of instrumentalism.

Chapter Nine is a further consideration of human knowledge as

causal, with special attention given to the differences between ontological and empirical causal analyses. Ontology verifies its causal
analyses by showing that their opposites are impossible. The principles of induction, simplicity and the search warrant, on the other
hand, show that it is unreasonable to believe the opposite of an empirical causal analysis given the evidence of experience. Differences
in ontological and empirical modes of concept formation are also
examined. Chapter Five's account of knowing "An F exists" shows
that ontological concepts are logically included in all our concepts,
and Chapter Six shows that the concept of disposition is ontological.
The ontological character of this concept explains the incompleteness
of empirical definitions using observation terms and logical relations
alone. Observation terms and logical relations are not sufficient to express the ontological background of empirical concepts. For "existence" is not an observation term in the sense of a term for an observationally distinguishable feature of experience.

In Chapter Nine it is also explained why knowledge of a thing's
causal relations gives us knowledge of what it is. It follows from the
necessity of the principle of causality that the natures of things *are*
causal dispositions, dispositions to produce and undergo certain
changes in certain circumstances. Contrary to Wittgenstein, it is not
grammar that gives essence; causality gives essence. This is true despite
the apparent triviality of examples like knowing that a drug has dormitive powers because it causes sleep. Another thing accomplished
in Chapter Nine is showing how philosophical issues, especially those
of interest to linguistic empiricism, which appear to have nothing at
all to do with causality, really are questions of causal analysis. The
common description of philosophy as conceptual analysis is not entirely wrong, however, inasmuch as philosophy verifies its causal
analyses by truths which are known from an understanding of how
their terms are being used.

There is one more unsolved empirical problem that the hypothesis
of necessary causal relations takes care of nicely, the problem of perception. Does perception put us in contact with sense data or physical
things? This problem is *not* best approached, as it so often is, by asking
how we know we are perceiving things rather than hallucinating about
them. It is best approached by asking what is the difference between
sensing something, a red patch, say, and imagining it. In Chapter Ten
I propose the hypothesis that in sensation we are aware of the causal
action of the environment on our sense organs, aware of it as causal
action. Sense data, in other words, are defined as the action of the

environment on our sensory apparatus, action perceived as such. Once
we are free of the epistemological concept of causality, we are able
to see that standard phenomenological descriptions of the difference
between sensing and imagining support this hypothesis.

But how does this hypothesis help solve the problem of perception? To show this Chapter Ten examines what the assumption that
the principle of causality is necessarily true implies concerning the
nature of causal action. From what has already been established about
causality, it follows that if we are aware of the action of the environment as action, we are directly, *not inferentially*, aware of the extramental existence of things in the environment as causes of that action.
To be aware of something as an action is to be aware of it as the action
of its cause and, therefore, to be aware of the existence of the cause
at least as term of the causal relation, that is, as that which the action
is the action of. I am aware of a red patch as a way the outside environment acts on my sense of sight. As such, I am experiencing the
red patch as something *of* the outside environment, specifically, as
characteristic of the causal dispositions of something in the environment. In sensations that result from artificial stimulations of the brain,
we are still, unlike when imagining, aware of the then existing action
of the environment on part of our sensory apparatus.

But from what has already been established about causality, it also
follows that if we are aware of the action of the environment on our
sense organs, what we are aware of in sensation must be relative to
the conditions under which the sense organs receive the action of the
environment. For the character of a change undergone by a component cause depends not only on the nature of the efficient cause but
also on the nature of the component cause and their relations to one
another. Where one person senses a square patch of red as something
of the outside environment, another person senses a rhomboidal patch
of gray as something of the outside environment. Yet both are directly aware of the existence of the same environment as cause of the action they are sensing as the action-of some cause.

In other words, the hypotheses that events must have causes and
that the senses are aware of causal action as such show that direct
sense consciousness of physical things and the relativity of sense consciousness are just different sides of the same coin. That which enables
us to be directly aware of the existence of physical things is the same
as that which requires what is sensed to be relative to the subject of
sensation. And that which explains the so-called illusions of the senses
does not imply that these illusions take place on a screen separating

us from the environment; it requires these illusions to be ways in which we are in direct contact with the environment.

But it has also been explained earlier that dissimilar causes can have similar effects. Hence hallucination can imitate sensation. I do not always know whether I am perceiving, and therefore sensing, or hallucinating, and therefore imagining. In deciding which, I take the coherence of present experiences with one another and with past and future experiences as evidence that I am perceiving. But the question whether I am perceiving or hallucinating concerns the causal analysis of the experience I am undergoing: is my present experience what it is because it is awareness of the action of the environment on my sense organs?

The fact that the coherence of experience is relevant to deciding whether this causal analysis is correct does not mean that our belief in physical things is belief in the existence of something beyond that which our senses are aware of. It means the opposite. Coherence is evidence that our experiences are not chance copies of sensations but are what they are because in them we are aware of the received action of things as the action of things.

There are two other common motives, in addition to Hume's argument against causal necessity, for rejecting non-empirical knowledge, metaphysics in particular. One of these motives is that all concepts descriptive of what exists must be derived from the senses, and it is by no means clear how metaphysical concepts, like the concepts of substance and accident, can be derived from the senses. If metaphysicians did not get these ideas from their sense experience, where did they get them? Again, the explanation which best harmonizes with the presuppositions of empiricism is the linguistic explanation. Metaphysical concepts are projects of linguistic structures onto the things we refer to in language. The substance-accident distinction, for instance, derives from the subject-predicate structure of sentences.

The linguistic account of metaphysical concepts is criticized in Chapters Two and Six. That account is a good illustration of the kind of hypotheses which linguistic philosophers make concerning traditional philosophers, hypotheses which conform to preconceived ideas about human knowledge but which do not conform to the actual practice of non-linguistic philosophers. There have been some metaphysicians whose concepts of substance and accident can be explained by the subject-predicate sentence structure or by some other feature of language. But what is important is that there have been many metaphysicians whose concepts of substance and accident cannot be

so explained. When accident and substances are defined, respectively, as what does or does not exist in another, they are defined in terms
of existence. And existence is a linguistic category, or a projection of
a linguistic category, if and only if to exist is to be referred to in
language.

Whether the empiricist recognizes it or not, the doctrine that our
concepts derive from sense experience is a (partial) causal analysis
of our concepts. And it is an accurate causal analysis. If not, we must
have extrasensory sources for concepts.

At the end of Chapter Ten, however, I argue that substance, accident and cause are found in sense experience; they are not inferred
entities postulated to be behind or beyond what is sensed. What the
senses are aware of are things that sense experience itself enables us
to recognize as instances of these concepts. To find substance, accident and cause in experience we must analyze that experience
ontologically. But it is sense experience which allows us to form ontological concepts by providing the evidence for the truth of statements
about the existence of the things that are primarily referred to in
language, publicly observable things. In providing the evidence for
the truth of sentences like "An F exists", sense experience puts us
in possession of the meaning of the word "exists". From there we
can form other ontological concepts and, as Chapter Ten argues, find
instances of them in experience.

There is one more common motive for empiricism: only in the
empirical disciplines do we succeed in avoiding interminable controversies of the kind that have always plagued philosophy. Empirical scientists always have disagreements, but they also achieve long-lasting
consensus with a degree of regularity that is unheard of among
philosophers. Philosophers of the same tradition do achieve a measure
of consensus; that, after all, is what makes them members of the same
tradition. But even this much consensus is far from that of empirical
scientists. And when the existence of diverse philosophical traditions
is taken into consideration, there is no comparison whatsoever.

These facts cannot be denied. But the question is what causal
analysis of these facts should be given? Those causal analyses which
deny philosophy's legitimate claim to being a distinct mode of knowing suffer from a number of problems. It is a cliché to accuse them
of self-referential inconsistency. The final section of Chapter Six,
however, will point out a different, and more subtle, reason than is
usually offered for finding empiricists self-referentially inconsistent:
in rejecting intellectual pursuits which do not produce long-lasting

consensus, empiricists imply a necessary, and hence unempirical, causal connection between the conditions which make knowledge possible and the conditions which make consensus possible. A contingent causal connection won't do for eliminating non-empirical knowledge claims. And a necessary connection could be known only by a piece of non-empirical knowledge.

I am not suggesting that there is no connection between the conditions necessary for knowledge and the conditions necessary for consensus. But in Chapter Eight it will be shown that necessary causal relations are consistent with the existence of chance. The occurrence of an event is determined by the fact that things with certain causal dispositions exist in a certain configuration. Their causal dispositions necessitate that these things behave in certain ways in these circumstances. But the causal dispositions of no one of these things necessitates its being in these circumstances. The co-existence of these causes in the configuration necessitating an event is contingent from the point of view of the natures of the causes. And this is true of the circumstances necessitating the occurrence of any event.

Now the conditions which make knowledge, and hence consensus, possible everywhere co-exist with conditions which, in the right configuration, will produce error. It is a very well established empirical fact, furthermore, that it is more difficult to achieve consensus in philosophy than in other fields. Therefore, it is reasonable to conclude that conditions producing error are more likely to occur in philosophy than elsewhere. If so, there will be less consensus among philosophers than among others. But that fact does not license the conclusion that philosophy is not a means of obtaining communicable knowledge. For in all fields of knowledge, consensus is a matter of degree. No more is implied than that, in philosophy, conditions which would produce consensus, other things being equal, co-exist with conditions which limit the degree of consensus which can be achieved. The conclusion to be drawn, consequently, is much less extreme, and one that everyone should already know: one should not look to consensus among philosophers as a basis for one's philosophical beliefs, including one's beliefs about the nature and value of philosophy.

But a problem less subtle than self-referential inconsistency besets those who take lack of consensus as evidence for the illegitimacy of philosophy as a distinct mode of knowing. Their views about the nature of knowledge, and the arguments by which they justify them, have always produced as much controversy, disagreement and paradox as they were supposed to liberate us from. Every generation offers its own analysis of philosophy's troubles and in doing so gets into troubles of the same kind. This is another well established empirical fact: attempts to eliminate disagreement in philosophy by eliminating philosophy or by making its method an extension of the method of some other discipline always produce more philosophical disagreement. One cannot be blamed for wanting a different way of accounting for philosophy's troubles.

Chapter Eleven offers such a way, not an ad hoc account, but an analysis which follows from the ontological character of philosophical concepts. A logical property of those concepts which has always been recognized, though its implications in this context have not, explains why error is more likely in philosophy than in other fields. The ontological character of philosophy therefore explains the empirical fact that philosophy has more difficulty achieving consensus, but it explains this without making philosophy illegitimate or identifying it with an extension of some other mode of knowing, empirical, logical or mathematical. Among the errors that are accounted for in this way are the major empirical fallacies refuted in earlier chapters, especially the misunderstanding of causal necessity and the substitution of epistemological concepts for ontological. From the ontological character of philosophical concepts it will also be demonstrated that formal languages are of no direct use in the solving of philosophical problems. (References to further examples of ontological causal analysis and further discussions of the topics dealt with in this book will be given in Appendix II.)

Now it should be clear why I consider the so-called critiques of empiricism that come from linguistic philosophers conservative. In fact, they are positively reactionary. All attempts to reduce philosophy to an after-the-fact reflection on other disciplines cut us off from knowledge without which such reflection is condemned to unsolvable problems, problems created by denying any independent validity to philosophy. It will be objected that the proposals I am making to get us out of this vicious circle require us to think the unthinkable. And many of these ideas are unthinkable from the point of view of the assumptions our philosophic training commonly imparts. Much in that training is excellent. It is the remainder that is the subject of this book.

Chapter Two
Ontology and Language

Philosophy as I understand it embraces a number of enterprises known by such traditional names as metaphysics, epistemology, the philosophy of science, the philosophy of language. What, if anything, distinguishes the method of philosophy from the methods of other inquiries? Later I will be arguing that philosophical method deserves to be called ontological in a sense in which the methods of non-philosophical disciplines do not deserve to be so called. "Ontology" in its traditional meaning does not refer to just any kind of belief about what exists. It refers to a specific type of belief about what exists, beliefs about the ultimate categories, constituents and causes of what exists, *and not necessarily* about the ultimate categories of our conceptual or linguistic frameworks. With respect to a particular philosopher, the ultimate categories of reality may be related to the ultimate categories of his conceptual scheme in one way or another, but ontology as such concerns the ultimate categories of reality.

My use of "ontological" to describe philosophical method will be derived from, but have wider extension than, this traditional use of "ontology". By ontological method, I mean a particular way of forming and verifying beliefs about what exists. This method is the proper method in all branches of philosophy, the epistemological branches included. In other words, I will not be using "ontological" in contrast to "epistemological". It is possible, as we will see, for the epistemological point of view to fallaciously encroach on non-epistemological domains. But the epistemological point of view is perfectly valid in itself since knowledge is a reality which can be examined philosophically, that is, ontologically, as well as empirically.

The ontological method of analysis can hardly be understood, however, if the traditional concept of ontology is not understood. And that concept has become obscured through the influence of a group of philosophers I will call the "linguistic ontologists". Among linguistic ontologists, there are diverse opinions on the exact relation between language and ontology. These disagreements are important in themselves but are less so from the perspective of the quite different approach to the problems of ontology, and other philosophical problems, which I am proposing. Therefore the linguistic ontologists may be treated together for the purposes of this discussion.

By way of generalization, then, it can be said that linguistic ontologists believe the questions of traditional ontology are to be answered by the analysis of and, for many, the revision of language. For they believe the problems of traditional ontology result from the misinterpretation or misuse of language. Our languages have ontological beliefs built into them such that one cannot adopt a language without at least implicitly adopting the beliefs about what exists that are included in the structure of the language. And the explicit ontological beliefs of traditional philosophers derive in great measure from the linguistic backgrounds of their assertions.

This chapter will expose some of the shortcomings of linguistic ontology and thus prepare for my later explanations of ontological method. The linguistic approach to ontology is not the most serious weakness of contemporary philosophy. But beginning here will allow me to introduce two ideas that will play major roles in many of the subsequent arguments of this book: the distinction between "things" and "objects of knowledge" and a corollary of this distinction which I will call "the epistemological fallacy". Nor are the criticisms of linguistic ontology offered here meant to be the last word on the matter; they will be completed by the further arguments of sections 6.2 and 6.3.

2.1 Linguistic Ontology
2.1.1 Some examples

Here is one common view of the relation of language to ontology:

Language cannot be used to explain, describe, refer or narrate unless it implicitly contains a conceptualization of reality. This conceptualization serves to specify the types of things we can think about and the sorts of properties and relations we can attribute to these things. The sort of conceptualization of reality implicit in our ordinary language has been made explicit by Strawson and labeled "Descriptive Metaphysics". Our ordinary language pictures reality as an inter-related collection of objects in a spatio-temporal framework. These objects have properties, with both primary and secondary qualities considered real properties of objects. . . . Others, such as Aristotle in his philosophy of nature and Merleau-Ponty in his phenomenology have developed quite similar views. Each could be interpreted—with a little stretching—as an attempt to make explicit the common sense view of reality that structures and is transmitted through our ordinary language . . .

. . . The meaning of a proposition depends on its relation to other propositions and to the conceptual framework which structures the network of propositions. In categorizing the prerequisites for the meaningfulness of a proposition we may make a facile first-order distinction between linguistic and ontic presuppositions. The linguistic presuppositions are the rules, whether of surface grammar or depth grammar, which structure the meaningful units within a language. . . . The ontic presuppositions concern the conceptualization of reality implicit in the language used, i.e., what sorts of things are accepted as real and what kinds of properties and relations are attributed to them. (MacKinnon, 1969, pp. 30-31)

By the very fact of using a language we are committed to certain presuppositions about what does or does not exist. The beliefs about reality which our language commits us to constitute an informal ontology. Ontology in the formal sense, philosophical ontology, makes these presuppositions explicit. This is what thinkers like Aristotle, Kant and Merleau-Ponty have been doing all along whether they were conscious of it or not. And how could it be otherwise since, to think, the philosopher must think in a language? To claim that one's knowledge of what exists is independent of the structure of one's language is to claim to have done the impossible, to have transcended language.

Thus we are *bound* by the ontological commitments built into our conceptual scheme; we cannot abstract ourselves from them. This binding is not absolute, however, since we can change our conceptual schemes. But between different conceptual schemes there is an incompatibility which implies that you cannot shift from one linguistic framework to another without altering your ontological presuppositions about the world. A convenient example of this kind of incompatibility is provided by Hanson (1969):

We say "The sun is yellow", "The grass is green", "Sugar is sweet", "Bears are furry". In this adjectival idiom, yellowness, greenness and sweetness are properties which inhere (passively) in the sun, grass, sugar and bears. They are built into the objects of which we speak. Now convey such information by means of verbs, as in Arabic and Russian: say "The sun yellows", "The grass greens", "Sugar sweetens", and "Bears fur" . . . .

That it is yellow is a passive thing to say about the sun, as if its colour were yellow as its shape is round and its distance great. Yellow inheres in the sun, as in a buttercup. "The sun yellows", however, describes what the sun does. As its surface burns so it yellows . . . .

. . . This is not merely to speak differently and to think in the same way. Discursive thought and speech have the same logic. How could the two differ? Speaking with colour-words as verbs just is to think of colours as activities and of things as colouring agents. . . .

If a conceptual distinction is to be made between a bear's activities when climbing and its activities when "furring", the machinery for making it ought to show itself in language. If a distinction cannot be made in language, it cannot be made conceptually. (pp. 32-34)

Philosophic knowledge deals with what is true of objects of our experience only as a result of their being referred to in language; being an activity, for example, or being a passively inherent quality. Is it left for *scientific* knowledge to deal with the things we experience as they are in themselves? No. Linguistic ontology casts doubt on the ability of science to supply us with facts holding true of things independently of the manner in which we conceptualize them in our languages:

Imagine us on Castle Hill this morning at dawn. I say: "It is a fact that the sun is on the horizon, whether or not there is any language in which to say so. And this grass at my feet is green. Whether everyone (or no one) knows these things they remain stubborn, brute facts." . . .

. . . Now convey such information by means of verbs, as in Arabic and Russian: say "The sun yellows", "The grass greens", "Sugar sweetens" and "Bears fur" . . .

. . . In such a language could it be stated as a fact that the sun is yellow, the grass is green, sugar is sweet? . . .

What if information about colours were expressed adverbially? We would then say "The sun glows yellowly", "The grass glitters greenly", "The chapel twinkles greyly". If everyone spoke thus, how could one insist on its being a fact that the sun is yellow, that grass is green, or that the chapel is grey? Could such "facts" be articulated at all?

It may be objected, "However we speak, one could always see the difference between a bear climbing and grass greening. Language could not blind us to differences between the way the sun brings its colour to us and the way the waiter brings tea to us''. This is not obvious; it may not even be true. If we had no possible way of communicating about differences between bears climbing and grass greening, what would be the force of insisting that there were such differences? (Ibid.)

The expression of a ''fact'' in language brings into play the whole conceptual scheme which is the condition for the meaningfulness of the sentences of the language. And ''it is not possible to specify the precise degree to which, in affirming a proposition, we also intend to affirm the presuppositions, framework features, and entailments on which the meaningfulness of the proposition depends'' (MacKinnon, p. 31). But if there are no language-independent facts, by what standard do we judge that one conceptual scheme is superior to another? It appears that we are left with merely subjective standards. I will argue below that ontology in my sense of the word, a method of forming concepts by reference to existence and verifying truths employing those concepts, can provide us with standards for evaluating different conceptual schemes (assuming for the sake of argument that there are genuine ontological conflicts between language frames — more on this question later). Before getting to my own views, however, I wish to point out some of the more obvious difficulties with the linguistic view of ontology we are presently considering.

It is clear that the history of philosophy gives little or no support to the view that philosophical ontology is (consciously or unconsciously) derived from language. Among English-speaking philosophers, for example, there have been Platonists, realists, Hegelians, empiricists, process philosophers, Kantians, Marxists, pragmatists, etc. Conversely, Aristotelians are to be found among philosophers whose native tongues were as diverse as Greek, Latin, Hebrew, Arabic, German, French, English, Russian and Japanese. I agree with MacKinnon that it would take a ''little stretching'' to interpret these facts as cases of philosophers explicating the conceptual framework of their ordinary language. In these cases the philosopher adopted his ontology not on the basis of the implicit assumptions of his language but on the basis of explicit arguments which by and large had explicit premises. Where these premises are mistaken, it may be that the philosopher has been misled by language. But his ontology itself is not thereby rendered linguistic unless he is committing the same fallacy I will shortly show the linguistic ontologists to be committing, the fallacy to be described as the epistemological fallacy.

A specific example will be helpful before we go any further. Austin,

Ryle and Strawson are supposed to have shown that Aristotle was a prototype Oxford analyst. His doctrine of substance, for instance, was an understandably clumsy way of registering the fact that the spatio-temporally distinct individual is at the basis of our conceptual scheme. But if that is the case, why have Aristotelians been unanimous in agreeing that such spatio-temporally distinct individuals as tables, chairs, buildings and mountains are not substances? And at the same time why have they always had such difficulty in discriminating unit substances within our experience, that is, in deciding such questions as whether the whole universe is one substance or whether each individual atom or proton or quark is a substance?

The linguistic reading of the Aristotelian doctrine of substance satisfies the requirements of a priori assumptions about what non-empirical philosophies must have been doing rather than the requirements of the evidence provided by the philosophies themselves. Current assumptions require that what philosophers have called ontology is linguistic in the sense that it has its source in the structures of our languages. But there may be more things on heaven and earth than are dreamed of in our metaphilosophies.

While on the subject of substance, it should be noted that the two most important examples of the view that the specific ontological beliefs of philosophers derive in great part from pre-philosophic linguistic structures will be discussed, at length, in later chapters. One is the view that substance-property ontologies, Aristotelian or otherwise, somehow result from the use of the subject-predicate or argument-function grammatical forms. (This will be dealt with in sections 6.1.2 and 9.3.2.) The other is the view that philosophers have been misled into thinking that existence is a property of things by the fact that "exists" functions as a grammatical predicate. (This will be the main topic of Chapter Five.)

Here it should be pointed out that there is at least as much danger of reading our ontological presuppositions into our interpretation of language as there is of reading our linguistic presuppositions into our ontology. The former is what Hanson seems to be doing. Consider his statement that if a conceptual distinction is to be made, "the machinery for making it ought to show itself in language", otherwise there would be "no possible way of communicating about differences". What does the machinery for making a conceptual distinction consist of? What does it mean for a language to have the ability to show a distinction? Hanson thinks it means that the distinction must somehow be built into the grammatical structure of the language.

But why cannot the ability of language to make an ontological distinction amount to the fact that, within the language, one is able to formulate a sentence to the effect that this distinction does obtain? For such a sentence to be formulated, the distinction need not be built into the grammar of the language. Of course formulating the sentence does not prove it true. But the issue here is not how such a sentence might be verified. Hanson's position is not a theory of how ontological distinctions are verified but of how they are expressed within a language.

The facts of the history of philosophy, again, provide proof that a philosopher's asserted distinctions need not correspond to distinctions made in his grammar. The fact that they use the English language has not prevented philosophers from denying that there are specific actions corresponding to active verbs like "thinking". (See, for example, Wittgenstein, 1965, p. 7.) Conversely the fact that we refer to thought by means of active verbs has not prevented philosophers from recognizing that proof is necessary to justify classifying thought as action. (See Simon, 1934, pp. 57-95.)

If Hanson's view of the way distinctions should show themselves in language were correct, it would be because philosophical assumptions he brings to his analysis of language happened to be correct; it would not be because an examination of the ontological assertions of philosophers shows these assertions to either derive from or imply the presence of certain distinctions and categorizations in grammar. Hanson's question begging is even clearer when he describes "The sun is yellow" as suggesting passivity. What licenses him to interpret "is yellow" this way? Some analytic truth or categorical imperative? And what evidence is there for asserting that "The sun yellows" suggests activity? Compare: "He just sits there all day long and doesn't do a thing", "That log just takes up space". Nothing intrinsic to the verb forms "sits" and "takes up" requires that we interpret them as suggesting either activity or passivity. But the hypothesis that our language determines our ontology (in the formal, that is, philosophical, sense) commits us to holding that certain grammatical forms call for certain ontological interpretations. Linguistic ontologists, in other words, have a theory-laden perception of our conceptual frameworks.

And still the criticism has not gone deep enough. There is one and only one way to judge a man's philosophical ontology: propose an ontological statement and ask him if he agrees or disagrees. By an ontological statement I do not mean a statement like "The sun is yellow"; I mean a statement like "Yellow is a property adhering passively in the sun". And there is no necessity whatsoever for a person who employs the first statement to assent to the second. A clever linguist like Whorf can achieve something analogous to a philosophical ontology by placing a philosophical interpretation on some grammar and then constructing assertions about the world on the basis of that interpretation:

> The Hopi metaphysics. . .imposes on the universe two grand cosmic forms . . . objective and subjective . . . . The subjective realm . . . is in a dynamic state, yet not a state of motion—it is not advancing towards us out of the future, but *already with us* in vital and mental form, and its dynamism is at work in the field of eventuating or manifesting, i.e., evolving without motion from the subjective by degrees to a result which is the objective. (Whorf, 1950, p. 173.)

That the result is only analogous to a philosophical ontology is shown by the fact that the constructed statements have never been held by anyone—least of all by the native speakers of language in question—and probably never will be.

Now teach one of those native speakers English. Admittedly, he acquires a new conceptual framework. But he also acquires the ability to understand the philosophical sentences about the world Whorf has constructed in *English*. Therefore we can now ask the native whether these sentences express what he formerly believed. As a control we should find some already existing English philosophical sentences which are genuinely incompatible with, not merely different from, Whorf's sentences. Then we would have an interesting test of the native's ontology. If I am right, the test would show that Whorf's sentences express the native's former grammar but not his former beliefs about the world.

2.1.2 The indeterminacy of translation

I would not have to mention that logical incompatibility between statements is not the same as mere difference between statements were it not for some of the moves made by Quine in defending his version of linguistic ontology. He holds that translations which are incompatible in the translating language can render the same sentence of the translated language with equal success. Each of the incompatible translations can be consistent with the linguistic responses to sensory stimuli of the speakers of both languages. And the differences in the translations will amount to the imputation of different ontologies to the speakers of the translated language. (It is true that Quine rejects Carnap's distinction between selecting a linguistic framework and selecting an empirical hypothesis. But that does not disqualify him as a linguistic ontologist in my sense. For he believes that in adopting languages of different structures, we are adopting different beliefs about what exists.)

But it is not easy to see how this incompatibility is possible if, as Quine also holds, "there are no meanings, nor likenesses nor distinctions of meaning, beyond what are implicit in people's dispositions to overt behavior" (1969, p. 29). Since the supposedly conflicting translations are each compatible with all the relevant behavior and since there is nothing to meaning other than what is implicit in behavior, in what respect are the translations in conflict? If the meaning of sentences involved the kind of extra-behavioral mental entities Quine rejects, there would be something with respect to which behaviorally equivalent translations could be incompatible. Quine calls extra-behavioral meaning inscrutable because "there is nothing to scrute". What he should have said is that there is nothing for behaviorally equivalent translations to be incompatible, and therefore indeterminate, about.

The examples Quine uses do not make the incompatibility any easier to see. In one place, he asks us to take "nothing" and "not anything" as conflicting translations of "*ne . . . rien*". (Ibid., p. 30) He admits that the example is trivial. But the question remains what it is a trivial example of. Then he asks us to believe that "five head of cattle" and "five oxen" are incompatible translations of certain Japanese classifiers. (Ibid., p. 36) But how is this alleged incompatibility any less trivial than the last? Quine's artificially devised examples fare no better. There is no incompatibility between the assertion that rabbits exist and the assertions that undetached rabbit parts or time slices of rabbit or instances of rabbithood exist. In fact, these sentences imply one another. As understood in English, if one is correct, the others must be correct. If the existence of rabbits, rabbit parts, etc. were not compatible with one another, Quine could not suggest those terms as possible alternative translations of the same expression. Consequently Quine's examples do not illustrate any incompatibility of a kind that would be interesting as far as philosophical ontology is concerned.

Quine would probably respond that the conflict he sees occurs in the rules of translation ("'gavagai' is to be translated by 'rabbit'" as opposed to "'gavagai' is to be translated by 'undetached rabbit part'") rather than in the sentences resulting from the use of those rules. He means his examples as examples of incompatible *translations*, not as incompatible assertions. This response does not show what ontological interest the differences in the rules of translation have if the sentences resulting from these rules do not make conflicting assertions about what exists. It is not clear, furthermore, how rules of translation can be incompatible if meaning is behavioral and the rules are consistent with the same behavior.

The rules in question concern the translation of a language's "apparatus of individuation": articles, pronouns, singular and plural endings, numerals, expressions for identity and set membership, etc. The apparatus of individuation is the source of the supposed ontological significance of diverse rules of translation. For it is by means of such apparatus that we make distinctions like those between rabbits, their parts and their time slices. But if there is nothing more to meaning than dispositions to linguistic behavior, why does Quine think conflicting sets of hypotheses for the translation of the apparatus of individuation are possible? Because he thinks behavioral evidence would be insufficient to settle a dispute about which of two conflicting sets of hypotheses was correct.

Buy why should it be insufficient? If the meaning of the apparatus of individuation amounts to no more than the fact that the speakers of a language respond in certain ways to certain stimuli, the meaning of the apparatus of individuation is fixed by behavior. We behave in certain ways with each language-form in our apparatus of individuation. The way we behave with each of these language-forms has certain relations to the way we behave with the others and to sensory stimuli. The set of these relations constitutes the behavioral significance of the apparatus of individuation. Different languages not only have different language-forms in their apparatus of individuation, but these language-forms can be characterized by different sets of behavioral relations to one another and to sensory stimuli. But whether the behavioral relations of some of our language-forms for referring to individuals are the same, in whole or in part, as those of forms in another language is something that is either true or false. There is something to scrute.

Then how do we scrute it? According to Quine, we can allow for radically incompatible translations of parts of an apparatus of individuation by making drastic enough adjustments elsewhere in our set of translation rules. But could a language-form which one set of rules succeeds in translating by "one" (as in "There is one rabbit") be successfully translated, according to another set of rules, as "two" or "more than one" (as in "There were two minute-long time slices of rabbit" or "There was more than one rabbit part")? If so, where one set of rules renders a sentence into English by "X multiplied by one is X'', the other set of rules would render the same sentence by ''X multiplied by more than one is X''. Whatever the truth-value of the sentence being translated, it could not be the case that both sets of rules preserve that truth-value in translation.

Or could one set of rules succeed in using ''all'' where others would use ''some'', ''most'' or even ''all but one''? Not if the logical validity of arguments employing universal predication is to be preserved. And rules of translation must work both ways. The logical validity of arguments in English must be preserved when translated into the other language.

Still, there is no denying that Quine has a point. A drastic enough adjustment elsewhere in the rules would make room for such radically different translations. All that is required is that one set of rules translate ''Yes'' where the other translates ''No''. For one of the behavioral tests of our translations of ''X multiplied by one is X'' or ''From the beliefs that all men are mortal and that Socrates is a man, it follows that Socrates is mortal'' or ''There are more rabbit parts than rabbits'' or ''Rabbits last longer than time slices of rabbits'' is to pose our translations to the speaker of another language as questions, asking him whether these sentences are true or false. If Quine is saying that incompatible rules of translation are possible if we strategically substitute ''Yes'' for ''No'' in our translations of the responses to these questions, no one would want to disagree with him. From contradiction, everything follows (Quine's caveats about the necessity of the principle of non-contradiction will be considered in due course.) The only trouble is that we have independent behavioral evidence for the translations of ''Yes'' and ''No''. For our behavior is evidence of whether or not we agree or disagree with the truth of a sentence, for example, the sentence ''This building is on fire''.

I am not denying anything that linguists know about the differences in the grammatical structures of diverse languages. It has been suggested, for instance, that in some cases logical validity cannot be preserved from language to language. If so, however, it would not follow that translation is indeterminate. It would follow that direct translation is not possible, that to the behavioral role of some language-form, nothing corresponds in another language. But it remains true that the behavioral role of any language-form either is or is not equivalent, in whole or in part, to that of some other language-form. There is something to scrute. If the results of the scrutinizing are fuzzy, the fuzziness is ordinary empirical fuzziness, not that of the absence of any determinate function for the apparatus of individuation or other language-forms. Consequently, where direct translation is not possible, empirical evidence can tell us that this is the case and why this is the case.

And it is possible for one language to speak of rabbits where others speak of instances of rabbithood, rabbit parts, etc. But once again, the existence of rabbits, instances of rabbithood and rabbit parts are perfectly compatible with—even imply—one another. We still lack a connection between differing linguistic structures and differing ontologies understood in some philosophically significant sense. If we make the assumption that there is no more to philosophical ontology than such differences between languages, those differences become philosophically significant by fiat. It then becomes necessary to find incompatibilities where there are only differences; otherwise the differences would not be significant philosophically. Hence the compatibility of beliefs in the existence of rabbits, rabbit time slices, etc. argues the gratuitousness of the assumption that philosophical ontology is a function of one's language. (Chapter Six will argue that if linguistic structures were to make a significant difference in our beliefs about what exists, philosophical or empirical evidence could determine which beliefs were true.)

Nothing in this discussion implies, however, that it is always unreasonable to hold that some grammatical forms are particularly appropriate for expressing certain relationships between realities while other grammatical forms are more appropriate for expressing other relationships. When a philosopher or grammarian points to an association between forms of language and ways of being, he may be doing any of several legitimate things. For example, he may be pointing to the cultural fact that a certain language-form is generally used for a certain purpose by speakers of the language. Thus a certain kind of inflection may be used when referring to men, another kind when referring to women. Or the structural analogy between certain relations among grammatical forms, on the one hand, and certain relations among objects of our experience, on the other, may be sufficiently strong to make it useful to name the grammatical relation after the experiential one—hence grammatical categories such as active and passive verbs. In these cases, however, beliefs about the realities with which we are associating the language-forms are presupposed to the association itself. The words "active" and "passive" were in the language before grammarians found it appropriate to *extend* their use for the sake of characterizing grammatical types; and they were in the language because they helped us communicate about experience as we underwent it, not language as we used it.

2.2 Things and Objects

This section will lay the groundwork for further criticisms of linguistic ontology and related doctrines; it will also lay the groundwork for many of the discussions concerning knowledge and philosophical method that will come in subsequent chapters.

If ontology in the philosophical sense were a matter of linguistic frameworks, ontology would be confined to dealing with things from a point of view that is contrary to the very meaning of the word: the study of what exists. Ontology would not deal with things as existents but as objects of human knowledge. For it is only as a result of being made objects of knowledge that realities become referred to in language. Consider the following sentences:

> The cherry tree was chopped down.
> John is ill.
> Sarah was reluctant to go.
> Water boils at 100 degrees centigrade.

In contrast consider the following:

> The cherry tree was the last thing I saw.
> John's illness has not been identified.
> Sarah's reluctance was the topic of conversation.
> The boiling point of water was discovered before 1800 A.D.

Let us say that the predicates of the first set are true of their subjects insofar as their subjects are things, and the predicates of the second set are true of their subjects insofar as their subjects are objects of knowledge. This distinction, the distinction between things as things and things as objects of knowledge, requires explanation and justification. For it is at the heart of philosophical problems concerning knowledge and will be referred to throughout this study.

In the process of explaining the distinction, I will show that what is first known about objects of knowledge is not that they are objects of knowledge and that to exist is not to be an object of knowledge. Is it beating a dead horse to argue that *esse non est percipi*? No. In the first place, the distinction between being and being-known needs to be firmly established because that distinction will be crucial to a number of the problems we will be dealing with. In the second place, some recent philosophers have used formulas which imply, however unintentionally, that to be is to be known.

2.2.1 The thing-object distinction

This terminology could be misleading. The use of the word "thing" is not meant to rule out an ontology of processes, events, states of affairs or whatever. The word is chosen simply because its ordinary meaning, as opposed to that meaning of "object" which I will be relying on, is non-relational. To say that something is a thing is not to say that it is related in any way to what is not itself. Something is an object of knowledge, on the other hand, only because the relation knowing-this-object is true of some entity.

"Thing" would be a relational word if Carnap's analysis of "A is a thing" were correct, that is, if "A is a thing" were the material mode of speech for "'A' is a thing-word". Since "A is a thing" would then be understood as a syntactical statement, being a thing would amount to being the term of a linguistic relation. Things would be what are signified by one kind of word, properties what are signified by another kind of word.

If Carnap's analysis were correct, I could avoid any difficulty simply by pointing out that I am using "thing" in a different sense. In fact, however, Carnap was guilty of the same circularity we have seen in Hanson. What it is to be a thing-word cannot be defined by grammar or syntax alone; it must be defined by the extra-linguistic term of the relation of designating. (This criticism of Carnap is worked out in Kaminsky, 1969, pp. 65-79.) In reality, to say that "W" is a thing-word is to say that "W" is a word used for designating things. Carnap's analysis is another example of an a priori hypothesis about philosophers' uses of language, an hypothesis so circular that the acclaim it received can only have one explanation: those who believed it did so because they *wanted* it to be true.

Why a non-relational word such as "thing" is needed will become clear as I explain my use of the word "object". In the first place, I will use "object" only to refer to objects of knowledge, not objects of desire or action. As the second set of sentences above illustrates, many descriptions describe the objects of our knowledge precisely as terms of knowledge relations. But not all predicates we can attribute to objects can be of this nature, not all of them can describe objects of knowledge as objects of knowledge. To say that something is an object of knowledge is to say that it is known, and the first thing known about our objects cannot be the fact that they are known. The word "knowledge" expresses a relation; the word "known" describes something as term of that relation. These words enter the vocabulary to describe something, call it "A", as known because something, call it "B" (though it may be identical with A), has knowledge of A. And if A is the first object of our knowledge, what is known about it cannot be that it is term of a knowledge relation.

The alternative would put us in an infinite regress. To recognize that something is known is to recognize that there is a knowledge relation of which it is the term. Therefore if what is first known about something is that it is a "known", the first object to which our knowledge is related is itself a knowledge relation to some term. And then we must ask what is the term that is known by the knowledge relation that is supposedly what is first known. If this term is not itself a knowledge relation, then what is first known is not that something is known. But if this term is a knowledge relation, we must repeat the question. What is the term of *that* knowledge relation? Either what is first known about something is an endless sequence of relations to terms which are themselves relations to terms or what is first known is not that something is known.

When objects of knowledge are here contrasted with things, it should be noted, "knowledge" is not understood in the sense of certitude caused by awareness of evidence sufficient to exclude the opposite from truth. It is understood in the more inclusive sense of cognition in general, awareness of some kind. On the other hand, our awareness of the truth of sentences, especially of philosophical sentences, is the subject of this book. This is the kind of cognition we will be mainly focusing on and for the understanding of which we will be making use of the thing-object distinction.

Cognition itself cannot be the primary object of cognition. A knowledge relation can be *recognized* to exist only if there is knowledge of some term other than knowledge itself. For a knowledge relation can *exist* only if knowledge initially has some term other than knowledge itself. To become what-is-known our first objects must be recognized other than as what-is-known. What-is-seen is not seen *as* what-is-seen; it is seen as red or large or moving. And if something were not capable of being recognized as red or large or moving, it would not be capable of becoming what-is-seen. "Objects", in other words, become objects first by our recognizing them other than as "objects"; if we did not know something about the first objects of our knowledge other than that they are objects, we would not have any objects.

With reference to sentential knowledge in particular, before predicating of our objects descriptions of them as terms of knowledge relations, we must be able to attribute to them predicates that do not describe them as terms of knowledge relations. The predicates "vegetable", "lighter than air", "composed of two parts hydrogen and one part oxygen", do not describe anything as term of a knowledge relation. It is only because we can attribute such predicates to things that we can also describe them as terms of knowledge relations. Predicates for sense qualities, "red", "sweet", "warm", etc., may as a result of scientific or philosophic sophistication come to include in their meanings a relation to sensation, the sensations of the average observer, for example. But they cannot be learned that way to begin with.

So-called act-object analyses of knowledge are unacceptable to some philosophers. But nothing that controversial is implied here by speaking of objects. An object is simply that to which we can truthfully attribute predicates which describe terms of knowledge relations as terms of such relations, predicates like "seen", "remembered", "referred to", "described", "meant", etc. In contrast to "object" we need a word that helps express the fact that what we know first about our objects is not that they are terms of knowledge relations. Hence the importance of opposing to the relational word "object" a non-relational word such as "thing".

It is not implied, however, that the features known about things when they become our objects do not include relations. Nor am I at the moment making any commitment to the existence of relations as entities of a class distinct from the things that they relate. Knowledge-of and desire-for are examples of existents which deserve to be called "relations". Whether they belong to a separate class from entities that are not relations or whether they are simply "absolute" entities which must be *described* relatively is a question that does not have to be answered here. But in order to become objects, objects must be known by features which are other than being-an-"object". Whatever it may mean for relations to characterize what we know insofar as these are other-than-"objects", it is certain that being-an-"object" is not among these relations. And it is in contrast to being-an-"object" that I am using the word "thing".

2.2.2 To be is not to be known

Objects of knowledge are more-than-objects in another sense as well. I have just argued that they are more-than-"objects" *conceptually*, that is, that attributing predicates like "known" to objects is dependent on our first knowing them other than as terms of knowledge relations. But our initial objects are also more than *objects* in the unequivocally ontological sense that, for them, to exist is other than being known. Against the idealist it has often been shown that his conclusion does not follow from his premises. But to my knowledge, no one has previously shown, except in barest outline, that the idealist position is impossible. I will argue this now.

To say that A is an object is to describe A as the term of a relation something (again call it "B" even though it may be the same as A) has to A; it is not to ascribe a relation or any other characteristic to A itself. It is to ascribe a relation to B. A can be said to be known because B knows A. It may be the case that A is the bearer of many relations to B. It may be the case that these relations are relevant to the fact that A is known by B. But that is not what we *say* when we say that A is known by B. And that A is known by B may imply, in conjunction with other statements about A and B, that other things are true of A also. But that these other things are true is not what is said when we say that A is known by B. All that is said is that the relation of knowing A is true of some entity called B.

"Being known" is what has been called an extrinsic denomination, a description of something not from the point of view of any of its features or characteristics but from the point of view of a relation something has to it. As another example, suppose we see Senator D nominating Governor C for President of the United States. What we are observing is D behaving in a certain way. We express this behavior by saying D is nominating C. But we could express the *same* behavior on the part of D by using the extrinsic denomination "being nominated by D" as in "C is being nominated by D". We thus describe C from the point of view of a relation that D has to C. Therefore "being nominated by D" does not express any of C's own characteristics. It is possible that, as a result of D's nominating him, C is really characterized by some new relation to D. But that is not what we know when we see D behaving in this way and express his behavior by saying that he is nominating C. Therefore, it is not what we know and express in "C is being nominated by D".

Similarly, because B knows A, we can view A as the term of B's relation and construct a description by which we describe A as such. We express the relation of knowing by means of an active verb, hence we describe A as the term of that relation by means of the passive verb form "is known". But to assert that A is known by B, we need know no more than that a state of knowing A is true of B. Describing A in this way no more requires that being known be a relation inhering in A than using an active verb requires that knowing be a causal operation on that which is known. If (*per impossible*) knowing were a causal operation on the known, that would still not be what is expressed by the use of the active verb "knowing". Likewise, A may be the bearer of many relations to B, identity included, but that is not what is said by calling A the object of B. To say that A is known by B is to saying nothing of A in itself.

One more distinction will be helpful in disposing of the view that to be is to be known. Recall that Berkeleyan and other forms of idealism do not deny the reality of the objects of perception; idealism is not skepticism. The objects of perception really exist for the idealist, but for these things really to exist is the same as for them to be known by the kind of knowledge we call perception. This is important, for our language contains resources for discoursing about all sorts of topics to which we do not want to attribute real existence: imaginary objects, logical relations, devices for simplifying other discourse such as "the average man", etc. I will call these topics of discourse "cognition-dependent objects" (after Deely, 1974, p. 862, with some modifications); or, where appropriate, I will speak of "logical constructs". About objects that do not have real existence, we may be able to say that to be is to be known. Whether or not this is the case, it is sufficient to note that the Berkeleyan dispute only arises between parties who agree that the objects, the nature of whose existence is in question, have real, as opposed to merely logical or imaginary, status. If an idealist wants to attribute real existence to *more* objects then the realist will, that is another matter.

A moment ago I made reference to the truism that, in conjunction with other statements, a statement may imply things that are not part of the claim made by the statement itself. I will now argue that the truthful attribution of the extrinsic denomination "is known" to a really existing thing necessarily implies that to be for this thing is really distinct from what is expressed by "being known". (The argument could also be put in terms of the attribution of existence to the *first* objects that we know, for we will see that it is because of our knowledge of really existent objects that we are able to talk about objects that have no real existence.) An extrinsic denomination treats the denominated purely as term of a relation and nothing more. It is impossible for what really exists to be *nothing but* the term of a relation something has to it. If the term of a relation had no reality other than that *expressed* (as opposed to implied in conjunction with other truths) by an extrinsic denomination, it would be nothing. For all the reality expressed by an extrinsic denomination is on the side of the relation of which the denominated is the term and on the side of the entity which is thereby related to this term. (And it is entirely accidental to the function of extrinsic denominations if that which is related and that to which it is related happen to be the same thing.) Logical constructs, like the average man, or imaginary objects, like a six-headed man, have relations to real existents. But to the extent that a cognition-dependent object is something to which real existence cannot be attributed, all the reality of the cognition-dependent object belongs to the psychological and social acts by which we think and discourse about it.

Getting back to real existents, consider an already existing reality, C. Suppose that subsequent to C's coming into existence, D becomes related to C in some way. Perhaps C has also become related to D, but as far as we know the only new reality in the situation is D's being related to C. We can express this reality by saying that D is R'ing C. And we can also form an extrinsic denomination describing C as that to which D is related: C is R'ed by D. The reality on which our construction of the extrinsic denomination is based lies entirely on the side of D, not C. Yet the logic of the extrinsic denomination by which we describe C as that to which D is related is the same as the logic of the extrinsic denominations "is known" or "is an object of knowledge". For in order to assert that A is known by B we do not have to know any more than that B is related to A by the relation knowledge-of. Since all the reality expressed by the extrinsic denomination "known by B" consists of features characterizing B's existence, not A's, to exist for A must be really distinct from what is expressed by "being known".

Recall our comparison of "being known" with "being nominated for President of the United States". That D is nominating C may imply that many things are true of C other than merely being term of D's relation. In conjunction with certain facts about the United States' constitution it may imply, for instance, that C is at least thirty-five years old. Similarly the fact that A really exists implies, in conjunction with the truth that all the reality expressed by an extrinsic denomination lies in the entity that bears the relation, not in the term of the relation, that to exist for A is not the same as being known.

I will briefly mention another way of putting this argument. An extrinsic denomination is, in itself, a logical construct. It is an object whose cognition results from the cognition of some other object(s) and which, insofar as it is distinct from the objects on whose cognition it depends, is a fiction having no real existence. Understanding the extrinsic denomination "being known", for instance, depends on understanding the relation knowledge-of. And what is expressed by "is known" differs from what is expressed by "has knowledge of" only in the logical device of describing the term of the knowledge relation, rather than the knower, by a relative predicate, a predicate to which something real must correspond in the knower but to which nothing real need correspond in the term on knowledge. To the extent that we have denominated anything extrinsically, we have predicated of it a fiction to which none of its features corresponds. Predicating of A an extrinsic denomination puts nothing real in A. Consequently, if the existence of A were what is expressed by extrinsic denomination, A would not really exist.

It should be noted that not every passive form of an expression for a relation is an extrinsic denomination. (Once again, grammar does not determine ontology.) Some words for relations are defined by features characterizing the *terms* of the relations. Compare the relations attempting-to-injure and injuring. The difference between them is determined by what is actually going on in the term of the relation, that is, whether or not something is actually sustaining an injury. It may be objected, therefore, that some criterion is needed to tell us that "being known" is not in this respect similar to "being injured". Not at all. If a relation is defined by features really characterizing its term, then, by hypothesis, what is expressed about the term of the relation is not simply that some entity has a relation to this term. In other words, a description of the term of the relation as term of the relation is not a purely extrinsic denomination: the term is not described simply as the term of a relation something has to it.

Consequently, even if "being known" were not a purely extrinsic denomination, the existence of known real existent A would still not be that of a mere term of B's relation of knowing A. For "known" would not express only the fact that B has a relation to A; it would express the reality belonging to A itself. (Since the relation borne by B would be described by reference to the reality belonging to its term, it would be the relation, not the term, that was extrinsically denominated.)

If the idealist is willing to concede that the existence of the known is not that of a mere term of a knowledge relation, or to concede that this relation is itself defined by reference to a reality which is other than that of the relation or of any characteristic of the bearer of the relation, he has no quarrel with realism. For then the existence of the known is other than the relation borne by the knower when the knower has knowledge-of something. The idealist is in a dilemma. "Being known" is either a purely extrinsic denomination or not a purely extrinsic denomination. On either hypothesis, the existence of the known is other than the knower's knowledge of it. (A further refinement of this argument will be made in section 11.3.2.)

2.2.3 Further notes on things and objects

Not all kinds of knowledge deal with real existents. Sentential knowledge, for instance, extends to both existents and non-existents. But the first objects of sentential knowledge must be really existent things. Even if the sentences we make about them are not always true, the primary objects about which we make sentences must be real existents. This is established by Wittgenstein's argument against private languages. Private objects, objects that cannot be shared by more than one person, are insufficient to cause usage to be correct or incorrect. Therefore, language requires public objects, objects that we can refer to in common. By private objects, Wittgenstein meant mental states such as a pain or the intention that an instruction be carried out a certain way. But as far as the ability to cause correctness and incorrectness in usage is concerned, merely imaginary or conceived objects are just as inadequate as pains. A language whose sole function was to describe one's fantasy life in a way that had no connection whatever with the descriptions we give real existents would be just as much a private language as a language whose function was to describe pains only to the person experiencing the pains. Therefore, a necessary condition for the public objects required by language is that they be real existents; fictions and logical constructs will not do. We can talk about the latter if and only if we make use of linguistic devices derived from those we develop for public, really existent, objects. (See sections 2.3.2 and 5.4.)

Since the first objects of sentential knowledge are really existent things, these objects are entities for whom existence is something other than being-an-*object*. (For those who do not accept Wittgenstein's critique of private language, another argument for the cognition-independent existence of our primary linguistic objects appears in section 10.5.) Real existents, again, are more-than-*objects* in two senses. On the one hand, their existence is not the same as being known. On the other hand, in order for something to be described as related to knowledge, it must first of all be describable by predicates that do not relate it to knowledge. For convenience I will call "object-descriptions" predicates describing an object of knowledge as related to knowledge, to some particular kind of knowledge or to some element in the knowledge process. Predicates attributable to real existents but which do not describe them as related to knowledge I will call "thing-descriptions".

Thing-descriptions do not cease being thing-descriptions when the things they are used to describe do not actually exist. The relevant consideration is not whether the thing a predicate describes actually exists. The relevant consideration is whether the predicate describes something as related to knowledge. A physical law, for instance, does not cease being true if no individual satisfying it happens to exist at the moment. But the predicates of physical laws do not, in general, relate things to knowledge.

In other words, I am including objects of knowledge which do not really exist in the extension of the word "thing". How can I do this when these objects do not have an existence describable as other than being-known? To say that an object of knowledge is a thing whose existence is other than being-known is to say that *if* and *when* this object actually exists, that existence is other than what is expressed by "being known". Any object which at some time in the past was a real existent as opposed to being merely an imaginary or fictional object deserves to be called a thing. And if an object is only a *possible* real existent, still it should be said that for it existence is not the same as being-known. For if and when the possibility of its really existing is fulfilled, its existence will be other than being the term of a knowledge relation.

Finally, being an object is not the same as being a thing, but when a thing, actual or possible, is known, that which is a thing (that to which thing-descriptions can be attributed) is the same as something which is an object (something to which object descriptions may be attributed). "Being an object" refers to a state of affairs really distinct from "being a thing". But that which is describable as an object may be identical with that which is describable as a thing. Likewise "being an apple" refers to a state of affairs distinct from "being red", but that which is an apple may also be something which is red. Although what is expressed by "being an object" is really distinct from what is expressed by "being a thing", when an actual or possible "thing" is "known", thing and object are distinct only conceptually, that is, the same individual satisfies the predicates "is a thing" and "is an object", but for different reasons.

2.3 The Epistemological Fallacy

The thing-object distinction will help us understand one of the major errors of linguistic ontology and of linguistic empiricism in general, the epistemological fallacy. Most philosophical questions (taking philosophy as it has been actually practiced, not necessarily as it should have been practiced) are epistemological. Most epistemological questions concern the relations of objects we are aware of and express in language to things existing otherwise than as terms of awareness and reference. Epistemologists ask how we can know (here in the sense of certitude caused by sufficient evidence) the identity between object and things. Some epistemologists hold there can be no questioning the truth of certain sentences about objects as objects (for instance, "It seems to me that I see a white patch"). But all epistemologists ask how we can know the faithfulness of what appears to us or what is communicated by means of language (objects) to what is really the case (things).

Not all philosophical questions have been epistemological. And the *epistemological fallacy* consists of treating objects as objects where the relevant concern is what is true of objects as things. It looks at things from the point of view of the conditions under which they become objects of knowledge or of the predicates which are attributable to them only as objects of knowledge where we should be considering things as things, as other-than-*objects.*

The fallacy takes many forms. It may lead us to read what is true of something only as a result of its having been objectified as characteristic of it in its extra-objective existence. (To "objectify" is simply to bring it about that an object-description may be truthfully attributed to something. Thus a language-act using words in the appropriate way may bring it about that something can be described as "referred to". No interior mental activity is intended by "objectify".) Or we may forget that in order for object-descriptions to be true of objects, objects must first be known by descriptions that do not relate them to knowledge. (Thus Husserl, 1960, p. 33, makes the starting point of philosophical knowledge *"Ego cogito COGITATUM"* — my emphasis.) Or the fallacy may take the form of confusing object-descriptions with thing-descriptions. This is not always the same as confusing what is true of things as objects with what is true of them as things. Logical relations, sense qualities and other attributes may characterize things only as a result of their having been made objects, but they are not object-descriptions if they do not express relations to knowledge.

It is often appropriate to distinguish the epistemological from the logical. For instance, Hume's theory of universality (a logical relation) as a defining note of causality can be distinguished from associated views of causal judgments and covering-law theories of explanation. And in discussing necessary truth, we are learning to distinguish the conditions of a sentence's truth from the conditions of our knowledge of its truth. (See Kripke, 1972, p. 35ff., and Plantinga, 1974, p. 4ff.) The notion of the epistemological fallacy, however, includes the logical—as well as the psychological and phenomenological—in the reference of "epistemological", since things terminate logical relations only as a result of our making things objects of knowledge.

2.3.1 Criteria and causes

Examples of the epistemological fallacy will appear at several points in this study. The following is a form of the fallacy that is necessary to deal with not only because it is pertinent to many of the arguments (and problems) of the linguistic empiricists, but because it is an obstacle to understanding the nature of both philosophical and empirical knowledge.

I have just said that it is possible to confuse object-descriptions with thing-descriptions. Desiring to avoid this confusion, someone might ask for a hard and fast *criterion* by means of which we can determine whether a given description should be classified as an object-description or a thing-description. Immediately attention is shifted away from the nature of these types of description to the manner in which we recognize them in particular cases, to the conditions under which a particular state of affairs becomes an object of knowledge. And knowing the conditions under which we recognize that particulars are instances of a certain class may tell us nothing whatsoever about the nature of that class. It will especially tell us nothing about the nature of the class when things are being classified according to features characterizing them as things.

Still, there are many situations in which it is clearly proper to ask for criteria in terms of which to distinguish Ps from Qs in our experience. Why not ask for criteria that will allow us to tell thing-descriptions from object-descriptions? What happens if, in order to find such criteria, we look back over the words already used to present this distinction? Should these words be interpreted as stating necessary conditions for a description to be called an object-description or thing-description? If so, are these conditions sufficient? As a matter of fact, it would be easy to produce ambiguous examples these conditions leave undecided. And it is not even clear that the necessary conditions themselves could be unambiguously determined to be present or absent in each particular case. If my formulas fail as criteria, must the conclusion be that the thing-object distinction is of little value? Only if we commit the epistemological fallacy.

The question that should be asked is not whether criteria for recognition can be provided but whether the use that has so far been made of these ideas, or any use that I will make of them in the sequel, requires that criteria be provided. Assuming that my arguments are in logical order, criteria of recognition would be needed if and only if some premise employed in these arguments could not be known true unless some other statement(s) expressing the appropriate criteria were known true. Not only is this not the case, to the best of my knowledge, but there is no reason why it should be the case. If a philosopher, or anybody else for that matter, cannot use a word unless he provides criteria for recognizing particulars for which the word is used, he is caught in an infinite regress. For he can provide criteria only by using other words for which criteria must also be provided.

So far I have argued that what is expressed by the object-description "known" cannot be identical with real existence and that object-descriptions can be truly predicated if and only if what are first known about our objects are thing-descriptions. In the argument against Berkeley it was agreed to by both sides, at least hypothetically, that we can describe A as the object of B's knowledge. If that or something similar had not been assumed, there could have been no argument. For no one would be claiming that to be is to be known or that being known is not the same as being. At this point, therefore, questions of criteria for recognition are irrelevant to the argument. From there the argument moved to a series of statements about what is involved in saying that A is known by B. Perhaps these statements are useful as partial criteria for distinguishing object-descriptions from thing-descriptions, perhaps not. What is certain is that these statements were not intended by their author to provide such criteria. As criteria they would have contributed nothing to the argument. For the stage at which criteria might be useful had to be already passed in order for there to be the factual agreement without which the argument could not have taken place.

The same can be said for the argument that the knowledge of thing-descriptions precedes the knowledge of object-descriptions. The infinite regress was developed by granting the opponent, for the sake of argument, that what is first known about A is that A is known. There followed statements about what is involved in recognizing that something is known together with the implicit claim that a description either expresses a relation to knowledge or it does not. Since either hypothesis was shown to destroy the opponent's position, there was no need for criteria telling us when a description does or does not express a relation to knowledge. Whatever it may be that an individual first knows about the first objects he attains in knowledge, it cannot be what is expressed in object-descriptions.

If my statements have not been intended to provide criteria, what is their purpose? They are intended as parts of *causal analyses* of certain kinds of sentential knowledge. They help us understand some of the causal factors that do, or some of the causal factors that do not, explain our awareness that something is an object or is a real existent. For instance, the argument that object-descriptions cannot be what are first known showed that something can be known to be perceived only as a result of our knowing it as red, or cold, or swift, etc. And in the argument against Berkeley I called attention to the fact that we attribute the predicate "known" to a thing as a result of recognizing that something is related to this thing by the relation, knowledge-of.

Some of the statements I have made turn on logical relations rather than causal relations (more on this distinction in Chapter Three). But I hold that analyses other than causal analyses enter philosophy only to assist us in achieving explanations in terms of causes. It is one of the theses of this book that philosophy, as well as empirical science, is causal knowledge and that most arguments, statements and definitions in philosophy are best understood as concerning the explanations of states of affairs in terms of their causes. I am fully aware of how vague this notion of causal analysis is at this point. For the moment I can only make assertions that will hopefully be both clarified and justified as we proceed. I need do no more than this now, however, because all that is required here is an idea of what I mean by claiming that criteria for recognition are, in general, irrelevant to philosophical argument. Demanding that every word used to describe be backed up by criteria for recognizing when individuals satisfy the description leads to an infinite regress, as we have seen. Requests for criteria do, as a matter of fact, come to an end at some point. And most philosophic arguments begin someplace subsequent to that point. They concern the explanation in terms of causes of something whose existence is granted—for example, our awareness of our self-identity, beliefs that others are in pain, successful predictions, reference to non-existents, etc.—granted at least for the sake of the discussion at hand. Therefore the level at which criteria operate is presupposed by the discussion. When philosophers disagree over an existence-claim, the disagreement can usually be settled only by appeal to the results of the causal analysis of things whose existence they do agree on. Again, criteria for recognition do not function.

I am not denying that clarification of language is a significant part of the philosopher's task. On the contrary, it is not only desirable but necessary for a philosopher's usage to be as clear as possible. But the ability to identify particular instances is only one of the goals which the clarification of language can have. What other goal is there? If, as I will argue in Chapter Three, the truth of some sentences is knowable simply by an understanding of the way the words of the sentences are being used, clarification of usage is important for our grasp of these truths, namely, necessary truths. And if, as I will argue in Chapter Seven, among necessary truths there are truths concerning causal relations, truths by means of which philosophy can establish its causal analyses, the clarification of usage allowing us to grasp these causal necessary truths is important for the discovery and verification of the causal analyses of things which have already been identified, at least hypothetically, as being of certain kinds. The goal of clarifying language in philosophy, therefore, is to help us grasp the necessary truth of causal explanations. (But how can we get an understanding of causal relations from an understanding of usage? See Chapters Three and Nine.)

I have pointed to the priority of thing-descriptions over object-descriptions as an example of a causal analysis. Another example was the analysis of object-descriptions as extrinsic denominations constructed in dependence on the recognition of relations like knowledge-of. Another important causal issue regarding the thing-object distinction concerns whether what is expressed by a predicate is true of something only as a result (effect) of its having been made an object (cause). In "The tree was ten feet from my eye" is "ten feet from my eye" an object-description because it relates the tree to an element in the process of knowledge? If there is any ambiguity about "ten feet from my eye" from the point of view of causal analysis, it is not an ambiguity brought about by lack of clear-cut criteria for identifying individual instances. To be ten feet from the eye is to be related to an element in the knowledge process. But being ten-feet-from-the-eye is not caused by being seen-by-the-eye, though the converse may be true. Therefore "ten feet from the eye" does not attribute to anything something that is true of it only as a result of its being an object of the sense of sight. If other questions are raised about "ten feet from the eye" from the point of view of the thing-object distinction, they are to be answered, if at all, by relating this description to the specific causal issues that are under discussion. (Again, I am using the terms "thing-description" and "object-description" solely for the convenience of compactness. In each case, what is important are the causes of the truth or falsity of the description.)

Allow me to respond to a possible objection. In using a phrase like "what is expressed by a predicate", I am not trying to introduce mental entities as bearers of meaning or truth. What I am trying to do is make room for the view that because language objectifies things only by casting what it expresses in a particular conceptual framework, language is unable to communicate what things are independently of the fact that they have become objects. On this view, what is expressed by *any* predicate is true of things only as a result of their being known. Unless we distinguish between words and what words are used for, however, this view becomes innocuous because trivially true, which is not, I believe, the intention. It is trivially true that to be referred to in language is to be an object of (a certain kind of) knowledge. Consequently all predicates become predicated of things only as a result of things being made objects. But more than this is needed to establish that what is communicated by means of predicates is not what something is independently of the fact that it is an object of knowledge, what something is as more-than-an-*object*. And according to the view we are considering, it is not only the fact that they are referred to in language that is true of things because they are objects; that which language communicates about things also results, at least in part, from the fact that things are made objects. For example, what "Bears are furry" communicates about bears is something passive while what "Bears fur" communicates is something active.

I will refute this view in Chapter Six. Causal analysis, either philosophical or empirical, regulated by necessary truths tells us what characteristics belong to things in their existence as things. Where neither philosophical nor empirical evidence would tell us which of two apparently conflicting beliefs about what exists is true, the differences between the beliefs are only on the side of what is true of things as objects, as a result of being made terms of knowledge relations, not on the side of what is believed about things as things, as more-than-terms-of-knowledge-relations. For instance, the differences can consist in things being objectified by means of different grammatical structures without anything different being attributed to things as things. In Chapter Six, I will also respond to objections against my claim that philosophical and empirical investigations presuppose the identification of some particulars as members of certain classes. One objection is that the way we classify a particular can change in the course of an investigation. Another is that the beliefs produced by any investigation are culturally relative since different languages can classify the same individual differently.

2.3.2 Linguistic ontologists and the epistemological fallacy

The linguistic ontologists can provide us with further examples of the epistemological fallacy. Consider one of Quine's early (1939) statements on the subject of existence:

> Here, then, are five ways of saying the same thing: "There is such a thing as appendicitis"; "The word 'appendicitis' designates"; "The word 'appendicitis' is a name"; "The word 'appendicitis' is a substitute for a variable"; "The disease appendicitis is a value of a variable". The universe of entities is a range of values of variables. To be is to be the value of a variable. (p. 50)

But things become describable as values of variables only as a result of being referred to in language. "Value of a variable" or "referred to in language" are object-descriptions. If to exist was to be the value of a variable in a true sentence, to exist would be to be known. ("Knowledge", again, is here taken in the general sense of cognition. We do not have to have certitude, supported by sufficient evidence, of the truth of a sentence in order for the sentence to be true. But to articulate things in language is to make them objects of linguistic cognition.) In effect, to exist would be true of things only as objects, not as things. *Esse* would be *percipi*.

In no way was it Quine's intention to imply this. Nothing could have been further from his mind. As his subsequent discussions have always tried to make clear, he was really concerned, not with what it is to exist, but with what it is to be *said* to exist: how existence claims are made and how we can tell which existence claims a theory is committed to. Such questions are epistemological in my sense of the word. They deal with a certain kind of linguistic objectification, assertion of existence, and with the objects of existence assertions considered as such, as terms of this linguistic relation. But Quine momentarily shifted from speaking of these epistemological topics to speaking about a non-epistemological topic, what it is to exist, without, however, dropping the epistemological point of view. As a result, he produced a formula reducing existence to being an object of knowledge by defining it from the point of view of the manner in which we make it an object of knowledge.

It is, of course, a truth about A's existence that if A exists, A can be the value of a variable in a true sentence. But being the value of a variable cannot be that something-other-than-being-the-term-of-a-knowledge-relation which existence has been demonstrated to be. The fact that A can be the value of a variable in a true sentence is an *effect* of A's existence, and effects are not the same as their causes. A's existing causes (by a mode of causality discussed in section 9.4.3) some sentences in which A is the value of a bound variable to be true. And that is another reason why being the value of such a variable cannot be what it is for A to exist. (That the epistemological fallacy discussed here is not peculiar to this momentary ill choice of words on Quine's part will be seen in section 5.2.)

But what about Quine's view that existential quantification commits us to the existence of the quantified objects? If we must quantify over classes in mathematics, does it follow that classes are real existents rather than cognition-dependent objects? No, and a so far unperceived implication of Wittgenstein's work shows why. Since language is public, the devices we employ to communicate about cognition-dependent objects must be derived from devices we employ for the sake of communicating about public objects. Public objects are real existents. And in communicating about public objects, we use existential quantification to attribute predicates to individuals, since it is only because these individuals are real existents that these predications are true. Again, it is A's existing which causes the truth of some of the sentences in which A is the value of a bound variable. Therefore in communicating about cognition-dependent objects we must use language which comes into being for the sake of objects to which we attribute predicates by means of existential quantification. It follows that in attributing predicates to cognition-dependent objects we must use existential quantification or some device definable by reference to existential quantification. (The impossibility of defining existential quantification itself by reference to proper names, even for finite domains, will be shown in section 5.2.4.)

But if we use existential quantification both in the case of realities and in the case of logical constructs, how can we express the difference between the ways these objects relate to extra-objective existence? To make the necessary distinction we do not have to have it somehow built into the grammatical structure of our language as Hanson apparently wants. In fact, whatever is built into grammatical structure is to that extent characteristic of objects only as a result of their being made objects. And what we want to express is the opposite, the existence which must be really distinct from anything true of objects only as objects. How then can we express the distinction between objects which can and do exist as more-than-*objects* and those which cannot? By saying so, no more, no less; by describing the existence of certain objects, namely, things, as "real", or "extra-objective", or "other than being known". And this is sufficient for distinguishing what existential quantification asserts in the case of things from what it asserts in the case of logical constructs.

We could, of course, adopt different symbols for existential quantification in the case of real existents and logical constructs. But there would be no difference in the logical relations between either of these symbols, on the one hand, and predicates, variables and names, on the other; the logic of quantification would be the same in both cases. Logical relations, as section 3.4.1 will explain, belong to the domain of objects, and of means of objectification, considered as such. They accrue to words and what are objectified by means of them as a result of the fact that we do so objectify things. Therefore it would be an epistemological fallacy to conclude from the fact that quantification over logical constructs has the same logic as quantification over things that extra-objective existence is asserted in both cases. No language-form can attribute real existence merely by means of its logical relations to other language-forms. If it did, to exist would be equivalent to being the term of some cognition-dependent relation.

But what tells us whether or not existential quantification is or is not imputing real existence to an object? The *nature* of whatever it is that earns the title "object" by being the term of a relation of existential quantification. And how does one judge that what I have vaguely described as the "nature" of an object is or is not the nature of an extra-objective existent? By causal analysis of the kind this book is attempting to explain.

Linguistic ontology in general is as much guilty of the epistemological fallacy as was Quine's early definition of existence. Grammatical structures are instruments for rendering *things* our objects, for making something the term of a knowledge relation which is more-than-the-term-of-a-knowledge-relation. To employ one grammatical structure as opposed to another, on the other hand, is to impose on our objects features true of them only as *objects*. (Being expressed by an active verb rather than a passive verb is an example.) Therefore adopting a particular linguistic framework need commit one to no ontological beliefs about things whatsoever. For whatever else they may be, ontological beliefs are beliefs about things as things, as existents. To exist is not the same as being an object of knowledge, so ontological beliefs are not beliefs about what is true of things as objects. It simply does not follow from the fact that a sentence describes the conditions under which something is made an object of Socrates' knowledge that the sentence describes what Socrates believes to be true of the thing in its status as a thing. Of course, knowledge, experience and linguistic behavior are existents; therefore we can form ontological beliefs about them and their causes. But it is the job of logic, linguistics and psychology, not of ontology, to make statements about, among other things, what is true of objects as objects rather than as things.

That is why the test of whether a person holds one ontology rather than another is not whether he expresses himself by saying "Grass is green" or "Grass is greening". The test is whether he assents to sentences like "Green is a property as opposed to an activity". As was said above, philosophers generally justify their ontologies by appeal to quite explicit premises. Where these premises are statements about things as objects, we have the epistemological fallacy. Often, however, these premises are statements about things as things, statements that are either true or false. When a false statement about things as things is made, the error may arise from the philosopher reading his grammar into his ontology. History shows that this does not happen nearly as often as the a priori assumptions of linguistic empiricists have led them to believe, but it can happen. And when it happens, an epistemological fallacy has been committed. Therefore those philosophers who have been guilty of reading grammar into ontology have only been making the same mistake that the linguistic ontologists themselves are making.

This is probably the reason why twentieth-century, English-speaking philosophers, when giving specific examples of how metaphysicians have been misled by language, so often cite examples from other twentieth-century, English-speaking philosophers rather than from more traditional philosophers. Although the epistemological fallacy need not be a confusion caused by language, or a confusion about language, it is understandable that it has frequently taken a linguistic form in a time when philosophers have been as preoccupied with language as we have been. But those twentieth-century philosophers who criticized others for being misled by language were just as often misled by language themselves. For they were treating questions as linguistic which are essentially extra-linguistic, questions that require linguistic tools in order to be solved only in the sense in which the answer to any question requires some linguistic tools.

It is probably unfair, however, to accuse any philosopher of being guilty of the epistemological fallacy. It is more accurate to say that he is a *victim* of it. For this fallacy is like something in the air we breathe. Or like original sin it is something we are born into when we begin to do philosophy in our times. It is endemic. It is part of the heritage that Descartes has bequeathed to modern philosophy. And no matter how much we may pride ourselves on standing in the tradition, not of Descartes, but of Locke, Berkeley and Hume, we have failed as yet to exorcize the Cartesian demon in this respect.

It is especially understandable for the linguistic empiricist to be a victim of this fallacy. For we have to account for what philosophers have been doing when they have made claims such as ''Green is a property as opposed to an activity'' or ''Each individual man is a substance, not an accidental grouping of substances''. Such claims cannot easily be classified as empirical nor explained as arising from confusion about the empirical facts. The only alternative seems to be to classify them as linguistic or at least to explain them as derived from language in one way or another. If not empirical, linguistic. What other alternative is there? For how can a philosopher who claims to be neither an empirical scientist nor a logician provide verification for statements like those about properties as opposed to activities or about substances as opposed to accidents?

The remainder of this book will attempt to answer these questions. It will do so by criticizing the assumptions which have led to the belief that there is no alternative to the linguistic account of philosophical ontology.

CHAPTER THREE

Truth and Necessary Truth

How can one go about distinguishing the true from the false in philosophy? This is the question of verification with which the present study is primarily concerned. And general principles pertaining to truth and verification have to be established before we can discuss truths of the ontological kind. In particular, the truth-value of a sentence is either contingent or necessary; it is either possible or impossible for a sentence to have the opposite truth-value. Many of the truths that enter into philosophy will be matters of contingent existential fact: knowledge exists; change exists; plurality exists; some things are similar to one another in various respects, etc. But can all the truths that enter into philosophy be contingent?

If so, the statements of philosophy will be verifiable mainly by reference to sense experience. (There are also statements about consciousness which are verified by introspection. While I do not deny their validity and their importance as *objects* for philosophical study, I would argue that their significance for the *method* of philosophy is limited.) How then can philosophy provide us with truths other than those known to science and common sense? Does philosophy possess some sophisticated technique for discovering facts of experience the sciences do not discover? While *philosophers* of science have too often been guilty of overlooking facts of experience—for instance, facts about what scientists and philosophers other than themselves have actually been doing—we can hardly make the same accusation against scientists. If philosophy can do something for us that the sciences cannot do, philosophy cannot consist entirely of truths verified by experience, contingent truths.

Since philosophy cannot consist entirely of contingent truths, it can advance our understanding of what we experience in a way different from that of science if and only if it is in possession of necessary truths that provide it with an additional but not conflicting way of interpreting and explaining what we experience. Further, although not all questions about what exists are matters for ontological analysis, ontological analysis as I understand it does approach things from the point of view of their existence. If my view of philosophy is correct, therefore, philosophy must be in possession of necessary truths concerning things as things, not things as objects of knowledge. Otherwise either philosophy becomes a study of what is known rather than what exists, or there is no difference between being and being known.

Many twentieth-century metaphysicians seem not to have appreciated the importance of necessary truth for their enterprise. Perhaps they felt secure in the knowledge that the verification principle could not overcome its many difficulties. But the verification principle was based on some fundamental truths: the truth-value of sentences is either necessary or contingent; each kind of truth has its own method of verification; and the method of verification appropriate to contingent truth leaves room for science and common sense but little more. If the logical positivists had said nothing else, no one could have faulted them. Their mistake was to read the division of truths into necessary and contingent as a criterion of meaning. The mistake was perhaps understandable in an era that has been attempting to use language as the point of view from which to approach traditional philosophical problems. But this mistake confused the nature of their attack on metaphysics both in their own minds and in the minds of their opponents.

The same presuppositions that produced the verification theory of meaning produced the theory that the value of necessary truths is wholly and entirely linguistic. And it is the linguistic theory of necessary truth, not the verification theory of meaning, that is the impediment to metaphysics and to any mode of philosophizing that would attempt to give us knowledge of things in their status as things. If necessity pertains only to the domain of the linguistic, it pertains to things only as terms of objectification in language. Philosophers, on the other hand, have a means for gaining knowledge of things as things that is distinct from that of science if and only if they can demonstrate their assertions by arguing from sentences that objectify what is necessarily true of things as things. Otherwise the assertions of philosophers may not be meaningless, but they are unverifiable.

Refuting the linguistic theory of necessary truth, then, is a prerequisite for a defense of philosophy as a distinct intellectual method. This chapter undertakes to accomplish that refutation and to present a new way of approaching the whole question of necessary truth. But there is no point in explaining necessary truth if there is no such thing as necessary truth. We must begin, therefore, not with the linguistic theory of necessity, but with its more recent progeny, Quine's denial that there are any necessary truths. From there we will move to the linguistic theory of necessity itself. In order to give an alternative account of necessary truth, I will make use of the distinction between things and objects to defend a theory of truth different from any that has been considered by linguistic empiricists, the identity theory of truth. Approaching truth in this way will allow us to explain necessity in terms of logical relations and causal relations. Finally, this chapter will give an analysis of the nature of logical relations. How this analysis sufficiently accounts for logical necessity and our knowledge of it will be explained in Chapter Four. With these issues out of the way, we will take up the specifically ontological character of philosophical truth in Chapter Five.

3.1 Quine on Necessary Truth

In "Two Dogmas of Empiricism" and elsewhere, Quine argues against the existence of necessary truths or, as he prefers to call them, analytic truths. What does "analytic" mean? After examining several alternatives, Quine concludes that this term cannot be satisfactorily explained or clarified. Since no satisfactory account of analyticity can be given, there is no reason to believe that any truths are analytic. But what kind of "account" or "clarification" is Quine looking for? What makes an "explanation" satisfactory and why?

"Two Dogmas" answers these questions only by example. It has been suggested, for instance, that "No bachelor is married" is analytic because it can be turned into a "logical truth" through substitution of synonyms for synonyms. The concept of a logically true sentence, that is, a sentence which remains true under all reinterpretations of its components but the logical particles, may have its own difficulties.

Waiving them for the sake of argument, what about the notion of synonymy which this explanation of the analytic relies on to translate sentences into the corresponding logical truths? Here we get an indication of the kind of "account" that Quine wants:

> Just what it means to affirm synonymy, just what the interconnections may be which are necessary and sufficient in order that two linguistic forms be properly describable as synonymous, is far from clear. (1963, pp.24-25)

And in the essay preceding "Two Dogmas" Quine had said:

> The problem of explaining the adjective . . . "synonymous" with some degree of clarity and rigor—preferably, as I see it, in terms of behavior—is as difficult as it is important. (p. 12)

Quine is looking for a *criterion* on the basis of which he can judge whether any given truth is or is not analytic, that is, some description of analyticity that will be useful for separating statements we are confronted with into those that are analytic and those that are not. The criterion cannot, of course, assign analyticity arbitrarily; at least some of the important characteristics traditionally ascribed to analytic truths must hold for all of the truths satisfying the criterion. The sought-for criterion is a sentence describing analyticity such that other sentences can be examined in the light of this one to see if they express truths that are analytic in some relevant sense. To confirm this interpretation of Quine, I quote from his essay "Carnap and Logical Truth":

> We at present lack any tenable general suggestion, either rough and practical or remotely theoretical, as to what it is to be an analytic sentence . . . Whenever there has been a semblance of a general *criterion*, to my knowledge, there has either been some drastic failure such as tended to admit all or no sentences as analytic, or there has been circularity . . . or there has been dependence on terms like "meaning", "possible", "conceivable" and the like which are at least as mysterious (and in the same way) as what we want to define. (1966, pp. 122-123, my emphasis)

It is small wonder that Quine fails to find the criterion he is after. It cannot exist. But the reason it cannot exist is *not* that there are no necessary truths. For there is no truth to the idea that if there are necessary truths, there is a criterion of this kind by which we can recognize them. The opposite is the case. If there are necessary truths, it is impossible that there be a criterion of necessity of the kind wanted by Quine. There is more than an epistemological fallacy here. Quine's critique of necessary truth is a pseudo-critique: it proposes a requirement for necessary truths that it would be self-contradictory for them to satisfy. If there are necessary truths, we cannot come to recognize them as such by making use of some previously known statement expressing a criterion of necessity. And *that* is a necessary truth as I will now try to show.

By what means can one acquire knowledge of necessary truth? One means would be reasoning from previously known truths. If the premises are necessarily true and the reasoning is valid, the conclusion is necessarily true. (We can overlook here the problems of defining validity. For if there are necessary truths known otherwise than by reasoning from previously known truths, we can use them to explain what it means for arguments to be valid.) But the process of deriving truths from previously known truths must begin from truths known otherwise than by such derivation. If not, reasoning is either part of an infinite regress of premises derived from prior premises or a circular process in which premises are derived from their own conclusions. For argument to begin from premises known to be true, there must be truths which we are capable of knowing without deriving them from truths previously known. Therefore if we know any necessary truths as a result of reasoning from others, some necessary truths must be known by a different method.

How else can they be known? A requirement for recognizing the truth of any sentence is an understanding of how its words are being used. To know whether "Snow is white" is true we must know how "snow" and "white" and "is" are being used. Understanding the use of the words, we judge the truth of this sentence on the basis of the evidence provided by our senses. But truths that depend on sense-experience for their verification cannot be known as necessary since what we are given in experience are contingent events. (I will argue in section 3.4.2 that truths verified by experience can be necessary, but verification by experience alone does not allow us to know that they are necessary.)

Knowing a necessary truth, like knowing any truth, requires understanding how the words of a sentence are used. But in the case of those necessary truths that are not derived from previously known truths, nothing more can be required than this understanding of usage. If they are not known true by arguing from other truths or by consulting the evidence of experience, they must be recognized as true solely by an understanding of the meanings of their words. When the truth of a sentence can be known solely from an understanding of the way its words are being used, that truth is *self-evident*: to understand the sentence is to know that it is impossible for it to be false, that is, that its opposite is contradictory.

Quine's argument against necessity is therefore beside the point. How can knowledge of the *self*-evident be derived from knowledge of *something else*, namely, a criterion of self-evidence? (And how is the criterion known to be necessarily true? Is it *self*-evident?) If our knowledge of the truth of a sentence results solely from our understanding of the way its words are used, it does *not* result from the application of a criterion expressible by means of some other sentence. There is knowledge of necessary truth if and only if there is knowledge of self-evidently necessary truth. And there is knowledge of self-evidently necessary truths only if they are not recognized as necessarily true by reference to a criterion for identifying particular instances of necessary truth or self-evidently necessary truth. Instead, they are recognized as necessarily true because the way their words are used makes their opposites contradictory and because we happen to be acquainted with the way their words are used.

Another way of putting it. To recognize that a truth is self-evident depends upon knowing how the words in which it is expressed are being used; it does not depend upon knowing the usage of any other words. Therefore unless the truth in question is a truth specifically about necessity or self-evidence themselves, recognizing that it is self-evidently true does not depend on our knowing the usage of (and much less our having criteria for) words such as "self-evident" or "necessary". In fact, we may not even find a need to have these words in our vocabulary until after we have discovered that some sentence cannot fail to be true as long as its words are used in certain ways. It is especially pointless, therefore, for Quine to search for an understanding of necessary truth in terms of criteria of recognition for the supposed cognates of "necessary" or "self-evident". Again, if there are no self-evident necessary truths, there is no way to discover any necessary truth. And a truth cannot become self-evident through the evidence of any other truth or through an understanding of any words other than its own.

Of course we do not learn how to use the words of a language in isolation from one another. In that sense, the understanding of other words may be necessary for understanding the words of a self-evident truth. But is the self-evident truth still *self*-evident if we must understand how to use other words in order to understand how to use its words? Yes. For it is not the case that knowledge of the use of these other words constitutes knowledge of *premises* from which the self-evident truth would be derived. Knowledge of a self-evident truth does not require an understanding of any words other than its own, but since we do not learn words in isolation from one another, the understanding of other words may constitute part of the understanding of the words of a self-evident truth. Furthermore, the knowledge we acquire in learning a new word by reference to words we have already learned is knowledge of rules governing linguistic usage. And the next section will demonstrate that the knowledge of usage required for the grasp of self-evident truth is not knowledge of linguistic rules.

To consider valid Quine's request for a criterion by which to recognize necessary truth is to render knowledge of necessary truth impossible before the argument has even begun. Please note, however, that this is not a repetition of the Grice-Strawson criticism that Quine has set his standards for clarification too high. My point is that no clarification of the kind wanted by Quine should be asked for. Philosophers who want to reject the necessary-contingent distinction will have to come up with a better reason than the lack of a criterion for necessity. One possible reason will be disposed of shortly. It is that the development of formal systems, in which nothing more need be understood than rules relating combinations of symbols, eliminates the need to appeal to self-evidence to explain our knowledge of logical and mathematical truths. (See section 3.2.2.)

Before going any further, I here present some examples of self-evident truth. The examples are taken from the arguments so far made in this book. This is for the sake of anyone who may be wondering whether I am willing to take my own methodological medicine.

> If an argument does not begin with premises that are not themselves derived by argument from other premises, the argument is either part of an infinite regress or is circular.

> If there are no truths that can be known without arguing from previously known truths, no argument can begin from truths that are known without arguing from previously known truths.

> If a sentence can be known true solely through an understanding of the way its words are used, knowing that it is true does not require knowing any other truth or understanding any other words except those required to understand the way its words are used.

> If a truth which is not a criterion for necessity or self-evidence can be known true without arguing from other truths, it can be known true without arguing from a criterion for necessity or self-evidence.

If a sentence can be known true only by arguing from other truths, the sentence cannot be known true solely from an understanding of the way its words are being used.

Every truth is either capable of being false or is not capable of being false.

If B knows A, then A is known by B.

A is known if and only if something knows A.

If something is described as knowing A, it is described as having a relation to A.

When real existent A is described solely as term of a relation not defined by features characterizing its term, that description does not express (as opposed to imply) any features characterizing A itself.

When A is described as term of a relation which is defined by features characterizing its term, A is not described as nothing but the term of a relation something has to A.

If all the reality expressed by "R'ed by B" in "Real existent A is R'ed by B" belongs to B, not A, to exist for A is not what is expressed by "R'ed by B".

To attribute to real existent A what is expressed by words for logical constructs is to attribute nothing really existing to A itself.

As several of these examples have hopefully made clear, being self-evident is not the same as being elementary. The truth of a sentence may be known solely from an understanding of how its words are used. But an understanding of how its words are used may not be easily acquired. In order to give a balanced picture of self-evidence, however, a few more examples are in order:

If A hits B, B is hit by A.
If A is walking, A is moving.
If A is equal to B, B is equal to A.
If A is red, A is colored.
If A is colored, A is not uncolored.

More examples will appear in later arguments.

To claim that the truth of a sentence is self-evident is not to claim that any user of the language to whom the sentence is presented will recognize that it is necessarily true. Chapter Eleven will explain that there is a feature specific to the use philosophy makes of language that causes a permanent tendency for us to misunderstand, in varying degrees, the meaning of philosophical sentences. Such misunderstanding is by no means inevitable. But the *tendency* to misunderstanding is an incorrigible result of the way philosophy, as opposed to other disciplines in which self-evident truths are found (logic and mathematics), uses language. This is the most fundamental reason why the self-evident may not be recognized as such, but there are others.

The most common mistake in this area, however, is to claim necessary truth for a statement that has none rather than to deny the truth of a self-evident statement. This is an instance of the human tendency to commit ourselves too hastily. And this is a tendency which I am under no obligation to explain here since it is not peculiar to philosophy.

When a self-evident truth is denied, on the other hand, it will often be for reasons extraneous to the understanding or the misunderstanding of the truth itself. Our philosophical education can have a corrupting effect on us. Just as it can produce the wrong kind of skepticism (and there *is* a healthy kind) about the existence of the external world, self-identity, the laws of science, etc., so it can introduce irrelevant considerations into the context of assent to a necessary truth. For instance, we can become committed a priori to certain models to which we think necessary truths or the processes of discovering and verifying necessary truths must conform. If a statement—especially a non-elementary one—does not conform to these models, we irrelevantly dismiss it. Or we may for reasons of theory dismiss the whole class to which a truth belongs rather than deal with the truth on its own terms. Or we may understand the ordinary usage which renders a sentence self-evidently true but, because of our philosophical background, add to this understanding and read more into the sentence than is consistent with its necessary truth.

No better example of a priori philosophical commitments diverting one from what is pertinent to judging necessary truth can be found than that provided by Quine himself. He apparently considers it an "obvious" truth that necessity can be found, if at all, only by employing a criterion by which to discriminate between it and contingency. And he assumes that "known to be true solely by an understanding of the use of words" is meant to provide such a criterion; that is, he interprets the phrase by using an uncriticized (and inappropriate) model.

"Known to be true solely by an understanding of the use of words" is a *criterion* for neither self-evidence nor necessity. It is a *causal analysis* of how we come to know the truth of certain sentences. It is not a rule to be employed in the discovery of new necessary truths. It is a description of the contingently occurring process by which some sentences have been, and in the future can be, known to be incapable of being false: it sometimes occurs that we do understand the usage of words; and in some cases this understanding is sufficient for us to grasp that the opposite of a sentence in which those words occur is contradictory. And this very causal analysis rules out the appeal to criteria in determining that these sentences are necessarily true. I do not pretend, however, that, as so far presented, this causal analysis is perfectly clear or that it has no difficulties; our discussion of necessity and self-evidence has only begun.

Given that we can fail to recognize self-evident necessity, is there any way of replying to an opponent who denies a self-evident truth? Self-evidence excludes direct derivation, but it does not exclude indirect proof, *reductio ad absurdum*. We can attempt to show an opponent that his denial of a self-evident truth yields a contradiction. This process, however, assumes that the opponent accepts other truths as necessary, truths which, in conjunction with the opponent's denial, yield the contradiction. At the very least, the opponent must grant the necessity of the principle of non-contradiction. And a philosopher like Quine will not shrink from suggesting that the principle of non-contradiction is not necessary after all.

But any denial of a self-evident truth is in effect, a form of *ignoratio elenchi* which rejects, not the self-evident truth itself, but something other than that truth. As we will see below, Quine winds up affirming exactly the same thing that is affirmed by saying that the principle of non-contradiction is necessarily true. In other words, he does not really deny the necessity of the principle of non-contradiction but instead rejects an *interpretation* of that necessity which he confuses with the genuine article. (See section 4.3.)

In replying to the denial of a self-evident truth, however, it would not be pertinent to show that the truth is *self-evident*. What is required in order for us to use it as a premise in an argument is to show that it is *necessarily true*, that is, that the opposite is contradictory. "Self-evident", again, is a reflexive causal description telling us how the necessity of some truths is grasped: a sentence is self-evident when an understanding of the way its words are used is sufficient to reveal that the opposite is contradictory. It is the grasp of necessity itself which is important to philosophical argument. And one can recognize that a truth is necessary without having carried out a causal analysis of the process by which that recognition takes place. We, on the other hand, must now pursue that analysis in more detail.

3.2 The Linguistic Theory of Necessity

In this section I will criticize the linguistic theory of necessity and argue for an alternative account of how the understanding of usage is related to the knowledge of necessary truth, an account which will show the irrelevancy of the issue of synonymy to the issue of necessity. Further, I will defend my position as needed for solving Lewis Carroll's Achilles-Tortoise paradox. And lastly, I will mention how my criticism of the linguistic explanation of necessity can be extended to the psychologistic explanation. With the ideas to be introduced here, we will be ready for the analysis of truth which will be undertaken in section 3.3. That analysis will be the basis for the completion of my explanations of necessity and self-evidence.

3.2.1 Lexicological and non-lexicological understanding of usage

The reason why one would mistakenly interpret "known true solely by an understanding of its words" as a criterion for judging necessary truth is that one has already interpreted "understanding of its words" as referring to lexicological knowledge: the knowledge that word "A" happens to have a particular use in a given language while word "B" happens to have another use. On this interpretation judging that a truth is necessary would require making a survey of the behavior of a linguistic community to determine how some of its language-forms were being used. If it happens to be the case, for instance, that in English "bachelor" is used synonymously with "unmarried man", our criterion tells us that "All bachelors are unmarried men" is a necessary truth. And Quine is surely right that no necessity can be found by this procedure. Our knowledge of how a word is being used can never achieve more than a high degree of empirical certitude.

But why read "understanding of its words" as referring to lexicological knowledge? One answer might be that the only alternative is to read it as referring to knowledge of abstract psychological entities such as meanings and concepts. Since knowledge of the meanings of words does occur, we cannot deny that it is knowledge about *some* facet of our experience. And if "knowing the meanings of words" involves more than knowledge of linguistic behavior, it appears that we are forced to introduce abstract entities to be the objects of that kind of knowledge. Fortunately these are not the only alternatives.

Assume that the truth of "No two colors can be in the same place at the same time" is self-evident. When we say that this sentence can be known true simply by understanding the meaning of its words, what do we mean by "meaning"? The meaning of a language-form is its use, its function in our behavior. So far, then, knowledge of meaning seems to be lexicological knowledge. But the phrase "use of a word" can refer to something other than a linguistic relation, on the one hand, or a psychological entity, on the other. "Use" can refer to "that for which a word is used". The meaning of "color", for example, would be color, that for which the word "color" is used. The meaning of "place" would be that for which the word is used, namely, the relation of being-in-place. The behavioral function of these words would be to objectify color and place for the purposes of communication.

If so, then the knowledge of use enabling us to grasp the self-evident truth of "No two colors can be in the same place at the same time" would be knowledge of what it is that can be described by the object-description "that for which a word is used" but knowledge of what it is *other than as described by this object-description*. If A is that for which the word "A" is being used, then the relevant knowledge of use would be knowledge—in the sense of awareness—of A, not knowledge of A's being that for which "A" is used. In this sense, understanding how "A" is used is awareness of A sufficient to enable us to use some word for A; it is acquaintance with that which can be described as "the use of 'A'" but not acquaintance with it as so described.

To know the meaning of "color" and "place" in this sense is to be acquainted with color and place. How being acquainted with color and place can enable us to grasp necessary truth remains to be seen. What does not remain to be seen is that knowledge of the meaning of "color" and "place" in the lexicological sense is knowledge of contingent facts only. Deliberate stipulation of usage can eliminate any uncertainty about meaning of the kind associated with the empirical observation of linguistic behavior. But stipulation can produce only a contingent relation between a word and its use and therefore only a contingent relation between the uses (in the lexicological sense) of various words. If color has a necessary relation to place, it is still only a contingent fact that "color" is used for something having a necessary relation to what "place" is used for. And this fact remains contingent whether we acquire our lexicological understanding of "color" and "place" from stipulation or observation of behavior or training.

There are two other reasons why necessary truth cannot be known from a lexicological understanding of the use of words. The first is that knowledge of necessary truth would become linguistic knowledge, not linguistic in the sense that it is knowledge of the truth of sentences—all knowledge of truth is linguistic in that sense—but linguistic in the sense that the sentences known to be true would be expressing nothing more than relations of language-forms either to other language-forms or to extra-linguistic things. But when a sentence is put forward as a necessary truth, the speaker or writer is not *mentioning* the words making up the sentence as he would be if the sentence expressed a belief about language or about things as terms of linguistic relations. He is *using* the words and is therefore communicating a non-linguistic belief, a belief about what is true of things as more-than-terms-of-linguistic-relations. As has often been pointed out, the linguistic theory of necessary truth commits the fallacy of confusing use with mention. (See, for example, Chisholm, 1966, p. 83; Veatch, 1969, pp. 118-125.)

The final reason. Knowledge of any truth, necessary or contingent, requires awareness of how the words of a sentence are being used. "Snow is white" is not true unless "snow", "white" and "is" have uses that it is not necessary for them to have. But a distinction must be made between the way the uses of words must be understood in order for someone to know a sentential truth and the ways the uses or words must be understood in order for someone to know how to express that truth properly according to the conventions of a particular language. Someone just learning English may think that "black" is used the way we actually use "white". When he says "Snow is black", he is expressing his knowledge of sentential truth. And it may even be possible for someone else to judge from observation of his linguistic behavior that he is trying to communicate the same truth the rest of us would communicate by "Snow is white". He can know this truth only if he is acquainted with that for which we happen to use the word "white". But he is acquainted with this even though he is not acquainted with the lexicological fact that the word "white" happens to have this use. (See Chisholm, ibid., pp. 36-37.)

An understanding of usage is required for the knowledge of truth, but not a lexicological understanding of the relation between a language-form and its function. For it is empirically and behaviorally meaningful for one to be in lexicological error while making a correct judgment about a sentential truth. And these considerations apply equally to contingent and necessary truth. If someone has confused the use of "or" with the use of "and", he is not to be accused of advocating a corrupt logic simply because he says "It is impossible for a thing to be or not be in the same respect at the same time".

The meaning of a word is nothing more than its use, its function. The meaning of a word is not some mental entity. Nor do we have access to any meanings other than those that can be articulated in language. Consequently it is impossible to be acquainted with a meaning that is not (or is not at least capable of being) the function of *some* word. But to be so disposed as to be able to use *some* word in a certain way is not the same as having accurate lexicological knowledge about the particular word or words that actually have this function in the language.

To know the relation of a given language-form to its function is what is meant by having an understanding of meaning in the lexicological sense. The awareness enabling us to use some language-form (not necessarily the correct one) in a certain way is what is meant by the non-lexicological understanding of meaning that is required for the grasp of sentential truth, necessary or contingent. In the case of meanings already present in the language, this non-lexicological understanding is acquaintance, not with the linguistic relation, is-used-this-way, but with the term of this relation—awareness of the use some language-form has been given, but awareness of it other than as the use *this* language-form has been given.

Let us refer to understanding meaning in the non-lexicological sense as being acquainted with a *word-function*. And where convenient I will write meaning$_T$ or usage$_T$ if the knowledge of meaning that enters into the recognition of sentential truth, non-lexicological knowledge of meaning, is being referred to, and I will write meaning$_L$ or usage$_L$ if it is a matter of knowledge of meaning in the lexicological sense. The phrases "word-function", "meaning$_T$" and "usage$_T$" are not chosen to express a new doctrine concerning meaning or to solve any philosophical problems concerning meaning. They are chosen to emphasize the fact that, although what is understood is not the relation of a language-form to its function, neither is it some entity of a psychological kind. Of course in a given case, a word-function, that for which some word is or can be used, may be a real or alleged psychological entity (for example, the super-ego or the collective unconscious), a linguistic relation (for example, being a subject or being the denotation of a word), a physical condition, a chemical reaction, or anything else that is really or fictionally under the sun.

These phrases are also chosen to underscore the fact that the doctrine of truth and necessary truth I will present does not presuppose a causal analysis of how language acquires meaning. Instead of presupposing a causal analysis of how language acquires meaning, the method I am presenting would be the method employed by any such causal analysis. My use of these phrases, therefore, is not meant to suppress questions traditionally associated with such terms as "sense", "reference", "connotation", "denotation", and "concept" (in the non-psychological sense). Nor am I recommending that "word-function" and "meaning$_T$" be used outside of this book to replace the more familiar terms, if it is clear that the traditional terms are not used for the relation of a language-form to its function or for some kind of psychological entity.

Word-functions can be performative as well as descriptive and referential. The logical relation of implication can be said to be the word-function both of the word "implication" and of "if...then" constructions. However, while "implication" mentions this relation, in "if...then" constructions, the relation is used.

And what it means to be acquainted with word-functions can be as varied as are word-functions themselves. At one extreme, acquaintance with word-functions is the same thing as acquaintance with those objects of our experience (physical things, sensible qualities, or whatever) that we are able to articulate in language. Here the word-functions always have (or have had) some status other than that of being the function of some language-form or of being, like a logical relation, a property of the way we use language-forms. At the other extreme from meanings$_T$ that are objects of prelinguistic experience, there are meanings$_T$, fictions and logical constructs, which have no status other than that of being the way *some* language-form is used. Still, being acquainted with such a word-function is not the same as having accurate knowledge of how a particular language-form is used by a linguistic community. A person can be mistaken about the lexicologically proper use of a phrase like "square root of -1" without being mistaken about any mathematical truth.

If the knowledge of usage needed for a grasp of self-evident truth is not familiarity with lexicological facts, then the issue of synonymy to which so much attention has been paid by Quine and others in their discussions of necessity is nothing but a red herring. The irrelevance of synonymy or of any other lexicological issue can be well illustrated by sentences employing constructions one does not find in ordinary language but which are based on the ordinary uses of certain words. The following is a version of the principle of sufficient reason of the kind some philosophers have constructed to ensure both that the principle is necessarily true and that God falls within its scope:

> Anything that exists is something for whose existence there is a sufficient condition or sufficient conditions: either itself or some other thing(s).

Anyone claiming that this is a self-evident truth would make his claim on the basis of his quite fallible opinions about the correct uses (meanings$_L$) of "exists", "sufficient condition", "there is", various pronouns, etc. If the words making up this sentence have the uses$_T$ he assumes they are ordinarily intended to have, what the sentence expresses is something he considers to be a self-evident truth. But he could be mistaken about the correct uses$_L$ of these words without the truth he is attempting to communicate ceasing to be self-evident because of the meanings$_T$, the word-functions, that enter into it.

In the above sentence "something for whose existence there is a sufficient condition" might be mistakenly given the use that "something for whose existence there is whatever may be required" would normally have for users of English. If so, the person putting this sentence forward would be in error about language but would still be knowing a self-evident truth. For the truth he had grasped and was attempting to communicate by means of this sentence would be the self-evident truth which standard usage would lead us to communicate in the sentence:

> Anything that exists is something for whose existence there is whatever may be required.

In defense of the linguistic theory of necessary truth, it is sometimes claimed that the problem with contradictory sentences is that they are linguistically pointless. To deny in one breath what one has affirmed in another breath is to deprive words of their usefulness. If we are using "bachelor" and "unmarried man" to refer to members of the same class and only that class, it is pointless to say "Some bachelor is not an unmarried man". What we accomplish by using the subject is cancelled by what we do with the predicate. A truth is necessary if and only if denying it produces a contradiction. And what is wrong with contradiction, in this view, is that it is linguistically self-stultifying. Can an account of necessity based on a non-lexicological understanding of meaning account for this *cul-de-sac* character of the denial of necessary truth?

When we affirm something in one breath and deny it in the next, we are depriving language of its function; we are preventing language from objectifying anything we might want to objectify by means of it. But in section 2.2.3, we saw that the primary function of language is to objectify things that are more-than-terms-of-linguistic-relations; and in section 2.2.1, we saw that the primary predicates that are known to be true of things cannot be predicates describing things as terms of linguistic relations. Since both the affirmation and the denial which together constitute contradiction are primarily matters of objectifying *things* by means of language, the self-stultifying character of contradiction proves nothing peculiarly linguistic about truths whose opposites are contradictory. For truth in general, necessary or contingent, is a matter of objectifying things by means of language. And if the meanings$_T$ of the predicates of a necessary truth are features characterizing things as things, the function contradiction deprives language of is that of stating what is true of things in their existence as things. Sentences whose opposites are contradictory objectify what is true of things if they are not to both be and not be in the same respect at the same time. (The self-stultifying character of contradiction will be explained in more detail in section 5.4.)

According to the linguistic theory of necessity, on the other hand, necessary truth concerns things only as objects, not as things. But when the word-functions of a necessary truth are features of things as things rather than as objects, that truth is just as much a piece of information about things as things as are contingent truths. The only difference between sentences of these kinds is that one kind tells us what is necessarily true of things as things while the other tells us what is contingently true of things as things.

By a sentence which tells us what is necessarily true of things as things, I do not mean what some have called a *de re* necessity. The necessity I am speaking of here is the necessity of a truth, *de dicto* necessity. The necessity of a truth can be grounded either in logical relations or in necessary causal relations. I will be arguing that even truths whose necessity is grounded in logical relations can be truths objectifying things as things, since the terms of logical relations like identity and otherness can be real existents.

3.2.2 What Achilles replied to the tortoise

Does the fact that we do much of logic and mathematics by constructing formal systems in which the understanding of meanings consists of nothing more than the understanding of rules relating combinations of symbols eliminate the need to appeal to self-evidence and the non-lexicological understanding of meaning to explain our logical and mathematical knowledge? If we think so, we have failed to learn the lesson of Lewis Carroll's Tortoise-Achilles paradox (Carroll, 1895).

Assume a system whose rules include *modus ponens*. Is it self-evident that in this system "q" is to be inferred from the premises "p → q" and "p"? If not, then we need another premise to justify inferring "q", namely, "((p → q) & p) → q". But is it self-evident that we should infer "q" from the conjunction of "((p → q) & p) → q" and "(p → q) & p"? If not, then to infer "q" we need the further premise "(((((p → q) & p) → q) & (p → q) & p) → q". And is it self-evident that "q" is to be inferred from the conjunction of the last premise with the others?

If you are skeptical of the occurrence of this infinite regress, I can do no better than refer you to Quine's (1936) presentation of it. Not only has Quine grasped Carroll's paradox, but from it he has also correctly drawn the conclusion that sentences cannot be rendered true by mere stipulation of the meaning of words. (Stipulation, again, gives us an "understanding of meaning" in the lexicological sense of that phrase, although awareness of the meanings$_T$ we have stipulated for some words may be sufficient for us to know the necessity of some truths employing those words.) But this is not the only lesson the Tortoise-Achilles paradox teaches.

The word-function of the constants of a formal system are relations, or sets of relations, between the formulas in which each constant appears and other formulas of the system, relations stipulated for the constants by the rules, axioms or definitions of the system. Carroll's regress can be avoided if and only if acquaintance with some of these word-functions (acquaintance, that is, with some of these purely formal relations) makes some truths about these relations self-evident and one or more of the rules or axioms of the system corresponds to a self-evidently necessary truth about these relations. Giving "&", " – " and " → " their standard formal definitions, for instance, to accept "((p → q) & p) & -q" as a theorem of the system would be equivalent to simultaneously affirming and denying that formulas using these symbols have the relations, the meanings$_T$, they are stipulated to have. For if they do have these meanings$_T$ (and do not simultaneously *not* have them), then "((p → q) & p) & -q" is a theorem only on the condition that at least one of these meanings$_T$ both is and is not what it is, that negation is not negation, for instance, or conjunction not conjunction.

If these relations are what they are (regardless of what symbols are stipulated to indicate them), given that formulas using the symbols " → ", "&" and " – " have the relations that have been lexicologically stipulated for them, it is necessarily true that "((p → q) & p) & -q" is not a theorem of the system. But this necessity can be known only if it, or some other necessary truths from which it can be derived, is self-evident. Without self-evidence, infinite regress occurs; with it, infinite regress need not occur.

Lexicological understanding of meaning is not sufficient for self-evidence since it concerns only the contingent fact that a particular symbol has been given a particular use. Therefore infinite regress can be avoided if and only if understanding the rules of a formal system includes, in addition to a lexicological understanding of the relation of symbols to their uses, a non-lexicological acquaintance with those uses. But a purely formal relation can be just as much an object of non-lexicological acquaintance as anything else can. Even though the word-functions of the constants are relations between groups of symbols, and not between symbols and things other than symbols, we do not have to use the particular symbols that we do use for these word-functions. An acquaintance with the formal relations that, as a matter of contingent fact, we happen to use these symbols for is sufficient for grasping that the denial of some statements about these uses$_T$ would be contradictory.

The contradictory character of these denials is rendered no less self-evident by the fact that a formula corresponding to the principle of non-contradiction of ordinary language may be derived rather than postulated in the system. That is a different question entirely. Since, as Carroll's paradox shows, understanding the purely symbolic rules of a formal system does not eliminate the need for logic to be based on the grasp of self-evident truth, it is not important that a system even *contain* a formula corresponding to the principle of non-contradiction either as postulated or as derived. What is important is that the system—even a system which has a many-valued logic for an interpretation, as we will see—be governed by the principle of non-contradiction, that is, that the system does not admit theorems which would imply that any of the statements to which its rules and axioms correspond is contradictory. And it is important that it be self-evident that the opposites of one or more of these statements is contradictory. Finally, the fact that formulas can be derived in one system that are equivalent to the axioms or rules of another system is irrelevant to the issue of self-evidence. We can construct valid arguments in which true conclusions are drawn from false premises; *a fortiori* we can construct valid arguments in which the self-evident is concluded from what is not self-evident. The only thing we cannot do is construct valid arguments in which the false is concluded from the true.

3.2.3 A note on psychologism

In the face of this criticism of the linguistic theory of necessity, it is possible, though unlikely, that someone may be tempted to resuscitate a psychological account. Grasping necessity depends on understanding the use$_T$ of words. Our understanding of the use of words (in either sense) requires a psychological explanation. That explanation may require the postulation of special psychological entities, for instance, entities corresponding to some uses of the word "concept". "Concept" is often used as equivalent to the meaning$_T$ of common nouns, verbs and adjectives; that is roughly the sense in which I use the term. But "concept" can also be used to refer to the *understanding* of meaning in the non-lexicological sense, to the *disposition* to understand meaning in the non-lexicological sense or to some *entity required to explain* either the understanding or the disposition to understand meaning in the non-lexicological sense.

Whether our ability to use a word in a particular way requires the existence of entities of any kind is a perfectly legitimate *causal* question answers to which should not be ruled out in advance. But we cannot identify the meanings$_T$, the understanding of which allows us to grasp necessary truth, with that understanding or with any entity explaining that understanding. The ability to use a word in a certain way is not the same as the way the word is used, and acquaintance with a word-function is not the same as the word-function. Therefore the knowledge of necessary truth does not result from the inspection or analysis of any psychological entities enabling us to use words the way we do.

Concepts in the psychological sense are not that which we understand when we understand what words are used for; they are *that by means of which* we understand what words are used for. Like the understanding of meaning in the lexicological sense, whatever psychological facts enter into the explanation of our knowledge of word-functions are one step removed from what we must know in order to know necessary truth. And like the linguistic theory of necessity, psychological accounts make knowledge of necessary truths, even when the word-functions of their predicates are features characterizing things in their existence as things, knowledge of what is true of objects only as objects.

For those still suspicious of the non-lexicological understanding of word-functions, I will be referring below to *empirical* evidence which shows that we can understand meanings capable of being expressed in language without having learned *any* words, much less having learned the words that are lexicologically correct for the expression of those meanings. (See section 6.3.3.) There should be no doubt in anybody's mind, however, that a merely lexicological understanding of meaning can account for neither necessity nor self-evidence. How meaning in the non-lexicological sense can account for necessity, and the understanding of meaning in the non-lexicological sense for self-evidence, has yet to be explained. That explanation will require a discussion of sentential truth, necessary and contingent, in general.

3.3 The Identity Theory of Truth

In this section I will analyze sentential truth from the point of view of the distinction between things and objects of knowledge. This analysis will provide the foundation needed for an explanation of necessary truth more exact than those associated with such traditional categories as "the analytic" and "the a priori". The final section of this chapter will outline how the explanation of necessity is built on that foundation, and subsequent chapters will fill in that outline for logical and causal necessity respectively.

3.3.1 Knowing sentential truth

Let us consider sentences of the forms $(x) (Fx \rightarrow Gx)$, $(\exists x) (Fx \& Gx)$, Fa, $Fa \& Ga$, $a = b$, any forms logically equivalent to these, and their negations. Although the principles to be developed here also apply to sentences of the form $(\exists x) Fx$, the problems associated with the assertion of existence deserve the separate treatment that will be given them in Chapter Five. Further, the sentences under consideration here will be sentences in which real existents, rather than logical constructs, are made objects of knowledge. The analysis will be extended to other sentences at the appropriate places below (section 3.4.4 and Chapter Four).

It is necessary to begin with sentences about real entities because the public character of language requires that all other uses of language derive from the language we use to make real entities the objects of sentential knowledge. Recall, however, that a sentence can communicate what is true of real entities as opposed to logical constructs without communicating what is true of *actual* existents. The truth of conditional sentences does not require the actual existence of any individuals satisfying the conditions. But the pertinent question is not whether these individuals actually exist. The question to be asked is whether the existence of these individuals is something other than being known *if and when* they actually exist. (This is not to deny however, that the chronologically first uses of language must be about actual rather than possible existents.) Finally, although negative truths are to be included in the analysis, I will at present confine the discussion to affirmatives. (For negatives, see section 4.1.2; see also section 5.5.2.)

Any affirmative sentence of the kinds under consideration involves linguistically distinct objectifications of one and the same thing or things. A thing may be an event, a process or whatever may be said to have an existence which is other than being known. In "$(\exists x)\,(Fx\ \&\ Gx)$", we objectify some x once as satisfying the predicate "F" and once as satisfying the predicate "G". For this sentence to be true, however, at least one x that is an F and one x that is a G must be the same x. And for "Fa" to be true one and the same thing must be made the referent of the name "a" and must satisfy the predicate "F". Affirmative truth, therefore, requires an identity at the level of things between objects that are non-identical as objects, an identity, in other words, between the terms of diverse knowledge relations, specifically, linguistic relations such as naming, referring, describing, articulating, etc. In traditional terminology, the truth of these sentences requires a logical distinction relative to a real identity. Even in "$a = a$" there are linguistically distinct objectifications of thing a in as much as a is twice made the referent of word-tokens occupying different positions in the sentence.

In all cases of knowledge, not only in the case of sentential knowledge, there is a real identity and no more than a logical distinction between that which can be described as an "object of knowledge" and that something-other-than-an-*object* which we are calling a "thing". It is the same x that "is an apple" and "is seen" when it is true that an apple is seen. Suppose that someone sees an apple, that the apple is sour, and that the person does not know it is sour. "He sees a sour apple" is true. "The object of his vision is sour" is also true. But the predicate "sour" is not true of the apple insofar as the apple is the object of the person's vision. The apple that becomes an object of perception in one way is the same thing that could, but does not, become an object of perception in many other ways. Therefore the distinction between that which terminates a knowledge relation in some way and the thing in its totality is a logical distinction only. The distinction between being-known and being is a real distinction. But if the distinction between that of which we are aware and that which is a thing were a real distinction, we would never truly be aware of cognition-independent things.

To return to sentential truth, if "Snow is white" is true, then that which is snow must also be something which is white. That-which-is-snow is a distinct conceptual object, a distinct meaning$_T$, from something-which-is-white. But when that-which-is-snow is our object, it is known as a thing whose reality (actual or possible) is in no way confined to the way in which it is thus made an object. Once again, the primary objects of sentential knowledge must be known to be more-than-*objects*. What is objectified by "that which is snow" cannot only be but can also be known to be what is objectified by "something which is white".

Every true affirmative judgment of the kinds we are investigating requires that things which are distinct when looked at from the point of view of the diverse ways in which they are made objects (logically or "conceptually" distinct) are not distinct but are identical as things (really identical). And to know the truth of such a sentence is to know the real identity of logically distinct objects. Sentences are instruments for objectifying things. When a relation of identity holds between thing and object as required by the sentence, the sentence is related to things by the relation *truth*, otherwise the sentence is related to things by the relation *falsehood*.

A word of caution. The identity theory of truth does not result from a misinterpretation of the function of the copula. For that matter it does not result from *any* interpretation of the copula. This point is worth making for only one reason. Among philosophers of the (hopefully) recent past, the favorite device for avoiding careful examinations of the bases for opposing views has been to accuse opponents of being misled by the incidental characteristics of their language. The facts of the history of philosophy show that, in general, this accusation is not well founded. But it is possible that someone might bring it out of moth balls in response to the identity theory of truth. For the copula has as one of several uses the function of expressing identity in the sense of "is the one and only". And philosophers have sometimes charged the copula with ambiguity on the grounds that its other functions can be confused with that of expressing identity. (See Russell, 1919, p. 172.)

But the logically distinct/really identical analysis is just as true of "$(\exists x) (Sx \& Wx)$" as it is of "Snow is white". And in the case of subject-copula-predicate sentences, to say that knowing their truth is knowing that diverse objects are really identical is not to say that the "is" has the function referred to as the "is" of identity. In "The east slope of Everest is the most dangerous climb", "is the" can be expanded to "is the one and only". This translation would not do for the "is" of "The east slope of Everest is more dangerous than any climb in Rhode Island". In general, sentences of the form "An F is a G" do not *say* that some F is the one and only G. But *knowing* that what is said by such sentences *is true* is knowing that something which has been objectified by "F" is the same as a thing which has been objectified by "G".

"The east slope of Everest" describes a thing that "more dangerous than any climb in Rhode Island" also describes. Granted, "more dangerous than any climb in Rhode Island" can describe more things than can "east slope of Everest". But this is to distinguish these descriptions from the point of view of their *logical* characteristics, that is, from the point of view of being *predicable-of* a larger or smaller number of individuals. If one of the individuals satisfying the more universal description, however, was not the same individual that satisfied the other description, it could not be true that the east slope of Everest is more dangerous than any climb in Rhode Island. Nor could this be known true unless it were known true that some individual satisfying each of these descriptions (an individual logically distinct from itself to the extent that it is a term of different knowledge relations) was the same individual. It is in this sense that knowledge of an affirmative truth, whether or not the sentence employs the "is" of identity, is knowledge of an identity.

In knowing "An F is a G" we do not, however, identify the word-function of "F" with the word-function of "G". "Snow is white" does not mean that "Snowness is whiteness", that what it is to be snow is the same as what it is to be white. What we identify are the things that are made objects by means of our giving "F" and "G" or "snow" and "white" certain word-functions. What we know when we know that "An F is a G" is that some things which is an F (or a member of the class of Fs) is also a thing which is a G (or a member of the class of Gs).

As Quine has reminded us (1960, pp. 52-54; 1969, pp. 1-4), we could have a language that made exclusive use of abstract terminology, as in "instance of rabbithood", where we now ordinarily use only concrete terms, as in "a rabbit". Using abstract terms we could do away with the copula of predication by doing away with direct predication altogether. Instead of reading "$(\exists x)(Fx \ \& \ Gx)$" as "Some F is a G", we would read it as "Something with F-ness also has G-ness". Again, the same thing is objectified diversely, once as having F-ness and once as having G-ness. Therefore the use of the copula in "Some F is a G" is incidental to the point that knowledge of sentential truth is knowledge of the real identity of the objectively distinct, the identity of thing and object. Finally, the identity known in knowing the truth of sentences which do not use the copula of identity can be expressed by using formulas like the following: *one* thing which is F is identical with one thing which is G; at least one thing has F-ness and the same thing has G-ness.

The point of the identity theory of truth is missed entirely, however, if its purpose is interpreted as the supplying of rules for the *translation* of sentences into other sentences. The theory is not intended to provide new sets of signs having the same function as other signs. Nor is it intended to represent the function of other signs, for example, the function of the "is" of identity, abstractly. A translation of any other use of the copula that rendered it as the "is" of identity would simply be an inaccurate translation. And an account of any other use of the copula that attributed to it the properties of the "is" of identity would be a false account. The identity theory of sentential truth is, on the contrary, part of the causal analysis of what takes place when we know the truth of a sentence.

That the formulas in which this theory is expressed are not intended as rules of translation is particularly evident in the case of sentences such as "Fa", "Alfred Hitchcock is a director" or "This is red". According to the theory, to know the truth of such sentences is to know that one thing which we are referring to by means of a name or an indexical term is also one member of a particular class. But would it be helpful as translation to render "*a*" or "Alfred Hitchcock" or "this" as "that which is referred to by '*a*' or by 'Alfred Hitchcock' or by 'this' "? Still, knowing the truth of such sentences requires us both to make something the object of the reference of a name or indexical term and to know that the thing so objectified is the same as one of the members of a certain class.

For convenience, I will henceforth refer to both proper names and indexicals as "names". This is not to imply any theory of the nature of names or indexicals. Such a theory is not necessary for this analysis of truth. Truth requires that we objectify the same thing in diverse ways. In deciding the truth of a sentence, we need to know what it is that is objectified by a name or indexical; we do not need to be able to explain how we succeed in so objectifying things. For many, the question of how names objectify is bound up with the question of whether we can refer to non-existents. I discuss the latter issue in sections 5.2.4, 5.5.2, and I.1.

What about one-word sentences, "Gavagai", for example? What about a language in which the job performed by "This is red" would be performed more economically by "Red"? Knowing the truth of one-word sentences in *our* language may or may not require, on the part of the user of the language, the linguistic *ability* to objectify the thing referred to in distinct ways (the ability to fill in the "understood" parts of the sentence). Why should this ability be required of the users of one-word sentences in all languages? Believing a one-word sentence does not involve believing that distinct objects are objectifications of an identical thing. Does it follow that the identity theory is not adequate for affirmative truth in general but only for sentences in which things are objectified in more than one way? No.

To know the truth of a one-word sentence is to know that what has been made an *object* by the sentence, what is describable as "referred to", "expressed", "meant", or "articulated" by the sentence, is identical with a *thing*, something more than what is describable as objectified by this sentence and something whose existence, if and when it exists, is not the same as being so objectified. For what makes believing the sentence different from merely understanding its meaning is that we hold that what is meant has a status other than simply being meant and what is understood has a status other than simply being understood. We hold that what has been linguistically objectified by the word is also something that is really the case. The most fundamental identity that is known when sentential truth is known is the identity between what has been made an object in some way and what is also a thing, not the identity of what has been made an object in diverse ways. For if there were no identity between that which has been made an object in some way and that which is something-more-than-what-is-so-objectified, there could be no identity between what is known by one mode of objectification and what is known by some other mode. (That knowledge of truth is fundamentally knowledge of the identity between that which has been objectified in some way and that which also has some status other than being *thus* objectified will be important for extending this account of truth to sentences about logical constructs.)

3.3.2 Correspondence and assertive-redundancy

To better understand the identity theory of truth, let us relate it to the correspondence and assertive-redundancy theories.

The "correspondence" of the correspondence theory of truth is, or should be, nothing more or nothing less than the strict identity we are discussing. There is truth when what is said *is* what is; read: there is truth when what is said is identical with what is, when the distinction between what has been linguistically objectified and what exists is no more than a logical distinction. Correspondence is identity, not any mere similarity, nor is it a relation between cognition-independent things and some kind of mental picture or concept (in the psychological sense). Again, I do not deny that psychological entities enter into the causal analysis of our grasp of truth. But they cannot enter that analysis as items we compare with things to determine whether there is any correspondence between them. We do not know truth by comparing things to thoughts; for how could such a comparison ever take place unless we had first learned what is true of things independently of comparing them to thoughts? And what properties of a mental image make it an image *of* this thing rather than that thing?

On the contrary, correspondence is a logical relation of identity between a thing and *itself*. For it is a relation between a thing and an object. And an object is not some third element interposed between language and the thing. It is the thing itself. Correspondence is a relation between a thing as thing and the *same thing* as object, between something for which existence is other than being the term of a knowledge relation and something which also happens to be the term of a knowledge relation. In other words, correspondence is not a relation between things and thoughts or descriptions. It is a relation between things and *that which* is thought or described. In judging the truth of "A is B", we judge the correspondence between the *thing* objectified by "A" and the *thing* objectified by "B". (But how does it come about that one thing rather than another is the term of some relation of objectification? Why is a description or concept a description or concept *of* this thing and not some other thing? That is a *different* question from the question of what terminates the relation of correspondence. And it can be answered correctly only after the question of correspondence has been separated from the relation of descriptions and concepts to their objects and located at another place.)

Similarly, falsehood does not imply a relation of non-correspondence between mental images and things. It is a relation of non-identity, or the absence of a relation of identity, between the term of a relation of objectification and extra-objective things. What is objectified in the sentence "This is red" is something red. If the thing objectified by "This" is not identical with a thing objectified by "red", the sentence is false. In the case of the one-word sentence "Red", one unexpressed piece of information that must be understood to judge its truth is what particular thing is asserted to be red, that is, what particular thing is being objectified as red by the assertion of the sentence. If that thing does not exist (as when "Red" is equivalent to "There is something red in the vicinity"), or if it exists and is not red (as when "Red" is equivalent to "This is red"), "Red" is false because there is no identity between the term of its relation of objectification and what exists extra-objectively.

But what is a term of a relation of objectification if it is not an existing thing? Terms of relations of objectification that are non-identical with what actually exists may be merely possible existents or logical constructs. But how can non-existents like mere possibles and logical constructs be terms of relations of objectification unless they are reducible to really existing mental entities?

Mental entities enter the discussion of knowledge relations not as terms of those relations, not as what we are aware of, but as the means by which something becomes the term of a knowledge relation, as that by means of which we are aware of whatever we are aware of. If mental entities have any function, it is to explain the existence of knowledge relations to terms other than the mental entities themselves (unless of course our awareness of mental entities themselves is what is under discussion). I will argue below (sections 5.5.2 and I.1) that, whatever kind of psychological entities may or may not be necessary to explain our objectification of non-existents, nothing is needed to explain our objectification of non-existents that is not also needed to explain our objectification of existents. Objectification of non-existents creates no special problem from this point of view.

How do we accomplish the feat of objectifying non-existents? In section 5.5.2, I will argue that, as far as language is concerned, we objectify non-existents by the same means that we objectify existents, by using language in certain ways. No more, no less. Certain modes of linguistic behavior are what constitute discourse about non-existents. And no psychological causal entities are required to explain such behavior that are not required to explain other linguistic behavior.

To get back to the question of truth, how is the identity of thing and object verified? By sense experience or by self-evident necessity. It is the purpose of the remainder of the book to explain this. Briefly, we recognize, for example, that something perception informs us to actually exist is identical with what is objectified by the word-function of "apple", namely, a member of the class of apples. Consequently we say "This is an apple" or simply "Apple". Or we recognize that the word-function of "red" is the same as the color of an area in our visual field. Knowing that the word-function of "red" objectifies that area, we say "This is red" or simply "Red". Or recognizing that what is present in perception is identical with something objectified by the word-functions of both "apple" and "red", we say "This apple is red". (Again, the word-functions of "apple" and "red" are not identified in knowing that an apple is red; it is things objectified by the fact that words have been given those functions that are identified.)

As the "apple" and "red" examples should make clear, the relation of correspondence is primarily between things and the objects of descriptions or names, not between things and sentences, except for one-word sentences. (I am using "description" for any predicative expression, general or particular. I do not confine its reference to definite and indefinite descriptions.) But when there is identity, as called for by a sentence, between things and the objects of descriptions and names, the sentence is true.

This theory of truth differs, therefore, from the correspondence theory criticized by Strawson (1950). For while denying that there is that in the world to which a statement corresponds, he admits

> that there is that in the world which a statement of this kind is about (true or false *of*), which is *referred to* and *described* and which the description fits (if the statement is true) or fails to fit (if it is false). (p. 561, n. 4)

and later that

> The quoted account (Austin's) of the conditions of truthful statement is more nearly appropriate as an account of the conditions of correct descriptive reference. (p. 566, n. 9)

Since Strawson admits the relation of accuracy-of-description, his arguments do not hold against the correspondence theory as I have presented it. But the theory I have presented, and which Strawson refers to in these footnotes, is what the classical correspondence theory really amounted to. As the most well-known recent representative of the classical position explained it (Maritain, 1959, p. 89, n. 1), correspondence is exactly the kind of relation Strawson refers to as that of a description fitting what exists in the world. And because of the correspondence between the object of a description and what exists, the sentence by which we articulate this thing-object identity is true.

The misleading plausibility of the assertive-redundancy theory of truth, by the way, was made possible by the fact that truth requires a relation of strict identity between what is said and what exists. *Truth is the logical relation attributable to a means of objectification, a sentence, correlative to the logical relation, namely, identity, between things and what is objectified by means of the descriptions and names of the sentence.* If truth did not require a relation of *identity* between what is said and what is, it would not appear to be the case that " 'p' is true" asserts no more than "p". But since truth is such a *logical* relation, a relation belonging to the domain of objects as objects, not *as things*, " 'p' is true" says no more about our objects as things than does "p". What " 'p' is true" expresses about things as things is identical with what "p" expresses.

But in knowing that a sentence is true we not only have knowledge of how things are in the world, we also know the identity of what has been made an object by means of language with what exists in the world. In saying only "p", however, we do not *refer to* the whole of our knowledge, we do not *mention* the fact that our knowledge concerns not only things as things but also things as objects. "This is an apple" is not a statement about things as objects but as things. The knowledge we have when we know its truth, on the other hand, extends to *both* things as things and as objects. " 'This is an apple' is true" is a statement about things as things *and* as objects articulated in language. And this statement does mention the fact that the knowledge we have when we know the truth of "This is an apple" concerns both things and objects.

3.3.3 Some difficulties

The preceding analysis can be further clarified by responding to some difficulties. The first two difficulties will be discussed at more length later, but it will be helpful to at least mention the solutions to them now.

Strawson's reference to the conditions for correct description raises a fundamental question that will not have escaped the reader. I have said that there is truth when there is the required identity between things and what is objectified by the descriptions and names of a sentence. But what constitutes this "required identity"? If truth depends on the identity between a thing and "that which is objectified by a word", what determines that which is objectified by a word? For names, this question is to be answered by the intentions of the community or individual using the names. However they succeed in doing so, names objectify the (existing or non-existing) individuals of which they have been made the names. But what does it mean for a thing to be objectifiable, that is, describable, by a description, or what does it mean for a thing to satisfy a predicate? What makes a description an accurate description?

The problem concerns the relation of things to the word-functions of predicates. That a particular predicate has the word-function it does have is the result of the intentions of its users to use it in that way. But why is one thing, or group of things, rather than another objectified once we have given a predicate a particular word-function? We could choose to use the word "black" the way we ordinarily use "white". But if the words "snow" and "black" are used the way they are ordinarily used, no amount of intending on our part will make what is objectifiable by "snow" identical with something objectifiable by "black". Why not?

As so far presented, the identity theory of truth is consistent with taking the word-function of a predicate, say "F", to be being-a-member-of-the-class-of-Fs. "F" would be an accurate description of a thing, and the thing would therefore be objectifiable by "F", if and only if the thing were a member of the class of Fs. This understanding of what it means for a thing to be objectifiable by a description is also sufficient for the theory of necessary truth given in section 3.4.2.

But what is it for a thing to be a member of the class of Fs, or, conversely, what is it for the members of a class to be Fs? If being a member of the class of apples is being one of the individuals referred to by "apple", then anything we wish may become a member of the class of apples since we may use the language-form "apple" any way we like. And if "being an apple" means "being a member of the class of apples", then things are apples only as a result of being made objects of knowledge. Class inclusion is a logical relation, and things are describable as terms of logical relations only as a result of having been made objects of knowledge.

And how is it that things are made objects of linguistic knowledge so that, as a consequence, they may be described as terms of logical relations, unless they are first objectified otherwise than as terms of such relations? If the meanings$_T$ of *all* predicates objectified things as terms of logical relations, nothing could terminate logical relations. The hypothesis that what first terminates the relation knowledge-of is another relation which results from the fact that there is a relation of knowledge-of-something generates the same kind of infinite regress as did the hypothesis that what is first known about things is that they are known. (Compare Parker, 1960, pp. 40-45.)

It will be argued in section 6.3.4 that there is only one interpretation of the function of predicates that can prevent any and all sentences from being true if we want them to be true. We need a summary of that argument here, however, in order to understand how the identity theory of truth works. Instead of being-a-member-of-the-class-of-Fs, the word function of "F" must be what-it-is-to-be-an-F (or F-ness, which is not a Platonic essence but is *nothing more than* what-it-is-to-be-an-F expressed in an abstract, rather than concrete, mode). For truth there must be identity between the word-function of a predicate and the nature of something that is more than a term of the predicate's relation of objectification.

Why is it that I cannot truthfully classify things any way I want to? The reason I cannot do this is that what things are determines what classes they belong to. Something is a member of the class of apples because it is an apple (or has appleness, to use the abstract way of expressing it). Therefore something is a member of the class of things referred to by "apple" because what it is, at least in part, is what the word "apple" happens to be used for. As a result, "apple" is an accurate description of this thing.

Thus things are objectifiable by descriptions if and only if the word-functions of descriptions are identical with what things are, at least in part (or are logical constructs so constructed that their truth is determined by word-functions identical with what things are—see section 6.3.4). Put otherwise, what exists extra-objectively is objectifiable by a predicate if and only if the word-function of the predicate is identical with what that which exists extra-objectively is. "This is an apple" is true because the word-function of "apple" is identical with what the thing designated by "this" is. "This is red" is true because the word-function of "red" is identical with what an area in our visual field is. (Even in the case of such notoriously subjective objects as sense qualities, acquaintance with word-functions is acquaintance with features of experience having some status other than being the way some word is used.)

In the case of extrinsic denominations, a thing is objectified by a predicate whose word-function is a logical construct based on a word-function identical with what some other thing is. The extrinsic denomination is truthfully attributed if there is identity between the word-function on which it is based and that which this other thing is. "B is known by A" is true because A knows B. And acquaintance with the logical construct requires acquaintance with what things must be in order for sentences using the logical construct as a predicate to be true.

One more way of putting it. Instead of being-a-member-of-the-class-of-Fs, the word-function of "F" must be that feature or group of features by which things are assigned to the class of Fs, the feature or features because of which it is true to classify something as an F. But the identity between word-functions and what things are does not require us to hypostasize attributes corresponding to the word-function of every predicate. For one thing, the word-functions of different predicates may differ only by logical relations, not with respect to the extra-logical natures with which they are identical; such are the differences between the word-functions of "scarlet", "red", and "color".

More importantly, the features that are the word-functions of predicates need not be really distinct from that of which they are the features. Where experientially verified separate existence does not establish a real distinction, causal analysis of the existence of things as things, rather than of the existence of the knowledge by which things are made objects, is necessary to establish such a distinction. To argue to a real distinction from the manner in which things are made objects by means of sentences would be to commit an *epistemological fallacy*. Neither the subject-predicate nor the argument-function sentence forms imposes on us an ontology of vacuous entities, on the one hand, and really distinct entities that are the characteristics of the latter, on the other hand. (This argument is developed further in sections 6.1.2 and 6.3.4.)

Note also that the alternative to taking the meaning$_T$ of a predicate to be being-a-member-of-some-class is not to make the meaning$_T$ some mental entity. Again, if mental entities are needed at all, they are needed as causes of our acquaintance with meanings$_T$. But meanings$_T$ themselves are to be equated neither with our acquaintance with them nor with the causes of that acquaintance.

But how can there be identity between what a thing is and the word-function of a predicate if things are individuals and predicates are universals? The property of being universal (of being predicable of more than one or of being that by which individuals are allocated to classes) is a logical relation accruing to word-functions as a result of our being so acquainted with them as to be capable of using words for them or, to put it another way, as a result of word-functions themselves being made objects of linguistic knowledge. (When they become the meanings$_T$ of predicates, word-functions become linguistic *objects* themselves, *and* the word-functions thus objectified become *means* for objectifying the individuals that satisfy those predicates.) Although universality accrues to something as the word-function of a predicate, the logical relation of universality is not itself the word-function of a predicate and is not what is attributed to things when the predicate is used. When predicates are used truthfully, there is identity between what predicates attribute, their word-functions, and the natures of anything to which these attributions are made. (On universality and other logical relations, see section 3.4.1. On universality, see also Peterson, 1976, and Conway, 1962, pp. 169-176.)

Another difficulty. How does the logically distinct/really identical analysis apply to contrary-to-fact conditionals? If "(x) (Fx → Gx)" is true but no x satisfying "F" and "G" exists, how can there be "real" identity of what is logically distinct? Nothing exists to provide a single term for the diverse relations of objectification. No, but "(x) (Fx → Gx)" means that *if and when* something which is an F *exists*, that thing will be identical with something which is a G. To know the truth of such a conditional is to know that possible existents that are objectifiable in one way are identical with possible existents that are objectifiable in another way. If you balk at calling the identity with itself of a possible existent "real", no matter. Call it whatever you want, as long as the actual existence for which the possible existent is considered eligible is an existence which is other than being-known.

On the other hand, this response does not answer the question why the possible existents which terminate diverse relations of objectification should be identical, why, in other words, a contrary to fact conditional is true. When something actually exists, its being what it is explains why it terminates the relations of objectification that it does terminate. Consequently its being what it is explains why sentences objectifying it by means of those relations are true. But when the terms of diverse relations of objectification are merely possible existents, what explains why these terms are identical and why the sentences employing these relations are true? The answer, as explained in section 5.5.2, will be that necessary causal relations link the word-functions by which the possible existents are objectified.

A third difficulty. How can an object be "really" identical with a thing if identity is a logical relation? "Really identical" was originally used, in contrast to "logically distinct", to describe the identity of diverse objects. The objects are not identical as objects (the sphere of the logical) but as things (the sphere of real existence). Still, diverse objects can be identical with the same thing only if each of the objects has a relation of identity with this thing. How can the term of a single relation of objectification be said to be "really" identical with a thing if identity is a logical relation?

Not only is there no contradiction here, but to say that thing and object are really identical is to imply that identity is a logical relation. For relations require terms that are in some way distinct. By definition, the relation of identity cannot be true of terms that are really distinct. Therefore, it is a relation between terms that are only logically distinct, and identity is a logical relation. Nothing would have been lost in our analysis of truth if instead of speaking of thing and object being *really* identical it had been said that they are distinct *only logically* or that there was *no* real distinction between them.

Still, speaking of real identity between thing and object points out something that is essential to the identity relation. Although a thing can be a term of an identity relation only as a result of being made the term of a relation of objectification, it must also be more than a term of this relation of objectification if it is to be the term of an identity relation. Since it is the nature of the identity relation that it pertains to things only as terms of relations of objectification and since it is the nature of the relation of objectification that its term be something-more-than-an-*object*, it is of the nature of identity that that which an object is identical with be something more than a term of a particular relation of objectification. And in the case of our initial objects, being more than a term of a particular relation of objectification means being a real existent. Therefore when we speak of objects and things being really identical, we are expressing the fact that our initial objects must be identical with real existents. Without real existents, there is nothing for them to be identical with.

Furthermore, the identity relation is part of our logical equipment for rendering things objects of knowledge. Things are not known to us as mere objects but as more-than-*objects*. And identity is a logical relation necessary for knowing that what is the term of a knowledge relation also has an existence that is other than being-known. One term of the relation of identity is a real existent, actual or possible, as a real existent. The phrase "really identical" is taken from this term of the relation. It is important to describe the relation by using the word for this term. For "real identity", identity with a real existent, makes reference to that which it is the precise function of the identity relation to objectify for us, namely, the extra-objective existence of our objects as things.

Finally can the identity theory itself be derived from self-evident truth? Consider the following:

"Fa" is true if and only if the same individual which is the referent of name "a" is one of the individuals which satisfy description "F".

"(∃x) (Fx & Gx)" is true if and only if some individual which satisfies "F" and some individual which satisfies "G" is the same individual.

"(x) (Fx → Gx)" is true if and only if each of the individuals satisfying "F" is the same as an individual satisfying "G".

If there were no identity between what has been made an object in some way and that which is something more than what-has-been-made-an-object-in-this-way, there could be no identity between what has been made an object in one way and what has been made an object in another way.

3.4 Logical Relations and Causal Relations

Kant's theory of judgment, and therefore of necessarily true judgments, has been criticized for not recognizing that the knowledge of any truth, even of so-called synthetic truth, is knowledge of the identity of diverse objects. Hitherto, this criticism has not been followed up by an analysis of necessary truth based on the thing-object identity from which sentential truth follows. Approaching necessary truth this way, however, will enable us to avoid many traditional problems, such as the problem of the synthetic a priori, and solve many others.

The analysis to follow will apply to necessary truth in all its forms. The main difference between kinds of necessary truth will be seen to derive from the use of logical relations or causal relations in diversely objectifying things. This analysis will require an explanation of logical relations and, more briefly at this point, of causal relations. But my description of necessary causal relations will be sufficient to show how they account for many of the hard cases philosophers of necessity have traditionally struggled with. Causal necessity will also be shown to be important for mathematics. This section will provide an introductory answer to the question how meaning in the non-lexicological sense can account for necessity. Subsequent chapters will work out that answer in detail as well as answer the question how knowledge of meaning in the non-lexicological sense can account for self-evidence.

3.4.1 Diverse objectification of the really identical

Although a true sentence may consist of one word, I am aware of no candidates for necessary truth that do not require things to be objectified in more than one way. Therefore we can focus on sentences diversely objectifying non-diverse things. Since the truth of sentences follows from the identity of objects with things, such sentences are necessarily true if and only if the identity of their diverse objects is necessary; if the identity of their diverse objects is contingent, such sentences are contingently true. Consequently, to understand necessary truth, we need to understand why what are diverse as objects must be identical as things, why, for instance, what is objectified by "a color" must be identical with what is objectified by "something occupying a unit of space distinct from every other color".

To understand the necessary identity of diverse objects, we need to understand the ways in which identical things can be diversely objectified. That is, we need a causal analysis of the diverse objectification of things that are not distinct as things. Even if there were one-word necessary truths, their necessity would have to be explained by the ways in which they make things objects; for the question concerning those truths would be why the terms of their relations of objectification must be identical with things.

A theory of necessary truth, therefore, comes from the identity theory of truth by way of an explanation of the ways in which things can be diversely objectified. Truth requires a real identity relative to a logical diversity. But to say that real things are logically distinct as terms of diverse relations of objectification is *not* to say that the logically distinct ways something is made an object cannot have their *source* in a real distinction. The logically distinct ways the same things is made an object in "This apple is red" have their source in a real distinction between features of our experience: being an apple is different from being red, as the sometimes separate existence of apples and red things proves. But the logical distinction that derives from this real distinction is not the same as this real distinction. A thing which is an apple is capable of being identified with a thing which is red, while being an apple and being red cannot be identified. In other words, the means by which we articulate the same thing in logically distinct ways may consist of the use of words whose meanings$_T$ differ by their reference to really distinct features of our experience. Although not identical with this real distinction, the logical distinction "corresponds" to it in the sense of being correlative with it.

But there is another source for logically distinct ways of objectifying the same thing. If the diversity in means of objectification does not derive from any real distinction, it can derive solely from *logical* characteristics of the means of objectification. What do I mean by these "logical" characteristics?

When we use language to objectify things, we are aware that things have been linguistically objectified. And when we are aware that things have been linguistically objectified, we are capable of recognizing logical relations of language-forms to other language-forms, of language-forms to their meanings$_T$, of meanings$_T$ to other meanings$_T$, and of both language-forms and their meanings$_T$ to the things they objectify. For we are aware of language-forms as means of objectification, of their meanings$_T$ both as means of objectification and as objects, and of things as what are objectified by these means. And by "logical relations" I mean relations we can recognize to hold between language-forms, their meanings$_T$ and things as means of objectification or as objects, respectively.

Our linguistic behavior is describable, in part, by relations between means of objectification and terms of objectification considered as such. The phrase "considered as such" is not an instrument of obfuscation, for these relations hold, and are recognizable as holding, *because* we use language to objectify things. Once again, what is at stake is a causal analysis, not a set of criteria for identifying individuals. Not that non-existents like logical relations have causes; what is caused is linguistic behavior. But that behavior is what it is because its causes have produced it and not something else. Since that behavior is what it is, it is describable by certain predicates. And the word-functions of these predicates include relations which are not themselves real existents but are constructs based on the really existing behavior by which we objectify things. Logical relations are themselves no more than objects, terms of relations of objectification, for they are attributable to language-forms, word-functions and things only insofar as we are able to perceive them as means of objectification or as objects.

In speaking of relations pertaining to language-forms as means of objectification, I have in mind relations resulting from the fact that language-forms are given word-functions. Word-tokens, for instance, can be related as used univocally or equivocally. They are terms of relations like these, and are recognizable as such, only to the extent that they are used as means of objectification and, therefore, only to the extent that we give them certain uses$_T$. The marks or sounds we recognize as word-tokens can also be related in non-logical ways, such as occurring before or after, to the north or south of, above or below one another. But to be so related, marks or sounds need not be used as means of objectification. If we are aware of the word-functions the series of marks "organism" and "animal" customarily have, we know that these words are related as more and less universal, that is, as predicable of a greater and smaller number of individuals. They are also related as being composed of a greater and smaller number of letters, and it is conceivable that these differences could affect their usefulness as means of objectification. But such differences would be true even if these series of letters were not used as means of objectification.

Therefore, to the causal analysis so far given, we can add that the logical relations attributable to a language-form are relations resulting from the fact that it has been given a particular meaning$_T$, not relations resulting from the fact that this language-form rather than another is so used. This excludes lexicological relations such as synonymy. These must be excluded because someone could make a lexicological mistake like thinking that "or" is used the way "and" is used without being mistaken about any truth concerning logical relations, for instance, that it is impossible for a sentence to be true and not true. And a person's behavior could be evidence of the fact that his mistake is lexicological and not logical. Logical relations result from using some language-form in a particular way, not from the fact that this language-form or that language-form is one that is so used. (A synonymy relation, by the way, can sometimes result from logical relations between the meanings$_T$ of various words. Because "bachelor", "unmarried" and "male" have the meanings$_T$ they do have and the meanings$_T$ of "unmarried" and "male" have the logical relations to the meaning$_T$ of "bachelor" that they do have, "unmarried male" is synonymous with "bachelor".)

Nor are the logical relations attributable to language-forms relations resulting from the particular grammatical structure of a given language. A language's grammatical structure may or may not enable it to employ or mention a certain logical relation. That is not the issue. Logical relations can occur between language-forms whether or not the language has a way of objectifying the relation itself. However, there are relations pertaining to language-forms as means of objectification, for instance, one way of expressing plurality's being synonymous with another way, that are not logical because they result solely from the fact that certain forms of the language have grammatical relations to other forms that they need not have had. (Synonymy relations between grammatical forms need not result solely from grammatical relations. Active and passive forms, as in "A knows B" and "B is known by A" happen to be used for word-functions that differ solely by logical relations. See section 9.3.3.)

But how do we tell whether a relation pertaining to means of objectification as such is logical rather than lexicological or grammatical? Here, again, criteria for identifying individuals will not be at issue. Logical relations, relations that do not depend on the fact that this language-form rather than some other is used in a certain way or has certain grammatical relations to other language-forms, do occur between means of objectification and objects. That logical relations between meanings$_T$ or words whose meanings$_T$ are logical relations can make sentences necessarily true follows from the definition of logical relation, as section 4.1 will show. When we are acquainted with such relations, therefore, we are acquainted with relations that can make sentences necessarily true. And acquaintance with those relations gives us the ability to recognize the necessary truth of those sentences.

But in order to know logically necessary truths, we do not have to know the definition of logical, lexicological or grammatical relations since we do not have to be in possession of a causal analysis of logical necessity. As we have already seen, knowledge of necessary truth is caused neither by applying criteria for identifying individuals nor by having an analysis of the causes of that knowledge. If we are acquainted with certain meanings$_T$, we cannot fail to be acquainted with relations between them that render some sentences necessarily true. (See section 4.2.) But acquaintance with those relations is one thing, the ability to explain their distinction from other relations, whether by way of causal analysis or criteria for identifying individuals, is another.

We are going into the nature of logical relations at this point, however, to show how they provide means for the diverse objectification of the same thing. Before going any further, therefore, let me give some examples illustrating how logical relations do this. Then I will return to explaining my definition of, as well as giving more examples of, logical relations. Any difference between the word-functions of "two multiplied by two" and "two multiplied by itself" or "married" and "not unmarried" is not derived from real distinction. The difference arises from the use of words whose functions are logical relations (identity and negation, respectively) as means of objectifying the same things we have objectified without the use of words having these functions. There is no difference between the functions of each member of these pairs of language-forms from the point of view of rendering things objects according to what is true of them as things. Whenever there is affirmative truth, the difference between objects is only logical; that is, objects differ as terms or diverse relations of objectification and not as things. But relations of objectification can be diversified by more than logical relations or words for logical relations. In these examples, they are not diversified by any more than that.

Or contrast the difference between "an apple" and "something red" with the difference between "something red" and "something colored". The difference between the word-functions of "red" and "colored" is not that "red" connotes some feature of experience really distinct from a color. It does not. The differences between these word-functions are properties true of them only as means of objectification and not as features of experience having some status other than that of being the function of certain words.

Some more words of explanation concerning logical relations are now in order. What does it mean to speak of relations being attributable to the word-functions of our language-forms *as means of objectification*? To be acquainted with the word-functions of "animal" and "vegetable" is to be acquainted with certain features of our experience. We are also acquainted with relations holding between them. We are acquainted with biological relations between them, for instance, the fact that in order for animal matter to exist vegetable matter must exist. But contrast that fact to what we are acquainted with in knowing that the word-functions of "animal" and "vegetable" are that by which individuals are assigned to different subclasses of the class of living things. In the latter case, relations between word-functions are logical, not biological. Animal life and vegetable life are features of our experience and cognition-independent existents. But as the word-functions of "animal" and "vegetable" respectively, they are used as means of objectifying the members of certain classes. And it is only as means of objectifying things (or as linguistic objects themselves, since it is as term of the relation that-for-which-some-word-is-used that they are means of objectifying things) that we can attribute to these features of experience relations like having-less-extension-than-the-word-function-of-"living".

The word-functions of "true" and "false" provide clear examples of relations characterizing language-forms as means of objectification. Truth and falsehood are characteristics of language-forms, of sentences specifically, but characteristics of them as instruments used in making things objects of knowledge. For truth and falsehood are determined by the relation to things of the function(s)$_T$ of the language-form(s) making up the sentence. Correspondingly, the word-functions of "identity" and "non-identity" are relations between things as things and things as terms of objectification by means of language-forms used

in certain ways. Whether a sentence using language-forms to objectify things is to be attributed the relation truth depends on whether
things as objectified by means of these language-forms are to be attributed the relation of identity with things as things. And the word-
functions of "if . . . then", "and", "or" "if and only if" are relations
between sentences as bearers of truth-value. Since truth and falsehood
are characteristics of means of objectification considered as such, so
are relations which are truth-functional.

What does it mean to speak of logical relations as only being objects and not having any real existence? Words for logical relations
describe the way we use language-forms to objectify things. But these
language-forms are real entities, the language-acts by which we use
them are real occurrences, the things objectified are real existents, and
the word-functions by means of which things are objectified may be
features belonging to things as real existents and, as in the case of
sense qualities, may at the very least have some status other than being
terms of linguistic relations. How can the meanings$_T$ of words
describing all of this truthfully not be features belonging to our
linguistic behavior as really existent?

Consider the word-function of "true". Assume a language-act making use of a sentence really occurs. Assume that there really exists
a thing objectified by the words of the sentence. What more must exist
in order for the knowledge that the sentence is true to exist? For it
to be known that the sentence is true a perception of the identity between what is objectified by the words of the sentence and some thing
must take place. The perception of the relation of identity must come
into existence, but does the relation of identity come into extra-objective
existence? No. The perceived relation has no status other than that
of object of this perception; the word-function of "identity" is nothing
but an object resulting from a comparison of some real existent with
that which has been objectified by means of some language-form. If
the relation of identity is not a real existent, neither is the relation,
holding between sentences and things, of truth.

The logical relations of extension and class inclusion illustrate the
same point. Particular acts of constructing classes, that is, of giving
a language-form a meaning$_T$ such that it may objectify more than one
individual, exist. But classes as such have no cognition-independent
existence. Individuals to which a predicate may be attributed exist.
But the relation between these individuals of agreeing in being that
to which the predicate may be attributed is a relation, perceived to
hold between these individuals and the predicate as used in a parti-

cular way, that has no status other than being an object of awareness. The terms of the relation are real existents, actual or possible, but the relation itself is nothing but the result of a comparison of these existents. These real existents, language-acts, language-forms, their meanings$_T$ and the individuals belonging to the class, become terms of relations of classifying and being classified only by being means of objectification or objects. (None of this implies that if a relation is *not* a logical relation in the sense of a relation attributable to linguistic objects and means of objectification as such, the relation is an extra-objective existent. The word-functions of "being loved", "being admired" or any number of other relative word-functions may be "logical" constructs; that does not make them logical relations in this sense.)

In the foregoing, I have attempted to clarify the meaning$_T$ for which I am using "logical relation", and I have made some claims about logical relations. I did not attempt to justify those claims by reduction to the self-evident because doing so would not be important for the use I will make of logical relations in the analysis of necessary truths. What will be important for that analysis is the self-evident truth of sentences like the following:

> The difference between the ways language-forms objectify one and the same thing either does or does not derive, at least in part, from a real distinction between terms having some status other than being linguistic objects.

> If the difference between the ways language forms objectify one and the same thing does not derive from a real distinction between terms having some status other than being linguistic objects, it derives solely from characteristics of the means of objectification as means of objectification or of objects as objects.

> Characteristics attributable to means of objectification and to objects either are attributable to them solely as a result of their being means of objectification and objects or are not attributable to them solely as a result of their being means of objectification and objects.

> The difference between the ways language-forms objectify one and the same thing either does or does not derive, at least in part, from characteristics of the means of objectification as means of objectification or of objects as objects.

> If the difference between the ways language-forms objectify one and the same thing does not derive, at least in part, from characteristics of means of objectification as means of objectification or of objects as objects, it derives solely from a real distinction between terms having some status other than being linguistic objects.

In short, it is necessarily true that differences in the ways language-forms objectify the same thing derive either from logical relations or from some real distinction and from no other source. Again, in all cases of affirmative truth, the differences between objects are "only *logical*" in the sense that objects differ only as terms of diverse relations of objectification, not as things. But these logical differences between objects need not be "*only* logical" in the sense that the diversity in relations of objectification derives solely from logical relations, not from any real distinction.

It might be thought that I have not taken into account differences like those between "Cicero" and "Tully" or "organism" and "living thing" as means of objectification, or the difference between the ways the same thing is objectified by the repetition of "a" in "$a = a$". But while "Cicero" and "Tully" or "organism" and "living thing" are different means of objectification, in their ordinary uses$_T$ they do not differ with respect to what I am calling characteristics of means of objectification as means of objectification, that is, characteristics resulting from the fact of their being used as means of objectification. They have differences like being composed of different letters and different numbers of letters but such differences would remain even if they weren't being used as means of objectification.

Similarly, if we are asking about the differences between the first and second "a" in "$a = a$" as means of objectification, we are looking at the series of marks "$a = a$" as a means of objectification, a sentence. This series of marks does not have to be looked at that way. There are differences between the first and second "a" that do not pertain to them as means of objectification. Looking at "$a = a$" as a sentence, however, the difference between the ways the same thing is objectified by repeating "a" consists in the difference between objectifying it as a and objectifying it as terminating a logical relation, identity. The diverse objectification accomplished by the repetition of "a" objectifies that for which "a" is used as terminating a relation of identity with itself. Hence in "$a = a$", there is no difference in the word-function of "a", but there is diversity in objectification that would not exist were "a" not used as a means of objectification. For identity pertains to things only insofar as they have been objectified. Therefore in "$a = a$" there is diversity in objectification resulting from the use of a logical relation.

3.4.2 Necessary truth and kinds of necessary truth

Now we can get on with the analysis of necessary truth in terms of the thing-object distinction and the identity theory of truth. It will be helpful, however, to begin with a brief explanation of necessary causal relations. This will enable us to appreciate better the implications of this account of necessary truth.

Many would admit that diversifying objectification solely by means of logical relations, as between "married" and "not unmarried", can result in necessary truth: "Whoever is married is not unmarried". But can truth be necessary if the diverse objectification is taken from the terms of some real distinction? The operation of removing twelve items from a group of sixteen is really distinct from that of adding two items to a group of two. Since the result of these operations is necessarily the same, we can make use of the diversity between them to construct a sentence informing us that the result of one is the same as the result of the other: "$16 - 12 = 2 + 2$". Likewise place and color are really distinct features of our experience; a place can be colorless and can have different colors at different times. Using that distinction we can articulate the necessary truth: "Each unit of color occupies a place different from any unit of any other color".

Why diversely objectifying one and the same thing by means of reference to really distinct features of experience can produce sentences whose truth is necessary is another matter. It can do so if and only if between these really distinct features there are what I will define as necessary causal relations. For the sake of defining a necessary causal relation I will anticipate the account of necessity in general which is to be given in a moment. Necessity is to be defined in terms of the contradictoriness of the opposite. And causal relations are relations between really distinct relata. Hence to say there is a necessary causal relation between the terms of a real distinction is to say of at least one of them that if it exists without the other existing, it both is and is not what it is, or both exists and does not exist. (An effect cannot come into existence if any of its necessary causes does not exist; and causes sufficient to produce an effect cannot exist without the effect coming into existence.)

For the sake of brevity, we can say that a necessary causal relation holds between distinct realities when at least one of them is such that it would not exist without the other existing. This way of putting it is equivalent to the first since if one of the things would not exist without the other and the other did not exist, it would be contradictory for the first to exist.

If a necessary causal relation does not hold between the terms of a real distinction that provides the means for diverse objectification, there is no reason why what are diverse as objects must be identical as things. There is no necessary connection between the terms of a real distinction unless at least one of them would not exist without the other; therefore any necessary connection between the terms of a real distinction is a necessary causal relation by definition. And if there is no necessary connection between the terms of a real distinction, why must things diversely objectified by reference to those terms be identical? If each of A and B can exist without the other, why must what are diversified as objects by reference to A and B be the same as things? The only other reason there could be is that both A and B have a necessary causal relation to some third thing, C, such that at least one member of each of the pairs, A and C, and B and C, would not exist without the other.

Instead of speaking here of necessary causal *relations*, I could have spoken simply of necessary causality holding between things. In discussions to come later, reference to causal relations could be replaced by reference to an effect's dependence on its causes, to a cause's dispositions to produce certain effects, and so on. Section 9.3.1 will discuss relations from the point of view of necessary causality and show that neither the definition of necessary causal relations nor the uses I will make of it presuppose the existence of relations as an ontological type distinct from the things they relate. I believe in the reality of ontologically distinct relations in certain cases. (See section 9.4.1, for example.) That belief is not an issue here. Real relations or not, if necessary causality holds between things, it derives from what these things are in themselves.

Likewise, in speaking of *necessary* causal relations, I am not entering the discussion of *de re* as opposed to *de dicto* necessity. The concern of this book is with *de dicto* necessity. And when authors discuss *de re* necessity, they are usually talking about necessity of a logical, not causal, kind. Instead of describing causality as "necessary", I could have introduced the concept of the kind of causality in which one thing would not exist without another and said that such causality is capable of grounding necessary *truths*.

Finally, I am not implying that all genuine causal relations are characterized by necessity. There are contingent causal connections, but they are not of direct relevance to the question of necessary truth. Let us now go on with discussion of that question.

Since diverse objectification must come either from a real distinction or from logical relations, ard since any necessary connection between the terms of a real distinction is a necessary causal relation, the identity as things of what are diversely objectified can be necessary for either of two and only two reasons: the way logical relations are

employed in diversely objectifying things or a necessary causal relation between the terms of a real distinction which provide the means
for diverse objectification. Thus there can be two and only two kinds
of necessary truths, truths whose necessity derives from logical relations and truths whose necessity derives from necessary causal relations. The significance of this distinction between kinds of necessary
truth will become clearer as we proceed with the analysis of necessary
truth itself.

I have just said that a truth is necessary if the identity between
what is made an object in one way and what is made an object in
another way is necessary. But what does it mean for this identity to
be "necessary"? The traditional understanding is that a sentence is
necessarily true if its denial is a contradiction or has contradictory consequences. Let us now try to be precise about what this means in the
light of the identity theory of truth. Recall that for diverse objects to
be identical as things, each object must be identical with the same
thing. For "(∃x) (Fx & Gx)" to be true some x must both be an existing individual and be identical with that-which-is-objectified-by the
word-functions of "F" and "G". In *necessary* identity, if a thing
objectified in one way (as an F, for instance) were not the same as
a thing that is objectified in another way (as a G), the thing objectified in at least one of these ways would both be and not be what
it is, would both be and not be identical with that which is made an
object in one of these ways. Given that "(x) (Fx → Gx)" is a necessary
truth, if "Gx" were false for some x, then "Fx" would be false.
Therefore if "(∃x) (Fx & -Gx)" were true, "(∃x) (Fx & -Fx)" would
also be true. To hypothesize that "Fx" is true for some x and "Gx"
is false is to imply that some x both is and is not what it is hypothesized
to be, namely, an F.

In both necessary and contingent truth, the same thing or things
are objectified diversely. But in the case of contingent truth, a thing
made object in one way would remain what it is, would remain identical with something-which-is-objectifiable in this way, even if it were
not identical with a thing made an object in another way. The entity
that is made an object as an F (or as having F-ness or as an instance
of F-hood or as an F-event or whatever) would remain identical with
what is expressed by "an F" even if it were not identical with an entity objectifiable as a G. The denial of a contingent truth, in other
words, is not contradictory. There is necessary truth, however, if and
only if a thing identical with what is made an object in one way (what
is expressed by "an F") would not be what it is if it were not iden-

tical with what is made an object in another way (what is expressed by "a G"). If an x that is F were not identical with an x that is G, an x that is F would not be identical with an x that is F; or, an x that is F would be identical with an x that is not F.

One more way of putting the necessary identity of things objectified by "F" and "G". Objects are identical with actual or possible existents. Consequently, if the opposite of "(x) (Fx → Gx)" is contradictory, an F that is not a G exists if and only if it both exists and does not exist. To hypothesize that an F would not exist if it were not also a G and that an F exists which is not a G is to imply that an F both exists and does not exist. These ways of putting it are equivalent because that which objects are identical with are what exists, actually or possibly. And all these ways of expressing the necessity of truth are consistent with understanding the objectifiability of things by predicates in terms of class membership. If it is necessary that members of the class of Fs are members of the class of Gs, a member of the class of Fs that is not a member of the class of Gs exists only if it also does not exist. Or, since things belong to the classes they do because they are what they are, if it is necessary that members of the class of Fs are members of the class of Gs, a member of the class of Fs is not a member of the class of Gs only if it also is not a member of the class of Fs and, therefore, both is and is not what it is.

This account of necessity leaves open the possibility of a truth being necessary without our being able to know that it is necessary, necessary in itself but not to us. It leaves open the possibility that what we can objectify as heat would not be heat unless it was also what we can objectify as something which expands solids. This would be the case if there are necessary causal relations between heat and the expansion of solids. If so, then for it to be *true* that what is objectifiable as heat is not also objectifiable as something which expands solids, it must be true that what is objectifiable as heat is at the same time *not* something objectifiable as heat. But it would not follow that we are able to *judge* that heat is the same as something which expands solids merely from our acquaintance with the word-functions of "heat", "something which expands solids" or of any other words.

Distinguishing between the necessity of a truth and our ability to judge its necessity protects us from the epistemological fallacy. Necessity and the contradictoriness of the opposite have not been described in terms of *knowledge* (in the sense of certitude caused by awareness of evidence). They have been described in terms of *things being what they are.* For necessary truth has been defined with reference to the identity of objects, and objects are not identical as terms of diverse relations of objectification but as actual or possible things. A truth is necessary only on the condition that, if it were false, a thing would both be and not be identical with what is objectified by some language-form; or, what amounts to the same thing, a truth is necessary only on the condition that, if it were false, a thing would both be and not be what it is. These amount to the same thing because what are objectified by language-forms are actual or possible things. Why are distinct objects necessarily identical with the same thing? Because otherwise a thing with which one of them is identical would both be and not be what it is. Notice, finally, that the necessity of truth and the necessity of causal relations have each been defined in terms of the contradictoriness of things being and not being.

Since an identity can be necessary without our being able to know it, a truth can be necessary without being either self-evident or derivable from truths that are self-evident. A truth is self-evidently necessary if and only if acquaintance with the meanings$_T$ of its words is sufficient to reveal that if its diverse objects were not identical as things, at least one of the objectified things would be and not be what it is. In other words, a sentence is self-evidently necessary if and only if it is self evident that the opposite is contradictory. And when we are discussing, not the necessity of a truth or the contradictory character of its opposite, but our *knowledge* of the necessity of a truth or of the contradictory character of its opposite, we are discussing self-evidence or derivation from the self-evident. And as we have just seen, we can consistently hypothesize the necessity of truths which are neither self-evident nor derivable from the self-evident so far as we know. To hypothesize that heat necessarily expands solids is to hypothesize that if heat existed without something-which-expands-solids existing, heat would be and not be.

For a truth to be self-evident, the way things are objectified by its word-functions must be such that acquaintance with the word-functions reveals the necessary identity of diverse objects. If the objects were not identical, the word-functions would both be and not be what they are. For it is the word-functions that determine what things are or are not rendered objects. But when the diverse objectification is drawn from really distinct features of experience between which there are necessary causal relations, it need not be the case that mere acquaintance with these features is sufficient to inform us of their necessary causal relations. Sometimes acquaintance with word-functions alone may be sufficient to make known a necessary identity between objects, sometimes it may not be sufficient. (Why it is sometimes sufficient and sometimes not sufficient will be explained in sections 8.3.2 and 9.1. But knowing the causes of acquaintance with word-functions sometimes being sufficient and sometimes insufficient to reveal necessary causal relations has nothing to do with our ability to grasp self-evident truth. For one can recognize that a truth is necessary without carrying out a causal analysis of the existence of that recognition.)

3.4.3 Solving some traditional problems

This section will defend my account of necessity by showing how the distinctions between logical relations and causal relations as bases for necessary truth and between the necessity of a truth and its derivability from the self-evident solve the difficult cases that the theory of necessary truth has always been hard put to handle. The success of these solutions will, of course, depend on the strength of the more detailed explanations of logical and causal necessity which are left for later chapters.

Why is "The number of planets is nine" a contingent truth while "The square of three is the triple of three" is a necessary truth? The way things and their characteristics are objectified in "number of planets" does not reveal the identity of what is so objectified with "nine". Nothing in the meaning$_T$ of "number of planets" informs us that some feature of our experience would both be and not be what is objectified by means of this phrase if it were not also objectifiable by "nine". In contrast, consider "The square of three is the triple of three". If the square of three were not identical with the triple of three, it would both be and not be the square of three. Why the difference between these cases? In the first case, we make use of really distinct features of our experience—being a planet is different from being a number—to articulate the same number. The difference between "three multiplied by three" and "three multiplied by itself" as means of objectification, on the other hand, consists solely of the use of the logical relation expressed by "itself". Since the only difference falls on the side of characteristics of means of objectification as means of objectification and of objects as terms of relations of objectification, there can be no difference on the side of that which terminates these relations of objectification insofar as it has some status other than being that which terminates either of the relations of objectification. Thus the identity of what is objectified by "the square of three" with what is objectified by "the triple of three" is necessary. (How do we know the necessity? Simply by having the word-function of "itself" as part of our logical equipment. See section 4.2.)

For "The number of planets is nine" to be a necessary truth there would have to be necessary causal relations between the features of experience which provide the meanings$_T$ of "planet" and "nine". And for "The number of planets is nine" to be a self-evidently necessary truth, these causal relations would have to be knowable from a mere acquaintance with these features of our experience. Now consider "3 × 3 = 9". Here the same quantity is objectified as term of diverse causal operations (as the result of adding three objects to three objects to three objects and as the result of counting to "9" according to the rules of the Arabic number system) which are so related that the quantity objectified as term of one of these causal operations must be identical with the objectified as term of the other operation. And by being acquainted with the word-functions of the multiplication sign and of the Arabic number system, we know that were the results of these operations not the same, these operations would not be what they are, that is, would both be and not be what they are at the same time. Furthermore, the number objectifiable as the result of removing four items from a group of thirteen is also necessarily identical with the number objectified by "9" in the Arabic number system. Consequently, if the operation of adding three items to three items to three items or the operation of removing four items from a group of thirteen takes place, the same result necessarily occurs. These operations are not causally related to one another but to the same term really distinct from both of them.

Now consider "Ruminants are cloven-hoofed". Here the logical diversification of objects is accomplished by reference to the terms of a real distinction between the process by which a ruminant digests and the number of its toes, rather than solely by the employment of logical devices to which no real distinction corresponds. Yet the statement may well be a necessary truth. If so, there must be relations between being a ruminant and being cloven-hoofed (or more likely between each of them and some other things) such that an animal could not be one without being the other. But the way things are objectified by the word-functions of "ruminant" and "cloven-hoofed" is not sufficient to reveal these relations.

Or consider "Ferdinand (an individual ruminant) is cloven-hoofed". Is this necessary or contingent? Assume it is necessary that ruminants have cloven-hoofs. Then a necessary connection exists between being cloven-hoofed and something else about Ferdinand, being a ruminant. But is it necessary that Ferdinand is a ruminant? Or is it necessary that Socrates is snub-nosed? To ask such a question about an individual is either to ask about an individual that is a unique configuration of really distinct characteristics or to ask about an individual that is absolutely simple, something having no part distinct from another part except logically.

Assume we are asking about a unique configuration of really distinct characteristics. Then when asking whether Ferdinand is necessarily a ruminant or Socrates necessarily snub-nosed, we are asking whether the remaining characteristics constituting these individuals, or a specific group of these characteristics, can be what they are without the additional characteristic of being a ruminant or being snub-nosed, respectively. In other words, we are asking whether necessary causal relations hold between the configuration of other characteristics and being a ruminant or snub-nosed. And perhaps such necessary causal relations are the case. But they can be the case without our being able to know they are the case, and, therefore, know that "Ferdinand is a ruminant" and "Socrates is snub-nosed" are necessary truths.

In asking these questions about Ferdinand and Socrates, we are taking "Ferdinand" and "Socrates" to have a set of characteristics as their word-function. This is not to say that proper names always express descriptions. It is merely to say that the questions about the necessary truth of "Ferdinand is a ruminant" and "Socrates is snub-nosed" cannot be answered unless we give proper names such word-functions at least for the purpose of asking the questions.

It might seem that we need not associate a name with a description in cases of what is misleadingly called the "essence" of an individual (see, for example, Plantinga, 1974). Instead of asking whether it is necessary that Socrates is snub-nosed, we can ask whether it is necessary that he is human. It seems that if Socrates were not snub-nosed, he would still be Socrates. But if he were not human, he would not be Socrates.

That depends, however, on what we $mean_T$ by "Socrates". If we mean the unique collection of (past and present) molecules that happen to be so organized that an individual human exists, then we can ask whether it is necessary that this collection of molecules is this collection of molecules. An affirmative answer is required by the logical relation of identity. But it does not follow that this collection of molecules is necessarily organized so as to constitute a human being. There is a real distinction between the unique collection of molecules in Socrates and its organization into something human, for change proves that the molecules in this collection could be related in some entirely different way. Therefore if "Socrates is human" means this collection of molecules has human organization, it is not necessarily true since no necessary causal relation links these molecules to this way of being organized.

On the other hand, in "A collection of molecules so organized as to be human is a collection of molecules so organized as to be human", objects are diverisified only as terms of the the logical relation of identity. Therefore the identity is necessary. So if by "Socrates" we mean a collection of molecules so organized, "Socrates is human" is necessarily true since the only diversity in objects, other than lexicological, is logical.

The real distinction between a collection of molecules and its mode of organization, however, does not imply that a mode of organization could exist independently of things that are so organized. A mode of organization has a relation of necessary causal dependence on that which is organized. The causality is the kind I will call component causality. It has long been recognized (see the general references in Appendix II) that the component cause is the cause of individuation. What makes this human *this* human is not the fact that the organization of its molecules makes it human. That fact is true of other human beings as well. What makes it *this* human is the fact that in it just these molecules and not some other group of molecules are so related as to be human.

Therefore causal relations make it necessarily true that Mary, this individual person, could not have had different parents since the parents supply the component causes, the sperm and the ovum, that made Mary *this* person. Here the name "Mary" does not have a description as its word-function. That for which it is used is an individual objectified as such. And the necessity derives from causal relations between that for which "Mary" is used, an individual objectified as an individual, and the word-function of "parents", the suppliers of component causes for the individual.

To take another example of individuation, could The Sears Tower be made of different materials? That depends on how we are using "The Sears Tower". If we associate it with a description such as "the tallest structure in Chicago", then no necessary causal relation links The Sears Tower with the materials it is made of. It could be made of different materials and still be the tallest structure in Chicago. But if we are using "The Sears Tower" for *this* tallest structure in Chicago, the individual building that is now taller than any other, The Sears

Tower could be made of different materials only on penalty of not being the The Sears Tower. For if it had different component causes, it would not be the same building as the building that is now taller than any other in Chicago.

Does it make sense to speak of real components as causes of *individuation* when individuality is a logical relation? It is wrong to argue from what is true of things as objects to what is true of them as things if the argument implies that what is true of things as object is the cause of what is true of them as things. But what is true of things as objects *can be* an effect of what is true of them as things. Thus what an elephant is and what a rose bush is determines that these things are species of the genus, living things. And in a sense everything true of things as objects is an effect of what is true of them as things since their real existence has causal priority over their being made objects.

Individuality is the correlative of universality. Therefore to ask what is the cause of individuation is to ask why the natures of things (cause) makes it possible to objectify them by predicates true of more than one thing (effect). Peter and Paul are both objectifiable by "man" because the what each them is makes them similar to the other in this respect. But each of them is also something distinct from what the other is, since Peter is not Paul. The cause of individuation is whatever it is about the extra-objectively existing nature of each that makes the humanity of each the humanity of something distinct from the other.

Necessary truths involving the "essences" of natural kinds should be handled the same way as those involving individuals. Is it a necessary truth that gold has the atomic number 79? If what we mean by "gold" is something that has the atomic number 79, then "Gold has the atomic number 79" is rendered necessary by diversely objectifying the same thing as term of the relation of identity. But if the word-function of "gold" is a collection of sub-atomic particles that happens to be organized into an atom with 79 protons, whether gold has that atomic number can be the question whether a collection of sub-atomic particles must be so organized. The answer is "No", since no causal relations require these particles to be so distributed.

A more likely candidate for the word-function of "gold", however, would be something that behaves in certain ways, especially something that behaves in certain ways in chemical experiments. In that case, "Gold has an atomic number 79" could be causally necessary. That is, the behavior could have as its necessary cause something with the atomic number 79. Since it is causal, this necessity does involve essence. (See section 4.3 and Chapter Nine.) Of course acquaintance with word-functions alone need not be sufficient to reveal these causal relations.

To return to individuals, what if we take being a ruminant and being snub-nosed as members of the configuration of characteristics that constitute what Ferdinand and Socrates are as unique individuals? Is it necessary that Ferdinand and Socrates, respectively, have these characteristics? Let us assume an individual, *a*, is constituted by the unique conjunction of characteristics, F, G and H. To ask whether *a* necessarily has H is then the same as asking whether it is necessarily true that the conjunction of F, G and H cannot exist without H. The answer is "Yes", but why? We have made the configuration of characteristics F, G and H the word-function of "*a*". In so doing, we make use of the truth-functional logical relation, conjunction. That relation makes it necessary that whatever is objectified as having F and G and H is identical with something objectifiable as having H. (Necessity and self-evidence in the case of truth-functions will be discussed in section 4.4.)

Now what if the individual in question, *a*, is absolutely simple? Then the difference between the word-function of any predicate true of *a* and the word-function of "*a*" derives either from logical relations or from some real distinction external to *a*. If from logical relations, the identity of what is objectified by "*a*" and by the predicate is logically necessary. And acquaintance with the word-functions will be sufficient to reveal the necessity.

Even though *a* is simple, diverse objectification could derive from reference to the terms of some real distinction. In most cases, a person's politics is distinct from his religion, but some times they are the same. Likewise, the word-functions of predicates F and G could be features of things that are sometimes distinct but are the same in *a*. Here the the necessity of the identity will depend on some necessary causal relation holding between the word-functions by which *a* can be objectified or between *a* and the terms of the real distinction from which the diverse objectification comes. And such a relation can hold without its being knowable to us from acquaintance with word-functions.

The preceding arguments, by the way, require us to make no commitments of any kind regarding the ontological analysis of complexes into simples. On *any* analysis of simple or complex entities, the necessity of truths concerning individuals must derive either from logical relations or from causal relations between the terms of some real distinction. Nor in order to know whether a sentence is necessarily true, do we need criteria telling us whether the necessity is logical or causal. For a sentence to be recognized as necessarily true, it must be self-evident or derived from the self-evident. And to grasp self-evident truths, we do not need a theory of logical and causal necessity; we need acquaintance with word-functions.

Another traditionally difficult case is whether sentences like "Cicero is Tully" are necessary truths. On any assumption concerning the way in which proper names objectify that for which they are used, word-functions of "Cicero" and "Tully" differ neither by logical relations nor by reference to the terms of some real distinction. The only diversity in objects, other than purely lexicological, results from objectifying the same thing as terminating the logical relation of identity. Therefore the identity of that which they objectify is necessary.

Logical relations, however, do not result from the fact that this or that particular language-form is used the way it is; it is lexicological relations like synonymy that depend on what language-forms are given what uses. And the synonymy of "Cicero" and "Tully" is a contingent lexicological fact that has nothing to do with the diverse objectifications of the same thing as terms of a relation of identity with itself in such sentences as "Cicero is Cicero". We can know that "Cicero is Cicero" is necessarily true without being acquainted, in either the lexicological or non-lexicological sense, with the usage of "Cicero", as long as we are acquainted with the meaning$_T$ that "is" has in this sentence. We cannot know that "Cicero is Tully" is necessarily true unless we know that each of these names is used for the same thing.

And why is it not necessarily true that the morning star is the evening star? What diversifies the ways "the morning star" and "the evening star" objectify the same individual, logical relations or reference to the terms of some real distinction? Well, are there or are there not real distinctions between something's being a star, something's being in a certain place in the sky, something's being visible in the morning and something's being visible in the evening? The separate occurrences of things satisfying these descriptions establish real distinctions. Consequently it is necessary that the morning star be the evening star if and only if necessary causal relations between the terms of these distinctions make the identity of what is objectifiable as the morning star with what is objectifiable as the evening star necessary. And that necessity would be knowable if and only if acquaintance with word-functions, at least the word-functions of "the morning star" and "the evening star", was sufficient to reveal those necessary causal relations.

Finally, what explains the necessary truth of sentences like "A square is not a circle" or "A categorical sentence is not hypothetical"? Logical relations. But the logical relations in question are best explained (in section 9.4.2) when the causal relations accounting for necessary truths like "No two colors can be in the same place at the same time" have been explained.

One question about causal relations that will be dealt with later should be mentioned now, however. If what it is to be an F is something really distinct from being a G, how can it be contradictory to deny "(x) (Fx → Gx)"; why must "(∃x) (Fx & -Gx)" be true if and only if "(∃x) (Fx & −Fx)" is true? The answer is that while what it is to be an F may be really distinct from what it is to be a G, being an F may be the same as being in such a relation to being a G that something could not be an F without being a G. As mentioned earlier, some realities, like knowing and loving, must be recognized as relative whether or not we want to admit the "reality of relations" in the sense of believing that relative things are relative only because of a class of entities distinct from them called "relations". And it will follow from the demonstration that every event must have a cause that caused realities are by nature relative to their causes. Their being related to their causes is not something over and above their being what they are.

A real existent cannot be *nothing but* the term of a relation, but it can be the term of a relation by its being what it is (as, for example, when a relation is defined by characteristics belonging to its term). Therefore being an F and being a G may be the same as being either a relation, a relative entity or the term of a relation such that something would not be an F unless it were also a G. And acquaintance with word-functions can be acquaintance with modes of being which are so causally related that, even though the diversity in the ways in which the word-functions objectify things consists of reference to the terms of a real distinction, what is objectifiable by one word-function, like that of "change", must be identical with what is objectifiable by another word-function, like that of "something having an efficient cause". (See section 9.3.2.)

3.4.4 Applications to mathematics

Since I have used sentences like "16 -12 = 2 + 2" to illustrate causal necessity, some remarks about causality in mathematics are called for. Describing numbers as terms of causal relations provides a good example of the point I was making in the last paragraph. To describe *four* as the result of removing twelve items from a group of sixteen is to describe it as term of a causal operation. But describing something as the effect of removing twelve items from a group of sixteen does not leave us ignorant of the nature of this effect, the number *four*. On the contrary, because we know the nature of the causal operation of which this effect is the term, we know the nature of the effect, namely, the number of remaining items. For effects are what they are as a result of their causes making them what they are. Therefore an effect's being what it is is precisely what terminates the causal relations by which the effect may be described. It should not be surprising, consequently, if the operation objectified by "the removal of twelve items from a group of sixteen" could not be what is so objectified unless it were also something objectifiable by "an operation which leaves four items remaining". Nor should it be surprising that we can know the truth of "16 − 12 = 4" by knowing truths which are self-evident to us because of our acquaintance with the rules for the Arabic number system, rules which determine the word-functions of the numbers, and our acquaintance with the word-functions of " − " and " = ".

To say that a causal operation of a certain kind necessarily has an effect of a certain kind is not to say that any effect occurs of necessity. The necessity is only hypothetical: if a specific operation occurs and no other change takes place, a specific effect will necessarily take place. Further, to point out that mathematics makes use of causal relations is not to accuse mathematics of being *about* causal relations in the sense of being an investigation-of causal relations. The teleonomic cause of causal investigations is the knowledge of why something really exists or of how it can come to really exist. But it does not matter to mathematics if any of the topics it discusses has or can have real existence in the sense of an existence which is other than being-known. As explained above (section 2.3.2), existential quantification need not imply an "ontological" commitment to the variables over which we quantify. Not that mathematics denies the real existence of the objects of its discourse; it is simply indifferent to the issue of real existence, actual or possible.

We do of course ask how certain numbers can come into cognition-independent existence, for instance, how wheat production can reach a certain number of bushels. These are causal investigations. But the answers to such questions always refer to causes defined otherwise than solely in terms of mathematical properties, for the effects whose existences are under discussion will always be defined otherwise than mathematically. Numbers can be said to exist extra-objectively only to the extent that numbers of things can be said to exist. And the causes on which things depend for their existence are not just numbers but numbers of things of certain kinds. The production of so much wheat requires so much land, water, etc.

Since mathematics does not seek to understand real existence, its goal is not the knowledge of causal relations. The teleonomic cause of classical mathematics, for instance, is the knowledge of relations of equality and inequality between quantities. To accomplish this, it constructs sentences in which the same quantities or quantitative relations are diversely objectified. And to accomplish the diverse objectification, it represents the identical quantity or quantitative relation as the term of diverse causal operations. The operations may be addition, subtraction, multiplication, division, geometric construction or simply the process of counting, as when the statements of arithmetic are explained as telling us the *results* of counting procedures carried out according to certain rules. Whatever the causal operation used, the important thing at the moment is that causality does not enter mathematics as that which is known but as the means employed to make known (to render an object) that which is known (that which is objectified): the quantity resulting from this operation is the same as that resulting from that operation; or the result of this operation is the same as something greater than the result of that operation; etc.

And since mathematics is not trying to know how real existence is to be explained, it makes no difference to it whether the causal relations it uses to diversify objectification are capable of cognition-independent existence. Cantor's proofs of the equivalence and non-equivalence of infinite sets, for instance, make use of rules for constructing matrices and series in which the members of infinite sets are enumerated. Of course, such effects as infinite matrices or series could never be produced by the operations Cantor's rules specify because in the finite time allotted to us we could not carry out the infinite number of operations required. But this does not bother the mathematician who is not interested in the real existence of these operations or their results. Even when simply adding or subtracting, the mathematician is not interested in whether the operations of joining to or removing from actually take place extra-objectively.

But even if the operations whose results the mathematician is interested in could not exist extra-objectively, they deserve to be considered causal operations in the sense that *if they existed extra-objectively*, these operations would be causally related to terms, their results, really distinct from themselves. To be more precise, if these operations existed extra-objectively, their relation to their results would satisfy our definition of a necessary causal relation. They would be really distinct from their results, but they could not exist without their results existing. These operations also deserve to be considered causal because, although they are cognition-dependent objects, we cognize them by combining word-functions that are really existing causal operations originally given in experience (like adding items to a group, removing items from a group, drawing figures, arranging things in series) with other word-functions. Thus we arrive at rules of construction defining geometric figures, rules for constructing a series of items standing in one-to-one correspondence with the natural numbers, etc.

It should be clear, therefore, that this understanding of the place of causal operations in mathematics has nothing to do with intuitionism. Describing Cantor's rules as rules of construction does not mean that his proofs are "constructive" in the intuitionist's sense of providing a realizable program for producing the objects defined. Proofs in mathematics need not be constructive in that way. Nor are the causal operations mathematics uses to diversely objectify its objects mental acts. They are word-functions which may or may not objectify something capable of cognition-independent existence. Any mental acts involved in using words for these functions and any causes of such mental acts are another matter.

That the mathematician is indifferent to whether the topics of his discourse are even capable of real existence has other significant implications. For one thing, causal relations are not the only means at mathematics' disposal for diversely objectifying its objects; it can also treat its objects as terms of purely logical relations such as class inclusion and exclusion. The causal operations mathematics uses may be "logical" constructs (cognition-dependent objects), but that does not make them logical relations. The meanings$_T$ of words for logical relations, unlike those of words for the cognition-dependent causal relations mathematics uses, are not constructed out of the meanings$_T$ of words for cognition-independent existents.

To say that mathematics can use logical relations as means of objectification is not to say mathematics need be an investigation-of logical relations any more than its use of causal relations makes it an investigation-of causal relations. Nor are there two kinds of mathematics, one describing its objects as terms of logical relations and one describing its objects as terms of causal relations. As indifferent to real existence, mathematics can diversely objectify its objects both by means taken from a class of which no members are capable of real existence, logical relations, and by means taken from a class of which at least some members are capable of real existence, causal relations.

Since logical relations are characteristics belonging to objects only as objects, it would be contradictory for logical relations to have real existence. This would imply that to be was to be known and therefore, as we saw in section 2.2.2, that to be was to be nothing. Yet there need be no contradiction in the definition of any logical relation. This illustrates another significant point about mathematics. As indifferent to real existence, mathematics can discourse about objects whose definitions contain no contradiction but to which the attribution of extra-objective existence would be contradictory. For the reason explained in section 2.3.2, mathematics will use existential quantification to assert that some logical construct satisfies a certain predicate. (For the same logical construct can be objectified in more than one way. "p → q" objectifies the same set of possible combinations of truth-values for "p" and "q" as does "-(p & -q)". See section 4.4.2.) But a predicate may be so defined as to be incapable of objectifying a real existent without being defined contradictorily. The only contradiction occurs if the object is asserted to have real existence, actually or possibly.

And this gives us an alternative way of handling paradoxes like that of parts of infinite wholes being equal in size to their wholes even though their wholes contain these parts together with additional parts. Why not say that this paradox proves that an actually infinite multitude cannot have extra-objective existence? That would not render the mathematics of transfinite sets invalid. The fact, for instance, that the set of odd numbers and the set of natural numbers satisfy non-contradictory mathematical definitions does not imply that it is not contradictory for the result of removing part, but not all, of a really existing whole composed of really existing parts to be equal to the size of the whole before the part was removed. For the parts of really existing wholes are causes (component causes) of those wholes. And causes are *other than* their effects. Therefore a component cause of a quantity cannot be the same as the quantity of which it is the cause.

On the other hand, logical constructs can be defined contradictorily. For the reason to be explained in section 5.4, a predicate so defined that its attribution to any object by means of existential quantification expresses or implies contradiction should not be attributed to any object, cognition-independent or cognition-dependent, by means of existential quantification. An example of a logical construct so defined as to yield contradiction when attributed to any object would be the class of all classes that are not members of themselves; hence we should not quantify over this class even though we do not intend the quantification to assert real existence.

This concludes my introductory treatment of necessary truth. In addition to the entire issue of causal necessity, I have yet to explain how logical relations render truths necessary. And I must address the question of how acquaintance with word-functions can cause the recognition of the necessity of truths, whether that necessity be logical or causal. The next chapter will deal specifically with truths rendered necessary by logical relations and our knowledge of these truths.

CHAPTER FOUR
Logical Necessity

Necessary truths can be known if and only if acquaintance with the meanings$_T$ of the words of some sentences is sufficient to make us aware that their opposites are contradictory. And a truth known through the application of a criterion expressed by some other sentence is not known simply through acquaintance with the meanings$_T$ of its words. A self-evidently necessary truth, therefore, is not known by using a criterion of necessity or of self-evidence. But how is it that word-functions render truths necessary and that acquaintance with word-functions is sufficient to make that necessity known? This chapter will answer these questions for logically necessary truths.

Logically necessary truths are those whose necessity results from logical relations characterizing diverse objects and means of objectification. The claim that logical relations can render truths necessary is not new. But I am unaware of any attempt to give an account of logical relations from which their ability to ground necessary truth can be deduced. I will attempt such a deduction on the basis of the analysis of logical relations given in the last chapter. We will find, however, that truths whose necessity derives from logical relations are not coextensive with truths of logic. Attention will also be given in this chapter to negation and to the necessary non-identity, rather than the identity, of diversely objectified things. The principle of non-contradiction will be discussed as will Quine's evaluation of it. And I will show how to apply my analysis of necessity and self-evidence to the formulas of symbolic logic.

Section 4.4.1 of this chapter explains a concept, logical inclusion, central to some of the later arguments in the book. Those readers not interested in logical necessity for its own sake may want to read only Section 4.4.1 and go on to the next chapter.

4.1 Logical Relations and Necessity
4.1.1 Necessary identity

Sometimes the meanings$_T$ of different language-forms do not differ even in respect to logical relations ("Cicero", "Tully"; "organism", "living thing"). Sometimes the meanings$_T$ of different language-forms differ by logical relations alone ("scarlet", "red", "color"; "B knows A", "A is known by B"). Sometimes words for logical relations are employed in such a way that there is no difference between the meanings$_T$ of different language-forms ("animate", "not inanimate"; "two multiplied by two", "two multiplied by itself"). *Whenever things are objectified by language-forms whose mean-ings$_T$ differ by no more than logical relations or by language-forms whose meanings$_T$ are the same because of the employment of words for logical rela-tions, there can be no difference in what is objectified by these means, no dif-ference in the terms of the diverse relations of objectification.* That is a necessary truth. And if for "logical relations" we substitute "characteristics attributable to objects only as objects or to means of objectification only as means of objectification" we can derive this truth from the self-evident. For by hypothesis, there is no difference in that which is objectified in diverse ways other than differences attributable to it as something terminating diverse relations of objectification; there is no difference in the terms of these relations insofar as they are some-thing-more-than-*objects*. Therefore if what is objectifiable in one way were not identical to something objectifiable in the other, it would both be and not be what it is.

In all affirmative sentences the diversity between objects consists, at least, in their being terms of diverse relations of objectification. But here the diversity can consist of no more than their being terms of diverse relations of objectification. There can be no difference in that which terminates the diverse relations of objectification insofar as it is something more than a term of relations of objectification, since all the differences fall in the category of characteristics with which ob-jects become associated only as a result of having become terms of relations of objectification.

This reasoning applies equally to sentences objectifying cognition-independent things and sentences objectifying logical constructs. A logical construct has no status other than being a term of *some* relation of objectification (specifically, being the way some language-form is used or a characteristic of the way some language-form is used). But a logical construct can be objectified in more than one way and, therefore, can have a status other than being the term of this or that relation of objectification. Logical constructs objectified in diverse ways are necessarily identical if there are no differences between them other than differences resulting from their being terms of these diverse relations of objectification. For by hypothesis, there is no difference between the terms of either of these relations of objectification insofar as that term has some status other than being what terminates this relation of objectification or that. If the logical construct terminating one relation of objectification were not the same as the logical construct terminating the other, it would both be and not be what it is. (Section 4.4.1 explains this argument further.)

Let us return to sentences objectifying cognition-independent things. Because all the differences between objects may fall into the category of characteristics pertaining to objects as objects, not as things, and because this necessitates that it be the same thing that is diversely objectified, it follows that there are necessary truths to the effect that certain ways of making things our objects yield truths that are incapable of being false. In other words, there are sentences that inform us that certain ways of making things objects of sentential knowledge yield other sentences that are necessarily true. And the sentences that inform us of this are themselves necessarily true. They are truths of logic. It is a necessary truth of logic, for instance, that any sentence of the form (x) (Fx $\rightarrow$ $-(-Fx)$) is necessarily true.

But a necessary truth about the way in which we make things objects is one thing; a necessary truth in which we make things objects is something else. "Every animate body is a body that is not inanimate" is a necessary truth because, given that the logical relation of negation is what it is, what is objectified by the subject could not fail to be what is also objectified by the predicate without ceasing to be what is objectified by the subject. But the fact that the diversity between subject and predicate consists in the way in which negation is used in the predicate does not imply that this sentence objectifies animate things according to what is true of them as objects rather than as things. What are objectified by "animate" and "inanimate" are things for which to be is other than to be known. Hence "Every animate body is a body that is not inanimate" is a statement about (that is, objectifying) things as things, not as objects. The identity known in knowing this truth is the identity with themselves of certain cognition-independent things.

On the other hand, a necessary truth to the effect that whatever is made an object in manner A differs only by logical relations from what is made an object in manner B characterizes things by predicates attributable to them only as terms of knowledge relations. And the identity known in knowing this truth is the identity with itself of something described purely as the term of different knowledge relations. (Both real entities and cognition-dependent objects can be described truthfully as terms of knowledge relations. But this does not contradict what has been said concerning the function of the identity relation in objectifying the real existence, actual or possible, of what has also been made term of a knowledge relation. The public character of language guarantees both that identity is primarily a relation to real existents and that the logical characteristics of the language used for discussing cognition-dependent objects is derived from that employed to render real existents objects of knowledge.)

Consequently a necessary law of logic tells us that anything we are able to objectify as "animate" is something we are able to objectify as "not inanimate". And the necessity of "Every animate body is a body that is not inanimate" results, not from causal relations, but from characteristics of ways in which we make things our objects. But it does not follow that "Every animate body is a body that is not inanimate" objectifies animate bodies as objects and not as things. If it did follow, we would be in contradiction. On the one hand, the necessity would derive from the ways the sentence renders an object of knowledge that something-other-than-an-*object* which we are calling a "thing". On the other hand, the sentence would not objectify anything as something-other-than-an-*object* but only as an object.

Necessary truths of logic inform us that sentences of the forms $a = a$ and $(x)(Fx \rightarrow Fx)$ are necessarily true. Such logical laws are truths about the manner in which we make things objects, namely, by means of sentences with various logical properties. But in sentences of either of these forms, sentences like "Snow is snow", for instance, things can be objectified as things, not as objects. Although "Snow is snow" objectifies snow as terminating a logical relation, "snow" objectifies snow as a thing. Things become terms of the relation of identity only as a result of being objectified. But they are objectified because they are things. And what terminates the identity relation are things as more-than-*objects*; the status of things as diverse objects is precisely the respect in which they are *not* identical. (Being an object is a necessary but not sufficient condition for terminating the identity relation.)

If there are necessary truths about our processes of objectification, they are necessary truths about the processes by which things whose existence is other than being-known, and which are known by predicates other than those describing them as terms of knowledge relations, are made objects. We have already seen that in the case of our first objects of knowledge there can be no more than a logical distinction between that which is an object and that which has or can have an existence other than being-known. And we have seen that the ways in which we objectify logical constructs must be derived from the way we objectify extra-cognitional things. It follows that if there are necessary truths concerning the way we objectify in sentences, either they are truths concerning the way we objectify *things* in sentences or they are derived from necessary truths about the way we objectify things in sentences.

In other words, laws of logic (necessary truths about the way we objectify in sentences) apply to sentences that are logically necessary but are not truths of logic. They are logically necessary because their necessity derives from logical relations. They are not truths of logic because they objectify things as things. (Logically necessary truths that are not truths of logic correspond to what Plantinga, 1974, p. 2, calls "broadly logical necessity".) That the necessary truth of sentences about things as things can derive solely from properties of the apparatus by which we make things objects should come as no surprise. For it is the very fact that the lack of identity is found solely on the side of characteristics belonging to the means of objectification as such that makes it necessarily true that there can be no lack of identity in that which is objectified. (That logical necessity can characterize sentences about things as things has important implications, brought out in section 5.4.2, for our understanding of philosophical method.)

4.1.2 Negation and necessary non-identity

We have been talking about logically necessary identity between diverse objects. What about logically necessary non-identity? In affirmative truth, what are non-identical as objects are identical as actual or possible things. In negative truth, what are non-identical as objects are also non-identical as things; no relation of identity holds between the terms of diverse relations of objectification as actual or possible things. (The problem of "negative facts" is to be handled in the same way as is the problem of reference to the non-existent in sections 3.3.2 and 5.5.2.) But why should it be the case that some non-identical objects are *necessarily* non-identical as things? As I have already mentioned, necessary non-identities like that of a square not being a circle will be accounted for by a kind of logical relationship to be explained later (section 9.4.2). Here I will discuss the necessary non-identity which derives from the use of the logical relation of negation, other-than. For this kind of necessity can appear to contradict what has been said so far about logical necessity.

Between "animate" and "not inanimate" there is no difference in meaning$_T$ and therefore no difference in things objectified by them. But what about the difference between "animate" and "inanimate" as means of objectification? The only difference between these language-forms is the presence of the particle "in" whose word-function is a logical relation, namely, negation. Does it follow that the word-functions of "animate" and "inanimate" differ at most by a logical relation? If so, animate things and inanimate things are necessarily identical rather than necessarily non-identical.

But in accounting for necessity by logical relations, the crucial question is not whether two language-forms differ by the occurrence in one or both of language-forms whose word-functions are logical relations. The question is whether the word-functions of the two language-forms differ at most by logical relations or, if their word-functions are the same, whether this sameness results from the way language-forms for logical relations are employed. In the case of language-forms differing only by the occurrence in one or the other of a sign for negation, it is *by hypothesis* not the case that the word-functions of the language-forms are the same or that the sole difference in their word-functions is one of logical relations. That is precisely what is prevented by the use of the negation sign. "F" and "not non-F" say the same thing in different ways. "F" and "non-F" do *not* say the same thing. That for which "animate" is used is not that for which "inanimate" is used, and the distinction is more than logical. The distinction between the word-functions of "animate" and "inanimate" is so real, in fact, that things objectifiable by means of them *must* be different things.

But how can the difference in word-functions and objectified things be more than one of logical relations if the difference in language-forms amounts to no more than a sign for a logical relation? Why do the word-functions and things terminate the relation of negation as more-than-*objects*? Simply because the word-function of negation signs, the relation other-than, is what it is. Why can the difference between the animate and the inanimate not consist only in their being terms of diverse relation of objectification? Because of the job that negation performs as a logical relation.

Like identity, the relation other-than is part of the logical apparatus by which we objectify things. Things terminate the identity relation only as a result of becoming objects. Still, the identity relation does have *things* among its terms. Likewise, the relation of non-identity has things among its terms even though it is a logical relation. If real existents, actual or possible, are not included among the terms of relations characterizing objects as a result of becoming objects, then there can be no real existents, actual or possible, among our objects, no identity between objects and things.

Logical constructs terminate logical relations as well. But the relation of non-identity first occurs in the objectification of cognition-independent things, for that is where the relation of identity first occurs. The primary terms of the relation which is the word-function of negation signs, therefore, are distinct as more-than-*objects*; otherwise they would be related as identical rather than as non-identical. As the relation of identity objectifies things as no more than logically distinct, negation objectifies things as more than logically distinct, more than distinct merely as objects.

For instance, when we negate that for which a thing-description is used, we objectify whatever is really distinct from the meaning$_T$ of that description. Using a language-form which has negation as its word-function, we construct a means of objectification, say "non-F", distinct from another means of objectification, "F". But the difference between what are objectified by these means cannot consist only of a logical relation. Relations are relations to terms. The terms of that relation which happens to be the word-function of "non" are really distinct from one another. One of those terms is that for which thing-description "F" is used: what it is to be an F. Therefore the word-function of "F" is really distinct from the word-function of "non-F"; being-an-F is really distinct from not-being-an-F. (And if the terms of a distinction are a real existent and a cognition-dependent object, the distinction is a real distinction. For example, such is the distinction between the word-functions of "existent" and "non-existent".)

Consequently the fact that negation is a logical relation does not imply that the distinction between Fs and non-Fs is only logical. Again, if this were implied, it would be possible for Fs and non-Fs to be the same as things. And that is just what we deny when we say that no F is a non-F. Call some non-F a "G". Objectifying it as a G does not tell us that it is a non-F. The function of negation is to tell us about the G what "G" does not tell us, namely, that it is other than an F. The function of negation is to render it an object of knowledge that things are not only diverse as objects, as described by "F" and "G", for instance, but as things. Hence the non-identity of what is objectifiable by "F" and what is objectifiable by "non-F" is rendered necessary by the logical relation which signs like "non" happen to be used for, the relation we call "negation". Given that signs like "non" are used for negation, what is objectified by "F" can be identical with what is objectified by "non-F" if and only if it both is and is *not* what it is.

4.2 Logical Self-evidence

Logical relations allow us to construct sentences that are necessarily true both because of the necessary identity of diverse objects and because of the necessary non-identity of diverse objects. And sentences of both kinds can objectify things as things. You may feel that the $64 question concerning these sentences is yet to be answered, however. How do we know they are necessarily true?

The cause of our knowledge of any self-evident truth is our understanding of its word-functions. We are talking about sentences in which diversity in objectification of things is achieved through logical relations or words for logical relations. In one case the identity is necessarily true, because the diversity between objects consists at most of diverse logical characteristics. In the other case the identity is necessarily false, because one objectified thing is related to the other by the logical relation of negation. Logical relations by which we achieve diversity in objectification can be understood through an understanding of word-functions in either of two ways. We may be acquainted with the meanings of words like "not", "itself", "and", words for logical relations. Or we may be acquainted with non-logical word-functions, such as those of "red" and "color", between which there are logical relations that we cannot fail to be acquainted with when we are acquainted with these word-functions. In either case, because we know the logical relations involved, we can know that certain sentences must be true. No cause for our knowledge of these necessary truths other than our acquaintance with the logical relations involved could be sought or should be sought.

But have we sufficiently accounted for our acquaintance with logical relations themselves? There is no other way to acquire an understanding of logical relations than to become acquainted with them in and by the fact of linguistically objectifying things other than logical relations. If they became objects of knowledge in any other way, they would be something other than logical relations, that is, relations attributable to linguistic objects as a result of being objects or to means of objectification as means of objectification. For it is self-evident that there is that to which a predicate attributable to objects as objects (or means of objectification as such) can be attributed only if there is an object (or a means of objectification). And it has already been established that there are objects only if they are first known (and thus objectified by some means) otherwise than as objects. Because the word-function of "logical relation" is what it is, logical relations become our objects if and only if we objectify things in certain ways.

And finally, being acquainted with logical relations amounts to being able to use some language-forms (not necessarily the lexicologically correct ones) in certain ways, either having the ability to use language-forms like "non", "if . . . then", "itself" whose meanings$_T$ are logical relations or words like "scarlet" and "red" whose meanings$_T$ are characterized by logical relations. That is why I said no cause of our knowledge of logically self-evident truths other than our ability to use words in certain ways could be sought or should be sought. There are relations characterizing our linguistic objects and means of objectification such that if things are objectified in certain ways, these relations are known; and if they are known, many self-evident truths can be known.

Once again, criteria for distinguishing logical relations from non-logical relations or words for logical relations from other words are not the issue. It happens to be the case that if we use language in certain ways, we cannot avoid being acquainted with certain logical relations. And it happens to be the case that if we are acquainted with certain logical relations, we cannot avoid being able to recognize the necessity of certain truths. This is established by the preceding analyses which constitute sufficient causal explanations of logical necessity and self-evidence. Our analysis of the necessary identity and non-identity of diversely objectified things is a sufficient explanation of why some characteristics of objects and means of objectification as such generate necessary truth. And our analysis of how we become acquainted with logical relations is a sufficient explanation of why some necessities generated by logical relations are self-evident.

In using words in certain ways, we become acquainted with lexicological and grammatical as well as logical relations. But to recognize necessary truth, we do not need to first distinguish logical relations from lexicological and grammatical. If there is some relation capable of making a sentence necessarily true, acquaintance with that relation allows us to know the sentence is necessarily true. Knowledge of the necessary truth does not require an understanding of the terms "logical relation", "lexicological relation", or "grammatical relation", nor does it require the ability to distinguish logical relations from relations of other kinds. Knowing the necessary truth only requires acquaintance with the relation that is, in fact, the source of the necessity. It is more appropriate to use the fact of grounding necessity as a means of distinguishing logical relations from the lexicological and grammatical than to use the distinction between these kinds of relations as a means of judging necessity.

If it is objected that these analyses cannot be described as causal since logical relations do not have causes, recall what was said in section 3.4.1. While logical relations do not have causes, the uses of language which they characterize do have causes; those uses of language have the logical relations they do because they are what they are; and they are what they are because their causes make them what they are. The effects of certain language-acts, for instance, are sentences characterized by the logical relation truth. The effects of certain uses of language-forms whose meanings$_T$ are, or are characterized by, logical relations are sentences characterized by the logical relation of necessary truth. And necessary truth also characterizes the results of certain uses of language-forms between whose meanings$_T$ there are necessary causal relations. It will be seen in section 5.4.2, finally, that this explanation of logical necessity and self-evidence by characteristics of the manner in which *things* are objectified is an *ontological* analysis.

4.3 Non-contradiction and Self-evidence

But how can any of the sentences under consideration be self-evident if their necessity has been denied by philosophers? According to our definition of necessity, to call a truth necessary is to say that if it were not true, something would both be and not be what it is. Therefore no truths are necessary if the principle of non-contradiction is not necessary, if it need not be the case that $-(p \& -p)$. And self-evident necessity has been defined as the self-evidence that the opposite is contradictory. Since philosophers have denied the necessity of the principle of non-contradiction itself, how can any truth be considered self-evidently necessary?

This problem gives me a chance to illustrate what was said above about denying self-evident truths. If a sentence really is self-evidently true, its denial must be a case of ignorance of the question; what the philosopher is denying is something other than the self-evident truth he thinks he is denying. Quine's treatment of the principle of non-contradiction makes this very clear, especially if we compare an earlier statement on the subject with a more recent statement. Here is the position of *Word and Object*:

> Consider the familiar remark that even the most audacious system-builder is bound by the law of contradiction. How is he really bound? If he were to accept contradiction, he would so re-adjust his logical laws as to insure distinctions of some sort; for the classical laws yield all sentences as consequences of any contradiction. But then we would proceed to reconstrue his heroically novel logic as a non-contradictory logic, perhaps even as familiar logic *in perverse notation*. (1960, p. 59, emphasis mine)

But if we can construe the new logic as a non-contradictory logic, the new logic does not deny the principle of non-contradiction. It may at most contain a formula such as "p & −p". But since the logic can be construed as a non-contradictory logic, that formula cannot have the meaning$_T$ that standard rules for the use of signs like "−" and "&" would give it.

From the point of view of standard notation, the notation of the new logic is lexicologically incorrect, that is, it *is* perverse notation. But this is the only thing perverse about the new logic. Quine apparently thinks he is countenancing a rejection of the principle of non-contradiction because he is countenancing accepting into a logical system a group of marks combined in a certain way. Therefore he apparently thinks that belief in the necessity of the principle is belief that marks combined in a certain way should not be accepted. But this is not what belief in the necessity of the principle is, and therefore he is not denying what supporters of necessity believe. To believe in the necessity of the principle is not to believe that sentences of the form −(p & −p) cannot be true; it is to believe that they cannot be true *on the hypothesis* that the marks making them up are being used in certain ways, are given certain word-functions. That Quine does not deny this belief is shown by his admission that the new logic would be construable as, and so consistent with, a non-contradictory logic.

But even more, when Quine admits that the new logic would be

construable as non-contradictory, he is admitting precisely what supporters of necessity believe, namely, that notation may change, but
no use of notation can succeed in *truthfully* denying what is expressed
in current notation by means of the formula $"-(p \ \& \ -p)"$. In this
passage, therefore, Quine is assenting to the necessity of the principle of non-contradiction even though he thinks he is denying it. If
you still have any doubt about this, I ask you to consider Quine's later
(1970) statement on the matter:

> . . . neither party (the proponent nor the opponent of the necessity
> of the principle) knows what he is talking about. They think they
> are talking about negation, $"-"$, "not"; but surely the notation
> ceased to be recognizable as negation when they took to regarding
> some conjunctions of the form "p & -p" as true, and stopped
> regarding such sentences as implying all others. Here, evidently,
> is the deviant logician's predicament; when he tries to deny the doc-
> trine he only changes the subject. (p. 81)

First let us ask why Quine should accuse *both* sides of not knowing what they are talking about. Who, after all, are the "they" that
think they are talking about negation signs but are really changing
the subject? Only the opponent of necessity deprives negations signs
of their standard uses by accepting contradiction. The proponents of
necessity know they are talking about negation signs in the sense of
signs whose word-function is the relation of negation. For they are
the first to agree with Quine that "p & -p" cannot be accepted as
long as, but only as long as, $"-"$ has the word-function it now has.

And notice that while at the beginning of the passage both sides
are accused of being ignorant of the question, at the end of the passage
it is only the deviant logician who is accused of being in a predicament. It is not the proponent of necessity who fails to understand
what the proponent of necessity is talking about; it is Quine who fails
to understand what the proponent of necessity is talking about. For
Quine and the proponent are saying exactly the same thing.

This passage, then, can be quoted as a defense of the view that
self-evidently necessary truths are deniable only by *ignoratio elenchi*,
only by changing the subject. It is itself a self-evident truth, incidentally, that when an understanding of a sentence's word-functions is
sufficient for knowing the truth of the sentence, we can fail to know
that truth only through ignorance of the functions of the sentence's
words. It is only in appearance, as Quine implies, that one denies
a self-evident truth. What is denied *appears* to be the same as the self-
evident truth, but only because the same language-forms occur in both

cases. Quine's deviant logician, for example, uses "p & −p". But the denial can only be in appearance since the language-forms are not being used in the same way. The deviant logician cannot be using them in the standard way because whoever understands the function that " − " is ordinarily given knows that −(p & −p).

But what is it that *forces* the deviant logician to succeed in doing nothing more than change the subject? It is not the contingent fact that certain language-forms are ordinarily given certain functions. Two historians can differ in their understanding of how the word "Waterloo" is used in "Napoleon was defeated at Waterloo". It does not follow that if one of them refuses to accept that sentence as true, he is *only* changing the subject. He may not only think that "Waterloo" is being used the way we ordinarily use "Moscow" and hence that Napoleon was *not* defeated at the place others understand as the referent of "Moscow". He may also believe that Napoleon was not defeated at the place others understand as the referent of "Waterloo" even though he is not aware that the place is so named.

What forces the deviant logician to change the subject is that one cannot assert "p & −p" without giving negation signs a function other than they now have. For given that their current word-function, the relation of negation, is what it is, to assert " −p" is to cancel what one asserts when one asserts "p". Therefore "p & −p" can be true if and only if the relation of negation is not the relation of negation.

Why does Quine fail to see that his position on non-contradiction is the same as that of the supporters of necessity and self-evidence? There could be many reasons. But at least one of them is demonstrably present in his writings; he is guilty of reading into the necessity/self-evidence position not only more than is required by it but more than is consistent with its truth. For he identifies that position with the linguistic theory of necessity. At one point he even implies that the only alternative to explaining necessity linguistically is "some doctrine of ultimate and inexplicable insight into the obvious traits of reality" (1966, p. 106).

But knowledge of the necessity of the principle of non-contradiction is a matter neither of lexicological knowledge nor of any inexplicable insight into anything. It is a matter of our very explicable acquaintance with the relation of negation. Quine is no doubt influenced by the causal connection between acquaintance with logical relations and the fact that we use words in certain ways. But he apparently concludes from this that to ground necessity in logical relations is to ground it in the lexicological contingency that the relevant word-functions are the functions of certain language-forms and not of others.

If my explanation of necessary truth and self-evidence does not require any inexplicable insights, neither does it make appeal to possible worlds, on the one hand, or essences, on the other. Why it can be said that a truth is necessary if and only if it is true in all possible worlds will be discussed in section 5.4.2. But something is true in all possible worlds because it is a necessary truth; it is not a necessary truth because it is true in all possible worlds. Truth in all possible worlds, in other words, must be explained in terms of necessity rather than necessity being explained in terms of it. (Compare Kripke, 1972, p. 19, n. 18.)

And when necessity is grounded in logical relations, it is grounded in something to which *traditional* concepts of essence are diametrically opposed. (I do not consider philosophical tradition to have begun in the late nineteenth century.) On the traditional definitions, essence is the exact opposite of a characteristic of things *as objects*. Essence is either considered a real causal principle accounting for what something is or considered the same as what something is. In either case, it cannot be a cognition-dependent object as logical relations are. Things as things constitute the sphere of essence as traditionally defined, while things as objects constitute the sphere of logical relations.

Paradoxically, the traditional association of essence with necessity comes by way of causal, not logical, necessity, the necessity that involves a real distinction between the terms of the relation. And this kind of necessity is not admitted by many who want to invoke essence as the ground of necessary truth. The often-cited Aristotelian essences have the job of explaining why things act the way they do (in other words, why they produce the kinds of effects they do), and why their existence requires the kinds of causes that produce them. The properties that an Aristotelian substance has necessarily are either identical with the substance (and hence the necessity is logical only), or distinct from the substance as accidents of it (and hence linked to the substantial nature by causal necessity). Of course "properties" in Aristotle's own sense are a type of accident, and so their necessity is always causal.

The relation of causality to what things are (essence) is the subject of Chapters Seven, Eight and Nine. It should be said now, however, that knowledge of necessary truths based on causal relations involves no more "inexplicable insight" into the natures of things than does the knowledge of logically necessary truths. It requires no more than acquaintance with word-functions, like those of "color" and "place" or "change occurring to something" and "that to which a change occurs", between which there are causal relations such that one would not exist without the other.

Today "properties" and similar terms are often used for anything that can be the word-function of a predicate. For example, Plantinga (1974, p 60ff.) calls such logical constructs as the word-functions of "being a prime number or else something else", "being snub-nosed in possible world W" and "being identical with Socrates" properties. If we wish to use "property" this way, we cannot endow it with any ontological, that is, extra-objective, significance. To do so would be an epistemological fallacy since, as thus defined, "property" is an object-description.

Plantinga tries to associate the property, being identical with Socrates, with the "essence" of Socrates. Being identical with Socrates is a property only of Socrates, while being identical with itself is a property of everything. True, but this difference lessens neither the logical character of identity nor the mutual irrelevance of such properties and necessities, on the one hand, and essence in the traditional ontological sense, on the other.

4.4 Further Elucidations

It will not be obvious how this analysis accounts for many necessary truths, including important truths of logic and mathematics, not yet considered. This section will extend the analysis to formulas of symbolic logic and to such truths as "If A is less than B and B is less than C, C is less than A" which at first sight do not appear amenable to the logical relation/causal relation account of necessity. Here I will also explain the significant relation, mentioned several times already, illustrated by the word-functions of "scarlet", "red" and "color", a relation that can be called one word-function's being logically included in another. Explaining this relation will be needed for understanding the argument of this section and later arguments as well.

4.4.1 Set membership and logical necessity

The formulas of propositional logic do not objectify things as things. Therefore we cannot analyze their truth in terms of an identity relation between that which has been made an object and that which actually or possibly has an existence which is other than being an object. Still there is an identity relation which determines their truth or falsity. These formulas objectify logical relations holding between terms. Such a formula is true if the relation between terms expressed by the formula is identical with a relation that does hold between these terms. "p → q" is true if and only if the relation between the truth-values of "p" and "q" is identical with the relation which is the word-function of "→". What this identity amounts to will become clear as we examine the necessary truth of formulas in symbolic logic.

What is the word-function of a truth-functional operator? A truth-functional operator expresses membership in a set of sets truth-values for atomic propositions. "p → q" for instance, means that one of the following sets of atomic truth-value combinations is true: "p" and "q" are both true; "p" and "q" are both false; "p" is false and "q" is true; and it means that the following set is false: "p" is true and "q" is false. Consequently, to understand the identity that is known when a logical truth is known and the necessity of the identity, we must examine some characteristics of sets, in general, and of the sets with which the logical operators are associated, in particular.

Set membership is a logical relation, a relation between the elements of the set and a language-form by means of which the elements are objectified. Sets have the following logical property (among others): the extension of the language-form expressing set membership must be equal to or greater than the extension of any language-form whose word-function is a particular member of the set; anything that is objectified by a language-form for a particular member of the set is objectified by the language-form for set membership, although the converse may not be true. Whatever we can articulate as "red" we can articulate as "color". But since "color" has greater extension than does "red", whatever we articulate as "color" may not be what we can articulate as "red". Whatever we can articulate by "square of 2" we can articulate by "even number", but not vice versa.

In other words, where there is a relation of set membership, there is only a logical distinction between what is objectified by a language-form for a particular member of the set and the language-form for set membership. To say that a distinction is only logical, however, is not to say that it is *necessarily* only logical. It may happen to be the case that there is no real distinction between that which is objectified by "gasoline" and a certain member of the set objectified by "commodities whose price went up last week". But this lack of real distinction may not be necessary since the diversity in word-functions consists of references to really distinct aspects of our experience, chemical and economic phenomena respectively, between which there may be no necessary causal relations. (Recall that for a distinction between objects to be "only logical" is for objects to be distinct only as terms of diverse relations of objectification; it is not for their objectification to be diversified only by logical relations.)

On the other hand, the difference between "red" and "color" as means of objectification consists solely of a logical relation. When we have an experience we can express by means of "red", we can express the same experience less precisely by means of "color". The characteristic of being less-precise-than is a logical relation. And as a result of "color" expressing less precisely the same feature of experience that "red" expresses, "color" has greater extension than does "red". That what it means for one word-function to objectify an experience less precisely than another may not be easily definable is not what is important here. What is important is that this relation between word-functions does occur.

No experience consists of one feature called "color" and a really distinct feature called "red". If that were the case, to be the visual quality red would not be to be a color. Anything that could be called an instance of red would be one thing; anything that could be called an instance of color would be another. Therefore the difference between the word-functions of "color" and "red" does not consist of reference to a real distinction; there is no real distinction between the redness of some experience and the color of some experience.

The logical relation between the word-functions of "color" and "red" is such that whatever information is conveyed by "color" is also conveyed by "red", but "red" conveys more information than does "color". The person who knows we are referring to red knows as much as and more than the person who only knows we are referring to a color. Consequently the relation between these word-functions can be called the logical inclusion of the more universal word-function in the less universal. The less universal word-function can also be described as being more explicit, determinate, concrete or informative than the more universal.

Logical inclusion can occur in more than one way. Compare the relation between "red" and "color" to that between "'p' is true" and "'p' or 'q' is true". Whoever knows that "'p'" is true has all the information conveyed by "'p' or 'q' is true" and more. In "'p' or 'q' is true" the lesser precision is achieved by the use of a word for a logical relation, "or". This is not how "color" becomes less precise than "red". The word-function of "color" is not a logical relation; it is just as much a feature of our experience as is the word-function of "red".

The relation between the word-functions of "color" and "red" can be described as logical abstraction. The word-function of "color" abstracts from and is more abstract than that of "red". "Abstraction" is here used for *this* logical relation and not for any of the other uses it has acquired in the vocabularies of philosophers, specifically, not for any psychological operation. A psychological process describable as abstraction may or may not be involved in the acquisition of logically abstract word-functions. (A third way in which logical inclusion occurs will be explained in section 5.3.2.)

What all cases of logical inclusion have in common is that whatever information is conveyed by the less inclusive language-form is conveyed by the more inclusive. The word-function of "used by Picasso" is less precise than the word-function of "red" but is not logically included in it. And it is important that the inclusion is logical, not epistemological. A person can know how "red" and "'p' is true" are used without knowing how "color" and "'p' or 'q' is true" are used. It remains the case that the uses$_T$ of the latter are logically included in those of the former.

Because the word-function of "color" differs only by a logical relation from that of "red", "Red is a color" is necessarily true. The difference between these word-functions lies entirely on the side of characteristics of objects as objects; therefore there can be no difference between what is objectified by "red" and "color" insofar as they are other-than-*objects*. Because the word-function of "color" is logically included in that of "red", something objectifiable by "red" could fail to be objectifiable by "color" only at the price of being and not being what it is. And acquaintance with these word-functions is all that is required to know that whatever is objectifiable as red is objectifiable as a color; "Red is a color" is self-evidently true.

On the other hand, although whatever is objectifiable as red is objectifiable as a color, something objectifiable as a color may be distinguished by more than logical relations from what is objectifiable as red. The word-function of "red" logically includes that of "color"; hence it is necessarily true that red is a color. The word-function of "color" does not logically include that of "red"; hence whatever is a color need not be red. Since the word-function of "red" is not logically included in that of "color", something objectifiable by "color" can fail to be objectifiable by "red" without being and not being what it is. Therefore the argument of section 4.1.1 demonstrating that logical relations can make the identity of diverse objects necessary should be amended as follows: when word-functions differ by logical relations alone, the identity between the things objectified by one of them and at least some of the things objectified by the other is necessary. In other words, since the logical relations distinguishing word-functions can be asymmetric, so can the necessary identity they generate.

What has logical inclusion to do with the formulas of symbolic logic? "→" is a language-form which in "p → q" expresses the membership of the set of the truth-values of "p" and "q" in a set of such sets. Assume that the set of truth-values of "p" and "q" is one of the members of the set which is the word-function of "→". Anything objectified by a language-form whose word-function happens to be, whether necessarily or contingently, a particular member of a set is also objectified by the language-form for set membership. Therefore what is objectified by "both 'p' and 'q' are true" is identical with one of the sets objectified by "p → q". The term of the first relation of objectification is identical with something that terminates the second relation of objectification.

In a moment, we will see that this identity is necessary for reasons similar to the necessity of the identity between what is objectifiable by "red" and what is objectifiable by "color". But first let me take the opportunity this provides to explain what it means to say there is only a "logical" distinction between objects that are themselves nothing more than logical relations or other logical constructs. Here "logically distinct" cannot be opposed to "really identical". In the absence of this contrast, the claim that two cognition-dependent objects are only logically distinct might appear to be empty. But it is possible for the same cognition-dependent object to be objectified in different ways. The meanings$_T$ of truth-functional operators, for instance, are cognition-dependent objects, in fact, sets of cognition-dependent objects. For the operators express membership in sets of sets of truth-values. But each truth-value set can be a member of different sets of such sets. And given the meanings$_T$ for which we use "→", "&" and "−", the set of truth-value sets objectified by "p → q" will be the same as the set objectified by "−(p & −q)". Thus a set of truth-values can be objectified as belonging to different sets of such sets, and the same set of truth-value sets can be objectified by different combinations of language-forms.

Even in the case of cognition-dependent objects, therefore, there can be diverse objectification with no difference in that which is objectified. The difference in mode of objectification may even consist of references to really distinct features of our experience. Consider "the cognition-dependent object I thought of on waking up this morning" as opposed to "the cognition-dependent object I will think of before going to bed tonight". Here the identity between cognition-dependent objects may be contingent. But when the diversity in objectification consists of the use of language-forms whose meanings$_T$ differ at most by logical relations, characteristics attributable to what is objectified in a particular way as objectified in that way, there can be no difference in that which is diversely objectified insofar as it is something capable of being objectified in more than one way.

Can it be objected that this argument would identify the word-functions of, for example, "&" and "V" since the word-functions of "&" and "V" differ solely by logical relations? No; these word-functions do not differ solely by logical relations attributable *to them* as what are objectified by "&" and "V" respectively. As truth-functional relations, the meanings$_T$ of "&" and "V" *are* relations attributable to means of objectification, sentences, as means of objectification. But when these relations are themselves objectified, they do not differ only by relations characterizing *them* as a result of the way in which they are objectified. They differ by relations characterizing other objects, for they differ *as being* different relations between the truth-values of sentences. "&" and "V" express membership in sets of sets of truth-values. These sets of sets differ from one another. And they do not differ solely by characteristics attributable to them as a result of being objectified, respectively, by "&" and "V".

A particular set of truth-values, on the other hand, may belong to both sets of sets of truth-values. And if a set of truth-values is objectifiable by the word-function of both "&" and "V", the diversity in objectification consists of the use of language-forms for diverse logical relations, characteristics attributable to what is objectified in a certain way only as objectified in that way; the identity of the objectified set of truth-values is therefore necessary. Let us now consider that necessity in more detail.

4.4.2 Necessary truth in symbolic logic

Even though, in the case of any set, what is objectified by a language-form for a particular member of the set is identical with something objectified by a language-form for set membership, this identity may be contingent. We are interested in *necessary* identities like those between what is objectified by formulas using different truth-functional operators or between what is objectified by such a formula and a particular set of truth-values for its component formulas. The identity between what is objectified by " 'p' and 'q' are true" and one of the truth-value sets objectifiable by "p → q" is necessary due to logical inclusion. Just as the person who knows that what is being referred to is red knows as much as and more than the person who knows that what is being referred to is colored, so the person who knows that both "p" and "q" are true knows everything the person who knows "p → q" is true knows and more. For the meaning$_T$ of "p → q" is the disjunction "p" and "q" are both true, both false or "p" is false and "q" is true. And the person who knows that "p" and "q" are both true not only knows the truth of that disjunction, but he knows which member of the disjunction is true. Given that "→" has the word-function it happens to have, all the information communicated by "p → q" is communicated by "both 'p' and 'q' are true", but the latter communicates more than does the former.

"→" does not have to have the word-function it does, nor do "red" and "colored" have to have the word-functions they have, but we cannot be acquainted with the word-functions these language-forms happen to have been given and fail to be aware of their logical relationships. In both cases, the word-function for membership in the set is logically included in the word-function for a particular member of the set. The set of truth-values objectified by "both 'p' and 'q' are true" is one of the sets objectifiable by "p → q". And since the word-function of "both 'p' and 'q' are true" differs only by logical relations from that of "p → q", it is necessarily the case that if "p" and "q" are true, "p → q" is true.

Applying the same analysis to the word-functions of other logical operators reveals interlocking series of identities between particular sets of truth-values of atomic propositions and what is objectified by means of different logical operators. And since the differences in the word-functions of the operators consist of characteristics attributable to objects only as objects, the identity of particular sets of atomic truth-values and what is objectified by the operators is necessary. Thus when "p" and "q" are true it is necessarily true that "p → q", "p & q", "p ∨ q", "−(p & −q)", "−(−p & q)", "−(−p & −q)", "p ∨ −q", "−p ∨ q", "−(−p ∨ −q)" are also true. And there is necessarily an identity between the entire set of truth-value sets objectified by "p → q" and the entire set objectified by "−(p & −q)". For given the word-functions of the operators involved, in every instance in which a particular set of truth-values is distinguished only by a logical relation from what is objectified by "p → q", it is distinguished only by a logical relation from what is objectified by "−(p & −q)", and in every instance in which a particular set of truth-values is distinguished only by a logical relation from what is objectified by " − (p & −q)", it is distinguished only by a logical relation from what is objectified by "p → q". Consequently "p → q" and " − (p & −q)" are language-forms objectifying the same sets, and the way signs for diverse logical relations are employed in these language-forms makes their word-functions identical. Therefore the identity of the sets they objectify is necessary.

Of course the formulas in which truths of logic are customarily expressed can be read as uninterpreted formulas of a formal system. If so, the sets of sets which are the word-functions of the constants are not sets of sets of truth-values but sets of sets of uninterpreted symbols, say "T" and "F". The word-function of an operator can be understood as a set, specifically, a disjunction, of sets of T-F table entries for the component formulas of a formula using the operator, such that certain sets of T-F assignments to the component formulas assign the formula using the operator T and the remaining sets of T-F assignments to the component formulas assign the formula using the operator F. The set of those sets of T-F table entries which assign T or F to an operator differs for each operator. Assigning T or F to "p" assigns F or T, respectively, to " − p". Assigning T to "p" and F to "q" assigns T to "p V q" but F to "p & q", etc.

A formula using an operator is assigned T when there is identity between the T-F assignments to its component formulas and a member of the set of component T-F assignments which assigns the operator T. A formula using an operator is assigned and F when there is identity between the T-F assignments to its component formulas and a set of component T-F assignments which assigns the operator F. Consequently the difference between the assignment of T or F to a formula using an operator and each set of T-F table entries for its component formulas is nothing other than the logical relation, attributable to each set of T-F table entries, of being a member of a particular disjunction of those sets, the disjunction of those sets which assigns the operator T or F. And these disjunctions are the word-functions of the operators.

Therefore the word-functions of the constants of a system whose formulas can be interpreted as truths of logic yield the same interlocking series of formulas as we have just seen the truth-functional operators to yield. Where the same entries in the T-F tables for component formulas are only logically distinct from the assignment of T to different formulas using the operators, there is logically necessary identity between the sets of T-F table entries assigning T to both formulas, either identity in the sense of strict equivalence between all the sets of component T-F assignments which assign both formulas T or, like the identity between what is objectified by "red" and what is objectified by "color", identity between all the component T-F assignments which assign one of the formulas T and some of the component T-F assignments which assign the other formula T.

But how can we speak of necessary *truth* with reference to uninterpreted formulas of a formal system? That the words "true" and "false" may occur neither in the system nor in that part of the metalanguage used to construct the system makes no difference here. Carroll's paradox showed us that the use of formal systems does not eliminate the need for self-evidently necessary truths to which some of the rules or axioms of the system correspond. If you like, we can formulate our problem by asking whether the truth-value of sentences like the following is necessary: "If the word-functions of '-' and '&' are those given them by the standard T-F tables, '−(p & −p)' is to be assigned T''; or "It is inconsistent with the standard T-F tables not to assign '−(p & −p)' T''; or "The standard T-F table definitions imply that '−(p & −p)' is to be assigned T''; or "These rules and definitions (standard ones) yield the formula '−(p & −p)' ''. All these formulations rely on natural-language word-functions such as those of "if . . . then", "inconsistent", "imply", "yield". But it does not matter whether the word-functions of the self-evident truths required by the use of formal systems belong to ordinary or to technical language.

To illustrate how my analysis works, let us apply it to non-contradiction and *modus ponens* read as uninterpreted formulas of a formal system. Why is it *necessary* to assign "−(p & −p)" T rather than F? Given the word-function of "−", "−(p & −p)" is to be assigned T if "p & −p" is to be assigned F. Therefore it is necessary to assign "−(p & −p)" T if it is necessary to assign "p & −p" F. Why is it necessary to assign "p & −p" F?

The word-function of "&" is a set of sets of T-F assignments to its left-hand and right-hand formulas such that one set of component T-F assignments assign "&" T and the others assign "&" F. Therefore the question is why it is necessary that any set of T-F assignments to "p" and "−p" be a set which assigns "p & −p" F. The word-function of "−" is a set of T-F assignments determined by the T-F table entries for the component formula. "−p" is assigned T if and only if "p" is assigned F and "−p" is assigned F if and only if "p" is assigned T. No necessity forces "−" to have that word-function, but that is the word-function it happens to have. Given that word-function, the only difference between the assignment of T to "p" and the assignment of F to " – p" or the assignment of F to "p" and the assignment of T to " – p" lies in the logical relation of being a member of the set of T-F table entries assigning either T or F to " – p".

And whatever the T-F table entry for "p" the set of entries of "p" and " – p" is one which assigns "p & – p" F. The only difference between each set of T-F table entries for "p" and " – p" and a set assigning F to "p & – p" is that to be a set of T-F table entries assigning F to "p & – p" is to be a member of a particular disjunction of T-F table entries, the disjunction which is the word-function of "&". Since the only difference is the logical relation of being a member of a disjunction, the identity between each set of T-F table entries for "p" and " – p" and a member of the set of T-F table entries for component formulas which assigns F to formulas using "&" is necessary. And from the word-function of " – ", if it is necessary to assign "p & – p" F, it is necessary to assign " – (p & – p)" T.

Examining *modus ponens* will show us how to extend the analysis to more complex formulas. Why is it necessarily true that, given the standard word-functions for its constants, "((p → q) & p) → q" is to be assigned a T rather than an F? The second " → " tells us that the set of T-F assignments to the formulas to the left and right of it is a member of a set of such sets. Why should the T-F table entries for the left-hand and right-hand formulas necessarily be identical with entries which assign " → " T? To answer this question we will consider both the possibility of the T-F entry for the left-hand formula being T and the possibility of its being F. On either hypothesis, it will necessarily be the case that the whole formula must be assigned a T.

What if the entry for the left-hand side is F? Then no matter what the entry for the right-hand side, the whole formula is assigned a T. For each entry for the right-hand side together with the entry of F for the left-hand side constitutes a set of T-F table entries which necessarily assigns " → " T. Each of these sets differs from a set which assigns " → " T only by the logical relation of being a member of a disjunction of component T-F table entries assigning T or F to " → " according to the word-function of " → ". Therefore the identity of the assignment of F to the left-hand formula of *modus ponens* together with any T-F assignment to the right-hand formula and a set of component T-F assignments which assigns *modus ponens* T is necessary.

What if the entry for the left-hand side is T? "(p → q) & p" is assigned T if and only if the formulas to the left and right of "&" are assigned T. That happens to be the function which as a matter of contingent fact "&" performs. When is "p → q" assigned T? "p → q" is assigned T by any of the following sets of T-F assignments to "p" and "q": "p" assigned T and "q" assigned T; "p" assigned F and "q" assigned T; "p" assigned F and "q" assigned F. And "p → q" is assigned F by the following set: "p" assigned T and "q" assigned F. But for "(p → q) & p" to be assigned T, the formula to the right of "&", "p", must also be assigned T. And "p" is assigned T in only one of the T-F table entries for "p" and "q" which assigns "p → q" a T, the first set of entries listed above. In that set both "p" *and* "q" are assigned T. If "p" is assigned T and "q" is assigned an F, "p → q" is assigned F. Consequently "(p → q) & p" is assigned T if and only if the entry for *both* "p" and "q" in the T-F tables is T.

The identity between only one set of T-F assignments for "p" and "q" and a set which assigns "(p → q) & p" T is necessitated by the fact that each set of T-F assignments for "p" and "q" is only logically distinct from a set assigning either T or F to formulas using "→" and "&" and that only one set of T-F assignments for "p" and "q" is logically distinct from a set which assigns T to formulas of both kinds. The set which assigns T to both "→" and "&" is the set constituted by assigning T to both "p" and "q". But the assigning of T to "q" is the assigning of T to the right-hand formula of *modus ponens*. The only difference between the assigning of T to "(p → q) & p)" and the assigning of T to "q" is that the employment of signs for logical relations ("→" and "&") makes the assigning of T to "(p → q) & p)" equivalent to assigning T to *both* "p" and "q". Therefore the assigning of T to the right-hand formula of *modus ponens* is logically included in the assigning of T to the left-hand formula.

But the assignment of T to the left-hand and right-hand formulas of a formula using "→" is distinct only by a logical relation from a set assigning T to the whole formula. Therefore whether the left-hand formula of *modus ponens* is assigned a T or an F, a necessary identity obtains between each set of T-F table entries for its component formulas and a set which assigns *modus ponens* T. For each set of component T-F table entries is distinct from a set assigning *modus ponens* T only by a logical relation.

All of this can be expressed in the more familiar terminology of the necessary being that which is assigned T on all T-F assignments to atomic formulas or that whose opposite is assigned F on all atomic T-F assignments. By our definition of necessity, it is necessary for a formula using an operator to be assigned a T if and only if assigning

it an F would be contradictory. Assigning F to such a formula is contradictory if and only if, for the assignment to be made, the set of all
atomic T-F assignments must both be and not be what it is, for the
word-functions of the operators are sets of atomic T-F assignments.
Therefore, if *all* sets of atomic T-F assignments are identical with sets
that assign a formula T, the formula cannot be assigned F without
the set of all atomic T-F assignments both being and not being what
it is. Conversely, a formula cannot be assigned F without the set of
all atomic T-F assignment both being and not being what it is only
if *no* set of atomic T-F assignments is identical with a set that assigns
the formula F.

And why *must* there be an identity between each set of atomic T-F
assignments and a set which assigns some formula using operators
T? Because each set of atomic T-F assignments is distinct only by a
logical relation from a set which assigns the formula T. Therefore either
the set of all atomic T-F assignments both is and is not what it is or
the word-functions of the operators both are and are not what they
are. And it can happen that each set of atomic T-F assignments is
distinct only by a logical relation from a set which assigns a formula
using operators T because the difference between any set of atomic
T-F assignments and a set which assigns T or F to any operator is
nothing more than the logical relation of being a member of a disjunction of atomic T-F assignments, a disjunction which happens to
be the word-function of the operator.

The procedure by which we have accounted for the necessity of
modus ponens can be extended to all the formulas of the propositional
calculus. In effect, then, we have explained the necessity of truths
concerning logical relations to which correspond rules of inference
and axioms that can be used in proofs of formulas of logic other than
the truth-functional. These formulas express relations between terms
(the terms, again, being language-forms alone, or their word-functions
or whatever is objectified by means of them). And the identity of the
relation between terms objectified by a formula and a relation which
does hold between those terms is necessary, or at least is a necessary
consequence of some set of premises, if the formula is inferred by
means of rules of inference or axioms to which correspond necessary
truths concerning logical relations.

4.4.3 Objections to logical inclusion

Two possible objections to the logical inclusion analysis of truth-
functional necessity need to be answered. The first attacks the notion

of logical inclusion itself. The second attacks its application to truth-functional operators.

Kripke (1972, p. 134) apparently thinks that, as applied to general terms, his theory of fixing the reference of a term undercuts "the hoary tradition of definition by genus and differentia". The idea is that the collection of properties ordinarily associated with the definition of terms like "cow" or "gold" do not constitute the meaning or connotation of these terms. These terms have no connotation. Instead they have reference to natural kinds. We use the "defining" properties, the yellow of gold, for instance, to establish the connection between the term and the natural kind that is its referent. But once that reference is fixed to this kind, empirical discoveries can make the original identifying properties irrelevant to the use of the term or even no longer true of the referent. Since the term has its reference independently of any set of identifying properties, a genus-difference definition composed of such properties does not give the meaning of the term.

My account of logical relations—not to mention my use of "word-function"—is not a theory of definition. Where a genus-difference definition is successful, we have an example of logical inclusion. But the converse is not true. We need not be able to provide definitions of "color" and "red" to recognize that the first articulates the same feature of experience as the second though less explicitly. Still, Kripke's argument that many general terms have no connotation may give some readers pause.

Without commenting on the merits of Kripke's theory of fixing reference, all one needs to point out is that relations of logical inclusion do sometimes occur and occur in cases that are important for necessary truth in philosophy and logic. Nothing I have said requires that they always occur, whatever that would mean. Each instance must be examined on its own evidence, as I have tried to do.

On the other hand, it should also be pointed out that nothing in Kripke's argument shows that logical inclusion does not occur. For the sake of argument, I grant him that a term like "gold" has no connotation, and therefore nothing it logically includes or is logically included in. It remains true that we are able to articulate some (at the least) of the properties that originally fixed the reference of "gold" by means of predicates of greater and lesser explicitness such that anyone who knows what is asserted by means of one of these predicates knows everything asserted by another predicate and more. And anyone who knows how both predicates are being used knows that if the assertion of one is true, the assertion of the other is true. Thus it is necessarily true that if yellow is one of the (apparent) properties by which we originally fix the reference of "gold", one of the properties by which we originally fix the reference of "gold" is a color.

Some of Kripke's examples may also cause confusion concerning logical inclusion. If it is necessarily true that red is a color, is it also necessarily true that cats are animals (p. 122)? What if empirical investigation shows that cats are automata? How could we maintain that the word-function of "animal" is logically included in that of "cat"?

The problem assumes, correctly, that we have acquired our use for "animal" independently of our experience of cats. But what if that were not the case; what if our mechanical cats were the only animal-like things we were acquainted with? (We are animal-like ourselves. But the revered ancestors who gave us these words may not have known, when they brought these words into their vocabulary, that they themselves were not automata. And they may have taught "animal" to their children, who certainly did not know that they were not automata, exclusively by reference to cats.) In that case, "animal" could easily mean something logically included in the word-function of "cat", for example, something whose underlying structure (whatever that may be) gives it the ability to grow fur or produce its own covering, meow or make sounds, climb trees or move itself about, etc.

The point is that our experience of mechanical cats would be one that we could articulate by means of terms of related to one another as more or less explicit expressions of the same object of our experience. And some of these terms or some combination of them might be equivalent to our pre-scientific meaning for "animal". In other words, the question of whether the word-function of "animal" is logically included in that of "cat" depends, self-evidently, on how we are using "animal" and "cat". Even though we acquired our use of "animal" independently of our experience of cats, perhaps we do use it in a way that is logically included in our use of "cat". If so, we would not be using "animal" in its scientific sense. But what requirement is there that we use it in this sense when we were far from being scientists when we learned these terms?

Kripke would respond that science does not change the ordinary connotation of terms for natural kinds since they have no connotation. For example, he believes the discovery that whales are not fish did not require a change in the concept of fish (p. 138). Science simply finds better sets of properties for identifying the kind. But that brings us back to where we were before; the word for the kind might not have a connotation that logically includes or is logically included in others, but the words for (some of?) the properties must. If properties enable us to have connotationless words by enabling us to fix reference, words for properties cannot themselves be connotationless without infinite regress in the fixing of reference. And if a word has connotation, why cannot that connotation be articulated in ways that differ only as more and less explicit or vague?

The second objection. Supposedly the word-function of a logical operator is a set of sets of T-F assignments to atomic formulas. But each set of T-F assignments is something really distinct from the other T-F assignments in the word-function of the operator. Therefore when we objectify one set as a member of a set of such sets, we objectify it by reference to something really distinct from itself. If diverse objectification is achieved by reference to the really distinct, we are no longer in the domain of the merely logical; so the necessity of the identity cannot be accounted for solely by relations like logical inclusion.

Nothing I said, however, when introducing diverse objectification by means of logical relations (section 3.4.1) implied that logical relations do not terminate in things. In fact, the opposite is the case. It is because things terminate logical relations that logical relations can be used to diversely objectify extra-objective things. And it is the nature of logical inclusion that logical relations can be terminated by things asymmetrically. Thus whatever is in the extension of "red" is in the extension of "color" but not vice versa. Therefore a logical relation used to objectify something can be a relation also terminated by things other than the thing we are using it to objectify. This does not affect necessity, nor make a necessity causal, if the necessity derives from the logical relation rather than any characteristic belonging to the other terms of the relation as things.

The meaning$_T$ of "color" includes colors other than red in its extension, but it does not make reference to colors other than red. If red were the only color we had experienced, we could still be acquainted with the meaning$_T$ of "color". Colors form a set of which "color" can be predicated, but the logical relation of set membership is not the meaning$_T$ of "color". (See sections 3.3.3 and 6.3.4.) On the other hand, the meaning$_T$ of truth-functional operators make reference to really distinct T-F sets. We could not understand the meaning$_T$ of the operator without being acquainted with each of those sets. Still, the necessary identity between what is objectified by "this set of T-F assignments" and by "a member of this set of sets of T-F assignments" is logical, not causal, for the relation of set membership *is* the meaning$_T$ of the operator.

The really distinct T-F assignments that are referred to by the meaning$_T$ of a truth-functional operator are there referred to as terms of the relation of membership in a set of sets rather than solely as extra-objective things. The same thing is objectified by "both 'p' and 'q' assigned T" and "a set of atomic T-F assignments that assigns T to 'p → q' ". The difference is that in the second case the T-F assignments are objectified as members of a set of sets. In other words, these really distinct T-F assignments are objectified by the meaning$_T$ of a truth-functional operator as terms of a logical relation, and the necessity of truth-functions using the operator derives from this relation.

To take another example, we might call something an "X-book" if it is a member of the set of books with 50 pages or a member of the set of books with 100 pages. If a book has fifty pages, it is necessarily true that it is an X-book, and if we are acquainted with the word-function of X-book, we know the necessary truth of "A book with 50 pages is an X-book". The word-function of "X-book" includes a reference to something really distinct from books with 50 pages, but it refers to books with 100 pages as terms of a logical relation, alternation, with books of 50 pages. And the necessity of a book with 50 pages being an X-book derives from that logical relation. For that necessity to hold, it does not matter what other things terminate the relation of alternation with books of 50 pages. It does not matter what characteristics these other things have as extra-objective things or even whether they actually exist. It only matters that the diversity in the ways the same thing is objectified by "book with 50 pages" and "X-book" consists solely of the fact that "X-book" objectifies the thing as term of a logical relation.

Since the necessity is indifferent to the nature and existence of the other terms, the fact that we can objectify a thing using a logical relation terminated by other things does not put us at risk of confusing logical and causal necessity. The issue in causal necessity is whether one thing could exist without the existence of something really distinct from itself. The necessity of red's being a color does not require the existence of other colors, nor does the necessity of a book with 50 pages being an X-book require the existence of books with 100 pages.

4.4.4 Logically mutual relations

How is the identity theory of truth and the logical relation/causal relation theory of necessity to be applied to the many garden-variety necessary truths in ordinary language and mathematics concerning relations which are other than identity and which are not logical relations? Examples: whatever A hits is hit by A; if A is lower than B, B is higher than A; if A is less than B and B is less than C, then A is less than C. Applying the identity theory of truth to examples such as these is no problem. "A hits B" is a language-form articulating the same event as does "B is hit by A". The same relation between A and B is objectified by "A is lower than B" and by "B is higher than A". And anything that can be objectified as "less than B" is identical with something that can be objectified as "less than anything B is less than".

The above sentences are true if and only if these identities between the terms of diverse objectifications hold. And in general, if the identity theory of sentential truth can account for the truth of one-word sentences, it can account for the truth of any sentence. A sentence expressing a relation or a set of relations, no matter how complicated, holding between terms is true if and only if the objectified relations are identical with relations which do hold between the objectified terms.

But why is it the case that some of these identities are *necessary*? Identities involving logical relations have been dealt with; how causal relations account for necessary identity has been discussed above and will be discussed below. What about identities involving non-logical mutual relations? As we have seen above, in order for logical relations to explain the necessary identity of the diversely objectified, that which is being objectified need not itself be a logical relation. "Every animate body is a body that is not inanimate" objectifies things as things, not as objects. No matter what object is diversely articulated by different language-forms, if the word-functions of the language-forms differ at most by logical relations, what is objectified by one of the language-forms is necessarily identical with what is objectified by the other. A's being less than B is not a logical relation as here defined (which is not to say that it may not be a cognition-dependent object of another kind). Still "A is less than B" and "B is greater than A" articulate the same situation in ways which are distinct only by logical relations.

Any doubt about this can be dispelled by the fact that the ordinary language functions of "less than", "equal to", and "greater than" can be read as interpretations of the symbols of a formal system, say "<", "=" and ">" respectively. And within a formal system, the word-functions of such symbols are defined by their logical relations to other symbols by means of such formulas as $(X)(Y)(((X<Y)\rightarrow -((X=Y)V(X>Y)))$. But we did not have to wait for the invention of formal systems to grasp the self-evidently necessary truth of sentences like "If A is less than B, B is greater than A". How do we know that the situation objectified by "A less than B" is identical with that objectified by "B greater than A"? Only by being acquainted with the word-functions of these language-forms, that is, by having the ability to use some language-forms in the way these are currently used in English.

The possibility of relations being real may appear to cause a difficulty for my statement that "A less than B" and "B greater than A" articulate the same situation. Perhaps there are really distinct relations, objectified by "less than" and "greater than", respectively, in A and B. On this reading the necessary truth of the sentences we are considering would derive from causal relations. B's being what it is, for instance, would be a necessary cause of A's having the relation less-than-B and vice versa.

But recall our example of knowing that D is in the act of nominating C for President of the United States. We can express the same knowledge of D's behavior either by "D is nominating C" or by "C is being nominated by D". In order to use the second form we do not have to know whether or not there is in C a real relation distinct from, yet corresponding, to D's behavior of nominating C. Much less do we have to know whether or not there is a causal relation between D's behavior and some real relation characterizing C. Even if there is no such causal connection and no such real relation in C, it remains true that if D is nominating C, C is being nominated by D. The necessity of this truth is logical. (See section 9.3.3.)

This does not in any way deny the reality of relations nor the possibility of causal connections between a relation and its term, on the one hand, and its bearer, on the other. Within one and the same situation which is diversely objectified by, say, active and passive verbal constructions, there may well be really distinct relations which happen to correspond to these different means of objectification. But this does not imply that the terms of these diverse objectifications are the two really distinct relations. It means that a single event which is objectified diversely calls for a complex causal analysis, a causal analysis with elements which may include really distinct relations. But no matter how complex, the causal analysis of a situation cannot destroy the situation's identity as term of diverse relations of objectification if and when it is so objectified. If the causal analysis of a situation does call for the positing of distinct relations which happen to correspond to the active and passive verbal construction, that fact is *not* established simply by our ability to objectify the same situation by these diverse means. (For an important recent defense of the reality of some relations, see Deely, 1974, 1975b and 1977a.)

4.4.5 Conclusion

This has been a causal explanation of logically necessary and self-evident sentences. Causal analyses presuppose, at least hypothetically, the effects to be explained. I have not begged the question of existence, however, since I have used Carroll's paradox to argue for the existence of self-evidently necessary truth. On the other hand it is worth pointing out that even if the existence of the effects to be explained had not been argued for in that way, this account would still not be guilty of question begging. For analysis may reveal that causes of a certain kind would produce the hypothesized effect, and it may be the case that causes of this kind are not themselves hypothetical but actually occur. And if there actually occur causes which would produce the hypothesized effect, that effect must occur also. But our analysis has shown that causes for necessity are found in logical relations which occur, not in the sense that they have an existence which is other than being-known, but in the sense that certain language acts do have such an existence and that these acts make use of language-forms in such ways that they, their word-functions and what is objectified by means of them, are so related. And our analysis has shown that causes for self-evidence are provided by our acquaintance with these relations, an acquaintance that actually occurs whenever we learn to use words in the appropriate manners.

I need say nothing more, then, in refutation of the arguments that would make necessity and self-evidence impossible. But a word of caution is in order for any who would continue to search for such arguments. Any argument against necessity or self-evidence must satisfy a condition which will render it inconclusive. This condition is that the argument must fail to demonstrate that the non-existence of necessary or of self-evident truths is necessarily true. (Note the self-evident necessity of this condition.) Neither the premises nor the conclusion of such an argument can be necessarily true, and therefore the premises cannot contain self-evident truths. The most powerful ammunition that could be employed by the argument would be contingent truths tending to show that belief in any kind of truth other than contingent would be unreasonable. The argument could not even show that the non-existence of necessary truth was *hypothetical-*

ly necessary, that is, that the existence of necessary truth, although not contradictory in itself, would contradict some contingently true state of affairs. To show this, the argument would have to show that the non-existence of this state of affairs follows logically from the assumption that necessary truth exists and the assumption of some additional contingent truths. But if there are no necessary truths, the logical laws by which this conclusion follows from these assumptions are not necessarily true.

It is possible, therefore, to maintain consistently the existence of necessity and self-evidence while admitting as true any evidence that is brought against them. If one considers the truth of some sentence self-evidently necessary, he will be more convinced of the truth of that sentence than he will be of any empirical hypotheses tending to make the existence of necessary truth unreasonable. And he will be more inclined to accept modifications of the empirical hypotheses than to cease believing in the truth he considers self-evident. But logic does not force him to modify either kind of belief; the occurrence of necessity can be both highly unlikely and true. In the face of empirical evidence to the contrary, the burden of proof would be on him who thinks there is necessary truth. But that is not news; the burden of proof has been there all along. For to show that there is necessary truth one must show that some truth is necessary, that were it not true, what is objectified by means of some language-form would both be and not be what it is.

CHAPTER FIVE

Existence as an Object of Sentential Knowledge

In Chapter Two we noted that linguistic ontology is usually associated with a relativistic account of sentential truth: different conceptual frameworks yield different and conflicting assertions. And in Chapter Two I promised to show that, even supposing that the differences between conceptual schemes result in genuine conflicts between beliefs (something I will be questioning), we can know truths that provide standards for judging the value of different conceptual schemes for objectifying things as they exist cognition-independently.

It might seem that I have already made good on that promise, at least in part, by refuting the linguistic theory of necessary truth. There are sentences that communicate what is *necessarily* true of things as things, not just as objects of knowledge. These necessary truths would seem to escape the conceptual relativism associated with linguistic ontology even if contingent truths continue to be a problem. Implicitly, this is the case, but only implicitly. For it has been argued that there are truths which can be known from an understanding of their terms and yet are relative to the conceptual frameworks of the languages in which they are expressed. (See Sellars, 1963, pp. 298-320.) This view has been presented within the context of a linguistic theory of necessity. But one can imagine how it could be presented otherwise.

Where the actual existence of things objectified in necessary truths is contingent, necessary truths are conditional and can be expressed by sentences of the form (x) (Fx → Gx) (see section 5.5). Precisely because it is conditional, a truth can be necessary and to some degree conditioned by its conceptual matrix. For conditional sentences hypothesize that entities exist as described by the predicates of those sentences. And the way in which predicates describe things depends to some degree on the framework characteristics of the language. As things are described by the predicates of one language, it is a necessary truth that if something is a color, it is identical with something occupying a space distinct from every other color. But as things might be described by the predicates of another language, it would be a necessary truth that if something is a process of coloring, it is identical with an activity governed by a territorial imperative.

According to the linguistic ontologists, "it is not possible to specify the precise degree to which, in affirming a proposition, we also intend to affirm the presuppositions, framework features, and entailments on which the meaningfulness of the proposition depends" (MacKinnon, 1969, p. 31). Necessary truths, therefore, would seem to be of no help in evaluating the reality-index of different conceptual schemes. The necessity of a truth would not bestow on it a validity transcending that of the provincialism of the conceptual framework within which the truth is formulated. More argumentation is needed, therefore, if we are to show that by refuting the linguistic theory of necessity, we have disarmed conceptual relativism's version of necessary truth.

And what about contingent truths; is their value relative to that of their conceptual matrices? Since we manifestly cannot step outside of language to discuss what is the case, is not the value of any claim, necessary or contingent, about things as things limited by the fact that descriptions are attributable to things only as a result of our having objectified them linguistically? How could one verify the claim that the value of his knowledge of things as things is not limited by the fact that it reflects the idiosyncrasies of one mode of objectification? Unless such a claim can be verified, we cannot evaluate the reality-index of different systems of conceptualizing things.

As a matter of fact, there is more than one way to refute conceptual relativism. I will emphasize a way of doing this that will allow me to complete my discussion of philosophical method at the same time. The argument will appeal to some self-evidently necessary truths. That may appear to be a begging of the question since the reality-index of such truths is one of the things conceptual relativism casts in doubt.

But the necessary truths on which I will base this refutation of conceptual relativism will be necessary truths of a particular kind, and my argument will be based on properties peculiar to this kind of necessary truth.

The necessary truths I have in mind here I will call "ontological" necessary truths. These are the necessary truths that make philosophy possible as a distinct mode of knowing by providing it with a means of verification. Showing how ontological necessary truths refute conceptual relativism and make philosophical verification possible will require explaining my use of "ontology" more precisely than I have done so far. When that explanation is given in the next section, however, it will give rise to an objection that must be disposed of before I can go any further with my arguments against conceptual relativism or my account of philosophical method. For this notion of ontological truth will be accused of taking "exists" to be a predicate. And since it appears that "exists" cannot be a predicate, it will appear that no truths can be ontological in this sense.

This objection must be replied to before the refutation of conceptual relativism can continue. Replying to it will give me the opportunity for further clarifications concerning logical necessity, clarifications that should be made before we leave the topic of the last chapter completely and move on to other things. Therefore the refutation of conceptual relativism will be postponed to Chapter Six in favor of laying the groundwork for it here.

This chapter will be concerned with existence as an object of sentential knowledge and with relations between the meaning$_T$ of "exists" and the necessity that derives from logical relations. I will begin by explaining what I mean by ontology. This will lead directly to a discussion of the view that "exists" is not a predicate. I will not disprove the non-predicate view but will show that it poses an obstacle to ontology if and only if it is, like Quine's early definition of existence, crypto-Berkeleyan, implying that to be is to be known. Although the validity of ontology does not depend on whether or not "exists" is a predicate, it does depend on the meanings$_T$ of "exists" and "being" (that which exists). Explaining certain theses that derive from classical realism will facilitate our understanding of these meanings$_T$. When properly understood, they reveal the possibility of a non-empirical method of articulating and analyzing our experience, ontological method.

Our consideration of these word-functions will also allow us to complete the analysis of logical necessity. Specifically, we will see how the necessity of truths of ontology is prior to that of truths of logic, why discourse about cognition-dependent objects must be governed by the same logical laws as is discourse about real entities, and why necessary truths are true in all possible worlds. Because the non-predicate view has often been relied on as the main objection to Anselmian arguments for the existence of God, the last section of the chapter will show that nothing I have said about the non-predicate view lends support to those arguments. But our discussion of Anselmian arguments will not constitute a digression from our main concerns. It will provide the opportunity for further clarification of the meaning$_T$ of "exists" and the notion of possible existence, as well as the opportunity to deal with contrary-to-fact conditionals and modes.

5.1 Ontological Analysis

In the sense of the term that is familiar from Quine, "ontology" is concerned with the answer to the question "What exists?" But ontology, as I understand it, and as it has been traditionally understood, means more than this. Every empirical science is concerned with the nature of what exists in its own particular domain of investigation. But ontology in my sense, and in the traditional sense, is to be distinguished from the empirical sciences. They study things that exist from the point of view of their empirical characteristics. Ontology studies these same things not from the point of view of any of their empirical properties but from the point of view of their existence. In other words, ontology takes existence itself as the perspective from which to investigate things.

What does it mean to take existence as the perspective from which to investigate things? It means to articulate experience by means of descriptions based on the meaning$_T$ of "exists", and it means to discover truths, necessary and contingent, that employ these descriptions, truths about things as things. What does it mean for a description to be based on the meaning$_T$ of "exists"? A word or phrase can be a cognate of "exists" in the sense that is meaning$_T$ is a *function* of the meaning$_T$ of "exists"; thus the meaning$_T$ of "being" is that-which-exists. (Here "function" is not taken as in "word-function", that for which a word is used; it is taken in the sense of a value determined by its relation to that of which it is a function.) Or the meaning$_T$ of a word or phrase can be a member of a disjunction made by affirming and denying "exists" or some language-form whose meaning$_T$ is a function of the meaning$_T$ of "exists" as, for example, the disjunction between existing-in-another and not-existing-in-another. Or the meaning$_T$ of a word or phrase can differ from the meaning$_T$ of "exists", or of one of its cognates, or of some member of a disjunction made by affirming or denying either of these only because of its use of words for logical relations; such is the meaning$_T$ of "non-being". As this example illustrates, words or phrases defined by opposition to the meanings$_T$ of ontological words likewise deserve to be classified as ontological for that very reason. Thus the meaning$_T$ of "logical construct" is ontological.

For the meaning$_T$ of a word to be a function of the meaning$_T$ of "exists" or any of its cognates, it is not enough that the extension of this word fall under the extension of an ontological word. The meanings$_T$ of "kinetic", "potential", "male", "female", "guilty" and "innocent" are all ways of existing. But calling any one of them a way of existing tells us nothing about it that is not true of the others. Like empirical science, ontological knowledge is causal knowledge. And the fact, for instance, that a particular way of existing resulting from change is caused does not give us any information peculiar to that way of existing that is not true of any other way of existing that results from change.

Ontological analysis can give us knowledge of what is peculiar to a particular way of existing if and only if the difference between that way of existing and others can be expressed by reference to "exists", its cognates, or terms defined in opposition to or by logical relation to "exists" and its cognates. Only if so, should the meaning$_T$ of a word whose extension is included in that of an ontological word be itself considered ontological. (Contrast, for example, the disjunction between existing-in-another and not-existing-in-another with the disjunction between kinetic and potential, male and female, guilty and innocent.)

In section 5.3.2, I will argue that the meanings$_T$ of thing-descriptions logically include existence by being *logical* functions of existence. Being a logical function of existence does not make a meaning$_T$ ontological. Logical relations enter ontological meanings$_T$ only by terminating in meanings$_T$ that are ontological on other, non-logical, grounds, as in the meanings$_T$ of "non-being" or "possible existent".

To say that ontology seeks to discover necessary truths employing descriptions based on the meaning$_T$ of "exists" is to say that ontology seeks to discover necessary truths holding of things insofar as things are objectifiable by the meanings$_T$ of such terms. To the extent that philosophy can give us knowledge about the world and our experience of it that the empirical sciences cannot, philosophy's method is ontological. On the other hand, empirical words are defined, insofar as they can be defined, by reference to sensibly distinguishable features of experience, and existence is not a sensibly distinguishable feature of experience (which is not to say that existence is not knowable by sense experience).

Ontology does not answer the question "What exists?" except when that question arises within the specific domain of ontology. It is ontology's job to give us truths about existence as such and about characteristics belonging to real existents, causal relations in particular, which are objectifiable by words definable in terms of the meanings$_T$ of "exists" and of other ontological words. We have seen the necessity, for instance, of recognizing the causal primacy of real existents among the objects of our linguistic knowledge (real existence is something other than being an object of knowledge, and if real existence were not true of the primary objects of linguistic knowledge, nothing, real existent or otherwise, would be an object of linguistic knowledge) and, therefore, of recognizing that logical relations, like identity and otherness, have as their primary terms objects that are also real existents.

Obviously, ontological method requires further explanation and justification. More explanation, with many more examples, will appear as we proceed. Sections 9.1 and 9.2, for instance, will discuss the differences between ontological and empirical methods; the question of empirical definitions will be dealt with there. Sensory awareness of real existence and the relation of ontological word-functions to sense experience will be discussed in Chapter Ten. But the first thing we must do is confront the non-predicate theory of existence. Not only will this allow us to clarify the meaning$_T$ of exists, but if the objections that come from the non-predicate view cannot be met, further discussion of ontological analysis will not be necessary.

5.2 Is "Is 'Exists' a Predicate?" a Question?

The theory that "exists" is not a predicate has been used to justify the claim that existence does not provide a point of reference distinct from empirical characteristics from which to conduct legitimate inquiries. In what follows, I will not deny the assertion that "exists" is not a predicate. Nor will I deny any of the evidence offered in support of this assertion. Rather I will show that neither the assertion nor the kind of evidence used to support it can allow us to draw the conclusion that our knowledge that things exists does not provide a basis for descriptions that are just as informative about things as extra-objective things as are empirical descriptions.

5.2.1 What's in a predicate?

What is the non-predicate thesis saying? With Moore (1936), I have my doubts. I know what a predicate is grammatically, and in that sense no one would want to assert that "exists" is not a predicate. I also know that when "exists" is translated into standard logical symbolism, "exists" is not represented by what are there referred to as "predicates" but by what is called a "quantifier". But what do I know in knowing this? If nothing more is meant by the assertion that "exists" is not a predicate, it is difficult to see how philosophers are justified in drawing the conclusions they have tried to draw, or any other conclusions, from this assertion. Of the grammar of formal languages we can say what was said of natural languages in Chapter Two, they do not determine our philosophical commitments. Their philosophical implications are in the eyes of their beholders. In order to yield a philosophical conclusion, linguistic structures must be submitted to a philosophical interpretation. And to yield a conclusion validly, our interpretation must not commit an epistemological fallacy.

One common philosophical interpretation of the meaning of "predicate", for example, is that predicates are words whose meanings$_T$ are attributes of things. But what is an "attribute", and why is existence not an attribute? A philosophical analysis of the nature of attributes is implied here. Philosophers are not above circular reasoning and might attempt to define attributes as whatever it is that are expressed in logic by predicates. But then we are back where we began. Granted, "exists" is not expressed in logic by means of predicates. But the problem was how to get any ontological mileage out of that fact and how to do so without committing an epistemological fallacy, without basing our beliefs about what is true of things as things on what is true of the logical apparatus by means of which things are made objects of knowledge.

One kind of evidence offered in support of the non-predicate theory is the difference in function between the grammatical predicates of sentences such as "Some tigers are not tame" and sentences such as "Some tigers do not exist". The first sentence can and the second cannot be translated as "There are tigers which . . .". Noting this difference we might try to define "attributes" as whatever are expressed by those grammatical predicates whose use in non-universal affirmation or denial presupposes the existence of that of which they are affirmed or denied. By the definition of "attribute", then, the function of "exists" as a grammatical predicate could not be to express an attribute. But now our understanding of "attribute" and, therefore, our understanding of "predicate" in the theory that "exists" is not a predicate, depends on our understanding of existence, the meaning$_T$ of "exists". And we have gotten further toward understanding neither what it is that some, *but not all*, grammatical predicates other than "exists" presuppose, namely existence, nor the relation of existence to what is known about things as extra-objective things.

The fact that what is presupposed when some other words operate as grammatical predicates is not presupposed when "exists" so operates reveals a difference between the word-function of "exists" and the kind of word-function we give these other words. But as yet we have only pointed to this distinction between the word-functions of certain grammatical predicates and given one side of this distinction a name; the word-functions on one side of this distinction are called "attributes". Reading any further implications into this distinction or into the move of giving the members of one side the name "attribute" takes us beyond the evidence that has so far been presented. Consistently with this evidence, a philosopher might make attributes a sub-set of what he might want to call the set of "properties" or "characteristics" or "features", or even "predibutes" or "attricates". Existence would belong to one sub-set of this set, attributes to another. And how far can we go on this road toward advancing our knowledge of what is or is not true of things as things?

The objection I am making to the attempt to get ontological implications out of the non-predicate theory is the same objection Cornman brought against the view that ethical predicates like "good" do not refer to "properties" because they have different logical characteristics from predicates like "blue":

> What seems to be required is a premise that relates certain logical characteristics of predicates to properties. This is achieved . . . with the following: (1') If a predicate is logically unlike empirical predicates such as "blue" in respects A, B, C . . . then it is not used descriptively, i.e., it does not refer to a property. . . . But the reason he (Nowell-Smith) thinks that anyone who says goodness is a property is committed to this debatable assertion (the assertion that the logic of "good" is like that of "blue") seems to be that he accepts the equally debatable assertion that if P is a property then "P" functions logically like predicates such as "blue", "loud" and "round". This assertion is roughly equivalent to premise (1'). On what grounds would this claim by Nowell-Smith rest? If not on intuition

then only, it would seem, on the claim that certain logical characteristics are the linguistic symptoms of properties. Thus wherever we find these symptoms we can conclude there is a property referred to and wherever we find no such characteristics we can conclude there is no property referred to. But why should we accept this claim? (Cornman, 1964, p. 230)

Why indeed, unless we are committing an epistemological fallacy, or unless we are merely adopting nomenclature for a distinction whose ontological significance can be explained otherwise than by the non-property theory, as Cornman does not fail to point out? For instead of saying that grammatical predicates of one kind refer to Fs and grammatical predicates of another kind do not refer to Fs, we can just as well say that both refer to Fs but the first predicates refer to Fs of one type while the second refer to Fs of another type. So instead of saying that certain predicates do, while ''exists'' does not, express attributes, we can say that ''exists'' expresses an attribute of one kind while the other predicates express attributes of a different kind.

5.2.2 What's not in the non-predicate theory?

What has been said so far in favor of the non-predicate theory is that some grammatical predicates presuppose existence and that the use of ''exists'' as a grammatical predicate does not presuppose existence—something that is hardly surprising. The question is what implication these facts have for ontology, if any. A test of whether they have any ontological implications is whether they rule out any philosophical theories about the relation of the meaning$_T$ of ''exists'' to that which exists. If these facts do not rule out any theories about things as things that are ontological in our sense, that is, theories whose descriptions turn on existence and its functions, they do not support any anti-ontological implications claimed for the non-predicate theory. And as a matter of fact, the evidence usually presented for the non-predicate theory is consistent with both theories of the relation of existence to that which exists that have come to us from the medieval philosophers.

One of these theories is that existence is really distinct from that which exists. According to this view, causal analysis reveals that existence is one of two correlative co-principles entering into the makeup of things. The other principle is essence, which is sometimes referred to as what exists, that which has existence, or sometimes referred to as that by which an existent is what it is. (A more complete statement of the essence-existence distinction is found in section 7.3.)

However it is described, essence is the principle determining the answer to the question "What is it that exists?" The answer to that question would be the sum total of a thing's attributes. Therefore the sum total of its attributes is, roughly speaking, the essence of a thing. The differences between the word-functions of "exists" and of words for attributes would derive from and reflect the distinction of existence from essence. Words for attributes refer to essence. But apart from its conjunction with the distinct principle, existence, essence is nothing. Therefore words for attributes presuppose the existence of that of which they are predicated.

But the opposite ontological theory is equally compatible with the evidence for the non-predicate view. According to this theory, existence is not a factor entering into the makeup of things really distinct from essence. "Existence" would refer to the attributes of a thing taken in their totality, the sum total of a thing's attributes not being itself an attribute. On this hypothesis also, affirming of A any of its attributes presupposes that A exists. For in the absence of some of the attributes whose totality are referred to by "A exists", it would not be A that exists but something else. The following suggestions of Kiteley and Kaminsky are perfectly consistent with this second medieval view of existence and provide a good illustration of why it is unaffected by the non-predicate theory:

> Perhaps some very obvious fact about predicates has been overlooked, namely, that technically we have no right to speak about predicates unless we have some way of categorizing these predicates. That is to say, following Russell, we must indicate the level and degree of each predicate being used. Otherwise we are faced with the traditional paradoxes Russell and Whitehead sought to overcome. Thus even though on some level of predicates "exists" cannot be a predicate we have not shown that "exists" cannot be a predicate at some other level. In brief, we are constantly thinking of predicates in the sense of "green", "is larger than", etc., and neglecting the fact that there can be and are different types of predicates. I refer to such predicates as "useful" as in "The object is useful"; or "manufactured" as in "This automobile was manufactured by U.S. Steel"; or "non-empty" as in "I want a non-empty box"; or "packaged" as in "The chocolates are packaged". To say an object is useful or manufactured or non-empty or packaged is not to add some further properties to the properties it already has. It is to say something about the entire cluster of properties. In a similar way logicians distinguish distributive from collective predicates. If I say lions are numerous, I do not mean that each lion has the property of being numerous. But if I say that lions are carnivorous, then I do mean this to apply to each individual lion. In

normal usage no one confuses these different functions of predicates. We would not expect anyone to ask how it is possible for "numerous" or "manufactured" to be predicates. We simply do not look for a manufactured or numerous property in the same way we might look for a green property. Yet all these predicates serve important functions. (Kaminsky, 1969, pp. 203-204; and see Kiteley, 1964.)

It should also be noted that both of these theories of the relation between existence and that which exists are compatible with something else that has been taken as evidence for the non-predicate view, the fact that neither sense experience nor scientific analysis reveals the presence, among the components entering into the constitution of sensible things, of a distinct factor answering to the word "existence". This is just what is to be expected if "existence" does not refer to anything other than that which exists considered in its totality. But it is equally to be expected if existence is a distinct from *that which* exists. For the components that sense experience and the theories of empirical science reveal in the constitution of sensible things are components of that which exists. On the other hand, if in addition to that which exists, there is something else which is called its existence, it is ontological, not empirical, causal analysis that must inform us of this.

If the evidence for the non-predicate view is consistent both with the ontological theory that existence is really distinct from that which exists and with the ontological theory that existence is not really distinct from that which exists, why should the non-predicate view, even if true, rule out theories of the ontological kind? It will be objected that the non-predicate thesis is not intended to contradict any particular ontological theory, be it a theory about the relation of existence to what exists or any other specific ontological theory. Rather, what is intended by the non-predicate thesis is the ruling out of *all* theories of this epistemological type. That this is one of the implications drawn from the non-predicate thesis is not under dispute. But we have just seen that some of the facts offered as evidence for the non-predicate thesis do not support the drawing of this conclusion, since there are ontological theories with which they are compatible. And I am now going to show that no evidence for the non-predicate thesis can justify this conclusion. For in order to yield the conclusion that "exists" cannot play the role that ontology has traditionally given it, an argument must interpret the word-function of "exists" in a way that is *necessarily* false. Therefore there will be no reason for me to deny the non-predicate thesis or any of the facts that support it. If a meaning can be given that thesis to make it compatible with what is otherwise true of the word-function of "exists", that thesis cannot stand in the way of ontology as I conceive it.

5.2.3 What's not in existential quantification?

What is there to prevent the knowledge communicated by sentences such as "There is an F" or "Fs exist" from providing a point of view from which to discover necessary truths about things as things? Nothing, unless we interpret such sentences as communicating knowledge of things *only as objects* and not as things. Assume that the word-function of "F" is a feature belonging to our objects as extraobjective things. So far then, "Fs exist" objectifies certain things according to what is true of them as things. But what about the second word in that sentence, "exists"? What role does it play when things are made objects of sentential knowledge? How does it help us to complete a sentential objectification of the object of the description "F"? The sentence completed by "exists" may further objectify Fs either according to what is true of them as objects or as other-than-*objects*, that is, as things. Only if sentences in which "exists" is the grammatical predicate communicate solely what is true of things as objects of knowledge, can the word-function of "exists" not provide a basis for the descriptions of things as things that make ontology in the strict sense possible. If "An F exists" is about an F as a thing, it makes no difference whether or not we refer to existence as an "attribute". Call it an "attricate" or a "predibute" if you like. The validity of ontological method remains intact.

In other words, ontology as a method distinct from empirical method is nullified by the non-predicate thesis if and only if that thesis interprets the word-function of "exists" as an object-description, if and only if it identifies being with being-known. We have already seen an unintentionally Berkeleyan version of the non-predicate view, Quine's definition of "exists" as "being the value of a bound variable". To repeat what was said in section 2.3.2, there is no denying that one consequence of something's existing is that it can be the value of a variable falling within the scope of "($\exists$x)" in a true sentence. But that something is the value of a variable falling within the scope of "($\exists$x)" cannot be what is asserted by "($\exists$x)" or by "exists".

We may as well say that what is asserted by "Tigers exist" is that tigers can be referred to by the word "exists", thereby violating the distinction between mention and use. As we saw in discussing the assertive-redundancy theory of truth, when we have sentential knowledge of the fact that some tigers are tame, we possess knowledge both of things as things and things as objects. Our knowledge concerning things as objects is expressed by "The sentence 'Some tigers are tame' is true". But the sentence "Some tigers are tame" does not itself make mention of what we know about things as objects; it only mentions what we know about things as things. Likewise in knowing the truth of "Tigers exist", one of the things we know is that the word "exists" can be used for tigers. To that extent our knowledge concerns tigers as objects of linguistic knowledge, not as things. But no mention of that part of our knowledge is made by "Tigers exist".

To speak of something as the value of a bound variable is to relate what we are speaking of to language. And this is to describe what we are speaking of by an object-description. For things become terms of linguistic relations only by becoming objects of linguistic knowledge. And whether agreeing with Quine or not, all versions of the non-predicate theory that would make the knowledge communicated by "There is a . . ." incapable of providing a point of view for discovering truths about things as things interpret "There is a. . ." as communicating knowledge about things as objects. We are told that "An F exists" or "There is something which is an F" have the same meaning as sentences such as " 'Fx' is sometimes true", "The concept of F has an application", "There is a referent for the word 'F' ". (See, for example, Russell, 1919, p. 165; Sellars, 1963. p. 116. Apparently Frege is the originator of this way of interpreting existence.) "An F exists", therefore, is a statement relating an F to such elements of our sentential knowledge as concepts, descriptions and words used referentially. And it is only as objects of sentential knowledge that things are terms of such relations.

To put it another way, the non-predicate theory is an attempt to explain the function of the existential quantifier. "$(\exists x)$" can be rendered as "There is an x which . . .". But "There is an x which . . ." is meaningless unless "an x" has the same word-function that "something" ordinarily has . "$(\exists x)$ Fx" means "There is something which is an F" or "Something is an F". "Something", however ordinarily has the same word-function as "an entity" or "an existent". Therefore this explanation of the existential quantifier presupposes the word-function of "exists". To avoid the circularity, the "something" in "There is something which is an F" must be replaced by an object-description such as "that to which the concept of F may be applied", "that which satisfies the description 'F'", "referent for the word 'F'".

Moreover, "(∃x) Fx" informs us both that some x is an F *and* that that which is an F is an existent. So far, then, the non-predicate theory has not made "exists" any less informative about things as things than is "F". Replacing "an x" or "something" with an object-description is the only way out. But then to be is to be an object of knowledge, being is being-known.

This result may not be intended by the non-predicate theorist. Good intentions are not sufficient for good philosophy, however. The point I am making is similar to that made by Harris in his criticism of Ryle's "Systematically Misleading Expressions". Ryle was attempting to use the view that "exists" is not a "genuine predicate" to show that certain things are not "genuine subjects". Harris replies as follows:

> How then do we distinguish genuine subjects? Merely by the fact that we assert of them genuine predicates? If so and if "real", "existent", and the like are not genuine predicates, only that is a genuine subject of which reality, existence or genuine being is *not* asserted. . . . If I say "Mr. Churchill is a famous person", he is a genuine subject; but if I say "Mr. Churchill is a genuine entity", he ceases to be one. But "genuine subject", if it means anything, means "genuine entity". Professor Ryle's protest is against the multiplication of bogus entities by hypostasization of bogus subjects (as in "God exists" as opposed to "There is *something* satisfying the description 'God' "), so by genuine subjects he must mean to refer to genuine entities. It would seem, therefore, that a genuine entity is only genuine when it is not stated to be so and becomes bogus as soon as it is identified as a genuine existent. . . .
>
> . . .The condition of the distinction between genuine and bogus subjects is the possibility of predicating reality, or existence, or genuine being of certain subjects. It is, therefore, ridiculous to maintain that such prediction is bogus. It consequently transpires that the analysis of existence-propositions itself presupposes the logical priority to all genuine subject-predicate statements of existence-propositions, and it is therefore seriously misleading to allege that, because existence predicates are not characters, their subjects are not genuine subjects. (Harris, 1953, pp. 203-204)

5.2.4 The syntactical interpretation of "exists"

Now we are ready to discuss the syntactical interpretation of the existential quantifier. If "something" is equivalent to "an existent", then translating "(∃x)" by, "There exists something which . . ." produces the apparent redundancy; "There exists an existent which . . .". For finite domains at least, the syntactical interpretation of "(∃x)" offers a way both of avoiding this redundancy and of depriving the word-function of "something" of any ontological significance. According to this view, "There is something which is F" is shorthand for "Fa v Fb . . . Fn". The existential quantifier functions to translate sentences using language-forms of one syntactical type, proper names, into logically equivalent sentences using language-forms of another syntactical type, individual variables. "Exists" is now defined syntactically, by reference to proper names. And by availing ourselves of symbols for proper names we seem to avoid having to worry whether "something" has the same function as "an existent". For "There is something which . . ." was introduced only as an ordinary language interpretation of "There is an x which . . . ". But now we can interpret "There is an x which . . ." more precisely by replacing it with a disjunction using proper names. "An x" and "something" become syntactical variables.

Even for finite domains, however, this move manages to neutralize the ontological significance of "exists" and "something" only at the price of confusing being with being-known. For the word-function of "exists" is now defined by reference to that for which proper names are used. And what is the function of proper names? They are constants for individuals. In other words, "There is something which . . ." amounts to "There is an *individual* which . . .". But what is an individual? Do not answer that an individual is whatever is the referent of a proper name. That would be like the Carnapian explanation of "Fs are things" as " 'F' is a thing-word".

Nor does it help to understand individuals as the correlative opposites of universals. For universality is a logical relation attributable to things only as objects or means of objectification. "Universal" means "predicable of more than one". And whatever is said to be predicable of more than one is either a word or a word-function which has been objectified and used as a means for objectifying things. Consequently to define "individual" as the opposite of "universal" is to define it as term of a logical relation, namely, as that of which universals are predicable and which is not itself predicable of many. Instead of "There is something which is F" we have "There is that of which 'F' can be predicated". If that is all there is to the existential quantifier, being has nothing to distinguish it from being-known. For things terminate logical relations only as a result of being made objects of knowledge.

Assume that the word-function of "F" is a feature of things as things. If it is true that some individual is a referent of "F" or satisfies description "F" or is an individual to which the concept of F may be applied, then it is true that an F exists. But this F does not exist because it is the referent of some word or satisfies some description or provides an application for some concept. On the contrary, all of these other things are true of it only because it exists. All these object-descriptions *imply* that "exists" is true of this individual. But we cannot make the function of "exists" equivalent to any object-description without becoming disciples of good Bishop Berkeley. "An F exists" cannot be explained by "This individual is an F, or that individual is an F . . ." unless being an individual is understood, not according to the object-description "that of which 'F' can be predicated", but as a thing of which existence can be asserted just insofar as it is more-than-an-*object*.

Explaining existential quantification by appeal to the notion of proper names, therefore, does not help the non-predicate theorist. As Harris put it:

> We are told that . . . "Mr. Churchill is a genuine entity" is not about Mr. Churchill. But it is about something for we are explicitly warned (by Ryle) that it is "not only significant but true", that it does not mislead its naive user and *need* not mislead the philosopher. Accordingly it may be paraphrased somewhat like this: "There is somebody called Mr. Churchill." But this is only an oblique way of saying that somebody (who is called Mr. Churchill) is a genuine entity, since that is the whole force of the phrase, "there is". (p. 203)

In other words, "Mr. Churchill exists" can be translated "There is something named Mr. Churchill" or "There is some individual named Mr. Churchill" if and only if "something" and "some individual" mean "some actually existing entity". Syntactical interpretation or no syntactical interpretation, proper names or individual variables, the non-predicate theorist must either opt for Berkeley's account of existence or recognize the validity of ontological method.

But what about the redundancy of "There exists something which . . ." if "something" is equivalent to "an existent"? In the first place, the redundancy can be avoided, and the distinction between being and being-known preserved, just by translating "$(\exists x) Fx$" by "Something is an F" or "There exists an F", instead of by "There exists something which is an F". In the second place, "There exists something which is an F" can be saved from redundancy as the syntactical interpretation saves it but without the disadvantages of the syntactical interpretation. "Something" can be interpreted as an ontological variable, not a syntactical variable. For "$(\exists x) Fx$" is equivalent to "Either this existent is an F, or that existent is an F, or that other existent is an F, etc." In effect, the syntactical interpretation reads "something" as the object-description "one of the terms of the relation of naming". It should be read as the thing-description "one of the existents" and "($\exists$x) Fx" read as "At least one of the existents is an F".

Of course, relations like naming and referring can be, and often are, understood to be defined by the fact that their terms really exist. If they are taken this way, the non-predicate view does not reduce being to being known because descriptions like "that which is named by" or "the referent of" are no longer object-descriptions pure and simple. And they ceased being merely extrinsic denominations when these relations were defined by something that was true of their terms, namely, real existence. (See section 2.2.2.) Descriptions of things as terms of these relations, therefore, do not express only the reality which characterizes that which has, rather than that which is the term of, the relations. But at the same time, these relations can no longer be used to explain the word-function of "exists" since they are themselves defined by reference to that word-function. Therefore no use of these relations by the non-predicate theorist can pose an obstacle to ontological method.

But nothing requires us to so define naming and referring that it is necessary for names and referring expressions to objectify what actually exists. Being objectified in some way is *always something other than* really existing. Therefore to be objectified as named is other than to exist. Of course, a mode of objectification can make something an object precisely as being a real existent; sensation, introspection and judgments of existence objectify things as really existing. That naming does not objectify things as really existing, however, is proven by the fact that we use names for known non-existents. Since our primary linguistic objects are real existents, our primary *named* objects are presumably real existents. But this primacy is caused by the nature of linguistic objectification, not by the nature of names as such. And just as we can extend language to non-existent objects, we can use names to objectify non-existent objects.

But what are the names of non-existents used *for*? What terminates the relation of referring? If these are legitimate questions and if their answer is that some real existent is needed to terminate the relation, then why is not the same answer called for when we ask what is it that terminates the relation of imagining when we imagine something? (The reason is not that a mental representation of the object terminates the relation. It is one thing to imagine, say, a talking dog. It is another thing to imagine a mental representation of a talking dog. The dog we imagine may have four legs, a tail, and an accent. No psychological modification I acquire when imagining the dog has such characteristics. The representation is not *what* we imagine; it is the *means by which* we imagine what we imagine. And how does the representation become a representation *of* the dog? "Being-a-representation-*of*" is just another phrase for the relation we are inquiring about.) And what terminates the relation used-for in the case of general terms? If real existents are required to terminate the relation of being-used-for in the case of names, why must we not say that universals really exist since they termintate the relation of meaning for general terms?

I discuss reference to the non-existent in section 5.5.2. In the meantime, I do not assume that a name requires a real existent for its object. There is no problem about the existence of named objects that is not shared by other modes of objectification, linguistic and non-linguistic.

5.3 The Word-function of "Exists"

Whatever else the word-function of "exists" may be, it is a knowable value of things as extra-objective things. For the word "thing" was introduced in section 2.2.1 for the purpose of expressing that something-more-than-being-an-*object* which is first known about objects when they become objects. And it was shown in section 2.2.2 that things are more-than-*objects* not just in the conceptual sense that they must be objectified by thing-descriptions before they can be objectified by object-descriptions, but also in the sense that the existence of things, when they really exist as opposed to being merely fictional or imaginary, is something really distinct from being an object of knowledge. Hence the meaning$_T$ of "exists" is a means for objectifying things as things. Further, concerning the things that are the first to be objectified in language, it must be true that they really exist since language is public.

What more can be said about the word-function of "exists"? Many things. But I will confine myself here to saying only enough about existence to accomplish the following: in section 5.3, explain why it has not been obvious that the anti-ontological interpretation of the non-predicate thesis leads to idealism and, at the same time, why so many have found the anti-ontological interpretation plausible; in section 5.4, show the implications of our use of "exists" for the principle of non-contradiction and and other truths whose necessity derives from logical relations and also for our discourse about cognition-dependent objects. Accomplishing these objectives will require explaining certain peculiarities of the word-function of "exists" which have long been noted in classical realism, peculiarities of the manner in which we become acquainted with this word-function and peculiarities of the relation of this word-function to the rest of human knowledge.

5.3.1 Existence as known by judgment

The first reason why the idealism of the anti-ontological view has not been obvious and why this view is so plausible was alluded to in the preceding section. If A really exists, then characterizing it as term of relations like knows-A, describes-A, refers-to-A implies, in conjunction with other truths, that A's existence is other than its being the term of any of these relations. Knowing that this implication necessarily holds, we read it into what is asserted by sentences like "There is a referent for 'F'''". And we fail to notice that what is *said* rather than *implied* by such a sentence cannot be all there is to existence assertions. And if these relations are defined by the existence of their terms, we take the fact that this existence is extra-objective for granted and forget that these relations cannot be used to define "exists".

To understand the second reason we need some idea of what it means to say that, as classical realism has traditionally pointed out, we become acquainted with the word-function of "exists" only by means of the act of judgment. First a distinction must be made. Things are presented in sense experience as real existents. (This is the topic of Chapter Ten.) In that sense, we do not need to make judgments to become acquainted with existence. But in the case of any word-function, to be acquainted with it on the sense level is not equivalent to being acquainted with it as that for which some language-form is capable of being used. It is common, for instance, for victims of severe brain damage to be incapable of linguistically articulating their sense experience in ways in which others can normally articulate theirs; and this can be true even though other behavioral evidence indicates the victim's perceptions to be the same as those of the normal person. So sense contact with real existence or with anything else is not equivalent to being acquainted with it in the manner psychological analysis can show to be required to make it the function of some language-form.

But whatever psychological process may be required for us to become acquainted with the word-function of "exists", sense experience does present its objects as actually existing; this is so even if the experience itself is an hallucination. Consequently the senses cannot distinguish one object from another by the presence or absence of existence the way they can distinguish red objects from green objects or faster moving objects from slower moving objects.

But sense experience also presents its objects as being in space and time. In fact, the occupation of space and time is often taken to be the word-function of "exists". And things are sensibly distinguishable as being in different parts of space and at different times. If spaces and times are sensibly distinguishable even though everything is sensed as being in space and time, why can existence not be a sensibly distinguishable characteristic of things?

The word-function of "exists", however, is *not* the occupation of space and time. If it were, space and time would necessarily be nonexistent since they do not occupy space and time. Rather the occupation of space and time, and of different spaces and times, are *means* by which we judge existence and make distinctions between existents. They are not *that which* we judge when we judge existence and distinguish existents from one another; they are means by which the senses make the existence of things evident to us. (See section 10.3.) But if existence itself is not a sensibly distinguishable feature of experience, how do we become acquainted with the meaning$_T$ of "exists"?

Since existence is made evident to us through our awareness of features of experience other than existence, we become acquainted with existence, if at all, by being aware of the existence-of something other than existence, that is, the existence-of something *objectifiable* otherwise than as an existent. We are aware of the existence of something red, something moving, something hard, etc. And becoming aware, at the level of linguistic objectification, that something red exists is what is meant by a judgment of existence. To say that we do not become acquainted with the meaning$_T$ of "exists" in a judgment of existence is to say that we can become acquainted with that meaning$_T$ apart from awareness of the existence-of something other than existence. I do not know how to show the impossibility of our having an experience from which we can acquire the meaning$_T$ of "exists" except by being aware of the existence of something objectifiable otherwise than as an existent. But as long as our sense experience (and our introspective experience as well) is what it is, it is necessary that we become linguistically acquainted with existence only by means of judgments of existence. For the meaning$_T$ of "judgment of existence" is just the kind of thing we do when we become aware that what can be objectified by "something red", "something moving" or "something hard" can also be objectified by "exists".

But how can this be if, as it seems, we make judgments by comparing the things objectified by *already-acquired* word-functions (what is objectified by "apple" and what is objectified by "red", for example) and if, as it also seems, we become acquainted with the meanings$_T$ of words objectifying things as they are present in sense experience by way of contrast, since the function of these words is to allow us to distinguish things from one another, something "exists" does not do? To explain this we will return again—and not for the last time— to our remarks about the assertive-redundancy theory of truth.

In knowing a sentential truth about things as things, we have knowledge both about things as things (namely, what is expressed by the sentence) and about things as objects (namely, that they have been linguistically objectified as they are objectified in this sentence). A judgment concerning the truth of a sentence is therefore a comparison between things as things and things as objects. And as we also saw in our discussion of truth, the correspondence that is judged in judging the truth of sentences is primarily a relation between things as things and things as the objects of descriptions or names, and secondarily a relation between things and sentences. For sentences are instruments for knowing and communicating the relation of identity between things and the objects of descriptions and names. When we believe that such a relation of identity holds, we believe that the sentence is true.

And we judge existence by judging the identity between what is objectified by a description or name and what is present in sense experience (or in introspective experience). Therefore it is in the comparison of something objectified by a description or name and what is present in sense experience that we become acquainted with the meaning$_T$ of "exists". For it is in such a comparison between a thing objectified by a description like "something red" and a thing presented in sense experience that we grasp that what is objectified by "something red" not only terminates this relation of objectification, is not only so objectified, but also . . .

Also what? The answer to this question is the state the other term of the identity relation must be in order for objects to have something they are identical with. The word for this state is "exists". "Exists" is the language-form by which we distinguish realities from objects that are merely objects, merely imagined, remembered or referred to. In other words, "exists" comes into the language for the purpose of objectifying that because of which objects are more-than-*objects*. For whatever else it may be, existence is that because of which some objects are more-than-*objects* or, to put it another way, that because of which those predicates by which things are primarily objectified, thing-descriptions, can be *truthfully* attributed to things. Things have causal priority over objects. There can be no objects unless there are first extra-objective things that we can objectify as such. The word-function of "exists" is the state in which things have causal priority over our objectification of them.

This way of describing how we become acquainted with the meaning$_T$ of "exists" may make it appear that the meaning$_T$ of "exists" is the correlative opposite of the meanings$_T$ of object-descriptions like "designated by a name" or "described by a predicate" (the crypto-Berkeleyan view, in effect). In making the judgment that something red exists, we do not use the object-description "what is objectified by 'something red' ". (It is in giving a causal analysis of this judgment, not in making the judgment, that we use the corresponding object-description.) But when we use a thing-description to make the judgment, we *know* that things are objectified, just as in knowing any sentential truth about things as things, we also know the truth that things have been made objects of knowledge. (This point about judgment is presented in different terminology by Maritain, 1959, p. 89, n. 1. Where I speak of not *using* object-descriptions but knowing that things have been objectified, Maritain speaks of the knower being aware of himself in exercised act but being aware of things in signified [read: *sign*-ified, as by means of language] act.)

Does it follow that the meaning$_T$ of "exists" is the correlative opposite of the meanings$_T$ of object-descriptions and, therefore, that to exist is to be the term of a knowledge relation? On the contrary. Our awareness that something present in experience has been objectified by a description or name provides the *contrast* we need to become linguistically acquainted with the meaning$_T$ of "exists". Although we cannot contrast two sensed objects as existing and not existing, what is objectified by a language-form need not be a real existent. We need judgment to objectify which linguistic objects do exist cognition-independently.

Our awareness that what we judge to exist has been objectified is a psychological fact that does not enter into that which is judged. *It would be an epistemological fallacy to reduce the meaning$_T$ of any word to the psychological conditions under which that meaning$_T$ enters the language.* The condition under which existence comes into the language is a comparison of what is presented in sense experience as existing with what has been objectified by a description like "something red".

But existence does not enter the language as the correlative of the meaning$_T$ of an object-description like "what is objectified by 'something red' "; it enters the language as the correlative of the meanings$_T$ of thing-descriptions like "something red". For "something red" objectifies things only to the extent it is used for some meaning$_T$. And it is because real existence is correlative to the meaning$_T$ of "something red" that it is attributable to what is objectified by "something red". Conversely, it is because real existence is not correlative to the meaning$_T$ of "logical construct" that it is not attributable to what is objectified by "a logical construct".

The meaning$_T$ of "something red" is what some actual or possible existent is. When existence is truthfully attributable to something red, it is because the meaning$_T$ of "something red" is what some actual existent is. In other words, what-is-objectified-by-"something red" can have existence attributed to it only because the meaning$_T$ of "something red" is what some actual existent is. If existence were not correlative to the meaning$_T$ of "something red", being a *thing* would not be causally prior to being an *object*, since existence is the state in which things have causal priority over their objectification. There is identity between what-is-objectified-by-"something red" and what-is-objectified-by-"an existent" because there is identity between something red and an existent. But to linguistically objectify existence as correlative to the meanings$_T$ of thing-descriptions like "something red", we must be aware that things have been objectified by means of such thing-descriptions.

Nor does this analysis imply that we become acquainted with the meanings$_T$ of such object-descriptions as "What is objectified by 'something red' " at some time *before* we become acquainted with the meaning$_T$ of "exists". Keeping in mind the distinction between lexicological and non-lexicological acquaintance with meaning, we can say that we become acquainted with these meanings$_T$ simultaneously. First we are made sensibly aware of the existence of something. Then we linguistically objectify it by making some of its sensibly distinguishable characteristics the meanings$_T$ of language-forms. But at the time when we have thus linguistically objectified it, we are not only sensibly aware of the objectified thing; we are also aware of the fact that it has been linguistically objectified. And when we are aware of the fact that it is thus objectified, we are linguistically aware of something else the senses were aware of all along: that the thing is not only what is objectified by means of some word-function, is not only something red or moving or hard, but is also a real existent. (In other words, we judge that the thing exists.)

On the other hand, learning the meaning of "exists" in the non-lexicological sense is not the same as learning it in the lexicological sense. "Exists" and its cognates are far from being the first words that enter our personal lexicons as we learn the language. But before learning the meaning$_L$ of "exists" we have for a long time known countless sentential truths knowledge of which logically includes what we later learn to express as the knowledge that things exist. By means of this previous knowledge of sentential truth, therefore, we are linguistically acquainted with something, namely, existence, for which we as yet have no special means of objectification but which is capable of being so objectified. And there can even be languages in which there are no words equivalent to our "exists". A language could, for instance, make exclusive use of one-word, or one-phrase, sentences such as "Apple" to communicate what we communicate by "An apple exists". (For more on this, see section 6.2.1.) The users of that language would, therefore, be non-lexicologically acquainted with the word-function of "exists".

It follows from what was said in the last paragraph that we could learn to use object-descriptions before acquiring a lexicological understanding of any words equivalent to our word "exists". As far as non-lexicological understanding is concerned, becoming acquainted with existence as something *capable* of linguistic objectification is simultaneous with the acquaintance (also capable of linguistic expression) with things as *objectified* by means of thing-descriptions. Three important qualifications accompany this assertion of simultaneity, however. First, the fact that awareness of the meanings$_T$ of object-descriptions is simultaneous with the objectification of things by means of thing-descriptions is not in contradiction with the fact that things must be known by thing-descriptions prior to their being known by object-descriptions. The priority is causal, not temporal. Awareness of things as described by thing-descriptions is something without which we would not be aware of the meanings$_T$ of object-descriptions.

The second qualification. In the non-lexicological sense, becoming acquainted with the meaning of "exists" is simultaneous with our acquaintance with the meaning of some object-description. But when we recognize that what is objectified by "something red" also exists, we are recognizing something that was true of the red thing before it became a term of this relation of objectification. The word-function of "exists" is true of things before the word-function of object-descriptions is true of them, and our acquaintance with the word-function of "exists" makes us capable of recognizing this. As a result of making judgments of existence, we can recognize that, unlike the meanings$_T$ of linguistic object-descriptions, the meaning$_T$ of "exists" is something we have been acquainted with all along, although not acquainted with it as a linguistic object. For we recognize that sense-experience has always presented things as really existing. We have always been in contact with existence at the level of sense knowledge and become acquainted with it at the level of linguistic knowledge as soon as we begin to articulate things in language.

The third qualification elaborates on something that has already been stressed. Becoming acquainted with the meaning$_T$ of "exists" is simultaneous with the knowledge, which can later be expressed by object-descriptions, that something has been linguistically objectified. But what we know when we know the meaning$_T$ of "exists" has a *causal* priority over the meaning$_T$ of any object-description. Language being public, if there were no real existents to objectify in language, there would be no linguistic knowledge and hence no meanings$_T$ of object-descriptions for linguistic objects. When we know the truth of "That exists" our knowledge encompasses the relations of the thing objectified by "That" both to the meaning$_T$ of "exists" and to the meaning$_T$ of the object-description "referred to by 'That'". But the relation of what is objectified by "That" to existence is a condition really distinct from being the term of a knowledge relation and a condition without which there would be no terms for knowledge relations to be true of. Existence, again, is what we know about things when we know they are distinct from objects not only conceptually but really. And without that distinction there are no public objects for language to objectify.

The plausibility of the non-predicate theory derives, at least in part, from the fact that we become acquainted with the word-function of "exists" through judgment. We cannot judge existence unless we have already objectified things by means of predicates other than "exists". And we judge existence by grasping the identity between something objectified by another predicate and something that is *more than* what is objectified by the other predicate. Hence the word-function of "exists" appears to contrast with those of the predicates whose objects are judged to exist. The source of the contrast is psychological, however, and implies nothing about these word-functions in themselves.

We have yet to explain, however, why the fact that we learn to use "exists" by means of making judgments differentiates the way we learn it from the way we learn other words for things as things. If we acquire our understanding of the word "exists" by comparing what is objectified by some other word, say "F", with things as things, can our understanding of the word-function of "F" be acquired in the same way? That is, can it be acquired through a process comparing sense-experienced things as things to what is objectified by means of some other word, say "G"? Then how did we acquire the use of "G"? An infinite regress can be avoided if and only if the process of comparing things as things and things as objectified by word-functions does not begin by using word-functions acquired by means of such a comparison. The publicly communicable thing-descriptions which are first to enter the language and without which the language could develop no further cannot be learned, like the meaning$_T$ of "exists", through the process of making judgments.

The various causal factors entering a child's acquisition of a word like "dada" (which is apparently learned as a description before becoming a name) may render it impossible to learn such a word without *at the same time* having knowledge of a sentential truth, that is, making a judgment. And when a child says "Dada", he may well be expressing knowledge of a sentential truth, knowledge we might express by "Dad is coming near" or even "Dad exists". But the argument of the preceding paragraph has shown that the correct analysis of these causal factors must allow for a real distinction between that process of comparing things and objects which takes place in judgment and the process of becoming acquainted with the word-functions of the thing-descriptions we use when we make judgments. The opposite is true of the process by which we learn to use "exists". That process is the same as the grasping of the identity between thing and object that is what knowing the truth of a sentence like "Something red exists" amounts to.

The fact that becoming acquainted with the word-function of "exists" is causally dependent on a knowledge of things as objects in a way that learning to use ordinary thing-descriptions is not tends to give credence to the anti-ontological interpretations of the non-predicate theory and to disguise its idealistic consequences. In the same process by which we become acquainted with the meaning$_T$ (not necessarily the meaning$_L$) of "exists", we become acquainted with the meanings$_T$ of such phrases as "referent of the description 'something red' " or "individual satisfying the description 'something red' ". Therefore we take existence for granted when we use these object-descriptions. And the existence we take for granted is extra-objective existence.

The tendency to take existence for granted will obviously be present if these descriptions are not purely extrinsic denominations but make use of relations defined by the real existence of their terms. But the tendency will still be present even if phrases like "referent for the word 'F' " are purely extrinsic denominations. In that case, the word-function of "referent" will not presuppose the real existence of that to which it is attributed, and it can be attributed to logical constructs as well as to extra-objective things. On this assumption the sentence "There is a referent for 'F' " objectifies things solely as objects and not as things.

Assume further, however, that the word-function of "F" is a feature characterizing things as extra-objective things. Then we have a situation which is the reverse of that encountered in our discussion of the assertive-redundancy theory of truth. The sentence "There is a referent for the word 'F' " makes no mention of things as things, but in knowing the truth of that sentence, we have knowledge that extends both to what is true of things as objects (that there is a referent for "F") and to what is true of things as things (that there is an F).

In knowing the truth of that sentence, we know that an F has an existence which is other-than-being-a-"referent". And because we know this we do not realize that our *philosophic use* of that sentence to explain the meaning of "exists" reduces existence to the state of being referred to in language. As with so many theories that suppress their own data, we do not see that the logical consequence of the theory is a denial of the data because we are taking the data for granted. Our inclination to take the data for granted is only increased by the fact that "There is a referent for 'F' " could be used as a substitute for "An F exists" in non-philosophic contexts where there is no danger that suppression of data will become an issue.

5.3.2 The word-function of "being"

Another source for the attractiveness of the anti-ontological view is found in the most important reason for taking extra-objective existence for granted when contemplating crypto-Berkeleyan definitions of existence. The word-functions of "exists" and its cognate "being" are logically the most fundamental word-functions in language; that is, they are *logically included* in the word-functions of all other predicates due to their causal relation to language. As logically included in them, the word-functions of "exists" and "being" are always present in the background of other predicates. Since they are always present in the background, when we consider the crypto-Berkeleyan definition of existence, we can fail to see that what is in the foreground ultimately contradicts them. This section deals with the logical inclusion of existence and being in the meanings$_T$ of the predicates for the primary objects of linguistic objectification. Section 5.4 will show how that inclusion applies to other objects.

What does it mean to call these meanings$_T$ most fundamental and what evidence is there for this assertion? When we are acquainted with the meaning$_T$ of "man" we are also acquainted with the meanings$_T$ of "animal", "organism" and "body". Not that we need be acquainted with the meanings of any of these words in the lexicological sense, but the meanings$_T$ of "animal", "organism" and "body" are necessarily distinct only by logical relations from the meaning$_T$ of "man" just as the meaning$_T$ of "color" is distinct only by logical relations from that of "red". It would appear, however, that the meaning$_T$ of "being", that-which-exists, cannot be distinct only by the logical relations of less explicitness and greater extension from the meanings$_T$ of thing-descriptions. Whatever object we can articulate by "man", we can articulate by "animal". Therefore it is necessarily true that man is an animal. If being is logically included in man the way animal is, it is necessarily true that man is a being, that is, an existent. The logical inclusion of being in the word-function of thing descriptions would give us an ontological argument proving the necessary existence of anything whatsoever.

When being is said to be logically included in other word-functions, "being" does not mean what actually exists but what is capable of existence, being with the logical relation of possibility. Possibility is a relation whose bearers are objectified as eligible, but only as eligible, to be judged identical with actual existents (or with something objectifiable non-contradictorily in the case of cognition-dependent objects). Thing-descriptions objectify things as possible existents rather than as actual existents, since actual existence is known in judgment. But when what is objectified by a thing-description actually exists, *that which* exists is the same as *that which* was objectified by the thing-description as a capacity for existence.

The first predicates to enter language are thing-descriptions. And the goal of objectifying things by means of predicates is to know, by means of sentences, the identity of what has been so objectified with what exists extra-objectively. Therefore the meanings$_T$ of these predicates are objectified as what some possible existent is, at least in part, (what-it-is-to-be-a-man, what-it-is-to-be-a-table). For things are so objectified by the meanings$_T$ of the first predicates that enter the language as to be capable of being judged real existents. This capability is not an incidental feature of the way things are objectified by these word-functions. The capability is necessary because of the teleonomic cause of using language in this way. These word-functions are logically structured to objectify things as capacities for existence because they are logically structured to be employed in judgments by which extra-objective existence is known. They must be so structured in order for us to achieve the goal of knowing the identity between what is objectified and what is more than an object, that is, what exists.

This fundamental character of the meanings$_T$ of "being" and, therefore, of "exists" is traditionally expressed by saying that being is what is first known about things and is included in all other meanings$_T$. Exactly the same point is made by the argument-function analysis of predication. Predicates can be analyzed as functions of that of which they are predicated. What are made our objects by means of words like "apple" or "red" are not merely the qualities of appleness or redness; if so, there could be no identity between what has been objectified by words with different meanings$_T$. Predicates are means for objectifying things. "Apple" and "red" serve to objectify some x, or some x's, of which "apple" and "red" may be true. But we know from section 5.2.3 that "x" is simply a substitute for "some*thing*", that is, "some existent". "Apple" objectifies (with the logical relation of possibility) some thing which is an apple or, equivalently, has appleness; the adjective "red" objectifies (with the logical relation of possibility) some thing which is red or, equivalently, has redness. That is what is meant when it is said that the meaning$_T$ of "being" is logically included in meanings$_T$ like those of "apple" and "red"; these other meanings$_T$ are objectified as *logical* functions of the meaning$_T$ of being.

The argument-function analysis of predicates does not make all meanings$_T$ ontological. To expand on what was said in section 5.1, for a meaning$_T$ objectifying things as things to be ontological, it must distinguish the things it objectifies from other things by an *extra-objective* function of existence, for example, existing-in-another, existing-in-itself. Given extra-objective functions of existence as meanings$_T$, a logical relation terminating in an ontological meaning$_T$, for example, the possibility for existence, is also an ontological meaning$_T$. But terminating the relation of possibility for existence does not itself make a meaning$_T$ ontological.

In passing we can take advantage of this reference to the argument-function analysis of predication to explain another doctrine from the realist tradition regarding what is most fundamental in language, being, yes, but being precisely as presented by sensible qualities. (*Ens concretum quiditati SENSIBILI* — my emphasis.) In other words, what is primary in language is not redness but something red, a red thing capable of being recognized to exist, not softness but something soft, not motion but something moving, not number but groups of things of various numbers. It is here that empiricism parts ways with philosophy conceived ontologically. Empiricism accepts only the second half of phrases like "something red", "something soft", "something moving" as descriptively significant of experience. "Something" has a merely logical or syntactical function, if any function at all. But then, whether we like it or not, we are in agreement with Berkeley.

To get back to our topic. "Being" objectifies something distinct from what "man" objectifies *only* by a logical relation of less explicitness. For a logical relation of possibility of existence is logically included in the word-function of man. This logical inclusion, however, takes place differently from the way color is logically included in red or animal logically included in man, namely, by abstraction. The logical relation of less-explicit-than is a property of animal in relation to man. But the word-function of "animal" is not something logical as is the word-function of "possibility". And to say that the relation of possibility of existence is logically included in the word-function of "man" is not to say that the word-function of "possibility" is a non-logical feature of our experience as is what-it-is-to-be-an-animal. Rather, the possibility of existence is logically included in other word-functions because they terminate this logical relation. (Being is abstractable from *some* of the word-functions in which it is logically included; but even there the abstractability differs from the genus-species kind. This is the topic of Chapter Eleven.)

It does not follow, however, that what is objectified by "possible existent" is something logical. What is objectified by "possible existent" or "being" is *that which* terminates the relation of possibility, that which is objectified as capable of existing. This is something non-logical, the non-logical value that is identical with word-functions like those of "something red" or "man". No logical relation is capable of extra-objective existence. And to objectify things as beings is not to objectify them as related to a cognition-dependent value. As objectified by "possible existent", what are objectified by the word-functions of thing-descriptions are related to that which is supremely extra-objective, existence. But we are able to so objectify the objects of thing-descriptions because the relation of possibility is a logical property of the word-functions of thing-descriptions.

Thus the word-function of "being" is not the logical relation of possibility. The word-function of "being" is that which terminates this relation, that-which-is-capable-of-existing. But the manner in which the word-function of "being" (taken as object or as means of objectification) relates things to existence is characterized by the use of the logical relation of possibility. For example, metaphysics, the study of beings as beings, objectifies things as possible existents. (See section 5.5.2.)

That the relation of possibility characterizes the word-functions of "being" and other thing-descriptions no more prevents these word-functions from objectifying actual existents than the fact that they are characterized by universality prevents them from objectifying individuals. When it is true that something exists, that which is objectified as capable of existing by the word-function of "being" is identical with that which is objectified as actually existing by the judgment of existence. Just as the word-function of "man" is what some extra-objective thing is, so the word-function of "being" is what our primary objects are, namely, existents.

That being objectifies things as capacities for existence implies nothing concerning the real distinction or real identity of what exists with its existence. That which exists may or may not be identical with its existence. It is not objectified as identical with its existence when objectified by thing-descriptions or by "being". In other words, *that which* bears the relation of capacity for existence as term of a certain kind of objectification may be identical with its existence in its state as more-than-an-*object*. Possibility is a logical relation terminating in existence as that which is objectified in judgment, not an ontological relation to existence as something really distinct from that which exists.

Even though the word-function of "being" relates things to what may be really distinct from them, the necessary truth of "If something is red, it exists", is logical, not causal. For the relation to existence that is in question is a logical relation. The reason this logical relation attaches necessarily to the word-functions of thing-descriptions is causal, the goal that the efficient cause of sentential objectification is trying to achieve. But the fact that the explanation of this and other logical necessities is causal does not make the effect being explained belong any less to the domain of the logical.

This analysis of "being" can be reinforced by replying to some objections. It may appear that the doctrine that existence enters the language by means of judgments contradicts the doctrine that existence and being are our most fundamental word-functions. For in order to judge that an apple exists we must have given "apple" a meaning$_T$. Therefore the meanings$_T$ of thing-descriptions like "apple" are cognized prior to the meaning$_T$ of "exists" and, consequently, to the meaning$_T$ of "being". And if acquaintance with meanings$_T$ like apple are prior conditions for becoming acquainted with existence and being, how can existence and being be the most fundamental word-functions in language?

As we saw in section 5.3.1, language-forms whose meanings$_T$ are the same as those of "exists" or "being" are not the first to enter language in the lexicological sense. But when these meanings$_T$ do enter the language lexicologically, we are able to see that the meaning$_T$ of "being", which is a function of that of "exists", is something logically included in the meanings$_T$ of other thing-descriptions. In other words, once in possession of means of expressing the meaning$_T$ of "being", we can enunciate the fact that other thing-descriptions have all along been objectifying things as beings. Likewise, we may not acquire the use$_L$ of "organism" until long after we have acquired that of "man". But when we do, we are capable of knowing that "organism" expresses something that "man" expresses in a more determinate and detailed manner.

If it were not the case that language had all along been objectifying things in such a way that they were capable of being judged to be actual existents, language could not exist because it could not be publicly communicable. Not only must the primary objects objectified in a public language be real existents, but they must be recognizable as such. If not, we could not know the truth of sentences about them, for it is because they exist that predicates can be truthfully asserted of them.

To say that the word-function of being is logically included in that of our primary thing-descriptions, is not to say we are acquainted with the word-function of being before we judge the existence of anything. Prior to judging existence (in the causal, not temporal, sense of priority), we are not acquainted with it as something linguistically objectifiable (although we are acquainted with it at the sense level). But the word-functions we are acquainted with prior to the judgment of existence are objectified with the logical relation of possibility. That is, they are objectified so as to be capable of employment in such a judgment. Therefore the relation of possibility—and the judgments for which meanings$_T$ are objectified—has existence for its term, as a matter of fact. Possibility is the possibility of existing. (This point apparently escaped Kant when he made causality and other ontological word-functions conditions for the possibility of something being an object of experience rather than, more simply, conditions for the possibility of something; and had Kant adopted the ontological point of view, he might have noticed that a condition for the possibility of experience is a condition for the possibility of the existence of experience, that is, a cause.)

Even though we are not acquainted with the word-function of "existence" as linguistically objectifiable merely through our acquaintance with the word-functions of thing-descriptions, when we are acquainted with the latter word-functions, a relation is present that has existence for its term. Since existence is its term, we cannot linguistically objectify that relation unless we linguistically objectify existence. But since that relation to existence is present all along, the word-function of "being", *that which has* this relation to existence, is logically included all along.

Another difficulty concerning the word-functions of "exists" and "being" is provided by what is known as the excluded-opposites argument. We have encountered this argument already. Supposedly a word cannot be descriptively significant unless its function is to distinguish some things from other things. A word that would be applicable to everything would serve all purposes and, therefore, serve no purpose. But "exists" and "being" distinguish their referents, quite literally, from nothing. Consequently they appear to be meaningless. When I discussed this argument above, I pointed out that it involves the epistemological fallacy of identifying the functions of words with the conditions under which word-functions enter the language. And while "exists" does not distinguish things from one another, it can distinguish linguistic *objects* from one another; some do and some do not really exist. Likewise, "being" distinguishes those objects that are actual or possible existents from those objects that are not actual or possible existents. (The sense in which being is logically included in a logical relation, for instance, does not make it correct to call a logical relation a being. See section 5.4.1.)

But there is a more fundamental defect in the excluded-opposites argument. For a word to be predicable of everything is not for it to serve all purposes (and therefore serve no purpose). A word can be predicable of everything without saying all there is to say about everything. Specifically, there are things to be said about being in general which "being" itself does not say. We need other words to serve those purposes. For example, all beings are identical with themselves, are terms of causal relations, are capable of being objects of knowledge. "Identical with itself", "term of a causal relation", and "capable of being an object of knowledge" do not tell us what "being" tells us. (For another example, see section 9.4.1; and see Quine, 1969, p. 52.)

To explain the plausibility of the crypto-Berkeleyan interpretation of the non-predicate thesis, we have been examining properties peculiar to the word-functions of "exists" and "being". It is not at all impossible that such properties, especially the fact that we become acquainted with existence by making judgments and the fact that ordinary predicates are functions of arguments subject to existential quantification, could provide the basis for an acceptable non-predicate theory. But a valid non-predicate theory would be one that did not make "exists" an object-description or some other kind of logical construct and allowed it to be true of things as things. Such a theory would support the legitimacy of ontological method rather than oppose it.

One final comment on the non-predicate theory. Sometimes associated with this theory has been the belief that sentences like "That exists" are necessarily true and sentences like "That does not exist" are contradictory. But the truth of "That exists" is contingent as far as our knowledge is concerned, because the identity of the thing which happens to be here and now objectified by "that" with something that exists is, as far as we know, contingent. It is no more necessary for what I am calling "that" to exist, than it is for me to exist.

What might lead us to think that "That exists" or "I exist" cannot be false are certain necessarily true conditional sentences of which these sentences are the consequents. It is necessary that if I am conscious, I exist, since the assertion that I exist is logically included in the assertion that I am conscious. Therefore, whenever I am in a position to consider the question of my own existence, it is necessarily true that I exist. But my being conscious, and therefore in a position to consider my existence, is a contingently true state of affairs.

Likewise, if we are in a position to use "that" to designate something currently present in our sense experience, and if we are not hallucinating, what we are using "that" to refer to exists. For the assertion that an object exists differs only by logical relations from the assertion that it is experienced as actually existing and the experience is not a *delusion*. But it is contingently true that something is present in sense experience and that we are not hallucinating. Just as we take the contingent fact of consciousness for granted when we say "I exist", we take the sensible presence of the object for granted when we say "That exists". Both "That does not exist" and "I am not conscious" are false, but they are contingently false as far as our knowledge is concerned.

5.4 Existence and Logic

Now we are in a position to complete the consideration of logical necessity in the light of our understanding of the word-functions of "exists" and "being". To accomplish this, I will first discuss the relations of cognition-dependent objects to the word-function of "being" and then look back at the analysis of logical necessity to see it as an example of ontological analysis.

5.4.1 Being and cognition-dependent objects

How can it be that existence and being are logically included in those word-functions that are cognition-dependent objects? In the case of objects attained by combining or deleting features of that which is present in experience, there is no difficulty. If a word-function combines features of what is present in experience, each of the component word-functions is a word-function objectifying things as capacities for existence. If a word-function deletes features of experience from other features of experience, the remaining word-functions objectify things as possible existents.

But what about cognition-dependent objects that are not objectified as even possibly extra-objective existents? The logical inclusion of being in such cognition-dependent objects can mean one of two things. The first concerns those cognition-dependent objects, including logical relations, which are relations terminated by real existents but which are not themselves real existents. Self-evidently, we objectify relations as such only by objectifying them as relations to terms, for reference to a term is the meaning$_T$ of "relation". Hence, when we linguistically objectify relations terminated by real existents, real existents are included among our objects. And although we can later attribute logical relations to other cognition-dependent objects, such relations are first perceived as characterizing real existents like language-acts, language-forms and what is objectified by their means.

The second way in which it can be argued that being is logically included in cognition-dependent objects points to the fact that our linguistic means of objectifying cognition-dependent objects must be the same as or derived from linguistic devices whose purpose is to objectify cognition-independent existents. Consequently the logical relations characterizing our discourse about cognition-dependent objects must be the same as, or at least derivable from, the logical relations characterizing our discourse about real existents. For logical relations are characteristics of means of objectification as means of objectification and of objects, not as capable or incapable of real existence, but as objects. Therefore it should be no surprise if cognition-dependent objects are characterized by the same logical properties as are real existents.

The word-functions of predicates for logical constructs, for example, do not logically include the possibility of extra-objective existence. But as in the case of predicates for extra-objective things, what is objectified by a predicate for a logical construct is objectified as possibly more than what-is-objectified-in-this-way; that is, it is objectified as eligible to be judged identical with what is also objectified in some other way. And as in the case of predicates for extra-objective things, this logical eligibility is eligibility for existential quantification. For we have already seen that we use existential quantification to attribute predicates to logical constructs because real existence is what causes the truth of attributions to those objects for which language comes into being.

What cognition-dependent objects and real existents have in common is the status of being objects and therefore of terminating logical relations; they differ with respect to being or not being more-than-*objects* and therefore with respect to things other than the terminating of logical relations. And if in dealing with cognition-dependent objects we invent language-forms and word-functions with logical properties not characteristic of the language with which we objectify real existents, we must be able to explain our neologisms by means of linguistic tools that are already available. Therefore the logical properties operating in our objectification of cognition-dependent objects at the very least *presuppose* the logical relations operating in our ojectification of real existents.

To illustrate, let us consider an example that might appear to argue for the contrary. The necessity of the laws of logic derives from logical relations. Therefore the same logical laws which govern our discourse about real existents must govern our discourse about logical constructs.

But the relations between the formulas of multi-valued logics are logical constructs that appear to constitute counter-examples to this claim. For in multi-valued logics, laws which are supposed to be necessarily true for sentences objectifying real existents can be neither true nor false.

But it remains the case that multi-valued logics are *governed* by the same necessarily true laws of logic, like the principles of non-contradiction and excluded middle, that govern our discourse about really existing things. The problem of the Achilles-Tortoise paradox is the same whether we are dealing with two-valued or multi-valued systems. Infinite regress in inferences can be avoided only by inferences whose validity is self-evidently necessary (that is, whose invalidity is self-evidently contradictory.) The validity of such inferences must be expressable by truths of logic which may or may not be interpretations of any formulas of the system. For a system to be governed by a law of logic is not equivalent to its containing a formula for which that law is an interpretation.

To this we can add that if a system does contain a formula for which a law governing the system is an interpretation, the system need not be interpretable as always assigning that formula the value truth. For the self-evident necessity required by the inferences of the system may be expressible only in sentences about a system and not in the system itself. Assume we are dealing with a formal system whose formulas can be assigned M in addition to being assigned T or F. Given the ordinary word-functions of "or" or "not", it is a necessary truth about such a system, and its opposite necessarily false, that a formula is either assigned a T or not assigned a T, either assigned an M or not assigned an M, etc. If not, the word-functions of "or" and "not" in ordinary language would both be and not be what they are; alternation would not be alternation, and negation would not be negation. And it can be necessarily true, and its opposite necessarily false, for such a system that a given formula is to be assigned an M and not a T or an F. For given the word-functions of the system's constants, all sets of T-F-M assignments to a formula's component formulas may assign the formula M. Therefore, the formula could be assigned a T or an F if and only if the set of all T-F-M assignments to the component formulas was also not the set of all T-F-M assignments to the component formulas, or the word-functions of the constants were also not the word-functions of the constants.

In other words, multi-valued logics are governed by two-valued logical laws in the sense that these laws govern sentences in the metalanguage that are *truths* concerning the formulas of the system, including sentences made necessarily true, and their opposites necessarily false, by word-functions established by the system's definitions, rules and/or axioms. A multi-valued logic that would not in this sense be governed by the principle of non-contradiction would be valueless.

Why? The necessity of the principle of non-contradiction derives from the word-function of negation signs, that is, the relation other-than. This logical relation cancels whatever it is that has been objectified in some way. Contradiction therefore deprives sentences of their goal, their teleonomic cause, which is knowledge of the identity of what has been objectified in diverse ways. Because contradictory sentences cannot achieve this goal, they cannot be true.

But what is it that is objectified by means of language in the first instance? Beings, real existents. It is because beings are objectified linguistically that negation enters the language. And it is because knowledge of the identity of what has been linguistically objectified with what exists extra-objectively is the primary goal of sentences (or because "being is the formal object of the intellect" in the terminology of the realist school) that all our sentences must conform to the principle of non-contradiction. Contradictory sentences cannot be true because they cannot achieve the goal of making sentences which, in the first place, is the objectification of real existents. But they cannot achieve this goal because it is an *ontological* truth, not a logical truth, that a thing cannot both exist and not exist. To understand this, we must understand the ontological character of our previous analysis of logical necessity.

5.4.2 The philosophy of logic as ontological analysis

In knowing the truth of the sentence "It is impossible for a thing to both exist and not exist", we also know the truth of the sentence "It is impossible for 'A thing both exists and does not exist' to be true". The first sentence is an ontological truth, a truth pertaining to things as existents. The second sentence is a logical truth about a means of objectifying things, specifically, about a sentence. In knowing the second, we know that a sentence using the logical relation of negation in a certain way cannot be true. Now if the first sentence could be false, that is, if a thing *could* both exist and not exist, the second sentence would be false, that is, a contradictory sentence could be true. But the reason things cannot manage to both be and not be is not that contradictory sentences cannot be true, that they cannot achieve the goal they are supposed to achieve. The reason "A thing both exists and does not exist" cannot give us knowledge of the identity of what is objectified in these diverse ways is that a thing cannot both be and not be. Otherwise, the way things exist would be an effect of the way we make them our objects, namely, by means of sentences characterized by truth.

Truth, or falsehood, results from the identity, or the lack of identity, between what has been objectified and what exists. That it is impossible for "A thing both exists and does not exist" to be true follows from the fact that it is impossible for what exists to be what does not exist. Since the goal of sentences is knowledge of the objectification of extra-objective existents and since it is impossible that a thing exists and does not exist, it is impossible for a sentence saying or implying as much to be true, that is, to achieve the goal of sentences. And if the sentence "It is impossible for a thing to both exist and not exist" is not an ontological sentence objectifying things as things, it is a logical sentence objectifying things as objects. But then to exist is to be an object of knowledge, for in this sentence, things are objectified by means of the word-function of "exists".

Granted, whether we are talking about the ontological or the logical principle of non-contradiction, the necessity of the principle derives from the *logical* relation of negation. But we know from section 4.1.1 that it cannot follow from the fact that a sentence owes its necessary truth to the use of a logical relation that the sentence objectifies things as objects rather than as things. Again, there are necessary truths about objects and means of objectification telling us that when sentences use logical relations in certain ways, they are necessarily true. These necessary truths about objects and means of objectification are laws of logic. But laws of logic pertain to sentences that in the first instance are sentences in which things are not objectified as objects but as things. Otherwise, truths about ways in which we objectify would not be truths in which we objectify *things*. If extra-objective things are not included among the terms of the relations that generate the logical necessity of sentences, then either we do not know extra-objective existents, or there are no extra-objective existents; that is, to be is to be an object of knowledge. Therefore sentences objectifying things as things can be as logically necessary as can sentences, like the laws of logic, objectifying things as objects.

The necessity of the *ontological* principle of non-contradiction (and of the ontological principle of excluded middle, a thing either exists or does not exist) derives from logical relations. Therefore laws of logic tell us that these principles are necessarily true. But in saying that laws of logic tell us that ontological principles are necessarily true, we are not saying that ontological principles are to be deduced from logical principles. That would be an epistemological fallacy. On the contrary, knowledge of things as existents (the sphere of ontological truth) is causally prior to knowledge of things as objects (the sphere of logical truth). To say that logical laws tell us that ontological principles are necessarily true is simply to say that the necessity of the ontological principles derives from the way they employ logical relations in objectifying things. And the objectification of things as things remains prior to the objectification of things as objects.

In generating necessary truths about things as things, however, logical relations also generate necessary truths about things as so objectified. And these truths pertain to anything that is so objectified, cognition-dependent objects included, because the same logical relations are involved. Our means of objectifying non-beings derive from, and presuppose the laws governing, our means of objectifying beings. Therefore contradictions cannot be true of cognition-dependent objects because, if they were, cognition-independent things could both exist and not exist. In both cases, it is the same relation of negation operating to cancel what has been objectified in some way. But negation can be used to cancel the objectification of cognition-dependent objects only because it has entered the language to cancel the objectification of real existents.

In other words, since being is that goal of our use of sentences without which they would be able to achieve no other goal, being is *logically* included in all our descriptions in the sense that the logical laws which govern our objectification of being must govern the objectification of all our objects. But the logical principle of non-contradiction governs sentences objectifying beings because the ontological principle of non-contradiction is necessarily true of all beings.

Reflecting further on the sentence "It is impossible for a thing to exist and not exist" will give us a clearer idea of what it means to call philosophy ontological analysis. This sentence not only informs us of something necessarily true of things as existents rather than as objects, but also informs us of something true of things as existents rather than as this or that kind of existent. "It is impossible for what is an apple to at the same time not be an apple" is a truth pertaining to apples not because they are a particular kind of fruit but because they are capacities for existence. And ontology informs us of what must be the case for things insofar as they are existents. It does not tell us what must be the case for this or that particular kind of existent unless what distinguishes that particular kind of existent from others can be defined, that is, causally analyzed, by means of ontological word-functions. Does "It is either raining or not raining" give us any information about the weather? It does not tell us about the weather as weather, as one domain of reality distinguishable from others. For it does not tell us anything true of the weather that is not also true of every other kind of being. But it does tell us about the weather as a kind of being (actually a collection of kinds of being), with no further qualification. For it tells us something that pertains to weather and to any other capacity for existence insofar as they are capacities for existence.

My analysis of logical necessity has clearly been an ontological analysis. Necessity itself has been defined in terms of the contradictoriness of something's both being and not being what it is. "Something's being what it is" enters the language to refer to extra-objective things and is extended to refer to any object objectifiable, like extra-objective things, by means of predicates. (A contradiction occurs in the domain of cognition-dependent objects if the truth of a sentence requires that such an object be both objectifiable and not objectifiable by some predicate. Because we use existential quantification to attribute predicates to cognition-dependent objects, we speak of such an object's being objectifiable by a predicate as its being what it is.)

And since language is public, the word-functions of "exists" and, therefore, of "being" have a necessary causal relation to the existence of language. Private objects are, at least, objects; therefore, for objects to be public, they must be more than mere *objects*. They must be real existents. The initial objects of our knowledge are not only existents; they are also red things, moving things, apples, hills, clouds, etc. But it is not as objectified by the meanings$_T$ of these descriptions that such objects have causal priority in knowledge—except insofar as the word-function of "capacity for existence" is logically included in these meanings$_T$.

Consequently my analysis of the causal priority of real existents over cognition-dependent objects among the objects of our knowledge has been an ontological analysis, an analysis in terms of causal relations terminated by ontological word-functions. And this causal analysis is the presupposition of the remainder of the account I have given of logical necessity. For logical necessity has been explained in terms of logical relations operating in the objectification of real existents, in terms of the achievement of the goal of sentences, which is knowledge of the identity of what has been objectified with what exists, and in terms of the need to objectify cognition-dependent objects by means of the same linguistic tools by which we objectify real existents. Note also that a causal analysis of logical necessity is not an analysis of being in general but of something associated with one particular kind of being only, linguistic knowledge. But the relevant properties of that particular kind of being cannot be adequately understood until they are analyzed by means of causal relations terminated by ontological word-functions. (For more on the specific kinds of causality involved, see sections 9.4.3 and 10.3.)

The ontological nature of this analysis explains why sentences whose opposites are contradictory are true in all possible worlds. Possible worlds are just a species of cognition-dependent objects, and we have just seen the connection between the impossibility of things both existing and not existing and the impossibility of contradictions being true of cognition-dependent objects. Sentences are not necessarily true because true in all possible worlds. They are true in all possible worlds because possibility is the logical relation of eligibility to be identical with something that exists, and contradictions do not objectify anything eligible for actual existence. Hence we say it is im*possible* for a thing to exist and not exist. "Possibility" without any further qualification ordinarily refers to the possibility of something's existing. To ask whether a sentence is true in a possibly existing world is to ask whether it is true *on the hypothesis* of the existence of that world. And to hypothesize that a world exists is to hypothesize that the ontological principle of non-contradiction is true of it.

Do these remarks about possibility in connection with necessary truth contradict what I said about possibility in connection with the word-functions of predicates? The logical inclusion of the possibility of existence in the word-functions of predicates means that we can use the predicate to form a judgment asserting existence. The judgment of course can be false. But can it be *necessarily* false if the word-function of its predicate includes the logical possibility of existence?

As a matter of fact, I have been using two senses of "possibility", one derived from the other. The primary sense is the possibility that what is objectified is identical with what exists extra-objectively. This is the possibility that is excluded by contradiction. The derived sense is the possibility of serving in logically well-formed judgments of existence. This is the possibility that characterizes the word-functions of thing-descriptions, and it is not excluded by contradiction.

Contradiction requires the objectification of something by more than one predicate and derives from the relation between the diverse ways in which the thing is objectified. Each of the diverse ways in which it is objectified, however, is itself non-contradictory. Therefore a single predicate can be given a word-function that is contradictory explicitly or by implication only by combining other word-functions that are not contradictory. A contradictory word-function includes the logical relation of possibility in the sense that it is logically eligible for use in a judgment of existence. It is not possible, however, that the word-function of a contradictory predicate objectifies something identical with what exists extra-objectively. Hence a sentence asserting existence of what is objectified by such a predicate is necessarily false.

It must be emphasized, however, that possibility in the derived sense is still a relation terminating in extra-objective existence. The possibility that characterizes the word-functions of predicates is a relation to extra-objective existence as objectified by judgment. That is what I mean by calling it derived. But the existence we objectify in judgment is extra-objective existence. (And again, the word-function of "being" is not this derived relation of possibility but is that which is objectified with this relation and, therefore, that which exists extra-objectively when sentences asserting existence are true.)

Finally, it should be understandable why the method of philosophy, essentially ontological and hence concerned with things as existents, is so often mistaken for that of logic, linguistics or some other discipline, like phenomenology, whose job it is to deal with objects as objects. Since its necessity derives from a logical relation, the principle of non-contradiction can appear to be a law of logic only. If the principle of non-contradiction does not pertain to things as things, how can a method which appeals to that principle to verify its assertions give us knowledge of things as things? Furthermore, how can the ontological principle of non-contradiction pertain to things as things if "exists" is an object-description? And if the crypto-Berkeleyan version of the non-predicate theory is not enough to cause us to confuse ontological sentences with logical sentences, the linguistic theory of necessity, with its failure to distinguish acquaintance with meaning$_T$ from acquaintance with meaning$_L$, is there to finish the job.

5.5 Anselmian Arguments, Conditionals and the Modes

Anselm introduced a way of arguing for the existence of God which has become known as the ontological argument. There is nothing wrong with describing arguments of Anselm's type as ontological. But in order not to overwork this word and to help make it clear that in defending a method which is specifically ontological I am not defending this kind of argument, I will refer to them as Anselmian arguments. Many consider the non-predicate view to be the definitive refutation of Anselmian arguments. To show that nothing I have said about the non-predicate view plays into the hands of those arguments, I will here present an alternative refutation. The refutation will call for further explanation of what has already been said about possible existence and conditional sentences. And these explanations will give me the chance to discuss reference to non-existents, "negative facts", contrary-to-fact conditionals and modal operators.

5.5.1 Anselmian arguments

In giving Anselm's name to these arguments, I am not unaware of the different formulations they have received. The refutation that follows is intended to hold for any arguments which claim that the existence of an all-perfect being is self-evident or can be derived from self-evident premises and from self-evident premises alone. That is the issue. The issue is not whether the existence of an all-perfect being is necessarily true. For we must distinguish between necessary truth and necessary truth that is knowable as such by us. Lack of identity between the terms of diverse relations of objectification may require that one of these terms both be and not be what it is. But this may be the case without our being able to know that it is the case simply by understanding (in the non-lexicological sense) the meanings of words. Our question is whether acquaintance with word-functions alone is sufficient to enable us to see a necessary identity between what is objectified by "an all-perfect being" and something objectifiable as "an existent".

Why are these distinct objects supposed to be necessarily identical as things? Because existence is supposed to be a perfection. And how do we know that existence is a perfection? By our acquaintance with the word-functions of "exists" and "perfection". This is where the non-predicate view comes in. The thesis that existence is not an "attribute" can be read as a denial that existence is a "perfection". Therefore acquaintance with the meanings$_T$ of "exists" and "perfection" would not force us to admit that it is necessary for an all-perfect being to exist.

In order to refute Anselm's argument, however, we do not have to deny that existence is a perfection. To demonstrate this, I will assume, subject to one crucial qualification forthcoming shortly, that existence is a perfection. But whether or not it is a perfection, to go from "all-perfect being" to "something that exists" we must make use of the meaning$_T$ of "exists". To disarm Anselm's argument, therefore, it is sufficient to attack it from the point of view of whether acquaintance with the meaning$_T$ of "exists" can render self-evident any truth from which it necessarily follows that something, an all-perfect being or anything else, actually exists.

In other words, since the question is not one of the necessary truth of the all-perfect's existence but of our ability to know necessary truths about existence, *the question must be answered in terms of the way or ways existence can be made an object of our knowledge*. Even though it may be necessarily true that heat expands solids, our acquaintance with the word-functions of "heat" and "expands solids" is not sufficient to show the necessity of this truth. Does our linguistic objectification of existence enable us to know the existence of anything as a necessary truth?

As a matter of fact, we must distinguish different ways in which existence is made object of linguistic knowledge. Existence as that which is expressed by the grammatical predicates of sentences such as "A exists" is existence objectified in one way. Existence as what is referred to by words such as "existence", "to exist" or "state of existing" is existence objectified in another way. In the first case, let us say we are dealing with existence *as asserted*; in the second case, with existence *as mentioned*. Existence as mentioned is the same existence that is the word-function of "exists", and we become acquainted with that word-function through the process of making existence assertions. In asserting existence we do more than mention it. However, when we ask questions like "Is existing the same as being known?", "Is existence an attribute?", "Is existence a perfection?", "Is existence distinct from that which exists?", we are using a word-function we acquired by means of making assertions, but we are not using it to assert existence of anything.

The difference between existence as asserted and existence as mentioned lies in the mode of objectification, the manner in which existence is made an object of knowledge, not in that which is objectified. It is the same extra-objective existence that is made an object in both cases. The existence we mention when we ask whether to exist is to be known or whether existence is a perfection is the same existence that we assert when we say that apples exist. These distinct objects are extra-objectively identical. But are they *necessarily* identical? In all cases of affirmative truth, necessary *and* contingent, there is identity between the terms of diverse relations of objectification. So far then, nothing has been said to indicate that existence as mentioned, the meaning$_T$ of "exists" which Anselmian arguments rely on, is *necessarily* identical with existence that is true of anything.

Nor is there anything that could be said about the meaning$_T$ of "exists" which would indicate that it must be true of something. For these are not necessary truths: existence exists; something has existence. Compare these statements to some statements using the meaning$_T$ of "exists" which are necessarily true: whatever exists, exists; if something exists, it exists. The latter illustrates another way in which existence can be objectified, namely, *as hypothetically asserted* rather than *as categorically asserted*. Like categorical existence assertions, hypothetical existence assertions do more than mention existence. And making use of our ability to objectify existence as hypothetically asserted, we can recognize the necessary truth that *if* something exists, then existence that is mentioned *is* identical with existence that can be categorically asserted.

But it is also necessarily true that *if* nothing exists, then existence as mentioned is not identical with existence that can be categorically asserted. Of these two necessary truths, it is the antecedent of the first, namely, that something exists, that is true. But that something exists is a contingent truth as far as our knowledge is concerned. The word-function of "exists" does not even render it self-evident that existence exists. It is self-evident that if we are acquainted with the word-function of "exists", something, ourselves at least, must exist. But the antecedent of this conditional, namely, that we are acquainted with the word-function of "exists", is itself a contingent truth.

Because it is necessarily true that if something exists, it exists, however, there is necessary identity between existence as mentioned and existence as *possible*. In section 3.3.3, we pointed out that conditional sentences are true when what they objectify diversely are identical as possible existents. And that is how we use the word-function of "exists" when objectifying existence as hypothetically asserted. We do not use it to assert the actual existence of anything. We use it to construct a conditional sentence true (or false) of some thing as a possible existent: if something exists, then . . . . I will explain possible existence further in a moment. But if existence as mentioned is necessarily identical with possible existence, then it is also *necessarily* the case that, as far our knowledge is concerned, existence as mentioned can be no more than *contingently* identical with existence as categorically asserted.

There can be necessary identity between the terms of diverse objectifications if and only if the diversity in objectification derives from either of two sources, logical relations or necessary causal relations. We can disregard causal relations here for a number of reasons. Causal relations are relations between really distinct existents, and Anselmian arguments appeal only to the all-perfect's identity with itself. And if they appealed to causal relations of some kind, what would distinguish them from cosmological arguments for the existence of God? But most importantly, in "existence exists" diverse objectification is not accomplished by referring to distinct realities between which causal relations could hold. This absence of reference to distinct realities is precisely what produces the illusion of necessary identity. And the difference between existence as mentioned ("Existence . . .") and existence as categorically asserted (". . . exists") will show us that acquaintance with the meaning$_T$ of "exists" cannot render any categorical assertion of existence self-evident or derivable from the self-evident.

What about logical relations? There is necessary identity between what is objectified in the antecedent and the consequent of "If something exists, it exists" since the only differences between these objects consist in the logical relations of being an antecedent and being a consequent. But *more* than logical relations can diversify the terms of the diverse relations of objectification, existence as mentioned and existence as categorically asserted, in "Existence exists". Not that existence as mentioned is one reality and existence as categorically asserted another; when existence can be categorically asserted, what is thus objectified is the same as what is objectified by existence as mentioned.

But existence as mentioned is existence as possible. And "possible" is a *logical* predicate whose meaning$_T$ characterizes something as having been made an object of knowledge in a particular manner. By means of the logical relation of possibility (in both the primary and the derived sense), we accomplish the diverse objectification of existence as mentioned, or as hypothetically asserted, from existence as categorically asserted. But it does not follow that the difference between these objects consists only of a logical relation any more than it followed, in section 4.1.2, from the fact that the language-forms "F" and "non-F" differ only by a sign for a logical relation that the distinction between what is objectified by these language-forms is not a real distinction.

The existence that is objectified by a truthful assertion of existence must be more than the term of a knowledge relation. But existence as possible, existence as mentioned or hypothetically asserted, is existence that may *or may not* be more than the term of a knowledge relation. As negation cancels the reality objectified by "F", existence as possible objectifies what assertion has already grasped as more than the term of a knowledge relation in such a way that it is not objectified as *necessarily* more than the term of a knowledge relation. For as mentioned or hypothetically asserted, existence is not objectified as actually true of anything. And unless it is actually true of something, existence is not more than the term of a knowledge relation. But existence that is actually true of something is really distinct from being-known. Therefore, since existence as mentioned is existence objectified as possibly no more than an object of knowledge, existence as mentioned *may* be really distinct from existence as categorically asserted (in other words, it may be that nothing actually exists), just as non-Fs are necessarily really distinct from Fs. In both cases, the diverse objectification is accomplished by means of logical relations, but the differences between what is objectified need not consist only of logical relations.

It should be added that, whether mentioned or asserted, existence is more-than-an-*object* conceptually; that is, the word-function of "exists" is always other than that of an object-description. It is a means for objectifying things as things. But existence as mentioned or as hypothetically asserted is existence that may or may not be *more than conceptually* other than the term of a knowledge relation. Existence as mentioned or hypothetically asserted is actually the term of a knowledge relation and may not be actually more-than-the-term-of-a-knowledge-relation. When existence can be categorically asserted, however, existence is not only the term of a knowledge relation but also must be more-than-the term-of-a-knowledge-relation both conceptually and in reality. For if and when a thing really exists, its existence is really distinct from being-known.

Another way of putting it. The difference between actual existence and the lack of actual existence cannot be the presence and absence of a logical relation; if so, to exist would amount to being-known. But neither can the difference between existence as the term of a relation of categorically asserting (actual existence) and existence as term of a relation of mentioning (possible existence) be the mere absence, in one case, and the presence, in the other, of the logical relation of possibility. That would be like saying that, since "existence" differs from "non-existence" only by a negation sign, existence is to be equated with the absence of the logical relation other-than. But existence can no more be equated with the mere absence of a logical relation than with the presence of one. Since existence is really distinct from being-known, the difference between the actual existence of something and its merely possible existence is not the same as the mere absence of a characteristic, like possibility, attributable to objects only as a result of being known. The difference between them is the presence, in the case of actual existence, and the absence, in the case of merely possible existence, of something extra-objective, namely the actual existence of the thing.

Consequently the identity of existence as mentioned with existence as categorically asserted is necessitated neither by necessary causal relations nor by logical relations. Existence as mentioned is identical with existence as categorically asserted but as a matter of contingent fact rather than as a necessary truth. For as a matter of contingent fact, something does exist. It happens that what we are acquainted with when we know the meaning$_T$ of "exists" is something that can be truthfully asserted of things. But existence as mentioned, the meaning$_T$ of "exists", is not existence objectified as actually true of something. Acquaintance with the meaning$_T$ of "exists", therefore, cannot render self-evidently true *any* categorical assertion of existence. Since existence as mentioned is existence as possible, any categorical assertion of existence may be false as far as we are able to judge on the basis of word-functions alone.

Incidentally, this also allows us to state why no one-word sentence can be necessarily true, at least as far as our knowledge of it is concerned. By hypothesis, the truth of the sentence is not determined by the identity of what has been objectified in diverse ways. Hence the identity which renders the sentence true can only be identity between what is objectified by means of the sentence and what actually exists. Without the actual existence of something, there would be no term for the relation of identity. But the actual existence of anything must be contingent as far as our knowledge of it is concerned.

It will be responded that Anselmian arguments do not establish *any* existence assertion; they establish the existence only of an all-perfect being. And they do so not only by appealing to our acquaintance with the word-function of "exists" but also to our acquaintance with the word-function of "perfection". In other words, the self-evident premise that existence is a perfection is the inference-ticket which allows us to pass from existence as mentioned to the assertion of existence for the all-perfect.

But we can only get out of an argument what we put into it. If all we have put into an argument is existence as mentioned and not existence as categorically asserted, we cannot get existence as categorically asserted out of the argument. We can, however, get out of the argument anything that is necessarily identical with existence as mentioned. And existence as hypothetically asserted is identical with existence as mentioned. For conditionals, too, objectify existence as possible. Therefore whenever a truth is self-evident to us because of our acquaintance with the word-function of "exists", that truth concerns existence as, at most, hypothetically asserted.

In other words, the most that can be self-evident or derived from the self-evident concerning existence as a perfection is that existence is a perfection *if it exists* or, if you prefer, that *if something exists*, then existence is a perfection for it. (This is the qualification I promised concerning the assumption that existence is a perfection.) Nothing else could be self-evident or derivable from the self-evident. For what is self-evident is known by acquaintance with word-functions. Acquaintance with the word-function of "exists" is not acquaintance with the existence of anything as categorically asserted. Acquaintance with the word-function of "exists" is acquaintance with what is necessarily identical only with the existence that is objectified by hypothetical assertions. Therefore the only necessity that this word-function allows us to recognize is necessity involving hypothetical assertions of existence. Existence objectified by categorical assertions is not among the givens from which Anselmian arguments proceed; therefore it cannot be among the conclusions at which it arrives.

If the conclusion is that the all-perfect exists *necessarily*, we must qualify this by adding that *if it exists*, it exists necessarily. This is not the place to argue about what sense "necessary existence" could have. In light of the distinction between the necessity of a truth and its knowability to us, the necessity of existence could mean that the assertion that an all-perfect exists, unlike other existence assertions, is necessarily true in itself even if not knowable as such to us. (See section 6.1.3.) The important thing to note here is that denying sense to necessary existence is not the way out of Anselmian arguments. The way out is to demonstrate that all necessary truths about the all-perfect's existence are hypothetical. Opponents have often claimed that Anselmian arguments prove only that *if* an all-perfect being exists, it exists necessarily. Now that claim has been demonstrated.

And in so demonstrating it, we have replied to that variation of the argument in which it is not existence but the necessity of existence that is a perfection. (See, for example, Malcolm, 1964.) Each perfection of the all-perfect is hypothetical in the sense that if the all-perfect exists, it possesses that perfection. If knowledge, power and immortality are perfections, it is necessarily true that if an all-perfect being exists, it has knowledge, power and immortality. Likewise, it is necessarily true that if the all-perfect exists, its existence is necessary; for the necessity of existence is a perfection. But the fact that the necessity of existence is a perfection no more gets us to existence as categorically asserted than does the fact that knowledge and power are perfections. For just as the statement that existence is a perfection uses existence as mentioned rather than as categorically asserted, the statement that the necessity of existence is a perfection uses necessary existence as mentioned rather than as categorically asserted. And just as existence as mentioned can be shown to be necessarily identical with existence as hypothetically asserted and, therefore, not with existence as categorically asserted, it can be shown that necessary existence as mentioned is necessarily identical with hypothetically asserted, and therefore not categorically asserted, necessary existence.

In addition, this type of Anselmian argument is meant to be innocent of the assumption that existence is a perfection. It is difficult to see, however, how the necessity of existence can be a perfection unless existence itself is a perfection. If the necessity of existence means, for instance, that the statement "An all-perfect being exists" is necessarily true, then it means that it would be contradictory for what is objectified by "an all-perfect being" not to be identical with what is objectified by "an existent". But where is the contradiction if the meaning$_T$ of "exists" is not a perfection? And on any interpretation of necessity, what perfection do we deny to the all-perfect if we attribute to it no more than necessary existence as hypothetically asserted? Only if *actual* existence, existence objectified by truthful categorical assertions, would be a perfection for the necessary existent, would the all-perfect's perfection require that necessary existence by asserted of it categorically rather than hypothetically. For when we have granted that an all-perfect being must exist necessarily *if it exists*, what perfection associated with existence have we failed to grant, unless the fulfillment of the hypothesis "if it exists" is itself a perfection? We are back at the premise that existence is a perfection. As a matter of fact existence would be as much a perfection for a necessary existent, if a necessary existent should exist, as it would be for anything else that might happen to exist. But existence, or the necessity of existence, would be a perfection of a necessary existent only on the hypothesis that a necessary existent exists.

Plantinga (1974) has argued that if the all-perfect's existence is *possible*, then it is necessary. But this gets us no further. From the fact that if an all-perfect being exists, it exists necessarily, it follows that if an all-perfect being does not exist, it is impossible for it to exist. If the all-perfect was capable of both being and not being, its existence would be contingent. Therefore, if it does not exist, it is not capable of existence. Plantinga's insight that possibility implies necessity in the case of the all-perfect is correct. But atheists do not deny the existence of God as a matter of contingent fact; they deny the possibility of God's existence. (I owe my refutation of Anselmian arguments to the Renaissance philosopher Cajetan.)

5.5.2 Possible existents, non-existents and conditionals

This refutation of Anselmian arguments has relied heavily on the ideas of possible existence and existence as hypothetically asserted. More needs to be said about possible existence in order to understand ontological truth, conditional sentences and reference to non-existents.

As we have just seen, the distinction between possible and actual existence is a distinction between diverse ways of objectifying the same extra-objective existence. To this we should add that when we use phrases like "actual existence" or "existence as categorically asserted" we may not be categorically asserting existence of anything; we may be only *mentioning* actual, categorically asserted, existence. If so, we are objectifying actual, categorically asserted existence *as possible*, not as actual. For there is no difference between the hypothetical assertion that something exists and the hypothetical assertion that something actually exists, since possible existence is the same existence that is sometimes actual.

Necessary ontological truths about existence can be said to objectify existence as possible, just as we can say that the opposites of these truths are *im*possible. Some philosophers are bothered by the assertion that necessary ontological truths objectify existence as possible. They think this prevents ontological analysis from knowing that which is outside the realm of the merely possible, actual existence.

The contradiction apparent in objectifying actual existence as possible is resolved by the fact that "actual" in "actual existence" refers to that which is objectified; it does not refer to a logical characteristic of the manner in which it is objectified. "Possible", as we have been using it, refers to a logical characteristic of a manner in which objects are objectified, regardless of the nature of that which is objectified. Describing its object as possible does not imply that ontological analysis fails to know that to exist is to be actual, not possible, and that existence is the mode of actuality without which there is no other mode. These latter truths are truths known about existence as extra-objective. Possibility is not that which is known about existence, it is a logical relation attaching to what is known about existence as a result of the fact that it is thus known.

If ontological sentences objectified existence in the same way that categorical existence assertions objectify it, these sentences could be true of what actually exists at the moment, but as far as we knew, they might not be true of what will actually exist tomorrow. For actual existence is contingent as far as our knowledge is concerned. Necessary ontological truths mention but do not categorically assert actual existence wherever actual existence is contingent. (See Cahalan, 1971.)

We saw earlier that to know the truth of a conditional like "(x) (Fx → Gx)" is to know that if and when something which is an F exists, it is identical with something which is a G; in other words, it is to know that possible existents objectifiable in one way are identical with possible existents objectifiable in another. About possible existents it can be asked what it is that terminates the relation of identity between diverse objects if the objects are not identical with something that actually exists? As terms of diverse knowledge relations, the objects are diverse. If, in addition to being objects, the objects do not exist extra-objectively, in what way are they identical?

The answer to this question is provided by the fact that existence is linguistically objectified by means of the act of judgment. In judgment we compare what is objectified by a description with what sense experience presents to us as actually existing. To the extent things are objectified by descriptions, they are objectified as capacities for existence but not as actually existing. Therefore things are objectified as possible existents from the very outset of their objectification in language.

To the extent that something is objectified as a possible existent, it is objectified as possibly identical with the terms of other relations of objectification, not identical with them as the term of this particular knowledge relation, but as something that is possibly more-than-the-term-of-this-knowledge-relation. (Diversely objectified cognition-dependent objects are possibly identical, not as what are objectified in this way or that way, but as possibly objectified in more than one way.)

What is it that terminates the relation of identity between diversely objectified possible existents? That which terminates any one of these diverse relations of objectification. For what terminates them is something objectified as possibly being more than that which terminates a relation of objectification. It is objectified as a possible existent, and as possibly an extra-objective existent, an object is possibly identical with other objects. (For a cognition-dependent object to be objectified as possibly more than what terminates this relation of objectification is simply for it to be objectified as capable of being judged identical with what is objectified in some other way.)

How, then, do we accomplish the feat of objectifying possible existents? We do so by behaving in certain ways, specifically, by using language-forms to perform the functions of predicates (and names, as I have argued). For by means of predicates, things are objectified as possible existents. Again, it is not the word-functions of predicates that are identical; it is things objectified by the fact that words are used for these functions that are identical. It is not what-it-is-to-be-an-apple that is identical with what-it-is-to-be-red; nor is being-a-member-of-the-class-of-apples identical with being-a-member-of-the-class-of-red-things. It is an apple, or a member of the class of apples, that is identical with something red, or a member of the class of red things.

The meanings_T of descriptions, in other words, are means for objectifying things. But must the objectified things be actual existents, possible existents, or can they be one or the other indifferently? The relevant fact here is not that the first objects attained in language must be actual existents. That is true. But that something actually exists does not enter our *linguistic* knowledge by means of using words as predicates or names. It enters by way of judgments. And what is judged is whether or not a thing objectified by a description or name actually exists. (Of course once we have grasped the actual existence of things in judgment, we can form descriptions of them as actual existents, for example, "the now existing trouble in the Middle East".)

Descriptions and names objectify things as possible existents. *It follows that we objectify non-existents by means of the same behavior with which we objectify actual existents.* For we use descriptions and names in objectifying actual existents, although descriptions and names do not objectify them as such. And to objectify non-existents is just to use language-forms as descriptions and names that do not objectify actual existents. Moreover, why should we not objectify non-existents by means of the same behavior with which we objectify existents? We first objectify things as possible existents; and a possible existent is one that, as such, *may not* be identical with any actual existent.

Hence no more is involved in the objectification of non-existents by means of descriptions and names than is involved in the objectification of existents. The same kind of behavior that constitutes the objectification of existents is the kind of behavior that constitutes the objectification of non-existents. The difference between the use of descriptions and names for objectifying existents and for objectifying non-existents is not a matter of the way objects are objectified but of whether or not objects are also *more-than-objects*. In speaking of the objectification of non-existents, to say that something terminates such a relation of objectification is just to say that the word-function of a language-form is, in the case of predicates, a means for objectifying merely possible existents or cognition-dependent objects or, in the case of names, an individual possible existent or cognition-dependent object.

When what is objectified by means of a thing-description is not something that is more-than-an-*object* other than conceptually—as in the case of false affirmative sentences ("A perpetual motion machine exists") or true negative sentences ("There is no perpetual motion machine")—there is no identity between the term of a relation of objectification and what exists extra-objectively. But we do not have to postulate, over and above what actually exists, a realm of negative facts to terminate relations of identity with what is objectified in negative sentences. To do so would be to confuse what it means to speak of something terminating a relation of objectification by means of a language-form (namely, that the language-form is used for a particular meaning$_T$) with what it means for what is objectified by means of a language-form to terminate a relation of identity with something really existing (namely, that what is objectified also has an existence which is other than being-an-*object*.)

But how does a merely possible or fictional object become that for which a name is used? A cognition-dependent object, for instance, has no status outside of the way we are using certain words. Must we not give a cognition-dependent object a name only by associating the name with a description, since the object is nothing more than what is objectified by a description? Thus Tolkien associated the name "Gandalf" with a fictional object described in various ways. And this account would imply that names objectify individuals by having descriptions or disjunctive sets of descriptions for their meanings$_T$—a view whose difficulties are well known.

There are at least two ways to avoid those difficulties. (Since the theory of names is not crucial to my analysis, I will not choose between these ways.) First, if some names objectify individuals by having descriptive meanings$_T$, it does not follow that all names must objectify in this way. Most of the difficulties with descriptive accounts of names concern names for actual existents. Why cannot names for (some?) actual existents objectify individuals otherwise than by way of description and names for cognition-dependent individuals objectify by way of description? This difference in the ways names objectify would correspond precisely to ontological and epistemological differences in that which is objectified.

The second way to avoid the difficulties with descriptive accounts of names is to point out that the relation between a name for a cognition-dependent object and the description it is associated with need not be that the description is the name's meaning$_T$ (or sense, or connotation, or whatever we may want to call it). Kripke (1972) has distinguished using a description to fix the reference of a name from making the description the meaning of the name. While I do not intend to endorse every application Kripke makes of this distinction, I want to suggest an application to a case where Kripke has not applied it, the case of fictional names. Why can we not use a fictional description to fix the reference of a name?

It might appear that, if cognition-dependent objects amount to no more than what are objectified by descriptions, there is nothing for a description to fix the reference of a name to. But the same cognition-dependent object can be objectified in more than one way, as we have seen already. It can even be objectified by non-cognition-dependent descriptions (as when we describe Gandalf as a character created by Tolkien rather than as the holder of the gray rank in the Order of Wizards). Therefore, even for cognition-dependent individuals, a description can fix the reference of a name without the description's being the meaning of the name. (A word-function is that for which a word is used. Therefore, when a name does not have a descriptive meaning$_T$, its word-function is nothing other than the individual, real existent or not, the name is used to objectify.)

My point here, however, is not to provide a specific explanation of reference to the non-existent. My point is that whatever causal factors may be needed to explain the linguistic objectification of non-existents are needed to explain the linguistic objectification of existents, for it is the same behavior that is being explained. Some have held, for instance, that in order to explain reference to objects that do not exist extra-objectively, a type of existence other than the ordinary has to be postulated, a mental existence described by such adjectives as "intentional" or "cognitional". That existence would provide a term for a knowledge relation to attain when ordinary existence is not available and, therefore, a way in which what are diverse as objects can be identical even if they are not identical as extra-objective existents. In this context, I must reemphasize that possible existence is *not* existence of another kind than actual extra-objective existence. It is the same existence that can truthfully be asserted of things as things, but it is that existence objectified in another way than as categorically asserted. Therefore possible existence is not what is meant by "intentional" or "cognitional" existence.

And the postulation of a specifically mental form of existence would not help us solve the problem of the identity of diversely objectified non-existents. When relations of objectification are diverse, cognitional relations are diverse; therefore cognitional existence does not provide an identical term for these relations. Rather, the terms of these relations are identical as possible extra-objective existents or as possible terms of other relations of objectification. The existence we attribute to possible existents when we quantify over them is real existence objectified as possible. The existence we attribute to logical constructs that cannot exist extra-objectively is just a replica of real existence, a cognition-dependent object that replicates the logical role real existence has as a result of causing our primary objects to truthfully terminate relations of objectification.

I am not denying, however, that there is such a thing as intentional existence, any more than I am denying the existence of concepts (in the psychological sense of that word). What I am denying is that anything is required to explain our objectification of non-existents that is not required to explain our objectification of existents. Since being an object is *other than* being an extra-objective existent, the fact that something exists extra-objectively does not explain how it terminates a relation of objectification, even objectification by "proper names". Therefore, before we explain how we objectify non-existents, we must explain how we objectify existents. When we have done that, there should be no additional problem about objectifying non-existents. (On the question whether intentional existence is required from this point of view, see section I.1.)

But what is it we are aware of when we are acquainted with the word-function of a language-form that does not objectify anything that exists? We are aware of the word-function of the language-form, what-it-is-to-be-an-F or what-it-is-to-be-a-member-of-the-class-of-Fs or the non-existing individual for which we use the name "*a*", etc. And what is it that exists when our awareness of the word-function of a language-form, or of what is objectified by means of that word-function, exists? That awareness itself. But how can such a knowledge relation be terminated by what does not exist?

As I argued in section 2.2.2, an expression like "D is nominating C" informs us only of D's behavior and not at all of the reality belonging to C. It may *imply* something about C but only on the assumption that C really exists. Our assumption, on the other hand, is that the terms of the relations we are dealing with do not really exist. Nor does D's nominating C imply that C exists. If, unknown to D, C dies while D is in the act of nominating C, D's behavior, the behavior objectified by "D is nominating C", will not change. Relations, in other words, do not have to have real existents for their terms any more than "C's being nominated by D" must express a characteristic belonging to the reality of C. To say that C "terminates" D's relation is not to say that something is really happening to C. (For more on reference to non-existents, see Deely, 1975b.)

We still have not answered the question *why* there is a relation of identity or non-identity between the terms of diverse knowledge relations in the case of merely possible existents, that is, when there is no actual existent that terminates these identity relations because it is what it is. Why is it true that if something were an F, it would also be a G? Or why is it true that if something were an F, it would be a non-G? When an F actually exists, there is something which either is or is not objectifiable as a G. But if there is no F, what is the reason for the truth or falsity of asserting "G" of a hypothetical F?

This is really the question of the truth of contrary-to-fact conditionals. There is no problem about counterfactuals when the identity or non-identity between the possible existents that are objectified is *necessary*. If logical relations or necessary causal relations between word-functions render the identity or non-identity of Fs and Gs necessary, those relations are the reason for the truth or falsity of the counterfactual. It is true that if something is an F, it is also a G because, if anything were an F without being a G, it would both be and not be an F.

But causal relations can be necessary without being knowable as such by deduction from the self-evident. Consequently belief in a counter-factual can amount to belief in a necessary causal relation, or to a conclusion drawn from such a belief, even if the relation cannot be deduced from self-evident truths. For the truth of a counter-factual can result from a necessary causal relation between word-functions even if the necessity of the relation cannot be known from mere acquaintance with word-functions. In addition, section 8.2 will show that induction provides evidence for necessary causal relations. For induction itself is justified by truths concerning necessary causal relations, truths that can be deduced from self-evident premises.

What about the much-discussed distinction between "lawlike" and "accidental" universals in connection with the problem of contrary-to-fact conditionals? Our discussions of causality and induction will show that causality is not to be defined by reference to the universality of laws. Instead, the validity of universal laws is a result of the necessary connections between causes of certain natures and effects of certain natures. And the same discussions will show how chance, which gives rise to accidental universals, is compatible with causal necessity. Hence causal relations both justify beliefs in the counterfactuals which are associated with lawlike universals and at the same time leave room for accidental universals. The epistemological distinction between the lawlike and the accidental universal, that is, how we know the accidental is accidental, can be accounted for similarly. (See section 8.3.1.)

Notice also that I am claiming no more than that the truth of counter-factuals *can* be a consequence of necessary causal relations and that belief in counterfactuals *can* amount to beliefs that such relations do obtain. Obviously, I am under no obligation to justify every use that has ever been made, or every use that one could attempt to make, of counterfactuals.

Finally, if it is asked why a cognition-dependent object objectified in one way is identical with a cognition-dependent object objectified in another way, the answer is to be sought in the means of diverse objectification that are used. Again, cognition-dependent objects can be diversely objectified both by means of logical relations and by reference to the terms of some real distinction. Logical relations can account for the necessary identity or non-identity of diversely objectified cognition-dependent objects. And objectification by reference to the terms of a real distinction can account for contingent identity or non-identity. Thus the identity of the cognition-dependent object I referred to last night with the cognition-dependent object I referred to this morning is a consequence of the contingent fact that I behaved in certain ways last night and this morning.

5.5.3 Logical modalities

In the foregoing, I have been using "possible" with reference to our objectification of things by means of names and descriptions (and by grammatical predicates such as "exists", if you do not want to call "exists" a description). Ordinarily, however, "possible" and other modal operators are defined with reference to the truth-values of sentences. But the truth-value of a sentence is a function of the identity with one another, or with actually existing things, of what are objectified by means of descriptions and names. Therefore modes should be understood as logical properties of the identity or non-identity of objects; and as a consequence of the fact that truth and falsity are determined by these relations of identity and non-identity, the modes also characterize the truth-values of sentences. For example, where the identity required for the truth of a sentence is possible (in the primary sense), it is possible that the sentence is true; where the identity is impossible, it is impossible that the sentence is true.

And since the modes are modes of the identity and non-identity of objects, we must say of them what we have said all along about identity and non-identity. Where there is truth, there is no real distinction between what is objectified, and hence terminates these logical relations, and what is also more than what is so objectified. Things terminate these logical relations only as a result of becoming objects; still things *do* terminate these relations. Relations of identity and non-identity have as one of their terms that which is objectified but as their other term that which is more than what is so objectified. So just as cognition-independent things terminate relations of identity and non-identity, they terminate modal relations like possibility. This is what is expressed by the phrase "possible existent". Because what is objectified in some way is a possible existent, a sentence asserting its existence is possibly true. And when the objectified thing actually exists, what is describable, insofar as it is an object, as a possible existent is identical with something existing extra-objectively.

The fact that things do terminate logical relation is what makes it possible for us to use words for relations like negation, conjunction, disjunction and, therefore, implication in descriptions of things as things, either empirical or ontological. Modal operators are likewise eligible for use in such descriptions. It is not the use of logical operators that makes such descriptions thing-descriptions. What allows them to objectify things as things is that the word-functions of the logical operators are relative to word-functions, and to what is objectified by means of them, by which things are objectified as things. And logical relations must be relations to such word-functions and their objects. If they were not, there would be nothing for them to be relative to. For it is by means of such word-functions that cognition-independent things become objects of linguistic knowledge.

Using logical operators in thing-descriptions is not the same as attributing logical relations to things as if they were features characterizing things in their extra-objective existence. Identity, for instance, is the relation by which we cognize the extra-objective existence of our objects as things. It does not follow that identity is a characteristic of things in their extra-objective existence rather than a characteristic attributable to them as a result of being mode objects. (A logical relation's property of having things for terms without being attributable to things as real existents might be described metaphorically as its transparency, the property of letting into knowledge, and of disappearing before, that which is extra-cognitional. Identity has this property and communicates it to other logical relations.)

From that point of view of this study, the most important examples of the use of modal operators in descriptions that are true of things as things occur in the formulas by which we objectify "necessary" causal relations; a *necessary* causal relation holds between A and B if and only if at least one of them *would not* exist without the other. To say that the modality of necessity can function in a description of things as things is not to say that the *existence* of these things is necessary. But among the features characterizing things in their cognition-independent existence are causal relations describable as necessary.

The use of modal terminology in describing these relations does not in any way compromise their cognition-independent nature. To say that a necessary causal relation holds between A and B is to say that if at least one of them exists without the other existing, it both is and is not. But that it is impossible for a thing to both be and not be is an ontological, not a logical, statement. It is a statement objectifying things as things, for it expresses the impossibility of a thing's being and not being, not the impossibility of a sentence's being true. Rather, it is the necessary non-identity between that which is objectified by "exists" (what exists) and that which is objectified by "does not exist" (what does not exist) which prevents a sentence whose truth would require their identity from being a true sentence. Therefore the use of the modal "necessary" in the description of a causal relation no more prevents the described from being a relation characterizing things as things than does the fact that the ontological principle of non-contradiction is characterized by the logical relation of necessary *truth* prevent that principle from being an ontological principle. Again, what allows a modal operator to be used in a description of things as things is the fact that the logical relation is terminated by a word-function objectifying things as things, in this case, the word-function of "exists".

The appropriateness of using modal operators in thing-descriptions can be better understood if we take note of another result of our analysis of logical modalities: our objectifications of things are characterized by modes even if we do not express this fact by means of modal operators. From the start, predicates and names objectify things as *possible* existents (in the derived sense). Even the indicative mood always has a modal function. In our initial judgments, we grasp the identity or non-identity of objects with actual existents. It is the function of the indicative in the categorical sentences that communicate these judgments to express the fact that the identity or non-identity required for the truth of the sentence is the identity or non-identity of objects with *actual* existents. But the truth of existence assertions, and therefore of any sentences in whose meanings$_T$ the assertion of existence is logically included, is *contingent* as far as our knowledge is concerned. (In different categoricals, for instance, in universal and particular categoricals, the modal significance of the indicative can be interpreted in various ways. But it always has some modal significance.)

Subjunctive constructions and the use of the indicative in conditionals, on the other hand, objectify identity or non-identity between possible existents. Therefore, when we are objectifying the kind of causal relation I am calling "necessary", the use of such a modal operator or of a modal construction like "would not exist without" is appropriate. For the relation being objectified is such that (to use a conditional with the indicative), if one of the terms, say A, exists without the other, B, existing, A both is and is not. And the identity between what exists and what does not exist is to be denied not only in the case of A but for all possible things; for anything, if it exists, it does not not exist.

In other words, the *kind* of identity being denied here is not the kind that is denied by the use of the indicative to express the identity or non-identity of an object with an actual existent. When the described relation holds between A and B, if what is objectified by "A" exists, it can fail to be identical with what is objectified by "something having this relation to B" only on a condition which excludes A from the possibility of existing, the condition that it both exists and does not exist. The diverse objects are therefore identical not only as actual but as possible existents. The non-identity of these objects is to be denied even if A does not actually exist since, if and when it exists, it is something having this relation to B.

It is precisely the job of hypothetical indicative constructions or subjunctive constructions to so objectify things that their identity or non-identity as possible existents is objectified. The word-function of "would not" in "A would not exist without B" is a logical relation indicating the necessity of the non-identity of A with something that exists without B also existing. If A is something that would not exist without B, then if A exists without B, A both exists and does not exist. The use of this kind of modal language-form in a description of a relation pertaining to things as things is a necessary *effect* of the fact that the word-function of the description is known to be the kind of relation that it is. Nor is there a contrast to be made between the sentential use of language-forms with modal significance and without modal significance, since all of our linguistic objectifications of things are modally characterized in one way or another.

But in philosophy it cannot be assumed that whenever we encounter words like "necessary", "contingent" and "possible", they are being used as modal operators. In the next chapter, we will see that such words have been used for meanings$_T$ that are unequivocally ontological, not logical.

CHAPTER SIX

Ontological Truth and Linguistic Relativity

Philosophical analysis is ontological analysis. Much empirical and logical knowledge enters philosophy, of course; it is not the case that all arguments found in a work of philosophy should be ontological. But to the extent that philosophy can do something for us that other modes of knowing cannot, philosophy is ontological. Ontological analysis constitutes a way of knowing what exists that is distinct from empirical knowledge. The words whose meanings$_T$ are fundamental to empirical analysis, that is, the words with reference to which other words are defined, are words for sensibly distinguishable features of experience. The words whose meanings$_T$ are fundamental to philosophical analysis are "exists" and its derivatives. Thus extra-objective existence provides philosophy with a point of view from which to discover truths that it is not the business of empirical science to discover, for existence is not a sensibly distinguishable feature of experience.

The preceding chapters have given examples of ontological analysis in epistemology, particularly in the philosophy of logic. We have seen the necessity of recognizing the causal primacy of extra-objective existents among the objects of our knowledge and of recognizing that the goal of sentential knowledge is identity between objects and extra-objective existents. The latter recognition is essential to the understanding of logical relations (like identity and otherness) of truths whose necessity derives from logical relations (like the principles of non-contradiction and excluded middle) and of the modes. Succeeding chapters will provide a further account of ontological method, its causal character, its distinction from and relations to empirical causal analysis, its relation to sense experience.

This chapter will make use of the ontological character of philosophical knowledge to refute linguistic relativism's account of truth, both necessary truth and contingent truth. In dealing with contingent truth, I will make use of the results of some ontological reasoning that can only be developed later when we are discussing causality. Specifically, it will be shown in section 8.2 that induction from experience and the requirement of simplicity in our theories have a basis in necessary truths of the ontological type, truths I will call "the principle of induction", "the search warrant" and "the principle of simplicity". Here it will be shown that, together with sense experience, these principles provide a non-relativistic basis for deciding between conflicting empirical hypotheses. Linguistic relativism can be criticized without appeal to ontological truths, however. And I will also refute it by pointing out its insurmountable internal difficulties.

6.1 Necessary Ontological Truths

To appreciate the power of ontological method in connection with conceptual relativism, however, we must first become familiar with a few more examples of necessary ontological truths and the ontological word-functions they employ. The examples to follow have not been chosen arbitrarily. Each of them is important for issues we have been or will be discussing; and each of them has played a significant role in the empiricist critique of metaphysics. These examples, finally, will illustrate something that was mentioned in section 5.1. Not every word for a possible way of existing is a word with an ontological word-function. To be an ontological word-function, a way of existing must be *distinguished* from other ways of existing by cognates of "exists".

6.1.1 Dispositions

Let us begin with the distinction between potency (capacity, ability, disposition) and act (fulfillment, achievement, accomplishment). To attribute dispositions to things is not, contrary to both some opponents and some *proponents* of the doctrine, to admit a halfway house between being and non-being. A given thing may be only potentially an F. But whatever is potentially an F is actual in other respects and is therefore a full-fledged existent. And the capacity for being an F is identical with an actually existing state characterized by features other than F. If not, the capacity for being an F would be nothing; for what is only potentially an existent is, absolutely speaking, nothing.

But precisely because to exist is to be actual in some respect, potentiality may appear to be a mere logical construct. How do we know that things have dispositions? By their actual behavior. Therefore disposition statements appear to be shorthand for statements about the actual behavior of things. Not, however, for categorical statements about behavior, for disposition statements can be true even if no categoricals asserting the existence of the relevant behavior are true. Disposition statements must be shorthand for contrary-to-fact conditionals to the effect that if certain conditions obtained, certain behavior would take place. And the word-functions of dispositional predicates are logical constructs used to make claims about the truth of contrary-to-fact conditionals. (See Ryle, 1949, Chapter Five.)

Now it is the case that if something has a disposition to be or do F, then some conditional assertion to the effect that it would be or do F in certain circumstances must be true. But if that were all the word-functions of dispositional predicates amounted to, dispositions would be defined by a knowledge relation, specifically by a relation to sentences of a certain logical form; and things would acquire dispositions only as a result of their being made objects of knowledge by means of such sentences. Dispositional predicates, in other words, would be object-descriptions.

Defining dispositions by reference to the truth of falsity of conditionals is *not* analogous to making use of words for logical relations in thing-descriptions. Logical relations have a place in thing-descriptions only to the extent they are relative to non-logical word-functions which, in effect, anchor the word-function of the description as a whole in the domain of the extra-objective. No such anchor is provided when we describe something solely by reference to the truth-values of antecedents and consequents. In conjunction with other things, such descriptions may *imply* truths about the described as something extra-objective. But if what is *expressed* by such descriptions is all there is to the described, to be for the described is to be an object of knowledge.

Concerning this way of explaining dispositions, I second Geach's remark that:

> I need hardly comment on Ryle's view that "the rubber has begun to lose its elasticity" has not to do with a change in the rubber but with the (incipient?) expiry of an inference-ticket. (1957, p. 7)

The same criticism would apply to any attempt to interpret dispositions as logical constructs or terms of knowledge relations. If A's capacity to become an F is no more than the term of a knowledge relation
or a cognition-dependent object, it is only because A has become an
object of knowledge that it has this capacity. (And does A have the
capacity to become an object of knowledge only because it has become
an object of knowledge?)

The meanings$_T$ of predicates which describe things as they are initially experienced by the senses are not dispositional. (See section
2.2.1.) Therefore acquaintance with the meanings$_T$ of dispositional
predicates involves an element of construction on our part that is not
true of those meanings$_T$ that are causally most fundamental, especially that of "exists". But this is "construction" in a psychological rather
than a logical sense. And it is not implied that acquaintance with our
most fundamental ontological and empirical meanings$_T$ requires no
construction in the psychological sense. It is not implied here, for instance, that we acquire our original meaning$_T$ for "red" by merely
performing the psychological act of abstracting it out of our sense experience. But whatever constructive activity might be involved in the
acquisition of our most primitive word-functions, the construction
necessary for dispositional predicates cannot be entirely of the same
kind.

In particular, dispositional predicates make reference to something
other than the described and to something that does not as yet even
exist. If A is describable as only having the capacity to acquire
characteristic F, A's being an F is a state of affairs that does not exist.
In other words, to objectify A as having this disposition, it *appears*
that we must make reference to a cognition-dependent object. A's
being an F is unlike a cognition-dependent object in that it is able to
exist extra-objectively. But A's being an F is like a cognition-dependent
object in that, *as long as* A is describable only as having the capacity
for F, that is, as long as this disposition is true of A, A's being an
F is something that *cannot* exist.

But it no more follows that a disposition which is objectified in this
way is a cognition-dependent object than it follows, from the fact that
the meaning$_T$ of "infinite" includes the logical relation other-than,
that an infinite space is a logical construct. Space may not be infinite.
But that is not proven by the fact that "finite" has a positive mean-
ing$_T$ and "infinite" a negative. For a distinction must *always* be made
between what characterizes that which is objectified and what charac-

terizes the means by which it is objectified. If this distinction could not be made, we could not know anything that was more than the term of a knowledge relation.

Rather than being cognition-dependent objects, the word-functions of most dispositional predicates are features characterizing things in their existence as things. A does not have the capacity for F because something has made A the object of its knowledge; A has the capacity for F because that capacity is one of the features constituting what A is. Specifically, dispositions are causal relations, relations of efficient causality in the case of dispositions to do something, active dispositions, relations of what I will call component causality in the case of dispositions to become something, passive dispositions. (Active and passive dispositions for the same achievement can be found in the same being, but the dispositions must be really distinct from one another. The same disposition, however, can be active and passive in different respects. To become the efficient cause of change B, a thing may need to undergo change A; hence the disposition that is active in respect to B is passive in respect to A. And sometimes in using the active voice to speak of the disposition to do something, we mean the disposition to passively undergo some change.)

The causal nature of dispositions makes it clear why the reference to non-existents in their objectifications does not reduce dispositions to cognition-dependent objects. A dispositional predicate relates the described to something other than itself. But that other enters the word-function of a dispositional predicate precisely as a possible way of existing to which the existent so disposed is causally related. Dispositions, again, are identical with actual states of things. But describing these states by dispositional predicates reveals something about them that simply describing them as actual states of things does not reveal: they are identical with causal relations to other (possible) ways of existing.

Explaining causal relations and, therefore, what it means to call dispositions causal relations will be the main business of the second half of this book. What is important to note now is that the meanings$_T$ of "disposition", "capacity", "potency", etc. and correspondingly of "achievement", "fulfillment", "act", etc. are ontological meanings$_T$. For the capacity to become something is the capacity to *be* something as the result of a change, the capacity to exist in a certain way. And the capacity to do something is the capacity to bring some state of affairs into existence. The fulfillment of any disposition, that to which the disposition is a causal relation, is the existence (or non-existence in the case of a disposition to cease being or doing something) of what was previously non-existent (or existent).

In this section, I have not been speaking of the capacity to exist but of the capacity to exist in some particular way, as an F or as something that does F. On the other hand, when I said descriptions and names objectify things as capacities for existence, "capacity" was used for the logical relation of possibility. But even with reference to existence itself, "capacity" and "possibility" need not be used only for a logical relation. On the view that essence and existence are really distinct, essence can be described as a capacity or possibility for existence. In that context, the meaning$_T$ of these words is a causal relation; they describe essence as a kind of component cause for existence. Finally, acquaintance with these ontological word-functions gives rise to knowledge of such necessary truths as: nothing becomes F unless it has the capacity to become F; nothing can be both potential and actual in the same respect at the same time.

6.1.2 Substance and accident

For linguistic empiricists and others, the substance-accident distinction is the classic example of a metaphysical theory that results from an epistemological fallacy, that is, from reading the manner in which things are known into our beliefs about the things themselves. The substance-accident distinction has been accused, for instance, of being an ontological projection of the subject-predicate sentence form. And it has been accused of being an extrapolation from an unsophisticated correspondence theory of truth, a correspondence theory which does not take into account the dependence of what is said in a language on that language's conceptual framework:

> There is an abiding temptation to read into "correspondence" a significance that transcends the limitations of the framework within which it functions. A proposition that is true and known to be true must, it is argued, correspond to what is the case in reality. Hence, the argument continues, by analyzing what a proposition says we can determine what reality is. This is essentially *modus tollendo tollens* argument. If the object did not itself objectively have the property attributed to it then the proposition attributing this property would be false. Therefore the object must have this property as an objective ontological determination of its mode of existence. And therefore, by implication, a metaphysics of substance and properties is justified. (MacKinnon, 1971, pp. 50-51)

Since MacKinnon cites Aristotle in this connection, he apparently means the substance-"property" distinction to be equivalent to the substance-accident distinction. But a substance's properties are not all accidents for Aristotle. If so, substance itself would be propertyless. However, it is not substance that is propertyless for Aristotle; it is a part of substance, prime matter. Form makes prime matter a substance of a particular kind and thereby gives it properties like being vegetable, animal or human. (Of course neither "property" nor "accident" are here understood in the sense of the predicables.)

And whatever may have been true for Aristotle, it is certainly not the case for such recent substance philosophers as Gilson (1956, pp. 30-31), Maritain (1937, pp. 217-238), Veatch (1952, pp. 95-97; 1969, p. 33) and Wild (1948, p.324) that the substance-accident distinction is made by reference to object-descriptions like "that of which something is predicated" and "that which is predicated". Nor is their way of making the distinction between substance and accident based in any way on the manner in which things are known. Instead, these philosophers use definitions like "that which exists in another" and "that which does not exist in another" for accident and substance respectively. The meanings$_T$ of these definitions are ontological; they are functions of the meaning$_T$ of "that which exists".

On the other hand, those committed to the view that all significant thing-descriptions are empirical have no choice but to explain "substance" and "accident" as words which have an epistemological or logical origin. But how can this kind of explanation be made to fit "that which exists in another" and "that which does not exist in another" (or "that which does not exist in itself" and "that which exists in itself")? In one and only one way. "Exists" must be explained as an object-description mistaken for a thing-description. And we have already seen where that interpretation of "exists" takes us.

The epistemological explanation of the substance-accident distinction would, however, apply to doctrine like that of the *Tractatus Logico-Philosophicus*. And in general, it is easier to demonstrate that the mistakes linguistic philosophers accuse classical metaphysicians of were made by other linguistic philosophers than it is to demonstrate that they were made by classical metaphysicians. In accusing traditional metaphysicians of the epistemological fallacy, linguistic philosophers are accusing them of what, by the very fact that they reduce metaphysical questions to questions of language, they are guilty of themselves.

Associated with the epistemological explanation of the substance-accident distinction is the idea that, Aristotle notwithstanding, substance would have to be a totally featureless entity since its features, the word-functions of the predicates attributable to it, are all accidents. It can be argued, for instance, that predicates whose word-functions are ostensibly what some Aristotelian substance is really do no more than relate the substance to its accidents. For example, if "animal" means something having sense faculties, the only feature "animal" attributes to things is the possession of a particular accident, since faculties are accidents for Aristotle. The same analysis must be given for the predicate "man" if "man" means an animal with the faculty of reason.

But predicates describing a substance as related to its accidents describe the substance, not the accidents; nor need such relations to accidents be something extrinsic to what the substance itself is. As will be explained below (section 9.3.2), a substance has at least a relation of component causality to its accidents; and that relation is *not* something other than the substance itself. Even in the case of accidents that accrue to a substance contingently, a substance is identical with a capacity for such accidents. For Aristotle, a human child is a substance that may have the capacity to become six feet tall. An insect is also a substance, but it may not have the capacity to acquire the accident of being six feet tall. This difference in capacities for accidents is not itself an accident. It consists in the presence and absence of a feature identical with the nature of one of the substances. Therefore, when we learn about a substance, say Socrates, that he is six feet tall, we are learning something about the substance of Socrates. We are learning that the substance has the capacity for this accident.

An Aristotelian substance is likewise identical with its relation to the causal principles, form and matter, that enter into its make-up. Being composed of matter and form is a feature of substance that is neither an accident nor a relation to accidents. Rather than being featureless, substance is the mode of being that is identical with the word-functions of descriptions like "capacity for being six feet tall" and "composed of matter and form". Such word-functions succeed in diversely objectifying the same substance by making reference to what is not identical with the substance, its matter, its form, its accidents. But it would be an epistemological fallacy to conclude from the manner in which diverse objectification is achieved that it is not the same thing that is being objectified. Each diversely objectified feature is really identical with the same substance.

This allows me to distinguish my views from so-called "ontologies of attributes" that populate the world with supposedly abstract entities like, features, qualities, and characteristics. Features are just what concrete things are, substantially or accidentally. Any abstractness associated with features results from their being made the word-functions of predicates and belongs to their mode of objectification, not to the word-functions themselves or to any entity objectified by their means. The word-function of "human" is what-it-is-to-be-something-human; the word-function of "musical" is what-it-is-to-be-something-musical. What exists in any given case is a concrete substance with substantial or accidental features like being human and being musical. In other words, it is an epistemological fallacy to hold that features must be abstract entities.

When a feature is accidental, the word-function of a predicate can be what the accident itself is, and not the substance that has the accident, as when "red" is used as a noun for a color and not an adjective for something having the color. In the first sense, the word-function of "red" is what-it-is-to-be-the-color-red. In the second sense, the word-function of "red" is what-it-is-to-be-something-having-the-color-red. In the latter sense, the word-function of "red" is what something having red is, at least in part. For what being red (adjective) amounts to is having the color red (noun) as an accident. Just as both the accident and the having of the accident can be the word-function of a predicate, so they can both be called features of a thing. (Features can also be logical constructs based on substantial and accidental features; see section 6.3.4. And logical relations are cognition-dependent features attaching to objects and means of objectification in the manner of accidents.)

It would be wrong to conclude from the last example that corresponding nouns and adjectives always objectify different things, one the accident, the other the having of the accident. In "Dave Brubeck is a musician" and "Dave Brubeck is musical", the word-function of both predicates can be what-it-is-to-be-something-having-the-accident-of-musical-ability. The differences need only be in the modes of objectification, not in that which is objectified.

Notice also that a feature a thing is said to *have* need not be an accidental feature really distinct from it. We can say that something is a man and has humanity (or is a substance and has substantiality). Again, the difference lies in the mode of objectification, not in that which is objectified. In the case of accidental features, the word-function of "having" happens to parallel a relation between really distinct terms; in the case of substantial features, it does not. Features need not be really distinct from that of which they are the features. (See sections 3.3.3 and 9.3.) These remarks on features in relation to word-functions, incidentally, illustrate that the identity theory of truth is independent of the substance-accident, thing-property or any other analysis of things as extra-objective things.

How do we decide whether a feature is substantial or accidental? By causal analysis. For accidents are causes; and their distinction from substance is asserted, not as the result of interpreting experience from an epistemological point of view, but to satisfy the demands of a causal analysis of experience. (See sections 9.4.1 and 10.6.)

Since substance and accident are ontological word-functions, the following self-evident truth is ontological: whatever exists exists either in another or not in another. (The necessity of this disjunction derives from its use of the logical relation of negation. But the terms of the disjunction are the presence or absence of the causal relation—component causality—objectified by "exists in another".)

And it follows from self-evident truths that if anything exists, substance exists. If there were nothing that did not exist in another, then everything must exist in another *ad infinitum* or circularly. But then such an infinite or circular series would be an existent that did not exist in another. In other words, the series of accidents existing in other accidents would be a substance.

Note that this has not been an Anselmian argument for the existence of substance. It does not prove that the existence of substance is a necessary truth. It proves only that the existence of substance is a necessary *consequence* of the hypothesis that something exists. But that anything at all exists is, for us, a matter of contingent fact. Note also that "substance" is not equivalent to "thing". As we are using it, "thing" is opposed to "object", not to "accident", and is consistent with a variety of ontological theories about what exists: events, processes, states of affairs, substances and their accidents, etc. On most philosophies of substance, for instance, not only is the color of the table an accident, but the table is an accident also. This would be true if the whole universe were one substance or each sub-atomic particle were a substance. Note also that "essence" or "nature" does not refer only to substance; for accidents also answer the question "What is it?"

6.1.3 Necessary and contingent existence

The reference to Anselmian arguments brings up the question whether necessity and contingency are only logical, and never ontological, categories. It is sometimes argued that necessary existence is a contradictory notion since necessity is a characteristic of truths and not of the things which truths are about. This is to accuse the concept of necessary existence of embodying an epistemological fallacy: necessity is a logical relation, not a feature characterizing the extra-objective existence of things. Once again, however, it is the accuser, not the accused, who is guilty of the fallacy.

If necessity is only a logical relation, so is contingency; contingency can be attributed to the truth-value of the sentence "A exists", but it cannot be attributed to the existence of A. It is the opposite that is the case, however. That the existence of the things we experience, and of our experiences themselves, is contingent is demonstrated by the fact that they have not always existed and can cease to exist. In other words, they are capable of not being, and that is what it means for their existence to be contingent.

A state of affairs may exist forever and yet be capable of not existing. The reason we know that the states of affairs we experience are capable of not existing is that they come into existence and go out of existence. And the reason we know that the existence of these states of affairs is contingent is *not* that sentences asserting their existence are capable of being false. On the contrary, the reason these sentences are capable of being false, and the reason we know these sentences are capable of being false, is that the states of affairs whose existence they assert are capable of not existing. Otherwise, the way a thing exists would be an effect of the sentences in which it is objectified. "Contingency" here refers to a way of having cognition-independent existence. Therefore the same must be true of "necessity", a necessary existent being one which is incapable of not existing.

It may be objected that the word-function of "capable of not existing" is to be classified as a logical construct, not because of the word-function of "exists", but because of the word-function that "capable of" has in this context. For such a capacity does not seem to be a disposition of the kind we have already discussed. Things cannot be disposed to total non-existence the way they can be disposed to cease being in this respect or that, for instance, to cease sitting or standing. The capacity not to be sitting or standing is an actual state of affairs characterized by features that can remain actual when the capacity in question is fulfilled. But the capability of not existing is not a capacity of this kind. For the fulfillment of that capability leaves nothing actual that could be identified as what was previously a capacity for non-existence. Rather, for a thing to be capable of not existing seems to mean that it is not impossible for the thing not to exist. And that it is not impossible seems to mean that it would not violate the principle of non-contradiction for the thing not to exist. Therefore the expression "capable of" in the definition of contingency refers to logical possibility, not to an ontological disposition.

But the truth of the statement that it is possible for a thing not to exist is an *effect* of what the thing is. If A's non-existence does not require that the word-function of "A" both be and not be what it is, the reason lies in the word-function of "A", namely, what-A-is. The word-function of "A" is not related, either logically or causally, to the word-function of "existent" such that it is contradictory for A not to be an existent. If we extend the use of the word "contingent" from truth to the extra-objective cause of that truth, we are not commiting an epistemological fallacy. Nor is it an epistemological fallacy to extend the use of the word "possibility" from the possible non-identity of what is objectified and what exists to the objectified itself, whose extra-objective nature causes this relation of possibility to characterize it as an object. An epistemological fallacy would occur only if we took characteristics of the object as object to be the cause of its characteristics as a thing.

A's existence is contingent, therefore, if and only if the following is true: if A exists, for A to have not existed or to cease existing is not for the word-function of "A" to both be and not be what it is. A's existence is necessary, on the other hand, if A exists and for A to have not existed or to cease existing is for the word-function of "A" to both be and not be what it is. For if A's non-existence requires that the word-function of "A" both be and not be what it is, it is the extra-objective nature of A that causes the necessary truth of "A did not not exist and will not cease to exist".

Like "Heat expands solids", "A did not not exist and will not cease to exist" may be a necessary truth even though we cannot verify it from acquaintance with word-functions alone. But acquaintance with word-functions is sufficient for us to grasp the necessity of such ontological truths as "Whatever exists is either capable of not existing or is not capable of not existing".

It is simply not the case that when "modal" words occur in philosophical discourse their meanings$_T$ are logical. One reason why so many philosophers have thought the opposite is their tendency to covertly idealize existence as in the usual readings of the non-predicate theory. But another reason is that necessary truths objectify things as possible existents rather than actual. And since our experience makes us aware only of contingent existents, the objects to which we most commonly attribute necessity are truths. Therefore "necessity" and, consequently, "contingency", "impossibility" and "possibility" come to be understood exclusively with reference to things as objects rather than as existents.

6.2 Reply to Relativism I:
The Ontological Reply

Now that we are more familiar with the nature of ontological necessary truth, the reply to linguistic relativism can proceed, first from the point of view of necessary truths and then from the point of view of contingent truths.

6.2.1 Necessary truths

How can we know whether the necessity of ontological truths has a value which transcends that of the quite contingent conceptual frameworks of the language in which they are expressed? The relation of any knowable necessary truth to extra-objective existence is hypothetical; if something is an F, then it is not a G. And according to the relativist, to claim that anything exists exactly as it is described by "F" or "G" is to attempt to transcend the limits of language. Descriptions "F" and "G" are linguistic devices whose use is valid on the assumption of the background features of the language which is their matrix, but any validity beyond that is accidental at best, not necessary. Consequently not even necessary truths would enable us to know that the meaning$_T$ of some description is identical with what something is in its extra-objective existence.

But in the case of ontological necessary truths, what is hypothesized to exist is existence itself or some function of existence. Such ontological meanings$_T$ can fail to be identical with what is extra-objectively the case only on penalty of contradiction; the only things they would not be identical with would be things that could not even possibly exist. If ontological word-functions are not more-than-*objects*, nothing is; for nothing exists extra-objectively. At the very least, ontological truths provide us with exhaustive divisions of possible ways of existing into which all things must fall. Whatever exists exists either in another or not in another, exists either contingently or necessarily, is caused to exist or is uncaused, etc.

And necessary truths of the ontological variety do more for us than give us exhaustive divisions of possible ways of existing. They license us to infer from one fact to another. From the fact that something exists, it follows necessarily that substance exists. From the fact that things undergo changes, it follows that they have passive dispositions.

From the fact that states of affairs come to be and cease to be, it follows that they exist contingently. (Their own relation to existence is contingent. Whether that existence is contingent in relation to the set of all its causes is another question.)

The linguistic relativist will no doubt balk at arguments which cite "facts". I will return to this point in a moment. First we must face the difficulty that word-functions like those of "existing in another" or "capable of not existing" are relative to those languages *in which they are able to be expressed*. In a language which does not contain word-functions of this kind, is it a necessary truth that everything exists either necessarily or contingently, or that everything exists either in another or not in another?

No. But it does not follow that truth is language-dependent in the sense that it changes from language to language. (And if it did follow *that* would be a statement which could cease being true in another language.) In the language of Euclidean geometry, it is not a truth that Napoleon was defeated at Waterloo. But this tells us nothing whatsoever about the identity or lack of identity between the meaning$_T$ of "Napoleon being defeated at Waterloo" and any of the events in European history. In the language of physics, it is not a truth that increased demand with constant supply will bring a rise in prices. Are the laws of thermodynamics true in the language of psychology? The laws of chemistry in the language of linguistics?

To establish that a truth is relative to its language *in the sense required by conceptual relativism* one must do more than note that there may be languages in which a truth cannot be stated. This deprives no terms of linguistic objectifications whatsoever of their identity with extra-objective things. In order for the truth-value of a sentence to be "absolute" or "objective", it is not necessary for the sentence to be translatable into every language. All that is needed is identity between what is objectifiable by the meanings$_T$ that, as a matter of contingent fact, the language-forms of the sentence happen to have been given and what actually or possibly exists. And this identity is to be judged by the evidence either of experience or of the impossibility of the opposite or a combination of both.

These remarks apply to all truths but especially to those of ontology. In ontology we are not dealing with hypothetical truths about the existence of extra-terrestrial life or of different kinds of non-Euclidean space; our hypotheses concern existence itself and ways of existing objectifiable by the affirmation and denial of functions of existence. Here there can be no question of reading our linguistic categories into the evidence. If some language cannot express the necessary truths of ontology, so much the worse for that language; there are truths about cognition-independent reality which human beings are capable of knowing but which that language cannot articulate for us. But we can with equal justice say so much the worse for the language of ontology because of all the truths it is not able to express.

All languages are *limited* in the sense of not being able to express every truth we are capable of knowing. But this does not imply that the word-functions of the descriptions in a given language are not identical with what exists extra-objectively. A language in which none of the language-forms has the function ''exists'' has in our language is lacking the lexicological capacity to do something our language is able to do. And the word-function for which lexicological resources are lacking happens to be that without which there would be no objects for any language to objectify.

6.2.2 Contingent truths

What about sentences whose truth-value is known not by the impossibility of their opposites but by the evidence of experience: sensation or introspection? The language-independent character of such truths is one of the alleged myths that linguistic relativism is trying to dispel. For the moment let us think of contingent truths of the ontological variety: something exists; more than one thing exists; things undergo changes, etc. If such facts are challenged by the relativist, several replies can be made. It can be shown that the relativist's conclusions concerning truth do not follow from his premises. This line of attack will be pursued in section 6.3. Or it can be shown that necessary truths, truths whose necessity is knowable from word-functions the relativist must be acquainted with in order to state his own case, disprove his conclusions. Denying these necessary truths while maintaining the relativist's conclusions will yield absurd consequences including the denial of facts that the relativist's case depends on.

My argument for the necessity of every event having a cause will assume, for example, that a change, either instantaneous or continuous, occurs to something to which it has not always been occurring. (The last clause excludes an eternal change such as Aristotle's eternal circular motion.) The analysis of change will turn out to be central to philosophy although it has been almost totally neglected in empiricism. To show how relativism can be replied to, therefore, let us use the assertion that such a change occurs as our example of a contingent ontological truth. (The reason the assertion is ontological is that the word-function of "change" is a form of coming into existence or ceasing to exist, creation out of nothing or annihilation into nothing being the other possible forms.)

By a change occurring to something, I mean a change undergone by something that remains throughout the change. Could a relativist argue that experience does not inform us that such changes exist? The relativist might have in mind the possibility of interpreting our experience either by means of a process philosophy or by some form of phenomenalism. But does a process philosophy really refute my claim that a change can occur to something that survives the change? No. If the objects of experience, or experience itself, are to be analyzed as continuously occurring processes of change, then it must be admitted that *changes themselves* undergo changes such as variations in velocity, acceleration, and direction. For as a matter of fact, changes which have not always been taking place occur in our experience. If a process view of reality were correct (that is, if processes were that which did not exist in another, or in other words, if processes were what satisfied our definition of *substance*), processes themselves must be undergoing changes. Otherwise, no variations would occur in our experience.

What if the relativist appeals to phenomenalism to support the view that we do not experience change occurring to something that remains throughout the change? A phenomenalism that presents itself as a description of experience as we undergo it must admit motions, such as that of a red patch moving from one place to another in my visual field, among the units of experience. When we see a red patch moving from point A to point C, we do not perceive the object as stationary at point B, somewhere between A and C. We perceive it as passing through point B. And when such a motion is perceived, a change is occurring to something which remains throughout the change, if not to the red patch, then at least to the perceiving subject in whose perceptual field this variation is taking place.

To deny this is to claim, in effect, that an experience takes place in an infinitesimal point of time, a durationless instant, and that successive instants of experience are totally discrete, rather than linked in a continuum. But this is not a description of experience as we are unsophisticatedly aware of it; this is a philosophical theory which can be arrived at only by argument. And what would the premises of the argument be? Necessary truths and necessary truths alone? It will hardly do for a *phenomenalist* to maintain that necessary truths can give us knowledge of the nature of what exists, namely, the objects of sense experience. Or are the premises contingent truths, either alone or in conjunction with necessary truths? What would the evidence for these truths be? Not evidence of the ordinary empirical kind, for that presupposes changes occurring to things that remain in existence throughout the change. Thus the verification of scientific hypotheses presupposes that things like measuring instruments and specimens remain in existence through various processes.

Or the argument may be that no more is needed to *explain* the apparent duration of an experience than an infinitesimal present accompanied by an apparent memory of the immediate past. Neither of these explanations of phenomenological duration, however, do away with change occurring to the *subject* of experience. As my apparent memory recalls one object after another, I am undergoing a change. An apparent memory cannot make me aware of a change like a red patch moving from A to C without a change occurring in my consciousness. A series of static objectifications of the patch at different points between A and C is *not* a memory of *change*, especially if the objectifications exist in my consciousness at the same time, as the infinitesimal present/apparent memory hypothesis requires. The apparent memory must objectify the patch as *moving through* some point or points between A and C. And that requires a change within my perceptual field, a change in the locations where the red patch is objectified as being.

It would be irrelevant, however, to introduce the infinitesimal-present-plus-immediate-past form of phenomenalism into the discussion of the relativity of contingent truths. The evidence for both ontological and empirical beliefs in contingent truths requires the existence of change and things remaining throughout change. If this radical form of phenomenalism were true, there would be no truths whose relativity was worth discussing.

Radical phenomenalism, in other words, should come up, and be refuted, at a different point. The refutation would be causal. For example, Wittgenstein showed that even a *real* memory would not be a sufficient cause for the language in which this phenomenalism is expressed. What are needed are public language-acts, which are themselves changes, and perceiving subjects who remain in existence long enough both to observe these changes and to perform similar acts themselves at other times.

To get back to ontological facts in general, it can be argued that they can be relativized only from the point of view of theories based on facts that are less certain than are these ontological facts themselves. Ontological facts are more certain because the word-functions of "exists" and "being" are logically included in all other word-functions; therefore all other factual claims will imply some ontological factual claims. And these word-functions are not only logically included in all others, they are also the causally primary terms to which the knowledge of sentential truth relates us. Therefore even if a language has no resources for objectifying existence and being separately from other word-functions, these word-functions are still made our objects by all the thing-descriptions of the language.

And as Parker (1953, 1960, 1962) has well argued, the relation knowledge-of cannot be a relation which alters the term of the relation, that which is known. Constructive activities, both psychological and social, may be necessary conditions for knowledge, but knowing itself does not modify the object known. If all our word-functions were guilty of altering things, all linguistic objectification would be falsification. There would be no identity between what exists and what we communicate in language, and nothing communicated in language would qualify as accurate knowledge. The only candidate for a relation of accurate knowledge would be something incommunicable: raw, unconceptualized sensation.

The coming into existence of knowledge requires many alterations to take place on the side of the knower. But if to make something an object of knowledge was to alter it, that which is an object would be other than that which exists extra-objectively. Therefore, if we are able to know any truths about extra-objective things—including truths about human knowers and human knowledge for they are things—we must have some word-functions that do not distort the nature of these things. And among these word-functions must be the primoridal ontological word-functions. Since they are logically included in all other word-functions, if any word-functions are capable of objectifying things as they exist extra objectively, ontological word-functions must be capable of doing it. At the very least, sentences using these ontological word-functions will have more certitude than will sentences using word-functions like those of "conceptual framework" or "ontological commitment". For acquaintance with the latter presupposes acquaintance with the former. And if none of our word-functions succeeded in being identical with what extra-objective existents are, the sentences of the relativist would be no more capable of communicating knowledge of what is the case than are any other sentences.

The arguments of this section and the last have replied, from the point of view of contingent and necessary truths respectively, to an objection that was posed in section 2.3.1. Self-evidently, it can be said of all predicates that they are true of things only to the extent that things have been objectified in language. Does it follow that the meanings$_T$ of predicates cannot be what things are in their extra-objective existence? In the case of ontological word-functions, that cannot follow unless to exist is to be an object of knowledge.

Now let us turn to contingent truths employing empirical word-functions. If the same sensations can be objectified differently in different systems of conceptualization, does it follow that conflicting conceptualizations of the same sensations could each be true relative to their own linguistic frameworks? No. Section 8.2 will show that to decide between conflicting empirical hypotheses, it is sufficient to view experience in the light of necessary ontological truths, the principles of induction, simplicity and the search warrant. Two equally simple theories could not describe our experiences in conflicting ways and yet each be capable of explaining all variations in our experience; so inductive reasoning would enable us to decide between them.

Even if we impose systems of conceptualization on sensation, the function of any conceptual system will be to mediate between necessary truths concerning causal relations and what is present in our sense experience. For whatever is present in sense experience will be either a change or something whose existence is the result of a change. And by their identity with themselves changes are realities that would not exist if things other than themselves did not also exist. Understanding the existence of changes and their results, therefore, requires understanding the relations between changes and their causes. Conceptual systems do not simply impose order on a multiplicity of experiences by means of logical relations like set membership. Logical relations are extrinsic to things as things, as cognition-independent existents. Conceptual systems allow us to put order into experience by means of relations belonging to the domain of things as things, causal relations. They allow us to understand the cognition-independent existents our senses put us in contact with by relating changes to their causes. And doing this is the same as revealing what things are, for it is according to what they are that things have necessary causal relations with one another. (See sections 8.2.1 and 9.3.)

This is not to imply that conceptual systems are *originally* developed with the conscious intent of applying the principle of efficient causality and its corollaries to experience. But understanding our experience requires relating causes and effects to one another according to the demands of necessary truths. And if our conceptual system does not allow us to so understand our experience, we modify the system. For if sensation does not impose all our concepts on us, different conceptual systems are possible.

Let us assume that between two such systems there is a genuine conflict with respect to what they assert about things as things. (A genuine conflict, recall, is not one between systems with merely grammatical differences, for grammatical differences pertain to things only as objects. Thus examples like Hanson's ''Bears fur'' versus ''Bears are furry'' will not do unless arbitrary interpretations are imposed on them.) Any conceptual system we use will call for each experience and each thing presented in experience to be classified in one way or another. And any such system of classification will have implications for the causal analysis of the changes we experience. This may not seem obvious at first sight. But under any such system some events will be classified as similar to others in certain respects. Therefore the use of any such system bears directly on the success of our inductions. For inductions concern similarities in sequences of events.

Given our experience as a whole, could two conflicting theories be equally simple and yet classify at least some experiences differently? If so, inductive evidence would allow us to decide between them. For a ''conflict'' between descriptions given by different theories to be empirically significant, the theories must make conflicting similarity classifications of the same events. Where one theory classifies event A as similar to event B but not to event C, the other theory must classify A as similar to C but not to B. Different similarity classifications will consequently produce conflicting predictions about which events will follow which and, therefore, about the similarity of future sequences of events to past sequences of events. Theory T_1 will predict that A will be preceded or followed by the kind of event that preceded or followed B while theory T_2 will predict that A will be preceded or followed by the kind of event that preceded or followed C. And experience would tell us which prediction was true.

On the other hand, if the same kinds of events are predicted to precede and follow A in both theories, the laws governing events B and C are the same in both theories, at least as far as their conformity to empirical evidence is concerned. Then what does the supposed difference between T_1 and T_2 amount to? They were said to consider B and C as belonging to different classes of events. But if this classification makes no empirical difference, what difference does it make?

Could T_1 and T_2 differ, not because they classify events different-ly, but because they postulate causes which, though the same in number, are of different kinds? The only rational bases for beliefs about what exists are experience and causal reasoning from experience. (For if an alleged entity is not itself present in experience, we can know that it exists if and only if something that is present in experience would not exist without it, the definition of a necessary causal relation.) And causal reasoning is governed by necessary truths of the ontological variety. If T_1 and T_2 differ neither with respect to experience nor with respect to the conclusions necessitated by ontological causal principles, what can the differences between the causes postulated by the theories amount to?

Since the only rational bases for beliefs about what exists are expe-rience and reasoning licensed by ontological truths, *where neither em-pirical nor ontological evidence would be relevant to deciding between theories, any differences in the theories must fall on the side of what characterizes objects as objects, not on the side of what we believe about these objects as things.* There will be no difference in what the theories attribute to things as extra-objective things. The only differences will be in linguistic or logical attributes accruing to things as terms of diverse relations of objectification. Such would be the difference between "Bear fur" and "Bears are furry", to use Hanson's example, and between "rabbit" and "instance of rabbithood", to use Quine's. Whether something is objectified by means of a verb ("fur") or by means of the copula with an adjective ("are furry"), in the concrete mode ("rabbit") or in the abstract mode ("instance of rabbithood") is a question concern-ing characteristics of diverse means of objectification, not characteristics of whatever it is that is objectified thereby.

Recalling what was said in section 2.3.2, to adopt a particular linguistic or logical structure as an instrument for rendering things objects is to commit oneself to no beliefs whatsoever concerning things as things; it is to impose on things a set of traits characterizing them not as things but as objects. The test of whether a person holds one ontology or another is not whether he expresses himself by saying "Bears fur" or "Instances of rabbithood reproduce frequently". The test is whether he assents to some ontological, rather than empirical, causal analysis of the things objectified in these sentences.

But what determines whether the meaning$_T$ of "furry" is a qual-ity, an action, a relation or some other kind of entity? Such questions can be answered, if at all, by ontological necessary truths whose necessity does not derive from the framework features of some language. These truths must be expressed in an ontological vocabulary. But it is not arbitrary to give preference to an ontological vocabulary when it comes to determining one's ontological beliefs.

And as was noted in section 2.3.1, neither philosophical nor empirical investigations begin by providing criteria for identifying individuals as members of classes. They presuppose belief in the existence of individuals of certain kinds and seek the causes of that existence. In the course of our investigation, we may be led to revise a previous categorization of some individual or some groups of individuals. But underlying such revisions are experience, on the one hand, and ontological truths, like the principles of induction and simplicity, on the other. Therefore these revisions are undertaken for the sake of achieving identity between what is attributed to things as things and what exists extra-objectively; and the possibility of achieving this identity is presupposed when such revisions are undertaken. Section 8.2.4 will show that a more complex causal hypothesis will require more variations (diversity in effects to be accounted for by diversity in causes) in our experience than will a less complex hypothesis. Therefore, if a particular classification of an individual calls for a more complex causal hypothesis and if the variations required by that hypothesis do not occur, it is unreasonable to believe that classification is true. And we have just seen how to determine the truth of conflicting classifications of individuals when these classifications call for equally simple causal hypotheses. (For an example of the use of inductive reasoning to determine how to classify an event, see sections 8.2.5 and 10.5.)

As based on experience, inductive reasoning does not show that a particular word-function *must* be identical with what extra-objective things are, but since reasonable beliefs about what exists are based on experience, induction can show that it is unreasonable to believe the opposite. And revising previous classifications may involve enriching our language by incorporating new categories, for there may be questions we cannot answer because language does not contain sufficient word-functions. If language L_1 can express more variations in experience than can L_2, the use of L_1 can affect the results obtained by using the principles of induction and simplicity, provided more variations in experience do actually occur.

Nothing I have said here, finally, implies that we can do the impossible and stand outside of language. We do not have to abstract ourselves from all conceptual schemes to know things in their existence as more-than-linguistic-*objects*. Language is precisely our instrument for knowing and communicating what is true of things in their existence as things. That we can talk about things only insofar as we conceptualize them in language is true. But it is also a truism. It simply does not follow that the meanings$_T$ of the predicates by which we describe cognition-independent existents are something other than what those existents are in their cognition-independent existence. The error of linguistic relativism, in other words, is the classic error of idealists: a thing is known only insofar as it is known (as others have pointed out, this is what everybody probably suspected); therefore it cannot be known as it exists outside of our knowledge. Granted, for a thing to be known is for it to be the term of a knowledge relation. Still, the term of a knowledge relation may be identical with, and may be known to be identical with, something having an existence which is other than being-known. As ontological truths illustrate, we are able to express in language conditions that must hold, not just if things are to be objects, but if they are to have that existence which is other than being-known.

6.3 Reply to Relativism II: Truth and Contradiction

But one does not have to accept my ideas concerning ontological truth to free himself from the extravagances of linguistic relativism. These extravagances, however, come packaged in a wide variety of assertions whose connections with one another are often unclear. I will not try to deal with all of these assertions or to clarify their interrelations. By responding to a few key relativist claims, I will establish the language-independence of truth in the sense in which my account of knowledge and of philosophical method requires it to be established. Some other relativistic claims having to do with the relation of language to sense experience will be brought up in section 10.4.

6.3.1 Meaning-variance

(Since I am here dealing with theories other than my own, I will drop the subscripts on "meaning" except when presenting my own views.) It is said that the meaning of words in scientific discourse is theory-laden; an individual description is meaningful only as part of an overall theory so that change in the theory produces changes in the meanings of words. As a result, words cannot be used in exactly the same way in conflicting theories. Another result is that the sentences of a theory do not contain truth-value on their own; only total theories can be called true or false. And just as meanings vary from theory to theory, the meanings of descriptions from different languages are said to vary with the background structures of the languages. Consequently truth does not consist in the conformity of the meanings of a sentence's descriptions with cognition-independent reality. Truth is a matter of our organizing experience by means of a cognition-dependent conceptual structure that reality itself does not impose on us.

It is also said that the use of different languages commits us to different beliefs about what exists, beliefs that are built into the conceptual framework of the language. Therefore no sharp distinction can be drawn between changes in our languages and changes in our theories. Changes in meaning are changes in theory and vice versa. (In the following discussion, however, I will sometimes speak solely of relations between different theories or between different languages, depending on which is more appropriate or perspicuous in the context.)

Let us consider apparently conflicting theories T_1 and T_2 in the light of the thesis that words cannot have the same meanings in different theories. If that thesis is true, what is most obvious about the relations between T_1 and T_2 and what is most relevant to the relativity of truth is also what is least often pointed out: if the meanings of T_1 are different from those of T_2, no sentence of T_1 can contradict any sentence of T_2. If T_1 contains "p" and T_2 "$-p$", these sentences are not in contradiction since what is asserted by "p" cannot be the same as what is denied by "$-p$"; it cannot be the same because the meanings of one sentence's words cannot be the same as those of the other. But then what is all the fuss about? How is the truth of any sentence in T_1 or T_2 relativized by the fact that the meanings of the sentence's words derive from the place of the sentence in its theory? Since everything asserted by T_1 is compatible with T_2, why cannot the sentences of both be true?

It may be responded that what is in question is not the truth of any or all sentences of T_1 and T_2 but the very nature of truth, whether or not the truth of a sentence consists in its plucking objective facts out of experience or in organizing experience in ways that are not determined by experience itself. For the relativist, truth is a matter of organizing experience according to the requirements of some conceptual system, and conflicting systems for organizing experience can be adopted.

Different systems for articulating our experience, however, are not the same as *conflicting* systems. Where is the conflict if the sentences produced by these systems do not contradict one another? No contradiction occurs between ''Bears fur'' and ''Bears are furry'' unless conflicting ontological interpretations are imposed on these differences of grammatical structure. Belief in the existence of rabbits does not contradict but implies belief in the existence of undetached rabbit parts, instances of rabbithood, time slices of rabbits, and time slices of instances of undetached-rabbit-parthood.

Nor are beliefs in the existence of these objects beliefs in different states of affairs. If so, I would be denying contradiction between different methods of conceptualization only at the price of multiplying entities *ad absurdum*. Again, the difference between ''rabbit'' and ''instance of rabbithood'' as means of objectification is not a difference in that which is objectified but in logical characteristics of diverse methods for rendering the same thing an object. The distinction between a rabbit and its parts is real but is a distinction between the terms of necessary causal relations, for a rabbit cannot exist without its parts. So the distinction does not multiply entities *without necessity*. On the contrary, it is just the necessary connection between the terms of this distinction that allows Quine to believe that they would serve equally well in translation.

Whether there is a real distinction between rabbits and time slices of rabbits depends on our ontological analysis of time. If there is a real distinction both terms of which exist (that is, if time slices are not cognition-dependent objects), there is a necessary *causal* relation between rabbits and their time slices, and entities are not multiplied without necessity. If there is no real distinction, the word-functions of ''rabbit'' and ''time slice of rabbit'' differ only by *logical* relations.

If it is asked how it can be judged whether the difference between what is objectified in ''Bears fur'' and ''Bears are furry'' or by ''rabbit'' and ''instance of rabbithood'' is logical or real, the reply is simple. Unless the evidence either of experience, or of the impossibility of the opposite of some ontological truth or of a combination of both requires us to recognize a real distinction between terms of diverse relations of objectification, there is no reason to do so. For those who accept only empirical evidence, where there is no empirical evidence for a real distinction, there is no reason to believe a distinction amounts to more than something's being the term of diverse logical or linguistic relations.

It is not as easy as some think, therefore, to demonstrate that differences between linguistic frameworks imply conflicting beliefs, either empirical or ontological, about what exists. The identity that determines the truth of a sentence is identity between an object of linguistic knowledge and what exists; it is not identity between the manner in which the objectification of something comes about (the process of objectification or the instruments used) and what exists.

To paraphrase one of the arguments Geach (1957, p. 39) has drawn from medieval philosophy, "to understand something otherwise than it is" can refer either to the goal attained by an attempt to understand or to the means by which the goal is attained. In the first sense, to understand something otherwise than it is amounts to understanding it incorrectly. But to understand something simple by means of a complex word-function, something concrete by means of a word-function expressed in the abstract mode, something individual by means of a universal word-function is not to attribute complexity to something simple, abstractness to something concrete, universality to something individual. When an extra-objective existent becomes an object of linguistic knowledge, it becomes the term of many linguistic and logical relations. *But in using thing-descriptions, we do not attribute such relations to things in their extra-objective existence.* These relations are, and are knowable as, attributable to things only as a result of their being made objects. Consequently all sorts of relativity may affect the processes by which things become objects of knowledge. But that is not relativity in what is known as a result of these processes.

6.3.2 Hesse's defense of the meaning-variance thesis

Hesse (1970) is one of the few who have attempted to face squarely the objection that the meaning-variance thesis prevents theories and languages from being in contradiction. She holds that the sense of "meaning" required for the truth of

(1) The meaning of a term in one theory is not the same as its meaning in a prima facie conflicting theory

is not the sense required for the truth of

(2) Therefore no statement, and in particular no observation statement, containing the predicate in one theory can contradict a statement containing the predicate in the other. (p. 221)

If so, however, the change of meaning in question would be vacuous. To say that "red" has different meanings in T_1 and T_2 but that an experience which would confirm "This is red" of T_1 would disconfirm "This is not red" of T_2 and an experience that would confirm "This is not red" of T_1 would disconfirm "This is red" of T_2 is to say that the meaning change between T_1 and T_2 has no empirical significance. In other words, if "This is red" of T_1 and "This is not red" of T_2 are in contradiction, how has the meaning of "red" changed? As Hesse asks (p. 222) "What then is the relevant identity of (predicate) "P" presupposed by the possibility of asserting (1) which will also make (2) false and hence dissolve the paradoxes?"

To judge from her answer, the relevant *identity* of meaning, the identity supposedly falsifying (2) by allowing theories to be in contradiction, is identity of meaning in the non-lexicological sense; two theories share at least some word-functions (although the language-forms which are given these functions may vary from theory to theory, of course.) And the *variance* of meaning, the variance which allows (1) to be true, is change of meaning in the lexicological sense only; two theories happen to use the same language-forms but give these language-forms different functions.

But that variance amounts to a trivial meaning change. And since the same word does not have the same meaning in both theories, sentences using the same word cannot contradict one another. Sentences using other words, however, can be in contradiction. Sentences are in contradiction if and only if what is asserted by one is denied by the other. In order for what is asserted and what is denied to be the same, it is not necessary for sentences to use the same words. But it is necessary for them to use words having the same meanings$_T$.

There is no escaping it. Either the meaning-variance asserted by (1) is variance of meaning in the non-lexicological sense, in which case the sentences of two theories cannot be in contradiction, or it is not variance of meaning in the non-lexicological sense, in which case some sentences of two theories can be in contradiction because meaning-variance between theories is trivial at most. To be significant (1) must refer to change of meaning in the non-lexicological sense. But that is a change which would nullify relativism by making (2) true.

That the meaning-variance by which she saves (1) while falsifying (2) is lexicological only (and hence trivial) is demonstrated by the sole example she provides, the fact that it is incorrect in Newton's physics, while correct in Aristotle's, to use the word "light" of air. But in Aristotle's meaning of the word, or, to avoid an historical dispute, in a meaning that we can attribute to him that accords with his known usage, it has not ceased to be true, even observationally, that air is "light". (If a meaning for "light" cannot be found such that the evidence of which Aristotle could have been aware makes "Air is not light" false, then, contrary to the assumption which allows Hesse to invoke this example, "Air is light" is false even in Aristotle's sense, and no change in the background theory is necessary to make it false. Rather, it would be the falsehood of "Air is light" that required a change in the background theory.) Therefore it is false to describe air by the word "light" if and only if the word is given a different meaning$_T$ than it has in Aristotle, if and only if a lexicological change takes place so that Aristotle's meaning$_T$ ceases to be ours.

Such a change has taken place. Calling it a change of a trivial kind does not imply that there was not good reason for it. It was justified by facts available to us of which Aristotle was not aware. But these facts do not make Aristotle's word-function for "light" false of air; they just show that there is little purpose to be served by using a word in that particular way.

Changes in theory often produce lexicological changes. But it should be noted that the fact that we have ceased to use any word for a particular meaning$_T$ does not imply that we must cease being acquainted with that meaning$_T$. If that were implied, however, we could no longer understand the sentences which used words for that meaning$_T$. And not understanding those sentences, we would never know something that as a matter of fact we do know, the specific lexicological changes that have taken place as a result of changes in theory.

Hesse has other things to say in defense of the meaning-variance thesis. But they seem to be based on the belief that the opponent of the thesis accuses it of precluding "substitutability with retention of truth-value" (p. 225) of predicate "P" in one theory for predicate "P" in the other. No, we who oppose the meaning-variance thesis accuse it of *not* precluding substitutability with retention of truth-value; since the meaning of "P" varies from theory to theory, the apparently contradictory sentences of each can all be true. It is the relativist who must show that meaning-variance between theories precludes the retention of truth-value by showing how the hypotheses of one theory can contradict those of the other. And that is precisely what the relativist's premise, meaning-variance, does not allow him or her to do.

6.3.3 The theory-ladenness of meaning

What, then, of the belief that acquaintance with meaning depends on acquaintance with theory? Acquaintance with meaning in the lexicological sense does not depend on theory except genetically. As children we first learn to use words for meanings$_T$ in the process of being taught that certain sentences are true. Subsequent changes in beliefs about the truth of those sentences may cause us to make lexicological changes in our vocabularies, that is, to cease using language-forms for certain meanings$_T$. But any meaning$_T$ with which we can be acquainted has a potential use in theory. Whether we find it worthwhile to so use it, and therefore make it the meaning of some word in the lexicological sense, does depend on other parts of our theory.

Evidence for the linguistic relativism of truth and the theory-ladenness of meaning comes from cultural linguistics as much as from the history of science. Where we would say "It thundered", ancient Babylonians would have said "En-lil roared". And it has been held (MacKinnon, 1969, pp. 30-31) that in using that sentence as an observation report, Babylonians would not have been able to extricate themselves from the belief in the existence of En-lil which the description "En-lil's roar" presupposes.

But the condition of having derived a description from a belief concerning a matter of fact is not sufficient to commit users of that description to that belief. An heretical Babylonian can continue to use "En-lil roared" for thunder just as we use "Achilles' tendon", "the rising sun", "prairie dogs", "battle of Bunker Hill", "malaria" (see Harré and Madden, 1975, p.21) and, for the natives of the lands explored by Columbus, "Indians".

It would be no objection that our language provides other ways of describing the referents of these expressions while the Babylonian language might not have had another way of describing thunder. Losing his faith would not require a Babylonian to lose his intelligence. He could use a metalinguistic device like "the so-called 'En-lil's roar'". And if the language did not possess the required metalinguistic tools, he could always invent them. Although the converse is held by some philosophers, necessity is still the mother of invention.

Do not think that inventing metalinguistic devices would be beyond the capacity of a poor, ignorant Babylonian. At a *very* early stage in their learning of language even chimpanzees can learn to use meta-linguistic language like "'X' is the symbol for . . ." and "'Y' is not the symbol for . . .". (Premack, 1971, p. 812) And the device needed by the heretical Babylonian might be no more than a mocking smile or a sneering tone of voice.

Associated with the view that the meanings of words derive from their relation to a larger linguistic matrix is the belief that having a concept is the same thing as knowing how to use a word in a certain way. For "having a concept" refers to acquaintance with a word-function. And it is sometimes held that we become acquainted with word-functions only in the process of learning the languages to which the words of which they are the functions belong. Empirical evidence argues the opposite, however. In Premack's experiments, chimpanzees have demonstrated acquaintance with the word-functions of "same" and "different" before they have been taught to use symbols for them (p. 810). The chimpanzees, for example, can learn to earn a reward by grouping things of the same visual appearance and afterwards learn to be similarly rewarded by using a symbol for sameness. Hence we can be acquainted with that for which a certain language-form happens to be used without learning the language and adopting the "built-in conceptual framework" that goes with the language. (And since there can be behavioral evidence other than linguistic of someone's acquaintance with a word-function, there should be even less reason to suspect meanings in the non-lexicological sense of being surreptitious mental entities.)

6.3.4 The nature of thing-object identity

The relativistic account of truth can also be attacked from the point of view of the thing-object identity that the truth of any affirmative sentence requires. In section 3.3.3, we raised the question of what constitutes the thing-object identity required for truth. If truth depends on the identity between a thing and that which is objectified by a word, what does it mean for a thing to be objectified by a word? In this context, to be objectified by a word means to be described or named. But why does a word describe or name one thing or group of things and not some other? A sentence is true if its use of descriptions or names is *successful* in achieving the goal of identity between the terms of diverse relations of describing or naming or between the term of any such relation and what exists extra-objectively. But what does success in achieving this goal consist of? What makes the difference between the mere intention to succeed in correctly describing or naming what exists and the actual attainment of this goal?

If relativism were true, successful objectification would be measured by the rules of the language such that "En-lil roared" is true for the Babylonian while "It thundered" is true for us. For "En-lil's roar" is the Babylonian's way of objectifying what we objectify by "thunder". Therefore when what we call "thunder" occurs, there is *identity* between what exists extra-objectively and what is objectified by "En-lil's roar".

But that kind of thing-object identity, identity between an extra-objective existent and something which a linguistic community *intends* a language-form to objectify, is not sufficient for sentential truth. In the case of names, the identity required for truth is a matter of intention; the identity is between things and the intended objects of the names. "Mt. Everest is taller than any other mountain" and "This is taller than any other mountain" are true or false depending on the identity or lack of identity between something that is taller than any other mountain and something a linguistic community or individual intends as the referent of "Mt. Everest" or an individual intends as the referent of "this". But we cannot leave at that the identity between things and what is objectified by means of a description.

"Taller than any other mountain" does not have to have the word-function it does. But given that word-function, Mt. Washington is not described by "taller than any other mountain"; we can succeed in describing Mt. Washington by "taller than any other mountain" only by giving the language-forms making up this phrase uses other than they now have. Where general terms are concerned, and therefore descriptions of individuals which employ general terms, what word-function a language-form has is a matter of the intentions of the users of a language. But given their word-functions, what thing or things are objectified by means of these language-forms is not a matter of intention. A nuclear explosion could make "Mt. Everest is taller than any other mountain" false no matter how honest the intentions of anyone continuing to think it true.

Making successful description a matter of intention to describe runs into the same difficulty as does the view that the knowledge we communicate in sentences is knowledge of no more than our subjective mental states. If so, everything, including contradictions, could be true. If, according to my idea, government ownership of the means of production is compatible with freedom of the press, then it is compatible with freedom of the press. But if, according to your idea, government ownership of the means of production is not compatible with freedom of the press, then it is not compatible with freedom of the press.

We get the same result if the identity required for truth is identity between what exists and what we intend to be described by means of a particular description. For if we *think* a description is accurate for a certain thing, we will use the description in sentences with the intention of accurately describing that thing. Someone believing that Jimmy Carter got more votes than Ronald Reagan could use the description "got more votes than Ronald Reagan" with the intention of describing Carter; he would consider Carter objectifiable in this way. And a whole linguistic community might intend thunder to be described by "what a supernatural being does when he is angry and awake" while another might intend to describe it by "what a supernatural being does when he is happy and asleep". The identity required for truth cannot be identity between things and what an individual or a community intends to be the term of the relation described-by-predicate-"F".

It is at this point that we may be tempted to interpret the word-functions of predicates as the assigning of individuals to classes. If so, what things are objectified by using a predicate with a particular word-function would be a matter of intention. For the intention to give a predicate a particular word-function would be equivalent to the intention to objectify just those individuals that are members of a certain class.

But let us assume some existing thing, A, is describable by predicate "F". Can what it means for A to be describable by "F" amount to A's being a member of the class of Fs. Over and above A's being what it is (and it is something since it really exists), what is it for A to be a member of a class? And why is A a member of the class of Fs but not of Gs? We cannot answer that A is a member of the class of Fs, but not of Gs, because A is one of the things we refer to by means of "F" but not one of the things we refer to by means of "G". For what is in question is why predicates refer to certain things and not to others and why any use of a predicate is not truthful if we intend it to be truthful.

The accuracy of using "F" to describe A was to be explained by A's membership in a class that happens to be the class for which we use "F". But now A's membership in that class is being explained by the use of "F" to describe A. If class inclusion is thus explained, anything can be made a member of the class of Fs simply by our intention to succeed in describing something by "F".

If class inclusion is to explain the relation between a description and the described, the membership of a thing in a class cannot be explained by the use of a particular language-form to describe the thing. Therefore, given that things are what they are and that our linguistic behavior is what it is, classes enter the explanation of descriptions as a third element (a *tertium quid*) standing between what the described things are and the linguistic behavior by which we describe them. Then what is the relation between what the described things are and the classes to which they belong?

I will now argue that no relation pertinent to the explanation of description is possible between a thing and a class or any other *tertium quid,* unless the word-function of a description is not such a *tertium quid.* Rather, the word-functions of descriptions must be identical with what possibly existing things are, at least in part (or in the case of word-functions which may not be identical with what things are in their existence as things but which have, at least possibly, some status other than what is objectified by this or that language-form, word-functions are identical with what some feature of experience or cognition-dependent object is.)

"This is a man" is true if and only if what is objectified by "This" is identical with one of the things objectified by "man". But something is identical with a thing objectified by "man" if and only if there is identity between the meaning$_T$ of "man" and what the thing we are intending to describe by "man" is as an extra-objective existent. And when there is no identity between what the thing we are intending to describe is and the word-function of the description, there is falsehood. *What is "objectified by a description", therefore, is a possible thing whose nature is, at least in part, identical with the meaning$_T$ of the description.*

Very often, of course, descriptions relate what something is to what something else is and cannot be replaced by descriptions not relating the described to something else. We cannot explain the truth of "A is longer than B" except in ways which relate the lengths of A and B to something else, as we do in "A is three feet long and B is two feet long". In such cases, there is accurate description because there is identity between the word-function of a description and a relation which does hold between the terms mentioned. It does not make any difference whether the relation in question is itself a real existent. If it is, then the identity is between a word-function and what some real existent is. If it is not, then the identity is between a word-function and a cognition-dependent object.

In the latter case, a description is true because one cognition-dependent relation, rather than other possible cognition-dependent relations, holds between the terms. But if these relations are not real existents, what determines which relations hold? The word-functions of the predicates in question are relations terminating in things being what they are such that what things are determines what relations hold between them. Only if the word-functions of these predicates are relations which, though cognition-dependent, are determined by things being what they are could these predicates by used to describe things. Thus if relations like longer-than or twice-the-length-of are cognition-dependent, still they are relations between things having length, relations determined by what the lengths of the things that terminate them are. Even such arbitrary relations as the word-functions of "left" and "right" are relations terminated by what things are, left being, for example, the side on which the heart is located in most humans.

Logical constructs, therefore, can be used to objectify *things*. Perhaps the proper ontological analysis of the United States of America will show it to be a garden-variety accident. If not, however, the word-function of "United States of America" is a cognition-dependent object, a set of cognition-dependent relations terminating in extra-objective things such that what those things are as real existents determines the truth of sentences about the United States of America.

This is not to say that sentences about the United States, or any other logical construct used to objectify things, can be exhaustively translated into sentences not using logical constructs. The existing states of affairs that determine the truth of these sentences may be objectifiable otherwise than by logical constructs. It does not follow that a logical construct is equivalent to what is objectified by a set of sentences not using logical constructs. The logical construct is precisely something not objectified in such sentences, namely, a cognition-dependent relation.

Sections 9.3.1 and 10.1 will show that causal analysis, verified by necessary truths of the ontological type, can in many cases tell us that a certain relation is a real existent. If so, the word-function of a relative predicate is identical with what some real existent is. But even if a relation like longer-than is cognition-dependent, the reason why "longer than" describes a relation of A to B cannot be that the ordered couple (A, B) is a member of a certain class of ordered couples. The same questions about classes and descriptions apply here as elsewhere. Why is (A, B) a member of this class and not the class that is supposedly the word-function of "shorter than" or "equal in length to"? The answer is that, because A and B are what they are and because the word-function of "longer than" is a relation which holds when A is what it happens to be and B is what it happens to be, (A, B) is among the ordered couples one of whose relations can be described by "longer than". (Recall that cognition-dependent relations are not coextensive with logical relations, as they would be, since class inclusion is a logical relation, if being the term of a cognition-dependent relation were the same as belonging to a couple of which the relation is a class. The ordering of such a couple, on the other hand, *is* a logical relation.)

What, finally, about the meanings$_T$ of words for features of experience to which we may not want to grant cognition-independent existence? I discuss the ontological status of sense qualities in Chapter 10. But whatever their ontological status, that for which the noun "red" or "redness" is used, for example, is what some color in our visual field is. That for which the adjective "red" is used is what it is for an area in our visual field to be something having redness. (What about a language which uses "redding" where we would use "red"? Even if they are not cognition-independent objects, the word-functions of "red" and "redding" are capable of being more than terms of this or that linguistic relation. As such, they do not differ if the evidence for the sentences using them is the same.)

This analysis of describing in terms of the identity of the meaning$_T$ of the description and what it is that is being described can be demonstrated as a necessary consequence of the fact that truth requires identity between what is objectified by some language-form and that which actually or possibly exists (or, at least, has some status other than being that which terminates this or that relation of objectification). The identity required for truth is identity between a thing and *itself*, between a thing as thing and the same thing as that which is objectified by some language-form (or between something as what is objectified in some way and as capable of some status other than being what is objectified in this way.) We are considering the case in which "what is objectified" is what is described. What a language-form describes is determined by its word-function. A language-form does not describe by being what it is but by being used in this or that way. As we saw in section 3.2.1, it is acquaintance with word-functions that puts us in a position to judge the truth of a sentence. Hence it is acquaintance with word-functions that allows us to determine what it is that is objectified and what it is that is not objectified by a description.

Therefore the relation commonly designated by "means" or "is-used-for" must be a relation terminated by that which exists, actually or possibly (or by that which can have some status other than being term of this relation). If predicate "F" accurately describes some really existing thing, A, "F" 's relation of being-used-for must be terminated by what exists when A exists. If it is not a relation terminated by what A is, it is terminated by something other than what A is; if it is terminated by something other than what A is, the identity required for truth is not between a thing and itself but between a thing and something other than itself. Since the identity required for truth is identity between a thing and itself, "F" 's relation of objectification, and therefore its relation of being-used-for that determines what it objectifies, cannot terminate in something other than that which the thing we are calling "A" is. Therefore that which "F" is used for, its word-function, is what A is.

The same conclusion follows from section 5.3.2's point that being is logically included in the word-functions of thing-descriptions. To achieve the goal of objectifying extra-objective existents, the word-function of a thing-description must be objectified as what some possible existent is, at least in part. The things we objectify have a multiplicity of (substantial or accidental) characteristics, including the characteristic of being composed of really distinct parts. In saying that the word-function of a description may be identical with what something is in part, I do not mean that the word-function of a description is what one part of the objectified thing is. If so, only that part, not the thing, would be objectified by the description. For example, "vertebrate" does not describe vertebrae; it describes things which have vertebrae as parts. Here, to objectify what a thing is in part is to objectify it as something having these parts. And to say that a word-function is identical with what a thing is in part is to say that the word-function is identical, not with the part, but with what it is to be something having such a part.

Likewise, a thing can be multiply objectified by reference to its accidents or its relations to other things. The meaning$_T$ of such a description is what a thing is, in part. But the meaning$_T$ is not what it is to be the accident or relation (what-it-is-to-be-the-color-red or what-it-is-to-be-the-relation-taller-than-X). The meaning$_T$ is what it is to be something having the accident or relation (something having redness, something having the relation taller-than-X), or something having the capacity for the accident or relation. Thus a meaning$_T$ that is what a thing is *in part* objectifies the *whole* thing but does not objectify it *by means of* reference to all of its parts, its accidents or its relations to other things.

We should also recall that not every distinction between the word-functions of predicates true of the same thing derives from reference to really distinct parts or features of the thing. Indefinitely many word-functions distinguishable only by logical relations can be identical with the same thing. One and the same feature of our visual experience is identical with the word-functions of "scarlet", "red" (and "redness") "chromatic color", "color". These word-functions are just logically distinct ways of articulating the same sensible object. Consequently identity between what something is and the meaning$_T$ of a description is compatible with all degrees of generality, vagueness, inexplicitness and abstractness on the part of descriptions.

Logical characteristics accruing to what something is as a result of its being objectified by a description are neither what the thing is nor what the word-function of the description is in their extra-objective state. Logical characteristics are what an object is as a result of being made an object, and characteristics attributable to something as that which is objectified in some way are not the same as that which is objectified in this way. To speak of identity between that which is a thing and that which is an object is one thing. To speak of the non-identity between the characteristics belonging to things as things and the characteristics accruing to things as objects is another. Diacritical realism distinguishes what is objectified (including word-functions) from characteristics attributable to it as that which is objectified, with the result that all distinction is eliminated between that which is objectified in some way and that which is more-than what is objectified in this way.

One logical property attributable to what things are as a result of being made the word-functions of predicates is that of being the means by which we allocate things to classes. For if we do not allocate things to classes because of what they are, class membership must be conceived as something other than a relation terminated by what things are. And any relation not terminated by what things are will not explain the relation of being-used-for because of which, as opposed to any mere intention on our part, a predicate can be truthfully asserted of some things and not of others.

To the direct arguments for identity between the meaning$_T$ of a description and the nature of the described, we can add a *reductio ad absurdum* parallel to the argument that sentential knowledge is not knowledge of our subjective states. We are trying to answer the question why all descriptions are not true of everything. And if the identity required for truth can be achieved in any other way than by identity between the meaning$_T$ of a description and the nature of what we are intending to describe, everything can be true, contradictions included. The reason why is the same one the later Wittgenstein (1965, p. 33) gave for rejecting the picture theory of truth. Any picture can be an accurate representation of any object according to some rules of projection, rules which can be so different that incompatible representations can be equally accurate.

In the relativist context, the rules of projection are the framework features of different languages, and they allow contradictory descriptions to be true of the same thing. Different languages may assert of the same thing descriptions with contradictory word-functions: "En-lil's roar" (what En-lil does when he is awake and angry) and "En-lil's snore" (what En-lil does when he is asleep and contented). The picture theory of truth and any version of conceptual relativism fail for the same reason; they attempt to understand truth *solely* by means of relations between really distinct terms, a sentence and the state of affairs it pictures or that for which a description is used and what the things of which we assert the description are. If the relation that determines whether thing A is described by a predicate in a particular language is a relation between A itself and something really distinct from what A itself is, say B, then why cannot some other language make the relation between A and B a relation determining that A is *not* described by a predicate whose meaning$_T$ is B?

And even a particular language's rules of projection, whether expressible or not, would not be sufficient to establish a connection between linguistic behavior and A if the relation that determines whether A is described by a predicate is a relation between A and something really distinct from itself. As Wittgenstein's argument emphasizes, rules of projection are themselves subject to various interpretations. What makes one interpretation the correct one? In the case of descriptions objectifying certain things and not others, even though their word-functions are more than logically distinct from what these things are, the framework features of the language supposedly determine what is or is not objectified by the descriptions. But even if these framework features are not expressed and are only "understood", what makes one understanding of them the correct one?

If interpretations of rules of projection are themselves subject to interpretation, an infinite regress opens up. The regress can be prevented if and only if to interpret language-forms is not to relate them to some *tertium quid* over and above what the things objectified by means of these language-forms are. Therefore understanding a language's relations of objectification is not a matter of relating its language-forms to such a *tertium quid*; it is understanding what the objectified things themselves are. *Correctness* in understanding a language's relations of objectification is a lexicological matter, a matter of knowing the contingent behavioral facts that certain language-forms have been given certain functions to perform. But in knowing what functions descriptions have been given, we are acquainted with that which the possible existents they describe are. (The arguments against the *tertium quid* explanation of the *word-functions* of descriptions, like my other arguments concerning meanings, are made without prejudice to the question of what psychological factors may or may not be needed to explain our *acquaintance with* word-functions.)

If the word-function of some predicate is not identical with the nature of whatever the linguistic community intends to be objectified by means of that predicate, the sentences in which that predicate is asserted of things are *false*. Like ''"En-lil's roar" a predicate may be lexicologically correct within a language group. But unless it is used for a word-function other than a noise-made-by-a-supernatural-being, it cannot be truthfully asserted of any real existent. (Again, what meaning$_T$ a word is or is not given is to be determined by behavioristic methods, including the asking of questions.) And to achieve the truth, a language may need to be enriched by the addition of the pertinent word-function or word-functions.

But how can we know whether or not the word-function of a description is identical with what something is? Since this identity is what determines the truth of sentences, the evidence for it is the same as the evidence by which we judge the truth of sentences, the evidence of experience and of the impossibility of the opposite. Where no evidence would be relevant to deciding which of two apparently incompatible word-functions is identical with what something is, the incompatibility is only apparent. (We have been concentrating on thing-object identity. For more on their *diversity*, see section I.1. A qualification of the identity between things and objects in the case of theories using mathematical language will be mentioned in section 8.3.3.)

It follows from the identity theory of truth that the meanings$_T$ of the predicates of a sentence can have a direct relation of either identity or non-identity with what exists. Therefore it is not the case that sentences do not have truth-value on their own, that truth and falsity are functions only of the language or theory that is the matrix of the sentence. But it does not follow from this that we can learn the meanings$_L$ of words without simultaneously acquiring knowledge of a broader linguistic and theoretical background. Nor does it follow that we can judge the truth-value of a sentence apart from a consideration of its links to other sentences. But it would be an epistemological fallacy to conclude, from the fact that we may not be able to judge the truth of a sentence in isolation, that the sentence is not true or false as a unit. The question of the relation of a sentence to extra-objective existents is not the same as the questions of how we go about determining what that relation is or how we learned to understand the sentence in the first place. On the other hand, I know of no reason why some contingently true sentences should not be considered directly knowable as units in the sense that mistakes about them are "merely verbal", that is, lexicological. (See Chisholm, 1966, pp. 36-37, and see section 10.4.)

In sum, if there are ontologically or empirically significant differences between conceptual schemes, that is, if one scheme commits its users to a belief about things as things which another scheme commits its users to denying, then one of these schemes commits its users to a belief that is true and another to a belief that is false. The truth or falsity of these beliefs depends on the identity between the word-functions of their descriptions and the cognition-independent nature of what exists. Not that it is easy to achieve the linguistic objectification of what real existents are. Commonly it takes centuries to develop acquaintance with the necessary word-functions. And the changes that must take place in order for the necessary word-functions to enter language include the invention, as in mathematics, of totally new linguistic structures; the new word-functions may be too complex or abstract for the old linguistic structures to handle. The identity theory of truth does not imply that we just read the truth off our experience the way we read a computer printout. Knowledge of the truth requires mental work on our part. But that work is required precisely in order to prevent what is objectified in our sentences from being something other than what things are as extra-objective things.

6.4 Methodological Imperialism

Note that I have contradicted none of the *facts* about differences in our languages from which relativists draw their conclusions concerning truth and our knowledge of it. What has been contradicted is the philosophic *significance* relativists attribute to those facts. My arguments have shown that significance to be read into the facts, not imposed by them. And how could it be otherwise? If truth were language-dependent in the relativistic sense, the "facts" on which the relativist relies would have no validity outside of the relativist's own peculiar linguistic framework. My analysis, on the other hand, allows any facts the relativist may cite to have the status of being objectifications of reality as it exists language-independently. And only as such can facts be cited in rational argument.

There are valid conclusions to be drawn from the relativist's facts. On the one hand, there is the precariousness of our relation to the truth; on the other hand, there are the oversimplifications of which most philosophic treatments of that relation are guilty. If the relativist would content himself with this kind of remark, he could not be gainsaid. Instead he goes beyond them and in so doing claims an exaggerated importance for certain facts about human language. Why?

Linguistic relativism is the latest, but far from the last, in an undistinguished series of attempts to give the method of some *other* discipline regulative significance for settling philosophic disputes. In the past we have been told that the key to philosophic wisdom was to model philosophy on mathematics, or that philosophy was higher psychology, or, with reference to particular philosophic issues, that there is nothing more to be said about determinism and indeterminism than what the physicist tells us, or that the social sciences have the last word on ethics, etc. Most recently one or another approach to language has been hailed as the way out of our philosophic problems. Logic done by the method of constructing formal languages has been considered the path to an understanding of either the ultimate structure of things or, at least, of our knowledge of things. Austin's method of doing philosophy bore unmistakable resemblance to the method of the classical philologist. Currently at the center of the philosophic stage is linguistics, structural, psychological and cultural.

These philosophic inflations of the significance of a particular method and that method's results have much in common with the economist's undoubting confidence in the efficacy of economic planning, the successful entrepeneur's trust in the justice of free enterprise, the biologist's belief that the most important features of human behavior can be explained genetically, the sociologist's refusal to accept genetic explanations of human behavior, etc.

Such parochial optimism is especially to be expected while the excitement of a new science, or of radically new discoveries in an established science, is still fresh. This is the case with linguistics today. Although it cannot be predicted what will come next, it can be predicted that as our excitement with linguistics dies down our judgment about its significance for philosophy will become more balanced. Someday there will be as many linguistic relativists (or Chomskean rationalists) as there are logical atomists.

And one other thing can be safely predicted: something will come next, and something else after that. Something will replace linguistics as that for which normative philosophic significance is claimed. It may be the next discovery in logic, mathematics, physics, biology, psychology, or the development of some hitherto undeveloped science.

Whatever it is, we can be sure that it will come and that it will be replaced in its turn as the freshness of its discovery wanes and new discoveries are made.

There is a difference, however, between simply being over-confident about one's method and making a philosophy out of something that is not a philosophy. Philosophic questions differ from other questions in being foundational, presuppositional. Whatever else it may do, philosophy attempts to examine what it is, if anything, that underlies the asking of other questions and the achieving of other kinds of knowledge. The best way to express this is to say that philosophy seeks to answer *ultimate* questions. Not every investigation that can be called, in some legitimate sense, foundational belongs to philosophy, but as long as an investigation is not philosophic, there remains some more ultimate way to examine the foundations of the branch of knowledge in question. Even a statement like "To speak paradoxically, there are no ultimate questions: only penultimate ones" (Hook, 1963, p. 225) answers an ultimate question in this sense, for it is an answer to a question about ultimates. Likewise to say that knowledge has no foundations is to answer an ultimate question. And it is an answer to an ultimate question to assert that there is no more to be said about truth or knowledge or causality or moral obligation or what exists than is said by such and such a science.

Overzealousness about a particular method has been accurately described as methodological imperialism. We need a name for the specifically philosophic form of this affliction, however. And since philosophy deals with ultimate questions, I suggest that we call it the fallacy of the "U-turn". To make a U-turn is to turn into a way of solving philosophic problems some method which, although adequate for dealing with other matters, is unsuitable for answering philosophic questions. (The "U" in "U-turn" can be taken to stand not only for the ultimacy but also for the universality that fallacies of this kind often claim for a less than universal method. Think of the beliefs, for instance, that the *only* genuine certitude concerns logically necessary truths or that *all* knowledge about what actually exists is empirical.)

Looking at philosophy sociologically, from the point of view, that is, of how it exists most of the time rather than how it should exist, philosophy might be defined as the continuously repeated attempt to make non-ultimate methods of inquiry ultimate. This is "metaphysics" in the pejorative sense of the word. A practitioner of a particular science is not satisfied to have a valid intellectual method. For whatever psychological reasons, he feels the need to endow his method with an all-transcending significance. (I recently heard a well-known linguist remark in apparent candor that each language constitutes a *totally* different way of looking at the world.) Each time a U-turn is made, however, the questions philosophy has always dealt with are translated into different questions. (For examples, see section 11.6.) And if it is pointed out to the U-turner that the results he is getting by applying his method do not answer the philosophic questions he intends them to, the U-turner will ask, ingenuously, what other *valid* questions could there be; what more is there to know about something than his method can reveal? (Thus methodological imperialism in its philosophic form can yield an epistemological fallacy; in a philosopher's mind, something is reduced to its status as object of a less than ultimate mode of inquiry.)

But in claiming philosophic authority for a less than ultimate method, the U-turner necessarily deprives his position of any substantiating evidence. For any such claim outreaches the evidence appropriate to the method for which the claim is being made. The U-turner's position does not fall *within* the particular domain of investigation which infatuates him but is a claim *about* that domain of investigation. And his assertions communicate no state of affairs other than the existence of his own subjective attitude toward the importance and power of that particular method of inquiry.

That kind of criticism has always been brought against the view that the sum total of our knowledge of what exists must be empirical knowledge. In reply to the charge that they violate their own rules of evidence, some contemporary empiricists would be careful to explain that they consider their own task as philosophers to be a branch of empirical knowledge. But what empirical evidence is there for the belief that all knowledge of what exists must be empirical? Ironically, while many philosophic, and hence non-empirical, justifications for this belief have been offered, the empirical basis for its widespread acceptance is rarely given as a justification: the fact that the empirical sciences do, while philosophy does not, achieve long-standing consensus among experts on a regular basis.

But what is the connection between the cultural phenomenon of consensus and the empirical philosopher's statements about the nature of knowledge? No one disputes that empirical evidence supports the belief that empirical scientists agree more often and for longer periods of time than do philosophers. But what has that evidence got to do with the belief that no philosophers have achieved any knowledge about reality over and above their empirical knowledge?

The answer to this question must be that there is either a necessarily true or a contingently true connection between the existence of knowledge and the existence of consensus among experts. A contingently true connection would be insufficient for ruling out the possibility of non-empirical knowledge, and for determining whether such knowledge has ever been achieved, one could not require that it be accompanied by consensus. But if the connection is necessarily true, knowledge of its truth would constitute an example of non-empirical knowledge about something that exists, namely, knowledge.

Their philosophic theories to the contrary aside, what really propels empiricists from facts about consensus to conclusions about knowledge is a non-empirical belief in a *necessary causal connection* between the *inter-subjective* evidence (cause) required for knowledge and the achievement of consensus (effect). If there is evidence for a belief, in other words, that evidence should be able to produce agreement among experts, those who have learned how to evaluate that kind of evidence.

There is nothing wrong with this causal analysis, but it fails to prove the empiricist's point. For how do we determine who is an expert and who is not an expert? Here a sociological definition (Ph. D. from an "accredited" university, articles in "scholarly" journals, etc.) will not do. Not that philosophic knowledge is not a product of culture and intersubjectively communicable, but the point at issue is whether there may be a form of truth about cognition-independent reality whose discovery and communication is more difficult to achieve, and about which it is easier to fall into error, than is the case with empirical truth. If so, there would be agreement among experts if by experts we mean those who best succeed in avoiding errors when examining the evidence, but not necessarily among experts if we mean those who have earned approval of a sufficient number of their colleagues to earn a degree or publish an article.

In the final chapter, I will argue that, due to the nature of ontological word-functions, this is exactly the situation philosophy is in. For the time being, it should be noted that the empirical evidence itself supports the conclusion, but no more than the conclusion, that it is more difficult to achieve long-standing consensus on philosophical questions than on empirical questions. For experience shows that we cannot rationally suppress philosophic inquiry; attempts to demonstrate the invalidity of philosophy as a human activity always lead to more philosophizing. And experience shows that attempts to eliminate philosophic disagreement by making U-turns always generate, among those making U-turns, as much disagreement as ever. U-turns with the methods of other disciplines are usually made, however, out of a desire to reduce philosophic disagreement at least to the point that philosophy can achieve the same degree of sociological success that the other disciplines have achieved. Whether this is possible without making U-turns will be looked into in the last chapter.

But we will avoid the fallacy of the U-turn if and (to be realistic about human nature as exhibited in our past philosophic behavior) only if we are acquainted with a method which has a legitimate claim to ultimacy, a method for which the claim of ultimacy does not exceed the evidence which this method is itself competent to investigate. Unless we are aware of such a method, some other method will, as has always happened in the past, take its place in our thinking as the proper way to deal with philosophic questions. For nature abhors a vacuum in our intellectual life.

U-turns are inevitable, therefore, as long as we lack an understanding of the ontological perspective. For ontological analysis is a method for which the claim of ultimacy does not require evidence of another kind than that for which the claim is being made. The ultimacy of ontological analysis is guaranteed by a fact those who deny that existence is a predicate know well: existence (actual or possible) is presupposed by whatever else may be true of things as things. If existence is not true of a thing, nothing is true of it. Really existing things are ultimate (as primary) among the objects of our knowledge, and recognition of this primacy is necessary for doing epistemology.

Real existence is ultimate not only from the perspective of things as objects, but also from the perspective of that which is most important in our knowledge about things as things, causal relations. For existence is ultimate both on the side of the effect (causes cause effects to exist) and on the side of the cause (to be causes, causes must exist). To say philosophy deals with ultimate questions, consequently, is to say philosophy's method must be ontological. If any other kind of investigation may be described as presuppositional or foundational, to the extent that it is other than ontological, its examination of foundations is less than ultimate.

We have already seen some examples of the ontological analysis of other disciplines' presuppositions. By tracing the foundations of truths of logic back to ontological truths, for instance, we explained why truths of logic extend to all possible objects. Ontological necessity, therefore, is also at the foundation of those presuppositions of mathematics whose necessity derives from logical relations. If "two quantities each equal to a third are equal to each other'' were not true, it would be possible for a thing to be and not be at the same time. If the quantity objectifiable as A and the quantity objectifiable as B are each identical with the quantity objectifiable as C but the quantity objectifiable as A is not identical with that objectifiable as B, then the quantity objectifiable as C is not identical with the quantity objectifiable as C; for quantity C is identical with non-identical quantities A and B.

In this chapter, ontological analysis has shown that linguistic knowledge can inform us of what things are as more-than-*objects*, the relativity of the manners in which different languages make things objects notwithstanding. In succeeding chapters, ontological analysis will show us how truths whose necessity derives from causal relations provide foundations for empirical science and allow us to solve the problem of perception. It is because identity with extra-objective existents is the goal of linguistic objectification that the ultimate analysis of the presuppositions of any kind of knowledge, ontology included, must be ontological. Consequently, when the U-turner asks what kind of knowledge we could want beyond that provided by his method, the answer is an ontological analysis of anything experience makes us aware of.

Such an analysis will also be a causal analysis. So far I have supported my assertions about causal analyses and the causal necessities that verify them only by way of examples. Now we are ready to address the issue of causality.

CHAPTER SEVEN

Causal Necessity

It is time to make good on my claim that we can know necessary causal relations. It has been shown that, when diversity between objects amounts to nothing more than a diversity of logical relations characterizing their objectification, it is necessary that these objects be no more than logically distinct. And we know the necessity of their identity if and only if we are acquainted with the logical relations involved, that is, if and only if we possess the appropriate linguistic skills. On the other hand, when the diversity between means of objectification derives from really distinct elements of our experience, as in "Every color occupies a unit of space distinct from every other color", how can we know that if the term of one relation of objectification were not identical with the term of the other, at least one of these terms would both be and not be what it is?

To say that there is a necessary causal relation between distinct realities A and B is to say that at least one of them, say A, would not exist without the other. If such a causal relation were true and if A occurred without B occurring, A would both be and not be at the same time. But can we make really distinct features of our experience objects in a manner which allows us to grasp necessary causal relations between them? If so, we are capable of knowing that means of objectification whose diversity consists in references to these distinct features

273

of experience necessarily objectify the same thing. We are capable of knowing, for example, that "A would not exist without B" is necessarily true or that a color is necessarily identical with something which occupies a unit of space distinct from every other color.

But most authorities would deny that we can know necessary truths concerning causal relations. Due to the influence of Hume, it is virtually self-evident for most philosophers that no statement known by us to be necessarily true can license us to infer the actual existence of one thing from the actual existence of another. We know that a statement is necessarily true if and only if we know that denying it requires us to affirm and deny the *same* thing at the same time. The principle of non-contradiction enjoins us only from denying a thing's identity with itself, but causality relates a thing to what is not identical with itself. For most of these same philosophers, necessary truths are by nature "analytic" or "logical" or "linguistic" or "conceptual" and therefore pertain to what we say (objects), not what exists (things). "A exists" informs us about A as a thing, not as an object. If necessary truths inform us only about objects as objects, necessary truths cannot inform us about real existence. Consequently no causal principle licensing us to assert the existence of something not otherwise known to exist can be necessarily true.

I am arguing, on the other hand, that once we have freed the principle of non-contradiction from its confinement to the domain of objects as objects and are ready to use it in our examination of things as things, we can discover necessary truths informing us of causal relations between things. An a priori prejudice against this claim is understandable but not justifiable. For the Humean argument is a non-sequitur. Nothing in it shows that what A is cannot include a relation to distinct reality B such that to affirm A and deny that relation is to affirm and deny the *same* thing. And before Hume objected to the necessity of truths about causal relations, it would by no means have been considered self-evident that the power of necessary truth extended only to the known as known and not to things as things. For before Hume it was believed—correctly, as we will see—that statements like "Every event has a cause" were necessarily true. It is only because of the widespread acceptance of the Humean critique of causal necessity that we today live in an atmosphere in which it appears undeniable that necessity pertains only to objects as objects. My earlier arguments against the linguistic theory of necessity aside, if the Humean critique of causal necessity is in error, our prejudice against sentences both informing us of real existence and being necessarily true is without rational foundation.

Possibility is best proven by actuality. To establish my claim that we can know necessary causal relations I will present a direct demonstration of the necessary truth of "Every event has an efficient cause". In the next section, I will prepare for the demonstration by explaining the meaning of this principle, establishing the terminology required for the argument and pointing out some self-evident truths about events and about causality as here defined. Section 7.2 will demonstrate the principle of efficient causality by showing contradictions that result from its denial. The chapter will conclude with replies to objections. Subsequent chapters will deal with the epistemological implications of this principle for science, philosophy and perception.

7.1 The Principle of Efficient Causality

7.1.1 Hume's reply to Clarke and Locke

For the strength of my argument to be better understood, let us recall Hume's critique of causal necessity in more detail. First, the issue confronting Hume was *not* whether events can be covered by laws of some epistemological type; that understanding of causality developed only *after the fact* of his critique of causal necessity. Hume, rather, was addressing the hitherto universally held belief in causality as a relation holding between things (where "thing" continues to be used in opposition to "object" but not necessarily in opposition to "event"). According to Hume, since causality is a relation between *distinct* things, denying a causal relation cannot produce a contradiction. It follows that any argument supporting the necessity of events having causes must be fallacious. And in particular, Hume found (*Treatise*, 1, 3, 3) that the arguments of both Clarke and Locke committed the fallacy of begging the question.

Locke had reasoned that unless there were a cause for what begins to exist, things would be caused by nothing as if "nothing" were the name of an agency capable of generating things. And Clarke had argued that in the absence of a cause distinct from whatever it is that begins to exist, whatever begins to exist would be the cause of itself as if it could exist before itself, in order to be the cause, and after itself, in order to be the effect. Hume responded that these absurd conclusions do not follow unless it has been assumed that what begins to exist does have a cause. If we do assume this and also that there is nothing distinct from what begins to exist which actually functions as a cause, absurd conclusions follow. But that assumption is the very point at issue: why must we assume that things have causes? The absurd conclusions can be avoided as easily by denying that things must be caused as by postulating the existence of efficient causes.

Hume's response can be generalized to cover most subsequent attempts to establish the ontological (as opposed to the epistemological, as in Kant) necessity of the principle of efficient causality. They usually go something like this. A contingent thing is capable of being or not being. Therefore the contingent cannot be its own sufficient reason for existing. For something whose nature is capable of being or not being F is not actually F through the fact that its nature is what it is. If contingent things are not their own reason for existing, they must have a reason for existing in something other than themselves. What does not exist through the fact that its nature is what it is must exist through something else's being what it is.

Whatever interpretation may be given phrases like "reason for existing" or "exists through its own nature", Hume's position need not be weakened at all by an admission that contingent things are not their own sufficient reasons for existing or do not exist through their own natures. Being one's own sufficient reason is not the contradictory opposite of having something else as a sufficient reason; it is the contradictory opposite only of not being one's own sufficient reason. The opposition between being one's own sufficient reason for existing and having another for a sufficient reason is not an opposition between being and non-being but between members of a particular class of beings, namely, the class of things that have sufficient reasons for existing. Likewise, the opposition between what owes its existence to itself and what owes its existence to another is an opposition between members of a particular class, the class of things that owe their existence to something. The principle of non-contradiction alone, therefore, does not allow us to conclude from the fact that a thing is not its own reason for existing that there is something else which is the thing's reason for existing. That conclusion is justified only if we assume that things do have reasons for existing, that they do exist through something. The logic of Hume's response to Clarke and Locke remains intact. The question at issue is begged unless it is shown that things do owe their existence to something.

My argument, on the contrary, will not assume that events owe their occurrence to anything. It will show that they owe their occurrence to something by showing directly that they are caused, that they depend for existence on something non-identical with themselves.

And it will show that it is an event's identity with itself that makes necessary its dependence on what is other than itself. It is true that a statement is known to be necessary if and only if we know that denying it requires us to affirm and deny the *same* thing at the same time. But as the analysis to follow will demonstrate, to deny that events owe their occurrence to what is not identical with themselves is to deny their identity with themselves. Therefore my argument will not beg the question by assuming gratuitously that events depend on causes. (On the principle of sufficient reason, see Cahalan, 1969, pp. 139-168.)

7.1.2 Change and component causality

What is an event? An event is a *change*, either instantaneous or continuous, occurring to something which previously either was not changing at all or at least was not changing in this particular way. I am not denying that an eternally continuous motion would be caused; I am excluding it from the argument for dialectical reasons which will become clear. But change will be the key notion in the argument for efficient causality. It is the occurrence of previously unoccurring change that will be shown to require an efficient cause. (And since changes require efficient causes, it is also entirely appropriate to speak of the results of changes as having efficient causes.)

Before I go any further, it will be helpful to point out a particular feature of the events of our experience. Changes in our experience consist of and result in complexes, compounds of diverse elements which were not conjoined before the change the way they are conjoined at the time of or after the change: a car moving down the street, Ronald Reagan becoming President of the United States, a leaf changing color or swaying from place to place in the breeze. Whatever kind of existents our ontology admits, if our ontology conforms to experience, existents will be recognized as complexes composed of non-identical parts, non-identical not only logically but really. And the existents we experience come into being because components— themselves complex—of already existing complex states of affairs undergo changes resulting in new complex states of affairs.

Since the events of our experience and their results are complexes, they could not exist unless things not identical with them also existed. For a complex whole is not identical with any of the parts of which it is composed. That is a self-evident truth, and here is another. A complex whole would not exist if any of its parts did not exist. If any of its parts are lost or replaced, it is a different whole. The complex whole CD, composed of really distinct elements C and D, is not identical with either C or D; nor would it exist if either C or D did not exist. In other words, the relation of a complex whole to its parts satisfies our definition of a necessary causal relation: if CD exists and either C or D does not, CD both exists and does not exist. This is not yet efficient causality, but it is causality.

Still, I have deliberately framed the definition of a necessary causal relation (if A and B are really distinct and A exists without B existing, A both exists and does not exist) so as to be true both of the relation of causes to their necessary effects (if sufficient causes for an effect exist without the effect coming into existence, causes sufficient for the effect's existence are not sufficient for the effect's existence) and of the relation of effects to their necessary causes (if an effect occurs in the absence of a cause without which it cannot occur, the effect both occurs and does not occur). This definition, therefore, does not tell us whether a thing is cause or effect of that which it cannot exist without. The difference between cause and effect is that an effect *depends* upon, derives its existence or some condition necessary for existence from, its cause. But this notion of dependence seems vague. Complex whole CD would not exist without its parts; therefore there is a causal relation between them. But what if it were also true that C and D could not exist unless CD existed? Which would be the cause on which the existence of the other depends, the whole or the parts?

Here change begins to take its central place in the argument. We are not talking about any complexes, we are talking about changes and their results. The hypothesis is that the components of these complexes existed before the changes occurred. Without that hypothesis, this discussion could not take place. But with that hypothesis we can settle the question of whether CD depends on C and D or whether C and D depend on CD. Since C and D existed before the change bringing about CD, it is not the case that C and D derive their existence from CD. What does not exist is nothing. If C and D depended on CD before CD existed, they would depend on nothing; they would depend and not depend. Their existence would be derived from another and not derived from another, since it would be derived from nothing. Where there is a necessary causal relation between A and B and where A does not depend on B for its existence or some condition necessary for existence, B depends on A; B is the effect and A is the cause. For if it were also true that B did not depend on A for existence or some condition necessary for existence, between A and B there would be no necessary causal relation, no relation such that one would not exist without the other. Since C and D do not depend on CD but CD would not exist without C and D, CD depends on C and D.

There is, however, another reason why it can be true of two really distinct things that one of them would not exist without the other; each can be a necessary effect of the same third thing. But the necessary causal relation expressed by "CD would not exist without C and D" is a relation of CD to C and D, and not a relation of each of these to some third thing T. And if this relation were a causal relation to some third thing, it would amount to a relation to an efficient cause. As I am going to describe that relation, if both C and D, on the one hand, and their union in CD, on the other, are necessary effects of T, then T is the efficient cause of CD. Therefore to claim that CD does not depend on C and D on the grounds that they all depend on T would be to concede the point at issue. (And interestingly enough, it would not be an epistemological fallacy to argue that the truth of "CD would not exist without C and D" could not be known from acquaintance with that for which "C", "D" and "CD" are used if the necessary causal relation being expressed were a relation to a *tertium quid* for which "T" is used. This is an argument from an effect, knowledge of a particular self-evident truth, to one of its necessary causes, causal relations between that for which certain words are used. It would be an epistemological fallacy to argue that knowledge causes its objects to be what they are. But it may be the case that what the object being known is causes the knowledge to have certain characteristics.)

I in no sense claim that this is a complete analysis of the idea of causal dependence. But this account is sufficient to allow us to proceed with the argument for efficient causality. The dependence of a complex whole on its parts is an instance of what is traditionally known as material causality. I will refer to it as *component causality* in order to underscore the fact that my argument does not rely on the Aristotelian ontology from which the name "material causality" comes. It is worth mentioning that component causality is one of the relations describable by the word "cause" and its cognates in ordinary language. What a thing is made of is a cause of (at least) some of its characteristics. To a question like "What caused the first automobile to suffer more damage than the second?" we accept an answer like "The first was made of aluminum, the second of steel". And at the very least, the notion of causal dependence as so far developed here is closer to the ordinary usage of "cause" than is the highly artificial definition (regular succession between events of certain kinds) forced on philosophers by their acceptance of Hume's arguments.

Mindful of the influence of Hume's critique of causal necessity, I emphasize that it is a complex whole's identity with itself that establishes its dependence on what is not identical with itself. The principle of non-contradiction would be violated if a complex whole were identical with any of its parts or if it existed while any of its parts did not exist. Since, by hypothesis, the parts existed before the complex whole, they can exist without the whole existing; therefore the whole's relation of not-existing-without-them is a relation of an effect on at least some of its causes. (The objection that the unity of distinct elements in a complex whole may be a logical construct will be dealt with in section 7.3.)

What if there were a world of absolute simples in no way conjoined to one another? Would it be necessary to recognize any causal relation in such a universe? If any of these simples undergoes a change which at some time it was not undergoing, the answer must be yes. By hypothesis, the simple entity is really distinct from its state of change, for at some time the simple entity existed without its state of change occurring. Therefore it is non-identical with its state of change. Furthermore, the state of change could not exist without the simple entity that undergoes it. For it is contradictory for a change occurring to S to exist if S does not exist. Therefore a necessary causal relation links the state of change with that which undergoes it. Which is the cause and which the effect? Does the change depend on that which undergoes it or does that which undergoes it depend on the change? Just as CD was not necessary for the existence of C and D, so the change is not necessary for the existence of the entity undergoing it, S, for S existed before the change. Therefore it is S that is necessary for the occurrence of the change rather than vice versa. The necessary causal relation linking the change and that which undergoes the change is a relation of dependence of the former on the latter. (Again, the relation we are knowing here is a necessary causal relation between S and a change, not yet a relation between either of them and some third thing T. If it were a relation to T that we were dealing with here, efficient causality would already by known.)

In other words, the fact of change occurring to something that at one time was not undergoing the change establishes the dependence of the change on a cause, namely, that which undergoes it. What undergoes a change will be called a component cause of the change whether the change is occurring to something complex or to something simple. For it is change which establishes that the causal relation between a complex and its components is a relation of dependence of the former on the latter. And if a change is occurring to something to which it was not previously occurring, it is the change which has a relation of dependence on that which undergoes it. (Notice also that by appealing to the fact of changes which have not always been occurring, the argument avoids any philosophical disputes about what to count as a real distinction, which the definition of causal relations calls for. What can exist without undergoing a certain change is really distinct from that change. Similarly, the components of a complex whole, if they at one time existed without being united to one another, are really distinct from each other and from their union in this whole.)

The notion of component causality, however, can be extended to any case of a relation of a capacity, such as a capacity to become part of a whole or to undergo any sort of change, to the fulfillment of the capacity, as long as the fulfillment in question is not the fulfillment of a capacity to act as an efficient cause. We said earlier, for example, that if what exists is distinct from its existence, it is a component cause of its existence. The extension of "component cause" beyond the case of complex events constituted by components which are themselves complex runs the risk of creating confusion. For a simple-undergoing-a-change or an essence-with-existence are legitimately describable as unions of components. But we are directly concerned only with causality in the case of change. And since all the changes we experience occur to and result in complexes, the technical sense we have given "component causality" has an intuitive value. Nor do I know any terminology with an equivalent intuitive value which does not run, for various reasons, an equal or greater risk of confusion.

The analysis of change reveals one more thing which is crucial to the demonstration of efficient causality: that which undergoes the change, and which therefore is a cause on which the change depends, is an *insufficient* cause for the existence of the change; and the components are *insufficient* causes of the existence of the complex. For the sake of familiarity I will limit myself to the use of the component-complex example; the same argument will apply to anything undergoing a change it was not previously undergoing. The insufficiency of the components as causes of the complex follows from the hypothesis that the components existed before the change bringing about their union in this complex whole. If the necessary can be defined as that without which something would not exist, the sufficient can be defined as that with which something does exist. If A's being what it is is sufficient to cause the existence of B, B must exist when A exists. Components can exist before the change bringing about their union exists. And if C and D exist, but CD does not exist, the existence of C and D is necessary for the existence of CD, but it is not sufficient. Simply by existing and by being what they are, the parts of those complex wholes which are changes or the results of changes are not sufficient to cause the existence of those complexes.

7.1.3 Component causality and efficient causality

Since the existence of the components is not sufficient for the existence of the complex, we can ask whether some causal function other than component causality must be fulfilled in order for an event to take place. Is there some thing or things, other than the event itself or its components, without which the components, which are not associated in an event by the mere fact they they are what they are, would not become so associated as to constitute the event? An event does not occur simply because its components are what they are. Does it occur because something other than itself and its components is what it is? That is what I mean by an efficient cause, something non-identical with an event that supplies what is lacking in the event's components in order for the event to occur. What is lacking in the components is that, to the extent that their existence is compatible with the non-existence of the event, their being what they are is not a sufficient cause of the event's taking place. The efficient cause adds to a situation whatever the component causes themselves lack in order for there to be sufficient causes of the occurrence of an event. Efficient causality brings it about that it is the components' association in a particular event, rather than some other possibility compatible with the nature of the components, that takes place.

This notion of efficient causality is vague. But its indefiniteness will neither invalidate the argument nor render it trivial. A more complete understanding of efficient causality requires additional information about the various kinds of complexes that come to be through change and the various kinds of components that make them up. If it can be shown that the principle of efficient causality is necessarily true, then when we pursue such additional information, we are only acting on the basis of what we already know, namely, that there do exist relations of efficient causality about which there is more information to be gained. But if we do not believe that efficient causes are necessary for changes to take place, we do not have to worry about how efficient causality works. Hence we can postpone further study of the nature of efficient causality in favor of establishing the existence of a causal function other than component causality which is necessary for the actual associating of the components in the composite.

The next two chapters will deal with the question of how we make progress in understanding the nature of causal relations. Clarity requires that something be said in anticipation of subsequent causal investigations, however. Since changes require causes, a change that has not always been occurring will not occur unless previous changes have brought into existence sufficient causes for its occurrence. But these previous changes need not be changes in which the sufficient causes are produced out of whole cloth. As we make progress in following up on the knowledge that the component cause of a change is not its only cause, we learn to make distinctions, as do Harré and Madden (1975), between *agents* by whose powers events are produced and those things whose only relation to an effect are the triggering of an agent's powers or the removal of an impediment to its action. Previous to the occurrence of a change, therefore, the agents and component causes necessary for the change may exist. But there may also exist some impediment to the agent's action. Or the agent may not exist in the proper spatial relation, whatever that may be, to the component cause or to some other thing required to trigger its action. Consequently, when we speak of sufficient causes for a change existing, we mean certain things both being what they are and existing in whatever spatial relations may be necessary for the change to occur. And such a situation comes into existence as a result of the existence of previous spatial arrangements in which agents caused changes to take place.

The $64,000 question is yet to be answered. The principle of efficient causality affirms a relation between distinct realities. If a sentence affirms a relation between distinct realities, how can its opposite be contradictory? How can denying a sentence concerning a relation between things that are *not* the same require us to affirm and deny the *same* thing at the same time? So far we have seen that a change is at least caused by the components that enter into it and that the components are not sufficient causes of the change. But we have learned these things by appeal to the principle of non-contradiction, to the identity with itself of a change undergone by something and to the identity with itself of something undergoing a change it previously was not undergoing. Nothing has yet shown how the identity of an event or its components would be violated if we deny the event's relation to an efficient cause distinct from itself and its components.

Even before the argument for efficient causality is made, however, we know that the back of Hume's argument against causal necessity has already been broken. Not only is it possible for there to be things which, by their identity with themselves, are related to others in such a way that without the others they would not exist, but we now know there are such things. Changes occurring to things are by their own nature relative to that which undergoes them. We have overlooked this obvious point just because it is so obvious (and for another reason explained in section 11.4). We cannot think of a change without thinking of that to which it occurs; consequently we do not take note of the non-identity between them.

But the process of learning what we have so far learned about causality has required more than abstracting (in the psychological sense) ideas from our sense experience. Complexes and changes are present in experience. But describing changes and complexes as having causes and describing component causes as insufficient for their effects required us to give the words "cause" and "insufficient" functions which are not just faint reproductions of the *manner in which what is experienced is objectified in sensation*.

Part of Hume's failure to see how the denial of causal dependence could produce contradiction stemmed from his inadequate appreciation of the extent of our powers of finding ways for words to articulate what we have experienced. "Would not exist without their components" is a description of the events we experience which relates them to what is not identical with themselves, their components. But because events are complexes made up of components, their identity with themselves guarantees the self-evident truth of this description.

And by acquaintance with the ways we are using their terms, other descriptions can be known to be necessarily true or false of what we have already described as "caused by its components" or "cause of the complex of which it is a part". For instance, it is necessarily true that what has causes is not one of its own causes, since causes are defined as not identical with that of which they are the causes. And it would be contradictory for that which is caused to have nothing for its cause, since the causal relation is defined as a relation between realities.

To describe events as efficiently caused is to describe them as related to what is not identical with themselves. And "not efficiently caused" is a description of events which denies a certain kind of relation between them and what is other than themselves. But on the basis of what we already know about the dependence of events on their components and about the components themselves, it can be shown that denying the kind of relation to the non-identical I am calling efficient causality leads to the denial of, among other things, some already established necessary truths about the dependence of events on causes. For example, it can be shown that if events do not depend on efficient as well as component causality, either they are caused and have nothing for their cause or they are caused and are causes of themselves. In other words, denying efficient causality leads to contradictions corresponding to the formulas of Clarke (nearly enough for our purposes) and Locke.

Denying the description "efficiently caused" has necessary implications for that which we have already described as dependent on the non-identical because dependent on components and for what we have already described as that on which something non-identical with themselves depends. It implies, for instance, that a caused event can be described as having necessary but not sufficient causes, since the components are insufficient and no other cause is available to supply what they lack. And, since no other cause is available to supply what is lacking in the causality of the components, it implies that an event's components can be described as the totality of the causes necessary for the event. If an event occurs without an efficient cause, there is nothing other than the components themselves without which they would not become associated in the event. And both of these implications of the denial of efficient causality lead in different ways to contradictions, including contradictions corresponding to the formulas of Clarke and Locke.

In other words, I am agreeing with Hume both that the contradictions pointed out by Clarke and Locke arise if and only if it is presupposed that events are caused and that the arguments of Clarke and Locke presuppose this gratuitously. But I have, in effect, supplemented their arguments with a demonstration that events are indeed caused; events are changes and changes are caused by that which undergoes them. The question before us, then, is *not* whether events are caused, whether they would not exist without what is non-identical with themselves. We already know that. The question before us is whether contradictions arise if component causes are the *only* causes that changes have.

7.2 The Demonstration

At last we come to the main attraction. Here rigor is more important than familiarity. And since change is the key notion, the demonstration will focus on a change's causal relation to that which undergoes it (which for the sake of argument we can assume to be either complex *or* simple), rather than on a complex event's causal relation to the elements whose association constitutes the event. First, I will show how contradictions follow from describing that which undergoes a change as the sum and total of the change's necessary causes. Secondly, I will show how contradictions follow from describing a change as having a necessary cause but not sufficient causes.

7.2.1 The first argument

Can the causality of that which undergoes a change be the sum total of the causality necessary for the occurrence of the change? Can that which undergoes the change be the change's only cause? Our hypothesis is that that which undergoes the change existed previously to the change. In making that which undergoes the change the only cause of the change, are we referring to this cause *as it exists before the change* or as it undergoes the change? Is it the causality of that which undergoes a change as it exists before the change that is the sum total of the causality necessary for the occurrence of the change? Before the change, that which undergoes the change is *only a potential cause* of the change. Only when the change is occurring is that which undergoes it an actual cause of it. Call something that undergoes a change "S" (since it may be something simple). If S does not exist, then a change-occurring-to-S does not exist. That which undergoes a change is something without which the change would not exist, that is, a cause of the change, at the time when the change is occurring.

Before the change, what will undergo the change does not actually have the relation to the change it will have at the time of the change. It is only potentially that on which the change will depend when the change actually occurs. And what is only potential in a certain respect does not exist in that respect. If the sum total of the causality necessary for the change is the causality of that which undergoes the change as it exists before the change, a change requires causes and has nothing to cause it.

Here it makes no difference whether or not we consider potentiality a logical construct. If you consider it a logical construct, all the better. Causality is a relation between distinct realities, and we recognize that change requires causing by recognizing its relation of dependence on a reality distinct from itself, that which undergoes the change. If change requires a cause and the sole cause available is such only as a logical construct, change is caused by something and by nothing.

On any interpretation of potentiality, if an F is only potential, an F does not exist; it is nothing. What is potentially an F may exist actually in many other respects, but it does not exist as an F. Change has a relation of causal dependence on that which undergoes it at the time when the change actually occurs. If the change's only cause were that which undergoes the change as existing before the change, the formula of Locke would apply. What requires something actually functioning as a cause would have nothing actually functioning as a cause.

On the other hand, if the sole cause necessary for the change is that which undergoes the change in the act of undergoing the change, a formula similar to that of Clarke (but without any temporal connotations) will apply; the change would be a cause of itself. We are asking what is the totality of things not identical with the change without which the change would not exist. By the principle of non-contradiction, we know that the change itself is not one of those things. And we also know that the change would not exist unless something not identical with itself existed. But this thing not identical with the change on which the change depends is that which undergoes the change *in the state of actually undergoing the change.* By making an actually changing thing the sole cause of the change, we have included the change itself among the causes of the change.

Lest anyone think some logical sleight of hand is going on here, let us look at the argument more closely. C has a relation of dependence on S. Unless the requirements of that relation are fulfilled, there is no change; C does not occur. Simply by being what it is, S is only a potential cause of the change; for S can exist before the change as well as at the time of the change. To be caused by what is only a potential cause is to be caused by something which may exist in many respects but which is not a cause. The mere existence of S, therefore, does not fulfill the requirements of C's relation of dependence on S.

The hypothesis we are refuting is that there is nothing distinct from either the change or the change's component cause that brings it about that the requirements of the change's relation of dependence on that which undergoes it are fulfilled. But C requires an actual component cause, and S becomes an actual component cause only by undergoing C. Therefore C is one of its own causes. For C is something without which S would not be an actual cause of C. And ''is something without which X would not exist'' is our definition of a necessary causal relation: a relation of a cause to a necessary effect, of an effect to a necessary cause or of two necessary effects to the same cause. Here ''would not exist without'' cannot refer to C's being a necessary effect of S, since

S can exist without C. And an additional cause, of which S's being an actual component cause of C would be an effect, is excluded by hypothesis. Therefore, "would not exist without" must refer to C's being a necessary cause of S's component causality of C.

C is hypothesized to be the effect of S. But where C itself is the only thing non-identical with S without which S would not be an actual cause of C, C's being something without which S would not be a cause of C implies more than that C is an effect of S. If the relation of C to S is *only* that of effect to cause, if C is not one of its own causes, C has no cause. For just by being what it is, S is *not* a cause of C. It is the fact that C occurs which makes S an actual cause of C. Therefore C is cause and effect in the same respect at the same time. It is an effect since it depends on S actually functioning as a cause. But consequently it also depends on anything making S an actual cause. And the hypothesis is that S is made a cause of C by nothing other than C itself.

Another way of putting it. To say that C depends on something other than itself is to say that it depends on something other than itself being what it is; C would not exist without the existence of the set of characteristics constituting the reality of something other than itself. But without C, the characteristics constituting S make S only a potential cause of C. C itself is the characteristic constituting S an actual cause of C. Therefore, if C's happening to S is not an effect of some third entity which *ipso facto* is the cause of S's becoming the actual cause of C, C causes itself, since S is constituted the cause of C solely by the fact that C is one of its characteristics.

The contradiction disappears if and only if there is something other than the change and what undergoes the change which, by being what it is, supplies what is lacking in the causality of that which undergoes the change; it disappears, in other words, if and only if S becomes the actual component cause of C as a result of some other thing's being what it is. That other thing, the efficient cause or agent, brings it about that what was only potentially changing actually changes. (Magnets being what they are, when previous changes have brought a magnet in sufficient proximity to an iron filing, the iron filing will change in position.) And by making something acquire the characteristic of undergoing a change, an efficient cause brings it about that what was only a potential component cause of change becomes an actual component cause of change, actually functions as something without which a change would not be occurring. In other words, because something other than S is what it is, S cannot remain what it is; that is, S must change.

S becomes a cause of C only by undergoing C. But no vicious circle of C causing itself occurs since something other than C causes C in S. S's being a cause is the same as S's undergoing C and so is an effect of the agent, not of C. C makes S a cause only in the sense that S becomes a cause by an agent's making S undergo C. But subtract the agent and C has a relation of dependence on itself since C depends on a total cause including C as the characteristic making it C's cause. Add the agent, and C does not depend on itself since the total cause of C does not include C. That S is a cause only when undergoing C then simply means that S becomes a cause by something else, which with S constitutes C's total cause, making S undergo C. The total cause of C, namely, the situation in which its efficient and component causes exist in the proper spatial relation, would not exist without C. But here "would not exist without" describes the relation of causes to a necessary effect. Potential component and efficient causes of C do not depend on C for being what they are. But given that they are what they are and that some change prior to C brings them into the proper relation, C will necessarily occur.

Needless to say, the same argument which establishes that something really distinct from C causes S to undergo C establishes that the cause of S's undergoing C is really distinct from S. It is possible for the same thing to be both a component and an efficient cause of a change, but these causal relations must terminate in really distinct characteristics of the thing. For example, the linking together of two magnets is an event that occurs through the causality of the magnets both as component causes and as the efficient causes which bring the components into union. But before being magnetized, a piece of metal has the characteristics (of having mass and being in a solid state) enabling it to undergo such a motion (whether induced by a magnet or by something else, since the same motion may be produced in many ways), without having the characteristics enabling it to induce a motion magnetically. Therefore the characteristics by which a magnet is an efficient cause and a component cause of a change are not the same, even though the latter may be necessary for the former.

Nor could such characteristics ever be the same. The necessity for the efficient cause follows from the fact that the nature of the component cause does not enable it to be the sole cause of a change. Consequently the characteristics making something eligible to be the component cause of a change cannot be identical with characteristics that would enable it to be the efficient cause of the change. To the extent that the nature of S is compatible with its either undergoing or not undergoing C, S's being what it is is not sufficient to cause C. And to that extent, something more than the nature of S is needed to prevent C from either being caused and having no cause or being cause and effect of itself.

Let us conclude this first argument by asking if the contradictions which require the postulation of the efficient cause could have been prevented in any other way. Could they be avoided by claiming that the change and that which undergoes the change are causes of one another, though not in the same respect? In what respect would that which undergoes the change depend on the change? It existed before the change, therefore it does not depend on the change in that respect. Now hypothesize that the only difference between S before C and S at the time of C is C itself. Then S depends on C for nothing other than the fact of its actually undergoing C. But for S to actually undergo C is what it means for S to be the actual cause that C requires for its existence. Consequently C is cause and effect in the same respect.

Next hypothesize that the difference in S before C and at the time of C is not only C but also C_1 in respect to which S depends on C. C_1 either is or is not that by which S becomes an actual cause of C. If the former, C is cause and effect of itself since S depends on C for C_1. If the latter, C alone is that by which S becomes cause of C, and the same conclusion follows. (Aristotelians have always held the principle "causes are causes of one another": the form causes the matter to have certain characteristics while the matter causes the individuation of the form. But this is possible only because the efficient cause, of which neither the matter nor the form is a cause, causes the matter to acquire a form—which is thereby individuated by the matter—and therefore breaks the vicious circle of a thing's existing by causing its own cause.)

But is it perhaps nothing more than a trivial truth that S is an actual cause of C only when undergoing C? Is this only a misleading way of saying that S actually undergoes C only when it is undergoing C? It might be if we did not know that C has a relation of dependence on S. C could not exist without S but S can exist without C. The only thing S cannot be without C is an actual cause of C. If C would not exist without S actually functioning as a cause and it is C on its own that constitutes S a cause, C is cause of itself.

Can the contradictions be avoided by interpreting the situation of S-undergoing-C in a different way? Instead of claiming that it is the change which is caused, why not say that it is the *union* of the change with that which undergoes it that is caused? Then it can be argued that since the change as such is not caused, we do not have to worry about the contradiction of the change being cause of itself. Rather both the change and that which undergoes the change make their own contributions to the event which is their union. And the fact that S actually undergoes C only when undergoing C assumes its rightful status as perfectly innocuous.

But the revised causal description of the event of S-undergoing-C merely states in different terms the same problem we have been dealing with. The event now is viewed as a complex whole, SC. And this whole depends on its components, S and C. Therefore we must ask the question whether these components are the totality of the causes necessary for the occurrence of the event. And here not only is S not a cause of SC just by being what it is, but also C does not even exist before the event occurs. In this case, therefore, the pointlessness of asking whether the totality of the event's causes are its components as capable of existing apart from the event is self-evident.

The alternative is to claim that the totality of the event's necessary causes are its components when they are actually causing the event, that is, when they are so united as to constitute the event. But then this union of diverse components is one of its own causes. For the components of the union function as actual causes only insofar as they are united in it, that is, only insofar as they each have that relation to the other that constitutes the event of which they are causes. (The responses to objections in section 7.3 will show the independence of this argument from the specific account one gives of the ontological status of the "union" or "association" that components have in a composite.)

It is only for the sake of argument, however, that I have granted the possibility that, with reference to the event of something undergoing a change, it is not the change that is caused but only the union of change with that which undergoes it. Even if this analysis of the causal structure of events were true, it would remain the case that events require efficient causes. But this analysis cannot be true. The event-of-S-undergoing-C could not exist unless S and C, which are really distinct from one another since S predates C, exist. Still, the change would not exist without something undergoing it, while that which undergoes it did exist without the change. Therefore C itself, not just the union of C and S, has a relation of dependence on S. And it is superfluous to posit an additional relation of dependence for the union composed of the change and that which undergoes the change as if whatever causes satisfy the requirements of the first relation would not by that fact satisfy the requirements of the second.

This concludes the first argument for the necessity of the principle of efficient causality. Before going on to the second let us stop to recall what this first argument has accomplished. At the beginning of the argument we knew that a change has a relation of dependence on, would not exist without, that which undergoes it. And it is about the change (or the complex made of the change and that which undergoes it, if you insist) that we are asking what is the sum total of that which is not identical with it without which it would not exist. But at the beginning of the argument we also knew that insofar as those causes which are the alleged sole causes were able to exist without the event occurring, their existence is not a sufficient cause of the occurrence of the event. Therefore, if that which undergoes the change (or the components of the event) is claimed to be the sole necessary cause, we have covertly made the effect into its own cause or we have implied that a caused event has nothing for its cause. For what is alleged to be the sole cause becomes a cause only by the occurrence of the event.

What the argument has proven is that for the event to occur a causal function other than that of what undergoes the change (or that of the components of the event) must be performed, a causal function without which what undergoes a change would not be something undergoing the change (or without which the components would not be united in the complex). Since an event has a relation of dependence on its component cause(s), it also has relation of dependence on whatever is required for its component cause(s) to actually undergo a change. Hence when we recognize a relation of dependence on a component cause, we are recognizing a relation which extends beyond the component cause to the efficient cause. If the relation does not extend beyond the component cause to the efficient cause, it cancels itself out, for the component cause cannot fulfill the requirements of that relation (namely, to be something that changes) alone.

7.2.2 The second argument

This argument will show that contradiction results from describing changes as having necessary causes, that is, the things that undergo them, but not sufficient causes. An objection to the contrary, directed against an earlier version of the argument, has been proposed by Milton Fisk. Perhaps composite CD is dependent as having components but is not dependent as a synthesis of components. CD is dependent in one respect but not in another respect. For that respect in which it is dependent, namely, as having components, CD requires necessary causes, namely, components C and D. These causes are not sufficient for CD, however, because there is a respect in which CD is independent of them. But in that respect in which CD is dependent on them, C and D may be not only necessary but also sufficient causes of CD. CD is dependent as having components and in that respect the components themselves may be sufficient causes of CD; CD is not dependent as a synthesis of components, and in that respect the components are not sufficient causes of CD.

The reply to this specific form of the objection is that if C and D can exist without CD existing, C and D are insufficient for CD precisely as having components. For C and D can be what they are without being components of CD; their own natures are compatible with either being or not being components of CD. But the objection can be stated in a more general form.

If a change has necessary but not sufficient causes, it is dependent on its causes in some respects but not in others. The causes must provide some condition(s) necessary for the existence of the change, conditions without which the change would not occur. (The causes would not be direct causes of existence itself, for then they would be sufficient for the existence of the change.) But if all a change's necessary causes are not sufficient for it, they can exist without the change existing. Therefore, when the change takes place, the occurrence of the change is the occurrence of *more* than whatever it may be the causes contribute to the change. And why can there not be more to a change than what it derives from its causes? If so, we can say the change is dependent on causes with respect to the necessary conditions they provide and independent of causes in other respects.

But let change C depend on causes in respect R. C's causes must be sufficient for C in respect R, sufficient to provide that condition for C's existence. To see why, assume the causes are not sufficient for C in respect R. If R is some condition necessary for the existence of C and all the causes necessary for R can exist without R existing, the existence of R is the existence of *more* than what is provided by C's causes. Consequently the causes do not supply R itself but some other condition necessary for R. In other words, C depends on its causes in respect R because it depends on them in some other respect, R_1, necessary for R. And are C's causes necessary but not sufficient for C in respect R_1? Then the causes supply some condition necessary but not sufficient for C in respect R_1. And C depends on its causes in respect R, because it depends on them in some other respect R_2 which is necessary but not sufficient for R_1. And are C's causes insufficient for C in respect R_2?

To prevent an infinite regress, we must hold that if a change has necessary causes in some respect, it has sufficient causes in that respect. If a change depends on causes for conditions without which it would not exist, the change would not exist without causes sufficient to supply those conditions. Otherwise, a change would be dependent on causes in a certain respect and at the same time not be dependent on causes in *that* respect but in some other respect necessary but not sufficient for the first. For the first respect would be a condition which is in part derived from the change's causes and in part not derived from the change's causes.

Therefore, if C depends on cause S in respect R but S is not sufficient for C in respect R, C also depends on other causes which, together with S, are sufficient for C in respect R. But we know that C is dependent with respect to the condition of having a component cause, having something to which it occurs. And we also know that S, the thing to which C occurs, is insufficient for C in precisely that respect; by being what it is, S is not a component cause for C. To recognize that C is caused by that which undergoes it is to recognize that it is caused by a thing which is itself insufficient to be something by which the change is caused. Consequently there must be another cause, or causes, whose existence, together with the existence of S, is sufficient for the event of S undergoing C to occur. In other words, efficient causality is necessary for the condition of S undergoing C to obtain. S does satisfy the requirement of C's relation of dependence on a component cause by providing C with that to which it occurs. S does this, however, not by being what it is but because something else's being what it is makes S undergo C.

And causes sufficient for S to undergo C are causes sufficient for C to occur. Therefore, from the existence of a necessary cause for C, the argument has shown the need for sufficient causes of C. (And in general, what has necessary but not sufficient causes *must* be a union of distinct elements, those elements which are derived from the causes and those that are not; and these elements are themselves causes of the complex of which they are components. But if the union of these elements is not brought about by sufficient causes other than the elements themselves, their union is one of its own causes. Therefore whatever has necessary causes must have sufficient causes.)

Perhaps it will be responded that I promised a contradiction but only delivered an infinite regress. And to establish the necessity of a statement it must be shown that denying it produces contradiction, not that it produces infinite regress. But infinite regresses are contradictory in the following manner. In order for the assumptions which generate the regress to be true, the regress would have to be finite or not occur at all. Since they generate an infinite regress, the assumptions could be true only on pain of contradiction. Thus C depends on necessary but not sufficient cause S in respect R if and only if it depends on S in respect R_n which is necessary but not sufficient for R. But there can be no such respect R_n. For the assumption is that S is only a necessary, not a sufficient, cause in respect R_n. Therefore S is a cause in respect R_n if and only if it is a cause in respect R_{n+1} which is necessary but not sufficient for R_n. In order for C to depend on S in respect R, therefore, the end of an unending regress would have to be reached. For if the regress does not terminate at R_n, which is a condition for C supplied by S, there is no dependence of C on S in respect R. As a result, to claim that C has necessary but not sufficient causes in respect R is to imply that C is causally dependent and causally independent in the same respect at the same time.

Can it be objected that S's being a *potential* component cause of C is a condition necessary for there to be an actual component cause, but a condition for which S's being what it is is sufficient? True, but it is not the case that C is dependent with respect to having something which potentially undergoes it and not with respect to having something that actually undergoes it. What actually undergoes it is something non-identical with C without which C would not exist. Therefore C's relation to what actually undergoes it is a relation of dependence on a cause, and C's causes must be sufficient for C in this respect. The absence of causes *sufficient* for the existence of a component cause of C is the absence of causes *necessary* for C's relation of dependence on its component cause to be satisfied.

Can the infinite regress be avoided by rejecting the assumption that S is not a sufficient cause of C? S is not sufficient to be a component cause of C before it undergoes C, but perhaps S undergoing C can be considered a sufficient cause of C. This way out, of course, merely repeats the error of making C part of that which causes it, only now the contradiction occurs because C makes S a sufficient, rather than just an actual, cause of C. It is true that S would not be an actual cause of C without C. But if S itself were a sufficient cause of C, the fact that S would not be an actual cause of C without C would mean nothing more than that C is a necessary effect of the existence of a sufficient cause for C. Since S by itself is not a sufficient cause for C, however, the fact that S would not be a cause of C without C means more than C's being a necessary effect of a sufficient cause. The fact that C differentiates S as a sufficient cause from S as an insufficient cause means that S is made a sufficient cause of C by C. Therefore, in the absence of something other than C to which S owes the fact that it is undergoing C, C becomes cause of itself. In fact, the occurrence of C depends on some thing or things non-identical with C functioning as sufficient causes. And whatever these things are, C itself cannot be among them.

If we try to avoid the infinite regress without positing an efficient cause, therefore, contradictions of the Clarke or Locke varieties are just around the corner. But if we posit an efficient cause, C would not be cause of itself even though it remains true that S would not be an actual cause of C unless it were undergoing C. For S undergoes C if and only if the existence of something other than C is sufficient for the occurrence of C in S. C then differentiates S as an actual from a potential cause only because S and the efficient cause together constitute sufficient causes of which C is a necessary effect.

To summarize the second argument. An event whose necessary causes can exist without the event occurring is an event with necessary but not sufficient causes. When such an event occurs, that which occurs must include something over and above what its causes contribute to it. For if the existence of the event derived entirely from its causes, the causes would be sufficient for the existence of the event. Therefore the event depends on its causes in some respects but not in others. And for whatever necessary conditions it derives from causes, an event must have sufficient causes. Otherwise the causes do and do not provide those conditions. But as capable of existing without undergoing C, S is not a sufficient cause of C in that particular respect in which C is known to depend on a cause, namely, as having something which undergoes it. Therefore something other than S must, together with S, be sufficient to cause the occurrence of C by causing S to undergo C. This something is what is meant by the efficient cause. C occurs only because things non-identical with itself, the efficient and component causes, are what they are.

Before turning to a discussion of difficulties, I want to mention another Humean argument against causal necessity which, though clearly not demonstrative, has been very persuasive. We are told that if it is necessary for events to have efficient causes, we should not be able to imagine an event occurring without also imagining a cause for that event. For the necessity of their opposites prevents us from imagining square circles, mountains without valleys, two colors occupying the same space, etc. But we can imagine an event occurring without imagining any efficient cause. Think of a billiard ball at rest. Now imagine it going from rest to motion and rolling across the table. In order to imagine this, we had to imagine no cue hitting the ball, no hidden triggers or magnets, no earthquakes or explosions. It seems, therefore, that the statement that events have efficient causes is not a necessary truth.

But in the situation just described there is an efficient cause operating to bring about the motion of the billiard ball. The billiard ball and the event of its going from rest to motion are *imagined*. And the mode of operation of the efficient cause of this event corresponds exactly to the kind of event of which it is the cause. The efficient cause of the imagined billiard ball going from rest to motion is the person doing the imagining and whatever psychological operations of his are required for this event to be imagined. When we imagine changes taking place, we are the causes of the fact changes are being imagined to occur.

It should come as no surprise that when we examine what is represented in the imagination, we do not find there a cause of the fact that it is so represented. For the fact that something is represented in the imagination is an *effect* of the activity of the imaginer. By hypothesis, we are examining the effect rather than the cause. Even if we imagined the cue hitting the ball, the cause of the ball's being represented as going from rest to motion would still lie on the side of the one doing the imagining and not on the side of what is being imagined. We could, for instance, imagine the cue hitting the ball without the ball moving. And what is the cause of the fact that the cue itself is imagined as being in motion rather than at rest?

Instead of imagining billiard balls, let us contemplate that really existent leaf that is swaying "in the breeze" outside the window. Hume was right; we do not *see* any efficient causality as we watch the leaf swaying. Yet what we are seeing is an effect of efficient causality. The motion in the leaf is induced by something (in all probability by the breeze although there could be other causes). If the motion in the leaf were not induced by something, the leaf would not be in motion. How do we know this if we do not see efficient causality? We know this because we can employ word-functions like would-not-exist-without to objectify relations holding between terms which are seen, specifically, a relation between swaying and that which sways. Word-functions like this allow us to understand the swaying as (not *see* the swaying as) something dependent, something that owes its existence to what is really distinct from itself, something in need of things which, by being what they are, are sufficient to bring it about that a leaf, which is not in motion simply by being what it is, goes from rest to motion.

7.3 Problems and Clarifications

Here I will take up some difficulties with the idea of efficient causality, in general, and my demonstration of its necessity, in particular.

The complexity of events has been presented as evidence that events are caused. But what kind of existence does a complex have over and above the distinct existences of the components making it up? What if the state of union or association between the parts of a whole is a logical construct resulting from our way of looking at the parts rather than a feature attributable to an object of our knowledge insofar as it is a thing. If this is the case, no really existing cause is needed to account for the association of components within a complex because what is being accounted for is not itself a real existent.

To bring the problem into sharp focus, imagine a world composed of only two entities each of which is absolutely simple. What kind of unity do we have here? What kind of *uni*-verse would be constituted by these two monads existing in splendid isolation from one another? Over and above the distinct realities of the two monads, what reality would the "union" of these entities have? Assume one of the monads is capable of cognition. It apprehends the fact that the two of them co-exist. Does their participation in a complex whole called a universe amount to anything more than the fact that they are apprehended as co-existing? If not, it seems that nothing more is needed to account for the existence of the "complex" that is "made up" of these monads than the separate existences of the monads themselves. An efficient cause would have nothing to cause since the union of the monads is, from the point of view of extra-objective existence, nothing.

My reply will be on two levels. First, in the universe just described there is an efficient cause operating to bring about a union of diverse elements. According to the objection, the monads constitute a unified whole only in the eye of a beholder. But then the unity of the whole requires an eye doing the beholding. In other words, we can make the same reply here that we made to the argument about our imagining changes without imagining causes. There is no really existing cause for a cognition-dependent object considered as such, for as such the object does not really exist. In this sense, the motion of the imaginary billiard ball has no real cause since the motion itself is not a real existent. But there are efficient causes for the knowledge acts by which cognition-dependent objects become objects. The person doing the imagining is responsible for the fact that the ball is being imagined as in motion. These efficient causes of cognition really exist because cognition really exists and because knowers undergo the change from not performing a certain act of cognition to performing it. The efficient causes in question can be physical, chemical, biological, psychological and sociological. Sociological causes are especially relevant in the case of *linguistic* objectification of cognition-dependent objects.

There is another level, however, on which we can respond to the objection. So far we have hypothesized the co-existence of two simple entities but have not hypothesized that they change in any respect. And since it is change, rather than complexity, which has been relied on to demonstrate the existence of efficient causality, let us assume some change really takes place in our hypothesized universe, a change undergone by one or both of the monads. A new state of affairs now exists in this universe which, by hypothesis, is not a cognition-dependent object. And the existence of this new state of affairs requires efficient causality. For it could not have occurred without that which underwent the change. And since that which underwent the change is hypothesized to have existed without the change occurring, its existence is not sufficient to produce the change.

Furthermore, any state of affairs produced or ended by a change occurring to a real existent must itself exist cognition-independently. For self-evidently, if something new has not come into existence or something old gone out of existence, a change has not occurred. Consequently, if what is new in the state of affairs produced by a change is an association the elements of which existed before the change, though not in this association, this new way for the elements to associate is *not* a cognition-dependent object. We may need to use a logical relation (specifically, conjunction as in "the union of C *and* D") to objectify this association of elements. But what is thereby objectified is not a cognition-dependent relation. (And to know this, we do not have to have completed an ontological analysis of the nature of the association as opposed to that of its elements.)

The next problem is the classic difficulty concerning the simultaneity or non-simultaneity of causes and their effects. Does the efficient cause act at a time prior to the occurrence of the event of which it is the cause? Then the production of the event does not exist at the time of the event. And how can something that no longer exists have any influence at all on what presently exists? On the other hand, if the action of the efficient cause and the occurrence of its effect are simultaneous, all events must be simultaneous and time disappears.

It is the second horn of the dilemma that must be grasped. Since the occurrence of a change is simultaneous with the existence of sufficient causes for it, the actual exercise of efficient causality must be simultaneous with the existence of its effect. (Section 10.1 demonstrates this from another point of view.) The act of sawing a piece of wood in two is simultaneous with the wood's undergoing the change of being sawed in two. The change produced by an efficient cause will result in the existence of a state of affairs that will succeed the action of the cause, but the action of the cause must co-exist with the occurrence of the change from which the new state of affairs results. What is it, then, that keeps all caused events from being simultaneous?

In the first place, what is there to prevent the exercise of efficient causality itself from existing continuously over a period of time? The effect of this kind of action will be a process of change existing continuously over the same period of time, for example, wood being sawed in two or water coming to boil over a source of heat. This allows time to elapse in the universe, but it does not solve our problem completely. Why do not all processes exist simultaneously? Why do some processes start or stop while others are still going on or after others have ceased? To see why, assume agent A is causing patient P to undergo continuous change C. At some time after the beginning of this change, patient P can achieve a state in which it becomes the agent for change C_1 which then comes into existence. C_1 may itself be a continuous process which eventually leads to something else becoming the agent of change C_2. Water being heated begins to give off steam, the steam gradually builds up in a chamber until it is able to cause a turbine to rotate, the turbine picks up speed until it is able to move a boat against the current, etc.

Or let us assume that the initial change, C, is a piece of wood being sawed in two. That change ceases with the complete separation of the wood into two pieces. But the cessation of that change may be simultaneous with the beginning of others. For instance, one of the pieces of wood may begin to fall as it separates from the other. It may fall into a fire that has already been ignited. The fire causes new changes in the wood as a result of which there is a larger fire than before, and a larger fire is an efficient cause capable of producing further effects which were not possible previously.

To sum up: at some point in the *continuous* action of agent A, patient P can have acquired sufficient new characteristics or new spatial relations to other things to be either the agent or the patient of a new change which will then come into existence. For a change will necessarily occur once there is an efficient cause and a component cause actually possessing the required characteristics and in the required relation to each other and to other things. The problem of how the simultaneity of cause and effect is compatible with time must be classified among the greatly overrated difficulties.

Before leaving this topic, however, I should point out another reason why processes brought into existence by efficient causes can succeed one another in time. As I have mentioned already, a change which is simultaneous with the action of an efficient cause will yield a state of affairs which continues in existence after that causality has ceased. My arguments do not require that efficient causality continue after the changes which yield these states of affairs have ceased. Efficient causality is not required again until a new change occurs which alters the already existing state of affairs. But component causality *does* continue after a change; a complex state of affairs would not exist without its parts. Hence that which is made to undergo a change by an efficient cause is potentially, not only a cause of the change, but a sustaining cause of the result of the change. The efficient cause is necessary because, by its own nature, what undergoes a change is only potentially a cause both of the change and of the result of the change. But once the change making something an actual component cause has occurred, no further change is required to make the thing a sustaining cause of the result of the change. For the efficient cause has already produced the change necessary to make the thing what it is not by its own nature, a component cause of the result of the change. (And if a further change were necessary, there would be an infinite regress.)

But the state of affairs resulting from a change can be either a continuous state of rest or a *continuous* state of *change*. By Newton's second law of motion, a moving body will continue to move with constant velocity and direction unless acted on by an external force. If a body is at rest, however, a change is required to put it in a state of motion; and that change requires an efficient cause, both by a law of physics and by a necessary ontological truth. But nothing in our arguments calls for efficient causality subsequent to a change which brings a body from a state of rest to a state of motion if that motion is in all respects continuous as it would be in a vacuum. For in a vacuum, no further change requiring additional efficient causality would take place.

In other words, if an efficient cause can make an actual component cause of a continuous state of rest out of something that is only poten-tially such a cause, it can make something an actual component cause of a continuous state of motion. The event of something going from rest to motion is a change that does not remain in existence for the duration of the motion; therefore the causing of that event does not remain in existence for the duration of the motion. And the need for an efficient cause ceased when it caused the change which made a potential component cause of the state of motion actual. (On the other hand, in whatever respects such a state of motion is *not* continuous, if there is a change in the velocity of a body's motion, for instance, an efficient cause is necessary. And when motion takes place in an environment of causes that alter velocity, for a body to move at constant velocity, efficient causality is required throughout the motion.)

A final objection comes from the Aristotelian school (to avoid historical controversies, let us think only of contemporary Aristotelians). Replying to it will allow me to clarify the ontological character of the concept of causality and to confirm the power of my arguments for efficient causality.

A necessary causal relation obtains between A and B if they are really distinct from one another, and if at least one of them would not exist without the other. Causality is defined in terms of existence; that is what makes the principle of efficient causality an ontological truth. Aristotelians make a distinction between existence and essence. "Essence" refers to that which exists, the answer to the question "What is it that exists". "Existence" refers to a factor in things really distinct from essence and related to essence as act to potency; realities are realities because that-which-exists exercises an act distinct from itself called existence. (Another way of putting it would be this: tak-ing that-which-exists not as essence but as a whole including existence, essence is *that by which* an existent is *what it is*; and existence is *that by which* an existent is an *actual existent*. I do not disagree at all with the merits of this way of putting it. But since it will not make any difference in what follows, I will rely on the first and, for our pur-poses, simpler formulation.) Distinguishing that which exists from its existence may appear to give a way out of the contradiction of a change being a cause of itself if it has no efficient cause.

Our argument began with the recognition of a change's dependence on a cause. By the definition of a necessary causal relation, what anything that depends on a cause depends on a cause for is existence. Consequently, if a change is identical with its existence, to include the change among the causes of its existence is to include the change among the causes of itself. Or if the union of a change with that which undergoes the change is identical with the existence of that union, the union is among the causes of its existence only on penalty of being cause of itself. But if the change or the union are distinguished from their own existence, the contradiction seems to disappear. It is the existence of the change or the union that requires causes. And if the change or the union are among those causes, they are not causes of themselves but causes of something other than themselves, their existence.

In the light of some of the things said earlier, it is necessary to elaborate on the idea that what an effect owes to its causes is its existence. If an event has necessary causes, what is it that we deprive the event of by removing or enjoining one of its necessary causes? We deprive it of existence; we prevent it from occurring. But it does not follow that in order to satisfy the definition of "cause" a thing must directly bestow on another a factor named "existence" which is distinct from that which exists. As we have seen, in order to be a cause, all a thing need contribute to its effect is some condition necessary for the existence of the effect. In Aristotelian philosophy, for example, only God can bestow on a thing that specific factor named "existence" without which there is nothing. God makes things by making existence-essence composites. But in the case of physical things, the essences which receive existence are themselves composed of matter and form. Matter and form are causes of one another, in different respects, because each supplies the other with conditions without which it would not exist.

And in addition to giving existence to essences composed of matter and form, God causes changes by which matter receives new forms by causing the existence of both the material and (created) efficient causes of change. The created efficient cause's being what it is induces the change bringing a new form to some already existing matter. Therefore the created agent is a genuine cause. Still the agent, the change and the matter exist by virtue of God's bestowal of existence on the relevant essences. The change, therefore, depends on God, the created agent and the matter but in different respects. (And after the change, God continues to hold the new matter-form union out of nothingness by giving it existence.)

This digression has given us an illustration of the idea that an effect can depend on causes for existence without those causes supplying an element named "existence" distinct from what the effect is. This is important because speaking of an effect as owing its existence to its causes does not presuppose a real distinction between existence and essence even though such a distinction is the premise of the current objection.

Now to respond. Rather than giving us a way to avoid the cause-of-itself contradiction, the objection merely provides a way to state that contradiction in different terms. What a change owes to its necessary causes is existence. But if the sole necessary cause is that which undergoes the change in the state of undergoing the change, the existence of the change, not just the change, is one of its own causes. The existence of the change depends on what is not identical with itself. The question is what is the totality of that which is not identical with the existence of the change and on which that existence depends. Whatever the answer is, the existence of the change cannot itself be part of that totality. Therefore that which undergoes the change, as actually undergoing it, cannot be the sole cause of the existence of the change.

The same conclusion would follow if instead of discussing the existence of the change we were discussing the existence of the union of the change and that which undergoes it. As long as existence is what an effect owes to its causes, existence cannot be among those causes. And this is true whether or not we distinguish existence from that which exists. Therefore an efficient cause is necessary on any interpretation of the situation; it is necessary if the change is identical with its existence, if the change is not identical with its existence, if the union of the change with that which undergoes it is identical with its existence, if the union of the change with that which undergoes it is not identical with its existence. This further reinforces the independence of the argument from the particular analysis one gives of the relation between the change and that which undergoes it or the relation of association of the components in a composite.

In conclusion, I should point out that no claim is being made that the arguments presented here are the only ways to prove that events have efficient causes. The ways of doing this may be indefinitely many. I believe, however, that the approaches I have taken have a fecundity that make them particularly useful. From the present reasoning a number of other important necessary truths about causes and their effects follow. Some of them, ontological principles with significant epistemological implications, will be explained in the next chapter. Nor has this chapter done more than touch on epistemological questions concerning the causing of our *knowledge* of necessary causal relations and self-evident causal truths. These issues are dealt with in Chapters Nine and Eleven.

CHAPTER EIGHT

Causality and Knowledge I:
Causality and Empirical Knowledge

Causality is neither an empirical nor an epistemological concept. It is an ontological concept. And lack of an ontological analysis of the causal relation has severely limited the tools we can bring to bear on the problems of philosophy and on the understanding of the philosophic process itself. Examples of the philosophic use of this concept have appeared at various points in this study: the contrast, exemplified by the concept of self-evidence, between a causal analysis and criteria for identifying individuals of a certain kind; the causal priority of things existing over things being terms of knowledge relations; the argument that learning to use words in certain ways is a sufficient cause of our acquaintance with logical relations and that this acquaintance is a sufficient cause of our knowing the truth of many sentences; the explanation that contradictory sentences cannot be true because contradictions cannot exist and knowledge of the identity of objects with real existents is the goal of making sentences. I have even pointed to causal relations in the sentences of arithmetic.

None of these uses of causality are justified *tout de suite* by the principle of efficient causality. Far from it. But demonstrating the principle of efficient causality shows that we have a way of verifying assertions about causal relations which is other than empirical. Every such assertion must be justified on its own merits by showing that its denial leads to a contradiction. But the demonstration of the principle of efficient causality proves that there is no logical or epistemological injunction against showing that the opposite of a causal assertion yields a contradiction. Therefore legitimate use of causal concepts and arguments is not to be confined to the phenomena of regular succession between events of certain kinds. And as was pointed out in section 3.4.2, a causal relation can be necessary without our being able to demonstrate the contradictory of its opposite from word-functions alone.

Most progress in human knowledge consists of attaining a better understanding of causal relations whose existence is known, but only vaguely known, at the beginning of the inquiry. Hume's arguments against causal necessity have prevented us from seeing this and, therefore, prevented us from appreciating what human knowledge really is. When we are undertaking an inquiry concerning really occurring events, we always have a vague grasp of the fact that the change or changes we are considering have a relation of dependence on the other. For we know events would not occur without their component causes. And we also know that the component causes can exist without the event occurring.

At the beginning of every such inquiry, therefore, we have a vague grasp both of component causality and of the other information we need to conclude to the dependence of events on efficient causes. Do we actually draw this conclusion? The least that can be said is that the psychological evidence indicates both that we often perceive things as if causally related and that this fact cannot be explained, in the manner of Hume, by repetition. Whether or not an individual actually goes through a process of reasoning analogous to our arguments for efficient causality is less important than the facts that a) we do perceive things as if related by efficient causality; b) we believe in the necessity of efficient causes unless we undergo the contrary philosophical conditioning; and c) valid reasons which are available to all can be given for this belief.

Not only is there epistemological and psychological evidence that inquiry begins from an implicit awareness that events are what they are because other things are what they are; there is evidence from the history of science as well. When we look at the very beginning of western science, Greek science, we find a search for component (or "material") causes. The birth of science is generally dated from the asking of the question "What are things made of?" Is it earth, air, fire, water or some combination of these? But it is not long before Greek scientists recognized that components which can exist without uniting with one another do not provide a sufficient explanation for the fact that they do unite. An efficient cause explaining why components enter into the combinations that actually occur is required also. And so Anaxagoras postulated his Nous.

There is no use speculating whether Anaxagoras arrived at the necessity of an efficient cause by following a line of thought similar to ours. What cannot be denied is that he was aware that events have component causes, he found the components insufficient to explain events, and he had evidence for this insufficiency available to him whether he made use of it or not. And if Anaxagoras had not grasped the insufficiency of explanation in terms of component causes, someone else would have had to do it. Where would we be today if we were still trying to explain events solely in terms of component causality without giving an account of why components which can exist without uniting with one another in a certain event do so unite?

Finally, the history of philosophy provides evidence that our unsophisticated belief that events have efficient causes is based on a vague grasp of valid reasons for that belief. Previous to Hume, the reasons most frequently offered by philosophers were analogous to those of Clarke and Locke. And like those of Clarke and Locke, most philosophic arguments work only on the presupposition that changes are caused in some way. But the frequency of that assumption in arguments for efficient causality indicates an inarticulate but firm grasp of the fact that changes are indeed caused in some way other than by efficient causality, a way that itself calls for the efficient cause.

Psychology and history aside, the demonstration of the principle of efficient causality implies that events occur in nature because the physical things that cause them are what they are. As we will see, it is because things have the active and passive dispositions they do have that events occur as they do. And knowledge of the natures of things is, in general, knowledge of the properties that must belong to things if they are to produce and undergo the changes we observe taking place. Knowledge of the natures of things, in other words, is an expansion and refinement of that vague knowledge which is at the beginning of our inquiries, the knowledge that events take place because some thing or some things other than themselves is what it is.

But how do we accomplish this improvement over our initial knowledge? Advances in the understanding of causal relations go on both in the empirical sciences and in philosophy; the next two chapters will discuss each of these in turn. This chapter will explain how empirical science accomplishes this, at least to the extent of giving the main outlines and resolving the main difficulties. I will begin by contrasting the ontological concept of causality with causality as it has been traditionally understood in the philosophy of science. The following section will deal with inductive reasoning and with simplicity as a basis for deciding between conflicting theories. For many readers that section will be one of the most important in the book. I will show that viewing progress in knowledge as progress in understanding causal relations dissolves difficulties over which much energy has been spent. Among the results of the discussion will be relations between inductive inference and the criterion of simplicity which to my knowledge have not hitherto been pointed out. But the most important result will be the demonstration that there are necessary truths about causal relations which not only solve the problems of induction and simplicity but in so doing provide the much-sought-for foundations of empirical knowledge.

The last section of the chapter will extend the analysis to the paradoxes of black ravens, grue emeralds and, to complete the explanation begun in Chapter Three, contrary-to-fact conditionals. The fact that knowing the natures of things is knowing their causal relations renders these problems null and void. But for those who do not admit necessary causal relations, these problems are unsolvabie. Finally, I will deal with some problems my own position gives rise to. If empirical knowledge is causal knowledge, why does the concept of cause find less and less favor among scientists? And if necessary causal relations can hold between word-functions, why is acquaintance with those word-functions so often insufficient to reveal the necessity? This question has been left unanswered since section 3.4.2 because it requires explanations to be given here.

8.1 Causality in the Philosophy of Science

It is in the philosophy of science that the style of philosophizing we are accustomed to differs most from the style that is being defended, and used, in this book. This difference is a direct result of our acceptance of the Humean critique of causal necessity. In this section, I will discuss the impact of that acceptance. The philosophy of science has traditionally had its own ''principle of causality'' quite distinct from the one I have defended. The most important difference is that acceptance of the Humean arguments has forced philosophers of science to make causality a cognition-dependent relation. Closely related to the "principle of causality" in the philosophy of science is the problem of causal determinism. It has often been pointed out that the epistemological point of view has wrongfully dominated the problem of determinism. I will show that the demonstration of the ontological principle of efficient causality reinforces that criticism.

It cannot be emphasized too much how dependent is the philosophy of science on Hume's critique of causal necessity. This should be, but is not, obvious to everyone. In correspondence concerning my arguments for causal necessity, a philosopher of science offered this as his main objection: one cannot talk about causality except by talking about how the concept of cause is used in science. If the Humean arguments were correct, this would be true. If statements of causal relations cannot be necessarily true, the only things for us to do are to pursue empirical knowledge and give logical analyses of the language-forms we employ in our empirical knowledge. But if the Humean arguments are not correct, if his disjunction between "relations of ideas", that is, logical relations, and "matters of fact" is not exhaustive, then we have a method other than empirical of knowing truths about causal relations. In other words, the view that all knowledge of things as things is empirical derives from the Humean critique of the necessity of the ontological principle of causality.

And from Hume, philosophers of empirical science have acquired their own "principle of causality" of which the following is a representative statement:

> The state of a physical system is known at a certain time. Then, by means of some scientific law, the state at a later time can be computed and thus predicted. When this kind of analysis is possible, modern science calls the earlier state the *cause*, and the later state the *effect*, and the law which mediates between them is spoken of as a causal law. Causality is the relation between the states; it is simply a methodological relation conferred upon a situation by virtue of the manner in which science is able to describe it.
>
> To say that causality holds in nature is at best an elliptical way of claiming that science succeeds in understanding temporal changes in its physical systems as a sequential unfolding or propagation of states of the kind just outlined. The statement refers directly to the procedural element of science, and indirectly to nature in holding that the procedure is successful when applied to nature. (Margenau, 1961, p. 204)

As Margenau points out, this makes causality an *epistemological* relation. For it is defined by the universality (meaning *true* of *all* of a kind) of laws (meaning a certain type of *sentence*). "Cause" and "effect", then, are object-descriptions, not thing-descriptions, since cause and effect are defined as terms of knowledge relations. Or at best, causality is a logical relation, since it is defined by universality. So defined, causal relations are not even possibly features of things as extra-objective existents. They can be no more than logical constructs characterizing things as a result of their being made objects of knowledge by means of laws.

But then we are prohibited from thinking what an acorn is as a thing has something to do with the fact that the tree that will grow from the acorn will be an oak and not a maple. We are prohibited from even speculating about this because the relation between the acorn and the oak must be solely in the eye of the beholder. Since "cause" and "effect" are object-descriptions or logical relations, it would be contradictory to suggest that things may depend on one another for their existence even though the way they depend on one another remains unknown to us. Surely this is the epistemological fallacy with a vengeance. We should recall again what Geach had to say about Ryle's attempt to analyze dispositional properties in terms of contrary-to-fact conditionals licensing us to make inferences:

> I need hardly comment on Ryle's view that "the rubber has begun to lose its elasticity" has not to do with a change in the rubber but with the (incipient?) expiry of an inference-ticket.

Whether we define causality by reference to laws or to contrary-to-fact conditionals, sentences about causal relations cannot inform us about acorns and rubber, they inform us about our knowledge of acorns and rubber. It would be contradictory for causal properties to characterize things as things, for causality is a knowledge relation.

Beauchamp and Rosenberg (1981, p. 282ff.) have sharply distinguished the epistemological relation of being explained by covering laws from the regularity theory of causation, which they call an "ontological" theory. They recall (p. 260) Hume's assertion that causes operate mind-independently. There is no doubt that Hume *intended* his theory of causation to make causality something cognition-independent, but that is not what his theory actually does. One sequence of events may be similar to another mind-independently, but similarity alone is insufficient for causality. The only thing that distinguishes Hume's view of causality from that most elemental of fallacies, *post hoc ergo propter hoc*, is that *all* events similar to A in certain respects have been followed by events similar to B in certain respects.

Universality, however, is a logical relation. Only individuals exist extra-objectively. Beauchamp and Rosenberg will reply (p. 281) that cause and effect are not logical entities but are that which terminate the relation of universality. Yes, logical relations terminate in non-logical things, but that does not make the relation any less logical. The question is what makes these things causes and effects; what constitutes the causal relation, something extra-objective or something logical. It might also be replied that logical relations can be used in thing-descriptions without reducing the word-function of the description to the logical. Yes, but using a logical relation in a thing-description is not the same as attributing the logical relation to the thing in its real existence. And to call a thing a "cause" for Hume is precisely to attribute to it the status of being an instance of a universal. All As may be followed by Bs extra-objectively. But for an A to be a cause cannot amount to being a member of the set of As.

Furthermore, the logical relations used in thing-descriptions cannot add anything extra-objective to what is being described. Let us agree that temporal succession, spatial contiguity and similarity are extra-objective. These three taken together do not make causality. And the only thing that universality adds to them is a logical relation.

The fact that Hume's concept reduces causality to a logical relation does not mean there is no connection between the universality of a causal law and what really exists. But to explain that connection, we need a concept of causality other than regular succession. For if something can be truthfully asserted of *all* events of a certain kind, the *cause* of the truth of the universal statement is what exists extra-objectively. And in general, the appropriateness of the use of a logical relation in a thing-description is an *effect* of the extra-objective nature of the thing being described. (See sections 5.5.3 and 8.3.1.) But the causing of truth or of the appropriateness of using a logical relation in a thing-description is not a matter of regular succession.

Corresponding to the difference between the ontological and empirical principles of causality, there is a distinction to be drawn between causal necessity as understood from the ontological point of view and causal determinism in physics. We are told by many that Heisenberg's indeterminacy principle commits us to the belief that causal determinism does not hold in nature. Determinists, of course, reply that the only indeterminacy required by quantum mechanics is epistemological, namely, the fact that we are barred from knowing except statistically both the position and velocity of particles. In rebuttal, the indeterminist points out that there would be little new in

Heisenberg's principle if it asserted no more than methodological in-determinacy. For it has always been admitted by scientists that a cer-tain degree of randomness in measurements is inevitable. What has not always been recognized by science is that laws of nature make representation of many crucial experimental results by non-statistical equations impossible. Therefore what is newly imposed by quantum mechanics is a commitment to physical (or "ontological" in the loose sense) determinism. (See, for example, Northrop, 1961, p. 204.)

But a commitment to physical indeterminism results only if we assume that the experimental method is the only method at our disposal for acquiring knowledge of things as things. For we must be relying exclusively on the methods of science to define "deter-minism", "cause", "position", etc. And of course we are free to define words in any way we like. But if we admit no other method of acquir-ing knowledge and defining terms, we are allowing our commitments concerning things as things to be governed by a prior commitment concerning things as objects of knowledge. Without the epistemological commitment that there is nothing more to be known than can be known by experimental methods, the state of classical physics can-not be contrasted to that of quantum physics as physical determinism to physical indeterminism. The contrast should rather be described either as the difference between methodological determinism and methodological indeterminism or as the difference between one kind of methodological indeterminism (one that described nature by means of non-statistical equations but recognized the inevitability of ran-domness in experimental results) and a new kind of methodological indeterminism (one for which the use of non-statistical equations is excluded by laws of nature).

Laws of nature rule out methodological determinism because exact measurement of position and velocity is rendered impossible by *causal* relations holding between physical existents, causal relations, specifically, affecting the conditions under which measurements are obtained from experiments. But that physical causal relations rule out certain modes of knowing by means of experiment does not imply that they rule out any modes of existing. (In particular, these causal relations do not rule out the existence of causal relations.) That deter-mined position and velocity cannot be *objects* of scientific knowledge does not imply that they cannot exist as *things*. On the other hand, scientific theory is so constructed as to be consistent with the kinds of experimental results that physical causal relations make possible. When science knows that conditions in nature require results to be of a definite kind, theory must be constructed accordingly. But neither the theory thus constructed nor the facts about nature on which it is based tell us that there is nothing true of nature other than what is known by means of such a theory. They tell us only that, to the extent our knowledge is acquired by experimental methods, deterministic results are impossible.

More and more, today's philosophers of science are trying to rid their discipline of dogmatic presuppositions. They have differing motives for doing so. Some are trying to be less empirical, while others are trying to be more consistent about their empiricism. Whatever the motives, the goal of freedom from dogmatic presuppositions is far from being achieved. And it will never be achieved as long as the doctrine that there can be no necessary causal relations between things remains unchallenged. This is an unempirical dogma if there ever was one.

Unless he has been deliberately conditioned to think otherwise by his philosophical education, the man on the street knows it is at least possible that, since oaks are what they are, an oak would not have come into existence unless there had been an acorn. He knows, in other words, it is possible that the coming into existence of oaks depends on acorns (and the soil, moisture, atmosphere, light, and temperature) being what they are. Other combinations of things might be capable of producing oaks, but it is possible that, in the world as it actually exists, those combinations never occur.

And why should the man on the street now know such things? When we are laughing at a joke, do we not know that, *ceteris paribus*, we would not now be laughing (effect) if we had not grasped the joke (cause). When we have counted the number of people in a room, do we not know that our knowledge of the number was caused by our act of counting? We know that assent to premises is what causes our assent to conclusions. I am aware that it was hearing of my friend's death that, together with certain psychological dispositions, produced my sadness, that it was his insult that gave rise to my wrath, his being late that made me impatient. Sometimes such incidents do not have these effects. That is exactly the point. When we are aware of these causal relations, we are not aware of them on inductive grounds. Causality is not generality.

Of course, unconscious causal factors may enter into the explanation of why we laugh at one joke and not at another, why we are saddened by the news of one death not another. Still, we are aware that getting the joke or hearing the news is one of the causes of our reaction. Perhaps we have specifically been hypnotized to laugh when we hear certain jokes; still, hearing the jokes is one of the causes of our laughter. I apologize for what I am going to do to you next, but it will make this point experientially. What do existentialist cows say? "Ca-moo, ca-moo." On inductive grounds, I cannot predict what your reaction to this pun will be. But *you* are aware that your pain (or pleasure) is at least in part due to your getting the joke. And it is not the constant conjunction of similar events that gives rise to (that is, causes) your awareness that you experienced pain (or pleasure) because of that joke. (I am indebted to the late Willis Nutting for pointing out this kind of experiential causal knowledge. He found it in the German philosopher Joseph Geyser.)

Awareness of such psychological causal relations should have made us skeptical of identifying causality with generality, and we have other grounds for skepticism as well. When we are asking what caused an event, we are asking what brought that event into existence. And when we know the cause but are asking why this cause produced this effect, we are asking for features of the existent which is the cause that are sufficient to bring the effect into existence. Previous to the Humean critique, philosophers were in agreement with the man on the street in being realists enough not to attribute what does or does not exist to a logical relation like generality or to the word-function of an object-description like "covered by a deterministic law". Being causes and being effects were recognized to be true of things as things. It is only because they now admit no other way of gaining knowledge of causal relations that philosophers define causality in terms of logical relations by means of which we summarize the results of accumulated experiences.

Since he is still a realist, the man on the street is able to attribute the growth of an oak, not to a logical relation, but to what an acorn is as a cognition-independent existent. When an ignited match sets fire to paper, he can attribute the event to what the flame and paper are. Not only that, but he can believe that the sciences tell us how acorns cause oaks by telling us what acorns are, that the sciences tell us why flames ignite combustible materials by telling us what flames and combustible materials are. Regarding the unobserved entities science postulates to explain observed behavior, the man on the street can think that the theories of science explain observations in terms of what these entities are supposed to be, not in terms of knowledge relations extrinsic to the natures of these entities.

These remarks lead to a suggestion. The arguments of Chapter Seven aside, let us conform to contemporary fashion and show our disdain for dogma by making the assumption that events necessarily have relations of dependence on causes. Do not object that necessity is strictly a matter of logical relations. That is the point at issue. Again, Hume's argument that the denial of a causal relation cannot produce contradiction is, at the very least, a non-sequitur. By its identity with itself, A may be so related to B, that were A to exist without B, A would both be and not be what it is. In other words, one reality may be essentially relative to another, as a change occurring to something is relative to that to which it occurs.

Therefore only an epistemological fallacy could rule out the assumption of causal necessity a priori, for we would have to identify the necessity of a truth with our ability to know that necessity from acquaintance with word-functions alone. And in order not to suspect that something is missing when the possibility of causal relations characterizing things as things is eliminated on the grounds that the elasticity of rubber or the combustibility of paper are nothing more than terms of knowledge relations, we have to have acquiesced to the all-sufficiency of the epistemological point of view and substituted it for the ontological.

Let us therefore treat the ontological principle of efficient causality as an hypothesis. What results do we get when we make the assumption that changes would not occur unless caused to occur? The following sections will show that the problems of induction, simplicity, contrary-to-fact conditionals, the foundations of empirical knowledge, and the raven and grue paradoxes are solvable when we make that assumption. The assumption would therefore recommend itself as the superior hypothesis even if our direct arguments for it were not conclusive. It is much more likely than not that when a change occurs to something, the change would not have occurred without the existence of realities other than itself, realities whose existence makes it impossible for the thing to remain as it is.

8.2 The Foundations of Empirical Knowledge

I will begin by deducing a number of consequences from the ontological principle of efficient causality. The deductions will rely on Chapter Seven's explanations of the word-functions involved in the demonstration of the principle of efficient causality, but will not presuppose that demonstration. The consequences deduced will prepare us to grasp the necessary truths that provide the foundations for inductive reasoning and for the belief that the simpler explanation is the superior explanation. They will also prepare us for the discussions of contrary-to-fact conditionals, black ravens and grue emeralds which will appear in section 8.3.

8.2.1 Preliminaries

From our previous discussion of the principle of efficient causality, we know that it asserts that when change C occurs, C has a relation of dependence both on that which undergoes it (the component cause) and on something else (the efficient cause) without which the component cause would be undergoing C only potentially. For by its own nature that which undergoes a change is not sufficient for the change even in respect to being its component cause. Let us assume the efficient cause of C is A and the component cause is S. To say that C is caused is to say that C is what it is by reason of the fact that realities other than itself, A and S, are what they are and have the spatial relation to one another that they do have.

Concerning the issue of causality and spatial relations, when we ask *where* the causality of the efficient cause must be, if anywhere, the answer is where the need for the efficient cause exists. If a thing has a relation of dependence on an efficient cause and that thing is a spatial thing, that is, has a location in space, then the relation of dependence on an efficient cause has the same location in space. Since the need for the efficient cause has a location in space, the fulfillment of that need must take place at that location. Therefore, the causality of the efficient cause exists at the location where the effect that needs this causality exists. This means there is no action at a distance. For an efficient cause is such just by being what it is. (See section 10.1.)

Since C is caused, then, its occurrence is *necessitated* by A and S (1) being what they are, that is, having the natures that they do have and (2) being spatially related to one another as they are related when C occurs. When a change takes place, in other words, it is necessary *both* that the change has efficient and component causes *and* that this change take place given that the circumstances in which it occurs are what they are.

Why? Where is the contradiction in the claim that the circumstances could be what they are and the change fail to occur? The contradiction lies in the fact that were C not to occur given that A and S are what they are and have a certain spatial relation to one another, A and S would be at most necessary and not sufficient causes of C, potential and not actual causes. And that contradicts the hypothesis that, when C does occur to S, A is C's efficient cause. For by definition, the efficient cause is what compensates for the component cause's insufficency to be a cause of the change; the efficient cause is what makes the component cause become a component cause.

If A and S can be what they are without C occurring, other causes are required which, together with A and S, are sufficient for S to undergo C; otherwise, either C is cause of itself or it has no cause. And given that all these causes, efficient and component, are what they are and are related to one another as they are related when C occurs, the occurrence of C is necessary. Two magnets must be in sufficient proximity if they are to cause each other to move. Other causes bring about this proximity. A buzz saw (efficient cause) may be running, but it cannot cause the event of a log's being cut unless the log (component cause) comes in contact with it. If other causes have brought about the proximity of the magnets or the contact of the saw and the log, the events of the magnets moving toward one another and the log being cut must occur. If these events fail to occur even though the magnets are sufficiently close and the saw in contact with the log, some other element of the situation must be present which prevents the event from happening. The teeth may break off the saw as it contacts the log, for instance. And when these events fail to occur, their non-occurrence is necessitated by the circumstances of their non-occurrence being what they are. (For more on these points, see section I.2.)

Therefore the occurrence of every physical event is determined by the configuration of circumstances in which it occurs. Since all such events are caused by other existents and since whenever an effect comes into existence its causes must exist, the circumstances in which events occur (and which include the state of the entire universe at that time) must contain their causes. And these causes cannot fail to produce these effects.

Further important consequences of the principle of efficient causality follow from this. C necessarily occurs because A and S are what they are and have certain spatial relations to one another. Therefore the natures of A and S (what A and S are) either *are* or *have* dispositions by which A and S are determined to behave in these ways in such circumstances. A's nature is (or if you prefer, has) a disposition such that A necessarily produces C in these circumstances. By its nature, S is so disposed that it necessarily undergoes C in these circumstances. For it is because A and S are what they are that they cannot fail to cause C in these circumstances. Therefore A and S are naturally determined to cause C by being what they are. If not, C would not occur of necessity in these circumstances, and A and S would not be sufficient causes of C. (These ideas are worked out in more detail, and difficulties overcome, in the following sections and section 9.3.)

The next point is a qualification on our previous results that we cannot afford to overlook; the occurrence of any event *is not necessitated* by the nature of any of its causes taken in isolation from the rest of the circumstances in which an event occurs. A's nature necessitates that A produce C in these circumstances. But nothing in A's nature requires that A actually be present in these circumstances. A does not produce C unless it has a certain spatial relation to something else, S, which is capable of undergoing C. But A's nature does not necessitate A's being in a situation in which S is present. A buzz saw can run without being in contact with a log.

It can be the case that the nature of a given efficient cause makes it necessary for it to exist only in conjunction with a component cause of a specific kind. But that would be a characteristic of an efficient cause of a particular type, not a characteristic of efficient causes as such. And if an efficient cause's nature requires its linkage with a component cause of a particular nature, the reason for this necessity must lie in causal relations between these natures or between things with these natures and some third thing. Therefore if we can ever know that such a linkage holds, it can only be as a result of the kind of causal investigation whose foundations we are now examining. And the justification of these methods of investigating causal relations cannot presuppose that such a linkage ever obtains. What the use of these methods will show, on the other hand, is that, in general, the natures of specific efficient causes do not necessitate that they exist only in union with component causes of particular kinds. Buzz saws can exist without logs.

In addition, it can be demonstrated that the occurrence of physical events always requires the existence, past or present, of a multiplicity of efficient causes. We have defined events as changes that have not always been occurring. If change C has not always been occurring, then sufficient causes for C have not always existed or have not always been in the proper spatial relation to one another. And a change prior to C is required to bring it about that sufficient causes for C exist in the proper relation to one another.

When there are two distinct changes, there are two distinct relations of dependence on efficient causes. Of course, both changes may have the same efficient cause, A. But why was A not always producing the prior change? Let us call the prior change C_1 and the subsequent change C_2. If A is capable of producing C_1 but is not always doing so, a prior change must be required involving either other efficient causes necessary for A to produce C_1 or C_1's component cause. If A's causing of C_1 requires the existence of other efficient causes, the occurrence of C_2 requires the past or present existence of more than one efficient cause.

Or A's causing of C_1 may require that C_1's component cause undergo a prior change, its being put in sufficient proximity to A, for instance. Again, A could be the efficient cause of that change, but then we must ask why A has not always been causing that change. Our cycle of questions is condemned to eternal return unless we admit that a multiplicity of efficient causes must have cooperated for the change with which we began, C_2, to occur.

But the nature of an efficient cause as disposed to produce certain effects in certain circumstances does not necessitate that it be in a situation where the other efficient causes, or the results of their past existence, are present. If, in a given case, necessary causal relations insure that A could not exist unless the other conditions required for C_2 had also been brought into existence, we could not know this except through the use of methods whose justification cannot take this for granted. And these methods will show that this is in general not the case.

In sum, causes are naturally determined so that they behave in certain ways in certain circumstances. But an individual event is not necessitated by the natural determination of any of its individual causes to behave in these ways. In addition to those natural determinations, the existential positing of a multiplicity of distinct causes is required. The upshot of this is that the world we have been describing as a world in which events are necessitated by the configuration of circumstances in which they occur can also be described as a world of chance and contingency. Yes, it follows from the principle of efficient causality that given the state of the physical universe at any time, the future course of natural events cannot be other than what it will be. But the future course of events is not due solely to the natures of the causes that exist in the universe, it is also due to whatever existential configuration of those causes happens to obtain at the time. And the existence of that configuration is not due solely to the natures of the causes that produced it but also to their existential configuration. And so on.

It is customary to define determinism by reference to the inevitability of the future course of natural events. Determinism in this sense is other than the necessity by which the natures of things dispose them to behave in certain ways. In relation to an individual event, that necessity is only hypothetical; if A is in a certain situation, C must occur. But if A had been in a different situation, its nature would still have been what it was and its dispositions to behavior the same, even though C would not have occurred. The occurrence of the situation in which A cannot fail to cause C has a contingent relation to A's being what it is. This allows us to describe the occurrence of any event as a "chance" event in the sense of something not necessitated by the natures of any of its causes. From this point of view it can be said that chance is non-contradictorily combined with necessity and determinism in every event.

8.2.2 The principle of induction

With this background we can now turn to some of the consequences of the principle of causality that are more directly related to inductive reasoning. Assume that A and S are the sole causes of the existence of C. Then if at some other time or place causes B and T, which have *the same dispositions to behave* as A and S respectively, are spatially related in the same way A and S are related when they cause C, and if no additional cause preventing its occurrence is present, an effect differing from C only numerically, or by space-time coordinates, will occur. To put it another way, if a cause with the same dispositions to behave as A is placed in circumstances which are the same, with respect to other causal dispositions and A's spatial relation to them, as the circumstances in which A produced C, the new cause will produce an effect which is in all respects the same as C except for the time or place of its occurrence. For that C should have occurred in the first place was necessitated by the fact that A's and S's causal dispositions were what they were and that A and S were placed in a certain relation. Therefore causes which are distinguished from A and S only by space-time coordinates will have an effect distinguished only by space-time coordinates from C.

Space-time coordinates are extrinsic denominations expressing, as opposed to implying, nothing of the reality of that of which they are asserted. The assumption we are making, therefore, is that whatever enters into the reality of the causes in these different circumstances would be the same except numerically. It follows that the effects must be the same except numerically. If not, effects being what they are would not be necessitated by the behavioral dispositions of their causes being what they are.

Like all necessary truths, the necessary truth that if the circumstances are the same in other respects, a cause with the same dispositions as A would produce an effect the same as A's is hypothetical. But in this case, the hypothesis is one whose fulfillment is quite probably impossible. And even if it were not impossible, it is unlikely that we could ever know that the hypothesis had been fulfilled. I will not stop to argue either of these points here, however. For the hypothetical necessary truth in question is not one on which inductive reasoning is founded. It is only a step in that direction.

In order for inductive reasoning to have a rational basis, it need never be the case that causes and circumstances differ only numerically from other causes and circumstances. Causes and circumstances need only be the same with respect to causal dispositions necessitating the occurrence of an effect having certain characteristics in common with another effect. If A and S are the sole causes of C, then for it to be necessary that an effect occur having certain characteristics in common with C, all that is required is the existence of causes B and T which are the same as A and S with respect to the dispositions that determined A and S to cause an effect with those characteristics. To this we must add a *ceteris paribus* clause with the following meaning: in the situation in which B and T are present there is no additional causal factor which will prevent the occurrence of an effect having those characteristics in common with C.

In sum, if causes exist whose dispositions to behavior are the same as those dispositions of the causes of C that necessitated the causing of an effect with certain of C's characteristics, and if these causes are spatially related as were C's causes, and if no additional cause is present which would prevent the occurrence of such an effect, then an effect having these characteristics in common with C must occur. This is *the principle of induction*. For brevity, let us use the following formula keeping in mind all the required qualifications: similar causes have similar effects. The principle of induction follows from the principle of efficient causality. If the principle of induction were not true, that A and S are what they are would not necessitate C's being what it is, and the occurrence of C would not be sufficiently caused by A and S being what they are.

Still, the principle of induction is hypothetical. If causes are similar, effects will be similar. Can we judge whether the antecedent of this principle is ever fulfilled, whether different circumstances are ever the same with respect to the existence and proper spatial relations of causes sufficient for the occurrence of effects with certain characteristics?

Yes. As hypothetical, the principle of induction taken alone tells us nothing whatsoever about what actually occurs in our experience.

But as necessary, the principle of induction is derived from a truth that does inform us about what happens in our experience, the principle of efficient causality. That principle informs us that events take place because their causes are what they are and consequently, that their causes' being what they are necessitates these events taking place. Since we know by experience that changes do take place, we know that there are causes whose natures determine them to take place. Not only that, but the principle of efficient causality informs us of two other truths about these causes which together with the principle of induction constitute the foundations of all reasoning on the basis of experience, the foundations, therefore, of empirical knowledge. These other truths are the principle of simplicity and the search warrant.

8.2.3 The search warrant

Another conclusion following necessarily from the principle of efficient causality tells us how to examine our experience to determine what is the cause of what. For we know that when a change occurs, sufficient causes for it must exist; and if a change is not occurring, sufficient causes for it must not exist. Hence C, a change that has not always been occurring, comes into existence if and only if the result of some previous change or changes is the existence of sufficient causes for the occurrence of C. (Except where clarity is at stake, it need not be repeated that C's sufficient causes must exist in the proper spatial relation to one another.) That is *the search warrant.*

In applying the search warrant to our experience, we must keep in mind the remarks made in section 7.3 concerning causality and time. First, the existence of sufficient causes for a change and the occurrence of a change are simultaneous; if the causes do not exist when the change comes into existence, the change is caused by what does not exist, caused by nothing. Second, the causing of a change may itself be a process which is extended through time. Third, a change which is continuous may remain in existence after its causes have brought it into existence; once the change putting a projectile in motion has occurred, further causes are necessary only for changes in its motion.

The search warrant is a license to examine experienced sequences of changes to determine which results of previous changes do and do not cause subsequent changes. For if change C_2 has not always been occurring and the only change of which it was the immediate successor was change C_1, then the result of C_1 must have a causal relation to C_2 either by way of introducing a new cause into the situation in which C_2 occurs, removing an impediment to a cause or bringing about a new spatial relationship among causes. If C_2 was not the immediate successor to such a change, C_2 would occur without a sufficient cause. Since C_2 has not always existed, sufficient causes for it did not always exist. But once sufficient causes for it exist, C_2 occurs immediately. Therefore C_2 is the immediate successor of a change or changes whose result is the existence of causes sufficient for C_2. (Note that the temporal directionality of the causal relation consists in the fact that a change that has not always been occurring cannot occur unless temporally prior *changes* bring its causes into existence. The causes themselves are simultaneous with the effect.)

In other words, the search warrant licenses us to look for causal relations by following the good old-fashioned empiricist advice to note variations, or the lack of variations, in sequences of events. For instance, if changes with certain characteristics in common are always followed by changes with certain other characteristics in common, and if no other changes are followed by changes of the second kind, we know that the result of changes of the first kind is the existence of causes sufficient for changes of the second kind.

I will explain why this and other inductive inferences are justified by replying to an obvious objection. If the only change of which C_2 is the immediate successor is C_1, it must be C_1 that brings sufficient causes for C_2 into existence. Is it ever the case, however, that a single change is the only one immediately preceding another? That is definitely not the case in our universe where uncountable changes are going on at every moment. And if it were the case, how could we ever know it? It seems, therefore, that the search warrant cannot help us decide what causes what.

Let us take a concrete example, the event of water boiling in a room with blue walls. The total set of circumstances in which such an event occurs can never be duplicated. But among these circumstances are sufficient causes for the event; the principle of efficient causality tells us that. What we are inquiring about is whether certain causal dispositions present in these circumstances necessitate the occurrence, not of an individual event considered as numerically distinct from other events, but of an event with certain characteristics. In other words, among these circumstances are there conditions present such that if the circumstances differed in other ways but these conditions were present, an effect having certain characteristics in common with the event of water boiling in a room with blue walls would be occurring? Or, if different circumstances contained causes whose dispositions to behavior were the same in some respects as causes present in these circumstances, must an event having some of the same characteristics as water boiling in a room with blue walls occur? The search warrant can help us make inductions if and only if using it will inform us that this is the case.

Let us therefore direct the inquiry toward certain characteristics of the event under consideration, namely, that it is an event of water boiling. Do all conditions holding in the circumstances in which this event occurs have necessary causal relations with its being an event of water boiling? The search warrant tells us that this is not the case. For if such an event can occur otherwise than in a room with blue walls, we know that sufficient causes for water boiling need not include blue walls. Blue walls are not necessary for the event of water boiling even though they are necessary for the event of water boiling in a room with blue walls. Noting variations in circumstances in the light of the principle of efficient causality and its implications, therefore, shows us that the color of walls is not a necessary cause of water boiling.

Although variations in the color of walls are not followed by water boiling or ceasing to boil, certain variations in temperature and/or atmospheric pressure are always followed by these changes. But a necessary consequence of the principle of efficient causality is the hypothetical truth that if there are causes whose dispositions to behavior are specifically related to the occurrence or non-occurrence of events with certain characteristics, changes bringing about the presence or absence of these causes will, other things being equal, be followed by the respective occurrence or non-occurrence of events with those characteristics (the principle of induction). And another necessary consequence is the hypothetical truth that if C_1 is the only change immediately preceding C_2, the result of C_1 must be the existence of sufficient causes for C_2 (the search warrant). Since variations in temperature and pressure are, and other changes are not, followed by the event of water boiling or ceasing to boil, noting variations in circumstances gives us evidence that temperature and pressure do, while other features of the situations in which water boils or ceases to boil do not, have necessary causal relations with these events.

Not only that, but examining variations in circumstances indicates that a mere numerical distinction of the current state of the temperature and pressure from the state an hour ago no more influences whether or not water will boil than does the color of the walls. Therefore we can conclude that in future situations in which the temperatures and atmospheric pressures are the same as those of past situations in which the event of water boiling has occurred, the boiling of water will again occur. For those situations contain causes naturally determined to produce an event of this kind.

But drawing this conclusion seems to beg a potential infinity of legitimate questions. We went into the example of water boiling in a room with blue walls to solve a problem: how can our knowledge that changes prior to C_2 are required in order for C_2 to have sufficient causes help us apply the principle of induction to our experience, for the number of changes going on prior to C_2 may be indefinitely great? When we are looking for the causes of water boiling, for example, how do we know that the real causes are not brought into existence by changes other than variations in temperature and pressure, changes that have been going on undetected whenever the temperature and pressure varied? No *observed* changes are so coordinated with variations of temperature and pressure. But the unobserved causes may be minute. Do we even know that the color of walls has nothing to do with the boiling of water? How do we know we do not systematically go color blind or suffer hallucinations every time we attempt to determine whether the color of walls is causally related to the boiling of water?

Since such hypotheses are logically possible, it seems that the search warrant does not aid us in finding a foundation for inductive reasoning. And therefore we seem to be back where we started. The principle of induction alone does not tell us anything about what actually transpires in our experience. The search warrant tells us something about what actually transpires in our experience, but the information it gives us is not sufficient to justify our use of inductive methods. Where do we go from here?

We are dealing with necessary consequences of the principle of efficient causality. And there is one more consequence which, together with the principle of induction and the search warrant, constitutes a rational foundation for empirical knowledge, the principle of simplicity. No one of these principles is sufficient by itself. But operating together, their mutual implications are sufficient to allow us to decide between conflicting empirical hypotheses. Put without the qualifications that will appear in the forthcoming discussion, the principle of simplicity states that there can be no more causes than are necessary for the events that occur. As we will see, this principle prevents us from invoking hallucinations or speculating about unobserved causes without paying an unacceptable price. Such hypotheses require us to give a causal analysis of the changes we experience that is more complex than that of another analysis which can account for the same changes. We therefore have a reason based on the principle of efficient causality for believing that these hypotheses are false. In what follows, I will first argue the necessary truth of the principle of simplicity and then show how it operates together with our other principles to provide foundations for induction and for deciding between theories that are based on the results of induction.

8.2.4 The principle of simplicity

First the truth of the principle of simplicity. The converse of the principle of induction is the claim that similar effects have similar causes. If this statement were necessarily true, we could know that whenever effects are the same in any respect, causes must be the same also. Postulating two causes where one would do or different kinds of causes for effects that are the same in kind could not be true. Effects, however, can be similar even if their causes are not. Wars can be caused by economic conditions, ideology, national pride, faces that launch a thousand ships, etc.

How can causes of dissimilar natures, and therefore dissimilar behavioral dispositions, have similar effects? The answer is provided by our analysis of chance. Where effects have multiple causes, their occurrence is not necessitated by the natures (or causal dispositions) of any of their causes taken separately. And by hypothesis, the occurrence of a similarity between effects of *different* causes is a *multiply-caused* state of affairs. Since chance, in this sense of the word, is not an impossibility, there is nothing to prevent an effect of cause A being similar to an effect of cause B even though the natures and causal dispositions of A and B are dissimilar. Should we say that the natures of A and B are similar at least to the extent of being dispositions to produce this kind of effect? Not necessarily. A can be what it is because composed of elements u and v while B can be what it is because composed of elements x and y. Their natures would then have nothing in common even though an effect of one was, by chance, similar to an effect of the other.

Does the occurrence of chance similarities between effects deprive us of any reason for believing that a theory which postulates no more causes than are necessary is the true theory? No. The effects of A and B may be alike in some respects. But it is impossible that all their effects be alike in all respects. If all the behavior, actual or possible, to which A and B are disposed is the same, their causal dispositions are the same, and the similarities between their effects are not by chance.

It may be objected that if we say that causes *have* dispositions to behavior, not that their natures *are* dispositions to behavior, two causes of different natures could have exactly the same behavioral dispositions, so that, by chance, their effects would be alike in all respects. To understand why this could not be the case, let us examine *the principle of simplicity* which we are now in a position to formulate with all the needed qualifications: there can be no more causes than would be necessary for the changes that would occur if all actual causes exercised all their dispositions to produce and undergo change. Assume that we have a choice between explaining change C in one of two ways, either by agent A or by the combination of agents D and E. C has not always been occurring and must have been preceded by changes bringing sufficient causes for it into existence. But if C is caused by the combination of D and E, the changes which brought sufficient causes for C into existence must *differ* from the changes that would precede C if A were its cause. Hence if we knew that all actual causal dispositions were exercised and we knew the results, we would also know that a theory more complex than is necessary to account for these results could not be true. For the more complex theory would call for changes other than those that occur when all actual causal dispositions are exercised. If not, the changes preceding C would be the same in both theories. But the changes preceding C are changes bringing sufficient causes for C into existence or are changes occurring to those causes if they already exist. Therefore, where there are no differences in the changes allowed by two theories, there are no differences in the causes these theories postulate.

Of course, we are never able to know all the actual effects of the causes that do exist and much less all of their possible effects. Consider changes of a kind having characteristic F in common. Assume they may all be caused by agents of a kind having characteristic G in common. Still in actual fact, some of them may be caused by agents with a different characteristic, J, which enables these agents to cause other changes of a kind which agents with characteristic G cannot cause. But because agents having J have not as yet manifested their disposition to cause changes which agents of kind G cannot cause, they appear to have characteristic G in common with the other causes of changes having F. Therefore the principle of simplicity would lead us to believe a theory which was false. How, then, does the principle of simplicity help us decide between conflicting hypotheses concerning the causing of the changes we experience?

Alone, the principle of simplicity no more informs us about what is actually taking place in our experience than does the principle of induction. But neither the principles of simplicity or induction are alone. For the search warrant licenses us to look for necessary causal relations by noting variations, or their absence, in the sequences of changes we experience. A theory more complex than necessary will allow changes to take place which differ from those of the simplest theory. In trying to determine which of the two theories is true, we vary circumstances, or simply observe variations in those circumstances over which we have no control, to see if any of the changes required by the more complex theory actually take place. If nothing different from what is predicted by the simpler theory can be found to occur, we have a rational basis for not believing the more complex theory and for believing the simpler theory true. Why?

The teleonomic cause of sentences is knowledge of the identity of what has been linguistically objectified and what exists. In plainer language, the goal of theories is knowledge of that which exists. But evidence for the existence of something is provided only by experience or by causal reasoning *from experience*. An alleged entity that is not itself present in experience can be known to exist if and only if something that *is* present in experience would not exist without it. And "would not exist without" is the definition of a necessary causal relation. Therefore the only rational application of necessary causal principles is to that which we have experienced or will in the future be able to experience.

One of the corollaries of the principle of efficient causality is that there can be no more causes than are necessary for the effects that would occur if all actual causes exercised all their causal dispositions. But in trying to determine what causes are indeed needed, we can do no more—and are justified in doing no more—than rely on experience to decide how wide a variety of effects actually occur as circumstances change. When we have observed what occurs in varied circumstances to the extent to which we are able, we rightfully believe the theory that explains what occurs by means of the fewest causes. For the only evidence we have of how many effects would occur from the exercise of all the dispositions of those causes that actually exist is our experience of what occurs when circumstances vary to the extent that it is within our power to observe. And the only rational bases for existence beliefs are such observations and inferences concerning the causes necessary for the existence of that which is observed to exist.

To the results of such reasoning it would be irrational to oppose the belief that there are undetectable changes going on which would confirm a more complex theory. But it would be equally irrational to refuse to look for new ways of getting experiential results relating to the confirmation of a theory which predicts changes we as yet have no means of detecting. For it would be irrational to reject a more complex theory if experiential evidence that would confirm it was possible of attainment.

If, on the other hand, a theory which apparently posits more causes and causal dispositions does not imply that its causes could produce any changes which are different from those producible by the causes of a less complex theory, there is no reason to believe in a real distinction between the causes and dispositions postulated by these theories. The greater complexity does not pertain to what the more complex theory asserts about things in their existence as things; it pertains to the objects postulated by the theory only as terms of knowledge relations. For example, a causal disposition may be *described* differently by reference to different effects. But a thing may be a cause of each of these effects by the reason of the same constituent of its make-up.

Let us now return to the hypothesis that the natures of two things could differ while their causal dispositions were the same in all respects. By hypothesis, causal reasoning on the basis of experience could not inform us of the existence of these "natures" alleged to be something over and above all the causal dispositions of the two things. Therefore there would be no reasonable basis for the belief in its existence. (For more on the points of the last two paragraphs, see sections 6.2.2 and 9.3.)

8.2.5 Simplicity and induction

We are now in a position to return to the problem of induction and see how the search warrant, the principle of induction and the principle of simplicity operate together to provide rational foundations for empirical knowledge. We were wondering how we could know that changes we have observed occurring before the event of water boiling, namely, changes in temperature and atmospheric pressure, were the changes that brought into existence sufficient causes for the boiling of water. The problem is that the number of changes going on at any given time is potentially infinite. But an examination of all the sequences of changes of which we are able to have experiential knowledge has revealed no other kind of change whose results either always accompany, or at least are always accompanied by, the boiling water. Therefore we can conclude that there are no causes in addition to temperature and pressure which are either necessary or sufficient for water to boil.

Knowing the truth of the principle of simplicity and knowing that reasoning from causal principles is rationally applied only to changes that are detectable in some way, we do not have to worry about the existence of undetectable changes and their unknowable causes. We can without fear make inductions from experience on the basis of the principle that changes occur if and only if previous changes have brought into existence sufficient causes—and *a fortiori* any necessary causes—for subsequent changes (the search warrant). In so doing, we know that our inferences have a rational foundation in the principle of efficient causality and its necessary consequences, and we know that any contrary hypotheses, though logically possible, are contrary to reason. Thus we can have *knowledge* that it is unreasonable to believe the opposite of an inductively established conclusion.

To illustrate further, let us apply our principles to the hypothesis that water will only boil in rooms with blue walls. Using the search warrant, we vary the circumstances to investigate whether there is a necessary causal relation between blue walls and boiling water. As we move our apparatus (water in suitable containers, heat source, instruments for measuring temperature and pressure) from room to room and out of doors, we find no correlation between water being in rooms with blue walls and water boiling or ceasing to boil. But according to the search warrant, there should be one or the other correlation if blue walls have causal dispositions which are either necessary or sufficient for the boiling of water in the areas they enclose.

In response, it may be claimed that blue walls have dispositions determining them to cause water to boil, but these dispositions are only manifested in circumstances where other causes of certain kinds are present, or where causes which have been present in all the circumstances that have been so far observed are absent. Perhaps, but here is were the principle of simplicity comes to our aid. If there are causes whose behavioral dispositions are such that in their presence or absence blue walls will cause water to boil, no changes that it has been within our power to observe have been able to bring blue walls into the required spatial relation with these other causes. Therefore we have no rational basis for postulating the existence either of such causes or of such dispositions on the part of blue walls.

Or could we say that, although blue walls do not always cause water to boil, if boiling happens to be going on in a blue room, it is not the temperature and pressure alone that cause the boiling but the temperature and pressure plus the blue walls? Simplicity rules this out also. If the combination of temperature, pressure and blue walls can produce an effect that temperature and pressure alone cannot, that effect will either be detectable or undetectable. If no such effect is detectable, it is unreasonable to believe that blue walls contribute anything to the boiling of the water.

But how do we know that whenever we are testing the relation between blue walls and boiling water, we do not systematically go color blind or hallucinate about whether we are indoors or out? Concerning two experiences, one normal and the other abnormal or one veridical and the other hallucinatory, which are phenomenologically similar, we can claim that they are the effects either of similar causes or of dissimilar causes. If the dispositions of the causes which produce such experiences are the same in all respects, the distinction between the normal and the abnormal and the veridical and the hallucinatory vanishes. The reason we make these distinctions is to allow us to escape apparent violations of the principle of induction by postulating different kinds of causes for these experiences even though the experiences are phenomenologically similar. For if the causes of abnormal and hallucinatory experiences were the same as the causes of other experiences, or if the objects present in these experiences have the same causal dispositions as the objects present in other experiences, the principle that similar causes have similar effects will call for further effects to be similar also. That is, the past and future experiences of ourselves and of other people will have to have certain characteristics. If these other experiences do not have these characteristics, either similar causes do not have similar effects or the causes are dissimilar.

We invoke maverick experiences, consequently, because additional causes are needed to account for certain kinds of variations in the sequences we experience. In claiming that one of two similar experiences is a maverick in this sense, we are claiming that the similarities between the experiences are chance effects of dissimilar causes. But there is no rational basis for believing in a more complex causal theory unless there occur, somewhere or sometime, observable variations which fewer causes could not account for. If our own past and future experience or other persons' reports of their experience do not make us aware of differences which call for explanations in terms of abnormal perceptions or hallucinations, it is irrational to refuse to make the inferences the search warrant and the principle of induction call for on the grounds that such maverick experiences are logically possible. For only when using the search warrant would otherwise force us to deny that similar causes have similar effects does the principle of simplicity allow us to postulate the existence of dissimilar causes. (The causal character of the hypothesis that an experience is an hallucination is explained more fully in section 10.5.)

This brings up one more important relation between the principles of induction and simplicity. Simplicity governs both the number of individual causes it is legitimate to posit and the number of kinds of causes, that is, causes whose common characteristics determine them to produce effects having certain characteristics in common. But there is an order of priority between the positing of individual causes and kinds of causes. Applying the corollaries of the principle of efficient causality reveals relations between individual effects and individual causes, but it does so only by revealing relations between effects with certain common characteristics and causes with certain common characteristics, relations which are expressible by inductively established laws.

That is because the knowledge we acquire when we examine sequences of changes in the light of the principle that a change occurs if and only if sufficient causes for it have been brought into existence by previous changes concerns only the relation between certain characteristics of the situation in which a change occurs and certain characteristics of the change. When a change occurs, it is necessitated by the existential configuration of its causes. It need not be the case, however, that everything existing at that time had a causal relation to the change. To isolate the causes, we vary the circumstances. But a configuration of individual causal entities which is the same in all respects as a previous configuration can never be achieved. For the individual causal entities will all be older than when the original change occurred. And at least one of these causes, the component cause, will have undergone a change which is other than the mere passage of time. For the component cause will have undergone the original change. Therefore the most that the search warrant allows us to determine is that there are causal relations between states of affairs with certain characteristics and states of affairs with other characteristics.

Furthermore, a configuration of causes necessitates the occurrence of an event only because the natural determinations of each of the causes necessitate that the causes behave in these ways in these circumstances. *Existential* necessity (which from another point of view deserves to be called chance) derives from the *natural* necessity of the behavioral dispositions of causes. To understand how an event is caused, therefore, we must understand these behavioral dispositions. And that understanding begins with inductively established laws telling us that causes with certain characteristics have effects of certain kinds in circumstances of certain kinds. For events are multiply caused, and the behavioral dispositions of any individual cause do not naturally determine it to produce a given individual effect. It is the configuration of causes that determines the occurrence of the individual. To understand the behavioral dispositions of the causes of an individual event we therefore have no method other than to examine different circumstances in the light of the search warrant to discover what effects the natures of individual things determine them to produce in different circumstances. The resulting understanding of why a particular change happened in a particular configuration of circumstances will consist, in addition to a description of the circumstances, of universal laws telling us that things of certain kinds produce or undergo changes of certain kinds in circumstances of certain kinds.

Simplicity makes induction possible by allowing us to use the search warrant free of any obligation to deal with hypotheses about undetectable changes and causes. And the reasoning that the principles of simplicity, induction and the search warrant license primarily concerns relations between causes with certain characteristics and effects with certain characteristics. But this is what should be expected. For the only evidence supporting existence beliefs is provided by experience and causal reasoning based on experience. And experience constitutes a starting point for causal reasoning only to the extent that it informs us of the existence of realities of certain kinds: changes and the results of changes. Our necessary causal principles concern realities of these kinds and apply to individuals only insofar as they are individuals of these kinds. And the reasoning that the corollaries of the principle of efficient causality license concerns what characteristics of a situation in which a change occurs are causality related to what characteristics of the change and the results of the change.

Hence the principle of simplicity enjoins us from unnecessarily multiplying the number of *laws* expressing relations between causes with certain characteristics and effects with certain characteristics. The hypothesis which postulates more kinds of causal relation than are needed implies the possibility of more events or of more differences between kinds of events than can actually be found to occur. (Conversely, each of the laws of the sufficiently simple hypothesis will cover a greater number of the events which actually occur than will the laws of the unnecessarily complex hypothesis.) Therefore it is unreasonable to believe in a more complex set of causal laws when a simpler set accounts for those changes which actually take place.

But a simpler set of laws can require us to multiply individual entities by postulating unobserved causes. Why is it reasonable to believe in a greater number of causal entities but not in a greater number of kinds of causal relations? Because our beliefs about the unobserved can be justified only by causal reasoning from the observed. And observation is a starting point for causal reasoning only insofar as it informs us of the existence of individuals of a certain kind, changes, and of the repetition or non-repetition of sequential relations between changes of certain kinds. Therefore there is no rational basis for belief in more kinds of causal relations than are necessary for the changes that we can find to actually occur. And if the existence of fewer causal entities would require more complex causal laws and hence imply that causes could produce and undergo more changes or more differences between kinds of changes than can be found to actually occur, it is unreasonable to believe in the existence of fewer causal entities.

Thus it has been shown that if the principle of efficient causality is true, those principles are also true by which, as explained in Section 6.2.2, we can settle disputes between genuinely conflicting empirical hypotheses. There remain questions about the other foundation of empirical knowledge, sense experience. But Chapter Ten will show that those problems can be handled by the same assumption from which we have deduced the principles of induction, simplicity and the search warrant.

8.3 If Non-grue Ravens Were Scientific Theories . . .

The preceding does not pretend to be a complete analysis of the structure of scientific theories. It is an attempt to lay a new foundation for such an analysis. The whole question has to be reconsidered on non-Humean grounds. What I will do in this section is show, briefly, why such a reconsideration will *not* have to deal with three conundrums which empiricism's dogmas concerning causality have generated, the paradoxes of black ravens and grue emeralds and the problem of contrary-to-fact conditionals. I will also explain why statements about physical causal relations can be necessarily true even though we may not be able to know them as such from an understanding of the ways their words are used and why the concept of causality itself is used less and less by science. The chapter will conclude with some brief but potentially important remarks about the use of mathematics in scientific theories.

8.3.1 Causality and logical relations

Inductive reasoning is based on the beliefs that events are caused, that similar causes have similar effects and that there are no more causes than are necessary to account for the events that occur. These beliefs license us to take regularities in nature as evidence for assigning effects of certain kinds to causes of certain kinds and vice versa. But this does not imply that all the laws used by science must be causal laws in the sense that the universal connection asserted by the law need be a connection between causes and effects. That all ruminants have cloven hoofs does not indicate that the digestive system of these organisms is either a cause or an effect of the number of their toes. But the regular connection between these features of our experience in all circumstances is evidence that the causal dispositions necessitating the coming into existence of animals that ruminate are regularly connected with causal dispositions necessitating the occurrence of animals with cloven hoofs. Therefore the universal truth that all ruminants have cloven hoofs has significance for our scientific knowledge of the causes of things.

Regularity is usually the only kind of evidence we have for specific causal connections. But not all regularities giving rise to universal truths need be, like the regular association of being a ruminant with having cloven hoofs, evidence for causal connections. For causality is not generality. And only to the extent that regularity gives evidence of causal connections does it provide a basis for inductive reasoning.

What distinguishes regularities that do provide such evidence from regularities that do not? Consider the raven paradox. Every non-black thing we have known has been a non-raven. If induction concerned nothing more than the logical relation of generality, each non-black non-raven we encounter should tend to confirm the belief that all ravens are black. But the fact that all known non-black things are non-ravens does not tend to confirm that belief. Why? Because that fact does not provide evidence for a causal relation between the other characteristics making ravens what they are and a specific way of reflecting light.

By definition, causal relations hold between cognition-independent existents, and they hold between existents because of features, namely, causal dispositions, characterizing causes as things. A word-function like that of "non-black", however, has two elements: "non" expresses a logical relation while "black" expresses a non-logical feature of experience. And only non-logical features of experience are eligible to be characteristics determining causal relations between things, for only non-logical features of experience could be characteristics belonging to things as cognition-independent existents.

If the search warrant yields knowledge of a causal relation terminated by being a raven and being black, we can know that all non-black things are non-ravens. But describing things as non-black and non-raven cannot add anything to our knowledge of causal relations over and above what we may already know about the causal relations associated with being a raven and being black. From the absence of causes with certain features we can sometimes argue to the absence of effects with certain features, and from the absence of effects with certain features we can sometimes argue to the absence of causes with certain features. But it is not by means of the logical relation "other than" that things become causes or effects. An unlimited number of things with an unlimited number of different kinds of causal dispositions and relations can be described as non-black and non-raven. The "non" in "non-black" or "non-raven", therefore, can add nothing to the knowledge we may or may not have of the causal relations into which a way of reflecting light and being a raven enter.

Another example is provided by the paradox of "grue" emeralds. Again, past regularities are significant for our expectations of the future only to the extent that they give rise to beliefs about connections between causes of certain kinds and effects of certain kinds. But that for which an effect depends on its causes is existence. Causes produce real existents and not, therefore, logical relations or other logical constructs. There are causes of the psychological and social occurrences without which there would be no discourse characterized by logical relations or discourse about logical constructs. But what is nothing needs no cause. There are no causes explaining why logical constructs have an existence which is other than being-an-*object* since they have no such existence.

Now both being green and being blue, in the sense of being disposed to reflect light in a manner normal observers refer to as "green" or "blue", are characteristics of things as things. And being inspected by today or being inspected after today are both cognition-independent events, an actual event in the first case, a possible event in the second. Consequently these are all modes of being that can terminate causal relations. And regularities in sequences involving them can constitute evidence for causal relations.

But what about the word-function of "grue", being green and inspected by today or being blue and inspected after today? This word-function makes use of a logical relation, disjunction. We noted in section 5.5.3, however, that logical relations can be used in thing-descriptions. Otherwise, no description using conjunction could be a thing-description. But logical relations can be so used only because they can be terminated by real existents and word-functions objectifying real existents as such. And word-functions using logical relations have causal significance only to the extent that their cognition-independent elements terminate causal relations. Consequently regularities involving things objectifiable by word-functions using logical relations are pertinent to causal inferences only to the extent that these regularities involve the non-logical elements of these word-functions.

Conjunction, for instance, is used to objectify the really existing union of parts in a complex whole. (Recall the discussion of the first difficulty in section 7.3.) And since the evidence for specific causal relations consists of the regular association of cognition-independent realities (either related as cause and effect or as effects of the same cause), the objectification of that evidence calls for the use of conjunction. Still, the fact that these cognition-independent realities can be objectified by the use of conjunction is a by-product of causal relations holding cognition-independently; things are not causally related by the fact of terminating conjunction or any other logical relation.

In contrast to conjunction, the relation of disjunction is entirely compatible with the absence of any cognition-independent association between the terms of the relation, or between these terms and any other thing. By logical inclusion, evidence that emeralds are green is also evidence that they are grue. But over and above the evidence induction provides that emeralds are disposed to reflect light in certain ways, it adds nothing to our knowledge of causal relations to know that emeralds are also grue. Since disjunctions are compatible with the absence of any cognition-independent association between their terms, they are compatible with the absence of causal relations between their terms. The fact that all emeralds so far known have been grue is evidence only for a causal connection between the nature of emeralds and one specific way of reflecting light; consequently it is evidence that emeralds will continue to reflect light in that way, not in some other way. For the only reasonable bases of beliefs about the future are inductively established *causal* relations.

Note also that a thing may have the capacity to be one or the other of several possibilities, for instance, to be either green or blue. The description "capacity to be either green or blue" makes use of a logical relation. The capacity to be either green or blue, however, is not a logical construct. As we explained in section 6.1.1, to be potential with respect to being F is the same as being actual in other respects. Otherwise, capacities would violate the principle of non-contradiction. They would not exist since they would be neither F nor G nor anything else actual; and they would exist since real existents do have capacities.

If something has a capacity for being either F or G because it is actual in some other respect H, when we ask for the cause of its being H, we are asking for the cause of its capacity to be either F or G. But asking for the cause of such a capacity is not the same as asking for a cause of the disjunction which forms part of the description of the capacity. The word-function of "either F or G" is a logical construct. The word-function of "capacity to be either F or G" is not a logical construct; it is a feature characterizing things as things which is identical with what we have alternatively described as "H".

To conclude. Our question was what distinguishes regularities that do from regularities that do not provide evidence of causal relations. Our answer is that only regular associations between real existents provide evidence of causal relations. And this fact disarms the raven and grue paradoxes.

Turning now to contrary-to-fact conditionals, I will complete the analysis given in section 5.5.2. Belief in the truth of a counter-factual can amount to a belief concerning, or a conclusion drawn from a belief concerning, a necessary causal relation. If the relation does obtain or the conclusion follow, the counterfactual is true; if not, it is false. In section 5.5.2, however, we knew only that it was possible for there to be necessary causal relations not deducible from self-evident truths. The arguments of section 8.2 have shown, in effect, that there are such causal relations and that understanding the natures of things is the same as understanding the necessary causal relations into which they enter. We now know, therefore, that it is entirely appropriate for us to express our knowledge of the natures of things by means of counterfactuals. We also know that the evidence for the truth of counterfactuals will be the same as that by which any empirical causal hypothesis is verified, namely, the evidence provided by the principles of induction, simplicity and the search warrant.

And one more remark about counterfactuals should be added.

Counter-factuals are said to be justified by "lawlike", but not justified by non-lawlike, universal sentences. I will let pass some objections that could be raised to this claim. What is of interest here is that the lawlike/non-lawlike distinction drives from the distinction between existential necessity (chance) and natural necessity. That all the coins in my pocket at the moment are silver is a necessary result of past configurations of causes that determined what entered and what left my pocket. But the truth of this universal is not evidence for any relations between *kinds* of causes and *kinds* of effects. Is there any kind of cause necessary for there being coins in my pocket? If so, does the nature of that kind of cause necessitate the coins in my pocket being silver? Experience reveals no regular association between the attributes being-a-coin-in-my-pocket and being-silver. Therefore there is no evidence whatsoever for a universal connection between causal dispositions necessary for coins coming into my pocket and causal dispositions necessitating silver things to come into my pocket.

To "All coins in my pocket are silver", contrast "All ruminants have cloven hoofs". The principles of induction, simplicity and the search warrant allow us to take the universal association so far experienced as evidence that the causes of the occurrence of ruminants, namely, other ruminants, necessitate the occurrence of cloven hoofed ruminants (which is not to say that no future experience, especially one that results from genetic engineering, will be to the contrary). Hence the universal "All ruminants have cloven hoofs" is "lawlike" because its truth is evidence of a universal connection between kinds of causes and kinds of effects. Causal dispositions necessitating each of the effects being-a-ruminant and having-cloven-hoofs are united in the natures of the causes of ruminants. That causes whose natures unite such dispositions should exist may be the result of genetic chance. But the *existence* of all causes of whatever natures is the result of chance, the causes of silver and of coins coming into my pockets included. In the case of the latter causal dispositions, however, there is no evidence that they are ever united other than existentially; that is, they are not united in the nature of any of the causes responsible for coins or silver coming into my pockets.

There is a universal connection between things describable as causes of silver coins coming into my pocket and effects describable as the existence of silver coins coming into my pocket. But experience shows that a given thing's being describable as a cause of something combining the characteristics of being-a-coin-in-my-pocket and being-silver is due to the circumstances in which the thing exists and not to any characteristics the thing retains from circumstance to circumstance. Nor among different things each describable as such a cause is there any common characteristic universally accompanied by the occurrence of such an effect *other than* the characteristic of being such a cause. Consequently there is no universal connection between the nature of any cause and the occurrence of such an effect. (And this illustrates how we avoid making necessary connections between kinds of causes and kinds of effects tautological by defining causes solely in terms of effects. See also section 9.3.) Since "All coins in my pocket" neither consists of, nor derives from, nor gives evidence for a belief in a connection between causes of a certain nature and effects of a certain nature, it is not a "lawlike" universal.

8.3.2 The causal opacity of empirical word-functions

I turn now to a question we have left unanswered since we began discussing causal necessity in Chapter Two: why the truth of a sentence can be necessary without our being able to know it as such by derivation from the self-evident. If the truth of a sentence like "Heat expands solids" is necessary, then it cannot be false unless some word-function both is and is not what it is. Why is it that we cannot know this from our acquaintance with word-functions? Why does acquaintance with some word-functions allow us to grasp the necessity of causal relations between them while acquaintance with other word-functions does not?

The next chapter answers that question for ontological word-functions. Empirical word-functions all derive to some extent from our experience of objects that are distinguishable by sense knowledge alone. By the sense of sight alone, we are able to distinguish the blue of one piece of litmus paper from the red of another, or the first mark on a calibrated scale from the second. Like all results of change, sensibly distinguishable objects terminate necessary causal relations. But to the extent that word-functions are such objects or include such objects, simple acquaintance with the word-functions is not sufficient to make us aware of those relations. Why?

Nothing presented in sense experience is what it is as the result of the causality of one cause alone. The objects of sense knowledge always result from the interaction of indefinitely many causes, efficient and component, which have a variety of causal dispositions relating them to an indefinite number of possible effects. Therefore our linguistic objectification of sensible qualities cannot alone guarantee that we will be able to grasp necessary relations between causes of specific kinds and effects of specific kinds even when such relations obtain. (This argument is adapted from Sikora, 1966, p. 92.)

Furthermore, similar sensible qualities can result from dissimilar causes whose effects have features in common by chance. For nothing prevents causes of dissimilar natures from producing effects having similar colors or shapes or sizes or velocities or numbers or weights or temperatures, etc. Therefore acquaintance with sensible qualities is not sufficient for us to assign causes of certain kinds to effects of certain kinds and vice versa. (See Cahalan, 1981, pp. 197, 198.)

When acquaintance with word-functions is insufficient to reveal necessary causal relations that may hold between them, those word-functions are *causally opaque*. Sensible qualities are causally opaque word-functions. To the extent other word-functions make reference to sensibly distinguishable objects, these word-functions will be causally opaque also.

It is possible to so construct theoretical concepts for heat and the expansion of solids that, as heat and the expansion of solids are thereby defined, it follows from the word-functions of the theory that heat expands solids. But what do these definitions have to do with what does nor does not take place in our experience? Sciences are not formal systems. For them to be empirically meaningful, some of their words must be defined, partially at least, by reference to the results of observations. The concept of heat as the energy of moving molecules must be related to the concept of heat as that which is measured by thermometers or in some other observable way. And the results of no observations give us word-functions making it self-evident or derivable from the self-evident that what is measured by thermometers causes solids to expand. None of this implies, however, that we cannot infer a necessary causal relation between heat and the expansion of solids by the use of the principles of induction, simplicity and the search warrant.

Empirical meanings$_T$ are not the only ones derived from sense experience. Ontological meanings$_T$ have their source there also. Because the meaning$_T$ of "cause" is a function of existence and not of any sensibly distinguishable objects, the meaning$_T$ of "cause" is not of direct use in empirical method, which verifies statements and forms meanings$_T$ by reference to qualities that, unlike existence, can distinguish one thing present in sense experience from another. As ontological, the meaning$_T$ of cause operates in the necessary truths that provide the *foundations* for empirical method, but it is only indirectly related to the *results* of empirical method.

Empirical science gets the word "cause" from ordinary language, and the function ordinary language gives that word is ontological. But since ontological considerations are the business of philosophy and since empirical science defines by reference to words whose functions are causally opaque, it is to be expected that science will make less and less use of the word "cause" and its cognates as it continues its historical movement away from philosophical preoccupations.

8.3.3 Simplicity and instrumentalism

A final word on the simplicity of scientific theories. Too little attention has been paid to the use of mathematics in science. As explained in section 3.4.4, mathematics is indifferent to the capacity of its topics of discourse for real existence. It does not matter to set theory whether transfinite multitudes can exist cognition-independently; what matters is that they can be so defined that properties can be demonstrated of them. Now science strives for experimental results that can be expressed quantitatively. Corresponding to the quantitative expression of its data, its theories attribute quantitatively expressed characteristics to entities (observed and postulated) in such a way that the theories will predict the same numbers arrived at by experiment.

But since objects incapable of real existence can be just as valid mathematical objects as can real existents, it has been held (see Appendix II for references) that scientific theories may sometimes postulate explanatory entities with mathematical properties sufficient to predict the numbers yielded by experiments but which are "fictional" in the strong sense of being incapable of extra-objective existence. (Recall that a topic of discourse, a logical relation for example, may be free of internal inconsistency even though its real existence would be contradictory. For the assertion of its existence may require the denial of some necessary truth concerning existence or its causes. Thus if logical relations had real existence, to exist would be the same as being an object of knowledge.) It has been held, for instance, that Minkowski's space-time is a fiction in this sense.

Should a scientific theory make use of explanatory factors incapable of real existence, we could have the following paradoxical situation: a theory postulating *fewer* causes than are *necessary* for all the known data could predict that data. On penalty of contradiction, there can be no fewer *real* causes than are necessary for the events that occur. But some fiction or group of fictions incapable of real existence may give a mathematically simpler means of deriving the results of our measurements. Since effects are what they are as a result of their causes being what they are, where there are differences in effects there must be differences in causes. But a theory may account for differences in effects either by more laws for kinds of causal relations or by more causal entities governed by simpler laws. Hence a mathematically expressed theory could achieve simplicity on the plane of law by postulating entities of a kind that could not exist.

Furthermore, simplicity may require empirical theory to refrain from positing modes of being, like absolute velocities and positions for particles or absolute simultaneity, which cannot be observed but which observation together with ontological considerations in addition to the principles of induction, simplicity and the search warrant may require us to posit. For example, the laws of physics do not allow absolute simultaneity between events. But assume event A, the second hand of a watch passing twelve, is taking place. If so, one of the following *must* be true: event A is taking place *and* event B, some event elsewhere in the universe is taking place, or event A is taking place *and* no event is taking place anywhere else in the universe. If it is true that both A and B exist, there is simultaneity between A and B. If it is false that both A and B exist, then nothing else is going on in the universe when A takes place; when A occurs, the universe is in a state of total rest. The second hand of one watch is passing twelve, but the hand of no other watch is passing any point on its dial. Observation and laws of science based on it, however, rule out the hypothesis that the universe is in a state of total rest when A is occurring. In the world we observe, processes coexist. Consequently there is simultaneity in the ontological sense of coexistence between temporal events (events which take place before and after other events). (This argument is from Maritain, 1933, pp. 91-92.)

For both of the above reasons, an empirical theory that is less complex than is necessary for physical events as they actually exist could give us a means of deducing the occurrence of everything knowable by empirical methods. The theory would employ fictions, *not* in the sense of linguistic instruments for abbreviating observation statements, but in the sense of postulated explanatory entities of a kind incapable of existence. (This is the way the question of "instrumentalism" should be posed.) And no empirical evidence would support a more complex theory. In explaining gravitational motion by changes in the geometry of space-time, for instance, everything empirically observable must be accounted for since the empirical objects explained are nothing more than events locatable by space-time coordinates.

But if truth is defined as the achievement of the goal of making sentences and if one's goal is the explanation of observed events by means of entities whose properties are expressed mathematically, a theory successfully employing simplifying fictions will rightfully be considered the true theory, the theory which achieves identity beween the results of prediction and the results of observation by the *simplest* mathematical representation of conditions yielding those results. In the case of mathematically expressed physical theory, consequently, it *is* appropriate to attribute truth to the theory as a whole rather than to its individual sentences.

But these consequences can be saved from the contradiction of the false being true and from the difficulties brought against conceptual relativism in Chapter Six if and only if there are other sentences whose truth is determined by strict identity between what is objectified and what exists. Instances of truth in the strict sense must provide the standard from which an attenuated use of "truth" may be derived for a particular purpose. (This is *not* a paradigm case argument for the existence of sentential truth. Chapter Eleven will analyze such attenuated predications, and show their capital significance for philosophy, independently of any connection with the paradigm case argument and the problems associated with it.)

This chapter has shown the great likelihood that there are necessary causal relations in nature. By refusing to recognize such relations, empiricism has rendered itself incapable of explaining the existence of empirical knowledge and has generated paradoxes about empirical knowledge that have proved immune to solution. In philosophical literature subsequent to Hume and not before, one finds paradoxes that cannot be solved as long as causality continues to be treated as logical or epistemological. This chapter has shown how the ontological approach to causality frees us from these difficulties, and Chapter Ten will show that it frees us from the main problems concerning perception as well. But before going on, we should remind ourselves that, in addition to all of these advantages, the hypothesis that events require causes has already been shown to have an even greater advantage, the advantage of being necessarily true.

CHAPTER NINE

Causality and Knowledge II: Philosophical Knowledge and Empirical Knowledge

The analysis of the preceding chapter allows us to throw light on philosophical method by contrasting it to empirical knowledge. We could not accomplish this had we not corrected ordinary interpretations of empirical method. Having achieved a more accurate understanding of empirical knowledge, we can use it to improve our understanding of philosophical knowledge. And that will lead in turn to more insight into empirical method.

The first two sections of this chapter will be concerned with contrasting empirical and philosophical method. Among other things, the discussion will explain the incompleteness of empirical definitions of theoretical terms. The remaining sections will deal with some problems which must be solved if my account of philosophical and empirical knowledge is to succeed. The explanations given should greatly clarify the causal character of philosophical and empirical knowledge. We will see, for instance, how philosophical arguments of a kind that may seem far removed from causal analysis actually are causal arguments, but at the same time we will see why it is valid to describe philosophy as conceptual analysis. Special attention will be given to problems concerning the view that causal knowledge reveals the nature of things, the problem, for instance, of the value of describing a sleep-inducing drug as having dormitive powers. Further, causal relations will be used to give an account of a particularly troublesome kind of necessary truth, the kind illustrated by "Nothing is both a square and a circle". And an account will be given of the place of modes of causality other than component and efficient causality in philosophical analysis.

9.1 Ontological and Empirical Knowledge Contrasted

Inductive reasoning does not show that the opposites of its conclusions are impossible. It shows that it is irrational to believe the opposites of its conclusions given the evidence available. Although inductive reasoning cannot exclude the opposite from possibility, it can give us *knowledge* that it is unreasonable to believe the opposite. On the other hand, philosophy tries to show that the opposites of its conclusions are impossible. It does this both by deriving conclusions from sentences whose truth is self-evidently necessary and by defending the necessity of self-evident truths by *reductio ad absurdum*. The methods of logic and mathematics also differ from empirical method in this way, however. How, then, does ontological method differ from logical and mathematical method?

Philosophy seeks to inform us of necessary truths objectifying things as possible cognition-independent existents. It analyzes experience in the light of truths whose necessity derives from causal relations entered into by the meanings$_T$ of "exists" and its cognates. Among the more important examples of ontological meanings$_T$ other than that of "exists" are those of "being", "essence", "cause", "effect", "substance", "accident", "act", "potency", "necessary", "contingent". Neither logic nor mathematics, on the other hand, are concerned with necessary truths objectifying things as real existents.

Logical relations accrue to things as terms of knowledge relations. Therefore the truths of logic pertain to all the truths of ontology and to the things objectified in them. But the truths of logic pertain to these things as a result of their being made objects of knowledge, not as extra-objective things. Mathematics is indifferent to the capacity of its objects for extra-objective existence. It does make use of causal relations, like adding-to and removing-from, for the purpose of diverse objectification. But it does so not to know conditions for the possibility of extra-objective existence but to know relations of equality and inequality between quantities diversely objectified as terms of causal relations.

Conditions for the possibility of extra-objective existence, that is, causal relations, are precisely what philosophy investigates, however.

The philosophies of logic and mathematics, for instance, examine the causes which bring these kinds of knowledge into existence, evaluate them in terms of the goals achieved (teleonomic causes) by their coming into existence and relate these goals to the goals achieved by the kinds of human knowledge brought into existence by other causes.

The ontological point of view is a necessary condition for seeing causal knowledge as it is. The empirical sciences do inform us of causal relations, but the sciences do not know them explicitly as such since causality is an ontological word-function. It is the philosopher who knows (what the man on the street believes, namely) that the sciences give us information about causal relations. For in order to recognize causal relations for what they are, ontological analysis is necessary.

This is the place, therefore, to address a question first raised in section 3.4.2. A causal relation can be necessary without our being able to know its necessity merely from acquaintance with word-functions. Sometimes acquaintance with word-functions can make a necessary causal relation known, sometimes not. Why? We explained the causal opacity of empirical word-functions in section 8.3.2. But if the most primitive word-functions derived from experience are causally opaque, how can acquaintance with any word-functions derived from experience reveal necessary causal relations?

Empirical word-functions make reference to sensible qualities that are multiply caused and that can be the effects of dissimilar causes. Both of these reasons prevent us from assigning specific causes to specific effects at the level of the details of our sense experience by means of acquaintance with word-functions alone. But nothing prevents us from discovering necessary causal relations by means of word-functions of higher degrees of universality than those for the details of sensible phenomena.

Chance and necessity are non-contradictorily combined in every event. It is a contingent fact that a particular configuration of causes occurs, but it is not a contingent fact that if a certain cause is placed in a particular relation with other causes, it will behave in a certain way. That is a necessity determined by the natures of the causes in question. Such natural determinations are what are expressed by universal causal laws. And the fact that singular events are chance effects of multiple causes does not prevent them from entering into necessary causal relations objectifiable by meanings$_T$ *more universal* than the causally opaque meanings$_T$ objectifying specific sensible qualities. In other words, the specific relations between kinds of causes and kinds of effects that are opaque to us can be instances of more universal causal relations that are not opaque to us.

More universal causal relations need not be opaque to us because word-functions revealing them can be *logically included* in less universal, causally opaque word-functions. "Color" is more universal than "red", and "place" is more universal than "surface of the book lying next to the telephone". But no matter how much chance enters into the explanation of there being a red book next to the telephone, it is not by chance that color and place are so causally related that no two colors can be in the same place at the same time. (See section 9.4.1.) "Change" is more universal than "transformation of a caterpillar into a butterfly". But no matter how ignorant we may be of the specific causes of such a metamorphosis, we can still be aware of the necessity of every change having both component and efficient causes.

When word-functions are related as logically included and logically including, they are logically distinct ways of articulating the *same* objects of experience. Because of the logical differences between them, however, such word-functions are useful in different ways. Whatever is objectifiable by "red" is objectifiable by "color", but the word-function of "color" is useful to us in ways that the word-function of "red" is not. Among other things, acquaintance with the word-function of "color" allows us to grasp that the word-function of "red" has a necessary causal relation to place.

Ontological word-functions are among these more universal word-functions which reveal necessary causal relations, since the word-function of "being" is logically included in that of every empirical thing-description. And it is especially true of ontological word-functions that they allow us to grasp necessary truths concerning causal relations. Ontological word-functions are *very* general, and causality is itself an ontological word-function. As section 9.3.1 will show, the demonstration of causal necessity has been a demonstration that effects *are* relations to causes and causes *are* relations to effects. Therefore nothing prevents an ontological analysis from revealing that were some causal relation not true, a thing, either the cause or the effect or both, would be and not be what it is.

With respect to the difference between word-functions that do and word-functions that do not allow us to know that the opposite of a sentence concerning causal relations is contradictory, it is important to recall what was emphasized so much in section 3.1: knowing a self-evident truth cannot be a matter of applying criteria for self-evidence. Consequently the fact that some meanings$_T$ do and some do not give rise to knowledge of necessary causal relations should not lead us to ask for criteria to distinguish these meanings$_T$ from one another, criteria that would operate to cause knowledge of the self-evident truths in question. Once such truths are known we can distinguish these meanings$_T$ by whether or not they generate such knowledge. But such truths are known only by our recognizing, from acquaintance with their word-functions, that their opposites would require something to both be and not be what it is.

Inaccurate or unclear statements of philosophers concerning what it means to know self-evidently necessary truths have led to accusations, like that of Quine, that belief in the existence of these truths is belief in a doctrine of "ultimate and inexplicable insight into the obvious traits of reality". And the idea that we can learn about the nature of reality by armchair deduction rather than by consulting experience does seem to be a bargain-basement approach to wisdom. But that is not the approach to wisdom I am defending. Although we do not depend on experience to *verify* that the opposite of a truth is contradictory, we do depend on experience to *discover* truths whose necessity is known from acquaintance with word-functions. Where do we get these word-functions from if not from experience or from operations performed on word-functions derived from experience?

Contrary to Quine, our knowledge of the self-evident is caused by our very explicable acquaintance with some meanings$_T$ that happen to be so related logically or causally that they yield such knowledge. "Explicable" is the key word here. For if it is impossible to give an a priori criterion for words that will generate knowledge of self-evident truth, it is very possible to give a causal analysis of our acquaintance with the meanings$_T$ of these words.

I gave this kind of causal analysis for necessary truths based on logical relations in Chapter Four. In the last chapter, I gave a causal analysis of the causal opacity of empirical word-functions. The discussions of ontological word-functions in Chapters Five and this chapter, together with the discussion of the problem of perception in Chapter Ten, constitute a causal analysis of acquaintance with ontological word-functions which can reveal necessary causal relations. But we do not need to be in possession of these analyses to know from acquaintance with word-functions that if some sentence were false, something would both be and not be what it is. Rather we need to know that kind of sentence in order to produce the causal analyses in question.

9.2 Ontological Definitions and Empirical Definitions

Further clarification of the differences between philosophical and empirical method can be achieved by comparing philosophical and empirical definitions as examples of causal analyses. Among other things, we will see why empirical definitions of theoretical terms *must* be incomplete, and why ontological analysis is required to understand, and compensate for, their incompleteness.

Contrary to Wittgenstein, grammar does not give essence; causal analysis gives essence. Wittgenstein was confusing meaning$_T$ with meaning$_L$. The most common kind of definition is one which establishes a lexicological relation of equivalence between the word-functions for which different language-forms are used. But sentences asserting a *definiens* of a *definiendum* can also serve to express causal relations between word-functions. For section 9.3 will explain that a necessary cause or effect *is* a relation to that of which it is a necessary cause or effect. Therefore understanding the essence (nature) of something amounts to understanding its causal dispositions.

Consider, for example, the classical philosophic definition of man, "rational animal". How is this way of expressing man's essence the result of a causal analysis? To appreciate the answer that is about to be given, let us ask ourselves how we know the truth of "All men are rational animals", and let us recall the paradoxes associated with non-lexicological interpretations of definitions of this kind. The universality of the statement might suggest that an extensional explanation is called for. We would learn that all men are rational animals the way we learn that all men in a certain place are under seven feet tall. In effect, we make a collection including all men and only men and examine the members of the collection to find out what characteristics they have in common. But how do we know we have collected all and only men unless we already know what features all men have in common? Our knowledge that all men are rational animals, therefore, is not simply a report of the fact that all and only men have been rational animals.

As a result, many philosophers have preferred an account like that of Kant. The predicate "rational animal" simply repeats in a more explicit way what is already contained, albeit in a more confused way, in the subject "man". But how does such a repetition advance our knowledge of reality? If we must know what man is to understand the word-function of "man", why is "All men are rational animals" any more informative of men as cognition-independent existents than is "All men are men"?

The causal approach, on the other hand, allows us to appreciate how "All men are rational animals" gives information about man as an extra-objective existent. A thing performs the activities it does because its nature disposes it to behave in these ways, and we acquire our understanding of its nature by learning what something must be in order to perform these activities. In our experience, we find some organisms performing activities we call "animal" as well as activities we call "rational". Such an organism is the meaning$_T$ of "man". But we can also call these organisms "rational animals". For "rational" and "animal" can be used not only for activities of certain kinds but for things *having the ability* to perform these activities. In this sense, for a thing to be described as rational, it is not necessary that its present activities be describable as rational; all that is necessary is that a thing have the ability to perform rational activities. Men do not cease being rational animals when they are sleeping.

If this analysis of the meaning$_T$ of "men" and "rational animals" is correct, then "All men are rational animals" means: everything performing activities like sensing or moving itself from place to place and like laughing at jokes or writing books is a thing that has the ability to perform such activities. For whatever performs activities of a certain kind has the ability to perform those activities—a self-evident truth licensing us to move from effects (activities) to causes (the dispositions to perform those activities). Therefore everything that performs rational and animal activities (every man) is a thing having the ability to perform rational and animal activities (is a rational animal).

Is the knowledge acquired by this movement from effects to causes vague? It could hardly be more vague. But everything else that we will ever learn about the nature of man will be an expansion and refinement of the kind of knowledge "All men are rational animals" expresses. For all of our further understanding of the nature of man will consist of knowledge of what his make-up must be in order for him to behave the way he does. And though vague, our initial knowledge of human nature has a knowable necessity that diminishes as we rely more and more on inductive reasoning to overcome the vagueness and explain the details of human behavior.

But another way to overcome the vagueness of this definition is by further causal analysis of the ontological variety. To the extent we can give ontological causal analyses of aspects of human behavior, it is possible to expand the kind of knowledge given by "All men are rational animals" without losing any of the necessity that comes from acquaintance with word-functions. And we will be developing the knowledge communicated by that definition of man along its own lines. For that definition is an ontological analysis of man as this passage from Simon makes clear:

Let us try a rigorous ascertainment of the meaning of a word found both in philosophical and in positive contexts. . . . To the question *what does the word man mean?* the answer will be "rational animal"; now, none of the elements of this definition presents a character of irreducible clarity. Take one of them, for instance, animal. What does this word mean? A correct definition would be: "a living body endowed with sense knowledge", and these are so many terms which badly need clarification. . . . In order to render the idea of life clearer, we would have to define it as self-actuation. . . . Its elements are identity and causality. Identity is the first property of being. Causality can be analyzed into potency and act. Identity, potency and act are so many concepts directly reducible to that of being, which is, in an absolute sense, the first and most intelligible of all concepts. We have reached the ultimate term of the analysis, the notion which neither needs to be nor can be defined and which does not admit of any beyond.

This is the kind of analysis that the word *man* suggests when it is used in certain contexts. Everyone would agree that a discourse which demands such an analysis is a philosophical one. But the same word *man* is often used in contexts which neither demand nor could stand such an analysis. . . .

. . . Both philosopher and zoologist consider man, but they have a different way of defining objects and of answering the question *what does it mean?* For the zoologist, man is a mammal of the order of Primates. How would he define such a term as mammal? A vertebrate characterized by the presence of special glands secreting a liquid called milk. How is milk defined? In terms of color, taste, average density, biological function, chemical components, etc.

Here the ultimate and undefinable element is some sense datum; it is the object of an intuition for which no logical construction can be substituted and upon which all the logical constructions of the science of nature finally rest. . . . It is the possibility of being ascertained through sense experience which gives the (elaborated scientific) concept its positive meaning. Every concept is meaningless for the positive scientist which cannot be, either directly or indirectly, explained in terms of sensations.

The philosophy of nature can be defined as a physical consideration whose conceptual instruments call for an ascending analysis, positive science as a physical consideration whose conceptual instruments call for a descending analysis. . . . According as this analysis goes up or down, according as the concept demands to be explained in more and more characteristically ontological terms or in terms which refer more and more directly to definite experiences, we know whether we have to do with a philosophic or a positive treatment. (1943, pp. 164-167)

This passage calls for several comments. First, and for the sake of the record, Simon elsewhere defines life more precisely as the nonfortuitous (in the sense of chance explained in section 8.2.1) coincidence of mover and moved. Second, the fact that he seems to make identity an ontological rather than logical relation does not weaken his analysis. The employment of a logical relation, again, need not make a description any less ontological. And this is especially true of identity which is the relation by which real existents are known as such.

Third, the passage illuminates further the difference between ontological and empirical analysis. An ontological definition seeks to objectify the defined as an essence, that is, as a way of existing, a capacity for existence. And ontological definitions are verified by truths concerning necessary causal relations; for necessary causal relations are conditions for the possibility of existence, since their opposites are im*possible*. (Whatever performs activities of a certain kind has the power to perform activities of that kind; therefore whatever performs rational and animal activities is a rational animal.) Since the truths by which they are verified state conditions for the possibility of existence, ontological definitions reveal their *definienda* as specific capacities for existence. "Essence" is another name for nature; it is nature understood in relation to existence rather than to behavior. But an analysis of behavior by means of necessary causal principles gives us an ontological understanding of behavior and of its causes as possible ways of existing, essences.

Empirical definitions, however, strive to objectify the defined as capacities for observation or as so related to that which can be observed that its existence can be determined by observation. Not that the meanings$_T$ of theoretical words are equivalent to the conditions under which sentences using them can be verified; that would be an epistemological fallacy. The meanings$_T$ of theoretical words are causal entities and dispositions. But to the extent that empirical word-functions do not give rise to causal analyses which can be verified by the principle of non-contradiction, the certitude of empirical causal analyses depends on the application of the principles of induction, simplicity and the search warrant to what is observed to exist by means of sense experience. Both ontological and empirical reasoning begin from experientially verified premises like "An F exists". But from there ontological reasoning goes on to show that a G exists because the word-functions of "F" and "G" make the opposite of "$(x) (Fx \rightarrow Gx)$" impossible. Inductive reasoning, on the other hand, shows only that it is not rational to believe the opposite of "$(x) (Fx \rightarrow Gx)$", given all other known facts of the form "An F exists". Hence empirical definitions must objectify the defined as something whose existence can be verified by observation.

This explains the relative importance for empirical knowledge of criteria for identifying particulars as members of classes and the relative unimportance of such criteria for ontological knowledge. The possibility of determining the presence of something in observation plays the role in empirical knowledge that the possibility of existence plays in ontological knowledge, the role of providing the means of verification. Empirical verification is justified, ultimately, by ontological principles whose opposites are impossible. But that justification is limited to the fact that the observations available to us make the opposite of certain beliefs unreasonable. Hence instead of distinguishing things from one another by the use of ontological word-functions, for example, that which is self-actuating as opposed to that which is not, empirical definitions refer, ultimately, to sensible qualities by which things can be distinguished from one another in perception. The senses do make us aware of existence. But existence, again, is not a quality by which one thing can be sensibly distinguished from another.

It may be objected, however, that the following are as much modes of being as anything else is: a thing shaped like → coinciding with the second mark on a calibrated scale; a thing shaped like → coinciding with the third mark on a calibrated scale. Since these are the kind of sensible objects to which empirical definitions refer and yet are states of affairs capable of real existence, why are empirical definitions less ontological than philosophical definitions? Because we cannot distinguish these modes of being from one another by means of ontological word-functions. (See sections 5.1 and 5.3.2.) Arrow-pointing-to-"2" and arrow-pointing-to-"3" have in common the fact that they are possible ways of existing. But that tells us nothing about each of them in particular since everything is a possible way of existing. Nor are we able to objectify what distinguishes arrow-pointing-to-"2" from arrow-pointing-to-"3" by means of the meaning$_T$ of "exists" and its cognates.

We cannot do this because each of these states of affairs is multiply caused each time it occurs and can result from dissimilar causal complexes at different times. Therefore necessary truths concerning conditions for the possibility of existence (causes) do not allow us to verify statements expressing what each of these things is as a distinct capacity for existence. We could grasp a necessary identity between what is objectified by "arrow pointing to '2' " and by some ontological words if and only if acquaintance with the word-function of "arrow pointing to '2' " made us aware of causal relations necessitating the identity. But the word-function of "arrow pointing to '2' " is causally opaque since it results from multiple causal relations which acquaintance with word-functions alone does not allow us to discriminate.

Of course, we can know the necessary truth of "The occurrence of an arrow pointing to '2' is efficiently caused" since such an occurrence is the result of change, and the word-function of "change" is not itself causally opaque. But "The occurrence of an arrow pointing to '2' is efficiently caused" tells us nothing about an arrow pointing to "2" which is not also true of an arrow pointing to "3" and true of each and every other result of change. Ontological analysis can tell us what is true of arrows pointing to "2" *as* results of change but not *as* this particular result of change as opposed to others.

And just as we use the word-function power-to-perform-rational-activities in the definition of man, we could use the word-function power-to-cause-the-pointer-of-some-scale-to-move-to-"2" in an empirical definition. Both of these complex word-functions are ontological, at least in part, for they make use of word-functions like those of "power" and "cause". But the question is whether these word-functions yield to further ontological analysis objectifying what is true of men as men and true of the causes of arrows pointing to "2" as the causes of arrows pointing to "2". (Simon showed that a part of the definition of man yields to further ontological analysis, but he did not attempt to do this for every part of the definition.)

The last example illustrates another important point. The distinction between ontological and empirical meanings$_T$ is not absolute in the sense that a meaning$_T$ cannot be partly ontological and partly empirical. And the meaning$_T$ of "change" shows that the same meaning$_T$ can be both ontological and empirical. It is empirical since change is a sensibly distinguishable feature of experience. It is ontological since the meaning$_T$ of "change" is a coming into existence or ceasing to exist relative to something which remains in existence. In other words, although existence is not a sensibly distinguishable feature of experience, nothing prevents the meaning$_T$ of a cognate of "exists" from being a sensibly distinguishable feature of experience.

Furthermore, the meanings$_T$ of all thing-descriptions logically include an ontological word-function since they logically include the meaning$_T$ of "being". And specific thing-descriptions logically include other ontological meanings$_T$, those of "change" and "cause", for example. Ontological meanings$_T$, in other words, constitute the logical background of empirical meanings$_T$. And that fact explains the incompleteness of empirical definitions of theoretical terms. It is well known that the theoretical vocabulary of science cannot be defined in terms of observation words and logical relations, truth-functional or modal, alone. What is missing in these definitions is what cannot be expressed by means of tools so limited, namely, the ontological background of empirical knowledge. In particular, what is missing is an understanding of the causal character of theoretical terms.

Why is this understanding missing? We must answer that question differently for the empirical scientist than for the empiricist philosopher of science. As already explained, it is not the business of the empirical scientist to understand causality as such. He makes use of causal principles as the bases of his reasoning. But the foundations of his reasoning are one thing; the results another. His results objectify causal relations by means of laws expressing regular association between terms so described as to enable them to be empirically distinguished, and by means of postulated entities whose descriptions so relate them to these laws that their postulation is able to keep the number of such laws to a minimum. Therefore the empirical scientist as such is not interested in the fact that cognates of the non-empirical term "exists" form the background of these descriptions.

The reason the empiricist philosopher has not appreciated the causal character of theoretical terms is his depreciation of the cognitive value of existence. Logical relations and observation terms alone cannot do justice to causality, an ontological word-function. Consider the word-function of "brittleness", a disposition to behave in a certain way if acted on in a certain way. So defined, the disposition is true of some things that are not now being acted on in the required way, but it is not true of *all* things that are not now being acted on in that way. The attempt to understand brittleness using observational word-functions and logical relations alone cannot account for that fact.

Because he appreciates the cognitive value of existence, the ontological philosopher knows that observational word-functions are important for science insofar as they can be known, by means of reasoning based on the principles of induction, simplicity and the search warrant, to enter into causal relations. And because causality is an ontological word-function, the ontological philosopher recognizes that dispositional terms attribute causal characteristics to things. The empiricist philosopher, on the other hand, must reduce causal relations to logical relations. If causal relations were logical relations, however, being, which causality is responsible for, would be being-known.

Before leaving the subject of ontological and empirical definitions, I should make it clear that, contrary to the impression that may have been given, I admit the existence of meanings$_T$ for things as things that are neither ontological nor empirical. We can be acquainted with mathematical, psychological, moral, aesthetic, social, and political word-functions without being able to define them by reference to sensibly distinguishable objects or to functions of existence. Acquaintance with such meanings$_T$ is able to make us aware of self-evident truths of both the logical and causal variety. For example, self-evidence itself is a psychological meaning$_T$ acquaintance with which reveals the impossibility of knowledge of the self-evident being caused by the application of a criterion for self-evidence.

Although the ontological and empirical exhaust neither the domain of word-functions for things as things nor the domain of causal knowledge, I believe that fully developed theories of causal relations will either be ontological or empirical and, therefore, that other word-functions and causal knowledge will tend to be subsumed under either ontological or empirical theoretical structures. For example, what the word-function of "self-evident" tells us about how knowledge of the self-evident is or is not caused has little interest for the empirical psychologist but is very important for the ontological analysis of necessary truth and of the causal factors that enter our knowledge of necessary truth. Likewise, the ontological analysis of necessary truth and the causes of knowledge of it is important for defending the notion of self-evidence.

9.3 Causality and Relations

Having argued that both empirical and philosophical knowledge is causal, I must now address a difficulty which has no doubt occurred to many readers and which seems to render impossible the view that knowledge of the nature of a thing consists of knowledge of causal relations into which the thing enters. If knowledge of a thing's nature is knowledge of its causal relations, knowledge of its nature is not knowledge of the thing itself but of its relations to things other than itself.

This may seem bad enough, but it is made worse by the fact that any other thing by relation to which the nature of something is known is in turn known not in itself but in relation to things other than itself. Knowing the nature of any one thing would seem to involve us either in an infinite regress of one thing known by its relation to a second known by its relation to a third or in a vicious circle of one thing known by its relation to another known by its relation to the first. And even if this causal view of progress in knowledge can avoid infinite regress and circularity, there is another charge it must escape, the charge of triviality. For what could be more trivial than explaining the fact that a drug causes sleep by attributing dormitive powers to the drug?

Examining these questions will not only remove the difficulties but will deepen our understanding of human knowledge and the causal necessities that are at the basis of progress in human knowledge. Among other things, replying to these objections will allow us to give a more complete answer to a question raised in section 3.4.3: if the meanings$_T$ of "F" and "G" differ otherwise than by logical relations alone, how can denying "Gx" require us to simultaneously affirm and deny "Fx"? I have already (section 9.1) answered the question why there can be word-functions that are not causally opaque, that is, word-functions from acquaintance with which truths whose necessity derives from causal relations can be known. But there is more to be said about why causal truths can be necessary (why there can be necessary causal relations between word-functions).

9.3.1 Relations

Answering these questions will require us to do some ontological analysis of relations. By establishing that things are causes and effects of one another, we have established that relations exist extra-objectively *in some way*. To describe something as a cause or as an effect is to describe it as related to something other than itself. The word-functions of such descriptions cannot be logical constructs. It is the Humean view that makes the dependence of effects on causes a logical construct. Since that dependence is something characterizing things in their extra-objective existence, causal relations have some extra-objective status. Causality is that without which an effect would not exist; no logical construct can be that if to exist is not the same as being-known.

But existence can be attributed to relations in more than one way. Let us assume that, like Aristotle, we have divided all modes of being into categories. Next assume that one of these modes of being is describable as nothing more than a way of referring modes of being other than itself to one another. This mode of being would exist in others as an accident exists in a substance, although accidents could be among the modes of being distinct from itself that it links. Assume, finally, we have chosen to give this mode of being the name "relation". By their possession of relations then, the remaining modes of being (which can be called absolute modes of being to distinguish them from relations) would become relative to things other than themselves in ways in which they would not be relative otherwise.

By hypothesis, an absolute endowed with a relation would not be relative in that particular way were it not for the relation. But there are modes of being that must be considered relative to others whether or not we believe that things become relative only by entities distinct from themselves called relations. Knowledge-of, love-for, trust-in, change are all relative to other things. Are they relative *only* because of their possession of a mode of being distinct from themselves? In a moment I will argue the opposite. To account for some ways in which things are relative to others, relations understood as a class of realities distinct from the realities they relate are not sufficient. Some realities which do not belong to the category of relations must be relative to others just by being what they are.

If there are such realities and if we have given the name "relation" to a class of realities distinct from them, we can say the former realities are *not* relations. But the word "relation" did not come into our vocabulary to designate a philosophical category. Rather, this philosophical use of "relation" is a narrowing of its use in pre-philosophical language. And there is nothing wrong with that. On the contrary, if there are beings whose whole reality consists of ways in which other beings are referred to one another, ordinary language supplies no other term to describe these beings than "relation".

But in ordinary language, "relation" can describe any way in which one mode of being is relative to another, even if a relative mode of being is not made relative by possessing a mode of being distinct from itself. In this sense, change, knowledge, trust, etc. may *be* relations. And if it can be shown that such things are related to others by being what they are, there is philosophical reason for continuing to predicate "relation" of them even if the existence of a class of things by which realities *distinct from* themselves become related also gives us philosophical reason to use "relation" to distinguish this class of things from others. (Apparent contradictions of this kind are both common and significant in philosophy. See Chapter Eleven.)

We would then have two kinds of cognition-independent relations. One kind of relation would consist of beings which are *nothing but* relations. Such a relation would have no existence beyond that of being a way of relating things other than itself. This mode of being would be distinguishable from others, therefore, precisely as a way in which other modes of being are related.

The second kind of relation would consist of beings that are relations but are *not just* relations. Their relativity would not consist of ways in which things *other than* themselves are related. Consequently they would not be distinguishable as ways in which modes of being other than themselves are related. Instead, they would be identical with relative *things*, things which have an existence other than that of being ways of relating realities distinct from themselves.

I will call relations of the first kind formal relations and relations of the second kind material relations. What is the cash value of calling a thing a material relation? Calling a thing a relation when its existence is not just that of a way of referring something distinct from itself to something else distinct from itself tells us that it is relative to others by being what it is, by its identity with itself. What is related to others by a formal relation is *caused* to be so related by something that is distinct from it as an accident is distinct from its substance. (This kind of causality will be explained in section 9.4.1.) But material relations are relative to other things in ways that are not caused by their having formal relations. This would be so even if a formal relation necessarily accompanied every material relation. In addition to being relative in the ways caused by these formal relations, things would still be relative in ways not caused by any formal relation.

It can be demonstrated that if things are cognition-independently relative, their being relative cannot be accounted for in terms of formal relations alone. Assume absolute entities A and B are related by formal relation R. By hypothesis, R exists in one of A or B as an accident, that is, as not existing in itself and hence as needing something else to exist in. Say R exists in A. (There may or may not be a corresponding relation existing in B. Recall the example of D nominating C and C being nominated by D.) Although A has an accidental mode of existence by which it is relative to B, this is not enough to explain A's relatedness; we must explain A's relatedness to R itself.

Does A have R necessarily or contingently? If necessarily, A would not be A if it did not have distinct reality R. Therefore A is related to R by being A. For if *R* is extrinsic to A, *the necessity of A's having R* is not extrinsic to A since, by the definition of necessity, A could not be A and not have its relation to R. And that necessity is a way in which A relates to something other than itself, R. The necessary truth of A's having R, in other words, is caused by a necessary causal relation to R which is not something other than the nature of A.

Could the necessity of A's having R be the result of another formal relation, R_1, distinct from the nature of A? Then why is it necessary for A to have R_1? If, without distinct reality R_1, A would both be and not be A, A is related to R_1 by its identity with itself.

What if A has R contingently? Then A can gain or lose R through change while remaining the same in other respects. But by being what it is, A has a capacity for having R; otherwise it could not acquire R as a result of a change. And a capacity is a relation to that for which it is a capacity. To repeat what was said in section 6.1.1, a capacity for R is identical with something that is actual in other respects. But describing a thing as a capacity for R reveals something about it that merely describing it as actual does not reveal, its identity with a potential component cause of R. For it is not the case that anything whatsoever has the ability to undergo any change whatsoever. It is by being what it is that a thing has the ability to undergo a particular change.

Again, we appear to make reference to cognition-dependent objects in describing dispositions as related to that of which they are dispositions. (See section 6.1.1.) Since R cannot exist when A only has a capacity for R, R can appear to be only a cognition-dependent object. But the relatedness of capacities for producing and undergoing changes cannot be cognition-dependent, cannot be solely a matter of the way the capacity is able to be *described*. It is a matter of the way the capacity *must be* able to be described, since the word-function of the description must be identical with the nature of the described. (All descriptions of material relations need not be explicitly relational. The inexplicitness of a description may be inexplicitness concerning the relative character of the described; for the nature of a material relation is *not just* a way of relating one thing to another. But the nature of a material relation makes *some* relational descriptions true of it by identity between the nature and the word-functions of the descriptions. For the relatedness in question pertains to the causality necessary for the existence of things. If this relatedness were cognition-dependent, a thing would, for example, have the capacity to become something else only as a result of being made an object of human knowledge.)

In the case we are considering, A has the capacity to be the component cause of R. And we must now ask whether it has this capacity necessarily or contingently. If contingently, A has the capacity for having the capacity for R; and we must ask whether it has *that* capacity necessarily or contingently. If contingently, the question repeats itself ad infinitum. If necessarily, A has a capacity for R by its identity with itself. That is, A is either identical with a capacity for R or identical with a necessary causal relation to a capacity for R.

On no hypothesis, then, can the relatedness of things be accounted for solely by formal relations. If things are cognition-independently related, there must at least be material relations. But the arguments of Chapters Seven and Eight have shown things to be related to one another causally. Change has a necessary relation of dependence on sufficient causes. And causes are so disposed as to necessarily produce certain effects in certain circumstances. These necessities are determined by the nature of change and the natures of things that cause change. Consequently changes and the causes of change are relative by nature whether or not they have formal relations. For even if their natures should require that change and the causes of change be related formally (a possible reason for believing so will be mentioned in section 10.1), still the *necessity* of these formal relations, or of the capacities of their bearers for them, would not be extrinsic to their natures. The bearers of these relations are materially relative to them or, at least, to their capacities for them.

Note that the existence of a material relation does not always require the coexistence of the term to which the relative thing is relative. Things have the capacity to acquire characteristics by undergoing changes; the capacities of things for these characteristics are material relations whose terms do not always exist. I doubt if it is true even of formal relations that their terms must actually exist. (See Deely, 1975b.) But if it were true, the reason would be that a formal relation is nothing but a way of relating things distinct from itself. *A fortiori*, a relation whose existence is more than that of a way of relating things distinct from itself can exist in the absence of a term.

The distinction between formal and material relations is not to be confused with what is commonly referred to as the distinction between ''internal'' and ''external'' relations. The latter distinction is based on assumptions about logical and causal necessity which, obviously, I do not share. The issues discussed in section 3.4.3 are closer to the problematic of that distinction than are the present issues. And the fact that, as here defined, a formal relation may be possessed by a thing necessarily and a material relation, such as a causal disposition, possessed contingently (see section 9.3.2) is enough to prevent any confusion between the two kinds of distinction.

Finally, as I mentioned in section 3.4.2, because causal necessity is based on material relations, we could have avoided reference to causal *relations* up to this point and have spoken instead of causality, causal dispositions, causal necessity, the necessity of something's having a cause or an effect, etc. Relations as entities distinct from their *relata* may or may not be required for causal necessity; and where they may be required, they are not the basis of causal necessity. If formal relations are anywhere causally necessary, that necessity is an *effect* of the material relations involved. Therefore, my theses concerning causal necessity do not need a theory of relations distinct from their *relata* as a premise. If they are shown to need it as a *consequence*, so be it.

On the other hand, to have not used the vocabulary of causal relations would have been to postpone the inevitable. Although the word "relation" need not appear in formulas about causality, the word-functions of these formulas are and must be relational, since the realities with which they are identical are relative. What things are demands that, if the truth about them is to be fully known, they be objectified by descriptions relating them to other things. For what things are are ways they stand in relation to other things.

Again, there can be excellent philosophical reasons for confining the use of the word "relation" to formal relations. After all, only a formal relation is a *pure* relation, consists exclusively of a way of relating one thing to another. Restricting the use of "relation" in this way would not eliminate the need for a way of expressing what formal and material relations have in common. We can, for example, describe a (formal) relation as a pure relatedness, and describe a thing whose relatedness does not derive from a relation distinct from its own nature as a relatedness that is not a pure relatedness, not exclusively a way one thing is related to another. Then, instead of speaking of formal and material *relations*, we could speak of pure and mixed *relatedness*, with only the former being called a "relation".

I will continue to use the terminology of formal and material relations. In doing so, I have no doctrinal disagreement with those who so use "relation" that only a pure relatedness can be a relation cognition-independently, while they recognize that the *truth* of relational descriptions of a thing that is not a pure relatedness can be imposed by the nature of the thing, that is, by *identity* between its cognition-independent nature and word-functions relating it to other things. Thus Deely distinguishes between things that

> cannot be explained save by reference to something not themselves; and in this sense . . .are relative according to the way their being must be *expressed* in discourse

and things that are

> relative according to the way they essentially (or definably) *have* being

the latter being things that consist

> *entirely* in a reference toward another. (Deely, 1977a, pp. 46-47)

Although Deely describes the former as things that "are not truly relations according to their way of being independently of the mind" (p. 51), his distinction is precisely the one I am making between formal and material relations. There is no disagreement between us.

9.3.2 Causal knowledge as relational

Now we can get to the problems raised at the outset. One problem was how the identity between the things objectified by "F" and "G" can be necessary when the diverse objectification is accomplished by reference to the terms of a real distinction. The necessary is that whose opposite is contradictory. Contradiction is the affirmation and denial of the *same*. When something is objectified by descriptions whose word-functions are not the same because they differ by more than logical relations, how can the opposite be contradictory?

The answer is that even though the word-functions are not the same, the things they objectify are the same. And these things are necessarily the same if the diverse objectification is accomplished by reference to really distinct terms at least one of which is identical with a necessary causal relation to the other term. The fact that the terms are really distinct does not prevent one of the terms from being identical with its relation to the other. A change, for instance, is really other than its causes but is not other than a material relation of dependence on its causes. A change *is* a material relation of dependence on its causes. Therefore, a change (Fx) without an efficient cause (-Gx) would both be and not be a change (Fx & -Fx). Hence "(x) (Fx $\rightarrow$ Gx)" is necessarily true.

In other words, since things are material relations to other things, a meaning$_T$'s being what something is amounts to its being what some material relation is. Sentences using descriptions with these word-functions can be necessarily true because the identity of what is objectified by these descriptions can be necessary. The identity can be necessary because the opposite would require a word-function to both be and not be what it is. And when word-functions are not causally opaque, acquaintance with them enables us to grasp the necessary identity of what they objectify. (Even causally opaque word-functions are material causal relations. Causal opacity is an epistemological question. Material relations concern what things are things as extra-objective things.)

The next problem is how learning about a thing's relations to others informs us about the thing itself. When what we know about a thing are its causal relations to other things, we know what the thing itself is. Hence the characteristics that constitute what a thing is include dispositions to produce or undergo certain changes in certain circumstances; and these dispositions *are* causal relations to their effects. When, for example, we describe a behavioral disposition of a drug as a dormitive power, reference is made to something, sleep, really distinct from what the described thing is. But the word "power" does not refer to anything other than what the described thing is. The meaning$_T$ of "power" is relational, but so is the reality it objectifies.

Since the natures of causes, of their causal dispositions and of changes are constituted by relations to one another, no infinite regress or vicious circle prevents our making progress in knowledge by moving from effect to cause. We broke the back of Hume's dilemma by pointing out that a change occurring to something is a reality with a necessary relation of dependence on what is other than itself. We now know that the necessity of that relation results from a change's being a relation to a component cause. From the change's relation to the component cause we move to the previously unknown relation of dependence on an efficient cause. From the recognition of a change's dual dependence on component and efficient causes we move to a recognition of the necessity of these causes producing and undergoing the already known change because their behavioral dispositions are what they are. Describing these dispositions by reference to the change they cause involves no infinite regress or vicious circle since the change was originally known by us independently of our knowledge of the existence of the dispositions necessitating the occurrence of the change. (We cannot be aware of a change without being aware of that which is its component cause, but it does not follow that we recognize component causality as such. Hume didn't.)

Returning to our dormitive power example, however, how do we escape the charge that the knowledge provided by descriptions of things as causes of certain effects is trivial? By pointing out that there is very little to escape from. That a chemical has the ability to induce sleep is obviously a very important piece of information to have. The objector will reply that this information does not tell us what there is about the nature of the chemical which gives it the ability to produce this effect. No, but we learn this only by discovering further causal relations entered into by the chemical and by the organisms in which it induces sleep and by relating these discoveries to the laws and theories that other causal investigations have produced. We get further information about the chemical from, for instance, reactions that occur when it is brought in contact with other chemicals and organisms. The results of such experiments acquire significance for understanding why the chemical causes sleep because they allow us to make causal inferences governed by the principles of induction, simplicity and the search warrant and because previous inferences justified by these principles are relevant to those results.

In other words, understanding the dormitive power of a drug amounts to understanding its chemistry and the chemistry of the organisms it puts to sleep. And knowledge of these chemical principles is the result of causal reasoning and hypothesizing guided by the principles of induction, simplicity and the search warrant. If changes and the behavioral dispositions of their causes were not themselves identical with causal relations, and if the things producing and undergoing changes were not in the last analysis identical with material causal relations, all of our efforts to obtain causal knowledge would result in nothing but descriptions of changes, causes and causal dispositions in terms of relations extrinsic to their natures. But the fact that these things are all identical with one or another kind of causal relation gives our causal reasoning a foothold in the natures of things.

To understand a thing's causal dispositions is to understand what the thing must be in order to behave, actively and passively, as it does. In practice, learning the natures of things amounts to discovery of that underlying causal structure that keeps the number of causal laws to a minimum. The postulation of an underlying causal structure is the postulation of an organized set of entities which are material causal relations. Some of a thing's causal dispositions will be either identical with or a necessary result of characteristics of this underlying causal structure. (An acid solution has the ability to turn litmus paper red because of the molecular structure of acids.) These are the causal dispositions which are taken to be essential to a "natural kind".

Others of a thing's causal dispositions are due to characteristics acquired from the action on it of external causes. (If an acid solution has been kept near a source of heat, it can warm the litmus paper.) Characteristics due to the action of external causes are individual modifications affecting the behavior to which a thing is disposed by its natural kind and include characteristics resulting from individual peculiarities of the causes that brought a thing of this natural kind into existence. But the action of external causes is ultimately due to their underlying causal structures and, therefore, to dispositions essential to their natural kinds.

How do we distinguish between those behavioral dispositions which are essential to a natural kind and those modifications of behavior which result from the action of external causes? In the same way that we arrive at the conclusion of any empirical reasoning, by examining variations in sequences of events in the light of the three principles of empirical knowledge.

Incidentally, I agree with Kripke (1972, p. 118ff.) that we spontaneously believe things to belong to natural kinds with certain internal structures that lie behind their phenomenal properties. But this is more than a spontaneous belief; it is an assent to self-evident, causally necessary truths. It may or may not be necessary that gold is yellow. But it is self-evidently certain that whatever is yellow (as gold sometimes is) has the capacity to be yellow (has a nature allowing it to be a component cause of yellowness).

I also agree with him that our concept of natural kind is detachable from the entire ensemble of phenomenal properties by which we originally identified the kind. As we apply the principles of empirical knowledge, we find that certain of a thing's behavioral dispositions are more informative about its internal structure than others. The fact that gold usually reflects light in a certain way, for instance, tells us little about the internal structure of gold as opposed to other things that can also reflect light in this way. Certain chemical reactions, on the other hand, require a unique atomic causal structure.

But none of this is evidence for extending Kripke's theory of fixing the reference from proper names to common nouns, thereby suppressing connotation. Rather than showing that the function of common nouns is not the connoting of certain features of kinds but the referencing of kinds non-descriptively, the evidence indicates that ontological word-functions, causal dispositions specifically, are logically included in the features that are the word-functions of common nouns. It is because causal dispositions are logically included that we can disassociate from the kind the original phenomenal properties in favor of other properties. Whatever the internal make-up of this lump we call "gold" may be, it gives the lump the ability to behave in whatever ways it does behave. (The fixing the reference theory is also not needed to solve Wittgenstein's problem with the meter stick, a commonplace epistemological fallacy. See Kripke, 1972, p. 54ff.)

Many other questions that can be raised about natures, causal dispositions, the causal character of theoretical definitions, etc. with reference to empirical knowledge are well discussed in Harré and Madden's *Causal Powers: A Theory of Natural Necessity*. This remarkable and important work came to my attention too late to discuss it at any length here. But the similarities and differences in our approaches are sufficiently obvious that I do not have to spell them out.

I will mention one difference, however, which is relatively minor from the point of view of their objectives but more significant for mine. They reject the concept of substance on the grounds that a substance would be a featureless entity. As a result, they do not consider it possible to identify a substance with any of its causal dispositions, while they quite correctly hold that explanation must begin with something whose nature is not distinguishable from a causal disposition (or, in my terminology, something which is a material causal relation).

I have already (section 6.1.2) discussed the view that substance is a featureless entity, and that discussion can now be put in terms of material relations. To describe a substance as related to its accidents or causes is not to describe something other than the substance itself, for a substance *is* a material relation to its accidents and causes. A substance has a particular accident either contingently or necessarily. If necessarily, then the substance is identical with a necessary causal relation to this accident. (Since it has a component cause, the accident also requires an efficient cause; the substance itself may be that efficient cause.) If a substance has an accident contingently, the substance is identical with a capacity for having that accident, a capacity for being that accident's component cause, or is identical with a causal relation to a necessary accident, which accident is the capacity for the contingent accident. A substance's causal relations to both its necessary and its contingent accidents, therefore, are features of the substance in the strong sense of being identical with the substance; they are what the substance is.

Could all the differences in the causal dispositions possessed by various things derive from the accidents of one underlying substance? If so, the entire universe could be one substance. (A natural kind need not be equivalent to a substance in the ontological sense.) Or are there differences in the dispositions of things to produce and undergo changes which require differences in the material causal relations that are identical with the substances to which these dispositions belong?

If so, we would be able to distinguish substances from one another. I will mention one possible way of doing this. Since my purpose is exclusively heuristic, I will outline the argument as briefly as possible without attempting to prove its assumptions.

There is such a thing as immanent activity. (See Parker, 1960, pp. 36-47; 1962; Simon, 1934, pp.57-95.) If a thing is enabled to perform an activity by an accident it receives from the causality of another thing, that activity is not an immanent activity. Consequently, where there are things capable of immanent activity and things not capable of it, there are substances of different kinds, substances which are different kinds of material relations to activity. On the other hand, differences between immanent activities may result from accidents that are not efficiently caused by their substances. But where the differences between immanent activities are themselves characterized by immanence, a thing that can perform one kind of immanent activity differs from one that cannot at the level of substance. It can be argued, for instance, that sense cognition and rational cognition are immanent activities whose differences cannot be explained by accidents received from causes extrinsic to the substances which perform them.

9.3.3 Extrinsic denominations

We have been considering how knowledge of a thing's causal relations gives us knowledge of its nature. To conclude this topic, I should mention that a description of a thing by its relation to a cause or an effect is not the kind of description we have referred to as an extrinsic denomination. An extrinsic denomination describes the denominated, not by its relation to some term, but as term of something's relation to it. To denominate something extrinsically is to describe it as *term* of a relation rather than as the *bearer* of a relation, the bearer of a relation being either a thing that is materially relative in this way or a thing in which a formal relation has its accidental existence.

A thing may be bearer and term of the same relation. (A knows A.) And the term of a relation borne by one thing may bear another relation corresponding to the first. (A is father of B; B is daughter of A.) But neither of these things is what is expressed by an extrinsic denomination; all that is expressed is that the denominated is the term of some relation. (The distinction between the bearer and the term of a relation does not have to be pointed out when their ontological status, or that of the relation, is not under discussion. At other times, it is preferable for reasons of simplicity to refer only to a relation and its terms.)

Even where the relation in question is cognition-independent, there are perhaps times when we are in doubt whether a description is attributing a relation to something or denominating it extrinsically. But that point would not be as significant as the following two. First, the fact that extrinsic denominations do not themselves express any of the characteristics making up the things they denominate does not prevent them from implying much about these things, the implications being based on necessary causal relations with which changes, causes and causal dispositions are identical. Second, there are many philosophically important cases where the causal relations that are the word-functions of descriptions leave no doubt at all whether a thing is bearer or term of a relation. When substance is described as the capacity for accidents there is no question whether it is the bearer of the relation; substance *is* the capacity for accidents.

Likewise, the word "knowledge" (in the general sense of awareness of some kind) happens to be used for a relative mode of being we are directly acquainted with as a relative mode of being. That for which we happen to use the word "knowledge" is awareness-of something; if it were not relative in this way, it would not be what it is. (Whether its relatedness is formal or material is another question.) And when we describe something as known, we are describing it as term of the knowledge relation. Therefore, we describe something as known by A because we believe that A knows it, that, in other words, the relative mode of being we call "knowledge" is a characteristic of A as the knowledge we are directly acquainted with is a characteristic of ourselves. Consequently "known by A" describes something as term of a relation of which A is the bearer. (And if it expressed anything more about the term of this relation, the reason would be that the meaning$_T$ of "knowledge" would include a reference to some characteristic of the term of the knowledge relation. See section 2.2.2.)

How is it, then, that we know which is the bearer and which the term of a relation? Sometimes acquaintance with the causality expressed or implied by a word-function is sufficient to answer the question. The word-functions of "substance" and "accident" imply that substance is a component cause of accidents. In "known by A", the function of "by" is to attribute causality, and hence a causal relation, to A. Sometimes awareness of the extra-objective cause of our acquaintance with the word-function is sufficient to answer the question. We acquire the word-function of "knows" from direct awareness of a relative mode of being. We become acquainted with the word-function of "being nominated by D" by observing D's behavior, not C's.

If any cases are left in doubt by our acquaintance with word-functions or our awareness of the causes of that acquaintance, the only significant question remaining would concern, not our *knowledge*, but the extra-objective causes of the states of affairs making sentences using those words *true*. In no case, however, is the question whether what a description objectifies is the bearer or term of a relation to be answered by criteria for distinguishing descriptions of bearers from descriptions of terms.

From the point of view of what pertains to things as objects, on the other hand, it can be said that "B is known by A" objectifies B as the bearer of the relation known-by-A. That is the sense in which the word-function of an extrinsic denomination is a cognition-dependent object. "Known by A" objectifies a really existing state of affairs, A's knowing B, but it does so by making B the *logical* bearer of a relation that is not borne by B in its extra-objective being. And there is nothing wrong with that since in objectifying things, we do not attribute to their extra-objective being the logical properties of the means by which we objectify them.

From the point of view of logical relations, in other words, it makes no difference whether a relation's *relata* are bearers or terms of the relation in their real existence and therefore whether a word-function like known-by-A is a real relation or a cognition-dependent relation based on a real relation borne by A. What is objectified by a relative predicate, say, "R", is a way one or more things relates to itself or others, as in "*a* R *b*". To achieve the goal of objectifying relation R, we must also objectify that which the relation relates, *a* and *b*. Therefore, the word-function of "R" is so objectified as to logically require that *a* and *b* be made terms objectifications distinct from the objectification of R, objectifications that allow *a* and *b* to be related to the word-function of "R" logically as well as extra-objectively.

But this distinction between the relation and each of its terms is strictly logical, strictly a matter of mode of objectification, and implies nothing about the extra-objective existence of the relation and its terms. The terms may be really identical (as in "*a* = *a*") or really distinct. The relation may be material, and hence really identical with one or more of the logical terms, or formal. *A fortiori*, what thing or things is the real bearer of the relation in its extra-objective state makes no difference to the thing's logical status as a term required by the word-function of a relative predicate.

Hence if we approach the question of extrinsic denominations solely from the perspective of logical relations, we will find it impossible to distinguish a bearer of a relation from a term. That is to be expected since the question is ontological and is to be decided by causal relations, not logical. When causal analysis shows a thing to be either a component cause of a relation or identical with a relation, the thing is the extra-objective bearer, not the term, of the relation.

9.4 Characterizing and Teleonomic Causes, Generic and Specific Word-Functions

Readers may have wondered why I have not discussed what is traditionally known as formal causality, for the analysis of changes and their results in terms of efficient and component (material) causality seems to be incomplete without formal causality. I will approach formal causality by what will appear to be the circuitous route of returning to an earlier question concerning our general theory of necessary truth. We raised the question in Chapter Three but left it unanswered for lack of the required background, which has since been provided.

The discussion of formal causality will also give me a chance to address some other problems mentioned earlier. When dealing with teleonomic causality in section 1.2, I said there was another reason why the goal of an agent's activity can be called a cause. And from section 2.3.2 on, I have been describing the real existence of things as a cause of the truth of sentences. An understanding of formal causality is necessary for explaining these causal relations.

9.4.1 Characterizing causes

The necessary non-identity of what is objectified by "married" and "not unmarried" derives from the use of the logical relation of negation. But whence the necessity of the non-identity of squares and circles, of sitting, standing and reclining persons, of places occupied by different colors? In such cases, the necessary non-identity is not traceable to the use of negation. The necessity of identity or non-identity, however, must derive from either logical relations or causal relations. What logical or causal relations account for this large category of necessary truths concerning the mutual exclusion of things diversely objectified otherwise than by the use of negation, a category that has sometimes driven philosophers to invoke that unexplanatory fiction, the synthetic a priori truth?

Let us take the "No two colors can be in the same place at the same time" example first. This is the classic example and has been discussed many times. Still, it has not yet been pointed out that the necessity of this truth derives from necessary *causal* relations. This example, then, is very useful for showing the power of the causal approach to necessary truth. What kind of causal relation guarantees that no two colors can be in the same place at the same time? Well what kind of causal relation holds between place and color? The kind of relation that holds between material (component) and formal causes. Place is the matter, color the form. Place is the potentiality, the capacity; color is the actualization of the potentiality, the fulfillment of the capacity.

Since we have replaced "material cause" with "component cause", let us introduce a corresponding neologism for "formal cause"; let us call it instead the "characterizing cause". Why use a neologism at all? For two reasons. In many contexts "form" is used for something quasi-empty, something for which what is called "matter" supplies the content, as, for example, when the logical form of an argument as opposed to its specific content. This is the exact opposite of the causal meanings of "form" and "matter". It is form that gives content and specification to otherwise unspecified matter. The material causes of a painting, for instance, are the hitherto empty canvas and unused paints; its formal causes are the colors and shapes of the completed work. The second reason is that classical realists have too often used the word "form" both for characterizing causes *and* for essence, thereby confusing both issues for those who do not happen to be experts in realism.

My reason for not mentioning characterizing causality before now? This book is being written at a time in the history of philosophy when most philosophers are unfamiliar with causal concepts of the ontological (as opposed to its epistemological substitute) variety, unfamiliar with necessary causal relations and unfamiliar with the causal character of philosophical arguments. In this cultural context, it would have been detrimental to communication to complicate the discussion any more than was necessary to settle the issues at hand. Furthermore, the fundamentals of characterizing causality have been adequately treated in many places, some of them referred to in Appendix II, and there is no need for me to add here to what the extensive literature already has to say on the subject. What has not been adequately discussed hitherto is the invalidity of the empirical analysis of efficient causality. That had to be done before taking up characterizing causality, for in the minds of most empiricists, causality is equivalent to efficient causality. Therefore if the necessity for efficient causality had not been demonstrated, it is hardly likely that characterizing causality would have been deemed worthy of consideration. Component causality had to be explained sufficiently to demonstrate the existence of efficient causality. But bringing characterizing causes in earlier would have served no purpose.

The existence of characterizing causality is demonstrated by an argument we have seen before. Change is the coming into existence of a state of affairs that did not previously exist. But unlike the total annihilation of one thing and its replacement by a completely different thing, change occurs to something which remains in existence throughout the change. What changes in some respects remains the same in others. Consequently what remains in existence must acquire or lose something by means of change. If not, a change would not take place because a new state of affairs would not come into existence. Whatever is acquired or lost by means of change is that which differentiates the new state of affairs from the old. This is the characterizing cause.

On any analysis of change, characterizing causality is necessary. If the results of change are assumed to be nothing more than new spatial arrangements of already existing things, the existence of (formal) spatial relations as accidents of these things must be admitted. Otherwise nothing new would exist as the result of change. The results of change, therefore, must be unions of component causes (which remain in existence throughout a change) with characterizing causes (which differentiate what is brought into existence by a change from what existed previously). But even though the result of a change is a whole of which both that which remains in existence and that which it acquires or loses through change can be called *parts*, I will continue to describe only that which remains in existence as a *component* cause of the change or its result.

If what remains through a change satisfies our definition of substance, the characterizing cause of the result is an accident. (The definitions of substance and accident are not only ontological but causal since "exists in another" refers to a relation of component causality.) But unlike the definition of substance most often used by empiricists, the definition I am using does not make it impossible for a change to bring a new substance into existence. The component cause of such a change could have no characteristics other than the characteristic of being a potential substance. (See Cahalan, 1970, pp. 413-415, 418-420.) But this component cause would never exist in a purely potential state since it would always have been made some actual substance by a substantial characterizing cause. (See Anscombe and Geach, 1961, pp. 70-71.)

The fact that one could not represent such a causal relation in the imagination is irrelevant. It need not be the case that we can imagine causal relations *as such* (things which *are* material causal relations can be imagined, of course). Causal relations are that by which we *explain* what we can imagine. They are necessary conditions for something we are acquainted with, not by means of imagination, but by means of perception and linguistic objectification: existence. We are sometimes inclined to think that what cannot be imagined cannot exist. On the contrary, what can be imagined could not come into existence without causal dispositions whose existence we are informed of by our acquaintance with word-functions, like would-not-exist-without, that cannot be represented in the imagination because they are not sensibly distinguishable features of experience.

Assume, for the sake of argument, that atoms exist just as they are pictured to exist in the traditional textbook models, namely, as clusters of spheres with other spheres in orbit around them. Assume further that each element is a distinct kind of substance. Then when we imagine an atom, we imagine a substance which has certain necessary accidents (the *shapes* of the subatomic particles and of their orbits, their *rates* of *motion*, the *number* of protons, etc.) and is a capacity for other accidents (ionization, for example). And what we imagine is the *result* of the union of something having no characteristics other than being a potential substance with a characterizing cause by which this potency is actualized in one way. The complex of substantial and accidental characteristics resulting from this union is made object of the imagination by means of accidents like shape, motion and number. But the fact that the objectification of substance is achieved *by means of* accidents does not imply that the objectification is only *of* accidents, that only accidents terminate the knowledge relation, any more than the fact that a substance is described by reference to its accidents implies that it is not the substance that is being described. (For more on the objectification of one thing by means of another, see section 10.3.)

To get back to the subject at hand, we need to understand characterizing causality to understand the necessity of no two colors being in the same place. Whether or not color exists extra-objectively, color is phenomenologically formal in relation to place. Any two-dimensional surface in our visual field is capable of being characterized by the visual object we call "color". An area of a surface is a visual capacity for which color is a visual fulfillment. But how does this matter-form relation between place and color make it necessary that no two colors be in the same place at the same time?

The answer is provided by the familiar realist principle that every being is one (undivided), or to put it differently, that unity (lack of division) is a word-function co-extensive with the word-function of "being". (Since such a word-function will transcend any categorization of beings, it is called a "transcendental".) If something is simple, it is undivided. If it is complex, it exists only as long as the diverse factors making it up are together. If they are separated, the thing does not exist. Therefore every existent is undivided.

From the fact that every existent is one, it follows that a passive potency can be actualized in one and only one way at a time. A passive potency, the potency by which something is eligible to be a component cause, is a potency for being, for existing in this way or that way. If a passive potency could be fulfilled in more than one way at a time, a being would be two beings and not one. The same entity may have several different passive potencies which are simultaneously actualized. But each of its passive potencies could not be simultaneously actualized in different ways. (An active potency can be actualized in more than one way only in the sense that by it multiple effects *external to the agent itself* can be produced.)

Therefore a component cause can have one and only one characterizing cause of a particular kind at any given time. For what makes two characterizing causes, like red and green, be of the same *kind* is that they are actualizations of the same potency. (In traditional terminology, the genus to which something belongs is taken from its matter.) In things whose intrinsic ontological structure consists of a union of component and characterizing causes, the characterizing cause is the intrinsic principle determining that the thing actually exists in a certain way. By itself, a component cause, for example, a surface, is only potentially a reality of a certain kind, for example, a colored reality. The characterizing cause unites with the component cause and determines that it actually exists in this way or that. But in so doing, the characterizing cause determines the result of its union with the component cause to be *one* in this respect or that, to be undivided as an actualized potency. For like all causes, characterizing causes are causes of existents and therefore causes of effects that are one. Any hue actualizing the potency of a surface for color causes the area it actualized to be *one* in color. If two colors could exist in the same place at the same time, any existent could be divided and undivided in the same respect at the same time.

9.4.2 Generic and specific word-functions

The component cause-characterizing cause relationship can explain other cases of the necessary non-identity of the members of certain classes, but can it explain all of them? That whoever is sitting is not standing is made necessary by the fact that sitting and standing are characterizing causes (spatial relations, to be exact) actualizing the same potency of their component cause, namely, the potency of the parts of a body to have determined spatial relations to one another. But what about the necessity of circles not being squares, of scalene triangles not being equilateral? The necessary mutual exclusivity of these classes is a matter of logical relations, not causal relations. What is peculiar to these logical relations, however, and allows them to generate the kind of necessary truths they do is that they are strictly analogous to that relation between component causes and characterizing causes which requires that a component cause have one and only one characterizing cause of a particular kind at a time.

The word-function of "enclosed figure" is logically included in those of "square" and "circle" the way the word-function of "color" is logically included in that of "red". Word-functions like those of "enclosed figure" and "color" differ respectively from those of "square" and "red", not just by logical relations of greater and lesser universality, but by the logical relations of more and less explicitness. Whatever information is communicated by the former words is also communicated by the latter, but the latter communicate more information than the former.

Contrast the relation between the meanings$_T$ of "color" and "red" to that between the meanings$_T$ of "color" and "color used to signify danger". The second member of each of these pairs can be looked on as an expansion of the meaning$_T$ of "color". But while "red" does not make reference to any feature of experience really distinct from the meaning$_T$ of "color", "used to signify danger" does make reference to things really distinct from the meaning$_T$ of "color". "Red" and "color used to signify danger" objectify the same feature of experience. But the diversity between objectifications of the same thing by means of "color" and "red" derives from logical relations alone. The diversity between objectification of the same thing by means of "color" and "color used to signify danger" derives from reference to really distinct features of experience. That is why the identity between red and color is necessary while the identity between red and a color used to signify danger is not.

The features of experience objectified by "red" and "green" are each objectified by "color", but what differentiates red and green from one another is only *potentially* objectified when either is objectified by "color". The explicit objectification of red and green as distinct from one another is potentially achievable but not actually achieved when we objectify each by "color". Still, we can say red is a color and green is a color because a feature of experience objectified by "color" as something containing differences like those distinguishing red and green in potency is only logically distinct from a feature of experience objectified by "red" or "green" as containing those differences in act. This logical potency is what constitutes the inexplicitness of the word-function of "color" relative to those of "red" and "green", and with the exception of this logical characteristic, the word-function of "color" and those of "red" and "green" are the same.

Now when we are acquainted with the word-functions of "red" and "green", we are thereby acquainted with that which distinguishes the color red from the color green. But that which distinguishes red from green has a different logical relation to the word-function of "color" than does the word-function of "used to signify danger". We cannot be acquainted with the difference of red without being aware of it as a fulfillment of the logical potency which constitutes the inexplicitness of the word-function of "color" relative to that of "red". For the logical relation the difference of red has to the word-function of "color" is that of an actualization of a certain potency. But we can be acquainted with the word-function of "used to signify danger" without being aware of it as a fulfillment relative to the inexplicitness of "color". Consequently there obtains between some but not all word-functions related as more and less universal the kind of potency-act relation that holds between component and characterizing causes.

When such a component-characterizing logical relation holds between word-functions, we call the more indeterminate word-function a "genus" and the more determinate word-function a "species" or "specific difference", as the case may be. Strictly speaking, it is not the species but the specific difference that stands to the genus as a characterizing cause stands to a component cause. The species corresponds to the union of characterizing and component causes. Since we often do not have a word for the specific difference distinct from the word for the species, however, and since it will not affect the argument I am making here, I will simplify by speaking of the species as characterizing relative to the genus. Thus a generic term like "figure" objectifies something in the manner of a potency for further actualization, and a specific term like "square" objectifies the same thing as a fulfillment of the logical potency that constitutes the indeterminacy of the genus.

When a component cause has a particular characterizing cause, it exists in a way in which it would otherwise only potentially exist. But that potentiality can be actualized in only one way at a time. A word-function for a set can be verified by the members of many subsets. But some subsets are such that their memberships must be mutually exclusive of one another. Why? Because the relation between the word-functions for these subsets is that of species of the same genus and, therefore, that of characterizing causes for the same potency of a component cause. That is why it is necessary that the same color not be both red and green though the same color can be used both to signify danger and to signify international communism. The differences of red and green are both related to the word-function of "color" as actualizations of its logical potency, since the function we give "color" is just that of communicating in a more indeterminate way what is communicated by "red" and "green".

Generic and specific word-functions are both means for objectifying things (or features of experience or logical constructs). But the generic word-function objectifies the thing as if it were in potency for that which the specific word-function objectifies in act. Therefore two specific word-functions cannot objectify the same thing. For the same potency, the logical potency accruing to something as objectified by the generic word-function, cannot be actualized in two distinct ways at the same time. The word-function for each species so actualizes and determines the potency which constitutes the indeterminateness of the genus that something objectified by both specific word-functions would be two things and not one. That the potency of the genus is only logical makes no difference. Both generic and specific word-functions, with all their logical characteristics, are means for objectifying things. Things must be one. And if potencies characterizing things as objects are fulfilled in more than one way, more than one thing is being objectified.

Why logical relations thus analogous to causal relations should occur is a valid question but one we do not have to answer. Nor would any purpose be served in looking for a criterion of determining the necessary truth of a sentence by determining whether such a relation does hold between word-functions. The fact is that some word-functions are so related, and we recognize this by being acquainted with these word-functions, that is, by having the ability to use words in certain ways. For it is by our acquaintance with the ways words are used that we recognize logical relations between word-functions. (An extended discussion of several of the issues in this section can be found in Bobik, 1965, pp. 61-115, 258-261.)

9.4.3 Teleonomic causes and extrinsic characterizing causes

A teleonomic cause is the term of the relation that determines an efficient cause to exercise its causality this way or that. In the case of sentences, men are the efficient causes, and one goal of making and using sentences, the goal of importance to epistemology and logic, is knowledge of the identity between what has been objectified by some name or description and what exists. And to know that a sentence is true, is to know that its use of language-forms has achieved the goal of identity between what is objectified by means of language forms and what exists. Thus in section 2.3.2, we said that the reason why the predicate "able to be the value of a bound variable in a true sentence" is co-extensive with that which exists is that the existence of something *causes* sentences asserting its existence to be true. For sentential truth consists in the achievement of the teleonomic cause of identity between an object and an existing thing.

Philosophers have debated whether describing the term of an agent's activity as itself a cause has any more than metaphorical value. But the term of any exercise of efficient causality is the acquisition of a new *characterizing cause* (or the loss of an old one) on the part of a component cause. In this way, at least, goals are genuine causes. What is teleonomic from the point of view of the efficient cause is characterizing from the point of view of the component cause. In the traditional formula, the formal cause and the final cause are the same.

The existence of what is asserted to exist causes the truth of the assertion by way of characterizing causality. Knowledge of thing-descriptions is causally prior to that of object-descriptions in the same way. (In these cases, there are also relations of efficient causality to consider. Since language is public, actual existents have relations both of characterizing and efficient causality to linguistic knowledge. For efficient causality, see the next chapter. And the use of language to objectify actual existents has a priority of efficient causality over its use for cognition-dependent objects, including object-descriptions.)

This kind of characterizing causality is a species of what is known in classical realism as extrinsic formal causality, the other species being the causality of the artist's idea relative to the work he produces. That a real existent is an *extrinsic* characterizing cause of the truth of an existence assertion follows from the fact that the existent does not enter into the make-up of the sentence objectifying it. (In the case of a sentence like "This sentence exists", the characterizing causality might be considered intrinsic but for the fact that as a bearer of truth, the sentence — or the language-forms making it up — is a means of objectification; the sentence is a cause of truth, however, not as a means of objectification but as that which is objectified. And as what is objectified, the sentence is an extrinsic characterizing cause of the *cognition* by which it is objectified.) That a real existent is a *characterizing* cause of the truth of an existence assertion follows from the fact that the object of any cognition is a characterizing cause of that cognition. (The fact that objects are extrinsic characterizing causes makes it possible for some of them to be efficient causes of cognition also.)

Although the knower is an efficient and component cause of his knowledge relations, these relations would not be what they are without something else with which they are not identical, their objects. The thought of Mr. Smith is what it is, in part, because of the nature of its object, the fact that Mr. Smith is what he is and not what Mr. Jones is. My perception of a patch of red differs from my perception of a patch of green for at least one reason: red differs from green. A perception of a red patch is what it is, and is not what a perception of a green patch would be, at least in part because red is what it is.

That this causal relation between a conscious state and its object is one of characterizing causality can be seen from the fact that it is the characterizing cause which differentiates the results of a change from what existed previously. As I watch a motion picture, many causes contribute to the fact that my perception has changed from being of one thing to being of another. But among those causes is the circumstance that the picture I am now seeing on the screen differs from the picture I was seeing a moment ago. The object I am now seeing is one of the things differentiating my current visual experience from past experience. And if no other change but this change of objects had taken place, it would still be true that my current visual experience was *thereby* differentiated from all previous ones.

The same analysis applies to any conscious relation. To describe a wish, one must include a description of what is wished for. In explaining a language-form's relation of "meaning" or "being-used-for", we must refer to that which is meant. This is because that for which a language-form is used is a characterizing cause of its status as a *language*-form, a characterizing cause of its relation of meaning or referring. Among the things making the use of the word "bat" for a species of rodent different from its use for a sporting instrument is the fact that what that particular kind of rodent is differs from what that particular sporting instrument is. And it is the identity of these characterizing causes of names and descriptions, namely, that for which they are used, with what actually or possibly exists that determines the truth of sentences. In other words, since truth is determined by identity between the word-functions of names and descriptions and what actually or possibly exists and since their word-functions are characterizing causes of the significance of these language-forms, the goal we call truth is achieved when what some actual or possible thing is is *identical* with a characterizing cause of the names or descriptions of a sentence. (On the object as a characterizing cause of knowledge, see Regis, 1959, pp. 254-256, 258-260. And see below, section I.1.)

9.5 Empiricist Arguments as Causal

At various places in this study, I have taken pains to point out that my own arguments exemplify the methodological principles I am defending. But how accurate is my account of philosophical method from the point of view of philosophy as it has been practiced by other philosophers, especially by philosophers outside of the realist tradition from which this work comes? Granted that more philosophers, both historically and in the twentieth century, have espoused metaphysics of the classical realist variety than any other single kind of metaphysics, and granted that philosophers of the classical realist persuasion acknowledge themselves to be doing causal analyses, what about philosophers from all those other traditions who collectively constitute the majority both historically and in the recent past? It seems that we can hardly classify all of their arguments as causal and much less as ontological in the sense in which that word is being used here.

In response, I will confine myself to commenting on arguments from the tradition which this book is addressing, the linguistic empirical tradition. To establish my point, it will be enough to glance briefly at a representative sampling of empiricist arguments. I will also take this opportunity to explain why philosophy is so easily interpreted, as it is interpreted in linguistic empiricism, as conceptual analysis rather than causal analysis. The reason is that in an important sense philosophical causal analysis *is* conceptual analysis.

Each of the examples that are about to follow will involve something which comes into existence through change and will involve a claim about a relation or lack of relation between this result of change and some cause. As it happens, in most of the examples, that which comes into existence through change will be a particular kind of knowledge. Consider the claim: a truth known only from an understanding of the way we use words is a truth which can give us no information other than information about the way we use words. The reasoning proceeds from a description of the cause of our knowledge of certain truths (known only from an understanding of the way we use words) to a claim about a characteristic this knowledge apparently must have as the effect of that cause (knowledge of nothing other than the way we use words). Or consider the claim: if a sentence is known to be true other than by reference to experience, the sentence does not give us any information about the actually existing world. The argument moves from the absence of a certain kind of cause for knowledge to the absence of a certain characteristic in the knowledge which lacks this cause. Or consider the claim: if a sentence is known to be true by reference to experience, it is a contingent truth. The claim is that a cause of a certain nature must produce an effect of a certain nature.

Quine's arguments against necessary truth presuppose that if knowledge of such truths can occur, the occurrence must be caused by the use of a criterion with which we distinguish necessary from contingent truths. Wittgenstein's argument against private language is an argument concerning a cause necessary for distinguishing correct from incorrect uses of language, the fact that doing so requires awareness of publicly observable language-acts in publicly observable circumstances. (Wittgenstein did not, however, show that this was *sufficient* for distinguishing correct uses of language from incorrect.) The traditional arguments for the existence of concepts and propositions in distinction from language-forms and linguistic behavior are arguments for causes necessary for otherwise meaningless entities to acquire meaning and for more than one otherwise meaningless entity to have the same meaning. Quine's theory of the indeterminacy of translation, on the other hand, argues against the existence of such causes on the grounds that an effect he thinks they should produce, namely, that our apparatus of individuation be interpretable in only one way, does not appear to be produced.

Some more examples. The paradigm case argument tried to show that certain things must exist since they are necessary causes of the occurrence of words for those things in our vocabularies. The excluded opposites argument reasoned to the existence of uses for the opposite of any description on the assumption that the teleonomic cause of descriptions was the distinguishing of one kind of thing from another. The important issue in the mind-body problem is whether matter is a sufficient cause for all kinds of consciousness. (And both sides need to realize that truths about causal connections can be necessary and that a truth can be necessary without our being able to derive it from the self-evident.)

And of course, we are still trying to solve the problems arising from alternative theories about the causes of our beliefs in the existence of other minds. Our view of the nature of these beliefs is determined by our view of what they can or cannot be caused by. For the nature of anything is determined by what its causes are capable of producing. Furthermore, the argument from analogy is a causal argument that takes on new significance once we are free from Humean prejudices about causality.

In each of these cases, something coming into existence through change is looked at precisely as having or not having a relation of dependence on something not identical with itself. And if the questions these arguments address can be answered philosophically, it is only to the extent that control can be exercised over the discussion by sentences whose opposites are capable of being recognized as contradictory. If we cannot succeed in demonstrating our answers by showing the impossibility of the opposite, we cannot resolve these questions philosophically.

This is not to imply, however, that philosophers spend their time in no other way than by trying to verify causal analyses by appeal to the principle of non-contradiction. Other activities can and should be found in philosophical literature. Much philosophical work is negative, not positive. In addition to establishing his own position, a philosopher must neutralize difficulties and refute opponents. To accomplish either, a philosopher often need do no more than propose an hypothesis consistent with his position and with the known facts, an hypothesis constituting a counter-example to an opponent's claim that there are no possibilities other than those covered by his argument. In the next chapter, for instance, an hypothesis will be presented which is perfectly consistent with my other positions, with other known facts and with the principle of simplicity and which will resolve the main epistemological problems concerning sense perception. Even on the positive side of philosophy, however, not all necessary truths employed will derive their necessity from causal relations. Many will derive their necessity from logical relations as do the principles of non-contradiction and excluded middle. Still philosophy employs arguments turning on logical relations only in the service of the causal analyses of things whose existence is verified by experience.

But if, as I have claimed, many of the main arguments of linguistic empiricists are causal, why do contemporary empiricists so frequently describe their activity as *conceptual* analysis? This is an example of a question that calls for an answer by way of reasonable hypothesis rather than by way of proof. For historical reasons too well known to need mentioning here, most English-speaking and some continental philosophy in the second half of this century has adopted language as its vantage point. Since dogmatic presuppositions prevented these philosophers from recognizing what they were doing as arguing on the basis of purported causal relations, the most natural thing for them to do was to describe their investigation of language as conceptual analysis. The linguistic theory of necessity reinforced this description; if not empirically verifiable, then linguistic.

But there is a reason more important than any collection of historical accidents why philosophy can be considered conceptual analysis. That reason is that philosophy *is* a form of conceptual analysis. In philosophy, unlike the empirical sciences, causal analysis is the same thing as conceptual analysis. For philosophy must verify by appeal to truths whose necessity is known from acquaintance with their word-functions and only from acquaintance with their word-functions. Philosophical knowledge of causal relations, therefore, arises from awareness of the meanings$_T$ of words. And it is only because we are aware of meanings$_T$ which have necessary causal relations between them that philosophy can make its discoveries and verify its conclusions. "Concept" can be used in many ways. In one of these ways, concepts are equivalent to meanings$_T$ of predicates, and in that sense, philosophical causal knowledge is conceptual analysis.

Finally, if the examples given have succeeded in showing that the arguments of empiricists concern causal relations, have they succeeded in showing that empiricists are doing ontological analysis, even though unknowingly? No, and they were not intended to. Doing causal analyses is not the same as doing them as they *should* be done.

CHAPTER TEN

Causality and Knowledge III:
Causality and Sense Knowledge

This chapter will deal with the philosophic analysis of sense experience. We would not have to go into the analysis of sense experience at all were it not for a difficulty which appears to undercut the very foundations of my arguments. In section 2.2, it was argued that the objects of our knowledge are first known other than as objects of knowledge and that the first objects of linguistic knowledge are cognition-independent existents. But those propositions appear to be flatly contradicted by the fact that whatever knowledge we have originates in sense experience. The objects of sense perception are notoriously relative to the perceiver and his subjective states. One person sees an elliptical area of red where another sees a round area of gray; one person is warm when another one is cold. If all knowledge is based on sense experience, how can cognition-independent existents even be known, much less be objects that are causally primary in knowledge? Clearly this problem is the same as that usually expressed in terms of the relation of sense data to physical things, the problem of perception.

The problem of perception has an additional relevance to this study. Dealing with it will provide further evidence of the power of the causal approach to philosophical problems and its superiority to the linguistic approach. Understanding the relation between sense experience and beliefs about physical things does not and *cannot* amount to under-standing the relations between physical thing statements and sense data statements. Learning the relations between two classes of sentences can at most show us the relations between two kinds of linguistic objectifications, not the relations between linguistic objectifications and sensory objectifications. The linguistic approach is capable of doing everything but solving the problem it is attempting to solve. The problem is a causal one. How can sense experience cause knowledge of the truth, or even belief in the truth, of sentences about extra-objective existents? The solution to the problem must be a causal analysis.

I have already given a causal analysis of how the meaning$_T$ of "exists" enters language. I will now offer a causal analysis explaining how sense experience makes us aware of real existence and, therefore, causes our awareness of the truth of sentences asserting existence. Explaining this will not only illustrate the power of the causal approach to philosophical problems but, in particular, the power of the theory of causal relations developed in the preceding three chapters. I hasten to add, however, that I will not be proposing anything like what is traditionally known as a "causal theory of perception". My account will have nothing to do with theories that reach the existence of physical things by reasoning to them as causes of our sense experience.

10.1 Acting and Being Acted On

In preceding chapters, I allowed myself to speak loosely of an efficient cause's "action" or "producing of an effect" or "exercise of its causal dispositions". In order to apply what we know about causal relations to the problem of perception, the word-functions of these phrases must be made clearer by determining their place in the system of causal relations whose necessity has been established. This having been done, the following sections will address the problem of perception directly.

Let us assume a potential efficient cause has everything it needs to produce a certain effect, C, but no component cause, S, exists in that relation to the efficient cause which is necessary for C to occur. It follows that C is not occurring. It follows also that the efficient cause's action, A, of producing C does not exist; this exercise, A, of the efficient cause's causal dispositions is not occurring. Now bring S into the required relation with the efficient cause. The production of C occurs necessarily. But no change has occurred in the efficient cause itself.

It had everything it needed for the production of C before that production occurred. No matter how many changes may have previously occurred to the efficient cause, the change by which A, its action of producing C, comes into existence is not a change occurring to the efficient cause. The only change occurs in the component cause. I do not mean the change that consisted of the component cause coming into the required relation with the efficient cause. I mean the change that occurred *as a result* of its coming into the required relation with the efficient cause. And that change is C.

The first conclusion we can draw, then, is that the action of an efficient cause is not something existing in the efficient cause as its causal dispositions exist in it. Action does not enter into the make-up of the agent. Where then does the action exist? It exists in the component cause. For, and this is the second conclusion, the efficient cause's action is the same reality as the component cause's being acted upon. The buzz saw's cutting of a log and the log's being cut by the buzz saw are one event, not two.

It is worth the effort to express this important point in some other ways. An agent's causing-of a change in S is the same event as S's being-caused to change, and S's being-caused to change is something happening to S, not to the agent. When an efficient cause is acting on S, S can be said to be undergoing a "passion", that is, to be undergoing something passively. But the event that is called a passion from the point of view of the component cause is the same as the event that is called an action from the point of view of the efficient cause. Action and passion are the same reality named differently from its relation to different terms.

But the most important conclusion is that an efficient cause's action of producing a change is identical with the *change* it produces. An agent's causing-of a change, a component cause's being-caused to change and the change itself are the same event. For in producing an effect, an efficient cause does not separately produce its production of the effect. If we thus distinguished the action of producing a change from the change itself, we would begin an infinite regress. If A is distinct from C, then when the efficient cause goes from not performing A to performing it, it produces two effects, A and C, not one. But if A is an effect produced by the efficient cause, then is the cause's production of A distinct from A? Infinite regress can be avoided if and only if efficient causes produce effects that are identical with the efficient cause's production of them.

In our initial example, an efficient cause was not actually producing C. Then S came into the required relation with the efficient cause, and C occurred. When C came into existence, the previously potential action of the efficient cause also came into existence. For C is that action. How can C be the same as the action by which its efficient cause produces it? C is a material relation of dependence on its efficient cause. And the action of the efficient cause is C itself *in its relation of dependence on that cause*. Action is change as dependent on the efficient cause, while passion is change as dependent on the component cause. With reference to the efficient cause, "dependent-on" is just another name for "produced-by" or "production-of" or "action-of". If action is the same as change in its relation of dependence on its efficient cause, it is identical to change as that which the efficient cause produces.

What a change depends on in particular are the specific behavioral dispositions of its causes. We now know that when we speak of the behavioral dispositions of the efficient cause, the behavior in question is behavior caused in the component cause. For it is the fact that it causes a component cause so to behave that makes something an efficient cause. Of course, something can be efficient and component causes of the same change by reason of diverse behavioral dispositions.

Some examples will make the point of this analysis less abstract. It has already been mentioned that the buzz saw's causing the log to be cut is the same as the log's being caused to be cut by the saw. And this is something going on in the log (for the fact that something is happening to the log is what makes the log a component cause). But the buzz saw can be running as it does when the action of cutting wood occurs without that action occurring. If the wood is not in contact with the saw, the action of cutting wood does not exist since the wood is not undergoing any change. Therefore the fact that the saw is running is not identical with its action of causing wood to be cut. Of course, other actions are occurring when the saw is running, the rotation of the blade, for instance, is an action. But this is not an action of the saw relative to the wood; it is the action of the motor relative to the blade. And if the blade is removed, the motor's production of motion in the blade ceases to exist even though the motor continues to run. The motions undergone by the motor's parts are actions but not the action of causing the blade to turn. They are actions because they are produced by other causes, electricity or exploding gases, for example. But remove the pistons from an internal combustion engine, and the action of causing the pistons to move cannot take place. Action is something that exists in the component cause because it is identical to the change the component cause undergoes.

One more example will be helpful. A magnet does not cause an iron filing to move toward it until the filing has been put in sufficient proximity to the magnet. Assume that has occurred and that the magnet is now causing the filing to move. "Now causing the filing to move" refers to no change occurring to the magnet itself. The magnet's causing of the motion is the same event as the filing's being caused to move, which is something happening to the filing. And the filing's being caused to move is the same as its undergoing the motion in question. Now consider the magnetic field in the vicinity of the magnet. The strength of this field is, in part, the result of the magnet continuously causing a change in the surrounding area. But if the magnet is shielded with lead, it will cease causing a field of that strength to exist at a particular place *even though no change has occurred to the magnet itself.* The magnet's causing-of the field, in other words, is identical to the continuous change that takes place in its environment to maintain the strength of the field.

An objection. If a change is identical with a material relation to its efficient and component causes, then is not a change's relation to its efficient cause identical to its relation to its component cause? And since the efficient and component causes are distinct, how can a change's relation to both be the same? I do not know a way to demonstrate that these relations are not sufficiently distinguished by the fact that their terms are distinguished. By being what it is, a change requires both an efficient cause and a component cause; an agent cannot produce a change without causing something to change, and a patient cannot undergo a change unless something causes it to change. And since a change is a *material* relation of dependence, it need not be considered a bearer of two distinct relations but as itself one relation with two distinct terms. Still, as a relation whose term is the efficient cause, the change is identical to an action; and as a relation whose term is the component cause, a change is identical to a passion.

But if an argument can be found to show that more is needed to account for a change's relations of dependence on diverse causes, we would have a reason for postulating the existence of formal relations, relations to the efficient and component causes respectively, borne by the change. This would mean that these formal relations are characteristics of a change which its causes bring into existence when they bring the change into existence. The action of the agent, however, would remain identical with the change as related to the agent; but now the change would be related to the agent formally as well as materially. The agent's production-of-a-change could not be identified with the formal relation as something distinct from the change. As we saw a moment ago, an infinite regress results if an agent's production-of-a-change stands between the agent and the change as a distinct effect produced by the agent. If a change is related to its agent formally, that formal relation is caused by the agent as a characteristic of the change; and the change, as bearer of a relation of dependence on the agent, is identical with the action of the agent. (The usual objection to the reality of formal relations is that they can come to be and cease to be because changes take place in their terms, even though no change takes place in their supposed bearers. The objection does not apply here. A change's formal relation of dependence on an efficient cause would exist as long as, but only as long as, the change is being caused. A continuous change occurring outside of a vacuum must be produced continuously. If the dispositions by which an agent is producing such a change are altered, and if no other agent so disposed as to continue causing the change enters the circumstances, the change itself must cease to exist.)

To repeat, the production of an effect by an efficient cause amounts to the fact that the component cause cannot remain what it is while the efficient cause is what it is. Given that the efficient cause is what it is, it is impossible for the component cause to remain the same in all respects. (When I press a seal onto some wax, the wax receives a new shape from the seal. That is how component causality works.) Now how does all this help solve the problem of perception?

10.2 The Sensation Hypothesis

This section will present and explain an hypothesis about causal action and sense experience which I will call the sensation hypothesis. Subsequent sections will develop the implications of the sensation hypothesis for the problem of perception.

Hypothesis: in sensation we are aware of sensible qualities as ways the environment is acting on the faculties of sensation; or, the operation of our sense faculties makes us aware of the actions of the environment on our sense faculties *as actions*. This hypothesis will explain both the subjectivity of sense experience and the occurrence of what are called "illusions" of the senses. (Let us group these problems together under the title of the relativity of sense experience.) At the same time, the sensation hypothesis will explain how the senses put us in contact with cognition-independent existents. Not only that, but the cause of the relativity of sense experience will be seen to be the very thing guaranteeing that the senses make us aware of cognition-independent existents.

Finally, this hypothesis will allow us to preserve the distinction, all-important but surprisingly neglected by epistemologists, between perceiving, on the one hand, and imagining and remembering, on the other. That distinction is expressed in the following passages:

> "Sensation", as opposed to perception, is more or less hypothetical. It is supposed to be the core, in perception, which is solely due to the stimulus and the sense-organ, not to past experience. When you judge that the table is rectangular, it is past experience that enables and compels you to do so; if you had been born blind and just operated on, you could not make this judgment . . . . From an introspective point of view, the elements due to the past experience are largely indistinguishable from those due to the stimulus alone. (Russell, 1926, p. 79)

> The worst difficulties of the present subject originate in our inability to achieve the experience of a sensation free from association with images, instinctive judgments, memories and thoughts. If it were possible for us to suspend, no matter how briefly, all such associated representations and processes, if it were possible to elicit pure sensations and yet watch ourselves sensing, the understanding of sensation would, no doubt, be greatly facilitated. But sensation is the center of a complex, and from this complex it cannot be extracted, except by rational analysis. Experientially considered, sensations always exist in the vital unity of wholes. By reason of this unity, we attribute to senses the apprehension of things which are neither sense qualities nor modes of sense qualities. Thus, the proposition, "I see the father of our friend" does not look like falsehood or nonsense. With equal sincerity we would say, "I smell ammonia," or "I touch scar tissue." Yet such a system of relations as "father of a friend," such a natural species as "ammonia," such an effect of accident and nature as "scar tissue," are things in the apprehension of which memory, imagination, instinct, animal intelligence and understanding obviously play decisive roles.
>
> It is good usage to call "perception" the complex act by which these things are apprehended and "sensation" the act, whatever its nature may be, which lies at the core of perception and makes the difference between having and not having things present in sense experience . . . . I can imagine my mother vividly, remember many events concerning her and achieve—better, perhaps, than when she was alive and present—an intelligent grasp of her personality. But the thing I am stubbornly denied is the privilege of seeing her, of hearing her voice, of holding her hand; in the words of a poet, "and, oh,/The difference to me!" *The study of sensation is, so to say, the study of the difference.* (Simon, 1960a, p. 56)

The problem of sensation is the problem of what makes the difference, on the one hand, between actually perceiving something and merely imagining or remembering it and, on the other hand, between perceiving and hallucinating. I intend to show also that the analysis of the difference between sensation and imagination contains the solution to the problem of whether we are aware of sense data or physical things. First, let us ask what it is that distinguishes a patch of red as I imagine it from a patch of red that I sense, if it is true that the object of sense awareness is the action of the environment on the sense faculties?

In imagination I am not aware of red as a way the environment is exercising an influence on me; I can imagine red without being acted on by the environment in that particular way. But I cannot sense red unless the action of the environment on my sense faculties is actually taking place. Furthermore, in being aware of the action of the environment as action, I am aware of action as existing cognition-independently. For I am aware of it as brought into cognition-independent existence by an efficient cause, since action is change as caused to exist by its efficient cause. And if the function of the sense faculties is that of making us aware of causal action exerted on them, sensing does not take place unless the sense faculties are undergoing this action passively. The cognition in question is itself dependent on the extra-objective exercise of efficient causality on the sense faculties because the object of the cognition is the extra-objective exercise of efficient causality on the sense faculties.

Action and passion are the same reality, and being aware of the environment acting on us requires us to be aware of ourselves undergoing its action. This is how we become aware of the existence of the action of the environment: we become aware of ourselves undergoing that action. That explains why the sense of touch gives us more certitude of the existence of its object than do the other senses; in our tactile experience of the resistance of the environment, we are most clearly aware that our bodies are undergoing causal influences. As I rub my finger on the edge of a board, I experience the pressure of the edge by being aware of a change being caused in my finger.

But we have the same kind of awareness in the other senses. The experience of the action of the environment is so constant, so pervasive and so fundamental to our consciousness that it is not easy to take note of it in normal circumstances as the experience of *action*. However, we are clearly aware of the object we sense as an influence we are undergoing when we hear very shrill or loud sounds, when we look directly at a bright light even from a distance, when we see a bright light reflected off a shiny surface, when we find our surroundings pervaded by an obnoxious odor. And these experiences differ only in degree from ordinary sense experiences. After being for a time in a dimly lit room, put on a very bright light, but one that does not shine directly in your eyes. For a short time before you become accustomed to the new light, your surroundings will not only be more clearly illuminated than before, but you can be aware that your sense of sight is undergoing the action of light more intensely than it did a moment before.

We still have a good distance to go before the problem of perception is behind us. Let us pause for a moment, however, to consider the question raised by the examples of the last paragraph: how do we know the sensation hypothesis is true? I do not know any way to show the impossibility of its opposite. But I must disagree with Russell when, to the remarks quoted above, he adds ''The notion of sensation as opposed to perception belongs, therefore, to the causal study of perception, not to the introspective study''. Humean scruples alone could justify *opposing* introspection to causal analysis. The only thing that would prevent us from describing the tactile experience of resistance, the visual experience of looking directly at a bright light, etc. as the awareness of causal action on our sense faculties is a superstition against calling anything a causal relation which is known as such otherwise than by constant conjunction. And even in normal experience, whenever an object is sensed rather than imagined and remembered, we are aware of the object as imposing itself on our consciousness, as coming to us *from* the outside environment. Our introspective awareness of this mode of presence is the reason we distinguish between sensation and other cognitional functions. And our awareness of objects as imposing themselves on us is what I mean by awareness of actions undergone by our sense faculties as actions.

Indirect but significant evidence that we are introspectively aware of sensible objects as actions is provided by the kind of language philosophers have found appropriate in contrasting sense experience to imagination, memory and thought. The terminology is almost invariably the terminology of action. The way in which the objects of sense experience are present is more *vivid*, *lively* and *forceful* than is the presence of other objects. Sense experience is something we *undergo*; we do not normally speak of undergoing the image, memory or thought of anything. Philosophers have found it appropriate to describe the objects of sense experience as *impressions* and to point out, as I just did, that they appear (how if not by introspection?) to *impose* themselves on us. Objects of sense experience are distinguished from other objects as *thrust* upon us; they are said to *dominate* our consciousness of them. Finally, consider the most common names for the objects of sense experience in recent science, *stimuli,* and in philosophy, *data,* that is, *givens.* (Giving is a causal operation, a transaction between an agent, the giver, and a patient, the receiver.) What makes this indirect evidence most significant is that such causal terminology has been freely employed by philosophers who are not only innocent of but even opposed to views of causality that would justify their language.

There are other arguments to support the belief that we are introspectively aware of undergoing causal influences from the environment. What is it, for instance, that distinguishes the elephant I now see to be charging at me from the elephant I am at the same time able to imagine charging at me? The elephant as object of my imagination is not present to me as actually able to do anything. When I am imagining it, the elephant does not terminate my knowledge relation as something that can produce an actually existing state of affairs. As term of a relation of sense awareness, however, the charging elephant is present to me as something that can cause something to happen to me. In other words, the elephant as object of sensation is something able to do the kind of thing the light reflecting from the elephant is now doing, namely, producing an effect in me. Seeing the elephant as a potential cause involves more than sensing; imagination plays an essential role in the process. But last night as I lay in bed, I was able to imagine the elephant charging at me without at the same time seeing it charge. Now I do see it charging. ''And, oh,/The difference to me!''

It will not be necessary, however, to prove the sensation hypothesis. That hypothesis will both explain the facts of, and remove the difficulties with, perception. If the sensation hypothesis solves the problems I claim it does, it will be up to an opponent to disprove it. The difficulties in question are those concerning how perception can put us in contact with physical things existing extra-objectively. Hence the burden of proof will be on the person who holds that we are aware of sense data *as opposed to* physical things. So far, however, we have explained neither the relativity of sensation nor our awareness of real existents other than the actions undergone by our sense faculties. Let us move to these questions now.

10.3 Sense Awareness of Physical Things

How do the senses inform us of the existence of the things whose actions they are aware of? What makes an event an action is its relation of dependence-on or being-produced-by an efficient cause. To be aware of an action *as an action* (the sensation hypothesis) is therefore to be aware of it *as related to that which produces it*; it is to be aware of an event as the action-of something that produces this event. If we are conscious of sense qualities as ways in which we are acted on, we are conscious of them as ways in which we are acted on by something (something other than the sense faculties themselves, since the sense faculties are passive with respect to them). We sense red, for example, as the red-of-something, specifically as the red of an extended, shaped area of our visual field, and we sense it is the red of something either moving or at rest relative to ourselves and to other colored areas in our visual field.

The difference between being aware of an event as an action or not as an action is the difference between being or not being aware of it as produced by some efficient cause. But to be aware of an event as related to some thing other than itself is to be aware of that other thing at least as the term of this relation and, if the relation is one that requires an actually existing term, as something that actually exists. And the occurrence of a change does require the actual existence of sufficient causes for the change; it is only while the efficient cause exists that the change's relation of being-produced-by the efficient cause exists. If the senses are aware of actions as such, therefore, they are aware of the existence of the things that are acting on us.

But how can awareness of one thing, the action the senses are undergoing, make us aware of another thing, the efficient cause of the action? The answer that we are aware of the first thing as related to the second may seem to beg the question. How can we be aware of one thing as related to another without being independently aware of the other?

It is the action, however, not the agent, which is the bearer of the relation of dependence-on the agent. Even if that dependence requires the existence of a formal relation as a characteristic of the caused event, to be aware of the relation we need only be aware of the event of which the relation is a characteristic. And an event's relation of dependence on an efficient cause is, ultimately, *nothing other than the event itself*. If a formal relation of dependence is required, it is required as a necessary consequence of an event's being a material relation of dependence. Thus being aware of an event as a material relation to a formal relation of dependence would be nothing more than a way of being aware of the event itself. In being aware of a change undergone by a sense faculty as bearer of a relation of dependence on an efficient cause, we are *ipso facto* aware of the existence of the term of this relation as term of this relation.

What do the senses tell us about the things that are acting on us? That they exist and are thus acting on us in various ways. But a thing acts in a particular way because it has certain causal dispositions. Therefore to be aware of a sense quality as *of* a thing acting on us is to be aware of the thing as causally disposed in a manner characterized by this way of acting. Or, in other words, to be aware of a sense quality as a way in which something is acting is to be aware of the quality as characterizing a thing's dispositions to act, since the sense quality is the thing's mode of acting. To sense an area of our visual field as red is to sense it as having a causal disposition characterized by the way of acting we experience as the color red.

Furthermore, to say that a thing acts in a particular way because it has certain causal dispositions is to say that its action is determined by what it is. For the causal dispositions that materially relate a thing to its effects are among the features constituting what the thing is. Therefore to be aware of a thing as acting in a particular way is to some extent to be aware of what it is, for it is to be aware that the thing's features include the dispositions by which it acts in this way. But in sensing something as acting in a particular way, we are aware of what its causal dispositions are only as dispositions for this way of acting, that is, only as having the characteristic of acting in this way. Therefore to be aware of a sense quality as a way in which something is acting is to be aware of causal dispositions having this manner of acting for a characteristic as *what* some thing in our environment *is*. To sense an area of our visual field as red is to sense it as having a red manner of acting as a feature, since this manner of acting characterizes the dispositions making the thing what it is. In short, it follows from the sensation hypothesis that we sense actions on our sense faculties as characteristics of the things acting on us.

As originally acquired from sensation, the word-function of the noun "red" is what it is to be a certain manner of acting or what it is for something to act in this manner. The word-function of the adjective "red" is what it is to have the disposition to be acting in this manner or what it is to have this manner of acting as that which one's causal dispositions are dispositions for. This use of the word "disposition" does not imply that this word-function is dispositional in the sense of being what something would do in certain circumstances. Dispositions are actual features, material relations, to be exact. The word-function of the adjective "red" is what it is to have an *actual* feature determining one to *be acting* in this manner. Words for sensible qualities may eventually acquire dispositional word-functions, but they do not have such functions originally.

Again, the hypothesis that the senses make us aware of the action of the environment as action amounts to the hypothesis that we are aware of sensible qualities, red, warm, soft, loud, etc., as ways in which things act upon us. To be aware of these qualities as related to something whose actions they are is to be aware of the existence of something as term of these relations. Awareness of one thing, in other words, can cause us to be aware of something other than itself *without any inference, construction, association or recollection being involved in the process.* One object can be the means by which another deserves to be called, in the strongest phenomenological sense, *given.*

This flies in the face of habitual ways of thinking. We assume that if perception involves awareness of more than the sensible qualities that are given in sensation, the explanation is the one we quoted from Simon a moment ago: sensation is part of a complex operation which relates what we are now sensing to the results of past experience. The hypothesis that sensation itself makes us aware not only of sensible qualities but also of other things to which these qualities are related may well go against common prejudice. What it does not go against, however, are facts about sensation and its objects that are constantly available to all of us.

As I mentioned above, sight is not aware only of qualities like red. By means of its awareness of colors, sight is also aware of extension, shape, number, movement and rest. For these are also modes of the action of the environment on us. Light reflecting from one place in my visual field will occupy an elliptically shaped area of that field; light from another place will occupy a circular area. Sometimes I see two areas of red; sometimes more or less than two, etc. And sight also allows us to judge that these features of our experience are really distinct from one another. We see the same color in different sizes and shapes, at rest or in motion. We see the same shape in different sizes and colors. We see objects change color yet remain the same size and shape, etc. But if everything in the universe remained the same as it is now, with the exception that all variation in color was removed, the eyes could detect nothing of the numerous moving and resting objects of various extensions and shapes that they now make us aware of. What color is to sight, resistance is to touch. If things did not offer resistance to our bodies, we would not be made aware of extension, shape, number and movement through the sense of touch. But these features of experience are no more identifiable with resistance than they are with color.

Therefore some objects of sensation, like color and resistance, can be the means by which other objects, like extension, shape, number and movement are *given* in sense awareness. It may require reference to past experience to learn that such objects are really distinct from one another. It does not require reference to past experience for us to perceive colors as occupying numerous areas of various shapes. Color and resistance are experienced precisely as related to objects which are really distinct from themselves. We do not infer the presence of such objects in that which we are aware of by means of our senses. Nor do associations resulting from past experience lead us to perceive color and resistance as related to these objects. Nor do we construct these objects out of objects of cognitions that are presumably more basic.

It is a fundamental and ubiquitous fact about sensation, therefore, that it grasps some objects as so related to others that we cannot be aware of the first without being aware of the second by means of our awareness of the first. The sensation hypothesis does nothing more than further specify this relational character of sense awareness. The analysis just completed shows that, contrary to a priori expectations, nothing prevents one object of sense cognition (like a sensible quality) from being a means by which another object (like a physical entity that causes the senses to be so acted on as to be aware of the sensible quality) is made present to the senses. All that is required is that the first object be sensed as having a causal relation which the second object terminates. Color and resistance are sensed as *characterizing* relative to extended surfaces. By means of color and resistance, shape is likewise sensed as characterizing extension. An object sensed as at relative rest or in relative motion is sensed as characterized by spatial relations to other objects or by change with respect to such spatial relations. Individual objects are sensed as *components* of groups characterized by number. The sensation hypothesis simply extends the relations by which one object can make us aware of another beyond component and characterizing causality to efficient causality. (The relation of any object, as such, to cognition is one of characterizing causality. But *within* an object that characterizes cognition, there may be causal relations of other kinds.)

To sum up: since sensible qualities are sensed as manners in which the environment acts on us, they are sensed only when that action really exists. And an action exists only as long as an efficient cause whose dispositions are sufficient for it actually exists, for only then is an event being produced by its efficient cause. To be aware of sensible qualities as ways we are acted on, therefore, is to be aware of real existents as acting on us in these ways.

To describe fully the objects of sensation as they are sensed, we must say that they are really existing unities of distinct features such as color, extension, shape, number, and movement and rest. The reason sight is aware of red as the red of an existing area of our visual field is that it is aware of red as the way something existing, extended and shaped is imposing itself, that is, acting, on us. Sensed as a manner in which something is acting, red is sensed as a characteristic of the thing whose action we sense. And an area of red is sensed as the active term of a relation of efficient causality, specifically, as an existent whose features dispose it to a red manner of acting.

Even in a case like seeing a dead star, we are aware of the action of a real existent occupying an area of our visual field, namely, the light from the star. The dead star example, however, illustrates how little a sensation can tell us about the nature of that which is acting on us. The paucity of information thus obtained, together with their misinterpretations of causality, are further reasons why philosophers have failed to see the truth of the sensation hypothesis.

I have been applying the results of our analysis of necessary causal relations to sensation. Do not let that mislead you into reading this account of our knowledge of physical things as an illative theory. We do not reason from the existence of actions on our sense faculties to the existence of their causes. What our analysis of necessary causal relations shows is that if we are aware of an action as an action, we do not need to reason to the existence of its cause; we are already aware of it as produced by something and, by that fact, aware of the existence of the thing producing it.

The eye no more reasons to the existence of an efficient cause of its experience of color than it reasons from its experience of color to the existence of extension. Just as sight makes us conscious of extension by making us conscious of color as extended, so it makes us conscious of things imposing themselves on our awareness by making us conscious of color as a way in which things act on the organs of sight.

Causal reasoning does not enter into sensation, but it does enter into the linguistic objectification of the ontological conditions making it possible for sense experience to be what it is. In describing how the senses make us aware of one object by means of another, I have spoken of objects being sensed as having causal relations. Sense awareness of objects as having causal relations, however, is not the same as linguistic objectification of these objects as entering into causal relations. Empirical word-functions are causally opaque for the reason already given: acquaintance with them is not sufficient for us to know necessary causal relations between effects of specific kinds and causes of specific kinds. The causal word-functions I have used to state the ontological conditions of sensation are among those very general word-functions logically included in the less general, causally opaque word-functions.

The sensation hypothesis, finally, explains another way, in addition to teleonomic and characterizing causality, in which the actual existence of things is causally prior to their being objects of knowledge. The actual existents that are the objects of sense knowledge are, along with the knower, efficient causes of that knowledge. Since sense knowledge is necessary for the existence of linguistic knowledge, the efficient causality of the objects of sense knowledge is necessary for their becoming objects of linguistic knowledge.

10.4 The Relativity of Sensation

The hypothesis that the object of sense experience is the action of the environment on our sense faculties not only explains our sense awareness of cognition-independent existents, it also explains illusions and the subjectivity of sensible qualities. From our discussion of causal necessity, we know that an effect's being what it is, as well as depending on its efficient cause being what it is, also depends on its component cause being what it is and on the spatial relations that obtain between the efficient and component causes. The same efficient cause can produce different effects in component causes with different natures or with different spatial relations to the efficient cause. The same heat source that will produce melting in wax will produce hardening in clay; it will produce one change in the temperature of an object near it and another change in the temperature of an object distant from it. In other words, whatever is received in a component cause from an efficient cause is received in a manner dependent on the nature of the component cause and on the spatial relation of the component cause to the efficient cause.

But causal action exists in that which is acted on; action is from the agent though in the patient, since it is something the agent does to the patient. Consequently the action of the environment on our sense faculties exists in our sense faculties. And what that action is depends on the conditions of the faculties receiving it and on the spatial relation of these faculties to the agent. The person with normal vision will see red; the color blind person will see gray. Both are aware of the physical environment as acting on their sense faculties, however. One sees an area of his visual field as characterized by a red manner of acting; the other sees it as characterized by a gray manner of acting. And the cause of their awareness of the existence of the physical environment is the *same* as the cause of the subjectivity of their experiences. They are aware of the physical environment because they are aware of action as action. But action is something existing in that which undergoes the action, and its manner of existence is dependent on the nature of that in which it exists. Hence the sensible qualities they see are phenomenologically different.

For this reason, incidentally, it is preferable to speak of sensible qualities as the manner in which things act on us rather than speak of them, unqualifiedly, as the actions of things. This allows us to distinguish action as produced by its efficient cause from the specific features an action assumes as dependent on its component cause. The red that I see and the gray that someone else sees can be the same insofar as they are related to an efficient cause (and hence are both sensed as characteristics of the same agent), but they differ because of differences in the conditions of the faculties receiving them. Still, acting and being acted on, what is from the agent and what is in the patient, are the same reality. And the source of the subjectivity of sensible qualities, the fact that they are actions undergone by the sense faculties, is also what allows us to become aware of extra-objective existents through our awareness of sensible qualities.

Notice also that in making sense qualities actions that exist in sense faculties, I am not implying that the sense faculties physically acquire those qualities by receiving the action. The eye does not become red just by seeing something red. The reason is that the sense quality is the action objectified as related to the agent, not the patient, that is, objectified as *of* the agent. The sense quality red is identical with an action the organs of vision are undergoing. But as an object of the senses, red is not what that action is in its relation to its patient.

Now I can respond to the difficulty mentioned at the beginning of this chapter, a difficulty that goes all the way back to our introduction of the distinction between things and objects in section 2.2. There I argued that what are first known about our objects are thing-descriptions, not object-descriptions, and that the first objects we know are real, cognition-independent existents. The objection is that whatever we know about our objects derives from our awareness of sensible qualities, and the subjectivity of sensible qualities hardly qualifies them to be bases for the knowledge of extra-objective things.

In response, the first thing to keep in mind is that the subjectivity of their word-functions does not disqualify words like "red", "warm", "loud" from being thing-descriptions; for as originally learned, these words do not describe things as terms of knowledge relations. Further, for sensible qualities to be relative to the sensing subject is not the same as to be relative to sense cognition itself. Their dependence on the state of the sense faculties that are undergoing the action of the environment is not dependence on the sense experience resulting from the fact that these faculties are undergoing this action.

Finally and most importantly, rather than preventing us from being aware of extra-objective existents, the reason for the subjectivity of sensible qualities, namely, the fact that they are actions undergone by our sense faculties, is also the reason why awareness of sensible qualities makes us aware of the existence of physical things acting on us. For that which is subjective because related to our sense faculties as undergone by them is also something related to other cognition-independent existents as produced by them.

Similar considerations dispose of the kind of sensory "illusions"— for instance, the fact that round coins look elliptical from most angles— that are usually brought up in connection with the sense data/physical thing problem. What an effect is is determined by the nature of its efficient and component causes *and* by their spatial relation to one another. The manner in which light reflecting off the coin acts on our eyes depends, in part, on the spatial relations of our eyes to the coin. Since the object of the senses is the action of the environment on the sense faculties, what we sense is determined by the causal laws governing that action. And physical causal laws governing the reflection of light require that if a subject sees a round coin from a certain angle, the action of the light on his eyes will be sensed as the action of something occupying an elliptically shaped area of his visual field.

Hence that which causes a round coin to be seen as occupying an elliptical area of our visual field is the same as that which allows our sense knowledge to have cognition-independent physical existents for its objects. Given that the senses make us aware of the action of extra-objective existents on us, there would be something *wrong* with our senses if from certain angles they did *not* sense light reflecting off the coin as acting on us in an elliptical pattern. For in so acting on our organs of vision, the light is only obeying the laws that express those causal relations that are identical with the nature of light. If sight were not aware of light as acting on the organs of vision in an elliptical pattern, it would not truly be aware of the way light is acting on the organs of vision. But if sight is aware of the way light acts on the organs of vision, then from most angles it will sense the light reflecting from the coin as the action of something taking up an elliptically shaped space in our visual field.

In other words, it is because sensation makes us aware of cognition-independent existents occupying areas of different sizes and shapes that the coin must look elliptical from certain angles. The coin may be round, or the star whose light is now reaching us may be dead. But the light from these things, the light which acts on our sense faculties, really exists, really occupies the space contiguous to our sense organs and really acts on the sense organs in the way determined by necessary causal relations. (This shows us, by the way, why color has a necessary causal relation to place even if it is not a quality existing in the surface of bodies. Both the light acting on our eyes and its action, which is experienced as color, occupy space.) And it is because the senses make us aware of the action of light reflecting from the coin in a law-governed manner that I know that the best way to judge visually whether the points on the edge of the coin are closer to being equidistant from one point (circular) than from two (elliptical) is to so situate the coin that the points on its edge are as close as possible to being equidistant from the point of vision, the point at which the light from the edge will act.

Again, this analysis consists of nothing more than necessary consequences drawn from previously established truths about causality together with the sensation hypothesis. Another previously established truth about causality is the fact that causes of different natures can have effects that are similar by chance. Such chance similarities take care of another kind of difficulty concerning sensation, a difficulty that might otherwise appear to undercut the sensation hypothesis.

The experience of being aware of sense objects, of seeing colors for example, can be produced, not by the action of the environment on our external sense organs, but by stimuli artificially introduced into the brain. In other words, causes of different natures can produce the same effect in our sense faculties. As the objection recognizes, however, our external sense organs are not our only sense faculties. We become aware of the action of the environment on our external sense organs only because that action begins a neurological process that ends with events occurring in our brains. Hence, when sensation is produced artificially, it remains true that we are then aware of the actually existing, cognition-independent *action* of the environment on *some* of our sense faculties.

The phenomenon of phantom limbs can be handled in the same way that we handle artificially produced sensations. When he experiences a sensation in a limb that has been amputated, the amputee is aware of an action some part of his nervous system is actually undergoing. That the action is in this case caused by another part of the same organism is incidental. What is not incidental is that one part of that organism is undergoing a causal influence from something and is making the amputee aware of that influence as such.

Nothing I have said, however, implies that we can always be certain that the object of our consciousness is the actually existing action of the environment on us. There are borderline cases where we cannot be certain of this:

> At night and in a silent place a friend is walking away. For a while we can hear the sound of his steps, but the time soon comes when we no longer know whether we are still hearing these sounds or only imagining and remembering them. Until he comes back, and perhaps throughout our life, we shall remember our listening to these steps, remember this last experience of a presence that nothing can replace. Again, we never knew exactly when presence and experience came to an end; it is true that a weak sensation and an image may be, on their borderline, empirically undistinguishable. Yet there is a world of qualitative difference between them . . . .
>
> Considering, again, the example of the steps in the night, I understand very well what it means to say that we do not know exactly when sensation ceases and imagination alone remains active. These two may be empirically undistinguishable in the vicinity of their borderline; they nevertheless constitute types whose intelligible diversity is unmistakable. By saying that I do not know when sensation comes to an end and imagination alone remains at work, I imply that, at an indeterminable moment, my relation to the sounds of the steps was no longer caused by the physical action of the sounding steps on my sense organs. (Simon, 1960a pp. 64-65)

In other words, the fact that borderline cases occur does not imply that cases where the distinction is clear do not occur. Nor does the philosophic account of the distinction between the two aim at producing criteria for identifying particular instances of each. It aims at understanding the distinction as between what Simon calls "intelligible types", that is, between things subject to differing causal analyses. (Where we can differentiate between borderline cases of sensation and imagination, we do it in the same way we distinguish perceptions from hallucinations. (See section 10.5.)

The fact that we can be in doubt about whether we are experiencing the action of things on our sense faculties calls for a clarification concerning the use of the word "given" in discussions of perception. Sometimes "given" does not refer to characteristics of sense cognition alone but to certain relations between sense awareness and our linguistic objectification of things. Thus when philosophers speak of "the myth of the given", they are referring to roles sense experience may or may not play in our use of words to describe what we experience.

Sometimes demythologizers of the given are asking whether any word-functions are given in the sense of being imposed on us by sense experience rather than being imposed on it by our conceptual schemes. At other times, they are asking whether the relation between any word-function and the objects of sense experience is such that we can never be mistaken in our judgments about the existence of what is objectified by the word-function. (These are both examples, by the way, of philosophical questions concerning causal relations. The second asks whether conditions exist which can cause us to be indefectibly correct about certain judgments.)

In this chapter, however, "given" is understood from the point of view of sense experience only, not from the point of view of the relation of language to sense experience. Of course, the present analysis is itself an instance of linguistic objectification of the objects of sensation. But understanding the relation between sense awareness and extra-objective existents is not a matter of understanding the relations between sense experience and language. It is a matter of understanding the causal relations, if any, which allow the senses to make us aware of real existents. The sensation hypothesis shows how real existents are given in sensation as being made our objects by sensation itself rather than by any inference, construction or association based on the fact that sensation has made us aware of *other* objects. But it does not follow from the fact that existing things are given in this way that it is always easy to judge whether sentences in which things are linguistically objectified as actually existing are true.

It is worth noting, by the way, that the two interpretations of the myth of the given just mentioned do not amount to the same thing. The fact that a word-function—for example, that of "think"—may not be expressible in all languages does not prevent the speakers of some language from having incorrigible knowledge of the truth of a sentence—for example, "I am thinking"—using it. Conversely, the fact that a word-function may be imposed on us by *some* experiences does not rule out the possibility of there being borderline cases where the truth of sentences using it is hard to determine.

To return to the relativity of sensation, most of the evidence supporting those who see an opposition between the awareness of sense data and the awareness of physical things come from so-called illusions of the senses and from the subjectivity of sensible qualities. But the sensation hypothesis shows that this relativity of the objects of sense awareness does not prevent physical things from being given in sensation. If sense data are actions we are aware of as actions, the problem of whether we are aware of sense data *or* physical things is reduced to a false dichotomy. Consciousness of an action as such *is* consciousness of an existing efficient cause as thus acting, for to be aware of an object as a way we are being acted on is to be aware of it as a way some really existing thing or things is acting on us.

Finally, since an action and its cause exist cognition-independently and are sensed as such, sensation enables us to recognize that its objects are at least *capable* of existing when they are not being sensed. (Even the action of a cause can exist in the sense faculties when sensation is not taking place, as is shown most dramatically by the use of anesthetics.) A sensation tells us very little about the natures of things that are acting on us, but it does tell us that they exist and are acting on us. And that is enough for sensation to provide us with the public objects that language requires.

The analysis in this section is intended to account for illusions resulting from the laws governing the physical action of the environment on the sense faculties, illusions like elliptical coins, sticks bent in water, Doppler's effect, the sun appearing smaller than an orange. It is not intended to account for the kind of illusion, more properly so-called in my opinion, that Gestalt psychology has so forcefully brought to our attention, illusions which are a function of the relation of a perceived object to a broader perceptual background. But if the first kind of illusion does not demonstrate a dichotomy between awareness of sense data and awareness of physical things, neither does the second. Two equal lines can be made to appear unequal by angles drawn at their ends. But the dichotomy theory has as much, and probably more, difficulty than does its opposite in explaining why two lines occupying equal segments of our visual field should appear unequal.

According to the sensation hypothesis, the two lines are present in our visual field because we are aware of the action of light on our organs of vision. Awareness of that action as such is awareness of real existents, the action and its agent. How the lines are perceived to relate to one another and to other things in our perceptual field is a different question, a question that does not suppress the sensation hypothesis. Illusions of the second kind provide no additional arguments for the dichotomy theory.

10.5 Hallucinations

The only evidence remaining for those who want to drive a wedge between our awareness of sense data and our awareness of physical things is the occurrence of hallucinations. Borderline cases are not the only reason our judgments about the real existence of the objects of sensation are not infallible. Hallucinations are introspectively indistinguishable from perceptions of real existents. Yet no one would want to say that when hallucinating, we are by that fact aware of the actually existing action of the environment on us. Since the objects of hallucinations appear qualitatively indistinguishable from the objects of perceptions, it seems that the objects of perceptions should not be described as the action of the environment recognized as such.

The occurrence of hallucinations, however, no more disproves that perception includes the element of sensation, which makes us aware of actions as such, than the existence of counterfeit works of art disproves the existence of originals, or the fact that invalid arguments can appear valid disproves the existence of valid arguments. Hallucination proves only that sensation can be imitated, that experiences other than sensation can present objects as if those objects were actions we are undergoing. And the fact that sensation can be imitated does not imply that sensation is not what it is.

Note that the point of the comparison between hallucinations and counterfeit works of art is not that there should be some way to tell a counterfeit from an original by internal evidence. The point is that in order for an art expert to recognize a counterfeit, more is required than the existence of some discernible difference between it and the original. Certain conditions, psychological and otherwise, must also be fulfilled on the part of the expert. The fact that he may misjudge the counterfeit when drunk or excessively tired or ill or in need of new glasses or emotionally distraught does not mean there is no difference between the counterfeit and the original.

Likewise, someone experiencing an hallucination is not able to distinguish between his awareness of the action of the environment on his sense faculties and his awareness of objects other than the current action of the environment on his sense faculties. The reason he, like the art expert, cannot make the appropriate distinction is either that causal factors necessary for him to make the distinction—causal factors in addition to the action of the environment itself—are missing or that additional causal factors interfering with the making of that distinction are present. But neither the presence nor absence of any additional causal factors can alter the nature of sensation itself or remove the difference between it and imagining, remembering and hallucinating. Or does the fact that the art expert may be drunk imply that there is no difference between the counterfeit and the original?

Nature, again, is given by causal analysis, and the reason we distinguish hallucination from the kind of experience which has genuine sensation at its core is to escape apparent violations of the principle of induction, a causal principle. Hallucinations are introspectively the same as perceptions. Since similar causes have similar effects, however, and since the effects of dissimilar causes cannot be alike in all respects, if hallucinatory experiences were of the same nature as perceptions, the course of events preceding and following hallucinations would be the same as the course of events preceding and following the corresponding perceptions. That not being the case, we know that the natures of these apparently similar experiences differ.

This does not mean that it is by inductive reasoning that we become aware of the action of the environment on the sense faculties. It is by sensation that we become aware of the action of the environment on the sense faculties. But we reason inductively to the conclusion either that a particular experience was one in which we were aware of the action of the environment as such or that it only appeared to be that kind of experience.

But there is another interpretation of what we imply in distinguishing between genuine perception and hallucination, the phenomenalist interpretation. According to the phenomenalist, since sense data are not the action of the environment recognized as such, the only difference between hallucinations and perceptions is the coherence with which experiences of either kind relate to the totality of our experiences. Among the many difficulties with the phenomenalist approach, however, are two that are particularly germane to this study. The phenomenalist must reduce being to being perceived or reduce belief in the extra-objective existence of physical things to a causal inference arriving at the existence of something we do not perceive but which stands behind what we do perceive.

For the phenomenalist, belief in whether or not an experience is hallucinatory can amount to belief in whether or not the objects of the experience have some kind of relation to unperceived real existents. But we have no way of justifying belief in the existence of the unperceived other than reasoning based on relations holding necessarily between what is perceived and what is not. Necessary relations between the non-identical are causal relations, by definition. Therefore belief in the existence of physical things would result from causal inference.

If the phenomenalist is willing to entertain necessary causal relations, however, he has no reason for rejecting the sensation hypothesis which gives us a much simpler explanation of our belief in the existence of physical things and one that avoids the problems traditionally associated with causal theories of perception. (The phenomenalist will also have to go some to justify his causal inferences. Appeal to inductively established laws is ruled out since we never have direct awareness of one term of the causal relation. Hence he must come up with self-evident causal truths to justify his inferences.)

The only alternative for the phenomenalist is to admit that perception is an awareness of real existents. But if so and if perception differs from hallucination *only* in fitting more coherently into the overall pattern of our experiences, then to be is to be the object of a certain kind of experience, that is, an experience with a certain kind of relation to other experiences. To be, in other words, is to be an object of knowledge of a certain kind.

These problems for phenomenalism allow me to mention the other argument I promised, in addition to the argument from the public character of language, in support of the contention that cognition-independent existents are what are first objectified in language. What we first objectify in language are what the senses make us aware of. The senses present things as really existing, not merely as characterized by sense qualities. If the senses did not also make us aware of things as existing cognition-independently, then either belief in the cognition-independent existence of things amounts to an unexplainable causal inference or to be is to be known.

The phenomenalist's position results from asking this question: if perception and hallucination are introspectively indistinguishable, how do I know whether I am perceiving or hallucinating? In the absence of an adequate understanding of causal relations, the answer seems to support the phenomenalist analysis of the distinction between these experiences. When the actual existence of a physical thing is under question, we do not let an individual sense experience settle the question for us; we rely on the concurring testimony of a number of experiences, including those of other people. Consequently the difference between perceptions and hallucinations seems to lie in the way they relate to other experiences.

But this is an *epistemological fallacy* on the part of the phenomenalist. How we know whether we are hallucinating or perceiving (that is, what causes the knowledge of whether we are hallucinating or perceiving) is one question; what constitutes the difference between the natures of hallucination and perception (that is, what are the different causal relations which make them what they are) is another. The answers to these two questions are related, no doubt. But the relation is not identity. As a matter of fact, the relation could be identity only under penalty of the difficulties with the phenomenalist account we have just discussed.

The reason we rely on the concurrence of many experiences to settle questions of existence is not that sensation does not make us aware of the existence of things acting on us. The reason is that we know we can err in judgments of existence based on sense experience, for we know there are such things as borderline cases and psychological states in which we can fail to distinguish sensation from what is not sensation. To determine whether an experience of red is a sensation we look for experiences which confirm or disconfirm that hypothesis. Confirming experiences are those which allow us to conclude, by inductive reasoning, that it is unreasonable to believe the opposite hypothesis.

The fact that this confirmation is inductive clarifies the relation between the answer to how we know whether we are hallucinating or perceiving and the answer to what constitutes the difference between these experiences. Induction is causal reasoning. In concluding that an experience was an awareness of things acting on us, we are rejecting an alternative causal analysis of the nature of the experience. But we are not reasoning to the existence of something not present in the experience. Rather we are concluding that an extra-objective existent was present and was experienced as an extra-objective existent *because our experience was an awareness of action as action.*

The key to whether our awareness of sense data is to be opposed to our awareness of physical things is not the distinction between perceiving and hallucinating, it is the distinction between sensing and imagining. The epistemological point of view, however, has led philosophers to focus on the first distinction to the neglect of the second. Philosophers have let their discussions be ruled by the question how we know whether or not we are hallucinating. But it is the distinction between sensing and imagining that provides the causal analysis which both closes the gap between sense data and physical things and explains how we know whether or not we are hallucinating.

The job of epistemology is to evaluate, to determine what goals we achieve in the various phases of our knowledge. (This is all that some realists meant by calling themselves *critical* realists. A critic evaluates; he does not necessarily evaluate negatively.) The difference between empiricism and realism can be expressed in terms of different goals by reference to which they evaluate the cognitive significance of language.

For the empiricist, cognitive significance is to be determined by reference to sensibly distinguishable features of experience. Whether he considers the objects of sense experience to be sense data or physical things, the function of language is to organize or predict experience in a manner that can be connected, ultimately, with occurrence of sensible qualities: blue here; motion there, etc. The empiricist's reason for evaluating language in this way is, whether he recognizes it or not, causal: knowledge is derived from and verified by sense experience; therefore cognitive significance is to be measured in terms of the objects that sensation enables us to distinguish from one another. As a result, the empiricist must assign "exists" a cognitive value subordinate to that of words for sensible qualities.

From the undeniable causal role of sense experience relative to linguistic knowledge, however, it does not follow that sensible qualities are that by which cognitive significance is to be measured. This is an epistemological fallacy of confusing the *means* (sensible qualities) by which knowledge achieves its *goal* (awareness of extra-objective existents) with that goal. *In the wake of Wittgenstein*, we must recognize what realists have always held, that the goal of linguistic objectification is identity with what exists extra-objectively. Since language is public, extra-objective existence is that by reference to which cognitive value is to be assigned language. And the sensation hypothesis shows us that words for sensible qualities, empirical words, are cognitively significant because their word-functions are the means by which the senses are made aware of extra-objective existence as such.

The epistemological point of view has prevented empiricists from making the ontological analyses necessary to understand causal relations. Consequently empiricists have been unable to recognize sensible qualities as the means by which we are put in contact with extra-objective existence. There was nothing left for them to do but make the manner in which we are made aware of real existence, rather than that which we are made aware of in this manner, the measure of cognitive value.

10.6 From Sense Experience to Metaphysics

Whether the sensation hypothesis is true or not, the senses do more than make us aware of sensible qualities. They present us with really existing unities of distinct sensible qualities. And the existence the senses make us aware of is cognition-independent; otherwise to be is to be perceived.

The senses, therefore, allow us to become acquainted with the word-functions of "exists" and "something existing" or "being" as linguistically objectifiable. Since we become acquainted with the word-function of "exists" in judgment, the psychological process by which ontological word-functions enter the language differs from the process for other thing-descriptions. But this does not prevent ontological word-functions from being related to others by logical inclusion. Any sensed object we can objectify as something red, we can objectify as something existing. In doing so, we are referring to no data other than that which allows us to objectify the sensed object as something red. "Being" does not put anything in sense experience that is not present when a red patch is present. Since being is logically included in something red, if something red is given in sense experience, something existing is given also.

The senses make us aware of existing unities of distinct sensible qualities. Some of these qualities are properties of others and are sensed as such; they do not exist on their own but exist, and are sensed as existing, in others. Shape, for example, is a sensible quality that has a relation of dependence on another sensible quality, extension. (Not vice versa; we do not experience extension without shape. But if the universe has infinite extension, it has no shape.) A shape is the shape of some extended thing, and that is how the senses make us aware of shape.

Shapes are realities. Changes occur bringing new shapes into existence. If shapes are not realities, there are changes that do not produce new states of affairs, changes that are not changes. Any attempt to analyze these changes to do away with the reality of shapes must replace shape with some reality equally describable as existing in another. And change itself is a reality the senses reveal as not existing in itself but as existing to the extent that it happens to something other than itself.

From sense experience, then, we can also derive the word-function of "something existing in another", or "accident". And the word-function of "accident" is logically included in that of "shape" or "change occurring to something" or "color", etc. Whenever an object satisfying the descriptions "red", "square" or "motion" is given in experience, an object satisfying the description "accident" is given in experience. These are just logically distinct ways of objectifying the same objects of experience.

But if sense experience enables us to acquire the word-function of "accident" (something-existing-in-another or something-not-existing-in-itself), it enables us to acquire the word-function of "substance" (something not existing in another or something existing in itself). The senses not only allow us to acquire this word-function, but they also make us aware of objects as not existing in others. For an object to be given in sensation as existing in another, the other must also be given, at least given as being that in which the first exists.

Even if there were an infinite series of things existing in other things, not everything given in sensation could be given as existing in another. An infinite series of accidents could not be sensed *as such* since our sense faculties are not powerful enough to grasp the infinite as such. At some point, one or more of the accidents in the series would be perceived as existing but not as existing in another.

And through our finite awareness of this series of accidents we would be made aware of something existing that has these accidents and does not exist in another, the infinite series itself, though we would not be aware of it as such. Therefore, when any accident is given in sensation as existing in another, we are made aware of the existence of something that has the accident and that as a matter of fact does not exist in another. Perhaps the whole universe is one substance. If so, in being aware of an accident as existing in something, we are aware of the existence of the universe, not as such, but as the something in which the accident exists.

Like the word-function of "accident", the word-function of "substance" refers to no data other than that from which we can derive empirical predicates. Every sensation presents us with *something* that does not exist in another. The difference between something existing that is red, curved, soft, and in motion and something existing that does not exist in another is not a difference in what is given in experience. It is a difference only of word-functions related to one another as logically including and logically included. The psychological processes by which we become acquainted with ontological and empirical word-functions are different. That does not prevent us from knowing that word-functions we are acquainted with as a result of these processes are so related that some are logically included in others.

How do words for causal relations derive from sense experience? Whenever sensation makes us aware of an object, for example, a change, as existing in another, a relationship of component causality is given in experience. The word-function of "accident" is only logically distinct from word-functions for sensible qualities. But "accident" expresses a relation to a component cause. Therefore the relationship of component causality is only logically distinct from the relation of an extended area in our visual field to its color, shape or motion.

If we are acquainted with component causality, however, we are acquainted with the relation of causal dependence in general, a relation that extends to modes of causality other than component. For causality in general is *logically included* in component causality. "Would not exist without something other than itself" attributes nothing to an object of experience that is not given when change or any other accident is given. Therefore, even if we had no other source for our acquaintance with efficient causality, sense awareness of component causality would allow us to acquire word-functions sufficient for achieving an understanding of efficient causality and for showing the necessity of every change having an efficient cause.

In addition to differing from empirical word-functions by logical inclusion, ontological word-functions *make use* of logical relations that are not found in experience. (See section 5.5.3.) To objectify something as existing in an*other*, we must use negation. To objectify that which would not exist without something other than itself, we use the modal phrase "would not". Ontological word-functions do not attribute logical relations to sensible things, but they use logical relations in objectifying what is logically included in empirical word-functions.

But no matter how much logical, linguistic or psychological work goes into understanding a meaning$_T$ like that of "something that would not exist without something other than itself", nothing prevents us from knowing that this word-function is distinct from that of "change occurring to something" only as a less explicit way of objectifying the same thing. Otherwise, a change occurring to something could exist without occurring to anything. But a change occurring to something could not be the same change if there were nothing undergoing the change (assuming such a change were possible). A change occurring to A is, by definition, a change having the result that A is different from before. If a change occurs that does not have such a result, it is not the same change as a change occurring to A. This is a necessary truth known by our acquaintance with the word-function of "change occurring to A", which is derived from sense experience.

How far from sense experience can the logical inclusion of ontological and causal word-functions in empirical word-functions take us? If "God" means the supreme being or the being that is cause of all else and that itself has no cause, then when it is asked what experience gives "God" its meaning, the answer must be plain, ordinary sense experience, the same experience from which we acquire our acquaintance with being and causality.

Chapter Eleven

Philosophical Fallibility

Philosophy verifies by appeal to truths known by understanding the way words are being used. Denial of such a truth, therefore, can only result from a failure to understand how words are being used, and ignorance of the question must be the reason there is so much disagreement in philosophy. In other disciplines that verify in this way, logic and mathematics, we are able to define our terms and proceed to our conclusions unambiguously. In philosophy, we do not succeed in settling questions just by giving definitions and reasoning from them. If there are self-evident truths in philosophy, why not?

The answer is found in a logical characteristic of most ontological, and some logical, word-functions. There is more than one way to be ignorant of these word-functions. Therefore the possibility of failing to understand how the words of a sentence are used exists in philosophy as it does not exist in other fields. I have in mind a fact that metaphysicians have long recognized about being and other word-functions on which their enterprise depends: these word-functions are not related to the kinds of which they can be predicated as genera are related to their species. Being is not a genus of which substance and accident are species; relation is not a genus whose species are formal and material relations.

Although this property of philosophical word-functions has long been recognized, what has not been pointed out previously is that this property explains the excessive difficulty philosophy has in achieving agreement on its necessary truths. In showing this, I will merely be drawing consequences from a classic discovery about the logic of philosophical concepts. And it is significant that those who have previously noted the non-generic character of philosophical word-functions have done so in innocence of the purpose of explaining the regular occurrence of ignorance of the question in philosophy. What follows is not an *ad hoc* strategy devised solely to get my theory of philosophical method off the hook.

There is something else that the non-generic nature of philosophical word-functions accounts for, the paradoxical character of so much philosophical discourse. Metaphysics regularly produces statements that strike many as strange or even meaningless. If a metaphysician's words are given an ordinary interpretation, his statements may appear to be self-contradictory or to contradict some obvious contingent fact. Often this is a sign that the metaphysician has committed a howler. But Simon showed that valid philosophizing, especially in metaphysics, must produce paradoxical sentences due to the non-generic word-functions philosophy deals with. He did not address the problem of ignorance of the question, but it is an extension of his analysis that will allow us to understand that fact of philosophical life.

This chapter will first describe the non-generic character of ontological word-functions and then explain how it generates philosophical paradox. Before applying the analysis to the problem of disagreement, some historical background will be given to explain the need for terminology I will be introducing and to enable us to bypass extraneous issues that have become associated with the question of whether being and other word-functions of importance to philosophy are genera. After having analyzed philosophical disagreement from the point of view of non-generic word-functions, I will note some other obstacles to philosophical consensus. And I will demonstrate that formal systems cannot be employed to solve ontological problems.

It would be wrong, however, to think that the problems I am addressing in this chapter are peculiar to a viewpoint that relies on verifiability by self-evident truths. Disagreement and paradox are problems that any treatment of philosophical method must face. And these problems are no more embarrassing for my position than they are for all those philosophical proposals, like the linguistic turn, that promise to reduce disagreement and paradox generated in philosophy to the proportions found in other disciplines. In fact, the problems of paradox and disagreement should be much more embarrassing for such proposals. For instead of reducing paradox and disagreement, such proposals always generate at least as much as the methodologies they are supplanting. My method, on the other hand, does *not* claim to eliminate these problems. It claims to explain why they cannot be eliminated and to explain this in a manner consistent with the fact that philosophical truth exists and is knowable by us.

11.1 Non-generic Abstraction

Why is being not a genus? Because it does not abstract from the difference distinguishing one kind of being from another the way a genus abstracts from the differences between its species. We saw in section 5.3.2 that the way being is logically included in the word-functions of thing-descriptions differs from the way animal is included in man or color in red. That difference resulted from the role of the logical relation of possibility in the word-function of "being". We could describe this difference by saying that being is not related to the word-functions of more explicit thing-descriptions by logical abstraction. However, this is not what I mean here by saying that being does not abstract from differences as a genus does.

On the other hand, there are word-functions from which being is distinguished by a relation of logical abstraction, for example, substance and accident. The relation between that-which-exists and either that-which-exists-in-itself or that-which-exists-in-another is that the first is abstracted from the other two. "Being" expresses part of what is expressed by "substance" and "accident" but leaves the rest unexpressed. What it leaves unexpressed is what distinguishes substances from accidents. Therefore being abstracts from the differences between these kinds of being. There is a crucial distinction, however, between the way a genus abstracts from its specific differences and the way being abstracts from differences between substance and accident. This difference is what I mean by non-generic abstraction.

11.1.1 The state of the question

I will begin by presenting what was understood about this issue previous to Simon and then explain his contribution. "Being" cannot express a feature common to all beings as "animal" expresses something common to both rational and irrational animals or as "triangle" expresses something common to isosceles, scalene and equilateral triangles. Isosceles, scalene and equilateral triangles are alike in having characteristics by which they satisfy the definition (that is, are objectifiable by the word-function) of "triangle", and they differ by having characteristics other than those by which they satisfy the definition of "triangle". But things cannot differ by characteristics that fail to satisfy the definition "that which exists". Whatever differentiates one being from another must be objectifiable by the word-function of "being". Outside of being, there is nothing.

The fact that being is not a genus is so important that it will pay us to take a closer look at the relation between generic and specific word-functions so as to leave no doubt about the relation of being to its kinds. A species is a *logically* complex word-function. It has a constituent of meaning$_T$ (the genus) which is shared by other species and a constituent of meaning$_T$ (the specific difference) which it does not share with other species, at least not with other species of this genus. We do not always have a word for the specific difference apart from the word which designates the species as a logical whole. For example, the meaning$_T$ of "red" is related to that of "color" such that it communicates everything that "color" communicates and more. This more is the difference distinguishing red from green as species of color.

Because the genus and the specific difference are logically included in the species, they are directly predicable of the species: man *is* rational, and man *is* animal. But the genus is not logically included in the specific difference such that it could be predicated of the specific difference as it is predicated of the species. Can "animal", for instance, be said of rationality the way "being" can be said of all the differences between beings? The context might occur in which we need a word to distinguish human intelligence from the intelligence of things belonging to other genera. We might then define "rationality" as the intelligence of animals (the kind of intelligence for which animals are the component causes). Does this imply that the generic meaning$_T$, animal, could be included in the specific meaning$_T$, rational, the way being is logically included in all its less universal meanings$_T$?

Because being is so included, whatever is objectifiable by a less universal meaning$_T$ is identical with something objectifiable by the meaning$_T$ of "being". But this definition of rationality does not identify rationality with being an animal; it identifies rationality with the *intelligence* of an animal. In the phrase, "intelligence of an animal", "intelligence" is the word for the genus (the *logical* component cause) and "of an animal" for the *specific difference* (the *logical* characterizing cause). But insofar as being can be predicated of all its modes, it is not a difference distinguishing one mode from another. Therefore even if "intelligence of an animal" did predicate animal of rationality, being would still not be related to its differences as a genus is to its.

But let us accept "intelligence of an animal" as a definition of "rationality". Then rationality is logically complex the way the meaning$_T$ of "man" is. One of its logical parts is expressed by "intelligence" and the other by "of an animal". And the question whether animal is logically included in the specific difference of man now becomes whether animal is logically included in the meaning$_T$ of "intelligence". If not, there is a constituent of the specific difference of man in which animal is not logically included, and the meaning$_T$ of "animal" would not relate to its differences the way being relates to its. For being can be predicated of all its differences because it is a less explicit objectification of what each of its differences is, namely, a way of existing.

But animal could not be predicated of intelligence short of making our definition of rationality redundant ad infinitum. If animal were a logical part of the meaning$_T$ of "intelligence" the way it is of "man", then intelligence is a logically complex meaning$_T$ whose parts are animal and some *other* meaning(s)$_T$. But of any other meaning$_T$ which is a logical part of intelligence we can ask whether the meaning$_T$ of "animal" is included in it the way it is included in the meaning$_T$ of "man". If so, this other meaning$_T$ is itself a logical complex one of whose parts is animal and another of whose parts is some further meaning$_T$. And this process of analyzing meanings$_T$ goes on ad infinitum unless there is some differentiating meaning$_T$ in which the genus is not logically included. If a genus is predicable of its differences the way being is predicable of its, every definition is infinitely redundant.

The same argument applies to all genus-species definitions. Therefore we would get no further if instead of defining man's specific difference in the abstract mode under the title of "rationality" we defined it in the concrete mode under the title of the "rational". The "rational" may be defined as an animal which is intelligent. Here animal is the genus, not the specific difference. But this definition works if and only if animal is not logically included in *its* specific difference, intelligence, or at least is not logically included in some other word-function which is a logical constituent of intelligence. Otherwise, the definition is infinitely repetitive.

Consequently being cannot abstract from its differences the way a genus abstracts from its. We cannot logically separate a constituent of meaning$_T$ which would be common to all beings from other constituents which would differentiate beings from one another. Being is just as much included in the differentiating constituent as it is in the constituent of similarity. For there to be a scalene triangle there must be a figure possessing the characteristics which satisfy the definition of "triangle" and *in addition* characteristics satisfying the definition of "scalene". But what is there in addition to being? Nothing. (Bobik, 1957, has pointed out, in effect, that what some have mistaken for the genus's being predicable of its specific differences as logically included in them is the fact that the genus is objectified as a logical component cause of which the specific differences are logical characterizing causes. See section 9.4.2.)

We have just walked the traditional path leading to the conclusion that being is not a genus. In a moment, we will have to go even further down this path, further than most others have gone. But this conclusion has never been an easy one to swallow. Where species can be said to be similar with respect to their genus, and thus have the genus predicated of them, they can be said to be dissimilar with respect to the differences of which the genus is not predicated. On the other hand, it seems that that with respect to which modes of being are similar is being and that with respect to which they are dissimilar is being, since being can be predicated of everything. But how can things be alike and unlike in the same respect at the same time?

To put it another way, it is because a genus abstracts from differences that it is a word-function with respect to which its species are alike. Many generic word-functions are related to that of "man" by logical abstraction. If any of these generic word-functions fails to abstract from certain characteristics of man, it cannot be predicated of things which do not share those characteristics with man. "Animal" can be said of men and horses, not men and molecules of water; "occupying space", on the other hand, can be said of men and molecules of water. The difference is that the word-function of "animal" abstracts less from the word-function of "man" than does the word-function of "occupying space". By abstracting from differences, a generic word-function becomes, though one word-function, predicable of many kinds. And to the extent that it does not abstract from differences, it is predicable of only some kinds and not of others.

Being is predicable of more than one kind also, and abstraction is what makes this possible. If we abstract being from its differences, however, they become nothing. So being seems to abstract and not to abstract in the same respect at the same time. As abstract, being is a word-function with respect to which things are alike, that is, a word-function capable of objectifying things as similar. As unabstract, it is a word-function with respect to which things differ, that is, a word-function capable of objectifying things as dissimilar.

How the same word-function can be something with respect to which things of which it is predicated are both alike and unlike has been a mystery since the time it was recognized that being is not a genus. It appears that being must be one and many in the same respect at the same time. If the things of which being is predicated were one in a certain respect but diverse in others, being would relate to its kinds the way a genus does. But if the things of which being is predicated are not one in a certain respect, in what way is the word-function we are predicating of them one word-function? Why is "being" not used in totally equivocal ways each time it is said of a different kind just as "bat" is used equivocally of an animal and a sporting instrument?

It is important to understand that the question how things can be alike and unlike in the same respect at the same time does not concern characteristics entering the make-up of things in their existence as things. The question is how the same word-function can *objectify* both a similarity and a difference between the same things. The word-function may be identical with some feature of reality. But the problem of how the word-function does or does not abstract from less universal word-functions which objectify the same feature of reality concerns a logical relation attaching to this feature of reality as a result of its having been made an object and of its being used as a means for objectifying the things of which it is a feature.

A thing does not have one extra-objective characterizing cause by which it is, for instance, square and another characterizing cause by which it is four-sided. The same extra-objective characterizing cause makes something both square, and hence unlike oblongs, and four-sided, and hence like oblongs. The meaning$_T$ of "square" is a species with reference to which some things are dissimilar; and the meaning$_T$ of "four-sided" is a genus with reference to which some of the same things are similar. But the same feature of reality may be objectified by "squareness" and by "four-sidedness".

Likewise, accidents are not beings, and hence similar to substance, by reason of one feature of themselves (whether existence or essence or whatever) and accidents, and hence unlike substance, by reason of another feature. It is the same reality that is objectified as a being and as an accident. Whether a meaning$_T$ logically included in less universal meanings$_T$ is generically abstracted or not, it will be identical with an extra-objective feature, or features, by reason of which a thing is both like and unlike other things.

Why some extra-objective similarities between things are, and some are not, objectifiable by means of generically abstracted word-functions, on the other hand, is a question that can be asked from two points of view, from the point of view of the status of what is objectified as object or the status of what is objectified as thing. We are considering the status of objects as objects. From the point of view of their status as things the answer must be found in the causal relations necessary for a feature of reality to be multipliable, that is, to have existence in more than one thing.

Briefly (and by way of bald assertions support for which will be found in the references of Appendix II), multiplication results from act being received by an otherwise potential component cause. A multipliable word-function is identical either with a particular kind of act-potency union or with a particular kind of act that can be united with potency. Why some multiplication allows generic similarity and some does not must therefore be traceable to the ways different potencies multiply and, hence, diversify their corresponding acts. Nothing about the nature of apples requires that it be the nature of this thing or that thing. For that to occur, matter existing at a particular place and time must be so organized as to be an apple. In other words, the diversification of act is the effect of its reception by potency. (Section 11.3.2 discusses these ideas further.)

Certain modes of being require a kind of component causality which allows for generic similarity between diverse individuals. A patch of red and a patch of green are similar in being patches of color. But these same modes of being are objectifiable by more universal word-functions whose extra-objective existence does not require (although it may have it in a given case) that particular kind of component cause. Red is objectifiable both by the generic term "color" and the non-generic term "being". That red can be an instance of a nongeneric word-function is made possible by the fact that all being does not require the kind of component cause required for the objectification of similarities by means of generic abstraction.

But we do not have to understand any kind of potency-act relation to solve the problem of how things can be objectified by a word-function with respect to which they are both alike and unlike. For of all realities objectifiable by more and less universal word-functions, whether generic or not, we can say that one and the same extra-objective feature can make a thing both like and unlike another thing with respect to different word-functions. The problem of how substance and accident can be similar and dissimilar with respect to the *same* word-function concerns the word-function of "being" not as something more-than-an-*object*, which it is, but as a means of objectifying different kinds of being.

11.1.2 The meaning of non-generic abstraction

It was Simon (1960b) who broke the back of the dilemma of unity and diversity in the word-function of "being" and other philosophical word-functions. The argument I will present here was not used by him, but it will complement and confirm his analysis.

To distinguish being from a genus, *it is not enough* to note that being is, while a genus is not, predicable of its differences. That is true, but it does not go to the heart of the matter. It only points to something more fundamental. There is one and only one way for a word-function to be something with respect to which things differ, one and only one way for a word-function to objectify a difference between things: that word-function must be affirmable of some things and *deniable* of others. If being is something with respect to which its kinds differ, it must be affirmable of some of its kinds and deniable of others. This is how being differs from a genus. Once a genus has been predicated of its kinds, they are objectified as similar. To objectify them as dissimilar we must affirm of some and deny of others a word-function other than the generic word-function. In the case of "being" and other words like it, we must use the same word-function to objectify kinds as similar by predication of each and to objectify kinds as dissimilar by predication of some but not of others. If not, being would be a genus.

This account of how being differs from a genus can be saved from contradiction. But in order to appreciate the solution to our problem, and the solution to this apparent contradiction, we must see why the statements just made are warranted.

If being is not affirmed of some beings but denied of others to express their difference, that is, if differences are expressed only by other word-functions *of which being happens to be predicable*, then things would be similar only, not different, with respect to being. Obviously, beings are distinguishable from one another by word-functions related to being as more explicit and less universal. But "being" itself must be among the predicates that can be asserted and denied of beings to express their differences. (Take "predicate" here in the grammatical sense if you balk at considering "being" a predicate in some other sense.)

To the extent that being is predicable of the *differences* between beings, being is something with reference to which these differences are *similar*, for they are all beings. But if these differences are alike in that they are beings, in what respect are *they* unlike? In other words, we must ask the same question about the differences between kinds of being that we have asked about the kinds: if they do not differ by being, since being is predicable of each, what do they differ by? They must differ by *nothing* since any word-function that does not logically include the word-function of "being" is incapable of extra-objective existence.

Therefore we cannot stop our contrast between the way being abstracts and the way a genus abstracts at the statement that being is, while a genus is not, predicable of its differences. If being is not itself a difference between kinds from which it is abstracted but is only predicable of those meanings$_T$ that are differences, being abstracts from *the differences betweeen its differences* as a genus does. But whatever being abstracts from is nothing.

In the same way that predicating a genus of its species objectifies the species as similar, predicating being of differences between kinds of being objectifies these differences as similar . Since it is abstraction that allows a generic meaning$_T$ to be something with respect to which things are similar, when being is related by abstraction to other meanings$_T$, what is it that distinguishes being from a genus? It must be that, in addition to abstracting from differences between its kinds, being in some way does *not* abstract from what differentiates one kind of being from another, with the result that being itself is something with respect to which things differ, that is, with the result that being itself is predicable of some things and deniable of others.

Another way of putting the argument. Being is logically included in all other word-functions for things as things. But if so, when we differentiate one kind of being from another with a word-function *other than* being itself, how do we avoid the same infinite regress we run into if a genus is logically included in its differences as being is included in its? What prevents the infinite regress in the case of a genus is that species are differentiated by word-functions in which the genus is not logically included. But there are no such word-functions to divide being. Therefore dividing being into kinds requires infinite redundancy. As a result, being could not be divided into kinds, and there would be no differences between beings.

The only way for the differences of being not to fall into nothingness is for being itself to be a difference between kinds of being. At some point (actually the first point since being is the most fundamental word-function) on a Porphyrean tree of kinds of being, being itself must be that which distinguishes the kinds; being must be divided into kinds by affirmation and negation of being itself. After that, kinds will be divided by word-functions in which being is logically included and which will therefore belong to one side or the other of the prior division. But these subsequent divisions will no longer be divisions of being as such; they will divide the particular kinds of being distinguished from one another by the original division of being. (We will see, however, that being can be divided into kinds by affirmation and negation of being itself in more than one way.)

A final way of putting the argument. We saw in the case of more and less universal genera that for a genus to fail to abstract from some features of its species means that the genus can be predicated of species with those features but must be denied of species without those features. In that way in which being does not abstract from differences between kinds from which it is otherwise abstractable, therefore, it can be predicated of some beings but must be denied of others. Because the meaning$_T$ of "animal" does not abstract from certain characteristics of man, it is not also predicable of molecules of water. To the extent that being is not abstractable from the differences of one of its kinds, it is not predicable of another kind. Further, because the meaning$_T$ of "occupying space" does abstract from certain characteristics of man, it is also predicable of molecules of water. And to the extent that being abstracts from differences between kinds, it is predicable of more than one kind. Consequently if being is not predicable of one kind of being and deniable of another, it abstracts from all differences between kinds just as a genus does. And if being is generically abstracted from its differences, they do not exist.

We must conclude that the only way for being to be something with respect to which its kinds differ, and the only way in which it can be said not to abstract from its differences, is for it to be attributable to some of its kinds and not to others. The way being objectifies differences between kinds is not the same way it objectifies similarities, namely, by being predicable of its differences. The only way for a word-function to be something with respect to which things differ is for the word-function to be predicable of some things and deniable of others. Things differ in respect to being, therefore, the way they differ with respect to any word-function, by being objectifiable or not being objectifiable by the word-function.

But how can this be? How can a word-function by means of which things are grouped together in a set also be used to distinguish members of the set from one another? How can we assert a predicate of a number of things and then deny it of some of the things of which we have just asserted it? I have been emphasizing this apparently contradictory conclusion in order to make clear that the solution which follows constitutes what it means, and *all* that it means, for being not to be a genus.

When an otherwise abstracted word-function is not related to the kinds of which it can be affirmed as a genus to its species, the difference between kinds must be expressed by a denial which amounts, not to a contradiction, but to an attenuation, an abatement, of what is affirmed. Of one kind, there will be, in effect, a reduplicative assertion of a predicate. Of the other kind, there will be an assertion accompanied by a hedge that will not quite contradict the assertion but will severely qualify it. If the difference expressed by denying the predicate were more than an attenuation of what is asserted by the predicate, there would be contradiction. But if the difference was something other than an attenuation of what is asserted by the predicate, it would be related to the meaning$_T$ of the predicate as a specific difference to a genus.

Assume a and b possess features F_1 and F_2, respectively, by which they are similar to one another. Assume also that at least one of these features, say, F_1, is not generically abstractable, that is, its nature does not include a necessary relation of dependence on the type of component cause that so diversifies the actuation it receives that the actuation is objectifiable by generically abstracted word-functions. Let us make F_1 the word-function of predicate "F". We could use some other predicate for F_2. But doing so would not allow us to objectify b as similar to a because of F_2, and by hypothesis F_1 and F_2 do make a and b similar. To objectify a and b as similar as a result of possessing F_1 and F_2, we must use "F" for F_2 as well as F_1. The word-function of "F", in other words, is that respect in which a and b are similar, what it is about a that is similar to b and what it is about b that is similar to a. And we objectify a and b as similar by predicating "F" of both.

Then how do we objectify a and b as dissimilar? a and b may differ in many respects. But if none of the respects in which they differ logically includes the word-function of "F", that is, if they do not also differ with respect to the word-function of "F", the differences between *a* and *b* relate to the word-function of "F" as specific differences to a genus. Since the word-function of "F" is not generically abstractable, we must be able to objectify *b* as dissimilar to *a* with respect to that word-function. The only way to do this is by affirming "F" of *a* and denying it of *b*.

Then how do we avoid contradicting what we said in predicating "F" of both *a* and *b*? We do so by saying *b* is an F but is not quite everything an F can be while *a* is an F and is an F fully. Or *b* has F-ness but does not have it in the strongest way F-ness can be had while *a* has F-ness and has it in the strongest way. And the standard by which stronger and weaker ways of having F-ness are judged is the nature of F-ness itself. If this way of distinguishing *a* from *b* with respect to the word-function of "F" can be replaced by some other way, the word-function of "F" is generically abstractable from its differences.

Some examples will show what I mean. When we predicate being of both substance and accident, we abstract from the difference between them; for we do not say whether the being in question does or does not exist in another. "In another", however, may look like a specific difference which can be affirmed and denied of what exists the way "rational" can be affirmed and denied of animals. But the phrase "exits in another" has the function of indicating that the existent in question is less than a full-fledged existent. "Another" means a *being* which is other. Accidents are existents but only to the extent that something other than themselves is an existent. They do not have an existence of their own, but an existence which belongs to something other than themselves. Consequently accidents are beings but incomplete beings, realities but not unqualified realities.

To make this clearer, let us contrast the way "exists in another" and "does not exist in another" distinguish kinds of being to the way "rational" and "irrational" distinguish kinds of animal. To express what differentiates a genus from a species, we use a word-function in which the genus is not logically included. If we define "rationality" as the intelligence of an animal, it is redundant to define "man" as an animal with the intelligence of an animal, rather than as an animal with intelligence. But to express what differentiates substance and accident, we cannot use a word-function in which existence, which is predicable of both substance and accident, is not logically included. The word-function distinguishing substance from accident is a logical complex including the word-functions of "exists" and of "in another". But the presence of existence in this logical complex distinguishing one kind of existent from another is not superfluous as the second "animal" would be if we defined "man" as an animal with the intelligence of an animal. It is not "in another" and "not in another" that distinguish substance and accident; it is "exists in another" and "does not exist in another".

In other words, being does not abstract from the difference between substance and accident and is therefore predicable of substance in a reduplicative, but not redundant, manner ("does not exist in another" amounts to "exists in itself"). And since being does not abstract from the difference of substance, when it is predicated of accident, the kind of being of which the difference of substance is *not* true, the predication is accompanied by a partial negation of what it asserts.

We can now reconcile the statement that being in some way abstracts from its differences with the statement that if it abstracts from them they are nothing. To say that a difference from which being abstracts would be nothing is to say that it would lack being. And it is a lack of being that differentiates accidents from substance. They lack existence in themselves, the difference of substance from which being does not abstract because that difference is being itself.

A moment ago I said that an accident is an *incomplete* being and that the difference of accident amounts to a *partial* negation of what is asserted when an accident is called a being. It is instructive to note an ambiguity to which words like "incomplete" and "partial" are subject in this connection. It can be said that molecules of water partially satisfy the meaning$_T$ of "animal" since one logical constituent of that meaning$_T$ is the meaning$_T$ of "occupying space". But the partial way in which accident satisfies the meaning$_T$ of "being" is not that of verifying one logical constituent and failing to verify another. The fact, after all, that part of the meaning$_T$ of "animal" is true of a molecule of water does not make water an incomplete animal. An accident satisfies the whole meaning$_T$ of "being" as a logical unit. But the way an accident satisfies this logical unit is so tenuous that it can only be expressed by a negation making use of the same logical unit. An accident is an incomplete being because its way of existing is a diminution of the meaning$_T$ of "being" considered as a whole.

This and this alone is the difference between being and a genus. A specific difference is neither a reaffirmation nor a watering down of its genus. If we take animal as included in the meaning$_T$ of "rational", then to say "rational" is to say "animal". But if so, something else must be included in the meaning$_T$ of "rational", something of which animal is not a logical part. Whatever that something else is, therefore, predicating it does not constitute a reaffirmation, nor does denying it constitute a negation, of what is asserted by "animal".

Another example of non-generic abstraction is provided by the division of being into potency and act (disposition and fulfillment). A being can exist as both actually something and potentially something. Although that which is potentially something can exist only to the extent it is actually something else, potency must still be recognized as a distinct mode of being. For a thing will not become F unless it is potentially F. And although what is potentially F must be actual in other respects, many things are actual in other respects that are not potentially F. But what is it that differentiates potency from act as a mode of being? Potency is a relation to that which does not exist; one is only potential with respect to that which one is not. Since potency is distinguished from act as a way of not being something, it is a negation of being that distinguishes these modes of being.

Being is the most obvious example of a non-generically abstracted word-function, but it is far from the only one. Other ontological and logical word-functions are non-generically abstracted as well. Is relation a genus of which material and formal relations are species? No; what differentiates material from formal relations is an abatement, in one case, and a reaffirmation in the other, of the force of the predicate "relation". A formal relation is a relation which is *just* a relation, a mode of being which relates other modes of being. A material relation, however, is a relation which is *not just* a relation; it is not a mode of being which does nothing but relate other modes of being. The non-generic character of what formal and material relations have in common remains even if we refer to what they have in common by a word other than "relation". If, for example, we speak of pure and mixed relatedness (see Section 9.3.1), the latter must be described as a relatedness that is not merely a relatedness.

Since non-generic abstraction is a logical relation, it should come as no surprise to find this relation characterizing logical word-functions. For an example, we need look no further than abstraction itself. What distinguishes generic abstraction from non-generic is the way in which non-generic word-functions do *not* abstract from differences between kinds. To the extent that they objectify something true of one kind and not of another kind, non-generic word-functions do not abstract from differences. But the same word-function which serves to objectify something true of one kind and not another also serves to objectify something true of both; and to that extent it does abstract from differences. Therefore non-generic abstraction is to be distinguished from generic abstraction by a negation of abstraction. Abstraction is a non-generically abstracted word-function predicable of kinds which can be differentiated by affirmation and negation of abstraction itself.

Non-generic abstraction has been described, not very perspicuously, as imperfect or incomplete abstraction. Worse than being unperspicuous, these descriptions can be read as referring to generic abstraction. An "incompletely abstracted" meaning$_T$ sounds like a logical complex of which one part is completely abstracted from something and another part is not. But that is an exact description of a species one of whose logical parts, the genus, is completely abstracted from another, the specific difference. And "imperfect abstraction" sounds like a lower species of a genus, the way an oyster, for instance, can be said to be a less perfect animal than a dolphin.

In order not to risk this kind of confusion, I propose to use the neologism "parageneric abstraction". The Greek prefix "para" sometimes has the pejorative connotation of something faulty, as in "paradox" and "paralogical". The pejorative connotation is in no way intended here. (Parageneric abstraction generates paradox but paradox in the sense of what is only apparently, not really, contradictory.) I am thinking, first of all, of the original meaning of "para", alongside-of; I am also thinking of the connotation, similar-to, that it has since acquired. Parageneric abstraction stands along side of generic as a distinct though similar type. Not, however, that they are similar with respect to being abstractions and dissimilar in some other respect; they are similar and dissimilar with respect to the logical relation of abstraction itself.

11.2 Philosophical Paradox

Using the same meaning$_T$ to objectify things both as similar and dissimilar creates paradoxes many find unacceptable. Again, the division of being into substance and accident provides a good example. Many cannot accept the idea of an existent which has its existence only in another. If an alleged existent has no existence in itself, it seems it does not deserve to be called an existent. Therefore it is denied that accidents (or whatever substitute, reasonable *or* unreasonable, for "accident" is used, "attribute", "quality" etc.) exist as something distinct from the things which have them. Instead, it is said that there only exist things (or events or processes etc.) describable as having qualities which are not really distinct from the things themselves. The only realities are, for instance, shaped and moving things, not shapes or motions. But to say that accidents have their reality only in others is not to say that they have no identity distinct from that of their substance or that the existence of an accident is the same as the existence of a substance. On the contrary, an accidental characterizing cause is an essence distinct from that of its component cause, substance. And describing the existence of an accident as in another distinguishes that existence, and that which so exists, from the existence of what is describable as not existing in another.

Therefore from one point of view, the point of view of accident's distinction from substance, it must be said that accidents have their own existence; but from another point of view, the point of view of an accident's relation of dependence on its component cause, it must be said that an accident's existence is not its own. Accidents are identical with relations of dependence on another mode of being such that they cannot exist except as characteristics of beings of that other mode. Therefore that which constitutes an accident as a reality distinct from substance is the same as that by reason of which we can describe an accident as having no reality in itself.

The statement that the only realities are things such as shaped things and moving things is not wrong. What is wrong is to think that attributing being to accidents claims any more than this. For what it means to say that accidents have their reality only in others is that they only exist to the extent that the things having them exist. But because of the parageneric abstraction of being, attributing being to accidents can appear to claim more than this. It can appear to make the contradictory claim that there is a reality which has no reality. No matter how paradoxical it is, however, the division of being into substance and accident is forced on us by an ontological analysis of experience. (See sections 9.4.1 and 10.6.)

In *The Blue Book* (p. 45ff.), Wittgenstein dealt with philosophical paradoxes of the "only my experiences are real" ilk. These are analogous to the statement that only things exist—not their qualities as in any way distinct from them—in at least one respect; each expresses a refusal to use a predicate to describe something it can legitimately describe, given its ordinary meaning$_T$, in favor of using it to describe only certain privileged cases. Since Wittgenstein claimed to cure philosophers of the temptation to make that kind of statement, it will be instructive to compare his explanation of philosophical paradox to the explanation parageneric abstraction gives us.

According to Wittgenstein, the person who says that only his experiences are real is victim of linguistic confusion. For some reason he is dissatisfied with the way ordinary language stresses similarities and differences between things, and he therefore desires a notation which allows him to stress them differently. But why should a desire for a new notation produce paradox; why does the person not just stipulate that his use of terms will differ from the ordinary? Because he mistakes his desire for a new notation with a disagreement over factual claims made by means of the old notation. Wittgenstein thinks the cure is to grant him his new use of words and then show him his disagreement with ordinary language is only verbal, by pointing out that we must now find another notation to do the job that the old notation used to do for us.

But why should a person who desires to stress likenesses and differences otherwise than they are stressed in ordinary language mistake his desire for a new notation with a disagreement over factual claims? Wittgenstein's answer is that a grammatical rule "states a logical impossibility" (p. 56). And confusing this logical impossibility with a "physical impossibility", the person thinks his use of the notation rules out certain factual claims made in ordinary language. But this explanation is insufficient since it relies on a linguistic theory of necessary truth, specifically, that logical necessity derives from meaning in the lexicological sense. Consequently Wittgenstein does not provide a sufficient reason why the desire for a notation stressing similarities and differences in a new way produces paradox instead of simply producing a new notation.

Parageneric abstraction, however, does provide a sufficient reason for being so misled as to refuse to objectify things as similar in a certain respect by (truthfully) asserting the same predicate of them. For when the meaning$_T$ of the predicate is parageneric, the *legitimate* use of the predicate, and not its misuse as a result of some linguistic confusion, will generate apparent contradictions. If a person thinks them contradictions, he will want to avoid them by refusing to use the parageneric predicate for that kind of thing of which it can both be affirmed and, in some way, denied. As a result, he will not see as similar things that language would ordinarily allow us to see as similar. And he will desire to use language that can express a similarity only to express a difference.

But this kind of confusion cannot be cured by granting the person his use of words and finding a new notation to replace the use that he rejects. For the apparent contradictions he wishes to avoid follow necessarily from a logical property of certain word-functions, not from our lexicological stipulations. It would do no good, for instance, to have one word for the parageneric word-function as objectifying similarity and another word for it as objectifying dissimilarity. If the meaning$_T$ of a word expressing dissimilarity is parageneric, then that word can also be used to express similarity. For the word-function with respect to which things are similar is also one with respect to which they are dissimilar. Therefore a word with such a meaning$_T$ will be affirmable of all of a number of things but at the same time affirmable of some of them and deniable of others. A change of vocabulary will not suppress the paradox.

The kind of apparent contradiction that results from parageneric abstraction is to be distinguished from the kind that results from people not being aware that a word is being used for different meanings$_T$. A philosophical use of a word which is appropriate in light of one of a word's ordinary uses may be inappropriate in the light of others. Here we can remove apparent contradictions by replacing the troublesome word with a phrase or clause that explains which use of the word the philosopher was relying on. But when a philosopher is using a word for a paragenerically abstracted meaning$_T$, whatever language-form is substituted will be capable of expressing both similarity and difference between the things of which it is said.

Even if we possessed language-forms as varied as the uses we have for them, our language would contain words subject to the kind of paradoxical uses we are discussing. For if words for paragenerically abstracted meanings$_T$ are missing from a language, that language is to that extent incomplete. It would be incapable of articulating some of the ways in which things are similar and some of the ways in which they are dissimilar, the same meanings$_T$ being needed to objectify both.

Since philosophy's word-functions are ontological or are logical relations whose terms are ontological word-functions, philosophical problems will always involve word-functions which are paragenerically abstracted or are the kinds of which a parageneric word-function is predicated. Therefore when a dispute concerns whether things are to be considered like or unlike in a certain respect, whether, for instance, material relations are relations, the dispute cannot be settled by arbitrarily stipulating that one word will be used for the parageneric word-function when objectifying things as similar and another for the parageneric word-function when objectifying things as dissimilar. The dispute must be settled as all philosophy's disputes must be settled, by appeal to truths whose opposites are self-evidently contradictory.

All one can do, consequently, is define his terms and argue that if his position were not true, something would both be and not be what it is. But just as parageneric abstraction can make statements appear to be contradictory when they are not, it can cause self-evidently necessary truths to be misunderstood and, therefore, denied. To explain this, I will introduce additional terminology whose usefulness is best understood in the light of some historical background.

11.3 Analogy

11.3.1 The vocabulary of analogy

We are discussing a logical relation that is usually treated in works on what is called the "analogical" use of words. The analogical use of words constitute a type which stands between univocity and equivocity. A word is used univocally when used in the same way, equivocally when used in entirely different ways, and analogically when used in ways that are somehow the same and somehow different. Since things are both in some way the same and in some way different with respect to parageneric meanings$_T$, parageneric words are used analogically when used to express both similarity and difference. But after centuries of experience, we should recognize that the vocabulary of analogy causes too much confusion to justify its continued use in this connection. The associations which this nomenclature carries with it, both those attaching to it because of its etymology and those deriving from its historical extensions, have prevented it from communicating what it is intended to communicate about philosophical language.

In the first place, one gets the impression from the typical ways the doctrine of analogical words is presented that its primary function is to solve the problem of religious language. This all but hopelessly confuses the issue. The primary problem for which the doctrine of analogical words is a solution is not the problem of religious language but the problem of the non-generic character of being and other important philosophical word-functions. Specifically, the problem is why "being" and other key philosophical words are not used equivocally given that their word-functions do not abstract from differences between their kinds.

Furthermore, in connection with the problem of religious language, the theory of the analogical use of words is constantly confused with the idea that we learn about God by analogical reasoning (human fathers love their children, so how much more must God love us), or with the idea that religious language is metaphorical (calling God a person is only an "analogy"). In fact, the exact opposites are meant. The doctrine of analogical language is not a theory about a particular kind of inference but of a particular kind of word-function. It is intended to describe word-functions which can appear in necessary truths that are premises of *formally valid* arguments and which can be *literally* true of God. (For example: whatever exists is undivided; God exists; therefore God is undivided.)

In theory, the confusion of the analogical use of words with analogical reasoning and with metaphor can be alleviated by patient explanation of what is meant by "analogy" in the discussion of philosophical language. In practice, this confusion is constantly made even by people who should know better, philosophers and theologians. If trained professionals cannot succeed in divorcing the technical use of the vocabulary of analogy from its more familiar use, there is no justification for retaining this vocabulary. Better to create an unfamiliar technical jargon than to have people mistake our use of a word for one that is more familiar to them.

These first two confusions are compounded by a third. Etymologically, "analogy" apparently refers to the similarity of two ratios, for example, 4 is to 2 as 6 is to 3. (See Simon, 1960b, p. 26.) Hence the logical form of a similarity between two ratios, proportion, has often been used as a model for explaining parageneric word-functions. (Because "proportion" can refer to a single ratio, "proportionality" is used in discussions of analogy for the similarity of two ratios.) There is a definite place for this model. But proportionality does not by itself show how things can be alike and unlike from the point of view of the same word-function. Obviously, the similarity between two ratios can be objectified generically, as "double" expresses the relation both of 4 to 2 and of 6 to 3.

In discussions of religious language, the model of proportionality has reinforced the confusion that the doctrine of analogy is a doctrine about a kind of reasoning. For the similarity of ratios is a logical device which allows us to determine an unknown value if the value of the other three terms of the relation are known. But proportionality is not intended as an explanation of the way we make inferences about God. It is intended as an explanation of word-functions which are not univocal because they are not abstractable from differences. Why these word-functions are not abstractable from differences is not explained by proportionality, however, but by the fact that their multiplication does not require the kind of component causality necessary for similarities to be objectifiable by generic abstraction.

If religious language is not the primary problem solved by analogy, might it still be the case that analogy is the solution to the problem of religious language? No. Since there can be no component causality in an uncaused being, any word-function attributed to both God and creatures must be paragenerically abstracted. But this shows, at the most, that the analogical use of words is a necessary condition for religious language, not that it is a sufficient condition. And far from being a sufficient condition, analogy should have a distinctly subsidiary role to play in the dispute about religious language. It is worth explaining why this is the case. Doing so will free our analysis of parageneric word-functions from extraneous issues that have always made the analysis of parageneric word-functions more difficult than it need be.

11.3.2 Digression on religious language

To make a long story short I will outline, without argument, Aquinas's solution to the problem of religious language. This will serve two purposes. First, since Aquinas is the source of the subsequent association of the doctrine of analogy with religious language, if that doctrine is not even *Aquinas's* solution to the problem of religious language, we have reason to suspect that it should not be anybody's. Second, Aquinas's account of religious language will illustrate the *reason why* analogy should not be the main focus of anyone's solution to the problem of religious language.

In the *Summa Theologiae*, Aquinas argues that the names of God are analogical only after he has argued that names can be applied to God *properly*. He follows this order consistently in other works. In his formal treatments of the names of God, I have not been able to find him arguing for the analogical character of religious language until after he has discussed the issues associated in the *Summa Theologiae* with naming God properly. In other words, when he asks whether the names of God are univocal or analogical, he is asking about names he has already established to be properly said of God. If we already know that names can be properly said of God, it makes sense to ask whether they are analogical. If we do not already know that, it does not make sense to use the doctrine of analogy to show it.

What does Aquinas mean by saying that names apply to God properly? He opposes proper to metaphorical application and holds that, in proper application, the perfection signified by a name (for example, life) does exist in God. He distinguishes that which is signified from the manner of signification and says that, while names do not properly apply to God from the point of view of mode of significa-tion, from the point of that which is signified, names can apply *more properly* to God than to creatures.

How does Aquinas justify this claim? To appreciate his justifica-tion, let us raise the following classic objection. Our words acquire their functions from our finite experience of finite, imperfect things. How can the meaning of any of our words be identical with that which an infinite and all-perfect being is? Aquinas's immediate answer is that while some of our words signify the imperfect ways in which God's perfections exist in creatures, what other words signify are the perfections themselves. The imperfect way that a perfection is received by creatures cannot exist in God, but the perfection itself can. And when that which is signified does not include the imperfect mode of reception in creatures, that which is signified is capable of existing in an infinite state.

This just seems to postpone the problem, however. Granting him his distinction between what is signified and the mode of significa-tion, how can that which is signified not include imperfection if it is an object drawn from our finite experience of finite and imperfect things? To find Aquinas's answer to the question how what is signified by a name can exclude imperfection, we have to go beyond his im-mediate discussion of religious language to its general metaphysical background.

What we find there is the doctrine that act (perfection) is limited only by being received in a potency. A word for a state of act, as op-posed to a word for the way act is received in potency, is a word for a perfection that can exist in an infinite state. Existence, for instance, includes potency in no respect since it is the supreme actuality to which everything else is in potency. When essence is distinct from existence, on the other hand, essence is a capacity for existence and hence the imperfect way in which existence is received. As such, essence is a principle of limitation allowing otherwise infinite existence to be multiply received. (Thus there are more beings but not more being, just as when truth is communicated, there are more knowers but not more truths known.) If there is a being that is a pure act of existence, therefore, it is infinite and all-perfect since it is unreceived by a limiting potency. But the argument showing that this being exists also shows that "essence" is the name for something that need not be distinct from existence and therefore can exist infinitely and without imper-fection.

As essence is the potency permitting many existences, prime matter is the potential limiting principle that permits many individuals to share the same kind of substantial essence. It is because a particular essence, like that of men or of hydrogen atoms or of quarks, results from the actualization of prime matter by substantial form, that there can be many individuals of the same generic or specific essence. Within the essence of each individual, the substantial form causes the essence to be similar to that of other individuals while the prime matter causes it to be a distinct, individual essence.

Since prime matter is the cause of limitation relative to essence, if a perfection of a finite essence can be shown not to require prime matter for its existence, we know that perfection can exist in an infinite state. That is, when what is signified by a name is a perfection for which prime matter is not a necessary cause, nothing in the nature of what is signified prevents it from existing in an infinite state. Infinite knowledge and love, for instance, would still be knowledge and love. But an infinite man or atom or quark would no longer be a man or atom or quark. What is signified by "man", "atom" or "quark" are what Aquinas calls imperfect ways in which perfection is received, because each of these names signifies a way in which prime matter is actualized.

It has often been debated whether proportionality or some other model for the analogical use of words explains how it is possible to attribute to God predicates expressing characteristics intrinsic to His being. Aquinas's justification for such intrinsic denomination, however, does not come from the doctrine of analogy but from an application of the doctrine that act is limited only by potency. If we have word for modes of being that are eligible for infinite existence, it will follow that these words are used analogically of God and creatures. But analogy is a secondary, after-the-fact issue.

The important thing to note about Aquinas's solution to the problem of religious language is that the question whether something could exist in an infinite state concerns the causal analysis of modes of being *as extra-objective existents*. Opponents of religious language, on the other hand, must try to prove that it is contradictory for the modes of being which are the functions of certain words to exist in an infinite state. Such a proof would require an *ontological*, not *epistemological*, causal analysis. It is an epistemological fallacy, not ignorance of analogy, that is behind the objection that finite experience of imperfect objects cannot make us aware of word-functions capable of existence in an infinite state.

As McInerny (1961) has perceived, the questions of whether a word is used analogically and its word-function is parageneric concern objects of knowledge *as objects of knowledge*, not as extra-objective existents. And to approach the problem of religious language from the point of view of properties attributable to word-functions only as objects of knowledge is to commit an epistemological fallacy. If ontological causal analysis can show that a word-function is a mode of being capable of existing in an infinite state, it follows that the word-function *as object of knowledge* has whatever logical and epistemological properties—analogy included—are necessary for it to be predicable of an infinite being. Any arguments to the contrary based on alleged necessary truths about objects as objects must be mistaken.

From the point of view of the manner in which they are made objects of human knowledge, our objects are necessarily characterized by finitude. Therefore a doctrine about objects as objects can express no more than necessary, not sufficient, conditions for religious language. No such doctrine could prove that words can be properly attributable to an infinitely perfect being. But what is true of the manner in which extra-objective existents are made terms of knowledge relations is one thing; what predicates describe extra-objective existents as such is another. The question of whether a predicate could be asserted of an infinite being concerns the word-function of the predicate from the point of view of that existence which is other than being-an-*object*. In all cases of knowledge, there is a difference between what is objectified and what characterizes the manner in which it is objectified. If such differences constituted contradictions, it could never be true of anything that it was an object of knowledge.

As we saw in discussing linguistic relativism, in no case of knowing the identity of that which is an object and that which is a thing do we attribute to the thing as thing the manner in which it is made an object. Of an infinitely good thing, for instance, we may want to say that it is not only good but is goodness itself, thereby using an abstract form of a predicate, "goodness", to identify the word-function of this predicate with a concrete existent. But the abstract form of the predicate is a characteristic of the mode of objectification, not of that which is objectified; so no contradiction arises when the predicate is asserted of a concrete being.

It is often held that, in Aquinas, analogy is not just a doctrine of how words signify; it is also a doctrine about that which is signified. Let me avoid this purely historical dispute by mentioning three things. First, whatever it may be elsewhere in his works, analogy enters Aquinas's formal treatments of the names of God as a doctrine of how words signify. Second, to show that analogy is Aquinas's explanation of how that which is signified can be properly attributed to an infinite being, it must be shown that he uses the vocabulary of analogy, not for just any ontological doctrine, but for the doctrine of the limitation of act by potency.

Third, if Aquinas or anyone else uses the vocabulary of analogy for a doctrine of things as things, he is using that vocabulary in a way otherwise than originally intended, since its original use was for a doctrine of how we use words. Of course we are free to modify our vocabulary any way we want. But if using the same vocabulary in different domains risks confusion, then we must do so only with caution and with appropriate clarification. Here the clarification must make clear that the problem of religious language requires an analysis of linguistic objects as extra-objective, not as linguistic objects. On the other hand, if confusion continues to exist even after appropriate clarification, it is better to forsake the new use of the vocabulary.

There is another problem that needlessly burdens paragenerically abstracted word-functions as a result of the vocabulary of analogy. Words for parageneric word-functions are sometimes used in expressing similarities between things, sometimes in expressing dissimilarities. The fact that a word-function is parageneric, however, does not imply that the word for it is used in these different ways each time it occurs in an argument. If so, the argument would be invalidated by equivocation.

But consider: whatever exists is undivided; God exists; therefore God is undivided. The words "exists" and "undivided" are used in the same way each time they occur in the argument. To say that a word-function is parageneric (or that a word is analogical) is to say that it is *capable* of being used sententially to objectify difference as well as likeness. But in this argument, parageneric word-functions are notused to objectify any differences between things of which they can be predicated; they are only used to objectify likenesses.

To show this, let us expand the sentences of the argument as follows: whatever exists (in one of the ways in which it is possible to exist) is undivided (in one of the ways in which it is possible to be undivided); God exists (in one of the ways in which it is possible to exist); therefore God is undivided (in one of the ways in which it is possible to be undivided). The parageneric words are used in exactly the same way in each case. The second premise does not specify the mode of existence that is peculiar to God; it does not, for instance, tell us whether His existence is identical with His essence. And the conclusion does not differentiate the way God is undivided from the way other things are; it does not tell us, for instance, whether God is undivided as something having no parts or as something whose parts are united. All words are used univocally *in this argument*.

Because they are parageneric, predicates affirmable of both God and creatures would also be in some way deniable of either God or creatures. (Creatures are *not* undivided as having no really distinct parts, but God is *not* undivided as having really distinct parts which are together.) Differences between God and creatures would be shown in the same way any argument shows a difference between things, by yielding a conclusion that denies a predicate of something. For example: whatever is composed of parts is efficiently caused; God is not efficiently caused; therefore God is not composed of parts. The word-functions of such an argument would be parageneric, but the words would be used the same way in each occurrence in the argument.

Before leaving the topic of religious language, let me add a footnote to the argument against Berkeley offered in section 2.2.2. Of a being which knows itself *and* whose knowledge of itself is identical with its existence, it can be said that to be is to be known; for such a being, to exist is to know, and therefore be known by, itself. Still, it is not the case that the existence is nothing more than what is expressed by the extrinsic denomination "known". The word-function of "known" remains a logical construct objectifying a thing merely as term of a relation something bears to it. The existence is identical with to-be-known, however, only because it is identical with to-know. Therefore the relation on which the logical construct is based implies that to exist is more than to be a *term* of a relation; the existence is identical with the *relation* itself, that is, the knowledge.

Furthermore, as Aristotle first noted and medieval philosophers discussed at length, necessary causal truths show that a thing whose existence is identical with its knowledge of itself must be unchanging, infinite, not composed of parts, etc. In other words, this thing must be God. Whenever knowledge is not identical with the knower's existence, to exist for the knower is not the same as being-known. And whenever the knower is subject to change, finite, composed of parts, etc., to exist for the knower is not identical with its knowledge of itself.

Hopefully, we can now continue our consideration of parageneric word-functions without having to worry about the problems of religious language or of equivocation in arguments.

11.3.3 An alternative to the vocabulary of analogy

The preceding discussion has been necessary to clear the field of extraneous issues and to justify the terminological suggestions I am about to make. Because of all the confusion from which it is too late to extricate the vocabulary of analogy, I propose to replace it with a vocabulary patterned after it but borrowing the prefix "para" from its use in "parageneric" and substituting it for the prefix "ana". Parageneric word-functions, for instance, have been called "analogues". I will call them "paralogues". The kinds of which analogues can be asserted have been called "analogates". I will call them "paralogates". A paralogate of which a paralogue can be affirmed with no accompanying negation is a primary paralogate; a paralogate of which the paralogue can be both in some way affirmed and in some way denied is a secondary paralogate.

For obvious reasons, I will not replace "analogical" with "paralogical" but will continue to use "parageneric" when an adjective is called for. It may be objected, however, that the use of "paralogue" and "paralogate" risks association with "paralogical" and "paralogism", and that would be a confusion as damaging as any that the vocabulary of analogy gets us into. But "paralogical" and "paralogism" are rarely used; the frequency of their use cannot even be compared to that of "analogy". And if used at all, they are used by specialists as part of a technical, academic vocabulary. Therefore we do not have to worry about our use of these terms being confused with some ordinary use, a use that does not exist for "paralogue" and "paralogate" and hardly exists for "paralogical" and "paralogism". The specialists who use the latter terms, finally, can be expected to be kept from misinterpretation by noting the differences between their terms and these neologisms.

11.4 Paralogues and Self-evidence

For a necessary truth to be self-evident, it must be knowable from acquaintance with word-functions and acquaintance with word-functions alone. Because it deals with parageneric word-functions and with the kinds of which they can be asserted, philosophy's knowledge of the necessary truths it relies on for verification takes place under the most disadvantageous conditions. Paralogues create a possibility for error concerning self-evident truths, a possibility of a kind that could not exist in the domain of generic abstraction. For if the word-functions of the truth are paralogues, it will be particularly easy to misunderstand how the words are being used.

Knowing a truth whose necessity derives from causal relations between word-functions requires abstracting the word-functions from differences whose association with the causal relation between the word-functions is contingent. It is incidental to the necessary relation between color and place that a particular color in a particular place be red or green. Consequently we could not recognize the necessity of the relation between red or green and place if we could not abstract the genus color from the differences of its species. Once we have become acquainted with color (and therefore have abstracted it from specific differences), however, we are capable of seeing it as entering a necessary causal relation to place. Once we have become acquainted with a paralogue we are also capable of seeing it as entering necessary causal relations. But to the extent that the paralogue does not abstract from differences, it is possible to be acquainted with the paralogue and yet fail to see it as entering its necessary causal relations.

The reason we fail to grasp a paralogue's necessary causal relations is not just that we may neglect to inquire about them as we might neglect to inquire about the relation of color to place. But just as parageneric abstraction can cause statements to appear to be contradictory when they are not, it can cause self-evident truths to be misunderstood.

Grasping a necessary causal relation is grasping that things objectifiable by some word-function would not be what they are if some really distinct thing objectifiable by some other word-function did not exist. If the necessary cause or necessary effect did not exist, one or the other of these things would both be and not be what it is, that is, it would both be and not be objectifiable by some word-function. But inasmuch as parageneric word-functions can be used to make both affirmations and denials regarding secondary paralogates, secondary paralogates are both objectifiable and not objectifiable by parageneric word-functions. That is why parageneric abstraction produces apparent contradictions. Apparent contradictions, however, make their opposites appear necessarily true. As a result of the parageneric abstraction of word-functions, therefore, we can think something is necessarily true when it is not. And self-evident truths or conclusions drawn from them which involve a paralogue being predicated of a secondary paralogate may appear to be necessarily false instead of necessarily true.

For example, it is not only denied but is even considered impossible for the principle of efficient causality to be derived from truths whose necessity is self-evident. For one more time, let us recall why.

The necessary is that whose opposite is contradictory, and contradictions are affirmations and denials of the same. But cause and effect are not the same; so there is no such thing as causal necessity. This argument is, in effect, a denial that things can be material relations to other things. For only if a thing is not related to another by its identity with itself does the non-existence of the other fail to require that the thing itself does not exist.

Why has it appeared necessarily true to so many philosophers that things cannot be material relations to one another? Because relation is a paralogue of which the primary paralogates are formal relations. Material relations are the secondary paralogates. If "relation" can be used to make an affirmation about them, it can also be used to make a denial about them. Because of the lack of perspicuousness with which material relations satisfy the meaning$_T$ of "relation" and because of the paradox of a thing which deserves to be called absolute, since it is not just a way of relating things other than itself, also being a relation, many take the meaning$_T$ of "relation" only as something that differentiates formal from material relations. As a result, it appears self-evident to them that one thing cannot be so related to another that without that other the thing would not be what it is.

This is how parageneric abstraction can mislead us into thinking that there *cannot be* necessary causal relations. Examining how parageneric abstraction prevents so many from seeing that there *must be* necessary causal relations will show us another way in which it can cause error regarding self-evident truth. My arguments for the principle of efficient causality depended on the truth of the following statements being knowable from acquaintance with word-functions alone:

> A change occurring to something other than itself is a change that would not exist without something other than itself.

> A change occurring to something that has existed without undergoing this change is a change occurring to something other than itself.

From these it follows that the relation between change and that which undergoes it is a causal relation. And that is what most philosophers since Hume have failed to see.

Why did they fail to see it? Because causality is a relation to the *other*. And otherness is a paralogue of which the relation between a component cause and its effect is only a secondary paralogate. If A is one thing and B is another, A's existence is not B's and B's is not A's.

But while the existence of a part, C, of a whole, D, is other than the existence of the whole (C's existence is not D's), the existence of the whole is, among other things, the existence of that part (D's existence *is*, among other things, the existence of C). Although otherness can be unqualifiedly asserted of two distinct things, it can be asserted of a whole and its parts only with a hedge that does not contradict the assertion but does not give what is asserted the full force it can have. Philosophers have failed to see the part as cause of the whole because they are thinking of otherness in terms of its primary paralogate. Since that kind of otherness must be denied of the part-whole relation, that relation has not been seen as a causal relation.

Perhaps it is even easier to fail to recognize that change is caused by what undergoes it than it is to fail to recognize that a whole is caused by its parts. Whatever the relation of a whole to its parts might be, change is an accident, and what undergoes it is, ultimately, substance. Although an accident is other than a substance, their relation instantiates the word-function of "other than" only in the most tenuous manner.

Otherness is a logical relation but a relation between existents. Since an accident is only a secondary paralogate of "existent", its otherness from its substance is only a secondary paralogate of otherness. The existence of an accident belongs to its substance. Therefore it does not differ from that of its substance as the existence of one substance differs from that of another or even as the existence of one accident would differ from that of an unrelated accident of the same substance. The paradox of an existent which does not exist in itself convinces some that there is no distinction to be drawn between an accident and the thing which has it. Therefore the relation of change to that which undergoes it is a relation to the other, and hence a causal relation, only in the least obvious and most paradoxical way.

Thus the parageneric abstraction of word-functions can incline us to fail to see a contradiction, and therefore the necessity of its opposite, where there is one to be seen. For if we do not recognize a secondary paralogate, like an accident, as a genuine instance of a paralogue, like the word-functions of "existent" or "other than", statements which imply that the paralogue cannot be attributed to this paralogate will appear not to contradict anything that is true.

To say that a change would not exist without that to which it occurs *and* that the change does not have a causal relation to that to which it occurs is to imply that the change is not *other than* that to which it occurs. It is self-evidently true, however, that a change occurring to something that has not always been undergoing change is other than that to which it occurs. But seeing this as self-evident requires using a paralogue to make an affirmation, rather than a denial, regarding a secondary paralogate. And that requires us not to take the paralogue as identical only with that which differentiates the primary paralogate. We can be dazzled by that difference, however, because of the apparent contradiction that occurs when the paralogue is predicated of a secondary paralogate. As a result, we understand the use of a parageneric word only in terms of this difference and fall into ignorance of the question.

In addition to apparent contradictions in the case of secondary paralogates, other things can influence us to understand a parageneric meaning$_T$ as a factor of dissimilarity between paralogates. We may have acquired the meaning$_T$ from only one of the paralogates. The fact that this paralogate is the cause of our acquaintance with the paralogue can be a strong influence on us. Or we may simply be more familiar with one of the paralogates than the other. (Section 11.5.2 will give other reasons for misunderstanding paralogues.)

Sometimes a misinterpretation of a self-evident truth resulting from the fact that its word-functions are paralogues will not lead us to deny the truth of a sentence. Instead, we may see that contradictions will follow if we deny the sentence, but we assign the sentence a meaning$_T$ other than that which renders it necessarily true. In other words, we can assent to a sentence even while misinterpreting the causal relations it asserts.

The necessary truth may be that the *secondary* paralogate terminates a causal relation specific to the secondary paralogate. (For the way the paralogue exists in its secondary paralogates may have certain necessary causes, may be the necessary effect of certain causes or may produce certain necessary effects.) But we may interpret the truth, while assenting to it, as attributing the relation to the primary paralogate. We would do this because we fail to recognize the secondary paralogate as a genuine instance of the paralogue. The result would be that we assign the right effects to the wrong causes.

It is a self-evident truth, for instance, that if a truth is knowable solely by knowing how its words are being used, no other evidence, whether that of sense experience or of some criterion of self-evidence, is needed to know its truth. But "knowing how its words are being used" is a parageneric expression descriptive of both lexicological and non-lexicological knowledge. In the case of non-lexicological knowledge of that for which a word is used, however, the assertion that it is knowledge of that for which a word is used must be accompanied by a hedge that constitutes an abatement of what is asserted. One can be acquainted with something which happens to be that for which some word is used without knowing what word has this use. To the extent that non-lexicological knowledge is compatible with ignorance of what words have what uses, non-lexicological knowledge is *not* knowledge of that for which a word is used.

Meanings$_T$ can be described otherwise than by object-descriptions like "meaning$_T$" or "word-function". It is such object-descriptions, however, that are relevant to the causal analysis of our knowledge of necessary truth. For it is acquaintance with linguistically communicable meanings$_T$ that allows us to judge necessity. Since necessary truths are known because we know meanings and since lexicological knowledge of meaning is the primary paralogate of this paralogue, many have been misled into taking lexicological knowledge as the cause of our knowledge of necessary truth, the linguistic theory of necessity.

The linguistic theory of necessity is reinforced if we have already, and as another result of parageneric abstraction, rejected causal necessity. Necessity based on logical relations will be the only kind left. Logical relations are simply relations between language-forms and their meanings$_T$ considered as means of objectification, or between either of these and the things objectified by them. In the case of words for logical relations, therefore, non-lexicological knowledge is knowledge of something that has no reality over and above the fact that we do use language-forms in certain ways.

Still, it is non-lexicological knowledge of meaning, not lexicological knowledge, which is the cause of our knowledge of necessary truth. Even in the case of words for logical relations, the knowledge of meaning that causes knowledge of necessary truth is not knowledge of which words happen to be used for which logical relations in a given linguistic community; for lexicological ignorance does not make one ignorant of any logical necessity. But because the non-lexicological variety is the secondary paralogate of knowledge of meaning, we mistakenly think it is lexicological knowledge, the primary paralogate, which is the cause under consideration. So even when we assent to the necessary truth of statements about these causal relations, we can be assenting to the wrong causal relations.

And since the problem concerns paralogues, it would not help to use one word for the paralogue as affirmed of both paralogates and another for the paralogue as affirmed of one and denied of the other. Whatever word is used for the paralogue will have a meaning$_T$ capable of both objectifying paralogates as similar and objectifying paralogates as dissimilar. We might try to avoid the confusion leading to the linguistic theory of necessity, for instance, by describing knowledge of meaning in the non-lexicological sense in a way that did not refer to language. But previous to the linguistic turn such descriptions were used. Knowledge of necessary truth was said to be knowledge of relations between ideas and to result from analysis of concepts. These words are also paralogues. And it makes all the difference to the causal account of our knowledge of necessary truth which paralogate of a word like "concept" we are thinking of. The "objective" concept is *that which* we are made aware of by means of the psychological disposition also known as a concept (the "formal" concept). And knowledge of necessary truth results from our acquaintance with objective concepts, not from acquaintance with the mental dispositions by means of which we are cognitively related to objective concepts.

But objective concepts are secondary paralogates of this paralogue. "Objective concept" is an object-description attributable to things that are *not just* objects, not just terms of knowledge relations. As a disposition for cognition, however, a psychological concept is a (formal or material) knowledge relation by definition. Still, thing and object are identical; so that which is not just an "object" can also be described by such an object-description as "objective concept". And what is expressed by this description, the fact that something has been made an object of knowledge by means of a formal concept, is what makes the knowledge of necessary truth possible. Consequently in giving a causal analysis of the knowledge of necessary truth, an object-description such as "concept" (or "meaning") is the relevant description to give. But we cannot give it without taking the risk that someone will attribute to the primary paralogate of the paralogue we are using the causal relation we are attributing to the secondary paralogate.

In sum, whenever a feature by which a thing enters a necessary causal relation must be objectified paragenerically, we are in danger of falling into philosophical error by identifying the paralogue with the difference between paralogates. Errors made possible by the parageneric abstraction of word-functions are correctable. We can explain at whatever length is required how a paralogue is operating in a particular instance of its use, and we can reduce the position opposite the truth to absurdity. Both of these methods, however, will make use of other parageneric words. *Reductio ad absurdum* requires that an opponent assent to some other truths which, together with his position, imply contradiction. These truths will likewise involve paralogues. And in explaining how words for paralogues are being used, we can do no more than make use of other words for paralogues.

At each step, therefore, conditions will be present that make fresh errors possible. Just how difficult is it to eliminate all such errors? The next section will give us some idea as we look at other sources of philosophical error, sources which reinforce the possibilities for error created by parageneric abstraction.

11.5 Paralogues and Other Sources of Error

These other sources of philosphical error are at least to some degree independent of parageneric abstraction even though they work together with it. I will not attempt to analyze them completely but to point out some important relations between them and the problems created by paralogues.

11.5.1 Epistemological fallacies and U-turns

Even if epistemological fallacies and U-turns are not in every instance caused by the fact that philosophy deals with parageneric word-functions, still the errors made possible by paralogues must be considered more fundamental. For they interfere directly with the process of philosophical verification, and they are what make it difficult to correct other errors once they have taken place. If someone has committed an epistemological fallacy or made a U-turn, the only way to enlighten him is by appealing to sentences whose truth is to be judged by our acquaintance with word-functions. When these word-functions are paralogues, the enlightenment will be far from automatic.

Explanations of how epistemological fallacies come about may differ in every instance. The only constant may be that when there is truth, object and thing are only logically distinct. This fact is a potentially endless source of ambiguities. "I am studying physics" can mean I am attempting to acquire scientific knowledge about the natural world or I am attempting to acquire epistemological or historical knowledge about the kind of human activity engaged in by people like Newton and Einstein. The philosopher of science might try to disambiguate by substituting "I am studying the subject matter of physics" if, for example, he is interested in what distinguishes the subject matters of physics and mathematics. But what else does the physicist do but study the subject matter of physics?

Or consider the description of a logical relation as characterizing a thing as that which is known. "Characterizing a thing as that which is known" can describe the extra-objective features known about a thing by a particular piece of knowledge. A similar ambiguity occurs in "A thing is known only insofar as it is known". "Only insofar as it is known" can mean only to the extent that something extra-objective is made the term of a knowledge relation, or it can mean that the known can only be the term of a knowledge relation, to the exclusion of also being something extra-objective.

The identity of thing and object together with our modern preoccupation with epistemological questions can make it appear that the kind of knowledge pertinent to philosophy is that expressed by object-descriptions. Even without a commitment to the epistemological point of view, however, philosophers must always be concerned with how we know our sentences are true. This concern together with the extensional equivalence of object-descriptions and thing-descriptions can cause us to look for, and be satisfied with, object-descriptions where knowledge of things as things is needed.

The possibility of substituting the point of view of what is true of things as objects for what is true of things as things is greatly reinforced if we are inclined to depreciate the word-function of "exists" as a means for objectifying things as things. And such an inclination can result from the parageneric character of existence. The sensible qualities through which we know whatever else we know are accidents. Accidents are secondary paralogates of existence. The most rarefied and paradoxical case of existence, therefore, is the existence that has a causal primacy in the genesis of our knowledge. This is even true of the knowledge of our own existence we acquire by awareness of our conscious states, for conscious states are accidents. Consequently it is possible for us, when philosophizing, to systematically overlook the existence of things as something that has causal priority over the objectification of things.

But the epistemological fallacy can also reinforce the tendency to error associated with parageneric abstraction. For it will be particularly easy to depreciate the cognitive value of existence if we have already adopted the epistemological point of view and are looking at things from the standpoint of the conditions under which they are made objects of knowledge. When we look at things from the ontological point of view, there will be a tendency to deny accidental existence in favor of substantial (or whatever the primary paralogate of existence may be called). When we look at things from the epistemological point of view, the tendency will be to reduce existence to the conditions under which it is made an object. And since secondary paralogates of existence are the cause of our acquaintance with this paralogue, it will be particularly easy to reduce existence to what is characteristic of it in the case of accidents.

But accidents are the paralogates of which existence must be not only affirmed but also denied. And since the cause of our knowledge of existence is the paralogate of which existence must in some way be denied, we can fail to appreciate existence as that by which things are causally prior to objects. As a result, we come up with covertly idealistic treatments of existence like the standard interpretations of the non-predicate theory. (The final answer to the question whether existence is a predicate will probably be yes and no. If "predicate" can be assigned a meaning$_T$ which is useful in this connection, that meaning$_T$ will likely be a paralogue which is in some way affirmable and in some way deniable of existence.)

In other cases, too, failing to recognize secondary paralogates as genuine instances of a paralogue can lead us into epistemological fallacies. When we have denied that potency is a mode of being or that causal relations are characteristics of things as things, we have to reinterpret these word-functions as logical or epistemological relations in the same way that standard non-predicate theories reinterpret existence. Since being is the teleonomic cause of sentential knowledge, logical relations and object-descriptions can have an extension as universal as that of being. Therefore we might be able to substitute such word-functions for descriptions of things as things while saving, with a lot of pushing and pulling here and there, the truth of all contingently true sentences. What we cannot save are necessary truths concerning causal relations. Our inclination to think in terms of what can be represented in the imagination will further reinforce the tendencies both to deny genuineness to certain paralogates and to redefine the paralogates in terms of logical or epistemological relations. For the imagination cannot represent potency or other causal relations or actual existence as such.

The error of overt idealism that *esse est percipi*, cannot be accounted for the way we have accounted for covert idealism. In Appendix I, however, I show how parageneric abstraction does account for it.

Concerning U-turns and paralogues, we can be brief. Like epistemological fallacies, U-turns are not necessarily caused by parageneric abstraction, but they can work hand in hand with it. U-turns provide philosophers with additional reasons for understanding paralogues as affirmable of only some of their paralogates. For the philosopher will think the only genuine paralogates are those dealt with by the particular method that infatuates him. Any use of a parageneric word which appears to contradict what that word asserts in the domain of knowledge with which he is making a U-turn will be rejected a priori. The classic example here is the confining of causality to the role it plays, if any, in the methods of empirical science.

Paradoxes resulting from the simultaneous use of paralogues to both affirm something and deny something of their secondary paralogates can incline us to understand a paralogue only as objectifying difference between paralogates. The least that can be said about epistemological fallacies and U-turns is that they can considerably reinforce, and can themselves be reinforced by, these inclinations.

11.5.2 Commitments to non-cognitive values

Epistemological fallacies and U-turns amount to commitments on the part of philosophers to the importance of certain facts about human knowledge, facts about the manner in which things are made objects or facts about the power of certain intellectual methods. We may therefore describe these fallacies as misguided value commitments, the values in question being values associated with cognition. But commitments to values not concerned solely with cognition can also put us in the position of misunderstanding sentences whose opposites are self-evidently contradictory. Religious or anti-religious commitments, moral, political and aesthetic commitments, commitments concerning the meaning of human freedom and fulfillment, all these can incline us toward a cyclopic understanding of a paralogue; for they can result in claims of sovereignty over the proper use of parageneric words.

Because of such commitments a philosopher will do more than *believe* truths in which paralogues objectify in certain ways. He will also assign a special importance to these truths and, therefore, to the ways in which paralogues operate in them. This importance will make these ways of operating appear to be the only genuine ones. And the philosopher will consider himself to have objective reasons for refusing to assent to any affirmation or denial of a paralogue which appears to contradict or weaken those affirmations or denials which are significant to him from the point of view of his value commitments. I am assuming, by the way, that the philosopher can be attaching significance to *truths*. The problem does not necessarily lie with the values a philosopher is committed to but with what be sincerely thinks he has to do to protect them. Affirming or denying a parageneric word of some paralogate may appear to contradict a statement necessary to articulate or defend a value to which he is committed.

Here are two of the many propositions in discussions of which it is very difficult for philosophers to leave their value commitments aside: freedom of choice is inconsistent with causality; the existence of God is inconsistent with evil. How many times have you walked away from a debate over such a question thinking something like "My opponent won't accept my position because he thinks it contradicts truth T. But I agree with T. Why can't he *see* that I am not contradicting T?" A sufficient reason for his difficulty in seeing this is that T affirms or denies a paralogue, say P, of something.

On the one hand, commitments to cognitive or non-cognitive values may make affirming or denying P of this thing specially important to the opponent. On the other hand, the premises of your argument may include or imply a truth in which the same thing is objectified by a denial made with the same paralogue that T affirms or an affirmation made with the same paralogue that T denies. Since P is a parageneric word-function, the apparent contradiction could not be removed simply by using a different word for P in each case. And the apparent contradiction looks all the more real due to the opponent's value commitment to the way P objectifies in T.

Or you may have walked away from this kind of debate thinking "My opponent's position contradicts truth T. But he claims to agree with me about T. Why can't he *see* that he is really contradicting T?" Again, T may affirm or deny P of some paralogate. And the premises of the opponent's argument may require him to affirm P of the paralogate as T denies it or deny P as T affirms it. He fails to see this, however, because his premises also require him to affirm P where T affirms, or deny P where T denies, but *otherwise* than as T affirms or denies it. Or the opponent's desire to avoid the apparent contradictions associated with P may lead him, in order to save T, to reinterpret P as a logical or epistemological relation. But he will not think of himself as distorting either T or P since the strength of his value commitments will have made him confident that his is the only valid understanding of what is and is not objectified by P.

In these debates, the person who understands the paralogue as something with respect to which paralogates are similar *knows* that he is not contradicting T or *knows* that his opponent is contradicting T. For he knows that contradictions follow if the truths both of certain affirmations and of certain denials involving the paralogue are denied. But powerful forces can cause the similarity objectified by a paralogue to be suppressed in our thinking. And because the same word-function that objectifies the difference which is not suppressed is needed to objectify the similarity which is suppressed, we fail to recognize necessary causal relations which all the paralogates have in common or which are specific to the secondary paralogate as an instance of the paralogue.

It will by no means be easy, therefore, for someone who has discovered a philosphical truth, and who indeed knows that it is a truth, to show all of his colleagues that it is the truth. Parageneric abstraction even makes it possible for *legitimate* value commitments to become obstacles to the knowledge of philosophical truth. (More examples of parageneric word-functions in philosophical discourse will be found in Simon, 1960b, Cahalan, 1971, and in the references of the latter article. Maritain, 1959, pp. 326-338—and see pp. 311-319, has explained another way in which parageneric language associated with value commitments can be in apparent contradiction to philosophical truths.)

11.6 The Philosophical Limits of Formal Systems

The nature of parageneric abstraction allows us to demonstrate that the methods of formal languages, so successful in logic and mathematics, cannot be extended to philosophy. This needs to be shown because the precision and clarity that formal systems offer make the formal approach to philosphical problems one of the most seductive versions of the U-turn. Fed up with the muddles, paradoxes and slipshod uses of language that are so common in philosophy, philosophers have sought a way out in formal method. That formal systems do provide precision and clarity cannot be doubted. But it is more than doubtful that the conditions necessary for formal systems to achieve these results are present when *ontological* issues, and logical issues associated with them, are under consideration.

In the first place, it should be understood by now that *no* attempt to solve philosophical problems linguistically can be adequate. Philosophical problems could be treated as linguistic if and only if the knowledge of meaning that is pertinent to necessity was lexicological knowledge, and the relations between meanings that were pertinent to necessity were exclusively logical. This fact is enough to deprive formal systems of any direct relevance to philosophy. But the *ontological* character of philosophical word-functions make their irrelevance even clearer.

Can we settle ontological questions by constructing systems of rules for manipulating symbols, rules yielding formulas which can be given interpretation by means of ontological sentences? A particular symbolic formula may, of course, have ontological interpretations. But the reason formal languages use symbols is to allow us to *abstract* from particular meaning$_T$ for which language-forms may be used. Formal systems abstract from the specific features characterizing their domains of interpretation. But that is precisely what the language of ontology cannot do. If the word-functions of ontological sentences abstracted from the differences between the things of which these sentences are true, being and other ontological word-functions would relate to their kinds as genera to species. Therefore addressing ontological problems begins somewhere after deriving formulas according to rules for manipulating symbols ends. (Recall in this connection the irrelevance to symbolic logic of distinguishing between quantifying over real existents and cognition-dependent objects, a distinction that is essential to ontological analysis. Recall also our discussion of the ontological as opposed to the logical interpretation of the principles of non-contradiction and excluded middle in section 5.4.)

Thus parageneric abstraction is a sufficient reason why we cannot solve philosophical problems by using formal methods. Ontological word-functions are paralogues or are the kinds of which paralogues are asserted and denied; the same is true of those logical word-functions, like abstraction and otherness, associated with ontological word-functions. Such are the topics philosophy deals with, and such are topics giving rise to problems immune to treatment by formal methods.

There is one more reason why formal languages are of no direct help in doing philosophy. Each logical operator of a formal system is defined solely by relations between the formulas in which it occurs and other formulas. And the variables of the system are treated *purely as terms* of such relations. Consequently we can answer questions by calculating results according to formal rules only in those areas, such as logic and mathematics, where we are interested in objects as nothing more than terms of relations. When we are interested in objects from a perspective which does not allow them to be treated merely as terms of relations, it is beside the point to try to answer questions by deriving formulas according to rules for manipulating otherwise meaning$_T$less symbols.

But philosophical method is ontological. It analyzes its objects in relation to cognition-independent existence. And, whatever else may be true of real existence, it cannot be that real existence is nothing more than the term of a relation. This is just another way of putting what we demonstrated against Berkeley in section 2.2.2. If to exist were nothing more than what is objectified by a description of it as a term of a relation, to exist would amount to being nothing. For all the reality asserted by describing something as term of a relation belongs to whatever bears the relation, not to that which terminates it.

If the relation happens to be one that existence bears to itself, still describing existence as term of the relation does not objectify the fact that it also bears the relation. It may imply that existence is also the bearer of the relation, but only if existence *is* something more than a mere term of a relation. And for the description to imply something about the nature of the term of the relation, it must enable us to describe the term other than merely as term of a relation. Or at least, we must be able to describe it as term of a relation that is defined by features belonging to its term, features themselves describable other than merely as terms of relations.

Philosophy, of course, investigates material relations (there is nothing else for it to study unless there are formal relations). But the relations that are the meanings$_T$ of parageneric words cannot be studied in abstraction from the natures of the different things to which they can be attributed. Formal method, on the other hand, hypothesizes that the relations between variables, the relations which constitute the meanings$_T$ of the constants of the system, abstract from the nature of whatever things may be taken as interpretations of the variables. Therefore, in the domain of ontological analysis, formal languages can do everything but tell us what we need to know.

The fact that formal method treats objects purely as terms of relations, by the way, explains the superficial similarity between logic and mathematics and the usefulness of formal systems in both disciplines. Both are interested in the individuals of their domains only as terms of relations, although the relations in question are of different kinds, logical relations in one case, quantitative relations in the other. As a result, both abstract from whatever is true of the terms of these relations other than as terms of these relations.

That is what makes it possible to do mathematics and logic by means of manipulating symbols according to systems of rules so constructed that the relations between the symbols correspond to logical and mathematical relations. But causal analysis of the way in which formal languages achieve clarity and precision shows that this method of obtaining these desirable results is foreign to the requirements of philosophy. Those who have used this method to bring clarity to philosophy have only succeeded in compounding confusion.

As involving paralogues, ontological issues are difficult enough on their own. Handling them with the methods proper to other objects requires redefining them and, to that extent, replacing our original questions with substitutes. Now we have two kinds of problems where we began with only one. We have our original ontological questions to answer, and we have the problem of explaining to the U-turner that his way of dealing with them misses the mark. How often have you had the experience of reading a philosopher whose thought was lucidly clear only to discover that the clarity was in strict proportion to his failure to solve—or even directly engage—the true difficulties of the subject he was addressing? The clarity achieved was of a kind irrelevant, or even inimical, to the requirements of the philosophical problem.

We do not have to look far for examples: the irrelevance of the non-predicate theory of "exists", the circularity of interpreting "A rose is a thing" as the material mode of speech for "'Rose' is a thing-word", the failure of Quine's critique of necessity, of Ryle's account of dispositions, of the linguistic ontologist's turning of linguistic differences into differences in beliefs about what exists, of Quine's making existential quantification the test of "ontological" commitment, of the formalist's attempt to read science as a formal system interpreted by means of correspondence rules and observation terms, especially of his attempt to define causal terms by means of logical relations and observation terms alone. And so on.

A final point. We sometimes hear it said that mathematical ability is a help in doing philosophy. In fact, it is often a hindrance or at least has proven so historically. The reason it is thought to be a help is that mathematics, like philosophy, uses abstraction. But the analysis just completed shows that the kind of abstraction which characterizes philosophy is radically different from that which characterizes mathematics. Simon tried to find paralogues in mathematics. But he could not succeed in showing a case in which the same word-function by means of which mathematics allocates objects to a class must be used in distinguishing members of the class from one another.

His example (1960b, p. 29) was the use of "circle" in Euclidean and in taxi-cab geometry. In both cases, "circle" refers to a set of points equidistant from a single point. What differentiates the circle in taxi-cab space is that the distance is measured by the meter of a taxi traveling square city blocks. But to describe the distance as measured or not measured by this means is to add a specific difference the way we add "rational" or "irrational" to "animal". "As measured by the meter of a taxi-cab traveling square city blocks" is neither a reaffirmation nor an attenuation of what is expressed by "distance", "equality" or "set of points". Therefore "circle" as here defined expresses a genus of which the Euclidean and taxi-cab varieties are species.

Unlike mathematics, philosophy must use word-functions that do not unqualifiedly abstract from differences between the kinds of which they are predicated, nor can philosophy deal with its objects as nothing more than terms of relations. This is why realists have always found wanting the philosophy produced by mathematically oriented thinkers like Plato and Descartes. But in candor, it must be admitted that this is also why realists have not made the contributions they should have made to the philosophy of mathematics.

11.7 Philosophy's Predicament

The upshot of our analysis of parageneric abstraction is that formidable obstacles stand in the way of the discovery and communication of philosophical truth. Self-evident truths whose word-functions are paralogues are prey to all sorts of misunderstandings, misunderstandings that can only be cleared up by means of other sentences whose word-functions are paralogues. Because a paralogue can be used to make both an affirmation and a denial regarding a secondary paralogate, philosophical truth lies on a razor-thin line between yes and no, is and is not. History shows that the slightest nudge, especially a nudge from a commitment to cognitive or non-cognitive values or from relying on the imagination as our means of understanding, can make us step off that line.

It follows that we cannot expect the same degree of consensus in philosophy that we find in other disciplines. Philosophy does know intersubjectively communicable truths, but our ability to recognize and communicate truth is determined by subjective conditions. The evidence verifying a philosphical statement, namely, the fact that its word-functions are what they are, is just as public as is the cognition-independent existence sensation puts us in contact with. But the ability to distinguish sensation from other modes of awareness requires the presence of enabling conditions, or the absence of interfering conditions, other than sensation itself. And the conditions under which the grasp of philosophical truth must take place make the likelihood of error greater in philosophy than elsewhere.

Can we expect to gradually improve our chances of avoiding error as time goes on? Progress in philosophy is much like progress in moral, political and social matters: there is progress in that which is good and progress in that which is bad. And it is not enough for a philosopher to assent to a truth; he must assent to the truth for the right reason. Therefore there are indefinitely many more ways of being wrong in philosophy than being right.

And as time goes on we invent new ways of being wrong. Like practitioners of empirical knowledge, philosophers are capable of learning from the errors of the past. But philosophers are also ingenious at producing new errors and at finding new ways to repeat old errors. Every generation produces new opportunities for epistemological fallacies as we learn more about human knowledge and new opportunities for U-turns as we develop new intellectual disciplines or make dramatic new discoveries in old disciplines. There is no final cure for these problems for the same reason that there can be no vaccine for all forms of influenza; the cause of the problem evolves too quickly.

Nor do philosophers necessarily learn to communicate better as time goes on. Occasions for misunderstandings among philosophers multiply as philosophical traditions break off into sub-traditions, each adopting their own definitions for the same stock of words. In the recent past, for instance, young students of philosophy have learned that the question of causality is *really* the question of the conformity of events to laws, that the question of necessary truth is *really* the question of what can be known from acquaintance with meanings$_L$, that the question of substance is *really* the question of an ultimate subject of predication, that the question of existence is *really* a linguistic question, etc. Again, this is not to say that philosophical knowledge is not communicable. It is. But as sociological phenomena, philosophy and empirical science differ in the degree of lasting consensus among experts (sociologically defined) they can achieve.

Previous analyses of philosophical method have offered, in general, two ways of responding to this fact of philosophy's life. One response has been to look for a method of doing philosophy that will eliminate its disputes and give it the same degree of sociological respectability that other disciplines have achieved. The other response has been to deny the validity of philosophy as a distinct mode of knowing. Philosophy has the difficulties it has because its very existence as a method distinct from other methods is due to some sort of mistake; the method we need is one that will expose the mistake, not one that will find solutions for problems that do not exist.

These responses are not so far apart. They both require us to U-turn

some other method either into the method of doing philosophy or
into the method that will take the place of philosophy as ultimate in
human knowledge. Like all U-turns, therefore, these remedies for
philosophy's ills suffer from self-referential inconsistency. But what
is especially embarrassing is that instead of saving us from the paradox
and disagreement that plague philosophy, these remedies always wind
up generating more. Empirical science achieves a much greater degree
of consensus than does philosophy. But philosophies holding that empirical methods are the only methods of acquiring knowledge about
what exists achieve no more consensus among empirical philosophers
than do non-empirical philosophies among non-empirical
philosophers. And one can hardly accuse empiricism of failing to provide us with paradoxes. The clarity and precision of formal languages
are unsurpassable. But the result of applying them to philosophical
questions has been philosophy that is just as fuzzy and muddled as
philosophy has always been.

Experience shows that we cannot suppress philosophical questions.
It also shows that trying to answer them in ways that are dressed in
the trappings of other disciplines or trying to give reasons why they
should be suppressed only succeeds in perpetuating the ills, namely,
paradox and disagreement, that were supposed to be cured. To borrow
some words Economos (1977) has used for a different purpose, the
history of attempts to eliminate paradox and disagreement in philosophy is the history of "excruciatingly reiterated re-explorations of certi-
fied dead-ends which have fair entrances . . . . dead ends . . . . so
appealing and so accessible that (philosophers) will always rediscover
them". The entrances are fair because of the virtues of the particular
method one is counting on to set philosophy straight. But the fact is
that all ways of doing philosophy, or of suppressing philosophy, produce paradox and disagreement and that all philosophers are willing
to consider solvable those paradoxes that follow from premises they
consider necessarily true, especially premises about what causes are
necessary or sufficient for knowledge of sentential truth.

I, too, wish there was less confusion and controversy in philosophy.
But if I wanted to hear as well as a dog or see as well as an eagle,
it would do no good pretending that my inability to do so was
psychosomatic in origin. And trying to straighten out philosophy by
importing methods from other disciplines is like treating an organically
caused condition as if it were psychosomatic. The treatment *can* have
a placebo effect, however. Philosophers can deceive themselves into
thinking they are solving, or dissolving, troublesome philosoph-

ical problems when they are only replacing them with other questions.

Imagine someone who knew nothing about philosophy prior to the *Philosophical Investigations* or *Word and Object* but who was familiar with the discussions subsequent to these works. That person could say what people have always said about philosophy, "You philosophers never agree on anything, and all you do is create paradoxes". But the methods of the linguistic turn were adopted because they were supposed to replace paradox with clarity and make agreement possible.

The self-deception of philosophers is reinforced by the fact that, at any moment in the history of philosophy, the majority of philosophers in a given culture can share a significant number of assumptions. Their degree of consensus will be far from that which characterizes other disciplines. But together with our propensity for wishful thinking, that much consensus can be sufficient for us to overlook the fact that *temporary* agreement on a large number of assumptions has *usually* been the case in philosophy. Consequently we will believe that our generation of philosophers is on the verge of the same kind of sociological success that our colleagues in other fields have achieved. Only tomorrow, however, philosophers will be saying of us, "Philosophy could not have come as far as it has without the work of our esteemed predecessors, but unlike them, we now know what we have to do to eliminate paradox and achieve lasting consensus in philosophy".

The methods that U-turners try to make ultimate in human knowledge are in themselves methods for acquiring rational knowledge. But the U-turners' belief that there are no legitimate philosophical questions other than those that can be posed and answered in terms of his method is just as much an act of *faith* as is any religious act of faith. There is this difference between philosophical and religious acts of faith, however; a philosophical act of faith is truly *blind* since it thinks of itself as rational knowledge.

But what if there was an explanation of philosophy's predicament that did not criticize other views of philosophical method for things it was equally guilty of. This explanation would not pretend to rescue us from the confusion and controversy which have always been the facts of philosophical life and to which it is itself subject. But at the same time it would not find in these facts a reason to consider philosophy invalid as a distinct mode of knowing, thereby falling into the inconsistency of philosophizing to show that one should not philosophize. This explanation would be consistent both with itself and with the history of contrary ways of dealing with philosophy's predicament.

Such an explanation is precisely what follows from our analysis of philosophical method as ontological. Ontological word-functions and key logical word-functions associated with them, are paragenerically abstracted. And parageneric abstraction shows why *valid* philosophizing must produce apparent contradictions and cannot produce the same degree of intersubjective communication of truth that is achieved by other modes of knowing. Philosophical evidence is supplied by meanings$_T$ for which we *jointly* use words. And like any technical language, philosophy's language derives from, and is explained in terms of, ordinary language. But philosophy's use of words for meanings$_T$ found in ordinary language produces paradoxes which the ordinary use of these words does not, paradoxes that follow from logical and causal relations between these meanings$_T$.

My explanation of philosophy's predicament does not claim to cure philosophy's diseases while suffering from them itself. All other accounts of confusion and controversy in philosophy have done just that. Just as ontological analysis is self-referentially consistent as a method of answering ultimate questions, so it is self-referentially consistent in explaining philosophy's predicament. Ontological analysis' showing that the nature of philosophical word-functions prevents us from achieving the same degree of consensus here as in other fields is not a reason to reject philosophy, and especially its core, metaphysics, as a mode of knowing that is valid in its own right. It is a reason to *continue* doing philosophy without substituting for its method the method of some non-ontological, and hence non-ultimate, discipline.

The issues philosophy deals with are so significant for mankind that there is only one goal worthy of the philosopher: certitude of truth caused by awareness of evidence sufficient to exclude the opposite from truth—in a word, knowledge. Philosophical method must be judged by that goal. And evaluating philosophical method by whether it can yield certitude based on sufficient evidence is not the same as evaluating it by the sociological standard of widespread and long-lasting consensus among philosophers. The evidence for philosophical truth is intersubjectively communicable. But communicability is one thing, success in communication is another. Successful communication of knowledge depends on the fact that the evidence (word-functions philosophers can be jointly acquainted with) is public, but it depends on the presence and absence of other causes as well.

To what degree do the causes of philosophy's predicament make communication of truth more difficult in philosophy than in other fields? The history of philosophy, including contemporary philosophy, is there to answer that question. What that history shows is not just that after 2500 years the most brilliant minds continually produce outrageous opinions, often as a result of simplistic errors. It shows that they do these things in the name of epistemological rigor, tough-minded thinking, skepticism toward metaphysical speculation—not to mention the precision and clarity they promise to bring to philosophy from the methods of other disciplines. That should tell us something about the tendency, when doing philosophy, to sub-stitute for evidence such things as excitement with the new, wishful thinking, the plausibility generated by consensus among our peers, and the desire to achieve preconceived results. That should also tell us something about how much hope there is for eliminating this tendency from philosophy.

Idealism, Wittgenstein and Freedom of Choice

In this appendix I will show how the error of overt idealism, that to be is to be known, results from parageneric abstraction. The analysis will allow me to comment on some of Wittgenstein's views concerning language and the mental. I will also apply the results of the analysis to the problem of freedom of choice.

I.1 Overt Idealism

Showing how parageneric abstraction contributes to the ultimate form of the epistemological fallacy will give me the chance to explain another way in which "exists" is used paragenerically, a way that is central to several of the philosophical problems we have encountered in this study.

My argument against the identity of being and being-known began by noting a difference between objects to which we do not attribute real existence and objects to which we do. The argument concerned the second kind of object. What I there called "real" existence (and "cognition-independent" or "extra-objective" existence), the existence attributable to a substance or accident, I could have called "entitative" existence, the existence things have for themselves, not just for us as terms of our knowledge relations. Then I could have said that to be known is to have an existence which *is* real but which is "inten-

tional" rather than entitative. For to be the term of a knowledge relation *is* to exist for the knower as its object.

Wittgenstein, unknowingly, stated why this is the case in the
following passage:

> The idea that that which we wish to happen must be present as a
> shadow in our wish is deeply rooted in our forms of expression.
> But, in fact, we might say that it is only the next best absurdity to
> the one which we should really like to say. IF IT WEREN'T TOO
> ABSURD (my emphasis) we should say that the fact which we wish
> for must be present in our wish. For how can we wish just this to
> happen if just this isn't present in our wish? It is quite true to say:
> The mere shadow won't do; for it stops short before the object; and
> we want the wish to contain the object itself. We want that the wish
> that Mr. Smith should come into this room should wish that just
> Mr. Smith, and no substitute, should do the *coming*, and no substi-
> tute for that, *into my room*, and no substitute for that. (1965, p. 37)

Precisely. How can there be *identity* between what is thought and
what exists or can exist extra-objectively unless what is thought *is* what
exists or can exist extra-objectively? But why should it be absurd, when
explaining what it means for something to be "in" thought, that is,
for an object to be a term of a knowledge relation, to say that
knowledge is a state in which the object really exists for the knower
with an existence that is other than the existence by which it is or can
be more-than-an-*object*? Why should it be absurd, that is, if the identity between object and thing concerns only *that which has* either kind
of existence, not the kind of existence it has?

There is a reason, however, why this should appear to be absurd.
For existence is the word-function which *distinguishes* what is only
an object of knowledge from what is more-than-an-*object*. Consequently, if this word-function is not a paralogue, it is contradictory to describe
an object's status as term of a knowledge relation as an existence of
the object. If existence is a paralogue, on the other hand, it may be
both in some way affirmed and in some way denied of being-an-*object*,
while it is unqualifiedly affirmed of its primary paralogate, extra-objective existence. If so, substantial and accidental existence would be
paralogates of entitative existence, and entitative and intentional existence would be paralogates of real existence. But why consider being
the term of a knowledge relation to be a paralogate of real existence?

Because, as argued in section 9.4.3, the object known is a
characterizing cause of the knowledge relation. That is what Wittgenstein's example shows. To describe a wish one must include a description of that which is wished for; the same is true of any conscious

relation. A thing's being what it is (actually or possibly) is entitatively other than our awareness of this thing's being what it is. But our awareness would not be what it is if this thing were not what it is. Therefore the object is a cause of our knowledge being what it is.

Section 9.4.3 showed that the object is a characterizing cause. Like any other characterizing cause, the object is something that provides the knowledge relation with characteristics it would not otherwise have, being the thought of Mr. Smith, for instance, and not of Mr. Jones. And since it provides the knowledge relation with characteristics it would not otherwise have, the object causes the knower to exist in a way he would not otherwise exist: as someone thinking of Mr. Smith.

But the object is not a characterizing cause of a knowledge relation insofar as the relation is an accident entitatively existing in the knower. For accidents themselves are characterizing causes. When an accident exists, a component cause, ultimately a substance, has received an accidental characterizing cause making that component cause exist, entitatively, in a way that it would otherwise not exist. But the object is not (or need not be as far as the nature of knowledge relations are concerned) a way in which the knower exists either substantially or accidentally. Being Mr. Smith, where ''being'' refers to that existence which is other than being-an-*object*, is something none of us accomplish simply by knowing him.

In what way then does the object cause the existence of knowledge? If it does not cause some existence, it is not a cause at all. On the one hand, Mr. Smith is something (as an actual or possible extra-objective existent) other than the knowledge relation and something without which the knowledge relation would not be what it is; Mr. Smith is a cause of the knowledge. On the other hand, Mr. Smith is a cause of neither substantial nor accidental existence. The knowledge-of Mr. Smith is a characterizing cause by which a substance exists accidentally as a knower. But the object is a characterizing cause of that knowledge, and therefore of the knower, that doesn't give substantial or accidental characteristics to the knower or his knowledge.

The object can be something other than the knowledge without which the knowledge would not be what it is, if and only if the object causes the knowledge to have characteristics that exist otherwise than by the substantial or accidental existence of either the knower, the knowledge or the object—other, that is, than the existence by which the knower, the knowledge and the object are more-than-*objects*. In other words, the object causes the knowledge to be what it is in a mode of existence other than entitative. And the characteristics that are given this mode of existence are identical with the object itself. The object itself is what exists in this non-entitative mode; for the effect that the causality of the object accounts for is nothing other than the fact that the knowledge is characterized by having this object and not some other. The effect of which Mr. Smith is the characterizing cause is the (non-entitative) existence of Mr. Smith as term of a knowledge relation belonging (entitatively) to the knower. (Mr. Smith is not a cause of himself but of an existence other than his entitative existence.) Consequently knowledge is, along with whatever else it might be, an existence of the object for the knower. It is this kind of existence that is called intentional.

This reasoning can perhaps be put more intuitively. We might be tempted to imagine the relation knowledge-of as if it were an antenna reaching out and touching objects external to us. The antenna analogy fails for two crucial reasons. First, the object touched by the antenna is completely external to the antenna. The antenna touches something that happens to be at a particular place, but if something else were at that place, the antenna would remain what it is. Knowledge of a particular object, however, is not the same as knowledge of another object. The word-function knowledge-of is *logically* included in both knowledges, but the knowledges are *really* distinct. The relation that exists when knowledge of X exists is similar to but different from the relation that exists when knowledge of Y exists.

Second, unlike an antenna that would be spatially exterior to the knower, knowledge remains within the knower as an entitative characteristic. My relation to the object has its existence entirely within me. However that relation manages to terminate in an entitatively external object, it terminates in the object without becoming external itself. If I am thinking of X at a particular time, I am different from what I would be if I were thinking of Y. The fact that X is my object is a characteristic of my being such that, were the object other than what it is, I would be to that extent other than what I am.

In other words, without being part of the entitative reality of the knowledge or the knower, the object is a characteristic of the knowledge and the knower. But a characteristic of something exists with the thing of which it is a characteristic, when that thing exists. X is a characteristic of that which exists when knowledge of X exists—a characteristic without which knowledge of X would *not* exist. Therefore X exists when knowledge of X exists but with an existence other than the entitative existence of the knowledge, the knower or the object. My relation to the object remains interior to me while terminating in what is entitatively exterior to me, because it makes that object exist interiorly to me in a non-entitative mode of existence.

Note that being, as that which exists entitatively, is still logically included in all other word-functions. For entitative existence is not only deniable but also affirmable of intentional existence. If knowledge did not have entitative existence, it would be nothing, absolutely speaking. But *that which* exists entitatively when knowledge exists is something that must itself be described as a type of existence distinct from the entitative type, a type of existence by which the object of knowledge exists not for itself but for another.

The same conclusion can be reached in at least one other way. In sections 3.3.2 and 6.3.4, I argued that truth requires a relation of identity between a thing and itself, not between a thing and something really distinct from itself. And in section 6.3.4, I argued that the relation between a description and a thing cannot be understood as a relation to some *tertium quid* standing between the description and what the described thing is. How, then, do sentences become so related to things that they are true?

We are enabled to use otherwise meaningless sounds and marks meaningfully by psychological states (namely, acquaintance with word-functions) really distinct from the things objectified by using sounds and marks meaningfully. Sentences can become so related to things that the identity required for truth holds if and only if a psychological state enabling us to use a language-form meaningfully is not a *tertium quid* relative to what the thing objectified by a language-form is. For if we explain the identity between things and what is objectified by language-forms in terms of our acquaintance with the meanings$_T$ of language-forms, how do we explain the identity between things and what is objectified by these relations of acquaintance?

At some point in the explanation of our knowledge of truth, the relation between a psychological state and the thing objectified by means of it must *not* be a relation between the thing and something non-identical with itself. From one point of view, a psychological state is a *tertium quid* between language and what is objectified by means of language. But from another point of view, such a psychological state must be identical with what is objectified by some language-form. However, this identity is not between what is objectified and the psychological state considered as an entitative existent. If so, we could use language to refer only to our subjective mental states.

What allows the identity required for truth to hold is that the existence of the psychological states enabling us to use language meaningfully (conscious states which are features entitatively existing in the knower) is at the same time the existence of something entitatively other than our psychological states (and entitatively other than the knower). Conscious states, in other words, are two-sided affairs having an entitative existence by which they are accidents of the knower and an intentional existence by which they are the existence of something entitatively other (actually or possibly) than the knower or his accidents. There is a real distinction between what is objectified by the language-forms of a sentence and what exists entitatively when our acquaintance with the word-functions of the sentence exists. But there need be no more than a logical distinction between what is objectified by a sentence and what exists intentionally when our acquaintance with word-functions exists. (Those who hold that all beliefs are subjective are thinking only of their entitative side; naive realists think only of their intentional side.)

It has often been argued that the postulation of psychological states (concepts, thoughts, images, etc.) does not advance our explanation of how consciousness and language relate to what is other than themselves. The reason the postulation does not appear to explain what it is supposed to explain is that it usually supplies these states with only entitative existence. And the mere multiplication of things with only entitative existence cannot explain knowledge relations. Psychological entities must have another mode of existence as well.

But the postulation of another mode of existence on the side of *the knower* still seems to leave the knowledge relation unexplained as long as *the known object* remains other than the knower and his knowledge. The same problem occurs for the new mode of existence that occurred for entitative existence: how is the relation to the *object* established; why is knowledge *of* X knowledge of **X**? A new mode of existence on the side of the knower solves the problem if and only if it is also a new mode of existence for the object, an existence by which the known itself exists within consciousness.

In short, conscious states differ from all other modes of entitative existence because, in them, something entitatively existing acquires a new mode of existence. Because a conscious state is the intentional existence of one thing rather than another, it is consciousness-of this thing rather than the other. And because consciousness is an existence of the object itself, the thing-object identity required for truth is possible. (Intentional existence is not a *presupposition* of my account of truth, however. It is a *conclusion* arrived at by a methodology I have defended independently of it.)

Truth is not the only issue for which the two-sided character of consciousness has implications. Since the object itself really exists in consciousness, there is no need for the acts by which we interpret language to be themselves subject to interpretation ad infinitum. In interpreting "red" as used for red, we do not relate the word red to some mental image that is really distinct from the color red, or rather we relate it to a mental image which is entitatively distinct from the color red but which also is the color red itself existing in us intentionally. And why do we accept one way of carrying out the order "Add 2!" as correct and consider all others incorrect? Because the entitatively existing psychological state by which we interpret these marks is at the same time the intentional but real existence of nothing other than that particular quantitative relation which is taken to be the meaning$_T$ of "Add 2!".

In other words, intentional existence is needed to complete Wittgenstein's account of language. Awareness of publicly observable objects (that is, actual entitative existents) is a necessary condition for language. But it is equally necessary that our acquaintance with the uses of words be nothing short of an existence of that for which words are used. Only the distinction between the entitative and the intentional existence of conscious states saves this requirement of language from contradiction. But that requirement saves language itself from contradiction.

Wittgenstein's disdain for "mental" acts in the explanation of language was due to his taking privacy or the conscious subject's *self*-awareness as what is characteristic of the mental. Thus his favorite example of sensation is pain, which is a form of self-consciousness. In self-consciousness, it is the entitatively existing subject of consciousness that acquires a new, intentional mode of existence as object known. But it is the fact that consciousness is equally able to be consciousness of what is entitatively other than the self that makes language possible. (Do not equate the question of what makes mental states capable of explaining knowledge with the question of whether it is privacy or intentionality that should distinguish the mental from the physical for the purposes of the mind-body problem.)

Why did Wittgenstein view the mental only as a relation to the self and overlook it as a relation to the other? One reason is the Cartesian, epistemological heritage of modern philosophy. Another reason, however, was Wittgenstein's *correctly* perceiving that consciousness' relation to the other could be helpful in explaining language only if that relation consisted in the other itself having a real existence in our consciousness. That appears to be the absurdity of the existentially other not being existentially other. And it would be an absurdity were existence not a paralogue fully affirmable of what exists entitatively while affirmable of what exists intentionally only with the hedge that what exists intentionally does not exist for itself but only for another.

It is important to note that the function of intentional existence is *not* to explain awareness of, or reference to, that which does not exist entitatively. Intentional existence is just as much needed to explain knowledge relations terminated by actual entities. Since to exist entitatively is always other than to be known, entitative existence is never sufficient for something's being objectified. When actual entitative existents are objects of knowledge, they have an existence for the knower that is over and above their entitative existence.

But since it is intentional, not entitative, existence that makes actual entitative existents objects of knowledge, there is nothing to prevent intentional existence from making non-actual entities objects of knowledge. Knowledge relations can terminate in what does not exist entitatively because these relations *are* ways in which their terms exist, even when their terms also have an entitative existence. This is what I meant by saying that nothing is needed for reference to the nonexistent that is not needed for reference to the existent. (It should be clear, therefore, that Russell's theory of descriptions is ontologically irrelevant. The fact that "there is someone who is king and who is bald" can be substituted for "The king is bald" may have some logical significance. It has nothing whatsoever to do with whether the meaningful use of language requires that what is objectified by a phrase like "someone who is king" have an existence within our consciousness.)

I have hitherto used "real existence" exclusively for entitative existence both to take advantage of our intuitive association of this paralogue with its primary paralogate and to avoid having to raise unnecessary problems. Problems cannot be put off forever, however, and we have here an excellent example of the fact that philosophical paradox cannot be resolved, as in *The Blue Book*, simply by using different words for the same paralogue. For want of using "existence" paragenerically, some existentialists found it necessary to describe consciousness as nothingness. They saw intentional existence *as opposed to* entitative and could not accept the apparent contradiction of consciousness being an intentional mode of existence and having an entitative mode of existence at the same time.

Their error is the mirror-image of that of the ontological idealists.

For the idealist, any existence other than the intentional is nothingness. They see what is other than the term of a knowledge relation as other than an existent because they recognize that being the term of a knowledge relation *is* a genuine mode of existence. And because there is nothing abstractably common to intentional and entitative existence that is not something which also distinguishes them from one another, idealists find it contradictory to describe the existence that terminates our knowledge relations when objects are sensed, rather than imagined or conceived, as other than being-known. Overt ontological idealism, in other words, is made possible both by the identity between things and objects and by the fact that existence is a paralogue that is a respect in which being an object and being an extra-objective thing are similar and at the same time is what distinguishes being an extra-objective thing from merely being an object.

I.2 Freedom of Choice

The discussion of the principles of empirical knowledge (section 8.2) showed that the necessity of a cause producing an effect with certain characteristics is grounded in the cause's having certain characteristics. Because a thing has certain causal dispositions, in a given set of circumstances it will produce an effect of a certain kind. By being what they are, in other words, things are oriented toward behavior of one kind rather than another. Since whatever exists must have some specific characteristics and lack others, every cause is oriented toward its behavior by necessity of its nature. For a cause not to be determined to behave in a certain way, it would have to be true that the cause was not one specific kind of thing.

This argument appears to exclude the possibility of freedom of choice in the sense of freedom from causal determination. An undetermined cause would have to exist in some sort of generalized way to escape the determination that specific natures impose on things. But nothing could exist in such a way. Whatever exists entitatively is concrete and individual. Generality has existence only as a logical relation, that is, existence as a perceived relation terminated by objects and means of objectification apprehended as such. (Logical relations are intentionally existing characterizing causes pertaining to objects and means of objectification as objects and means of objectification.)

That nothing can exist in a generalized way is true of entitative existence. However, the very presuppositions of the question show that it is not true of intentional existence. To say that generality has only a logical status is to say that it characterizes things only insofar as they are objects, that is, insofar as they exist intentionally in consciousness. Generality pertains to the word-functions of predicates as linguistically objectifiable rather than as that which extra-objective existents are. As linguistically objectifiable, word-functions of predicates exist in consciousness in a state of generality, a state of applicability to more than one entitative existent.

This state of generality allows conscious orientation toward behavior to escape causal determination without contradiction to the argument for determination, since that argument concerns entitative existence only. It is not the generality of just any word-functions that makes freedom possible. But in making decisions governing our behavior, we ask questions like "What is the meaning of life?", "What should my goal in life be?", "What is happiness?", "What is the good life?", "Are there any values worth pursuing for their own sake and not for the sake of anything else?" To ask these questions we must be acquainted with word-functions such as those of "meaning of life", "goal", "happiness", "good", "value". And the fact that we can be without answers to such questions shows that we can be conscious of these word-functions otherwise than as means for objectifying any particular state or states of affairs that might be an answer to the questions.

To the extent that our behaviour is consciously directed, we orient ourselves toward goals by our knowledge. But we can objectify what it is to be the meaning or goal of life, what happiness is, what it is to be a value worth pursuing for its own sake, etc., in abstraction from individual things that might be instances of these generalized objects. As oriented to behavior by this kind of knowledge, we are necessitated to consciously seek *some* meaning in life, to have *some* thing or things as goals we consciously direct ourselves to. But this kind of knowledge does not necessitate us to seek meaning in this particular kind of behavior or that, to have this or that particular thing as our goal, to pursue happiness in one way rather than another.

This sketch is not a full-fledged demonstration of freedom of choice. It is meant only to show that my argument for causal determinism does not exclude the possibility of freedom for intelligent beings (but only for intelligent beings). The sketch, however, allows me to respond to the most important objections drawn from the argument for determinism. I have said that the argument for determinism applies to entitative existence while it is intentional existence that opens the possibility of freedom. But intentional existence cannot occur independently of entitative. Knowledge must have entitative existence in order to be intentional existence. Likewise, intentional existence can occur only if the entitatively existing nature of the knower is a capacity for intentional modes of existence. Therefore it seems the same necessity that rules other modes of entitative being must rule the knower and his intentional states.

Precisely. It is not by chance that intelligent beings try to find *some* meaning in life, make *some* things goals they consciously pursue, seek happiness of one kind or another. This necessity is not only rigorous but is rigorously appropriate for the specific, entitatively existing nature that grounds the necessity, a nature that permits the intentional existence of general objects and that orients us to behavior directed by our knowledge of objects. We can even go so far as to say that were we experientially confronted with a concrete thing that fulfilled all possible hopes for happiness, contained all possible meaning, value and goodness, we would necessarily choose that thing.

Thus the very exigencies of the argument for determinism call for a kind of necessity in intelligent behavior that is compatible with freedom. For the argument requires that a thing's orientation to behavior be determined by its nature. An intelligent being's nature requires that its behavior be directed to goals and values as objectified by universal word-functions. This necessity itself, however, prevents us from being determined to seek a particular goal that does not contain all possible fulfillment of these universal word-functions.

But must not efficient and component causes that are *sufficient* for an event produce that event necessarily? Let A and S be the efficient and component causes, respectively, of event C. Since A and S are sufficient for C, when A and S are in the proper relation, C must occur. If C does not occur, the existence of A and S in that relation is not sufficient for C; the occurrence of C is the occurrence of something *more* than what is accounted for by the causality of A and S. They may provide necessary conditions for C, but the occurrence of C requires more than those conditions.

Another way of putting the objection would be that if A and S are sufficient causes of C but can exist without C occurring, when C does occur, C is cause of itself. A change without an efficient cause is an impossible entity because, without the efficient cause, the change has no component cause. A potential component cause is insufficient to be a component cause. The efficient cause provides for the insufficiency of the component cause since, given that the efficient cause is what it is, the component cause cannot remain the same. But if sufficient causes do not necessitate their effect, A and S can produce C one time and fail to produce C another time. When C does occur, however, A does not make S change just by being what it is, since A can exist without S changing. Consequently C is needed to make S an actual component cause. C is that by which S becomes a component cause, because A's being what it is does not by itself provide for S's inability to be a component cause.

Sufficient causes that do not necessitate their effect are therefore contradictory. Focusing on the efficient cause for the sake of the comparison with freedom, we see that a sufficient though non-necessitating agent would both be and not be what it is, for it would be both sufficient and insufficient by being what it is. At one time A's being what it is does not make S undergo a change; at another time A does make S undergo a change, with no other change in A or S having taken place. Hence what A is both is and is not sufficient to cause C. In other words, a change's need for a sufficient efficient cause is the need for something whose features determine it to produce this change in these circumstances. If the characteristics making up an agent's nature make it a sufficient cause of C, it can fail to cause C if and only if its nature is not what it is.

This connection between sufficiency and necessity holds as long as entitative existence alone is considered. It even holds for an entity oriented to behavior by goals intentionally existing in a universal state, if the entity is able to experience a concrete thing containing all possible value. But the connection does not hold for orientation to behavior by goals intentionally existing in a universal state, when the concrete courses of action among which we choose are not experienced as containing all possible value.

Again, the reason for the connection between sufficiency and necessity is that, if the agent's nature makes it sufficient to cause a change, the agent can fail to produce the change only if it both is and is not what it is. But what the agent is amounts to a particular, concrete mode of being, for only particular, concrete things can exist. In other words, the features making up the concrete being of the agent orient the agent to behavior in a specific, determinate way. If they do not necessitate this behavior, then either the agent both is and is not what it is, or it does not exist in a concrete, particular way.

The requirements of concreteness and particularity, however, apply to entitative existence only. Words for the opposites of concreteness and particularity have a place in our vocabulary because their word-functions *can* characterize what exists intentionally. When orientation to behavior consists of a relation to goals intentionally existing in a universal state, the entitative existence of the agent is insufficient for the occurrence of the change by which the choice of a limited good comes about. But it is insufficient in a paragenerically paradoxical sense that appears to, but actually does not, contradict either a change's need for sufficient causes or the determinacy by which a non-intelligent sufficient cause necessitates its effect. The existence of the free agent is *in*sufficient for the change in the sense that the agent can exist without the change coming into existence. But this insufficiency of a free agent's relation to its effect is a form of *super*-sufficiency, is the result of the agent's way of being more than sufficient for its effect. For the free agent *is* sufficient in the sense of having all that is necessary for the effect. But the fact that it has all that is *necessary* without *necessitating* the effect does not here mean that the existence of the effect is the existence of more than its necessary causes contribute to it. Instead, it is the effect that falls short of what the agent is oriented to by necessity of nature, namely, value in its universal amplitude.

In the case of non-intelligent agents, on the other hand, insufficiency implies that something is lacking in the agent. If a cause does not necessitate an effect, then the existence of the effect is the existence of more than what its cause contributes to it, and the cause would not have all that is necessary for the effect. In a given set of circumstance, if agent A does not produce change C in component cause S, then A's nature either determines it to produce some change other than C or makes A unable to produce any change in these circumstances. In a discussion of freedom, the relevant comparison is with the case in which A produces no change. For in order to choose freely between X and Y, a free agent must be able to non-act with respect to X and with respect to Y. Non-action in the case of a non-intelligent agent implies that among the orientations to specific behavior given it by its mode of being, an orientation having all that is necessary for producing C is lacking. For if such an orientation was present, it could fail to produce C only by not being what it is.

In intelligent beings alone is non-acting with respect to C consistent with an agent's having all that is necessary for C. For there and only there, all that is necessary for C amounts to the existence of a concrete individual whose entitative features include a determined and necessitating orientation that is able to extend to C but which can be what it is without causing C. Solely in the case of an intelligent being, in other words, does what the thing is determine its behavior by orienting it to goals objectified in a universal state. Such a causal disposition can be what it is without producing C because it is not an orientation to this concrete, particular effect. Wherever the concrete, entitative being by which an agent is oriented to behavior includes the intentional existence of the general, a cause that has all that is necessary for an effect can be what it is without producing the effect.

When a free agent does produce C, C is not among its own causes. C is a change consisting of the transition from not choosing to choosing a particular course of action. That change has sufficient causes in (1) the agent's necessary orientation to seek *some* concrete, limited good (the agent being both the efficient and the component cause of C by reason of distinct features of its makeup) and (2) the agent's consciousness of the value to be acquired by choosing this course of action. These causes are sufficient assuming that the agent does not prefer the state of affairs that exists when it does not choose this course of action. When sufficient awareness of the desirability of this course of action exists, the agent *necessarily* chooses it, if at that time the agent does not prefer to refrain from choosing it. Preferring to refrain, however, does not require the agent to produce some other change, a change that would need its own causes, thereby generating an endless repetition of our cycle of explanations. Preferring the state of affairs that exists when it is not choosing this course of action means letting something that already exists remain as it is without any change.

Preferring the existing state of affairs amounts to a non-action with respect to making a new choice. But this preference is more than something negative. It is a positive relation consisting of the agent's consciousness of the value embodied in the already-existing situation together with the agent's dynamic orientation to value objectified in the universal. That orientation makes it impossible for the agent to avoid making some concrete value its preferred value. That orientation also allows the agent to prefer the state of affairs that will exist when it makes a new choice. The agent accomplishes this by not non-acting at the time when sufficient awareness of the desirability of the choice exists. Not non-acting means the agent does not consciously prefer the opposite at that time. Therefore the agent must make the new choice since doing so is the contradictory of preferring the opposite—preferring the new choice being the same as causing the change bringing this choice into existence.

When that change occurs, it has sufficient causes (the agent's orientation to value objectified in the universal and its awareness of the desirability of this choice) that produce the change freely since the agent could have non-acted. Instead of non-acting, the agent deliberately lets its awareness of the desirability of the choice cause it to go from non-acting to acting, from not causing the change bringing the new choice into existence to causing it. Since the agent is not always causing this change, its disposition for doing so must itself be caused to go from potency to act. The awareness of the desirability of the choice is what causes the transition from potency to act, provided the agent does not deliberately non-act.

Another traditional problem with freedom of choice is pertinent to this study. Freedom seems irrational since a sufficient reason (teleonomic cause) cannot be assigned for choosing this rather than that. If a sufficient reason could be assigned, an intelligent being would choose this rather than that, not freely, but because determined by its knowledge of the reason for preferring this to that.

Freedom, however, is a type of causality. Its effects are choices. Causes are causes of entitative existents, not of logical constructs. Causes therefore cause this entity, or they cause that entity, but they do not cause this-rather-than-that. "Rather than" objectifies a logical relation, disjunction, and this-rather-than-that is a logical construct. Of course logical relations and constructs can be used in thing-descriptions, for the reasons I have given. But their use must be consistent with what the things being objectified are as entitative existents, nor can they add anything extra-objective to what is being objectified.

Therefore, the logical relation rather-than can add nothing extra-objective to the causal relation between a cause and this effect, if *this* is its effect, or between a cause and that effect, if *that* is its effect. The sufficient reason for making this choice *rather than that* is nothing over and above the reason for making *this* choice. The sufficient reason for this choice is whatever value I perceive in this course of action. The perception of that value does not determine me to choose it rather than some other value. But that value is the reason I made this choice and therefore the reason I made this choice rather than that.

APPENDIX II

Bibliography

II.1 Bibliographical Essay

(Complete bibliographical data on the works mentioned here will be found in the "List of Works Cited" which follows this essay.)

I owe the distinction between things and objects, the identity theory of truth and the distinction between ontological and empirical analysis to Jacques Maritain's *The Degrees of Knowledge* (hereafter, DK). DK is also my main source for the distinction between entitative and intentional existence. The pertinent sections of this difficult work should be read in the following order: first and foremost, the pivotal Chapter Three, and with it sections 8, 18-19 and 26-30 of Chapter Two, and sections 1-4 of Appendix I; then the rest of Chapter Two, Chapters Four and Five, sections 3-8 and 13-19 of Chapter Eight, and section 2 of Appendix V. (For the insight that the "correspondence" required for truth is the identity of a thing with itself, see p. 97, n. 2.)

DK is Maritain's most mature statement of his theory of knowledge. But helpful background can be found in his earlier *Réflexions sur l'intelligence et sur sa vie propre* and the "Preface to the Second Edition of *La Philosophie Bergsonnienne*" translated in *Bergsonian Philosophy and Thomism*. See also his (1937, pp. 154-62), (1941b) and (1957). The reader of Maritain should be warned that his footnotes are often as impor-

485

important as his text. (It was also Maritain, 1944, pp. 130-41, who made me aware of Cajetan's refutation of Anselm.)

A number of works are very helpful for the further study of diacritical realism. Simon's *Introduction à l'ontologie du connaitre* should be mentioned first. My arguments for intentional existence were suggested by this work (pp. 9-18). See also Simon (1960a) and Chapter Eight of his *The Great Dialogue of Nature and Space*. Several relevant essays are collected in *The Return to Reason*, edited by Wild; and see the essays of FitzGerald (1963), Parker (1953, 1960 and 1962), Phelan (1939), and Wild (1947). Many of the discussions in Veatch's *Intentional Logic* and *Two Logics* run parallel to or provide background for the views I have presented. The articles of Rasmussen (1980, 1982a, 1982b, 1983, 1984) are also very relevant, as are those in Henle *et al.* (1981). Peifer has collected many of the classic texts on realism's theory of knowledge in *The Mystery of Knowledge*. Peterson's *Realism and Logical Atomism* is a realist critique of Bergmann and his school.

The Tradition via Heidegger by Deely is a sustained comparison of Maritain and Heidegger concerning intentional existence and *Dasein*. Deely covers a variety of topics concerning language in the titles listed from 1972 to "Forthcoming". Much material is to be found in Deely's forthcoming edition of Poinsot's *Treatise on Signs*, and some material from Poinsot is already available in *The Material Logic of John of St. Thomas*. Poinsot is definitely not for the uninitiated, however. (What I have called material relations, Poinsot and others call transcendental or mixed relations; what I have called formal relations others call predicamental, categorical or pure relations.) One can also consult Hachey (1957) and Almeida Sampaio (1963).

Strangely, the crucial thing-object distinction has been little studied by anyone other than Maritain. Hopefully, this book has done something to remedy that situation. For applications of that distinction in other contexts, see Cahalan (1971; 1975, pp. 354-362; 1981, pp. 207-215; 1983, pp. 532-533). The reader should be aware, however, that Maritain's doctrine and his meaning for the word "object" include both epistemological and metaphysical (in that sense of "metaphysical" which is opposed to "epistemological") aspects. Since I have been concerned only with the epistemological side of the distinction, I have used "object" only in the epistemological sense of that which is describable as term of a knowledge relation. Still, nothing I have said using the word in this sense contradicts anything Maritain has said using the word in his more inclusive sense.

On ontological and empirical analysis and the philosophy of science, the primary source is DK. In addition, see Maritain's *The Philosophy of Nature*, and "The Conflict of Methods at the End of the Middle Ages". Again, important background will be found in *Réflexions sur l'intelligence* and in Chapter Six of *Theonas*, an essay on time. Simon's "Maritain's Philosophy of the Sciences" is essential reading. And see his *Prévoir et Savoir* and *The Great Dialogue of Nature and Space* (the latter contains some but not all of the material from the former). Chapter Five and Appendix II of Sikora's *The Scientific Knowledge of Physical Nature* should be read, and his (1957) and (1958) are also helpful. (Sikora does overemphasize the instrumentalistic side of Maritain, however.) Allard (1981) and Jaki (1984) can also be consulted.

A different realist approach to the philosophy of science is represented by works such as Ashley (1961) and Wallace's *From a Realist Point of View*. Cahalan (1981 and 1983) discusses the main issues disputed by these approaches. Martin's *The Order and Integration of Knowledge* also contains realist work on the philosophy of science.

De Koninck (1957) has discussions on the theory of knowledge in general and the philosophies of science and mathematics in particular. Discussions pertinent to the philosophy of mathematics will be found in the already cited works of Maritain, Simon, Wallace and Martin and in De Koninck (1956) and Conway (1962, pp 169-76). Although Conway strangely misunderstands the subject of his article, the barber paradox, he has significant things to say about Russell's paradox. Sikora (1965a) is a creative essay on the philosophy of logic.

Klubertanz's *The Philosophy of Human Nature*, Appendix K, discusses empirical psychology. For Freudian psychology, see Adler's *What Man Has Made of Man*, Dalbiez's *Psychoanalytic Method and the Doctrine of Freud* (but see also the emendation of Dalbiez in Simon, 1969, pp. 40-44) and Maritain's *Scholasticism and Politics*, Chapter Six. The discussion of evolution in Appendix N of Klubertanz is dated but still contains some relevant observations. See also Deely (1969) and the discussion of evolution as a scientific theory in Part I of Deely and Nogar's *The Problem of Evolution*. On the mind-body problem, see Chapter Twelve of Adler's *The Difference of Man and the Difference It Makes*. Adler points out, in effect, that while realists have given a clear *causal* meaning to the claim that rational consciousness is immaterial (rational thought is performed by a causal disposition of which matter is not a part), no such causal meaning has been given to the claim that sense consciousness is immaterial. In realist discussions of consciousness in general, however, immateriality has often been given priority over intentional existence. The result has been to make it more difficult than it need be to understand intentional existence.

On the distinction of metaphysics from the philosophy of nature, see DK, Chapter Two, and these other places in Maritain: *The Philosophy of Nature*, Chapter One, *A Preface to Metaphysics*, Lecture Four, and *Existence and the Existent*, Chapter One.

On causality and causal necessity, see Garrigou-Lagrange's *God: His Existence and His Nature*, vol. I, Chapters Two and Three. Other than the classical sources, this is without doubt the most dated of the works to which I am referring you. Still, it contains more detailed discussions of some issues than are available elsewhere. (It was this work, p. 203, that first made me aware of the connection between the principles of causality and induction.) See also Garrigou's *Le réalisme du principe de finalité*. Maritain deals with causality and necessity in (1942a) and in *A Preface to Metaphysics*, pp.80-81 and 96-142; see especially the analysis of teleonomic causality in Lecture Six. Harré and Madden's *Causal Powers* is certainly to be recommended. And one can consult Regis (1959, pp. 157-174), Sikora (1965, Chapter Six) and Wild (1949). The textbooks mentioned below also contain treatments of many causal issues. For more on causality in philosophical knowledge, see Cahalan (1969, Chapters One and Three).

Wallace's 2-volume *Causality and Scientific Explanation* contains valuable historical analyses. Comparisons of causality in ontological and empirical knowledge can be found in DK, Chapter Four and in Chapter One of *Prévoir et Savoir*. Simon discusses chance and determinism in the latter place and in Chapter Ten of *The Great Dialogue of Nature and Space*. Chapter Two of *Introduction à l'ontologie du connaitre* has an analysis of action from the point of view of the agent. Simon also deals with causality and determinism in his *Traité du libre arbitre*. (The posthumously published English translation, *Freedom of Choice*, leaves out material from the original; still, it should be used if the French is not available.) For freedom and causality, one should also see Maritain's *Scholasticism and Politics*, Chapter Five.

It would be wrong to leave the unique contributions of Etienne Gilson out of this survey. See especially *The Unity of Philosophical Experience* (the classic exposé of the U-turn) and its important sequel *Being and Some Philosophers*. The material of the latter's Chapter Five, however, is handled better by Gilson himself in *The Christian Philosophy of St. Thomas Aquinas*, Part I, Chapters One and Four, and Part III, Chapter Seven. For Gilson's epistemological insights, see *Réalisme thomiste et critique de la connaissance*.

For the general metaphysical background that is presupposed by most of the works already mentioned, one can see Bobik's *Aquinas on Being and Essence*. Also, a number of textbooks are quite competent within the limits of the genre. Even though it is dated, Phillips (1950) should be consulted as the most thorough text in English; it has things that are not easy to find elsewhere. Among the other texts that can be consulted are McGlynn and Farley (1966), Van Steenberghen (1952) and Grenet (1967), a précis. For philosophical psychology, there is Klubertanz (1953). Henle's *Theory of Knowledge* is a general epistemology.

On the concepts of being, essence and existence, see *A Preface to Metaphysics*, Lectures Two and Four, and *Existence and the Existent*, Chapter One. In connection with the former work, note that, while Maritain liked to speak of intuition, never does he make intuition more than a method of *discovery* in philosophy. He explicitly denies (p. 59) that philosophy *verifies* by intuition.

Those approaching realism from a phenomenological background should see Chapter Three of DK and Deely's book on Heidegger. Those with an existentialist background should see the latter work, *A Preface to Metaphysics*, Lecture Three, *Existence and the Existent*, Chapter Three (and the clarifications in Appendix IV of DK), and above all, *Existence and the Existent*, Chapter Five. And see the discussions of subjectivity in Chapter One, Seven and Twelve of Sikora (1965).

The following can be used as introductions both to realism and to philosophy: *The Unity of Philosophical Experience*, *The Great Dialogue of Nature and Space*, and Bobik's *Aquinas on Being and Essence*. But I also strongly recommend Aristotle's neglected *Physics* which should be read, as Sir David Ross pointed out, with Aquinas's commentary. Lack of attention to the *Physics* is one reason why Aristotle is not better understood.

The main influences on the realist tradition have been Aristotle and Aquinas. Unfortunately, the relevant texts of Aquinas are so diffused throughout his many works that it would not be practical to refer you to individual titles (except for *On Being and Essence*, which is contained in Bobik's *Aquinas on Being and Essence*). Most of the authors I have cited, however, provide you with ample references to specific texts in Aquinas.

Finally, I apologize for the unintentional omissions in this essay.

II.2 List of Works Cited

(Only dates of editions or translations used are given except in the case of older authors, where original dates of composition or publication are added for the reader's convenience.)

Adler, Mortimer J.
 1937. *What Man Has Made of Man*. New York: Longmans.
 1967. *The Difference of Man and the Difference It Makes*. New York: Holt, Rinehart and Winston.

Allard, Jean-Louis.
 1981. "Maritain's Epistemology of Modern Science." In *Conference-Seminar on Jacques Maritain's The Degrees of Knowledge*, pp. 144-173. Edited by R. J. Henle, S.J., Marion Cordes and Jeanne Vatterott. St. Louis: American Maritain Association.

Almeida Sampaio, Laura Fraga de.
 1963. *L'intuition dans la philosophie de Jacques Maritain*. Paris: Vrin.

Anscombe, G.E.M. and Geach, P. T.
 1961. *Three Philosophers*. Oxford: Blackwell.

Ashley, Benedict, O.P.
 1961. "Does Natural Science Attain Nature or Only the Phenomena?" In *The Philosophy of Physics*. Edited by Vincent Edward Smith. Jamaica, New York: St. John's University Press.

Beauchamp, Tom L. and Rosenberg, Alexander.
 1981. *Hume and the Problem of Causation*. Oxford: Oxford University Press.

Bergmann, Gustav.
 1964. *Logic and Reality*. Madison: The University of Wisconsin Press.

Bobik, Joseph.
 1957. "A Note on the Question: 'Is Being a Genus?'." *Philosophical Studies* (Maynooth) 6: 117-122.
 1965. *Aquinas on Being and Essence: A Translation and Interpretation*. Notre Dame: University of Notre Dame Press.

Cahalan, John C.
 1969. *Necessary Truth and Philosophic Method: A Re-examination*. Ph.D. dissertation, University of Notre Dame.
 1970. "Analogy and the Disrepute of Metaphysics." *The Thomist* 34: 387-422.

1971. Review of *The Paradoxical Structure of Existence*, by Frederick D. Wilhelmsen. *The Thomist* 35: 328-337.

1975. Review of *The Problem of Evolution*, edited by John N. Deely and Raymond J. Nogar. *The New Scholasticism* 49: 350-362.

1981. "Maritain's Views on the Philosophy of Nature." In *Conference-Seminar on Jacques Maritain's The Degrees of Knowledge*, pp. 185-218. Edited by R. J. Henle, S.J., Marion Cordes, and Jeanne Vatterott. St. Louis: American Maritain Association.

1983. "Metaphysics and Immateriality." *The New Scholasticism* 57: 528-533.

Carroll, Lewis (Charles Lutwidge Dodgson).
1895. "What the Tortoise Said to Achilles." *Mind*, n.s. 14: 278-280.

Chisholm, Roderick M.
1966. *Theory of Knowledge*. Englewood Cliffs: Prentice-Hall.

Conway, Pierre.
1962. "The Barber Paradox." *Laval théologique et philosophique* 17: 161-176.

Cornman, James W.
1964. "Uses of Language and Philosophical Problems." *Philosophical Studies* 15: 11-16. Page reference in the text is to the reprint in Rorty (1967).

Dalbiez, Roland.
1941. *Psychoanalytic Method and the Doctrine of Freud*. 2 vols. New York: Longmans.

Deely, John N.
1969. "The Philosophical Dimensions of the Origin of Species." *The Thomist* 33: 75-149, 251-342.

1971. *The Tradition Via Heidegger*. The Hague: Nijhoff.

1972. "How Language Refers." *Studi Internazionali Filosofia* 4: 41-50.

1974. "The Two Approaches to Language: Philosophical and Historical Reflections on the Point of Departure of Jean Poinsot's Semiotic." *The Thomist* 38: 856-907.

1975a. "Modern Logic, Animal Psychology, and Human Discourse." *Revue de l'Université d'Ottowa* 45: 80-100.

1975b. "Reference to the Non-Existent." *The Thomist* 39: 253-308.
1976. "The Doctrine of Signs: Taking Form at Last." *Semiotica* 18: 171-193.
1977a. " 'Semiotic' as the Doctrine of Signs." *Ars Semeiotica* 1: 41-66.
1977b. "The Use of Words to Mention." *The New Scholasticism* 51: 546-553.
1978a. "Semiotic and the Controversy over Mental Events." *Proceedings of the American Catholic Philosophical Association* 52: 16-27.
1978b. "Toward the Origin of Semiotic." In *Sight, Sound and Sense.* Edited by T. A. Sebeok. Bloomington: Indiana University Press.
1978c. "What's in a Name?" *Semiotica* 22: 151-181.
1980. "The Nonverbal Inlay in Linguistic Communication." In *The Signifying Animal.* Edited by Irmengard Rauch and Gerald F. Carr. Bloomington: Indiana University Press.
1981. "The Relation of Logic to Semiotics." *Semiotica* 35: 193-265.
1982. *Introducing Semiotic: Its History and Doctrine.* Bloomington: Indiana University Press.
1983. "Cognition from a Semiotic Point of View." In *Semiotics 1981: Proceedings of the Semiotic Society of America.* Edited by John N. Deely and Margot D. Lenhart. New York: Plenum.
Forthcoming. *Logic as a Liberal Art* (University of Toronto: Toronto Semiotic Circle Monograph Series, 1985).

Deely, John N. and Nogar, Raymond, J., eds.
1973. *The Problem of Evolution: A Study of the Philosophical Repercussions of Evolutionary Science.* New York: Appleton-Century-Crofts.

DeKoninck, Charles.
1956. "Random Reflections on Science and Calculation." *Laval théologique et philosophique* 12: 84-119.
1957. "Abstraction From Matter." *Laval théologique et philosophique* 13: 133-196; 16 (1960): 53-69, 169-188.

Economos, Judith.
1977. Letter to *the New York Times.* Tuesday, December 27. Reprinted in *Proceedings and Addresses of the American Philosophical Association* 51 (1978): 623-624.

FitzGerald, John J.
1963. "Maritain's Critical Realism." In *Jacques Maritain: The Man and His Achievement,* pp. 58-86. Edited by Joseph W. Evans. New York: Sheed and Ward.

Gallagher, Donald and Idella.
1962. *The Achievement of Jacques and Raissa Maritain: A Bibliography.* Garden City, New York: Doubleday.

Garrigou-Lagrange, Reginald.
1932. *Le réalisme du principe de finalité.* Paris: Desclée.
1939. *God: His Existence and His Nature.* St. Louis: Herder.

Geach, Peter.
1957. *Mental Acts.* London: Routledge and Kegan Paul.

Gilson, Etienne.
1937. *The Unity of Philosophical Experience.* New York: Scribners.
1947. *Réalisme Thomiste et critique de la connaissance.* Paris: Vrin.
1949. *Being and Some Philosophers.* Toronto: Pontifical Institute of Medieval Studies.
1956. *The Christian Philosophy of St. Thomas Aquinas.* New York: Random House.

Grenet, Paul.
1967. *Thomism: An Introduction.* New York: Harper & Row.

Hachey, Mary Mercedes.
1957. *An Investigation and Evaluation of Two Interpretations of St. Thomas' Doctrine of the Objectivity of the Concept.* Ph.D. dissertation, University of Notre Dame.

Hanson, Norwood Russell.
1969. *Patterns of Discovery.* Cambridge: The Cambridge University Press.

Harré, Romano and Madden, Edward H.
1975. *Causal Powers: A Theory of Natural Necessity.* Totowa, New Jersey; Rowman and Littlefield.

Harris, Errol E.
1953. "Misleading Analyses." *Philosophical Quarterly 3: 289-300. Page references in the text are to the reprint in Clarity Is Not Enough,* pp. 201-216. Edited by H. D. Lewis. London: Allen and Unwin.

Henle, R. J., S.J.
   1983.   *Theory of Knowledge.* Chicago: Loyola University Press.

Henle, R. J., S.J., Cordes, Marion, and Vatterott, Jeanne, eds.
   1981.   *Conference-Seminar on Jacques Maritain's The Degrees of Knowledge.* St. Louis: American Maritain Association.

Hesse, Mary.
   1970.   "Duhem, Quine and a New Empiricism." In *Knowledge and Necessity,* the Royal Institute of Philosophy Lectures, vol. 3, pp. 191-209. Page references in the text are to the reprint in *Challenges to Empiricism,* pp. 208-227. Edited by Harold Morick. Belmont, California: Wadsworth, 1972.

Hook, Sidney.
   1963.   *The Quest for Being.* New York: Dell.

Hume, David.
   1739.   *A Treatise of Human Nature.* Garden City: Doubleday, 1961.

Husserl, Edmund.
   1960.   *Cartesian Meditations.* The Hague: Nijhoff.

Jaki, Stanley L.
   1984.   "Maritain and Science." *The New Scholasticism* 58: 267-292.

Kaminsky, Jack.
   1969.   *Language and Ontology.* Carbondale: Southern Illinois University Press.

Kiteley, M.
   1964.   "Is Existence a Predicate?" *Mind* 73: 364-373.

Klubertanz, George P.
   1953.   *The Philosophy of Human Nature.* New York: Appleton-Century-Crofts.

Kripke, Saul A.
   1972.   *Naming and Necessity.* Cambridge, Massachusetts: Harvard University Press.

McGlynn, James V. and Farley, Paul Mary.
   1966.   *A Metaphysics of Being and God.* Englewood Cliffs: Prentice-Hall.

McInerny, Ralph M.
1961. *The Logic of Analogy*. The Hague: Nijhoff.

MacKinnon, Edward M.
1969. "The Role of Conceptual and Linguistic Frameworks." *Proceedings of the American Catholic Philosophical Association* 43: 24-43.
1971. *Truth and Expression*. New York: Newman.

Malcolm, Norman.
1964. "Anselm's Ontological Arguments." In *The Existence of God*, pp. 47-70. Edited by John Hick. New York: Macmillan.

Margenau, Henry.
1961. *Open Vistas: Philosophical Perspectives of Modern Science*. New Haven: Yale University Press.

Maritain, Jacques.
1926. *Réflexions sur l'intelligence et sur sa vie propre*. Paris: Nouvelle Libraire Nationale.
1933. *Theonas: Conversations of a Sage*. New York: Sheed and Ward.
1937. *An Introduction to Philosophy*. New York: Sheed and Ward.
1939. *A Preface to Metaphysics*. New York: Sheed and Ward.
1940. *Scholasticism and Politics*. New York: Macmillan.
1941a. "The Conflict of Methods at the End of the Middle Ages." *The Thomist* 3: 527-538.
1941b. "Sign and Symbol." In *Ransoming the Time*, pp. 191-224. New York: Scribners. Published in England as *Redeeming the Time*. London: Bles, 1943.
1942a. "Reflections on Necessity and Contingency." In *Essays in Thomism*, pp. 65-96. Edited by Robert E. Brennan. New York: Sheed and Ward.
1942b. *St. Thomas and the Problem of Evil*. Milwaukee: Marquette University Press.
1944. *The Dream of Descartes*. New York: Philosophical Library.
1948. *Existence and the Existent*. New York: Pantheon.
1949. *Neuf leçons sur les notions premières de la philosophie morale*. Paris: Téqui.
1951. *The Philosophy of Nature*. New York: Philosophical Library.
1955. *Bergsonian Philosophy and Thomism*. New York: Philosophical Library.

1957.   "Language and the Theory of Sign." In *Language: An In-quiry into Its Meaning and Function*, pp. 86-101. Edited by Ruth Nanda Anshen. New York: Harper.

1959.   *The Degrees of Knowledge*. Translated by Gerald B. Phelan. New York: Scribners.

Martin, William Oliver.
1957.   *The Order and Integration of Knowledge*. Ann Arbor: University of Michigan Press; reprint ed., New York: Greenwood, 1968.

Moore, G. E.
1936.   "Is Existence a Predicate?" *Proceedings of the Aristotelian Society, Supplementary*. Vol. 15: 175-188.

Northrop, F.S.C.
1961.   "Causation, Determinism, and the Good." In *Determinism and Freedom in the Age of Modern Science*, pp. 201-211. Edited by Sidney Hook. New York: Collier.

Parker, Francis, H.
1953.   "Realistic Epistemology." In Wild (1953, pp. 152-176).
1960.   "A Realistic Appraisal of Knowledge." In *Philosophy of Knowledge*, pp. 18-48. Edited by Roland Houde and Joseph P. Mullally. Chicago: Lippincott.
1962.   "A Demonstration of Epistemological Realism." *International Philosophical Quarterly* 2: 367-393.

Peifer, John.
1964.   *The Mystery of Knowledge*. Albany: Magi.

Peterson, John.
1976.   *Realism and Logical Atomism: A Critique of Neo-Atomism from the Viewpoint of Classical Realism*. University, Alabama: The University of Alabama Press.

Phelan, Gerald B.
1939.   "*Verum Sequitur Esse Rerum*." *Medieval Studies* 1: 11-22.

Phillips, R.P.
1950.   *Modern Thomistic Philosophy*. 2 vols. Westminister, Maryland: Newman.

Plantinga, Alvin.
1974. *The Nature of Necessity*. Oxford: Oxford University Press.

Poinsot, John.
1631-1635. *Cursus Philosophicus Thomisticus*. Edited by B. Reiser
3 vols. Turin: Marietti, 1930-1937.
1631-1667. *Cursus Theologicus*. Solesmes edition. 4 vols. to date.
Paris: Desclée, 1931-1953. Vivès edition, 10 vols., Paris, 1884.
1632. *The Material Logic of John of St. Thomas*. Translated and edited
by Yves Simon, John Glanville and G. Donald Hollenhorst.
Chicago: University of Chicago Press, 1955.
1632a. *Tractatus de Signis: The Semiotic of John Poinsot*. Translated
and edited by John N. Deely. Berkeley: University of California Press, 1985.

Premack, David.
1971. "Language in Chimpanzee." *Science*: 172: 808-822.

Quine, Willard Van Orman.
1936. "Truth By Convention." In Quine (1966, pp. 70-99).
1939. "Designation and Existence." *Journal of Philosophy* 36. Page
reference in the text is to the reprint in *Readings in
Philosophical Analysis*, pp. 44-51. Edited by Herbert Feigel
and Wilfred Sellars. New York: Appleton-Century-Crofts,
1949.
1960. *Word and Object*. Cambridge, Massachusetts: Massachusetts
Institute of Technology Press.
1963. *From a Logical Point of View*. New York: Harper and Row.
1966. *The Ways of Paradox and Other Essays*. New York: Random
House.
1969. *Ontological Relativity and Other Essays*. New York: Colum-
bia University Press.
1970. *Philosophy of Logic*. Englewood Cliffs: Prentice-Hall.

Rasmussen, Douglas B.
1980. "Deely, Wittgenstein, and Mental Events." *The New
Scholasticism* 54: 60-67.
1982a. "Necessary Truth, the Game Analogy, and the Meaning-
is-use Thesis." *The Thomist* 46: 423-440.

1982b. "The Open-Question Argument and the Issue of Conceivability." *Proceedings of the American Catholic Philosophical Association* 56: 162-172.

1983. "Rorty, Wittgenstein, and the Nature of Intentionality." *Proceedings of the American Catholic Philosophical Association* 57: 152-162.

1984. "Quine and Aristotelian Essentialism." *The New Scholasticism* 58: 316-335.

Regis, L. M.
1959. *Epistemology*. New York: Macmillan.

Rorty, Richard.
1967. "Metaphilosophical Difficulties of Linguistic Philosophy." In *The Linguistic Turn*, pp. 1-39. Edited by Rorty. Chicago: University of Chicago Press.

Russell, Bertrand.
1919. *Introduction to Mathematical Philosophy*. London: Allen and Unwin.

1926. "Perception." *Journal of Philosophical Studies*: 78-86.

Ryle, Gilbert.
1931. "Systematically Misleading Expressions." *Proceedings of the Aristotelian Society* 32: 139-170.

1949. *The Concept of Mind*. London: Hutchinson.

Sellars, Wilfred.
1963. *Science, Perception and Reality*. New York: The Humanities Press.

Sikora, Joseph J.
1957. "The Philosophy of Nature and Natural Science from a Thomist Viewpoint." *The Thomist* 20: 330-348.

1958. " 'Integrated' Knowledge of Nature." *The Thomist* 21: 171-183.

1965a. "Some Thomist Reflections on the Foundations of Formal Logic." *Notre Dame Journal of Formal Logic* 6.

1965b. *Inquiry into Being*. Chicago: Loyola University Press.

1966. *The Scientific Knowledge of Physical Nature*. Bruges-Paris: Desclée.

Simon, Yves R.
1934. *Introduction à l'ontologie du connaitre*. Paris: Desclée. Reprint edition, Dubuque: Wm. C. Brown.
1943. "Maritain's Philosophy of the Sciences." *The Thomist* 5: 85-102. Page references in the text are to the reprint in Maritain (1951, pp. 157-182). Reprinted with revisions in *The Philosophy of Physics*, pp. 25-39. Edited by Vincent E. Smith. New York: St. John's University Press, 1961.
1944. *Prévoir et savoir. Études sur l'idée de la necessité dans la pensée scientifique et en philosophie*. Montreal: Éditions de l'arbre.
1951. *Traité du libre arbitre*. Liege: Sciences et Lettres. Paris: Vrin, 1952.
1960a. "An Essay on Sensation." In *Philosophy of Knowledge*, pp. 55-95. Edited by Roland Houde and Joseph P. Mullally. Chicago: Lippincott.
1960b. "On Order in Analogical Sets." *The New Scholasticism* 34: 1-42.
1969. *Freedom of Choice*. Edited by Peter Wolff. New York: Fordham University Press.
1970. *The Great Dialogue of Nature and Space*. Albany: Magi.
1971. *Work, Society and Culture*. Edited by Vukan Kuic. New York: Fordham University Press.

Strawson, P.F.
1950. "Truth." *Proceedings of the Aristotelian Society, Supplementary* Vol. 24: 129-156. Page references in the text are to the reprint in *An Introduction to Philosophical Inquiry*, pp. 557-574. Edited by Joseph Margolis. New York: Knopf, 1968.

Thomas Aquinas, Saint.
c. 1268. *Commentary on Aristotle's Physics*. New Haven: Yale University Press, 1963.

Van Steenberghen, Fernand.
1952. *Ontology*. New York: Wagner.

Veatch, Henry B.
1952. *Intentional Logic*. New Haven: Yale University Press.
1969. *Two Logics*. Evanston: Northwestern University Press.

Wallace, William A., O.P.
1979. *From a Realist Point of View: Essays in the Philosophy of Science*. Lanham, Maryland: University Press of America.

1981.   *Causality and Scientific Explanation*, 2 vols. Lanham, Maryland: University Press of America.

Whorf, Benjamin L.
1950.   "An American Indian Model of the Universe." *International Journal of American Linguistics* 16: 67-72. Page reference in the text is to the reprint in *Philosophy of Knowledge*, pp. 171-177. Edited by Roland Houde and Joseph P. Mullally. Chicago; Lippincott, 1960.

Wild, John.
1947.   "An Introduction to the Phenomenology of Signs." *Philosophy and Phenomenological Research* 8: 228-233.
1948.   *Introduction to Realistic Philosophy*. New York: Harper.
1949.   "A Realistic Defense of Causal Efficacy." *Review of Metaphysics* 2: 1-14.
1952.   "Tendency." *The Journal of Philosophy* 49: 468-472.

Wild, John, ed.
1953.   *The Return to Reason*. Chicago: Regnery.

Wittgenstein, Ludwig.
1958.   *Philosophical Investigations*. Translated by G.E.M. Anscombe. 3rd ed. Macmillan.
1965.   *The Blue and Brown Books*. New York: Harper and Row.
1971.   *Tractatus Logico-Philosophicus*. Translated by D. F. Pears and B. G. McGuinness. 2nd ed. London: Routledge and Kegan Paul.

INDEX OF PROPER NAMES

INDEX OF TERMINOLOGY

At various points, this study introduces terminology, some of it new or at least unfamiliar, that subsequent discussions make use of. To assist the reader, the following list gives the places where those terms are introduced and/or principally defined.